3rd Edition

Understanding Organizational Behavior

DEBRA L. NELSON

Oklahoma State University

JAMES CAMPBELL QUICK

The University of Texas at Arlington

THOMSON

SOUTH-WESTERN

Australia · Brazil · Canada · Mexico · Singapore · Spain · United Kingdom · United States

THOMSON

SOUTH-WESTERN

Understanding Organizational Behavior, 3rd Edition
Debra L. Nelson and James Campbell Quick

VP/Editorial Director:
Jack W. Calhoun

Editor-in-Chief:
Melissa Acuña

Sr. Acquisitions Editor:
Michele Rhoads

Editorial Assistant:
Ruth Belanger

Developmental Editor:
Erin Berger

Marketing Manager:
Clint Kernen

Executive Marketing Manager:
Kimberly Kanakes

Content Project Manager:
Kelly Hoard

Manager of Technology, Editorial:
John Barans

Technology Project Manager:
Kristin Meere

Manufacturing Coordinator:
Doug Wilke

Production House:
LEAP Publishing Services, Inc.

Compositor:
ICC Macmillan Inc.

Printer:
Transcontinental Louisville, QC

Art Director:
Stacy Jenkins Shirley

Internal Designers:
Nick Gliebe
Diane Gliebe

Cover Designers:
Nick Gliebe
Diane Gliebe

Student Edition ISBN 13:
978-0-324-42302-0
Student Edition
ISBN 10: 0-324-42302-0

Library of Congress Control Number:
2007934901

For more information about our
products, contact us at:

Thomson Learning Academic
Resource Center

1-800-423-0563

Thomson Higher Education
5191 Natorp Boulevard
Mason, OH 45040
USA

CONTENTS IN BRIEF

CONTENTS

PART 1 INTRODUCTION

PART 2 INDIVIDUAL PROCESSES AND BEHAVIOR

PART 3 INTERPERSONAL PROCESSES AND BEHAVIOR

Change was the overarching theme for the first two editions of *Understanding Organizational Behavior,* and so it continues. For some people, change is experienced as a crisis. This is not necessarily bad when one understands that the Chinese symbol for crisis is a combination of the symbols for danger and opportunity. Yes, change may pose dangers for individuals and organizations. However, change also opens the door for new opportunities, new challenges, and new experiences. World-changing events have produced significant effects on organizations in all sectors of world economies, and in turn, these changes also have significant effects on peoples' attitudes, emotions, and behavior at work. Organizational behavior is at the heart of productive business, and it is the basis for taking advantage of the opportunities that change offers to us all. As leaders, our challenge is to harness the power of these opportunities. We have welcomed the opportunity to change *Understanding Organizational Behavior* while still retaining a solid research core.

Understanding Organizational Behavior, third edition, continues to reflect our core value of solid scholarly foundations on which the science of organizational behavior is built, our immersion into the realities of contemporary organizational life, and our firm belief that challenges are the pathways to taking advantage of the opportunities that change offers. The science of organizational behavior is anchored in broad, deep research roots in our discipline. Our book contains classic as well as leading-edge research in the field. Research and theory form the foundations of our knowledge. Organizational behavior is an applied discipline used by leaders at every level in organizations. Thus, we include examples from all types of organizations. Some of the examples show successes, while others show failures, of managers applying organizational behavior knowledge in the real world. Challenges are the opportunities we have to grow and develop both as individuals and organizations. In the book, they take the form of individual activities for proactive learning.

Organizational behavior is the study of individual behavior and group dynamics in organizational settings. It focuses on timeless topics like motivation, leadership, teamwork, and communication. Such issues have captured our attention for decades. Organizational behavior also encompasses contemporary issues in organizations. How do we encourage employees to engage in organizational citizenship behaviors, to go above and beyond the call of duty to exhibit exceptional performance? How can ethical behavior be encouraged among leaders and followers? How can trust be developed and nurtured within work relationships? How do we manage employee behavior in virtual organizations or teams? What happens when organizations with strong cultures and a need for constancy face the pressure to become current, competitive, and agile? *Understanding Organizational Behavior* thus engages both classic and emerging issues.

Our overarching theme of change is accompanied by three supporting subthemes: globalization, diversity, and ethics. Each subtheme presents its own challenges and encourages individuals to learn, grow, and adjust. A world without borders means that a broad understanding of differences as assets must be a part of any viable organizational culture. Personal integrity is a value of continuing importance to us all. In addition to emphasizing these themes, we have expanded our coverage of many important emerging issues in organizational behavior. Justice at work has become a critical issue, and so we have incorporated the most recent research on organizational justice. For example, we see that unfair treatment at work leads to adverse stress and health reactions. There has been an explosion of research on emotions at work; so much so that we have retitled Chapter 4 to be "Attitudes, Emotions, and Ethics" to incorporate this contemporary perspective. The coverage of emotions at work has been expanded throughout the book. We have also incorporated a new section on political skills, which, along with leadership skills, are crucial for a successful managerial career. In line with the above themes is an enhanced focus on healthy business practices and values-driven management.

Our book rests on our belief that learning involves not only acquiring knowledge but also developing skills. The rich theory and research in organizational behavior must be translated into application. Thus, our book presents the opportunity to know concepts, ideas, and theories, and to practice skills, abilities, and behaviors to enhance the management of human behavior at work. Both knowledge and skills are essential for our future managers. We hope the knowledge and skills presented here empower them to succeed in the changing world of work.

SPECIAL FEATURES

Several special features of the book extend the foundations, realities, and challenges to specific applications. These features are designed to enhance the application of theory and research in practice, to stimulate student interest and discussion, and to facilitate cognitive as well as skill-based learning.

FOUNDATIONS

Each chapter includes leading-edge research studies related to the chapter's topic. The book is based on extensive classic and contemporary research literature. At the end of the textbook is a lengthy chapter-by-chapter reference list that students can refer to for in-depth treatments of the chapter topics.

REALITIES

Focus Companies The third edition features extensive examples from four key organizations: Cisco Systems, Pixar Studies, Virgin Group, Ltd., and Whole Foods Market. The opening and closing vignettes for each chapter feature one of these organizations. By focusing on these four organizations throughout the book, students can familiarize themselves with the companies in greater depth than a single appearance would allow.

A host of relevant, recent examples are also included within each chapter. These examples spotlight contemporary organizational life. They are realities that reflect the themes of globalization, diversity, and ethics. They include not only examples of successes, but also examples of failures, which are also opportunities for learning.

◼ CHALLENGES

Challenge Exercises We've expanded the challenge feature by including two Challenges in the body of each chapter. These are self-assessment exercises that provide the student with feedback on one aspect of the topic. Examples are the learning style inventory in Chapter 1, in which students discover their own learning preferences, and applying force field analysis inventory in Chapter 16, which helps students assess forces affecting change. Each Challenge is designed to enhance self-knowledge or to promote skill development in the subject matter. The student is able to use the results of the Challenge for self-discovery or behavioral change.

"Think Critically" Dilemmas Ethics questions and dilemmas in the margins of each chapter provoke students to think critically about what is right and wrong as well as about the various ways to resolve ethical conflicts in organizations. Many of the ethical questions and dilemmas do not have a single answer; instead, they raise key issues for the students to think through. Critical thinking skills are also called for by AACSB in terms of arming our students for future success.

Experiential Exercises Two group-oriented Experiential Exercises are included at the end of each chapter. They are designed for students to work in teams to learn more about an important aspect of the chapter's topic. The exercises give students opportunities to develop interpersonal skills and to process their thinking within a teamwork setting. In the Chapter 15 exercise, "Contrasting Organizational Cultures," groups of students compare the cultures of two organizations and relate the dimensions of culture to the organizations' performance.

◼ CONCISE FORMAT

In a world of semesters and quarters that never seem quite long enough, a textbook that presents information to students in a clear, concise format becomes invaluable. *Understanding Organizational Behavior* provides an alternative to the larger OB texts on the market, coming in at 16 chapers, compared to longer 18-, 19-, and 20-chapter texts. This text, based off of the 18-chapter Nelson/Quick *Organizational Behavior* text, retains the benefits of the larger text—providing students with the foundations, realities, and challenges needed to understand the course area. These benefits, however, come in a compact package that provides instructors the flexibility to integrate additional learning aids to customize the course to their learners' needs. Instead of six focus companies, this text has been streamlined to include four focus companies. Instead of three or four examples to explain a concept, there may be two strong examples. This tightening allows students to focus closely on specific topics and presents material in a concise, thorough manner.

◼ SOME DISTINCTIVE FEATURES STUDENTS LIKE

Understanding Organizational Behavior offers a number of distinctive, time-tested, and interesting features for students, as well as new and innovative features. Each chapter begins with a clear statement of learning objectives to provide students with expectations about what is to come. Graphics and tables facilitate students' grasp of the topical material and involve students actively in the learning process.

Examples from diverse organizations (multinational, regional, nonprofit, public) and industries (manufacturing, service, defense) are included. These examples are integrated throughout the text. A unique feature of the book is its focus on the four organizations mentioned earlier. These represent many different types of organizations—large and small, for-profit and not-for-profit, product and service oriented. The purpose of this approach is to provide a sense of continuity and depth not achieved in single examples.

STUDY AIDS

To help students learn, understand, and apply the material in *Understanding Organizational Behavior,* the third edition provides unique and comprehensive study tools.

Web Site (http://www.thomsonedu.com/management/nelson-quick) A Web site complements the text, providing key terms, interactive quizzes, and other text-related information.

ThomsonNOW (http://www.thomsonedu.com/thomsonnow) This powerful and fully integrated online teaching and learning system provides instructors with flexibility and control, saves valuable time, and improves outcomes. Students benefit by having choices in the way they learn through a unique personalized learning path. This unique product includes:

> Homework, assignable and automatically graded
> Integrated eBook
> Personalized Learning Paths
> Interactive Course Assignments
> Assessment Options including AACSB learning standards achievement reporting
> Test Delivery
> Course Management Tools, including Grade Book
> WebCT & Blackboard Integration

SOME DISTINCTIVE FEATURES INSTRUCTORS WELCOME

Professors have demanding jobs. They should expect textbook authors and publishers to provide them with the support they need to do an excellent job for students. Among their expectations should be a well-integrated, complete ancillary package. *Understanding Organizational Behavior* has that package.

ANCILLARY PACKAGE

A comprehensive set of ancillaries supports the basic text: an instructor's resource manual with video guide, a test bank, ExamView (computerized testing software), PowerPoint® slides, a product support Web site, and a video program. The videos include a variety of short vignettes about real companies with which your students may already be familiar. Using video in the classroom will enhance the text presentation and reinforce its themes, adding continuity and integration to the overall understanding of organizational behavior.

Instructor's Manual with Video Guide *(available electronically on the Instructor's Resource CD-ROM and on the Product Support Web site)* The instructor's manual with video guide for *Understanding Organizational Behavior* was prepared by David A. Foote (Middle Tennessee State University) and BJ Parker. Each chapter contains the following information:

> Chapter scan—a brief overview of the chapter.

> Suggested learning objectives that are presented in the textbook.

> Key terms—a list of key terms from the chapter.

> The chapter summarized—an extended outline with narratives under each major point to flesh out the discussion and offer alternative examples and issues to bring forward. The extended outlines are several pages long and incorporate many teaching suggestions.

> Assignment materials, including review questions and discussion and communication questions.

> Answer guidelines for assignment materials—detailed responses to the review questions, discussion and communication questions, and "Think Critically" ethics questions, with suggestions for keeping discussion on track in the classroom.

> Challenges—suggested answers for the Challenges.

> Experiential exercises—a brief description of each exercise as well as a detailed summary of anticipated results. Discussion questions are provided with selected experiential exercises.

> Video cases are included for select chapters with accompanying video segments.

Test Bank *(available electronically on the Instructor's Resource CD-ROM)* The test bank, prepared by Jon G. Kalinowski (Minnesota State University, Mankato), has been thoroughly revised for this edition. The test bank contains more than 1,000 multiple-choice, true/false, matching, and essay questions. Each question has been coded according to learning objective, AACSB learning assessments, level of difficulty, and type.

ExamView *(available electronically on the Instructor's Resource CD-ROM)* This supplement contains all of the questions in the printed test bank. This program is an easy-to-use test creation software compatible with Microsoft Windows. Instructors can add or edit questions, instructions, and answers, and select questions by previewing them on the screen, selecting them randomly, or selecting them by number. Instructors can also create and administer quizzes online, whether over the Internet, a local area network (LAN), or a wide area network (WAN).

PowerPoint® Slides *(available electronically on the Instructor's Resource CD-ROM and on the Product Support Web site)* Ram Subramanian, Montclair State University, has updated more than 250 PowerPoint® slides for this text. These slides feature figures from the text, lecture outlines, and innovative adaptations to enhance the classroom presentation.

Instructor's Resource CD-ROM *(ISBN: 0-324-53693-3)* Key instructor ancillaries (instructor's manual, test bank, ExamView, and PowerPoint® slides) are provided on CD-ROM, giving instructors the ultimate tool for customizing lectures and presentations.

Web Site (http://www.thomsonedu.com/management/nelson-quick) *Understanding Organizational Behavior* has its own product support Web site. The full PowerPoint® presentation is available for you to download. The instructor's manual and video guide are also available for download. Web quizzing for students is available.

Video Program (ISBN: 0-324-53695-X) An extensive updated video program has been developed for use with *Understanding Organizational Behavior*. Video segments have been selected to support the themes of the book and to deepen students' understanding of the organizational behavior concepts presented throughout the text. Information on using the videos can be found in the instructor's manual.

◪ OUR REVIEWERS ARE APPRECIATED

We would like to thank our professional peers and colleagues who reviewed the first, second, and third editions and drafts of the manuscript to evaluate scholarly accuracy, writing style, and pedagogy. The many changes we made are based on their suggestions. We gratefully acknowledge the help of the following individuals:

David Adams, Manhattanville College
Terry R. Adler, New Mexico State University
Clarence Anderson, Walla Walla College
Carolyn Ashe, University of Houston—Downtown
Talya Bauer, Portland State University
Joy Benson, University of Illinois—Springfield
Constant D. Beugré, Kent State University, Tuscarawas Campus
Allan Bird, University of Missouri—St. Louis
Deborah Ramirez Bishop, Saginaw Valley State University
William R. Blackerby, Siena Heights University
Donna M. Bogle, Community College of Beaver County
Katharine A. Bohley, University of Indianapolis
Cindy Brown, South Plains College
Gilad Chen, University of Maryland
Beth Chung, San Diego State University
Jeanette A. Davy, Wright State University
David Drehmer, DePaul University
Sally Dresdow, University of Wisconsin—Green Bay
David A. Foote, Middle Tennessee State University
Jackie Gilbert, Middle Tennessee State University
Robert D. Goddard III, Appalachian State University
Andra Gumbus, Sacred Heart University
Nell Tabor Hartley, Robert Morris College
Fred Hughes, Faulkner University
Dong I. Jung, San Diego State University
John W. Lewis III, Boston College
John Mathieu, University of Connecticut
Jalane M. Meloun, Kent State University
Charlie Nagelschmidt, Champlain College
Dorothy Perrin Moore, The Citadel

William D. Spangler, SUNY—Binghamton
Charlotte Sutton, Auburn University
William H. Turnley, Kansas State University
Kate Walsh, Cornell University
Kathleen Wilch, Georgia Southwestern State University

▰ ACKNOWLEDGEMENTS

The third edition of *Understanding Organizational Behavior* represents a true team effort, and we are fortunate to work among a team of excellent professionals. Michele Rhoades provided much appreciated leadership as our editor. Mardell Glinski Schultz directed the early stages of the revision with ease and good humor, and then Erin Berger joined the team in a seamless transition and kept us right on track. Malvine Litten of LEAP Publishing Services took us through the polishing and delivery phases with great expertise and professionalism. Janaki Gooty of SUNY—Binghamton was an invaluable partner in the third edition, taking key roles in incorporating research on emotions and trust, as well as providing valuable updates on all chapters. Her voice and expertise come through clearly in this edition. Faye Cocchiara of Arkansas State University was wonderful in reviewing the most recent research and literature for many of the topics in the book, as well as ensuring the timeliness and accuracy of the information contained in the chapters. Her own research on diversity in the workplace along with her sensitivity to the issues of organizational culture and globalization enriched the perspectives we have on these important issues in organizational life and the workplace.

We are fortunate to have several colleagues who have made helpful contributions and supported our development through all three editions of the textbook: Mike Hitt of Texas A&M University; Lisa Kennedy of Baylor College of Medicine; Raj Basu, Robert Dooley, Ken Eastman, and Mark Gavin, all of Oklahoma State University; Bret Simmons of University of Nevada, Reno; Thomas A. Wright of Kansas State University; and David Gray, Dave Mack, Ken Price, and Jim Lavelle, all of the University of Texas at Arlington. Joanne H. Gavin of Marist College continues to be an important voice on issues of ethics, personal integrity, and moral reasoning related to ethical dilemmas.

Our families and friends have encouraged us throughout the development of the book. They have provided us with emotional support and examples for the book and have graciously allowed us the time to do the book justice. We are truly grateful for their support.

This book has been a labor of love for both of us. It has made us better teachers and also better learners. We hope it does the same for you.

Debra L. Nelson
James Campbell Quick

DEBRA L. NELSON

Dr. Debra L. Nelson is The CBA Associates Professor of Business Administration and Professor of Management at Oklahoma State University. She received her Ph.D. from the University of Texas at Arlington, where she was the recipient of the R. D. Irwin Dissertation Fellowship Award. Dr. Nelson is the author of over 70 journal articles focusing on organizational stress management, gender differences at work, and positive organizational behavior. Her research has been published in the *Academy of Management Executive, Academy of Management Journal, Academy of Management Review, MIS Quarterly, Organizational Dynamics, Journal of Organizational Behavior,* and other journals. In addition, she is coauthor/coeditor of several books, including *Positive Organizational Behavior* (Sage, 2007), *Organizational Behavior: Foundations, Realities, and Challenges* (5th ed., South-Western/Thomson Learning, 2006), *Gender, Work Stress and Health* (American Psychological Association, 2002), *Advancing Women in Management* (Blackwell, 2002), and *Preventive Stress Management in Organizations* (American Psychological Association, 1997). Dr. Nelson has also served as a consultant to several organizations including AT&T, American Fidelity Assurance, Sonic, State Farm Insurance Companies, and Southwestern Bell. She has presented leadership and preventive stress management seminars in a host of organizations, including Blue Cross/Blue Shield, Conoco, Oklahoma Gas and Electric, Oklahoma Natural Gas, and Preview Network Systems. She was honored with the Regents' Distinguished Research Award, the Greiner Graduate Teaching Award, the Chandler-Frates and Reitz Graduate Teaching Award, the Regents' Distinguished Teaching Award, and the Burlington Northern Faculty Achievement Award at OSU. Dr. Nelson also serves on the editorial review boards of the *Journal of Organizational Behavior and Leadership* and the *Journal of Leadership and Organization Studies.*

JAMES CAMPBELL QUICK

Dr. James Campbell (Jim) Quick is a John and Judy Goolsby Distinguished Professor at the University of Texas at Arlington and Visiting Professor, Lancaster University Management School, United Kingdom. He earned an A.B. with Honors from Colgate University, where he was a George Cobb Fellow and awarded a Harvard Business School Association Internship. He earned an M.B.A. and a Ph.D. at the University of Houston. He completed post-graduate courses in behavioral medicine (Harvard Medical School) and combat stress (University of Texas Health Science Center at San Antonio).

Dr. Quick is a Fellow of the Society for Industrial and Organizational Psychology, the American Psychological Association, the American

Psychological Society, and the American Institute of Stress. He was awarded a Presidential Citation by the American Psychological Association in 2001 and awarded the prestigious Harry and Miriam Levinson Award by the American Psychological Foundation in 2002.

Dr. Quick framed preventive stress management with his brother (Jonathan D. Quick, MD, MPH), a term now included in the *APA Dictionary of Psychology* (2007). He has received over $300,000 in funded support for research, scholarship, and intellectual contributions from the Society for Human Resource Management, Hospital Corporation of America, the state of Texas, and the American Psychological Association. His articles have been published in leading journals such as the *Academy of Management Journal, Academy of Management Review,* and *Journal of Management, Journal of Organizational Behavior, Air University Review, Stress Medicine,* and the *Journal of Medical Education.* He received the 1990 Distinguished Professional Publication Award for Corporate Warfare: Preventing Combat Stress and Battle Fatigue, coauthored with Debra L. Nelson and his brother for the American Management Association's *Organizational Dynamics.*

He is coauthor of *Preventive Stress Management in Organizations* (American Psychological Association, 1997), originally published in 1984 and released as *Unternehmen ohne Stress* in German. He is coauthor of *Managing Executive Health* (Cambridge University Press, 2007), released in seven languages other than English (Portuguese, Spanish, Russian, Greek, Chinese, Korean, and Thai), and *Stress and Challenge at the Top: The Paradox of the Successful Executive* (John Wiley & Sons, 1990). He is coeditor of the *Handbook of Occupational Health Psychology* (APA, 2002), *The New Organizational Reality: Downsizing, Restructuring, and Revitalization* (APA, 1998), *Stress and Well-Being at Work* (APA, 1992), and *Work Stress: Health Care Systems in the Workplace* (Praeger Scientific, 1987), for which he received the 1987 Distinguished Service Award from the UTA College of Business. He is a member of Beta Gamma Sigma and Phi Beta Delta honor societies and the Great Southwest Rotary Club, where he is a Paul Harris Fellow.

Dr. Quick was the American Psychological Association's stress expert to the National Academy of Sciences on National Health Objectives for the Year 2000. Dr. Quick was a scientific exchange delegate to the People's Republic of China. Dr. Quick was recognized with the Texas Volunteer Recognition Award (American Heart Association, 1985), a listing in Who's Who in the World, 7th Edition (1984–85), The Maroon Citation (Colgate University Alumni Corporation, 1993), and three Minnie Stevens Piper Professorship Award nominations (1995/2001/2007). He is a Main Panel Member for the Research Assessment Exercise 2008 (RAE2008) in the United Kingdom.

Colonel Quick, U.S. Air Force (Retired), was the Senior Individual Mobilization Augmentee at the San Antonio Air Logistics Center (AFMC), Kelly AFB, Texas, in his last assignment. He was Distinguished Visiting Professor of Psychology, 59th Medical Wing (1999). His awards and decorations include The Legion of Merit, Meritorious Service Medal, and National Defense Service Medal with Bronze Star.

He is married to the former Sheri Grimes Schember. Both are members of the Chancellor's Council of the University of Texas System and the President's Club of Colgate University.

To our students, who challenge us to be better than we are, who keep us in touch with reality, and who are the foundation of our careers.

1

Organizational Behavior and Opportunity

LEARNING OBJECTIVES

After reading this chapter, you should be able to do the following:

: 1. Define *organizational behavior.*

: 2. Identify four action steps for responding positively in times of change.

: 3. Describe the formal and informal elements of an organization.

: 4. Recognize the opportunities that change creates for organizational behavior.

: 5. Demonstrate the value of objective knowledge and skill development in the study of organizational behavior.

THINKING AHEAD :: Cisco Systems

Opportunity Calls for Cisco

Cisco Systems got a rude wake-up call in 2001 when its revenues were headed down and its top customers were threatening to revolt and bolt. Cisco's wake-up call came from some of the biggest telecom companies in the world, which included Level 3 Communications and AT&T. The call came in April 2001 when several Cisco executives were summoned to a conference on the Colorado campus of Level 3 Communications, the fiber-optic network operator. In addition to elite engineers from Level 3 Communications were their elite peers from AT&T and a half-dozen other big-time telecom players. These big telecom companies were all major buyers of Cisco networking gear, and their message was very clear—it jarred the Cisco executives. The engineers reported significant technological problems with Cisco routers. The telecom giants gave Cisco a choice: Either fix it or risk losing some of your biggest customers.[1]

The message from the telecom engineers was that the software on the Cisco routers that linked telecom networks stank. The software crashed parts of the networks as often as once a month, sometimes for as long as 30 minutes. Within the telecom industry, the acceptable crash standard was more like "a few minutes" about "once a year." Cisco's software was way off standard and therefore performing at a totally unacceptable level. This confrontation with Cisco by the major telecom companies came during a difficult time in the industry. For Cisco, spring 2001 was a rather dark time. The Internet and technology bubbles were bursting, taking Cisco off its pinnacle as the most valuable corporation on earth, worth more than half a trillion dollars.

Cisco was able to see opportunity in the wake-up call. Mighty Cisco was a proud young company built on the technological excellence and expertise of its computer science and engineering origins. Cisco saw, as did its rivals, a goldmine in Internet-based networks. In the telecom industry, phone companies had been accumulating multiple networks over several decades. One of these networks carried traditional phone traffic, another was connecting corporate headquarters with regional offices, while still another was carrying secure transmissions of data, voice, and video information. The phone companies were operating through traditional networks, but Internet protocol (IP) networks were vastly cheaper to build and operate. Cisco, which was founded on the Blue Box router that allowed corporations to connect their various computers, was ideally positioned to take advantage of the phone companies' transition to a new breed of phone company—the Internet service provider.

⚑ HUMAN BEHAVIOR IN ORGANIZATIONS

Human behavior in organizations is complex and often difficult to understand. Organizations have been described as clockworks in which human behavior is logical and rational, but they often seem like snake pits to those who work in them.[2] The clockwork metaphor reflects an orderly, idealized view of organizational behavior devoid of conflict or dilemma because all the working parts (the people) mesh smoothly. The snake pit metaphor conveys the daily conflict, distress, and struggle in organizations. Each metaphor reflects reality from a different perspective—the organization's versus the individual's point of view. These metaphors reflect the complexity of human behavior, the dark side of which is seen in cases of air rage and workplace violence. On the positive side, the Gallup

: 1. Define *organizational behavior*.

opportunities
Favorable times or chances for progress and advancement.

change
The transformation or modification of an organization and/or its stakeholders.

challenge
The call to competition, contest, or battle.

organizational behavior
The study of individual behavior and group dynamics in organizations.

Organization's Marcus Buckingham suggests that people's psychological makeup is at the heart of the emotional economy.[3]

This chapter is an introduction to organizational behavior. The first section provides an overview of human behavior in organizations, its interdisciplinary origins, and behavior in times of change. The second section presents an organizational context within which behavior occurs and briefly introduces the four focus companies used selectively in the book. The third section highlights the *opportunities* that exist in times of *change* and *challenge* for people at work.[4] The fourth section addresses the ways people learn about organizational behavior and explains how the text's pedagogical features relate to the various ways of learning. The final section of the chapter presents the plan for the book.

Organizational behavior is individual behavior and group dynamics in organizations. The study of organizational behavior is primarily concerned with the psychosocial, interpersonal, and behavioral dynamics in organizations. However, organizational variables that affect human behavior at work are also relevant to the study of organizational behavior. These organizational variables include jobs, the design of work, communication, performance appraisal, organizational design, and organizational structure. Therefore, although individual behavior and group dynamics are the primary concerns in the study of organizational behavior, organizational variables are also important.

This section briefly contrasts two perspectives for understanding human behavior, the external and the internal perspectives. The section then discusses six scientific disciplines from which the study of organizational behavior has emerged and concludes with a discussion of behavior in times of change.

■ UNDERSTANDING HUMAN BEHAVIOR

The vast majority of theories and models of human behavior fall into one of two basic categories. One category has an internal perspective, and the other has an external perspective. The internal perspective considers factors inside the person to understand behavior. This view is psychodynamically oriented. People who subscribe to this view understand human behavior in terms of the thoughts, feelings, past experiences, and needs of the individual. The internal perspective explains people's actions and behavior in terms of their history and personal value systems. The internal processes of thinking, feeling, perceiving, and judging lead people to act in specific ways. The internal perspective has given rise to a wide range of motivational and leadership theories. This perspective implies that people are best understood from the inside and that people's behavior is best interpreted after understanding their thoughts and feelings.

The other category of theories and models of human behavior takes an external perspective. This perspective focuses on factors outside the person to understand behavior. People who subscribe to this view understand human behavior in terms of external events, consequences of behavior, and the environmental forces to which a person is subject. From the external perspective, a person's history, feelings, thoughts, and personal value systems are not very important in interpreting actions and behavior. This perspective has given rise to an alternative set of motivational and leadership theories, which are covered in Chapters 5 and 12 of the text. The external perspective implies that a person's behavior is best understood by examining the surrounding external events and environmental forces.

The internal and external perspectives offer alternative explanations for human behavior. For example, the internal perspective might say Mary is an outstanding employee because she has a high need for achievement, whereas the external perspective might say Mary is an outstanding employee because she is paid extremely well for her work. Kurt Lewin captured both perspectives in saying that behavior is a function of both the person and the environment.[5]

■ INTERDISCIPLINARY INFLUENCES

Organizational behavior is a blended discipline that has grown out of contributions from numerous earlier fields of study, only one of which is the psychological discipline from which Kurt Lewin came. These interdisciplinary influences are the roots for what is increasingly recognized as the independent discipline of organizational behavior. The sciences of psychology, sociology, engineering, anthropology, management, and medicine have each contributed to our understanding of human behavior in organizations.

Psychology is the science of human behavior and dates back to the closing decades of the nineteenth century. Psychology traces its own origins to philosophy and the science of physiology. One of the most prominent early psychologists, William James, actually held a degree in medicine (M.D.). Since its origin, psychology has itself become differentiated into a number of specialized fields, such as clinical, experimental, military, organizational, and social psychology. Organizational psychology includes the study of many topics, such as work motivation, which are also covered by organizational behavior.[6] Early psychological research for the American military during World War I had later implications for sophisticated personnel selection methods used by corporations such as Johnson & Johnson, Valero Energy, and Chaparral Steel.[7]

psychology
The science of human behavior.

Sociology, the science of society, has made important contributions to knowledge about group and intergroup dynamics in the study of organizational behavior. Because sociology takes society rather than the individual as its point of departure, the sociologist is concerned with the variety of roles within a society or culture, the norms and standards of behavior in groups, and the consequences of compliant and deviant behavior. For example, the concept of *role set*, a key contribution to role theory in 1957 by Robert Merton, was used by a team of Harvard educators to study the school superintendent role in Massachusetts.[8] More recently, the role set concept has been used to study the effects of codes of ethics in organizations.[9]

sociology
The science of society.

Engineering is the applied science of energy and matter. Engineering has made important contributions to our understanding of the design of work. By taking basic engineering ideas and applying them to human behavior at work, Frederick Taylor had a profound influence on the early years of the study of organizational behavior.[10] Taylor's engineering background led him to place special emphasis on human productivity and efficiency in work behavior. His notions of performance standards and differential piece-rate systems have had lasting impact. Taylor's original ideas are embedded in organizational goal-setting programs, such as those at Black & Decker, IBM, and Weyerhaeuser.[11]

engineering
The applied science of energy and matter.

Anthropology is the science of human learned behavior and is especially important to understanding organizational culture. Cultural anthropology focuses on the origins of culture and the patterns of behavior as culture is communicated symbolically. Research in this tradition has examined the effects of efficient

anthropology
The science of the learned behavior of human beings.

cultures on organization performance[12] and how pathological personalities may lead to dysfunctional organizational cultures.[13] Schwartz used a psychodynamic, anthropological mode of inquiry in exploring corporate decay at General Motors and NASA.[14]

Management, originally called administrative science, is a discipline concerned with the study of overseeing activities and supervising people in organizations. It emphasizes the design, implementation, and management of various administrative and organizational systems. March and Simon take the human organization as their point of departure and concern themselves with the administrative practices that will enhance the effectiveness of the system.[15] Management is the first discipline to take the modern corporation as the unit of analysis, and this viewpoint distinguishes the discipline's contribution to the study of organizational behavior.

Medicine is the applied science of healing or treatment of diseases to enhance an individual's health and well-being. Medicine has long-standing concern for both physical and psychological health, as well as for industrial mental health.[16] More recently, as the war against acute diseases is being won, medical attention has shifted to more chronic diseases, such as hypertension, and to occupational health and well-being.[17] Individual behavior and lifestyle patterns play important roles in treating chronic diseases.[18] These trends have contributed to the growth of corporate wellness programs, such as Johnson & Johnson's "Live for Life Program." The surge in health care costs over the past two decades has contributed to increased organizational concern with medicine and health care in the workplace.[19]

management
The study of overseeing activities and supervising people in organizations.

medicine
The applied science of healing or treatment of diseases to enhance an individual's health and well-being.

◀◀**think critically**▶▶

Which disciplines are important for understanding the moral and ethical issues for organizations and management?

■ BEHAVIOR IN TIMES OF CHANGE

2. Identify four action steps for responding positively in times of change.

Early research with individuals, groups, and organizations in the midst of environmental change found that change is often experienced as a threat which leads to a reliance on well-learned and dominant forms of behavior.[20] That is, in the midst of change, people often become rigid and reactive, rather than open and responsive. This may be useful if the change is neither dramatic nor rapid because we are often effective at coping with incremental change. However, if significant change occurs, then rigid and well-learned behavior may be counterproductive. The challenge for Cisco System's people in the context of the opening case is to stay open, responsive, and flexible to learn from the opportunity. Big changes disrupt people's habitual behavior and require learning if they are to be managed successfully. Eric Brown of ProLine International offers some sage words of advice to see the opportunity in change.[21] He recommends adapting to change by seeing it as positive and accepting challenge as good rather than bad. His action steps for doing this are to (1) have a positive attitude, (2) ask questions, (3) listen to the answers, and (4) be committed to success.

However, success is never guaranteed, and change sometimes results in failure. If this happens, do not despair. Some of the world's greatest leaders, such as

Winston Churchill, experienced dramatic failure before achieving lasting success. The key to their eventual success was their capacity to learn from the failure and to respond positively to the opportunities presented to them. One venture capitalist with whom the authors have worked likes to ask those seeking to build a business to tell him about their greatest failure. What the venture capitalist is looking for in the answer is how the executive responded to the failure and what he or she learned from the experience. While change carries with it the risk of failure as well as the opportunity for success, it is often how we behave in the midst of change that determines which outcome results.

THE ORGANIZATIONAL CONTEXT

A complete understanding of organizational behavior requires both an understanding of human behavior and an understanding of the organizational context within which human behavior is acted out. The organizational context is the specific setting within which organizational behavior is enacted. This section discusses several aspects of this organizational context and includes specific organizational examples. First, the formal and informal organization is discussed. Next, four focus companies are presented as contemporary examples, which are drawn on throughout the text.

: 3. Describe the formal and informal elements of an organization.

THE FORMAL AND INFORMAL ORGANIZATION

The *formal organization* is the official, legitimate, and most visible part that enables people to think of organizations in logical and rational ways. The snake pit organizational metaphor mentioned earlier has its roots in the study and examination of the *informal organization*, which is unofficial and less visible. The informal elements were first fully appreciated as a result of the *Hawthorne studies*, conducted during the 1920s and 1930s. It was during the interview study, the third of the four Hawthorne studies, that the researchers began to develop a fuller appreciation for the informal elements of the Hawthorne Works as an organization.[22] The formal and informal elements of the organization are depicted in Figure 1.1.

Potential conflict between the formal and informal organization makes an understanding of both important. Conflicts between these two elements erupted in many organizations during the early years of the twentieth century and were embodied in the union–management strife of that era. The conflicts escalated into violence in a number of cases. For example, during the 1920s, supervisors at the Homestead Works of U.S. Steel were issued pistols and boxes of ammunition "just in case" it became necessary to shoot unruly, dangerous steelworkers. Not all organizations are characterized by such potential formal–informal, management–labor conflict. During the same era, Eastman Kodak was very progressive. The company helped with financial backing for employees' neighborhood communities, such as Meadowbrook in Rochester, New York. Kodak's concern for employees and attention to informal issues made unions unnecessary within the company.

The informal elements of the organization are frequent points of diagnostic and intervention activities in organization development, though the formal elements must always be considered as well because they provide the context for the informal.[23] These informal elements are important because people's feelings,

formal organization
The official, legitimate, and most visible part of the system.

informal organization
The unofficial and less visible part of the system.

Hawthorne studies
Studies conducted during the 1920s and 1930s that discovered the existence of the informal organization.

FIGURE 1.1

Formal and Informal Organization

Formal organization (overt)
Goals and objectives
Policies and procedures
Job descriptions
Financial resources
Authority structure
Communication channels
Products and services

Social surface

Informal organization (covert)
Beliefs and assumptions
Perceptions and attitudes
Values
Feelings, such as fear,
    joy, anger, trust, and hope
Group norms
Informal leaders

thoughts, and attitudes about their work do make a difference in their behavior and performance. Individual behavior plays out in the context of the formal and informal elements of the system, becoming organizational behavior. The uncovering of the informal elements in an organization was one of the major discoveries of the Hawthorne studies.

FOUR FOCUS ORGANIZATIONS

Organizational behavior always occurs in the context of a specific organizational setting. Most attempts at explaining or predicting organizational behavior rely heavily on factors within the organization and give less weight to external environmental considerations.[24] Students can benefit from being sensitive to the industrial context of organizations and from developing an appreciation for each organization as a whole.[25] In this vein, four organizations are featured in the Thinking Ahead and Looking Back sections of the chapters. Cisco Systems is illustrated in this chapter. We challenge you in each chapter to anticipate what will be in the Looking Back feature once you read Thinking Ahead.

The U.S. economy is the largest in the world, with a gross domestic product of more than $12.4 trillion in 2005. Of the major sectors of the economy, the largest sectors are service (44 percent), product manufacture of nondurable goods (21 percent), and durable goods (8 percent). Taken together, the production of products and the delivery of services account for 73 percent of the U.S. economy. Government and fixed investments account for the remaining 27 percent. Large and small organizations operate in each sector of the economy.

The private sectors are an important part of the economy. The manufacturing sector includes the production of basic materials, such as steel, and the production of finished products, such as automobiles and electronic equipment. The service sector includes transportation, financial services, insurance, and retail sales. The government sectors, which provide essential infrastructure, and nonprofit organizations are also important to our collective well-being because they meet needs not addressed in these economic sectors. We have chosen organizations that can reflect the manufacturing, service, retail, and nonprofit sectors of business. These four organizations are Cisco Systems, Pixar Animation Studios, Virgin Group, Ltd., and Whole Foods Market, Inc. Each of these four organizations makes an important and unique contribution to the manufacturing or service sectors of the national economy and/or to our national well-being. These organizations are not alone, however. Hundreds of other small, medium, and large organizations are making valuable and significant contributions to the economic health and human welfare of the United States. Brief examples from many organizations are used throughout the book. We hope that by better understanding these organizations, you may have a greater appreciation for your own organization and others within the diverse world of private business enterprises and nonprofit organizations.

CISCO SYSTEMS

Which is more impressive: Cisco Systems' 2004 sales of $22 billion or Cisco's 2004 cash and investments balance of $19.3 billion?[26] While the Internet and technology sector bubbles destroyed many companies and humbled others, Cisco's bread-and-butter business of selling the routers and switches that power the Internet continues to grow. In addition, Cisco is actively working to expand the worldwide online market from its corporate headquarters in San Jose, California. In 150 countries like Afghanistan, 10,000 Cisco academies are training more than 400,000 future network professionals to help their communities enter the Information Age. Networks are at the heart of Cisco's business and are essential for business, education, government, and home communications.

Cisco has had deep roots in technology from its founding in 1984 by a group of computer scientists from Stanford University. Cisco has grown to 36,000 employees worldwide, and its engineers have factored prominently in the development of Internet protocol (IP)-based networking technologies. We take many of these networking technologies for granted today. The firm currently pours 18 percent of annual revenues back into research and development, an investment it hopes will pay dividends in the future. Cisco operates on twin core values of customer focus and corporate citizenship, which are expressed through global involvement in education, community, and philanthropic efforts.

PIXAR ANIMATION STUDIOS

Combine cutting-edge technology and old-fashioned storytelling and what do you get? In the case of Pixar Animation Studios, you get movies that kids and parents love. With a shelf full of awards and a string of blockbusters including *Monsters, Inc.* and *Finding Nemo* as well as *Cars,* Pixar is the world's leading digital animation studio.

Founded in 1986, Pixar spent more than nine years bringing its first full-length film, *Toy Story,* to the screen. While best known for its high-tech animation tools and flashy CEO Steve Jobs, Pixar's culture is built solidly around great storytelling. At its eclectic California campus, 700 employees revise and refine the stories and characters that eventually become Pixar's movies. The formula has paid off handsomely for Pixar and its former release partner, Walt Disney Pictures; today, the firm has annual revenues of over $273 million.[27] But as the cutting-edge software tools it has developed become more common in the industry, how will Pixar keep its edge? Can it stay competitive by releasing only one movie every 18 months as it does now, especially if one of those releases is not a blockbuster? Will its renewed relationship with Disney help keep Pixar's creative juices flowing?

VIRGIN GROUP, LTD.

The Virgin Group may well be one of the most recognizable brands in the world. Founded in 1970 by Richard Branson, then a 17-year-old boarding school dropout, Virgin began as a mail-order record company aptly named "Virgin" because of Branson's lack of experience at the time. More than 30 years later, the Virgin Group can best be described as a conglomerate of consumer products and services selling everything from air and rail travel to soft drinks, though its biggest breadwinners are by far its travel operations led by Virgin Atlantic.

Knighted in 2000, Sir Richard Branson remains the chairman, president, and CEO of the Virgin Group family of companies. Though his holdings are mostly private, Sir Richard's net worth was estimated at $2.6 billion in 2003. Virgin's growth plan can hardly be described as deliberate or strategic. Branson had one simple goal— "to be a disrupter, taking on industries that either charged too much (music), held consumers hostage (cell phone companies), or treated consumers badly and bored them to tears (airlines)." By 2003, Branson had amassed an empire of more than 200 entertainment, media, and travel companies worldwide; operations in Africa, Asia, Australia, Europe, and North America; and revenues in excess of $5 billion.[28]

WHOLE FOODS MARKET, INC.

The world's number one natural foods chain, Whole Foods Market, operates more than 140 stores in 25 states, Washington, D.C., and Canada. Whole Foods has pioneered the supermarket concept in health foods retailing, offering more than 1,200 items in four lines of private label products. Led by John Mackey in 1980 with a $10,000 loan from his father, Whole Foods Market was born as a meager 11,000-square-foot supermarket in Austin, Texas. Capitalizing on the increased health consciousness among consumers coupled with their desire for natural and organic foods, Whole Foods became an instant success and expanded its operations to Houston, Dallas, and Louisiana in the mid- to late-1980s.

By 1992, the chain debuted its first private label products and went public with 12 stores. Soon, every competitor in the fragmented health foods industry became a potential acquisition for Whole Foods. Its biggest acquisition came in 1996 with the purchase of Fresh Fields' 22 stores on the East Coast and Chicago. By 2003, Whole Foods had crossed the border into Canada, opening its first foreign store in downtown Toronto. Whole Foods Market has since expanded into related businesses such as nutritional supplements and now sells online through a co-branding operation with Gaiam.com. Based in Austin, Texas, the chain has over 24,000 employees and reported revenues for fiscal 2004 of over $3.8 billion, the best year in its 24-year history.[29]

CHANGE CREATES OPPORTUNITIES

Change creates opportunities and risks, as mentioned earlier in the chapter. Global competition is a leading force driving change at work. Competition in the United States and world economies has increased significantly during the past couple of decades, especially in industries such as banking, finance, and air transportation. Corporate competition creates performance and cost pressures, which have a ripple effect on people and their behavior at work. While one risk for employees is the marginalization of part-time professionals, good management practice can ensure the integration of these part-time professionals.[30] The competition may lead to downsizing and restructuring, yet it provides the opportunity for revitalization as well.[31] Further, small companies are not necessarily the losers in this competitive environment. Scientech, a small power and energy company, found it had to enhance its managerial talent and service quality to meet the challenges of growth and big-company competitors. Product and service quality is one tool that can help companies become winners in a competitive environment. Problem-solving skills are another tool used by IBM, Control Data Services, Inc., Northwest Airlines, and Southwest Airlines to help achieve high-quality products and services.

Too much change leads to chaos; too little change leads to stagnation. What are your perceptions of change? What do you think is the perception of the Cisco Systems people given the challenge they faced as described in the opening case? In a different example, Xerox CEO, Anne Mulcahy, aims to drive changes in the work culture so that problems are more quickly identified and solved.[32]

: 4. Recognize the opportunities that change creates for organizational behavior.

CHALLENGES FOR MANAGERS RELATED TO CHANGE

Chapter 2 develops challenges for managers related to change in contemporary organizations: globalization, workforce diversity, and ethics and character. These are driving forces creating and shaping changes at work. Further, success in global competition requires organizations to be more responsive to ethnic, religious, and gender diversity as well as personal integrity in the workforce, in addition to responding positively to the competition in the international marketplace. Workforce demographic change and diversity are critical challenges in themselves for the study and management of organizational behavior.[33] The theories of motivation, leadership, and group behavior based on research in a workforce of one composition may not be applicable in a workforce of a very different composition.[34] This may be especially problematic if ethnic, gender, and/or religious differences lead to conflicts between leaders and followers in organizations. For example, the Russian military establishment has found ethnic and religious conflicts between the officers and enlisted corps a real impediment to unit cohesion and performance at times.

GLOBAL COMPETITION IN BUSINESS

Managers and executives in the United States face radical change in response to increased global competition. According to noted economist Lester Thurow, this competition is characterized by intense rivalry between the United States, Japan, and Europe in core industries.[35] Economic competition places pressure on all categories of employees to be productive and to add value to the firm.

CHALLENGE 1.1

Analyze Your Perceptions of a Change

Everyone perceives change differently. Think of a change situation you are currently experiencing. It can be any business, school-related, or personal experience that requires a significant change in your attitude or behavior. Rate your feelings about this change using the following scales. For instance, if you feel the change is more of a threat than an opportunity, you would circle 0, 2, or 4 on the first scale.

1. Threat	0	2	4	6	8	10	Opportunity
2. Holding on to the past	0	2	4	6	8	10	Reaching for the future
3. Immobilized	0	2	4	6	8	10	Activated
4. Rigid	0	2	4	6	8	10	Versatile
5. A loss	0	2	4	6	8	10	A gain
6. Victim of change	0	2	4	6	8	10	Agent of change
7. Reactive	0	2	4	6	8	10	Proactive
8. Focused on the past	0	2	4	6	8	10	Focused on the future
9. Separate from change	0	2	4	6	8	10	Involved with change
10. Confused	0	2	4	6	8	10	Clear

How positive are your perceptions of this change?

Source: H. Woodward and S. Buchholz, *Aftershock: Helping People through Corporate Change,* p. 15. Copyright © 1987, John Wiley & Sons, Inc. Reprinted by permission of John Wiley & Sons, Inc.

The uncertainty of unemployment resulting from corporate warfare and competition is an ongoing feature of organizational life for people in companies or industries that pursue cost-cutting strategies to achieve economic success. The global competition in the automotive industry among the Japanese, U.S., and European car companies embodies the intensity that can be expected in other industries in the future.

Some people feel that the future must be the focus in coming to grips with this international competition, whereas others believe we can deal with the future only by studying the past.[36] Global, economic, and organizational changes have dramatic effects on the study and management of organizational behavior. How positive were your perceptions of the change? Are you an optimist who sees opportunity, or a pessimist who sees threat?

■ CUSTOMER FOCUSED FOR HIGH QUALITY

Global competition has challenged organizations to become more customer focused, to meet changing product and service demands, and to exceed customers' expectations of high quality. Quality has the potential for giving organizations in viable industries a competitive edge in meeting international competition.

Quality became a rubric for products and services of high status. Total quality is defined in many ways.[37] Total quality management (TQM) is the total dedication to continuous improvement and to customers so that the customers' needs are met and their expectations exceeded. Quality is a customer-oriented philosophy of management with important implications for virtually all aspects of organizational behavior. Quality cannot be optimized, because customer needs and expectations are always changing. Quality is a cultural value embedded in highly successful organizations. Ford Motor Company's dramatic metamorphosis as an automotive leader is attributable to the decision to "make quality Job One" in all aspects of the design and manufacture of cars.

Quality improvement enhances the probability of organizational success in increasingly competitive industries. One study of 193 general medical hospitals examined seven TQM practices and found them positively related to the financial performance of the hospital.[38] Quality improvement is an enduring feature of an organization's culture and of the economic competition we face today. It leads to competitive advantage through customer responsiveness, results acceleration, and resource effectiveness.[39] The three key questions in evaluating quality improvement ideas for people at work are these: (1) Does the idea improve customer response? (2) Does the idea accelerate results? (3) Does the idea increase the effectiveness of resources? A "yes" answer means the idea should be implemented to improve quality.

Six Sigma is a philosophy for company-wide quality improvement developed by Motorola and popularized by General Electric. The Six Sigma program is characterized by its customer-driven approach, its emphasis on decision making based on quantitative data, and its priority on saving money.[40] It has evolved into a high-performance system to execute business strategy. Part of its quality program is a 12-step problem-solving method specifically designed to lead a Six Sigma "Black Belt" to significant improvement within a defined process. It tackles problems in four phases: (1) measure, (2) analyze, (3) improve, and (4) control. In addition, it demands that executives be aligned to the right objective and targets, quality improvement teams be mobilized for action, results be accelerated, and sustained improvement be monitored. Six Sigma is set up in a way that it can be applied to a range of problems and areas, from manufacturing settings to service work environments. One study compared Six Sigma to two other methods for quality improvement (specifically, Taguchi's methods and the Shainin system) and found it to be the most complete strategy of the three, with a strong emphasis on exploiting statistical modeling techniques.[41] Anne Mulcahy at Xerox is one chief executive who implemented Six Sigma as a productivity improvement tool.[42]

Six Sigma
A high-performance system to execute business strategy that is customer-driven, emphasizes quantitative decision making, and places a priority on saving money.

■ BEHAVIOR AND QUALITY AT WORK

Whereas total quality may draw on reliability engineering or just-in-time management, total quality improvement can be successful only when employees have the skills and authority to respond to customer needs.[43] Total quality has direct and important effects on the behavior of employees at all levels in the organization, not just on employees working directly with customers. Chief executives can advance total quality by engaging in participative management, being willing to change everything, focusing quality efforts on customer service (not cost cutting), including quality as a criterion in reward systems, improving the flow of information regarding quality improvement successes or failures, and being actively and personally involved in quality efforts. While serving as chairman of Motorola, George Fisher emphasized the behavioral attributes of leadership, cooperation, communication, and participation as important elements in the company's Six Sigma program.

Quality improvement continues to be important to our competitiveness. The U.S. Department of Commerce's sponsorship of an annual award in the name of Malcolm Baldrige, former secretary of commerce in the Reagan administration, recognizes companies excelling in quality improvement and management. The Malcolm Baldrige National Quality Award examination evaluates an organization in seven categories: leadership, information and analysis, strategic quality planning, human resource utilization, quality assurance of products and services, quality results, and customer satisfaction.

According to George H. W. Bush, "Quality management is not just a strategy. It must be a new style of working, even a new style of thinking. A dedication to quality and excellence is more than good business. It is a way of life, giving something back to society, offering your best to others."

Quality is one watchword for competitive success. Organizations that do not respond to customer needs find their customers choosing alternative product and service suppliers who are willing to exceed customer expectations. With this said, you should not conclude that total quality is a panacea for all organizations or that total quality guarantees unqualified success.

■ MANAGING ORGANIZATIONAL BEHAVIOR IN CHANGING TIMES

Over and above the challenge of quality improvement to meet international competition, managing organizational behavior during changing times is challenging for at least three reasons: (1) the increasing globalization of organizations' operating territory, (2) the increasing diversity of organizational workforces, and (3) the continuing demand for higher levels of moral and ethical behavior at work. In addition, technology and technological innovations may have an impact on people as we saw in the opening case with Cisco Systems. We see how the Internet helped Cisco leverage the opportunity and challenge it faced.

Each of these issues is explored in detail in Chapter 2 and highlighted throughout the text because they are intertwined in the contemporary practice of organizational behavior. For example, the issue of women in the workplace concerns workforce diversity and at the same time overlaps the globalization issue. Gender roles are often defined differently in various cultures, and sexual harassment is a frequent ethical problem for organizations in the United States, Europe, Israel, and South Africa. Human behavior is also impacted by technology, or vice versa. For example, process and technology innovations require attention to behavioral issues if they are to be successful. In one study of innovation in 47 German companies, organizational support and psychological safety were positively related to return on assets and goal achievement.[44] Therefore, students of organizational behavior appreciate and understand these important issues.

◄◄think critically►►

What are the most sensitive ethical issues facing your business, industry, or organization today? How would you go about addressing these issues?

LEARNING ABOUT ORGANIZATIONAL BEHAVIOR

Organizational behavior is based on scientific knowledge and applied practice. It involves the study of abstract ideas, such as valence and expectancy in motivation, as well as the study of concrete matters, such as observable behaviors and medical symptoms of distress at work. Therefore, learning about organizational behavior includes at least three activities, as shown in Figure 1.2. First, the science of organizational behavior requires the mastery of a certain body of *objective knowledge.* Objective knowledge results from research and scientific activities, as referenced in the many scientific references in each chapter. Second, the practice of organizational behavior requires *skill development* based on knowledge and an understanding of yourself in order to master the abilities essential to success. The Challenge features in each chapter help you to know yourself and apply what you are learning. Third, both objective knowledge and skill development must be applied in real world settings. This is illustrated in the opening and closing cases as well as many examples throughout the text.

Learning is challenging and fun because we are all different. Student diversity is best addressed in the learning process through more options for students and greater responsibility on the part of students as coproducers in the effort and fun of learning.[45] For those who are blind or have vision impairments, learning can be a special challenge. And, like these cases, agencies such as Canine Companions for Independence make important contributions. To gain a better understanding of yourself as a learner, so as to maximize your potential and develop strategies in specific learning environments, you need to evaluate the way you prefer to learn and process information. Challenge 1.2 offers a short, quick way of assessing your learning style. If you are a visual learner, then use charts, maps, PowerPoint slides, videos, the Internet, notes, or flash cards, and write things out for visual review. If you are an auditory learner, listen, take notes during lectures, and consider taping them so you can fill in gaps later; review your notes frequently; and recite key concepts out loud. If you are a tactile learner, trace words as you are saying them, write down facts several times, and make study sheets.

OBJECTIVE KNOWLEDGE

Objective knowledge, in any field of study, is developed through basic and applied research. Research in organizational behavior has continued since early research on scientific management. Acquiring objective knowledge requires the cognitive mastery of theories, conceptual models, and research findings. In this book, the objective knowledge in each chapter is reflected in the notes and references that support the text. Mastering the concepts and ideas that come from these notes enables you to intelligently discuss topics such as motivation, performance, leadership,[46] and executive stress.[47]

5. Demonstrate the value of objective knowledge and skill development in the study of organizational behavior.

objective knowledge
Knowledge that results from research and scientific activities.

skill development
The mastery of abilities essential to successful functioning in organizations.

FIGURE 1.2

Learning about Organizational Behavior

Learning Style Inventory

Directions: This 24-item survey is not timed. Answer each question as honestly as you can. Place a check on the appropriate line after each statement.

	OFTEN	SOMETIMES	SELDOM
5 1. Can remember more about a subject through the lecture method with information, explanations, and discussion.	✓		
5 2. Prefer information to be written on the chalkboard, with the use of visual aids and assigned readings.	✓		
5 3. Like to write things down or to take notes for visual review.	✓		
5 4. Prefer to use posters, models, or actual practice and some activities in class.	✓		
5 5. Require explanations of diagrams, graphs, or visual directions.	✓		
5 6. Enjoy working with my hands or making things.	✓		
3 7. Am skillful with and enjoy developing and making graphs and charts.		✓	
3 8. Can tell if sounds match when presented with pairs of sounds.		✓	
3 9. Remember best by writing things down several times.		✓	
5 10. Can understand and follow directions on maps.	✓		
3 11. Do better at academic subjects by listening to lectures and tapes.		✓	
3 12. Play with coins or keys in pockets.		✓	
5 13. Learn to spell better by repeating the word out loud than by writing the word on paper.	✓		
5 14. Can better understand a news development by reading about it in the paper than by listening to the radio.	✓		
3 15. Chew gum, smoke, or snack during studies.		✓	
3 16. Feel the best way to remember is to picture it in my head.		✓	
1 17. Learn spelling by "finger spelling" words.			✓
5 18. Would rather listen to a good lecture or speech than read about the same material in a textbook.	✓		
5 19. Am good at working and solving jigsaw puzzles and mazes.	✓		
3 20. Grip objects in hands during learning period.		✓	
3 21. Prefer listening to the news on the radio rather than reading about it in the newspaper.		✓	
5 22. Obtain information on an interesting subject by reading relevant materials.	✓		
5 23. Feel very comfortable touching others, hugging, hand-shaking, etc.	✓		
3 24. Follow oral directions better than written ones.		✓	

Scoring Procedures

Score 5 points for each OFTEN, 3 points for each SOMETIMES, and 1 point for each SELDOM.
Visual Preference Score 5 Points for questions 2 + 3 + 7 + 10 + 14 + 16 + 19 + 22 = __36__
Auditory Preference Score 5 Points for questions 1 + 5 + 8 + 11 + 13 + 18 + 21 + 24   = __34__
Tactile Preference Score 5 Points for questions 4 + 6 + 9 + 12 + 15 + 17 + 20 + 23 = __28__

Source: Adapted from J. N. Gardner and A. J. Jewler, *Your College Experience: Strategies for Success, Third Concise Edition* (Belmont, Calif.: Wadsworth/ ITP, 1998), pp. 62–63; E. Jensen, *Student Success Secrets,* 4th ed. (Hauppauge, N.Y.: Barron's, 1996), pp. 33–36.

We encourage instructors and students of organizational behavior to think critically about the objective knowledge in organizational behavior. Only by engaging in critical thinking can one question or challenge the results of specific research and responsibly consider how to apply research results in a particular work setting. Rote memorization does not enable the student to appreciate the complexity of specific theories or the interrelationships among concepts, ideas, and topics. Good critical thinking, in contrast, enables the student to identify inconsistencies and limitations in the current body of objective knowledge.

Critical thinking, based on knowledge and understanding of basic ideas, leads to inquisitive exploration and is a key to accepting the responsibility of coproducer in the learning process. A questioning, probing attitude is at the core of critical thinking. The student of organizational behavior should evolve into a critical consumer of knowledge related to organizational behavior—one who is able to intelligently question the latest research results and distinguish plausible, sound new approaches from fads that lack substance or adequate foundation. Ideally, the student of organizational behavior develops into a scientific professional manager who is knowledgeable in the art and science of organizational behavior.

▌ SKILL DEVELOPMENT

Learning about organizational behavior requires doing as well as knowing. The development of skills and abilities requires that students be challenged by the instructor and by themselves. Skill development is a very active component of the learning process. The Challenge features in each chapter give you a chance to learn about yourself, challenge yourself, and developmentally apply what you are learning.

The U.S. Department of Labor is concerned that people achieve the necessary skills to be successful in the workplace.[48] The essential skills identified by the Department of Labor are (1) resource management skills, such as time management; (2) information management skills, such as data interpretation; (3) personal interaction skills, such as teamwork; (4) systems behavior and performance skills, such as cause–effect relationships; and (5) technology utilization skills, such as troubleshooting. Many of these skills, such as decision making and information management, are directly related to the study of organizational behavior.[49]

Developing skills is different from acquiring objective knowledge in that it requires structured practice and feedback. A key function of experiential learning is to engage the student in individual or group activities that are systematically reviewed, leading to new skills and understanding. Objective knowledge acquisition and skill development are interrelated. The process for learning from structured or experiential activities is depicted in Figure 1.3. The student engages in an individual or group-structured activity and systematically reviews that activity, which leads to new or modified knowledge and skills.

If skill development and structured learning occur in this way, there should be an inherently self-correcting element to learning because of the modification of the student's knowledge and skills over time.[50] To ensure that skill development does occur and that the learning is self-correcting as it occurs, three basic assumptions that underlie the previous model must be followed.

First, each student must accept responsibility for his or her own behavior, actions, and learning. This is a key to the coproducer role in the learning process.

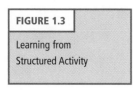

FIGURE 1.3

Learning from
Structured Activity

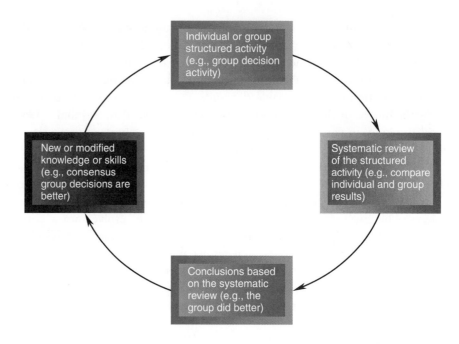

A group cannot learn for its members. Each member must accept responsibility for what he or she does and learns. Denial of responsibility helps no one, least of all the learner.

Second, each student must actively participate in the individual or group-structured learning activity. Structured learning is not passive; it is active. In group activities, everyone suffers if just one person adopts a passive attitude. Hence, all must actively participate.

Third, each student must be open to new information, new skills, new ideas, and experimentation. This does not mean that students should be indiscriminately open. It does mean that students should have a nondefensive, open attitude so that change is possible through the learning process.

■ APPLICATION OF KNOWLEDGE AND SKILLS

Our case examples throughout the text, in addition to the opening and closing cases in each chapter, give you a window into organizational realities and potentially assess your own knowledge of the real world at work. Understanding organizational behavior includes an appreciation and understanding of working realities, as well as of science and of yourself.

One of the advantages of structured, experiential learning is that a person can explore new behaviors and skills in a comparatively safe environment. Losing your temper in a classroom activity and learning about the potential adverse impact on other people will probably have dramatically different consequences from losing your temper with an important customer in a tense work situation. The ultimate objective of skill application and experiential learning is that one transfers the process employed in learning from structured activities in the classroom to learning from unstructured opportunities in the workplace.

Although organizational behavior is an applied discipline, a student is not "trained" in organizational behavior. Rather, one is "educated" in organizational behavior and is a coproducer in learning. The distinction between these two modes of learning is found in the degree of direct and immediate applicability of either knowledge or skills. As an activity, training more nearly ties direct objective knowledge or skill development to specific applications. By contrast, education enhances a person's residual pool of objective knowledge and skills that may then be selectively applied later—sometimes significantly later—when the opportunity presents itself. Hence, education is highly consistent with the concept of lifelong learning. Especially in a growing area of knowledge such as organizational behavior, the student can think of the first course as the outset of lifelong learning about the topics and subject.

PLAN FOR THE BOOK

Challenge and opportunity are watchwords in organizations during these changing times. Managers and employees alike are challenged to meet change in positive and optimistic ways: change in how work gets done, change in psychological and legal contracts between individuals and organizations, change in who is working in the organization, and change in the basis for organization. Challenges for managers are the global environment, workplace diversity, and ethical issues at work. These challenges, which are discussed in detail in Chapter 2, are shaping the changes occurring in organizations throughout the world. For example, the increasing globalization of business has led to intense international competition in core industries, and the changing demographics of the workplace have led to gender, age, racial, and ethnic diversity among working populations.

The first two chapters compose Part 1 of the book, the introduction. Against the backdrop of the challenges discussed here, we develop and explore the specific content subjects in organizational behavior. In addition to the introduction, the text has three major parts. Part 2 addresses individual processes and behavior. Part 3 addresses interpersonal processes and behavior. Part 4 addresses organizational processes and structure.

The four chapters in Part 2 are designed to help the reader understand specific aspects of human behavior. Chapter 3 discusses personality, perception, and attribution. Chapter 4 examines attitudes, emotions, and ethics. Finally, Chapters 5 and 6 address the broad range of motivational theories, learning, and performance management in organizations.

Part 3 is composed of six chapters designed to help the reader better understand interpersonal and group dynamics in organizations. Chapter 7 addresses communication in organizations. Chapter 8 focuses on teamwork and groups as an increasingly prominent feature of the workplace. Chapter 9 examines how individuals and groups make decisions. Chapter 10 is about power and politics, one very dynamic aspect of organizational life. Chapter 11 addresses the companion topics of leadership and followership. Finally, Chapter 12 examines conflict at work, not all of which do we consider bad.

The four chapters in Part 4 are designed to help the reader better understand organizational processes and the organizational context of behavior at work.

Chapter 13 examines traditional and contemporary approaches to job design. Chapter 14 develops the topics of organizational design and structure, giving special attention to contemporary forces reshaping organizations and to emerging forms of organization. Chapter 15 addresses the culture of the organization. Chapter 16 brings closure to the text and the main theme of change by addressing the topic of managing change.

■ MANAGERIAL IMPLICATIONS: FOUNDATIONS FOR THE FUTURE

Managers must consider personal and environmental factors to understand fully how people behave in organizations and to help them grow to be all they can be. Human behavior is complex and at times confusing. Characteristics of the organizational system and formal–informal dynamics at work are important environmental factors that influence people's behavior. Managers should look for similarities and differences in manufacturing, service-oriented, nonprofit, and governmental organizations.

Change may be seen as a threat or as an opportunity by contemporary managers. In the Looking Back feature, you see how John Chambers took advantage of the opportunity that called on Cisco Systems. Changing customer demands for high-quality outputs challenge companies to beat the global competition. Globalization, workforce diversity, ethics, and technology are four challenges for managers that are developed in Chapter 2. Another aspect of meeting the competition is learning. Managers must continually upgrade their knowledge about all aspects of their businesses, to include especially the human side of the enterprise. They must hone both their technical and interpersonal skills, engaging in a lifelong educational process. This is a fun and somewhat unpredictable process that can at times be frustrating while always challenging and exciting.

Several business trends and ongoing changes are affecting managers across the globe. These include continuing industrial restructuring, a dramatic increase in the amount and availability of information, a need to attract and retain the best employees, a need to understand a wide range of human and cultural differences, and a rapid shortening of response times in all aspects of business activities. Further, the old company towns are largely relics of the past, and managers are being called on to reintegrate their businesses with communities, cultures, and societies at a much broader level than has ever been required before. Trust, predictability, and a sense of security become important issues in this context. Reweaving the fabric of human relationships within, across, and outside the organization is a challenge for managers today.

Knowledge becomes power in tracking these trends and addressing these issues. Facts and information are two elements of knowledge in this context. Theories are a third element of a manager's knowledge base. Good theories are tools that help managers understand human and organizational behavior, help them make good business decisions, and inform them about actions to take or to refrain from taking. Managers always use theories, if not those generated from systematic research, then those evolved from the manager's implicit observation. Theories tell us how organizations, business, and people work—or do not work. Therefore, the student is challenged to master the theories in each topic area, and then apply and test the theory in the real world of organizational life. The challenge for the student and the manager is to see what works and what does not work in their specific work context.

LOOKING BACK :: CISCO SYSTEMS

Chambers Answers the Phone

John Chambers came to Cisco in 1991 riding a wave of high-powered sales positions at IBM and Wang. He was named CEO in 1995 and aimed to help Cisco cement its control in the Internet gear market. Even though the company enjoyed 70 percent control of the market for routers, switches, and related gear in large corporate computer networks, these markets had seen only single-digit growth for years. While positive, energetic, and optimistic, Chambers had no illusions concerning what the company was up against in spring 2001. He saw opportunity in tele-communications and with the phone companies. Therefore, the combination of the phone companies' fury and Cisco's internal bickering drove home the message to Chambers that change was needed and a certain amount of damage control was essential.

Cisco's base was as a networking powerhouse that built the most dominant equipment for routing data in corporations. Now the company had to remake that equipment to handle all different kinds of media that could be turned into digital data, especially voice media. The convergence of the computing and telecommunication industries over several decades had now created an exciting opportunity for the convergence of data, voice, and video. Chambers saw this convergence occurring over a single Internet protocol infrastructure,

the hottest being IP telephony—Internet phone calls—made possible by voice over Internet protocol (VOIP).[51] VOIP is growing rapidly for long-distance calls. For example, about 37 percent of international calls originating from India use VOIP. The software to manage Internet telephone calls improves daily, and costs are dropping. For instance, no additional charges are applied when using broadband connections.

When Internet-based telephony arrived in 2003, so too did Cisco's opportunity to regain its dominance in the market. The next step beyond VOIP is to combine it with Wi-Fi. Wi-Fi is wireless broadcast technology that allows digital devices within a several-hundred-foot range to connect at broadband speeds to the Internet. The combination of VOIP with Wi-Fi allows for free calling with mobility, a significant advance over the still expensive cell phone networks. In 2003, Cisco shipped its first wireless IP phone for offices with plans for phones for any Wi-Fi access point. In addition, free calling with mobility can be a money-saving feature on cell phones that use conventional cell frequencies when out of Wi-Fi range. By seeing opportunity in the midst of the tech sector downturn and phone company fury, John Chambers and Cisco were able to respond positively to market changes and lead with technological advances.

CHAPTER SUMMARY

1. Organizational behavior is individual behavior and group dynamics in organizations.
2. Change is an opportunity when one has a positive attitude, asks questions, listens, and is committed to succeed.
3. The sciences of psychology, sociology, engineering, anthropology, management, and medicine have each contributed to the organizational behavior discipline.
4. Organizations have formal and informal elements within them.
5. Manufacturing organizations, service organizations, privately owned companies, and nonprofit organizations all contribute to our national well-being.
6. The changes and challenges facing managers are driven by international competition and customer demands.
7. Learning about organizational behavior requires a mastery of objective knowledge, specific skill development, and thoughtful application.

KEY TERMS

anthropology (p. 5)
challenge (p. 4)
change (p. 4)
engineering (p. 5)
formal organization (p. 7)
Hawthorne studies (p. 7)

informal organization (p. 7)
management (p. 6)
medicine (p. 6)
objective knowledge (p. 15)
opportunities (p. 4)
organizational behavior (p. 4)

psychology (p. 5)
Six Sigma (p. 13)
skill development (p. 15)
sociology (p. 5)

REVIEW QUESTIONS

1. Define *organizational behavior.* What is its focus?
2. Identify the four action steps for responding positively to change.
3. What is an organization?
4. Briefly describe the elements of the formal and the informal organization. Give examples of each.
5. Discuss the four focus organizations used in this book.
6. Describe how competition and total quality are affecting organizational behavior. Why is managing organizational behavior in changing times challenging?

Discussion and Communication QUESTIONS

1. How do the formal aspects of your work environment affect you? What informal aspects of your work environment are important?
2. What is the biggest competitive challenge or change facing the businesses in your industry today? Will that be different in the next five years?
3. Describe the next chief executive of your company and what she or he must do to succeed.
4. Discuss two ways people learn about organizational behavior.
5. Which of the focus companies is your own company most like? Do you work for one of these focus companies? For which company would you most like to work?
6. (*communication question*) Prepare a memo about an organizational change occurring where you

work or in your college or university. Write a 100-word description of the change and identify how it is affecting the people, structure, task, and/or technology of the organization.
7. (*communication question*) Develop an oral presentation about the changes and challenges facing your college or university based on an interview with a faculty member or administrator. Be prepared to describe the changes and challenges. Are these good or bad changes? Why?
8. (*communication question*) Prepare a brief description of a service or manufacturing company, entrepreneurial venture, or nonprofit organization of your choice. Go to the library and read about the organization from several sources. Then use these multiple sources to write your description.

ETHICAL DILEMMA

The afternoon was as gloomy as Brian's mood. It had not been a very productive day. All Brian could think about was the decision before him. He found the current situation interesting in that he had never before struggled with decisions. In the past, he had always been able to make quick and good decisions. His gut gave him the answer and he trusted his instincts. This time he felt nothing, and he was unsure how to proceed without that guiding force.

Brian Cowell was 62 years old and the CEO of Data Solutions, a company he had run for the last 20 years. Brian had been very successful at the helm of the company. Data Solutions had grown from a small data processing business to one of the largest employers in the area. Brian's good instincts had guided it through the challenging times of the '80s and '90s, and the company was in just the right place to meet the challenges ahead. Or was it? This was the question that plagued Brian.

Changes in technology were providing some interesting possibilities for the future. A part of Brian said that he needed to step up and help Data Solutions move into the global environment. He could lead Data Solutions into the global marketplace and continue the growth he had begun so many years ago. That was a big step and would take Brian down a very challenging road. The other option was to continue on the company's current path. Not a bad one, the company had been the most profitable in its history last year and everyone was very happy. Deep inside, Brian knew the answer. Move the company forward to the next logical step: globalization. But Brian was tired and really wanted to spend his last years at Data Solutions reaping the benefits of his hard work, not gearing up for the biggest challenge of his career. Didn't he deserve the right to enjoy his final years at Data Solutions?

QUESTIONS

1. Does Brian have an obligation to lead the company to globalization?

2. What is Brian's responsibility to himself and his family?

3. Consider Brian's decision in light of rule, virtue rights, and justice theories.

EXPERIENTIAL EXERCISES

1.1 THE HOLLOW SQUARE EXERCISE

Materials: Each group should bring one pair of scissors and four envelopes unless the instructor will provide the necessary materials.

This exercise is designed to simulate the stage in the change process when the planners of a change must communicate it to the people who will implement the change. (Time allotted: 95 minutes)

Step 1. The class divides into groups of eight people. These groups will then further subdivide into four planners and four implementers. If there is an odd number of students, place three to five people on the planning team. The implementation teams, however, should always consist of exactly four people (5 minutes).

Step 2. Once the groups have decided who will be planners and implementers, the implementers will wait in a separate area until the instructor has given the planners their instructions. Please do not read the instructions for the other team.

Step 3. The instructor reads to the planning teams their instructions and either provides them with the materials they need to perform the exercise or explains how to obtain them.

Step 4. The planning teams have 30 minutes to plan how they will communicate the instructions to their implementation team (30 minutes).

Step 5. The instructor reads the implementation teams their instructions.

Step 6. All implementation teams begin the 15-minute assembly period at the signal of the instructor. The first team to complete the assembly wins. During this time, the planning team can only observe and must refrain from making any noises that might distract or influence the implementing team (15 minutes).

Step 7. When the assembly period is completed, each participant should complete both sections of the Team Evaluation Form that follows. Then each subgroup should average its scores for each question (i.e., the implementation team comes up with its own team average and the planning team does likewise) (5 minutes).

COMPARISON OF SCORES	IMPLEMENTATION TEAM SUBTOTAL	PLANNING TEAM SUBTOTAL
Planners		
Implementers		

Step 8. Group Discussion. The two subgroups that worked together compare their evaluation scores. Discuss the following questions and choose a representative to present your answers to the class during the plenary session. (10 minutes)

a. Are there any differences in the way the planning and implementation teams perceived and evaluated each other? Why or why not?

b. What did the planning team do that helped the implementation team? Did they do anything that hindered the implementers? Use the chart on the next page, Analysis of the Hollow Square Exercise, to record these factors.

c. What did the implementation team do that helped it succeed in this exercise? Did the team do anything that hindered its success?

TEAM EVALUATIONS FORM
EVALUATION OF THE IMPLEMENTATION TEAM

a. How well was the puzzle completed?   Team average

Not at all well   1   2   3   4   5   6   7   Very well   _____

b. How faithfully did the implementers follow the planning team's instructions?

Not at all well   1   2   3   4   5   6   7   Very well   _____

c. How well organized was the implementation team?

Not at all well   1   2   3   4   5   6   7   Very well   _____

d. How well did the implementation team understand the planning team's instructions?

Not at all well   1   2   3   4   5   6   7   Very well   _____

e. To what extent did the implementation team try to clarify the planning team's instructions (e.g., asking questions, paraphrasing instructions, etc.)?

Not at all well   1   2   3   4   5   6   7   Very well   _____

Implementation Team Subtotal (a–e)   _____

EVALUATION OF THE PLANNING TEAM

f. How clear (explicit, unequivocal) were the instructions given by the planning team?

Not at all well   1   2   3   4   5   6   7   Very well   _____

g. How well organized was the planning team?

Not at all well   1   2   3   4   5   6   7   Very well   _____

h. To what extent did the planning team involve the implementation team in their strategies?

Not at all well   1   2   3   4   5   6   7   To a large degree   _____

Planning Team Subtotal (f–h)   _____

ANALYSIS OF THE HOLLOW SQUARE EXERCISE

Planning Team Actions That		Implementation Team Actions That	
Helped	Hindered	Helped	Hindered

Step 9. Plenary debriefing (30 minutes). Each group presents its findings, and the class as a whole discusses the following questions:

a. What feelings and thoughts did the implementation teams experience while awaiting the instructions for an unknown task?

b. How did the implementation teams organize to accomplish this task?

c. How did the planners transfer the instructions? What was your strategy?

d. How much time did the planning teams devote to figuring out how to transmit their message to the implementation teams?

e. At what time did the implementation teams enter and how did that occur? Why did the planning teams bring or allow the implementation teams in when they did?

f. Did the time at which the planners brought the implementers into the process (early on or just before the assembly period) have an effect upon the proceedings? If so, what was the effect and why did it occur?

g. What can we learn about communicating an organizational change from this exercise?

h. What parallels can you draw between this simulation and organizational change efforts you have observed or experienced?

INSTRUCTIONS FOR THE IMPLEMENTATION TEAMS

1. You have the responsibility for carrying out a task for four people in accordance with the instructions given to you by your planning team. Your planning team can call you back to the classroom to receive these instructions at any time during their 30-minute preparation period.

However, if they have not called you by _____ (five minutes before you are scheduled to carry out your task), you should report to them. Your task is programmed to start exactly at _____. Once you begin, your planning team cannot provide you with any more instructions.

2. Your mission is to complete the assigned task as quickly as possible.

3. While you are waiting for the planning team to call you in to receive your instructions, please discuss and take notes on the following questions. Your notes will be useful during the plenary debriefing session.

a. What feelings and thoughts are you experiencing as you await the instructions for an unknown task?

b. How can the four of you organize yourselves as a team to accomplish this task?

LEARNING POINTS

1. Managing change has become a crucial skill for both managers and employees.

2. Incremental change is linear, continuous, and targeted at fixing or modifying problems or procedures. Transformative change is radical, discontinuous, multidimensional, and multilevel, and modifies the fundamental structure, systems, orientation, and strategies of the organization.

3. Critical mass is defined as the smallest number of people and/or groups who must be committed to a change for it to occur.

4. Successful changes often begin at the periphery of the organization with dedicated general managers who focus energy on work improvements rather than abstract principles.

5. Lewin described the process of change as unfreezing, moving, and refreezing.

6. Change is a process rather than an event or a managerial edict.

7. The essential components of the change process are determining the need for change, forming a guiding coalition, developing a shared vision, creating a tentative plan, analyzing potential resistance and obtaining participation, establishing an implementation plan, communicating the change, implementing the change, and evaluating the change.

8. To diagnose the situation, a force field analysis assigns pressures for change and resistance to change to opposite sides of an equilibrium state.

9. Creative tension, which sometimes motivates people to change, results from perceiving the gap between the ideal situation (vision) and an honest appraisal of its current reality.

10. Change agents are people who act as catalysts and assume the responsibility for managing change activities.

11. The role of a transformational leader consists of envisioning, energizing, and enabling.

12. Resistance to change is a natural reaction and part of the process of adaptation.

13. Managers should seek to understand the source of resistance and listen carefully to concerns employees have regarding proposed changes rather than seeing those who resist as adversaries.

14. Resistance to change can be caused by inadequate change goals, inadequate change processes, personal resistance, political resistance, and systemic resistance.

15. Tactics for dealing with resistance include empathy, education and communication, participation and involvement, facilitation and support, co-optation, negotiation and agreement, manipulation, and coercion.

16. Organization development (OD) is a system-wide process of data collection, diagnosis, action, planning, intervention, and evaluation aimed at enhancing organizational fit, problem solving, effectiveness, health, and self-renewal.

17. International OD interventions and change programs have to be contextualized so they fit the local cultural context.

ACTION SCRIPTS

For Employees

- Employees who are proficient at handling change recognize their own orientations and biases toward change. They take the time to understand the basis for their reactions to change and then respond appropriately.

- They also realize that they can be sources of change. When acting as change agents, these employees carefully survey the political landscape to determine allies and opponents and work to reinforce their allies and persuade their opponents.

- Expert change agents do not give up if their ideas are not immediately accepted. They focus on developing alliances at all levels of the organization. They recognize that peers and managers are important sources of support and can be critical for successfully implementing change.

For Managers

- Managers who are adept at implementing change don't make changes simply to be taking action or to look good. Too much change in a system is just as frustrating to employees as the feeling that any change is impossible. They think through the pros and cons of potential changes very carefully before taking action. For some people, making changes has more to do with their own need to impact the system than with the needs of the system.

- They analyze the political landscape and seek to understand why employees are reacting negatively to a proposed change. They deal with the specific sources of resistance for each employee.

- Employees often undergo a period of "mourning" in large-scale change projects. Accepting this difficulty, acknowledging it with employees, allowing them to vent their feelings, and planning ritual celebrations like farewell parties help people to get through this period more easily.

- Expert managers realize that trust is an important aspect of any change effort. Employees do not believe management's sense of urgency or new visions for the future unless their trust has been won. Experts know that making promises regarding a change that cannot be kept or promising too much diminishes trust.

- They understand that change is not always a rational, linear process. When major organizational transformation is required, change involves a leap of faith to move the organization to another plane that cannot always be seen from the point of departure. For this reason, such changes require shared values and symbolic gestures by managers.

- Expert managers recognize the importance of "small wins"—quick, tangible results that can be clearly linked to the change effort. These results provide needed reinforcement for supporters and help convince opponents. Smart change agents build those wins into their plan for change right from the start.

- They devote a great deal of time to communicating the change message and signal to others in the organization that the change is significant enough to warrant changing the previous rules of the game and making sacrifices.

For Organizational Architects

- Almost all organizations should focus energy on innovation and change on a regular basis. But not everyone in the organization needs to be involved in this. Expert organizational architects utilize parallel or collateral organization structures. Parallel organizations have the freedom and flexibility to do the innovating and problem solving, whereas the "maintenance organization" carries on with business as usual. People who dislike uncertainty and who cherish a fondness for the status quo are more satisfied in maintenance organizations, while the creative, entrepreneurial types prefer the parallel organization. Architects and managers who point out that both of these structures and types of employees are equally valuable to the organization can avoid potential conflict between these groups.

- New programs require careful attention and nurturing. Successful change designers often have the heads of major new programs report directly to the CEO or senior managers until the programs are well established.

- Expert organizational architects recognize that making change "stick" is one of the greatest challenges they face. They build reinforcements and continued resources for implementation in their change plan. They also monitor the progress of the change effort and make any needed adjustments based on the feedback they receive.

PERSONAL APPLICATION ASSIGNMENT

The topic of this assignment is to think back on a significant experience involving organizational change. Choose an experience that intrigues you and that you want to learn more about.

A. Concrete Experience

1. Objectively describe the experience (who, what, when, where, how information). (2 points)

2. Subjectively describe your feelings, perceptions, and thoughts that occurred during (not after) the experience. What did others seem to be feeling? (2 points)

B. Reflective Observation

1. Looking back at the experience, what were the perspectives of the key actors (including you)? (2 points)

2. Why did the people involved (including you) behave as they did? (2 points)

C. Abstract Conceptualization

1. Relate concepts or theories from the assigned readings or the lecture to the experience. Explain thoroughly how they apply to your experience. Please apply at least two concepts or theories and cite them correctly. (4 points)

D. Active Experimentation

1. What did you learn about change from this experience? (1 point)

2. What did you learn about yourself? (1 point)

3. What action steps will you take to be more effective in the future? (2 points)

E. Integration, Synthesis, and Writing

1. Did you integrate and synthesize the four sections? (1 point)
2. Was the personal application assignment well written and easy to understand? (1 point)
3. Was it free of spelling and grammatical errors? (2 points)

Instructions for the Planning Teams

Unless your instructor provides you with different materials, each member should cut out the shapes on either the A, B, C, or D diagrams found on the following page. Please do not mix these pieces up (keep all A pieces separate, etc.). Thus, each of the four members of the planning team will have a separate group of four shapes in front of them as we read the following instructions. (If there are five members on the team, two members can share one set of shapes.) These sets, when properly assembled with pieces from other participants, will make a hollow square design.

During the next 30 minutes, your task is to:

1. Plan how these pieces, distributed among you, should be assembled to make the design shown below.

I. Overall pattern

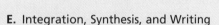

II. Detailed assembly guide

2. Instruct your implementation team on how to implement your plan so as to complete your task ahead of the other teams. You may begin instructing your implementation team at any time during the 30-minute planning period— but no later than five minutes before they are to begin the assembly process at _____.

General Rules

1. You must keep all four of your pieces in front of you at all times.
2. You may not touch the pieces of other planning team members or trade pieces with other members of your team during the planning or instructing phase.
3. You may not show the assembled square to the implementation team at any time. Nor may you provide them with written instructions or drawings.
4. You may not actually assemble the entire square at any time (this is to be left to your implementation team at the moment the assembly period begins).
5. You may not number or otherwise mark the pieces at any time during the exercise.
6. Members of your implementation team must also observe the preceding rules until the signal is given to begin the assembly.
7. Just before the assembly time starts, place your four pieces into an envelope and give the envelope to an implementer. This will allow the implementers on each team to start from an equal position.
8. When your instructor announces the start of the contest and your implementation team begins assembling the pieces, you may give no further instructions. Just step back and observe the implementation team at work without making any noises that might distract or influence the implementers.

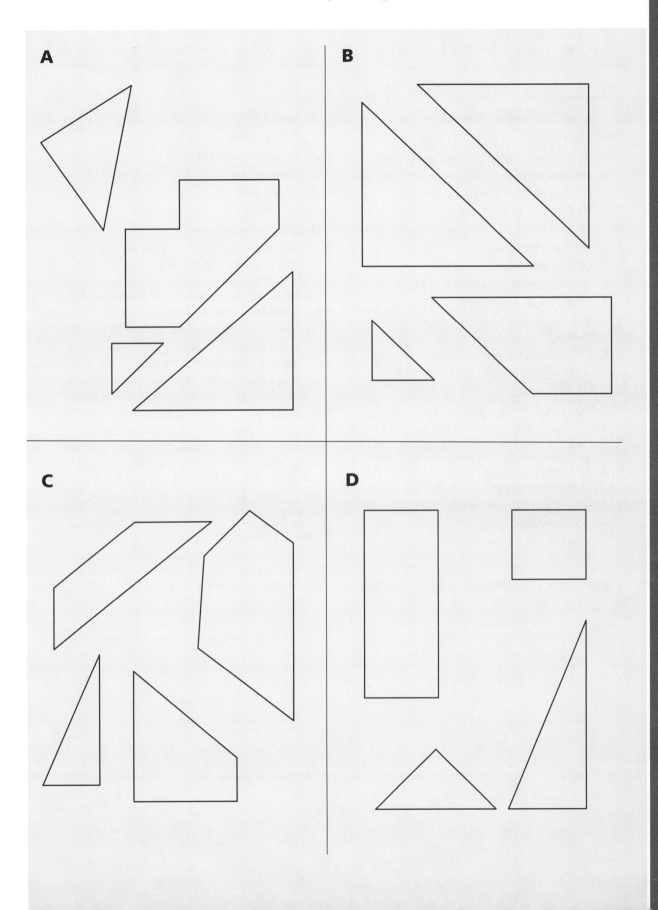

1.2 MY ABSOLUTE WORST JOB

Purpose: To become acquainted with fellow classmates.

Group size: Any number of groups of two.

Exercise schedule:

1. Write answers to the following questions:
   a. What was the worst job you ever had? Describe the following:
      (1) The type of work you did
      (2) Your boss
      (3) Your coworkers
      (4) The organization and its policies
      (5) What made the job so bad
   b. What is your dream job?

2. Find someone you do not know and share your responses.

3. Get together with another dyad, preferably new people. Partner "a" of one dyad introduces partner "b" to the other dyad, then "b" introduces "a." The same process is followed by the other dyad. The introduction should follow this format: "This is Mary Cullen. Her very worst job was putting appliqués on bibs at a clothing factory, and she disliked it for the following reason. What she would rather do is be a financial analyst for a big corporation."

4. Each group of four meets with another quartet and is introduced, as before.

5. Your instructor asks for a show of hands on the number of people whose worst jobs fit into the following categories:
   a. Factory
   b. Restaurant
   c. Manual labor
   d. Driving or delivery
   e. Professional
   f. Health care
   g. Phone sales or communication
   h. Other

6. Your instructor gathers data on worst jobs from each group and asks the groups to answer these questions:
   a. What are the common characteristics of the worst jobs in your group?
   b. How did your coworkers feel about their jobs?
   c. What happens to morale and productivity when a worker hates the job?
   d. What was the difference between your own morale and productivity in your worst job and in a job you really enjoyed?
   e. Why do organizations continue to allow unpleasant working conditions to exist?

7. Your instructor leads a group discussion on parts (a) through (e) of Question 6.

SOURCE: D. Marcic, "My Absolute Worst Job: An Icebreaker," *Organizational Behavior: Experiences and Cases* (St. Paul, Minn.: West, 1989), pp. 5–6. Copyright 1988 Dorothy Marcic. All rights reserved. Reprinted by permission.

Challenges for Managers

2

LEARNING OBJECTIVES

After reading this chapter, you should be able to do the following:

: 1. Describe the dimensions of cultural differences in societies that affect work-related attitudes.

: 2. Explain the social and demographic changes that are producing diversity in organizations.

: 3. Evaluate the actions managers can take to help their employees value diversity.

: 4. Discuss the assumptions of consequential, rule-based, and character ethical theories and explain how they help people in organizations make the "right" decisions.

: 5. Explain six issues that pose ethical dilemmas for managers and provide suggestions for handling them.

: 6. Explain the three types of organizational justice and how they affect ethical decision making in organizations.

THINKING AHEAD :: PIXAR ANIMATION STUDIOS

A Dream Challenged from the Start

Ed Catmull is president of Pixar Animation Studios, the outfit behind such cartoon classics as *Toy Story* and *Monsters, Inc.* His ascent to the presidency and the work he leads is in some ways an unlikely story. As with most healthy children, Ed had a dream while growing up. His dream was to be a Disney animator. Unfortunately, he was confronted with the reality of his limited drawing abilities. During Ed's childhood, animation was done by gifted artists who drew Mickey Mouse, Donald Duck, Minnie Mouse, and Goofy. These animators were the cornerstones for the whole fantasy and dreamworld that Walt Disney imagined and then created. Fortunately for Ed Catmull, animation did not remain trapped in a time warp, and his own career redirection became a detour that ultimately led him back to the fulfillment of his dream.

Pixar was the heart of the Walt Disney Pictures dreamworld and a household name synonymous with family entertainment at its finest.[1] While Disney had its fingers everywhere—in radio, television, and theme parks—Pixar had released only five features since its 1995 debut with *Toy Story*. However, Pixar had come to stand for traditional Disney values before their partnership ended. The promise of *Toy Story*, the first computer-animated feature film

with extraordinary creativity and intelligence, was further fulfilled with *A Bug's Life* (1998), *Toy Story 2* (1999), and *Monsters, Inc.* (2001). Pixar extends from a solid platform of computer-generated special effects with roots in the 1970s revolution in computer graphics.

While Pixar lives in a fantasy world of dreams first created by Disney, it would be a mistake to think it's all fun and games without substance. For example, Pixar's 2003 release, *Finding Nemo*, has sparkling visual clarity that also comes very close to realism. The witty humor, the adventure, and the dazzling excitement are all there. These eye-popping features aim to grab kids' attention, while the story line is built on a parable for their parents. Like the darkest of Disney's fairy tales, *Finding Nemo* begins with a barracuda devouring Nemo's mother and hundreds of his would-be siblings. Only Nemo and his father, Marlin, survive. The film is then the story of Nemo growing up, just as the kids in the theater are growing up. In *Finding Nemo*, Pixar delivers a message of substance and positive value for parents while entertaining their children.

Ed Catmull grew up to live out his dream. How did he do it when faced with his limited drawing abilities?

📌 MANAGEMENT CHALLENGES IN A NEW TIME

Most U.S. executives continue to believe that U.S. firms are encountering unprecedented global competition.[2] Globalization is being driven on the one hand by the spread of economic logics centered on freeing, opening, deregulating, and privatizing economies to make them more attractive for investment and, on the other hand, by the digitization of technologies that is revolutionizing communication.[3] The challenges for managers in this context are manifest in both opportunities and threats, as were briefly touched upon in Chapter 1. The long, robust economic expansion in the United States during the 1990s led to a bubble that burst and several years of economic difficulty. Managers are challenged to lead people in the good times and the bad times, as is Anne Mulcahy at Xerox Corporation, because business cycles ultimately produce both. Thus, the opportunities and threats for managers are history-dependent.

What major challenges must managers overcome in order to remain competitive? Chief executive officers of U.S. corporations cite at least three issues that are paramount: (1) globalizing the firm's operations to compete in the global village, (2) leading a diverse workforce, and (3) encouraging positive ethics, character, and personal integrity.[4,5]

Successful organizations and managers respond to these challenges as opportunities rather than as threats. Our four focus companies—Cisco Systems, Pixar Animation Studios, Virgin Group, Ltd., and Whole Foods Market, Inc.—and their managers have wrestled with one or more of these challenges as they pursue success and achievement. We see in the Looking Back feature later in this chapter how Ed Catmull responded positively to the challenge described in the Thinking Ahead feature. You read in Chapter 1 how John Chambers of Cisco Systems, in a similar vein, responded positively when opportunity called. In this chapter, we focus attention on these challenges that, when well managed, lead to success and healthy organizational outcomes.

Globalization has led to the emergence of the global village in the world economy. The Internet along with rapid political and social changes have broken down old national barriers to competition. What has emerged is a world characterized by an ongoing process of integration and interconnection of states, markets, technologies, and firms. This world as a global macroeconomic village is a boundaryless market in which all firms, large and small, must compete.[6]

Managing a diverse workforce is something organizations like Alcon Laboratories and Coors Brewing Company do extremely well. Both companies reap success from their efforts. The workforce of today is more diverse than ever before. Managers are challenged to bring together employees of different backgrounds in work teams. This requires attention to more than surface-level diversity; it requires attention to deep-level diversity.[7]

Good character, ethical behavior, and *personal integrity* are what managers in organizations like Johnson & Johnson are known. The company's credo guides employee behavior and has helped employees do the right thing in some tough situations. Ethical behavior in business has been at the forefront of public consciousness for some time now. Insider trading scandals, influence peddling, and contract frauds are in the news daily. It need not be that way. Many executives lead with a spirit of personal integrity.[8]

Organizations and managers who see opportunity in these challenges can remain competitive and thrive rather than just survive in today's turbulent environment. Throughout this book, we'll show you how organizational behavior can contribute to managing the challenges with optimism and hope.

THE GLOBAL VILLAGE

Only a few years ago, business conducted across national borders was referred to as "international" activity. The word *international* carries with it a connotation that the individual's or the organization's nationality is held strongly in consciousness.[9] *Globalization,* in contrast, implies that the world is free from national boundaries and that it is really a borderless world.[10] U.S. workers are now competing with workers in other countries. Organizations from other countries are

**transnational
organization**

An organization in which
the global viewpoint
supersedes national
issues.

locating subsidiaries in the United States, such as the U.S. manufacturing locations of Honda, Mazda, and Mercedes.

Similarly, what were once referred to as multinational organizations (organizations that did business in several countries) are now referred to as transnational companies. In *transnational organizations*, the global viewpoint supersedes national issues.[11] Transnational organizations operate over large global distances and are multicultural in terms of the people they employ. 3M, Dow Chemical, Coca-Cola, and other transnational organizations operate worldwide with diverse populations of employees.

■ CHANGES IN THE GLOBAL MARKETPLACE

Social and political upheavals have led organizations to change the way they conduct business and to encourage their members to think globally. Toyota is one Japanese company thinking big, thinking globally, and thinking differently in part by learning how to communicate with Generation Y.[12] The collapse of Eastern Europe was followed quickly by the demise of the Berlin Wall. East and West Germany were united into a single country. In the Soviet Union, perestroika led to the liberation of the satellite countries and the breaking away of the Soviet Union's member nations. Perestroika also brought about many opportunities for U.S. businesses, as witnessed by the press releases showing extremely long waiting lines at Moscow's first McDonald's restaurant.

guanxi

The Chinese practice of
building networks for
social exchange.

Business ventures in China have become increasingly attractive to U.S. businesses. Coca-Cola has led the way. One challenge U.S. managers have tackled is attempting to understand the Chinese way of doing business. Chinese managers' business practices have been shaped by the Communist Party, socialism, feudalistic values, and *guanxi* (building networks for social exchange). Once *guanxi* is established, individuals can ask favors of each other with the expectation that the favor will be returned. For example, it is common in China to use *guanxi,* or personal connections, to conduct business or to obtain jobs. The term *guanxi* is sometimes a sensitive word, because Communist Party policies oppose the use of such practices to gain influence. In China, the family is regarded as being responsible for a worker's productivity, and in turn, the company is responsible for the worker's family. Because of socialism, Chinese managers have very little experience with rewards and punishments and are reluctant to use them in the workplace. The concept of *guanxi* is not unique to China. There are similar concepts in many other countries, including Russia and Haiti. It is a broad term that can mean anything from strongly loyal relationships to ceremonial gift-giving, sometimes seen as bribery. *Guanxi* is more common in societies with underdeveloped legal support for private businesses.[13]

To work with Chinese managers, Americans can learn to build their own *guanxi;* understand the Chinese chain of command; and negotiate slow, general agreements in order to interact effectively. Using the foreign government as the local franchisee may be effective in China. For example, KFC Corporation's operation in China is a joint venture between KFC (60 percent) and two Chinese government bodies (40 percent).[14]

In 1993, the European Union integrated 15 nations into a single market by removing trade barriers. At that time, the member nations of the European Union were Austria, Belgium, Denmark, Finland, France, Germany, Greece, Ireland, Italy,

Luxembourg, the Netherlands, Portugal, Spain, Sweden, and the United Kingdom. As of 2004, Estonia, Hungary, Latvia, Lithuania, Malta, Poland, Slovakia, and Slovenia were also members. The integration of Europe provides many opportunities for U.S. organizations, including 350 million potential customers. Companies like Ford Motor Company and IBM, which entered the market early with wholly owned subsidiaries, will have a head start on these opportunities.[15] Competition within the European Union will increase, however, as will competition from Japan and the former Soviet nations.

The United States, Canada, and Mexico have dramatically reduced trade barriers in accordance with the North American Free Trade Agreement (NAFTA), which took effect in 1994. Organizations have found promising new markets for their products, and many companies have located plants in Mexico to take advantage of low labor costs. DaimlerChrysler, for example, has a massive assembly plant in Saltillo. Prior to NAFTA, Mexico placed heavy tariffs on U.S. exports. The agreement immediately eliminated many of these tariffs and provided that the remaining tariffs be phased out over time.

All of these changes have brought about the need to think globally. Managers can benefit from global thinking by taking a long-term view. Entry into global markets requires long-term strategies.

UNDERSTANDING CULTURAL DIFFERENCES

1. Describe the dimensions of cultural differences in societies that affect work-related attitudes.

One of the keys for any company competing in the global marketplace is to understand diverse cultures. Whether managing culturally diverse individuals within the United States or managing individuals at remote locations around the globe, an appreciation of the differences among cultures is crucial. Edgar Schein suggests that to understand an organization's culture, or more broadly any culture, it is important to dig below the surface of visible artifacts and uncover the basic underlying assumptions at the core of the culture.[16] His definition of organizational culture is the pattern of basic assumptions that a given group has invented, discovered, or developed in learning to cope with its problems of external adaptation and internal integration, and that have worked well enough to be considered valid. These basic assumptions are then taught to new members as the correct way to perceive, think, and feel in relation to those problems. We develop Schein's culture model of basic assumptions, values, visible artifacts, and creations more fully in Chapter 15.

Microcultural differences (i.e., differences within cultures) can play an important role in understanding the global work environment.[17] Knowing cultural differences in symbols is extremely important. Computer icons may not translate well in other cultures. The thumbs up sign, for example, means approval in the United States. In Australia, however, it is an obscene gesture. And manila file folders, like the icons used in Windows applications, aren't used in many European countries and therefore aren't recognized.[18]

Do cultural differences translate into differences in work-related attitudes? The pioneering Dutch researcher Geert Hofstede focused on this question.[19] He and his colleagues surveyed 160,000 managers and employees of IBM who were working in 60 different countries.[20] In this way, the researchers were able to study individuals from the same company in the same jobs, but working in different countries. Hofstede's work is important, because his studies showed that national culture explains more differences in work-related attitudes than do age, gender, profession,

FIGURE 2.1

Hofstede's Dimensions of
Cultural Differences

SOURCE: Republished with permission of Academy of Management, PO Box 3020, Briar Cliff, NY 10510-8020, from *Cultural Constraints in Management Theories* (Figure) by G. Hofstede, *Academy of Management Executive* 7 (1993); peremission conveyed through Copyright Clearance Center, Inc.

or position within the organization. Thus, cultural differences do affect individuals' work-related attitudes. Hofstede found five dimensions of cultural differences that formed the basis for work-related attitudes. These dimensions are shown in Figure 2.1 and are described next.

INDIVIDUALISM VERSUS COLLECTIVISM

individualism

A cultural orientation in which people belong to loose social frameworks, and their primary concern is for themselves and their families.

In cultures where *individualism* predominates, people belong to loose social frameworks, but their primary concern is for themselves and their families. People are responsible for taking care of their own interests. They believe that individuals should make decisions. Cultures characterized by *collectivism* are tightly knit social frameworks in which individual members depend strongly on extended families or clans. Group decisions are valued and accepted.

collectivism

A cultural orientation in which individuals belong to tightly knit social frameworks, and they depend strongly on large extended families or clans.

The North American culture is individualistic in orientation. It is a "can-do" culture that values individual freedom and responsibility. In contrast, collectivist cultures emphasize group welfare and harmony. Israeli kibbutzim and the Japanese culture are examples of societies in which group loyalty and unity are paramount. Organization charts show these orientations. In Canada and the United States, which are individualistic cultures, organization charts show individual positions. In Malaysia, which is a collectivist culture, organization charts show only sections or departments.

This dimension of cultural differences has other workplace implications. Individualistic managers, as found in Great Britain and the Netherlands, emphasize and encourage individual achievement. In contrast, collectivistic managers, such as in Japan and Colombia, seek to fit harmoniously within the group. They also encourage these behaviors among their employees. There are also cultural differences within regions of the world. Arabs are more collectivist than Americans. Within the Arab culture, however, Egyptians are more individualistic than Arabs from the Gulf States (Saudi Arabia, Oman, Bahrain, Kuwait, Quatar, United Arab Emirates). This may be due to the fact that Egyptian businesspeople tend to have longer and more intense exposures to Western culture.[21]

power distance

The degree to which a culture accepts unequal distribution of power.

POWER DISTANCE

The second dimension of cultural differences examines the acceptance of unequal distribution of power. In countries with a high *power distance*, bosses are afforded more power simply because they are the bosses. Titles are used, formality is the rule, and authority is seldom bypassed. Power holders are entitled to their privileges, and managers and employees see one another as fundamentally different kinds of people. India is a country with a high power distance, as are Venezuela and Mexico.

In countries with a low power distance, people believe that inequality in society should be minimized. People at various power levels are less threatened by, and more willing to trust, one another. Managers and employees see one another as similar. Managers are given power only if they have expertise. Employees frequently bypass the boss in order to get work done in countries with a low power distance, such as Denmark and Australia.

UNCERTAINTY AVOIDANCE

Some cultures are quite comfortable with ambiguity and uncertainty, whereas others do not tolerate these conditions well. Cultures with high *uncertainty avoidance* are concerned with security and tend to avoid conflict. People have a need for consensus. The inherent uncertainty in life is a threat against which people in such cultures constantly struggle.

Cultures with low uncertainty avoidance are more tolerant of ambiguity. People are more willing to take risks and are more tolerant of individual differences. Conflict is seen as constructive, and people accept dissenting viewpoints. Norway and Australia are characterized by low uncertainty avoidance, and this trait is seen in the value placed on job mobility. Japan and Italy are characterized by high uncertainty avoidance, so career stability is emphasized.

uncertainty avoidance
The degree to which a culture tolerates ambiguity and uncertainty.

MASCULINITY VERSUS FEMININITY

In cultures that are characterized by *masculinity*, assertiveness and materialism are valued. Men should be assertive, tough, and decisive, whereas women should be nurturing, modest, and tender.[22] Money and possessions are important, and performance is what counts. Achievement is admired. Cultures that are characterized by *femininity* emphasize relationships and concern for others. Men and women are expected to assume both assertive and nurturing roles. Quality of life is important, and people and the environment are emphasized.

Masculine societies, such as in Austria and Venezuela, define gender roles strictly. Feminine societies, in contrast, tend to blur gender roles. Women may be the providers, and men may stay home with the children. The Scandinavian countries of Norway, Sweden, and Denmark exemplify the feminine orientation.

masculinity
The cultural orientation in which assertiveness and materialism are valued.

femininity
The cultural orientation in which relationships and concern for others are valued.

TIME ORIENTATION

Cultures also differ in *time orientation*; that is, whether the culture's values are oriented toward the future (long-term orientation) or toward the past and present (short-term orientation).[23] In China, a culture with a long-term orientation, values such as thrift and persistence, which focus on the future, are emphasized. In Russia, the orientation is short term. Values such as respect for tradition (past) and meeting social obligations (present) are emphasized.

time orientation
Whether a culture's values are oriented toward the future (long-term orientation) or toward the past and present (short-term orientation).

U.S. CULTURE

The position of the United States on these five dimensions is interesting. Hofstede found the United States to be the most individualistic country of any studied. On the power distance dimension, the United States ranked among the

CHALLENGE   2.1

Planning for a Global Career

Think of a country you would like to work in, do business in, or visit. Find out about its culture, using Hofstede's dimensions as guidelines. You can use a variety of sources to accomplish this, particularly your school library, government offices, faculty members, or others who have global experience. You will want to answer the following questions:

1. Is the culture individualistic or collectivist?
2. Is the power distance high or low?
3. Is uncertainty avoidance high or low?
4. Is the country masculine or feminine in its orientation?
5. Is the time orientation short term or long term?
6. How did you arrive at your answers to the first five questions?
7. How will these characteristics affect business practices in the country you chose to investigate?

expatriate manager
A manager who works in a country other than his or her home country.

countries with weak power distance. Its rank on uncertainty avoidance indicated a tolerance of uncertainty. The United States also ranked as a masculine culture with a short-term orientation. These values have shaped U.S. management theory, so Hofstede's work casts doubt on the universal applicability of U.S. management theories. Because cultures differ so widely on these dimensions, management practices should be adjusted to account for cultural differences. Managers in transnational organizations must learn as much as they can about other cultures in order to lead their culturally diverse organizations effectively.

Careers in management have taken on a global dimension. Working in transnational organizations may well give managers the opportunity to work in other countries. *Expatriate managers*, those who work in a country other than their home country, benefit from having as much knowledge as possible about cultural differences. Because managers are increasingly exposed to global work experiences, it is never too early to begin planning for this aspect of your career. Challenge 2.1 asks you to begin gathering information about a country in which you would like to work, including information on its culture.

International executives are executives whose jobs have international scope, whether in an expatriate assignment or in a job dealing with international issues. What kind of competencies should an individual develop in order to prepare for an international career? There seem to be several attributes, all of them centering around core competencies and the ability to learn from experience. Some of the key competencies are integrity, insightfulness, risk taking, courage to take a stand, and ability to bring out the best in people. Learning-oriented attributes of international executives include cultural adventurousness, flexibility, openness to criticism, desire to seek learning opportunities, and sensitivity to cultural differences.[24]

Understanding cultural differences becomes especially important for companies that are considering opening foreign offices, because workplace customs can vary widely from one country to another. Carefully searching out this information in advance can help companies successfully manage foreign operations. Consulate offices and companies operating within the foreign country are excellent sources of information about national customs and legal requirements. Table 2.1 presents a business guide to cultural differences in three countries: Japan, Mexico, and Saudi Arabia.

Another reality that can affect global business practices is the cost of layoffs in other countries. The practice of downsizing is not unique to the United States. Dismissing a 45-year-old middle manager with 20 years of service and a $50,000 annual salary can vary in cost from a low of $13,000 in Ireland to a high of $130,000 in Italy.[25] The cost of laying off this manager in the United States would be approximately $19,000. The wide variability in costs stems from the various legal protections that certain countries give workers. In Italy, laid-off employees must receive a "notice period" payment (one year's pay if they have nine years or more of service) plus a severance payment (based on pay and years of service). U.S. companies operating overseas often adopt the European tradition of training and retraining workers to avoid overstaffing and potential layoffs. An appreciation of the customs and rules for doing business in another country is essential if a company wants to go global.

■ DEVELOPING CROSS-CULTURAL SENSITIVITY

As organizations compete in the global marketplace, employees must learn to deal with individuals from diverse cultural backgrounds. Stereotypes may pervade employees' perceptions of other cultures. In addition, employees may be unaware of others' perceptions of the employees' national culture. A potentially valuable exercise is to ask members of various cultures to describe one another's cultures. This provides a lesson on the misinterpretation of culture.

Intel wants interns and employees to understand the company's culture, but more importantly, it wants to understand the employees' cultures. In an effort to increase diversity, Intel's proportion of ethnic minorities in managerial positions increased from 13 percent in 1993 to 20 percent in 2003, and is still climbing.[26] Many individuals feel their cultural heritage is important and may walk into uncomfortable situations at work. To prevent this, Intel's new workers are paired carefully with mentors, and mentors and protégés learn about each others' cultures.

Cultural sensitivity training is a popular method for helping employees recognize and appreciate cultural differences. Another way of developing sensitivity is to use cross-cultural task forces or teams. The Milwaukee-based GE Medical Systems Group (GEMS) has 19,000 employees working worldwide. GEMS has developed a vehicle for bringing managers from each of its three regions (the Americas, Europe, and Asia) together to work on a variety of business projects. Under the Global Leadership Program, several work groups made up of managers from various regions of the world are formed. The teams work on important projects, such as worldwide employee integration to increase the employees' sense of belonging throughout the GEMS international organization.[27]

The globalization of business affects all parts of the organization, and human resource management is affected in particular. Companies have employees around the world, and human resource managers face the daunting task of effectively supporting a culturally diverse workforce. Human resource managers must adopt a global view of all functions, including human resource planning, recruitment

TABLE 2.1

Business Guide to Cultural Differences

COUNTRY	APPOINTMENTS	DRESS	GIFTS	NEGOTIATIONS
Japan	Punctuality is necessary when doing business here. It is considered rude to be late.	Conservative for men and women in large to medium companies, though pastel shirts are common. May be expected to remove shoes in temples and homes, as well as in some ryokan (inn) style restaurants. In that case, slip-on shoes should be worn.	Important part of Japanese business protocol. Gifts are typically exchanged among colleagues on July 15 and January 1 to commemorate midyear and the year's end, respectively.	Business cards ("meishi") are an important part of doing business in Japan and key for establishing credentials. One side of your card should be in English and the reverse in Japanese. It is an asset to include information such as membership in professional associations.
Mexico	Punctuality is not always as much of a priority in Mexican business culture. Nonetheless, Mexicans are accustomed to North Americans arriving on time, and most Mexicans in business, if not government, will try to return the favor.	Dark, conservative suits and ties are the norm for most men. Standard office attire for women includes dresses, skirted suits, or skirts and blouses. Femininity is strongly encouraged in women's dress. Women business travelers will want to bring hosiery and high heels.	Not usually a requirement in business dealings though presenting a small gift will generally be appreciated as a gesture of goodwill. If giving a gift, be aware that inquiring about what the receiver would like to receive can be offensive.	Mexicans avoid directly saying "no." A "no" is often disguised in responses such as "maybe" or "We'll see." You should also use this indirect approach in your dealings. Otherwise, your Mexican counterparts may perceive you as being rude and pushy.
Saudi Arabia	Customary to make appointments for times of day rather than precise hours. The importance Saudis attach to courtesy and hospitality can cause delays that prevent keeping to a strict schedule.	Only absolute requirement of dress code in the Kingdom is modesty. For men, this means covering everything from navel to knee. Females are required to cover everything except the face, hands and feet in public; they can wear literally anything they want providing they cover it with an abaya (standard black cloak) and headscarf when they go out.	Should only be given to the most intimate of friends. For a Saudi to receive a present from a lesser acquaintance is so embarrassing that it is considered offensive.	Business cards are common but not essential. If used, the common practice is to have both English and Arabic printed, one on each side so that neither language is perceived as less important by being on the reverse of the same card.

SOURCE: Adapted from information obtained from business culture guides accessed online at http://www.executiveplanet.com.

and selection, compensation, and training and development. They must have a working knowledge of the legal systems in various countries, as well as of global economics, cultures, and customs. Human resource managers must not only prepare U.S. workers to live outside their native country but also help foreign employees interact with U.S. culture. Global human resource management is a complex endeavor, but it is critical to the success of organizations in the global marketplace.

Globalization is one challenge managers must meet in order to remain competitive in the changing world. Imagination can be the spark for creativity in dealing with this and other managerial realities. Just as dreams and imagination are the spark for great animation as we saw in the Pixar opening case, so too can dreams and imagination help address managerial challenges. Related to globalization is the challenge of managing an increasingly diverse workforce. Cultural differences contribute a great deal to the diversity of the workforce, but there are other forms of diversity as well.

THE DIVERSE WORKFORCE

Workforce diversity is an important issue for organizations. The United States, as a melting pot nation, has always had a mix of individuals in its workforce. We once sought to be all alike, as in the melting pot, but we now recognize and appreciate individual differences. *Diversity* encompasses all forms of differences among individuals, including culture, gender, age, ability, race, religion, personality, social status, and sexual orientation. Catalyst's Sheila Wellington believes 2003 was the year in which business made the case for diversity and inclusion, and then matched it with action.

Attention to diversity has increased in recent years. This is largely because of the changing demographics of the working population. Managers feel that dealing with diversity successfully is a paramount concern for two reasons. First, managers need to know how to motivate diverse work groups. Second, managers need to know how to communicate effectively with employees who have different values and language skills.

Several demographic trends are affecting organizations. By the year 2020, the workforce will be more culturally diverse, more female, and older than ever. In addition, legislation and new technologies have brought more workers with disabilities into the workforce. Hence, learning to work together is an increasingly important skill. One study found that demographic dissimilarity led to positive outcomes when people were open-minded and to negative outcomes when they were close-minded.[28] Alcon Laboratories, the Swiss-owned and Fort Worth-based international company whose mission is to improve and preserve eyesight and hearing, creates an opportunity for learning to work together and for open-mindedness through diversity training.[29] Valuing diversity in organizations is an important issue.[30]

CULTURAL DIVERSITY

Cultural diversity in the workplace is growing because of the globalization of business, as we discussed earlier. People of diverse national origins—Koreans, Bolivians, Pakistanis, Vietnamese, Swedes, Australians, and others—find themselves

diversity
All forms of individual differences, including culture, gender, age, ability, race, religion, personality, social status, and sexual orientation.

: 2. Explain the social and demographic changes that are producing diversity in organizations.

cooperating in teams to perform the work of the organization. In addition, changing demographics within the United States significantly affect the cultural diversity in organizations. By 2020, minorities will constitute more than one-half of the new entrants to the U.S. workforce. The participation rates of African-Americans and Hispanic Americans in the labor force increased dramatically in recent years. By 2020, white non-Hispanics will constitute 68 percent of the labor force (down from 83 percent in 2002); 14 percent of the workforce will be Hispanic (up from 12 percent); African-Americans' share will remain at 11 percent, and 5 percent will be Asian.[31]

These trends have important implications for organizations. African-Americans and Hispanics are overrepresented in declining occupations, thus limiting their opportunities. Further, African-Americans and Hispanics tend to live in a small number of large cities that are facing severe economic difficulties and high crime rates. Because of these factors, minority workers are likely to be at a disadvantage within organizations. It does not have to be this way. For example, by monitoring its human resource systems, Coca-Cola has made substantial progress on diversity.[32]

The jobs available in the future will require more skill than has been the case in the past. Often, minority workers have not had opportunities to develop leading-edge skills. Minority skill deficits are large, and the proportions of African-Americans and Hispanic Americans who are qualified for higher level jobs are often much lower than the proportions of qualified whites and Asian Americans.[33] Minority workers are less likely to be prepared because they are less likely to have had satisfactory schooling and on-the-job training. Educational systems within the workplace are needed to supply minority workers the skills necessary for success. Companies such as Motorola are already recognizing and meeting this need by focusing on basic skills training.

The globalization of business and changing demographic trends present organizations with a tremendously culturally diverse workforce. This represents both a challenge and a risk. The challenge is to harness the wealth of differences that cultural diversity provides. The risk is that prejudices and stereotypes may prevent managers and employees from developing synergies that can benefit the organization.

■ GENDER DIVERSITY

The feminization of the workforce has increased substantially. The number of women in the labor force increased from 31.5 million in 1970 to 64 million in 2003. This increase accounts for almost 60 percent of the overall expansion of the entire labor force in the United States for this time period. In 2004, women made up over 60 percent of the labor force, and it is predicted that by the year 2010, 70 percent of new entrants into the workforce will be women and/or people of color. Women are better prepared to contribute in organizations than ever before. Women now earn 32 percent of all doctorates, 52 percent of master's degrees, and 50 percent of all undergraduate degrees. Thus, women are better educated, and more are electing to work. In 2004, almost 58 percent of U.S. women were employed.[34] However, women comprised only 13.6 percent of corporate board members in 2003.

Women's participation in the workforce is increasing, but their share of the rewards of participation is not increasing commensurately. Women hold only 16.4 percent of corporate officer positions in the *Fortune 500* companies.[35] In

2005, only seven *Fortune 500* companies had female CEOs.[36] Xerox CEO Anne Mulcahy is still the exception, not the rule. Salaries for women persist at a level of 78 percent of their male counterparts' earnings.[37] Furthermore, because benefits are tied to compensation, women also receive lower levels of benefits.

In addition to lower earnings, women face other obstacles at work. The *glass ceiling* is a transparent barrier that keeps women from rising above a certain level in organizations. In the United States, it is rare to find women in positions above middle management in corporations.[38] The ultimate glass ceiling may well be the corporate board room and the professional partnership. One study found no substantive increase in female corporate board members between 1996 and 2002.[39] While women account for 40 percent of the legal professionals, they are not 40 percent of the partners.

There is reason to believe that, on a global basis, the leadership picture for women is improving and will continue to improve. For example, the number of female political leaders around the world increased dramatically in recent decades. In the 1970s, there were only five such leaders. In the 1990s, twenty-one female leaders came into power. Countries such as Ireland, Sri Lanka, Iceland, and Norway all had female political leaders in the 1990s. Women around the world are leading major global companies, albeit not in the United States. These global female business leaders do not come predominantly from the West. In addition, a large number of women have founded entrepreneurial businesses. Women now own one-third of all American businesses, and these women-owned businesses employ more people than the entire *Fortune 500* combined.[40]

Removing the glass ceiling and other obstacles to women's success represents a major challenge to organizations. Policies that promote equity in pay and benefits, encourage benefit programs of special interest to women, and provide equal starting salaries for jobs of equal value are needed in organizations. Corporations that shatter the glass ceiling have several practices in common. Upper managers clearly demonstrate support for the advancement of women, often with a statement of commitment issued by the CEO. Women are represented on standing committees that address strategic business issues of importance to the company. Women are targeted for participation in executive education programs, and systems are in place for identifying women with high potential for advancement.[41] Three of the best companies in terms of their advancement and development of women are Motorola, Deloitte & Touche, and the Bank of Montreal.[42]

Although women in our society have adopted the provider role, men have not been as quick to share domestic responsibilities. Managing the home and arranging for child care are still seen as the woman's domain. In addition, working women often find themselves having to care for their elderly parents. Because of their multiple roles, women are more likely than men to experience conflicts between work and home. Organizations can offer incentives such as flexible work schedules, child care, elder care, and work site health promotion programs to assist working women in managing the stress of their lives.[43]

More women in the workforce means that organizations must help them achieve their potential. To do less would be to underutilize the talents of half of the U.S. workforce. Thus, creative and imaginative approaches are called for in dreaming up positive new pathways. If Pixar dreamers can create great animation, organizational dreamers can imagine positive new paths for women's careers.

glass ceiling
A transparent barrier that keeps women from rising above a certain level in organizations.

The glass ceiling is not the only gender barrier in organizations. Males may suffer from discrimination when they are employed in traditionally female jobs such as nursing, elementary school teaching, and social work. Males may be overlooked as candidates for managerial positions in traditionally female occupations.[44]

■ AGE DIVERSITY

The graying of the U.S. workforce is another source of diversity in organizations. Aging baby boomers (those individuals born from 1946 through 1964) contributed to the rise of the median age in the United States to 36 in the year 2000—six years older than at any earlier time in history. This also means that the number of middle-aged Americans is rising dramatically. In the workforce, the number of younger workers is declining, as is the number of older workers (over age 65). The net result will be a gain in workers aged 35 to 54. By 2030, there will be 70 million older persons, more than twice their number in 1996. People over age 65 will comprise 13 percent of the population in 2010, and 20 percent of the population by 2030.[45]

This change in worker profile has profound implications for organizations. The job crunch among middle-aged workers will become more intense as companies seek flatter organizations and the elimination of middle-management jobs. Older workers are often higher paid, and companies that employ large numbers of aging baby boomers may find these pay scales a handicap to competitiveness.[46] However, a more experienced, stable, reliable, and healthy workforce can pay dividends to companies. The baby boomers are well-trained and educated, and their knowledge can be a definite asset to organizations.

Another effect of the aging workforce is greater intergenerational contact in the workplace.[47] As organizations grow flatter, workers who were traditionally segregated by old corporate hierarchies (with older workers at the top and younger workers at the bottom) are working together. Four generations are cooperating: the silent generation (people born from 1930 through 1945), a small group that includes most organizations' top managers; the baby boomers, whose substantial numbers give them a strong influence; the baby bust generation, popularly known as Generation X (those born from 1965 through 1976); and the subsequent generation, tentatively called Generation Y or the baby boomlet.[48] Although there is certainly diversity within each generation, each generation differs in general ways from other generations.

Revisiting generational work values for the new millennium is based on a three-generations framework in which two generational groups are prevalent in the workforce.[49] These two groups are the Baby Boomers (Boomers) and Generation X (Gen X-ers). While there is agreement on these labels, the current thinking no longer agrees on the years encompassing them. These two generations are the experienced employees and managers in the American workforce. The next or third generation in the framework is alternately labeled the Generation Y-ers, the Millennials, or the Next Generation. Work values do differ between the generations, and work values change as workers grow older. This is seen in the increasing desire among American workers to balance work and personal goals.

One company that is succeeding in accommodating "baby busters" is Patagonia, a manufacturer of products for outdoor enthusiasts. Although the company does not actively recruit 20-year-olds, approximately 20 percent of Patagonia's workers are in this age group because they are attracted to its products. To retain baby busters, the company offers several options, one of which is flextime. Employees can arrive at work as early as 6 A.M., and work as late as 6 P.M., as long as they work the core hours between 9 A.M. and 3 P.M. Workers also have the option of working at the office for five hours a day and at home for three hours.

Personal leaves of absence are also offered, generally unpaid, for as much as four months per year. This allows employees to take an extended summer break and prevents job burnout. Patagonia has taken into consideration the baby busters' desires for more time for personal concerns and has incorporated these desires into the company.[50]

Younger workers may have false impressions of older workers, viewing them as resistant to change, unable to learn new work methods, less physically capable, and less creative than younger employees. Research indicates, however, that older employees are more satisfied with their jobs, are more committed to the organization, and possess more internal work motivation than their younger cohorts.[51] Research also indicates that direct experience with older workers reduces younger workers' negative beliefs.[52] Motivating aging workers and helping them maintain high levels of contribution to the organization are key tasks for managers.

ABILITY DIVERSITY

The workforce is full of individuals with different abilities, presenting another form of diversity. Individuals with disabilities are an underutilized human resource. An estimated 50 million individuals, or 1 in 5 Americans, with disabilities live in the United States, and their unemployment rate is estimated to exceed 50 percent.[53] Nevertheless, the representation of individuals with disabilities in the workforce has increased because of the Americans with Disabilities Act, which went into effect in the summer of 1992. Under this law, employers are required to make reasonable accommodations to permit workers with disabilities to perform jobs. Research indicates that 70 percent of workers with disabilities require no accommodations and for those who do, 71 percent of accommodations cost less than $500 while one in five accommodations costs nothing.[54] The act defines a person with a disability as "anyone possessing a physical or mental impairment that substantially limits one or more major life activities."[55] It protects individuals with temporary, as well as permanent, disabilities; many disabilities are invisible. The act's protection encompasses a broad range of illnesses that produce disabilities. Among these are acquired immune deficiency syndrome (AIDS), cancer, hypertension, anxiety disorders, dyslexia, blindness, and cerebral palsy, to name only a few. People with disabilities want to work, but are more likely to be unemployed and receive lower earnings than those who are not disabled. A common misperception about people with disabilities is that they have higher absenteeism than people without disabilities. Research indicates, however, that rates of absence and performance for people with disabilities are similar to those without disabilities.[56] Some companies recognized the value of employing workers with disabilities long before the legislation. Pizza Hut employs 3,000 workers with disabilities and plans to hire more. The turnover rate for Pizza Hut workers with disabilities is only one-fifth of the normal turnover rate.[57]

McDonald's created McJOBS, a program that has trained and hired more than 9,000 mentally and physically challenged individuals since 1981.[58] McJOBS is a corporate plan to recruit, train, and retain individuals with disabilities. Its participants include workers with visual, hearing, or orthopedic impairments; learning disabilities; and mental retardation. Through classroom and on-site training, the McJOBS program prepares individuals with disabilities for the work environment. Before McJOBS workers go onsite, sensitivity training sessions are held with store managers and crew members. These sessions help workers without disabilities understand what it means to be a worker with a disabling condition. Most McJOBS workers start part time and advance according to their own abilities and the opportunities available. Some McJOBS workers with visual impairments prefer to work on the back line, whereas others who use wheelchairs can work the drive-thru window.

Companies like Pizza Hut and McDonald's have led the way in hiring individuals with disabilities. One key to the success of these firms is helping able-bodied employees understand how workers with disabilities can contribute to the organization. In this way, ability diversity becomes an asset and helps organizations meet the challenge of unleashing the talents of workers with disabilities.

Another, more recently recognized form of individual difference in workers is the degree to which they are able to recognize and manage their own and others' emotions. Individuals with high levels of emotional intelligence (EI) have that little "extra something" that goes beyond cognitive ability that enables them to be successful. The concept of EI is defined and elaborated on in Chapter 4 and again in Chapter 11.

■ DIFFERENCES ARE ASSETS

Diversity involves much more than culture, gender, age, ability, race, or personality. It also encompasses religion, social status, and sexual orientation. The scope of diversity is broad and inclusive. All these types of diversity lend heterogeneity to the workforce.

The issue of sexual orientation as a form of diversity has received increasing attention from organizations. Approximately 1.5 million households in the United States are identified as homosexual domestic partnerships.[59] Sexual orientation is an emotionally charged issue. Often, heterosexual resistance to accepting gay, lesbian, or bisexual workers is caused by moral beliefs. Although organizations must respect these beliefs, they must also send a message that all people are valued. The threat of job discrimination leads many gay men and lesbians to keep their sexual orientation secret at work. This secrecy has a cost, however. Closeted gay workers report lower job satisfaction and organizational commitment and more role conflict and conflict between work and home life issues than do openly gay workers or heterosexual workers.[60] To counteract these problems, companies like NCR are seeking gay job applicants. Other companies like IBM, Ford Motor Company, J.P. Morgan Chase, and American Airlines are offering benefits, training, support groups, and marketing strategies in support of gay rights. These initiatives help gay employees become more integrated and productive organizational members. Education and training can be supplemented by everyday practices like using inclusive language—for example, using the term "partner" instead of "spouse" in verbal and written communication.

Part of the challenge in managing diversity lies in attempting to combat prejudices and discrimination. Whereas prejudice is an attitude, discrimination is behavior. Both are detrimental to organizations that depend on productivity from every single worker. Often, in studies of ratings of promotion potential, minorities are rated lower than whites, and females are rated lower than males.[61] The disparity between the pay of women and minority-group members relative to white men increases with age.[62] It is to organizations' benefit to make sure that good workers are promoted and compensated fairly, but as the workforce becomes increasingly diverse, the potential for unfair treatment also increases.

Diversity is advantageous to the organization in a multitude of ways. Some organizations have recognized the potential benefits of aggressively working to increase the diversity of their workforces. Yum! Brands' Kentucky Fried Chicken (KFC) has a goal of attracting and retaining female and minority-group executives. A president of KFC's U.S. operations said, "We want to bring in the best people. If there are two equally qualified people, we'd clearly like to have diversity."[63]

In an effort to understand and appreciate diversity, Alcon Laboratories developed a diversity training class called Working Together. The course takes advantage of two key ideas. First, people work best when they are valued and when diversity is taken into account. Second, when people feel valued, they build relationships and work together as a team.[64] Even majority group managers may be more supportive of diversity training if they appreciate their own ethnic identity. One evaluation of diversity training found that participants were more favorable if the training was framed with a traditional title and had a broad focus.[65] Further, women react more positively to diversity training than men. Companies can get positive payoffs from diversity training and should, therefore, measure the effect of training.

Managing diversity is one way a company can become more competitive. It is more than simply being a good corporate citizen or complying with affirmative action.[66] It is also more than assimilating women and minorities into a dominant male culture. Managing diversity includes a painful examination of hidden assumptions that employees hold. Biases and prejudices about people's differences must be uncovered and dealt with so that differences can be celebrated and exploited to their full advantage.

: 3. Evaluate the actions managers can take to help their employees value diversity.

▌ DIVERSITY'S BENEFITS AND PROBLEMS

Diversity can enhance organizational performance. Table 2.2 summarizes the main benefits, as well as problems, with diversity at work. Organizations can reap five main benefits from diversity. First, diversity management can help firms attract and retain the best available human talent. The companies that appear at the top of "Best Places to Work" lists are usually excellent at managing diversity. Second,

BENEFITS	PROBLEMS
• Attracts and retains the best human talent	• Resistance to change
• Improves marketing efforts	• Lack of cohesiveness
• Promotes creativity and innovation	• Communication problems
• Results in better problem solving	• Interpersonal conflicts
• Enhances organizational flexibility	• Slowed decision making

TABLE 2.2

Diversity's Benefits and Problems

diversity can enhance marketing efforts. Just as workforces are becoming more diverse, so are markets. Having a diverse workforce can help the company improve its marketing plans by drawing on insights of employees from various cultural backgrounds. Third, diversity promotes creativity and innovation. The most innovative companies, such as HP, deliberately put together diverse teams to foster creativity. Fourth, diversity results in better problem solving. Diverse groups bring more expertise and experience to bear on problems and decisions. They also encourage higher levels of critical thinking. Fifth, diversity enhances organizational flexibility. Inflexible organizations are characterized by narrow thinking, rigidity, and standard definitions of "good" work styles. In contrast, diversity makes an organization challenge old assumptions and become more adaptable. These five benefits can add up to competitive advantage for a company that manages diversity well.

Lest we paint an overly rosy picture of diversity, we must recognize its potential problems. Five problems are particularly important: resistance to change, lack of cohesiveness, communication problems, conflicts, and decision making. People are more highly attracted to, and feel more comfortable with, others like themselves. It stands to reason that diversity efforts may be met with considerable resistance when individuals are forced to interact with others unlike themselves. Managers should be prepared for this resistance rather than naively assuming that everybody supports diversity. (Managing resistance to change is presented at length in Chapter 16.) Another potential problem with diversity is the issue of cohesiveness, that invisible "glue" that holds a group together. Cohesive, or tightly knit, groups are preferred by most people. It takes longer for a diverse group of individuals to become cohesive. In addition, cohesive groups have higher morale and better communication. We can reason that it may take longer for diverse groups to develop high morale.

Another obstacle to performance in diverse groups is communication. Culturally diverse groups may encounter special challenges in terms of communication barriers. Misunderstandings may occur that can lower work group effectiveness. Conflicts can also arise, and decision making may take more time.[67]

In summary, diversity has several advantages that can lead to improved productivity and competitive advantage. In diverse groups, however, certain aspects of group functioning can become problematic. The key is to maximize the benefits of diversity and prevent or resolve the potential problems.

Pillsbury is one company that lays out the performance case for managing and valuing differences. Pillsbury's managers argue that the same business rationale for cross-functional teams is relevant to all kinds of diversity. Managing differences includes bringing race and gender, as well as marketing expertise, into a team. To open up a very profitable baked-goods market in a tough-to-crack niche, Pillsbury hired some Spanish-speaking Hispanics. The company lacked the language expertise and cultural access to the Hispanic community. Pillsbury's vice president of human resources conducted his own study of the food industry, asking an independent group to rate the diversity performance of 10 companies and correlate it with financial performance over a 10-year period. Along with many other studies, the Pillsbury research suggests that diversity is a strong contributor to financial performance.[68]

Whereas the struggle for equal employment opportunity is a battle against racism and prejudice, managing diversity is a battle to value the differences that individuals bring to the workplace. Organizations that manage diversity effectively can reap the rewards of increased productivity and improved organizational health. Another aspect of a healthy organization is employees of good character, ethical behavior, and personal integrity.

⬛ ETHICS, CHARACTER, AND PERSONAL INTEGRITY

In addition to the challenges of globalization and workforce diversity, managers frequently face ethical challenges and dilemmas in organizations. Some organizations display good character, and their executives show personal integrity in addressing ethical dilemmas. Johnson & Johnson (J & J) employees operate under an organizational credo, presented later in this chapter. Another organization that manages ethical issues well is Merck & Company. This pharmaceutical company's emphasis on ethical behavior has earned it recognition as one of America's most admired companies in *Fortune*'s polls of CEOs.

Despite the positive way some organizations handle ethical issues, however, unethical conduct does sometimes occur. A few of the ethical problems that managers report as toughest to resolve include employee theft, environmental issues, comparable worth of employees, conflicts of interest, and sexual harassment.[69]

How can people in organizations rationally think through ethical decisions so that they make the "right" choices? Ethical theories help us understand, evaluate, and classify moral arguments; make decisions; and then defend conclusions about what is right and wrong. Ethical theories can be classified as consequential, rule-based, or character.

Consequential theories of ethics emphasize the consequences or results of behavior. John Stuart Mill's utilitarianism, a well-known consequential theory, suggests that right and wrong are determined by the consequences of the action.[70] "Good" is the ultimate moral value, and we should maximize the most good for the greatest number of people. But do good ethics make for good business?[71] Right actions do not always produce good consequences, and good consequences do not always follow from right actions. And how do we determine the greatest good—in short-term or long-term consequences? Using the "greatest number" criterion can imply that minorities (less than 50 percent) might be excluded in evaluating the morality of actions. An issue that may be important for a minority but unimportant for the majority might be ignored. These are but a few of the dilemmas raised by utilitarianism.

In contrast, *rule-based theories* of ethics emphasize the character of the act itself, not its effects, in arriving at universal moral rights and wrongs.[72] Moral rights, the basis for legal rights, are associated with such theories. In a theological context, the Bible, the Talmud, and the Koran are rule-based guides to ethical behavior. Immanuel Kant worked toward the ultimate moral principle in formulating his categorical imperative, a universal standard of behavior.[73] Kant argued that individuals should be treated with respect and dignity and that they should not be used as a means to an end. He argued that we should put ourselves in the other person's position and ask if we would make the same decision if we were in that person's situation.

Corporations and business enterprises are more prone to subscribe to consequential ethics than rule-based ethics, in part due to the persuasive arguments of the Scottish political economist and moral philosopher Adam Smith.[74] He believed

---

4. Discuss the assumptions of consequential, rule-based, and character ethical theories and explain how they help people in organizations make the "right" decisions.

consequential theory
An ethical theory that emphasizes the consequences or results of behavior.

rule-based theory
An ethical theory that emphasizes the character of the act itself rather than its effects.

that the self-interest of human beings is God's providence, not the government's. Smith set forth a doctrine of natural liberty, presenting the classical argument for open market competition and free trade. Within this framework, people should be allowed to pursue what is in their economic self-interest, and the natural efficiency of the marketplace would serve the well-being of society. However, an alternative to those theories is offered through virtue-ethics.

character theory

An ethical theory that emphasizes the character, personal virtues, and integrity of the individual.

Character theories of ethics emphasize the character of the individual and the intent of the actor, in contrast to either the character of the act itself or the consequences of the act. These theories emphasize virtue-ethics and are based on an Aristotelean approach to character. Robert Solomon is the best-known advocate of this Aristotelean approach to business ethics.[75] He advocates a business ethics theory that centers on the individual within the corporation, thus emphasizing both corporate roles and personal virtues. The center of Aristotle's vision was on the inner character and virtuousness of the individual, not on the person's behavior or actions. Thus, the "good" person who acted out of virtuous and "right" intentions was one with integrity and ultimately good ethical standards. For Solomon, the six dimensions of virtue-ethics are community, excellence, role identity, integrity, judgment (phronesis), and holism. Further, "the virtues" are a shorthand way of summarizing the ideals that define good character. These include honesty, loyalty, sincerity, courage, reliability, trustworthiness, benevolence, sensitivity, helpfulness, cooperativeness, civility, decency, modesty, openness, and gracefulness, just to name a few.

Cultural relativism contends that there are no universal ethical principles and that people should not impose their own ethical standards on others. Local standards should be the guides for ethical behavior. Cultural relativism encourages individuals to operate under the old adage "When in Rome, do as the Romans do." Unfortunately, strict adherence to cultural relativism can lead individuals to deny accountability for their own decisions and to avoid difficult ethical dilemmas.

5. Explain six issues that pose ethical dilemmas for managers and provide suggestions for handling them.

People need ethical theories to help them think through confusing, complex, difficult moral choices and ethical decisions. In contemporary organizations, people face ethical and moral dilemmas in many diverse areas. The key areas we address are employee rights, sexual harassment, romantic involvements, organizational justice, whistle-blowing, and social responsibility. We conclude with a discussion of professionalism and codes of ethics.

◀◀ think critically ▶▶

Suppose, as a manager, you were ordered to implement a recruiting policy that limited the number of minority candidates who would be considered for job openings. Though the policy has been determined not to be illegal, you refuse to implement the policy for fear that it could lead to discrimination. Are you within your rights to refuse to follow company procedures? Explain.

■ EMPLOYEE RIGHTS

Managing the rights of employees at work creates many ethical dilemmas in organizations. Some of these dilemmas are privacy issues related to technology. Computerized monitoring, discussed later in the chapter, constitutes an invasion of privacy in the minds of some individuals. The use of employee data from computerized information systems presents many ethical concerns. Safeguarding the employee's right to privacy and at the same time preserving access to the data for those who need it requires that the manager balance competing interests.

Drug testing, free speech, downsizing and layoffs, and due process are but a few of the issues involving employee rights that managers face. Perhaps no issue generates as much need for managers to balance the interests of employees and the interests of the organization as the reality of AIDS in the workplace. New drugs have shown the promise of extended lives for people with human immunodeficiency virus (HIV), and this means that HIV-infected individuals can remain in the workforce and stay productive. Managers may be caught in the middle of a conflict between the rights of HIV-infected workers and the rights of their coworkers who feel threatened.

Employers are not required to make concessions to coworkers, but employers do have obligations to educate, reassure, and provide emotional support to coworkers. Confidentiality may also be a difficult issue. Some employees with HIV or AIDS do not wish to waive confidentiality and do not want to reveal their condition to their coworkers because of fears of stigmatization or even reprisals. In any case, management should discuss with the affected employee the ramifications of trying to maintain confidentiality and should assure the employee that every effort will be made to prevent negative consequences for him or her in the workplace.[76]

Laws exist that protect HIV-infected workers. As mentioned earlier, the Americans with Disabilities Act requires employees to treat HIV-infected workers as disabled individuals and to make reasonable accommodations for them. The ethical dilemmas involved with this situation, however, go far beyond the legal issues. How does a manager protect the dignity of the person with AIDS and preserve the morale and productivity of the work group when so much prejudice and ignorance surround this disease? Many organizations, such as Wells Fargo, believe the answer is education.[77] Wells Fargo has a written AIDS policy because of the special issues associated with the disease—such as confidentiality, employee socialization, coworker education, and counseling—that must be addressed. The Body Shop's employee education program consists of factual seminars combined with interactive theater workshops. The workshops depict a scenario in which an HIV-positive worker must make decisions, and the audience decides what the worker should do. This helps participants explore the emotional and social issues surrounding HIV.[78] Many fears arise because of a lack of knowledge about AIDS.

◀◀think critically▶▶

What are some of the concerns that a person with AIDS would have about his or her job? What are some of the fears that coworkers would have? How can a manager balance these two sets of concerns?

SEXUAL HARASSMENT

According to the Equal Employment Opportunity Commission, sexual harassment is unwelcome sexual attention, whether verbal or physical, that affects an employee's job conditions or creates a hostile working environment.[79] Court rulings, too, have broadened the definition of sexual harassment beyond job-related

CHALLENGE   2.2

How Much Do You Know about Sexual Harassment?

Indicate whether you believe each statement below is true (T) or false (F).

_____   1. Sexual harassment is unprofessional behavior.

_____   2. Sexual harassment is against the law in all 50 states.

_____   3. Sexual advances are a form of sexual harassment.

_____   4. A request for sexual activity is a form of sexual harassment.

_____   5. Verbal or physical conduct of a sexual nature may be sexual harassment.

_____   6. Sexual harassment occurs when submission to sex acts is a condition of employment.

_____   7. Sexual harassment occurs when submission to or rejection of sexual acts is a basis for performance evaluation.

_____   8. Sexual harassment occurs when such behavior interferes with an employee's performance or creates an intimidating, hostile, and offensive environment.

_____   9. Sexual harassment includes physical contact of a sexual nature, such as touching.

_____   10. Sexual harassment requires that a person have the intent to harass, harm, or intimidate.

All of the items are true except item 10, which is false. While somewhat ambiguous, sexual harassment is defined in the eyes of the beholder. Give yourself 1 point for each correct answer. This score reflects how much you know about sexual harassment. Scores can range from 0 (poorly informed about sexual harassment) to 10 (well informed about sexual harassment). If your score was less than 5, you need to learn more about sexual harassment.

Source: W. O'Donohue, ed., *Sexual Harassment* (Boston: Allyn and Bacon, 1997) for theory, research, and treatment. See http://www.eeoc.gov/stats/harass.html for the latest statistics.

abuse to include acts that create a hostile work environment. In addition, Supreme Court rulings presume companies are to blame when managers create a sexually hostile working environment. Some organizations are more tolerant of sexual harassment. Complaints are not taken seriously, it is risky to complain, and perpetrators are unlikely to be punished. In these organizations, sexual harassment is more likely to occur. Sexual harassment is also more likely to occur in male-dominated workplaces.[80] Managers can defend themselves by demonstrating that they took action to eliminate workplace harassment and that the complaining employee did not take advantage of company procedures to deal with harassment. Even the best sexual harassment policy, however, will not absolve a company when harassment leads to firing, demotions, or undesirable working assignments.[81] How much do you know about sexual harassment? Complete Challenge 2.2 to get an idea.

There are three types of sexual harassment. *Gender harassment* includes crude comments or sexual jokes and behaviors that disparage someone's gender or convey hostility toward a particular gender. *Unwanted sexual attention* involves unwanted touching or repeated unwanted pressures for dates. *Sexual coercion* consists of implicit or explicit demands for sexual favors by threatening negative job-related consequences or promising job-related rewards.[82] Recent theory has focused attention on the aggressive behavior of sexual harassers.[83]

Sexual harassment costs the typical *Fortune 500* company $6.7 million per year in absenteeism, turnover, and loss of productivity. Valeant Pharmaceuticals International has paid out millions to settle four sexual harassment complaints against former CEO Milan Panic. One U.S. airline reached a $2.6 million settlement with the EEOC in 2001 after the agency found widespread sexual harassment of female employees at the airline's New York JFK International Airport facility. Plaintiffs may now sue not only for back pay but also for compensatory and punitive damages. And these costs do not take into account the negative publicity that firms may encounter from sexual harassment cases, which can cost untold millions. Sexual harassment can have strong negative effects on victims. Victims are less satisfied with their work, supervisors, and coworkers and may psychologically withdraw at work. They may suffer poorer mental health and even exhibit symptoms of posttraumatic stress disorder in conjunction with the harassment experience. Some victims report alcohol abuse, depression, headaches, and nausea.[84]

Several companies have created comprehensive sexual harassment programs that seem to work. Atlantic Richfield (ARCO), owned by British Petroleum and a player in the male-dominated energy industry, has a handbook on preventing sexual harassment that includes phone numbers of state agencies where employees can file complaints. In essence, it gives employees a road map to the courthouse, and the openness seems to work. Lawsuits rarely happen at ARCO. When sexual harassment complaints come in, the company assumes the allegations are true and investigates thoroughly. The process has resulted in the firing of highly placed managers—the captain of an oil tanker was fired for sexually harassing coworkers. Other companies believe in the power of training programs. Some of the best training programs use role-playing, videotapes, and group discussions of real cases to help supervisors recognize unlawful sexual harassment and investigate complaints properly.

ROMANTIC INVOLVEMENTS

Hugging, sexual innuendos, and repeated requests for dates may constitute sexual harassment for some, but they are a prelude to romance for others. This situation carries with it a different set of ethical dilemmas for organizations. While some male-female cartoons or animations are deeply humorous to some individuals, they are raucous for others. Hence, Pixar animators must be sensitive and careful as they create images that speak to our deeper psychology.

A recent fax poll indicated that three-fourths of the respondents felt it was okay to date a coworker, while three-fourths disapproved of dating a superior or subordinate. In *Meritor vs. Vinson*, the Supreme Court ruled that the agency principle applies to supervisor–subordinate relationships. Employers are liable for acts of their agents (supervisors) and can thus be held liable for sexual harassment. Other employees might claim that the subordinate who is romantically involved with the supervisor gets preferential treatment. Dating between coworkers poses less liability for the company because the agency principle does not apply. Policing coworker dating can also backfire: Wal-Mart lost a lawsuit when it tried to forbid coworkers from dating.

Workplace romances may result, for the participants, in experiences that can be positive or negative, temporary or permanent, exploitative to nonexploitative.

The effects of office romances can similarly be positive or negative, or they can simply be mild diversions. Romances can be damaging to organizational effectiveness, or they can occasionally enhance effectiveness through their positive effects on participants. Two particular kinds of romances are hazardous in the workplace. Hierarchical romances, in which one person directly reports to another, can create tremendous conflicts of interest. Utilitarian romances, in which one person satisfies the needs of another in exchange for task-related or career-related favors, are potentially damaging in the workplace. Though most managers realize that workplace romance cannot be eliminated through rules and policies, they believe that intervention is a must when romance constitutes a serious threat to productivity or workplace morale.[85]

ORGANIZATIONAL JUSTICE

Another area in which moral and ethical dilemmas may arise for people at work concerns organizational justice, both distributive and procedural. *Distributive justice* concerns the fairness of outcomes individuals receive. For example, the salaries and bonuses of U.S. corporate executives became a central issue with Japanese executives when former President George H. W. Bush and American CEOs in key industries visited Japan in 1992. The Japanese CEOs questioned the distributive justice in keeping the American CEOs' salaries at high levels at a time when so many companies were in difficulty and laying off workers.

Procedural justice concerns the fairness of the process by which outcomes are allocated. The ethical questions here do not concern the just or unjust distribution of organizational resources. Rather, the ethical questions in procedural justice concern the process. Has the organization used the correct procedures in allocating resources? Have the right considerations, such as competence and skill, been brought to bear in the decision process? And have the wrong considerations, such as race and gender, been excluded from the decision process? Some research has shown cultural differences in the effects of distributive and procedural justice, such as between Hong Kong and the United States.[86]

Interactional justice concerns the fairness of the interpersonal treatment given in the course of explaining procedures and outcomes. For example, an employee's (Mike) supervisor may treat Mike in an unkind and uncaring fashion by showing him little dignity and respect by giving him limited information about the procedures about which Mike is so concerned. In this example, if a supervisor's comments include "Those are the breaks," and "That's our system, so get used to it," then this supervisor is demonstrating a low degree of interactional justice. By contrast, suppose Mike's supervisor acted in the opposite manner by showing great dignity and respect, and by giving him copious amounts of information about how the pay was determined. "I know that the system stinks," he may apologize, adding "Let me see what I can do to make things right." In this case, the supervisor would be sending Mike a message that he is a valued member of the organization, someone who is worthwhile and desirable. In this case, the supervisor would be demonstrating a high degree of interactional justice.[87]

WHISTLE-BLOWING

Whistle-blowers are employees who inform authorities of wrongdoings by their companies or coworkers. Whistle-blowers can be perceived as either heroes

---

6. Explain the three types of organizational justice and how they affect ethical decision making in organizations.

distributive justice
The fairness of the outcomes that individuals receive in an organization.

procedural justice
The fairness of the process by which outcomes are allocated in an organization.

interactional justice
The fairness of the interpersonal treatment given in the course of explaining procedures and outcomes.

whistle-blower
An employee who informs authorities of the wrongdoings of his or her company or coworkers.

or "vile wretches" depending on the circumstances of the situation. For a whistle-blower to be considered a public hero, the gravity of the situation that the whistle-blower reports to authorities must be of such magnitude and quality as to be perceived as abhorrent by others.[88] In contrast, the whistle-blower is considered a vile wretch if others see the act of whistle-blowing as more offensive than the situation the whistle-blower reports to authorities.

Whistle-blowing is important in the United States because committed organizational members sometimes engage in unethical behavior in an intense desire to succeed. Many examples of whistle-blowing can be found in corporate America. For example, one former Coke employee made a number of allegations against the company and issued an ultimatum: Coke must pay him almost $45 million or he would go to the media.[89] While a Georgia state court dismissed most of the allegations, Coke still had to defend itself against claims related to wrongful termination. One of the former employee's allegations relating to a falsified marketing test did have the effect of Coke making a public apology and offering to pay Burger King $21 million.

Organizations can manage whistle-blowing by communicating the conditions that are appropriate for the disclosure of wrongdoing. Clearly delineating wrongful behavior and the appropriate ways to respond are important organizational actions.

▮ SOCIAL RESPONSIBILITY

Corporate *social responsibility* is the obligation of an organization to behave in ethical ways in the social environment in which it operates. Ethical conduct at the individual level can translate into social responsibility at the organizational level. When Malden Mills, the maker of Polartec, burned down in 1995, the company's president, Aaron Feuerstein, paid workers during the months it took to rebuild the company. Although doing so cost the company a lot of money and was not required by law, Feuerstein said his own values caused him to do the socially responsible thing. Malden Mills recovered financially and continues its success with Polartec.

Socially responsible actions are expected of organizations. Current concerns include protecting the environment, promoting worker safety, supporting social issues, and investing in the community, among others. Some organizations, like IBM, loan executives to inner-city schools to teach science and math. Other organizations, like Patagonia, demonstrate social responsibility through environmentalism. Firms that are seen as socially responsible have a competitive advantage in attracting applicants.[90]

social responsibility
The obligation of an organization to behave in ethical ways.

▮ CODES OF ETHICS

One of the characteristics of mature professions is the existence of a code of ethics to which the practitioners adhere in their actions and behavior. An example is the Hippocratic oath in medicine. Although some of the individual differences we address in Chapter 4 produce ethical or unethical orientations in specific people, a profession's code of ethics becomes a standard against which members can measure themselves in the absence of internalized standards.

No universal code of ethics or oath exists for business as it does for medicine. However, Paul Harris and four business colleagues, who founded Rotary International in 1905, made an effort to address ethical and moral behavior right from the beginning. During the business struggles of the Great Depression of the 1930s,

The Four-Way Test
OF WHAT WE THINK, SAY, OR DO

1. Is it the TRUTH?

2. Is it FAIR to all concerned?

3. Will it build GOODWILL and better friendships?

4. Will it be BENEFICIAL to all concerned?

FIGURE 2.2

The Four-Way Test

Chicago Rotarian Herbert J. Taylor developed The Four-Way Test for doing business.[91] Now used in more than 166 nations throughout the world by the 1.2 million Rotarians in more than 30,000 Rotary clubs, The Four-Way Test (see Figure 2.2) focuses on key ethical and moral questions.

Beyond the individual and professional level, corporate culture is another excellent starting point for addressing ethics and morality. In Chapter 16, we examine how corporate culture and leader behavior trickle down the company, setting a standard for all below. In some cases, the corporate ethics may be captured in a regulation. For example, the Joint Ethics Regulation (DOD 5500.7-R, August 1993) specifies the ethical standards to which all U.S. military personnel are to adhere. In other cases, the corporate ethics may be in the form of a credo. Johnson & Johnson's credo, shown in Figure 2.3,

FIGURE 2.3

The Johnson & Johnson Credo

We believe our first responsibility is to the doctors, nurses and patients, to mothers and fathers and all others who use our products and services. In meeting their needs everything we do must be of high quality. We must constantly strive to reduce our costs in order to maintain reasonable prices. Customers' orders must be serviced promptly and accurately. Our suppliers and distributors must have an opportunity to make a fair profit.

We are responsible to our employees, the men and women who work with us throughout the world. Everyone must be considered as an individual. We must respect their dignity and recognize their merit. They must have a sense of security in their jobs. Compensation must be fair and adequate, and working conditions clean, orderly and safe. We must be mindful of ways to help our employees fulfill their family responsibilities. Employees must feel free to make suggestions and complaints. There must be equal opportunity for employment, development and advancement for those qualified. We must provide competent management, and their actions must be just and ethical.

We are responsible to the communities in which we live and work and to the world community as well. We must be good citizens—support good works and charities and bear our fair share of taxes. We must encourage civic improvements and better health and education. We must maintain in good order the property we are privileged to use, protecting the environment and natural resources.

Our final responsibility is to our stockholders. Business must make a sound profit. We must experiment with new ideas. Research must be carried on, innovative programs developed and mistakes paid for. New equipment must be purchased, new facilities provided and new products launched. Reserves must be created to provide for adverse times. When we operate according to these principles, the stockholders should realize a fair return.

SOURCE: Johnson & Johnson.

helped hundreds of employees ethically address the criminal tampering with Tylenol products. In its 1986 centennial annual report, J & J attributed its success in this crisis, as well as its long-term business growth (a compound sales rate of 11.6 percent for 100 years), to "our unique form of decentralized management, our adherence to the ethical principles embodied in our credo, and our emphasis on managing the business for the long term."

Individual codes of ethics, professional oaths, and organizational credos all must be anchored in a moral, ethical framework. They are always open to question and continuous improvement using ethical theories as a tool for reexamining the soundness of the current standard. Although a universal right and wrong may exist, it would be hard to argue that there is only one code of ethics to which all individuals, professions, and organizations can subscribe.

MANAGERIAL IMPLICATIONS: BEATING THE CHALLENGES

Organizational success depends on managers' ability to address the challenges of globalization, workforce diversity, and ethics. Failure to address the challenges can be costly. Think about Pepsi's losses to Coke in the global cola wars. Coke is winning the battle and capitalizing on the huge opportunities and profits from global markets. A racial discrimination lawsuit against Texaco not only cost the company millions in a settlement but also damaged the company's reputation. Mitsubishi suffered a similar fate in a sexual harassment scandal. Failure to address these challenges can mean costly losses, damage to reputations, and ultimately an organization's demise.

These challenges are important because the way managers handle them shapes employee behavior. Developing global mindsets among employees expands their worldview and puts competition on a larger scale. Knowing that diversity is valued and differences are assets causes employees to think twice about engaging in behaviors that are discriminatory. Sending a message that unethical behavior is not tolerated lets employees know that doing the right thing pays.

These challenges are recurring themes that you will see throughout our book. We show you how companies are tackling these challenges and how organizational behavior can be used to create opportunity in organizations, which is a must if they are to remain competitive.

LOOKING BACK :: PIXAR ANIMATION STUDIOS

The Dream Becomes Reality

Rather than moving forward in frustration given the limits of his drawing abilities, Ed Catmull turned in a new direction. He enrolled in the University of Utah's computer science program. His classmates included Jim Clark, John Warnock, and others who became the forefront of a revolution in computer graphics. Clark went on to become founder of Silicon Graphics and Netscape, while Warnock founded Adobe Systems.

Catmull was in the midst of this hotbed of change, challenge, and exciting times. He ultimately earned his Ph.D. and ran a research laboratory before landing at Lucasfilm in 1979. That was the time in which *Star Wars* was a recent phenomenon and George Lucas had recognized the value of computer-generated special effects. From Lucasfilm, Catmull truly began coming home to his dream of being an animator. Steve Jobs bought Lucasfilm's computer division for $10 million in 1986, and Catmull became one of the cofounders of a new, stand-alone company christened Pixar. Over the decades, Pixar has forged an innovative culture and distinctive competence.[92]

Embedding a culture of innovation in a fantasy industry can be a challenge in itself. When asked about whether he was concerned that others were stealing his ideas early on, Walt Disney responded by saying that he could create ideas faster than others could steal them. Disney planned to stay ahead of the curve. So, too, with Pixar; it stays ahead of the curve. Pixar recognizes that as soon as you are successful, competitors jump on the bandwagon. And, imitators can do a great job of replicating cutting-edge creations. Therefore, Pixar treats every one of its movie creations as a stepping stone on a positive learning curve in which it learns what works and what does not work. Pixar wants to be a stepping stone for itself, benefiting from its own learning, rather than a stepping stone for others who would aspire to climb over Pixar in their own ascent.

Pixar's distinctive competence lies in its creation of a variety of original software programs and wealth of technical wizardry. It is the only major studio working exclusively in computer-generated animation. Pixar's program can model surface textures, such as metal, cloth, or hair, and create lighting effects, such as bright sunlight or flickering candlelight. The studio's RenderMan program captures all the data and helps artists create the final images. RenderMan won an Academy Award for technical achievement in 2001. More than bells and whistles, Pixar has distinctive competence in the good stories that emerge from its movie scripts; that is the foundation of its business.

CHAPTER SUMMARY

1. To ensure that their organizations meet the competition, managers must tackle important challenges: globalization, workforce diversity, and ethical behavior.

2. The five cultural differences that affect work-related attitudes are individualism versus collectivism, power distance, uncertainty avoidance, masculinity versus femininity, and time orientation.

3. Diversity encompasses gender, culture, personality, sexual orientation, religion, ability, race, social status, and a host of other differences.

4. Managers must take a proactive approach to managing diversity so that differences are valued and capitalized upon.

5. Three types of ethical theories include consequential theories, rule-based theories, and character theories.

6. Ethical dilemmas emerge for people at work in the areas of employee rights, sexual harassment, romantic involvements, organizational justice, whistle-blowing, and social responsibility.

KEY TERMS

character theory (p. 50)

collectivism (p. 36)

consequential theory (p. 49)

distributive justice (p. 54)

diversity (p. 41)

expatriate manager (p. 38)

femininity (p. 37)

glass ceiling (p. 43)

guanxi (p. 34)

individualism (p. 36)

interactional justice (p. 54)

masculinity (p. 37)

power distance (p. 36)

procedural justice (p. 54)

rule-based theory (p. 49)

social responsibility (p. 55)

time orientation (p. 37)

transnational organization (p. 34)

uncertainty avoidance (p. 37)

whistle-blower (p. 54)

REVIEW QUESTIONS

1. What are Hofstede's five dimensions of cultural differences that affect work attitudes? Using these dimensions, describe the United States.

2. What are the primary sources of diversity in the U.S. workforce?

3. What are the potential benefits and problems of diversity?

4. What is the reality of the glass ceiling? What would it take to change this reality?

5. What are some of the ethical challenges encountered in organizations?

6. Describe the differences between distributive, interactional, and procedural justice.

7. Do organizations need to have formal codes of ethics?

Discussion and Communication QUESTIONS

1. How can managers be encouraged to develop global thinking? How can managers dispel stereotypes about other cultures?

2. What effects will the globalization of business have on a company's culture? How can an organization with a strong "made in America" identity compete in the global marketplace?

3. Why is diversity such an important issue? Is the workforce more diverse today than in the past?

4. How does a manager strike a balance between encouraging employees to celebrate their own cultures and forming a single unified culture within the organization?

5. Do you agree with Hofstede's findings about U.S. culture? Other cultures? On what do you base your agreement or disagreement?

6. (*communication question*) Select one of the challenges (globalization, diversity, ethics) and write a brief position paper arguing for its importance to managers.

7. (*communication question*) Find someone whose culture is different from your own. This might be a classmate, an international student, or a Native American at your university. Interview the person about his or her culture, using Hofstede's dimensions. Also ask what you might need to know about doing business in the person's country (e.g., customs, etiquette). Be prepared to share this information in class.

ETHICAL DILEMMA

Jill Warner, president of Ace Toys, sat looking at the monthly profit and loss statement. For the fifth month in a row, the company had lost money. Labor costs were killing it. Jill had done everything she could think of to reduce costs and still produce a quality product. She was beginning to face the fact that soon she would no longer be able to avoid the idea of outsourcing. It was a concept that Jill had done everything to avoid, but it was beginning to look inevitable.

Jill felt strongly about making a quality American product using American workers in an American factory. But if things continued the way they were, she was going to have to do something. She owed

it to her stockholders and board of directors to keep the company financially healthy. They had entrusted her with the future of the company, and she could not let them down. It was not her money or company to do with as she pleased. Her job was to make sure that Ace Toys flourished.

However, if she chose to outsource the production segment of the company, only management and the sales force would keep their jobs. How could she face the 500 people who would lose their jobs? How would the small community that depended on those 500 jobs survive? She also worried about the customers who had come to depend on Ace Toys to produce a safe product that they could give to their children with confidence. Would that quality suffer if she sent production halfway around the world? How could she ensure that the company she hired to produce their toys would live up to Ace's standards? Would the other company pay a fair wage and not employ children? The questions seemed endless, but Jill needed to decide how to save the company.

QUESTIONS

1. Is sending jobs out of the country unethical?
2. Using rule, virtue, right, and justice theories, evaluate Jill's options.

E X P E R I E N T I A L   E X E R C I S E S

2.1 INTERNATIONAL ORIENTATIONS

1. Preparation (preclass)
Read the background on the International Orientation Scale and the case study "Office Supplies International—Marketing Associate," complete the ratings and questions, and fill out the self-assessment inventory.

2. Group Discussions
Groups of four to six people discuss their answers to the case study questions and their own responses to the self-assessment.

3. Class Discussion
Instructor leads a discussion on the International Orientation Scale and the difficulties and challenges of adjusting to a new culture. Why do some people adjust more easily than others? What can you do to adjust to a new culture? What can you regularly do that will help you adjust in the future to almost any new culture?

OFFICE SUPPLIES INTERNATIONAL— MARKETING ASSOCIATE*

Jonathan Fraser is a marketing associate for a large multinational corporation, Office Supplies International (OSI), in Buffalo, New York. He is being considered for a transfer to the international division of OSI. This position will require that he spend between one and three years working abroad in one of OSI's three foreign subsidiaries: OSI-France, OSI-Japan, or OSI-Australia. This transfer is considered a fast track career move at OSI, and Jonathan feels honored to be in the running for the position.

Jonathan has been working at OSI since he graduated with his bachelor's degree in marketing 10 years ago. He is married and has lived and worked in Buffalo all his life. Jonathan's parents are first-generation German Americans. His grandparents, although deceased, spoke only German at home and upheld many of their ethnic traditions. His parents, although quite "Americanized," have retained some of their German traditions. To communicate better with his grandparents, Jonathan took German in high school but never used it because his grandparents had passed away.

In college, Jonathan joined the German Club and was a club officer for two years. His other collegiate extracurricular activity was playing for the varsity baseball team. Jonathan still enjoys playing in a summer softball league with his college friends. Given his athletic interests, he volunteered to be the athletic programming coordinator at OSI, where he organizes the company's softball and volleyball teams. Jonathan has been making steady progress at OSI. Last year, he was named marketing associate of the year.

His wife, Sue, is also a Buffalo native. She teaches English literature at the high school in one of the middle-class suburbs of Buffalo. Sue took five years off from teaching after she had a baby but returned to teaching this year when Janine, their five-year-old daughter, started kindergarten. She is happy to be resuming her career. One or two nights a week, Sue volunteers at the city mission where she works as a career counselor and a basic skills trainer. For fun, she takes both pottery and ethnic cooking classes.

Both Sue and Jonathan are excited about the potential transfer and accompanying pay raise. They are, however, also feeling apprehensive and cautious. Neither Sue nor Jonathan has ever lived away from their families in Buffalo, and Sue is concerned about giving up her newly reestablished career. Their daughter Janine has just started school, and Jonathan and Sue are uncertain whether living abroad is the best thing for her at her age.

Using the following three-point scale, try to rate Jonathan and Sue as potential expatriates. Write a sentence or two on why you gave the ratings you did.

RATING SCALE

1. Based on this dimension, this person would adjust well to living abroad.
2. Based on this dimension, this person may or may not adjust well to living abroad.
3. Based on this dimension, this person would not adjust well to living abroad.

JONATHAN'S INTERNATIONAL ORIENTATION

RATING DIMENSION	RATING AND REASON FOR RATING
International attitudes	
Foreign experiences	
Comfort with differences	
Participation in cultural events	

SUE'S INTERNATIONAL ORIENTATION

RATING DIMENSION	RATING AND REASON FOR RATING
International attitudes	
Foreign experiences	
Comfort with differences	
Participation in cultural events	

DISCUSSION QUESTIONS: OFFICE SUPPLIES INTERNATIONAL

1. Imagine that you are the international human resource manager for OSI. Your job is to interview both Jonathan and Sue to determine whether they should be sent abroad. What are some of the questions you would ask? What critical information do you feel is missing? It might be helpful to role-play the three parts and evaluate your classmates' responses as Jonathan and Sue.
2. Suppose France is the country where they would be sent. To what extent would your ratings change? What else would you change about the way you are assessing the couple?

3. Now answer the same questions, except this time they are being sent to Japan. Repeat the exercise for Australia.
4. For those dimensions that you rated Sue and Jonathan either 2 or 3 (indicating that they might have a potential adjustment problem), what would you suggest for training and development? What might be included in a training program?
5. Reflect on your own life for a moment and give yourself a rating on each of the following dimensions. Try to justify why you rated yourself as you did. Do you feel that you would adjust well to living abroad? What might be difficult for you?

RATING DIMENSION	RATING AND REASON FOR RATING FRANCE, JAPAN, AUSTRALIA (OR OTHER)
International attitudes	
Foreign experiences	
Comfort with differences	
Participation in cultural events	

6. Generally, what are some of the potential problems a dual-career couple might face? What are some of the solutions to those problems?
7. How would the ages of children affect the expatriate's assignment? At what age should the children's international orientations be assessed along with their parents?

INTERNATIONAL ORIENTATION SCALE

The following sample items are taken from the International Orientation Scale. Answer each question and give yourself a score for each dimension. The highest possible score for any dimension is 20 points.

DIMENSION 1: INTERNATIONAL ATTITUDES

Use the following scale to answer questions Q1 through Q4.

1	*Strongly agree*
2	*Agree somewhat*
3	*Maybe or unsure*
4	*Disagree somewhat*
5	*Strongly disagree*

Q1. Foreign language skills should be taught as early as elementary school. _____

Q2. Traveling the world is a priority in my life. _____

Q3. A year-long overseas assignment (from my company) would be a fantastic opportunity for my family and me. _____

Q4. Other countries fascinate me. _____

Total Dimension 1 _____

DIMENSION 2: FOREIGN EXPERIENCES

Q1. I have studied a foreign language.

1 Never
2 For less than a year
3 For a year
4 For a few years
5 For several years

Q2. I am fluent in another language.

1 I don't know another language.
2 I am limited to very short and simple phrases.
3 I know basic grammatical structure and speak with a limited vocabulary.
4 I understand conversation on most topics.
5 I am very fluent in another language.

Q3. I have spent time overseas (traveling, studying abroad, etc.).

1 Never
2 About a week
3 A few weeks
4 A few months
5 Several months or years

Q4. I was overseas before the age of 18.

1 Never
2 About a week
3 A few weeks
4 A few months
5 Several months or years

Total Dimension 2 _____

DIMENSION 3: COMFORT WITH DIFFERENCES

Use the following scale for questions Q1 through Q4.

1 *Quite similar*
2 *Mostly similar*
3 *Somewhat different*
4 *Quite different*
5 *Extremely different*

Q1. My friends' career goals, interests, and education are . . . _____

Q2. My friends' ethnic backgrounds are . . . _____

Q3. My friends' religious affiliations are . . . _____

Q4. My friends' first languages are . . . _____

Total Dimension 3 _____

DIMENSION 4: PARTICIPATION IN CULTURAL EVENTS

Use the following scale to answer questions Q1 through Q4.

1 *Never*
2 *Seldom*
3 *Sometimes*
4 *Frequently*
5 *As often as possible*

Q1. I eat at a variety of ethnic restaurants (e.g., Greek, Polynesian, Thai, German). _____

Q2. I watch the major networks' world news programs. _____

Q3. I attend ethnic festivals. _____

Q4. I visit art galleries and museums. _____

Total Dimension 4 _____

SELF-ASSESSMENT DISCUSSION QUESTIONS:

Do any of these scores suprise you?

Would you like to improve your international orientation?

If so, what could you do to change various aspects of your life?

*"Office Supplies International—Marketing Associate" by Paula Caligiuri. Copyright © 1994 by Paula Caligiuri, Ph.D. Information for The International Orientation Scale can be obtained by contacting Paula Caligiuri, Ph.D. at 732-445-5228 or e-mail: paula@caligiuri.com. Reprinted by permission of the author.

SOURCE: Dorothy Marcic and Sheila Puffer, *Management International*, West Publishing, 1994. All rights reserved. May not be reproduced without written permission of the publisher.

2.2 ETHICAL DILEMMAS

Divide the class into five groups. Each group should choose one of the following scenarios and agree on a course of action.

1. Sam works for you. He is technically capable and a good worker, but he does not get along well with others in the work group. When Sam has an opportunity to transfer, you encourage him to take it. What would you say to Sam's potential supervisor when he asks about Sam?

2. Your boss has told you that you must reduce your work group by 30 percent. Which of the following criteria would you use to lay off workers?

    a. Lay off older, higher paid employees.

    b. Lay off younger, lower paid employees.

    c. Lay off workers based on seniority only.

    d. Lay off workers based on performance only.

3. You are an engineer, but you are not working on your company's Department of Transportation (DOT) project. One day you overhear a conversation in the cafeteria between the program manager and the project engineer that makes you reasonably sure a large contract will soon be given to the ABC Company to develop and manufacture a key DOT subsystem. ABC is a small firm, and its stock is traded over the counter. You feel sure that the stock will rise from its present $2.25 per share as soon as news of the DOT contract gets out. Would you go out and buy ABC's stock?

4. You are the project engineer working on the development of a small liquid rocket engine. You know that if you could achieve a throttling ratio greater than 8 to 1, your system would be considered a success and continue to receive funding support. To date, the best you have achieved is a 4 to 1 ratio. You have an unproven idea that you feel has a 50 percent chance of being successful. Your project is currently being reviewed to determine if it should be continued. You would like to continue it. How optimistically should you present the test results?

5. Imagine that you are the president of a company in a highly competitive industry. You learn that a competitor has made an important scientific discovery that is not patentable and will give that company an advantage that will substantially reduce the profits of your company for about a year. There is some hope of hiring one of the competitor's employees who knows the details of the discovery. Would you try to hire this person?

Each group should present its scenario and chosen course of action to the class. The class should then evaluate the ethics of the course of action, using the following questions to guide discussion:

1. Are you following rules that are understood and accepted?

2. Are you comfortable discussing and defending your action?

3. Would you want someone to do this to you?

4. What if everyone acted this way?

5. Are there alternatives that rest on firmer ethical ground?

SOURCES: Scenarios adapted from R. A. DiBattista, "Providing a Rationale for Ethical Conduct from Alternatives Taken in Ethical Dilemmas," *Journal of General Psychology* 116 (1989): 207–214; discussion questions adapted with the permission of The Free Press, a division of Simon & Schuster, Inc. from *The Manager as Negotiator: Bargaining for Cooperation and Competitive Gain* by David A. Lax and James K. Sebenius 0-02-918770-2. Copyright © 1986 by David A. Lax and James K. Sebenius. All rights reserved.

Personality, Perception, and Attribution

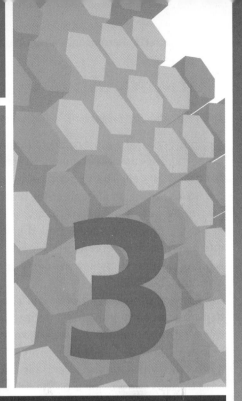

3

LEARNING OBJECTIVES

After reading this chapter, you should be able to do the following:

: 1. Describe individual differences and their importance in understanding behavior.

: 2. Define *personality*.

: 3. Identify several personality characteristics and their influences on behavior in organizations.

: 4. Give examples of each personality characteristic from your own work experience and how you would apply your knowledge in managing personality differences.

: 5. Discuss Carl Jung's contribution to our understanding of individual differences, and explain how his theory is used in the Myers-Briggs Type Indicator® instrument.

: 6. Evaluate the importance of the MBTI to managers.

: 7. Define *social perception* and explain how characteristics of the perceiver, the target, and the situation affect it.

: 8. Identify five common barriers to social perception.

: 9. Explain the attribution process and how attributions affect managerial behavior.

: 10. Evaluate the accuracy of managerial attributions from the standpoint of attribution biases and errors.

<u>THINKING AHEAD</u> :: Virgin Group Ltd.

A Different Individual: Sir Richard Branson

Virgin is one of the most respected brands in Great Britain and is rapidly becoming an important global brand as well. The Virgin brand was started in the 1970s with a small mail order record company that grew out of a student magazine. Since then, Richard Branson has developed the Virgin brand into a veritable entrepreneurial empire. Sir Branson is an interesting study in personality and its effects on human behavior.

Branson dropped out of school at an early age to pursue his entrepreneurial interests. In school, he was a pitiful student but a superb athlete. Though he was dyslexic and had vision problems, his inability to read, write, and spell and his poor performance on tests were blamed on stupidity or laziness. In commenting on Branson's academic miseries as a

child in relation to his athletic and future entrepreneurial successes, one observer noted:

In the end, it was the tests that failed. They totally missed his ability and passion for sports. They had no means to identify ambition, the fire inside that drives people to find a path to success that zigzags around the maze of standard doors that won't open. They never identified the most important talent of all. It's the ability to connect with people, mind to mind, and soul to soul. It's that rare power to energize the ambitions of others so that they, too, rise to the level of their dreams.

Want to learn more about what makes Sir Richard Branson unique? Read the Looking Back feature at the end of the chapter.

SOURCES: This case was written by Michael K. McCuddy, The Louis S. and Mary L. Morgal Chair of Christian Business Ethics and Professor of Management, College of Business Administration, Valparaiso University. This case was developed from material contained on the Virgin Group Web site at http://www.virgin.com and in the following articles: J. Hopkins, "Entrepreneurs Are Born, But Can They Be Taught?" *USA Today* (April 7, 2004), accessed from http://search.epnet.com/direct.asp?an=JOE398148936304$db=f5h; B. Morris, "Richard Branson: What a Life. 'I don't think of work as work and play as play. It's all living.'" *Fortune* (October 6, 2003), accessed at http://www.fortune.com; and J. Shepler, "Richard Branson's Virgin Success: The Incredible Triumph of an Enigmatic Entrepreneur," accessed at http://www.johnshepler.com.

: **1.** Describe individual differences and their importance in understanding behavior.

individual differences
The way in which factors such as skills, abilities, personalities, perceptions, attitudes, values, and ethics differ from one individual to another.

INDIVIDUAL DIFFERENCES AND ORGANIZATIONAL BEHAVIOR

In this chapter and continuing in Chapter 4, we explore the concept of *individual differences*. Individuals are unique in terms of their skills, abilities, personalities, perceptions, attitudes, emotions, and ethics. These are just a few of the ways individuals may be similar to or different from one another. Individual differences represent the essence of the challenge of management, because no two individuals are completely alike. Managers face the challenge of working with people who possess a multitude of individual characteristics, so the more managers understand individual differences, the better they can work with others. Figure 3.1 illustrates how individual differences affect human behavior.

The basis for understanding individual differences stems from Lewin's early contention that behavior is a function of the person and the environment.[1] Lewin expressed this idea in an equation: B = f(P, E), where B = behavior, P = person,

FIGURE 3.1

Variables Influencing
Individual Behavior

and E = environment. This idea has been developed by the *interactional psychology* approach.[2] Basically, this approach says that in order to understand human behavior, we must know something about the person and something about the situation. There are four basic propositions of interactional psychology:

1. Behavior is a function of a continuous, multidirectional interaction between the person and the situation.

2. The person is active in this process and is both changed by situations and changes situations.

3. People vary in many characteristics, including cognitive, affective, motivational, and ability factors.

4. Two interpretations of situations are important: the objective situation and the person's subjective view of the situation.[3]

The interactional psychology approach points out the need to study both persons and situations. We will focus on personal and situational factors throughout the text. The person consists of individual differences such as those we emphasize in this chapter and Chapter 4: skills, abilities, personality, perception, attribution, attitudes, emotions, and ethics. The situation consists of the environment the person operates in, and it can include things like the organization, work group, personal life situation, job characteristics, and many other environmental influences.

interactional psychology
The psychological approach that emphasizes that in order to understand human behavior, we must know something about the person and about the situation.

⚑ SKILLS AND ABILITIES

There are many skills and abilities that relate to work outcomes. General mental ability (GMA) was introduced by Spearman (1904)[4] almost 100 years ago. It is defined as an individual's innate cognitive intelligence. It was the single best predictor of work performance across many occupations studied both here in the United States[5] and across different cultures.[6] Emotional intelligence (EI) is an ability of particular importance for leaders. Leaders who have more EI are more effective because they can accurately perceive and manage the followers' emotions. We will revisit this concept of emotional intelligence in Chapter 11. Another important and fascinating individual difference is personality.

: **2.** Define *personality*.

personality
A relatively stable set of characteristics that influence an individual's behavior.

PERSONALITY

What makes an individual behave in consistent ways in a variety of situations? Personality is an individual difference that lends consistency to a person's behavior. *Personality* is defined as a relatively stable set of characteristics that influence an individual's behavior. Although there is debate about the determinants of personality, we conclude that there are several origins. One determinant is heredity, and some interesting studies have supported this position. Identical twins who are separated at birth and raised apart in very different situations have been found to share personality traits and job preferences. For example, about half of the variation in traits like extraversion, impulsiveness, and flexibility was found to be genetically determined; that is, identical twins who grew up in different environments shared these traits.[7] In addition, the twins held similar jobs.[8] Thus, genetics do appear to influence personality.

Another determinant of personality is the environment to which a person is exposed. Family influences, cultural influences, educational influences, and other environmental forces shape personality. Personality is therefore shaped by both heredity and environment. Sir Richard Branson is a prime illustration of this concept as his childhood was marked by his mom encouraging him to take risks and never be afraid. He attributes much of his entrepreneurial nature to such early influences.

BIG FIVE PERSONALITY MODEL

Personality theories have long argued that in order to understand individual behavior, people's behavioral patterns can be broken down into a series of observable traits. While several traditions of personality research exist, the most popular personality classification is that of the Big Five. The "Big Five" traits include extraversion, agreeableness, conscientiousness, emotional stability, and openness to experience.[9] Descriptions of the "Big Five" are shown in Table 3.1. The Big Five are broad, global traits that are associated with behaviors at work.

From preliminary research, we know that introverted and conscientious employees are less likely to be absent from work.[10] In making peer evaluations, individuals with high agreeableness tend to rate others more leniently, while individuals with high conscientiousness tend to be tougher as raters.[11] Extraverts tend to have higher salaries, receive more promotions, and are more satisfied with their careers.[12] Across lots of occupations, people who are conscientious are more motivated and are high performers.[13] When you view more specific occupations, however, different patterns of the Big Five factors are related to high performance. For customer service jobs, individuals high in emotional stability, agreeableness, and openness to experience perform best. For managers,

		TABLE 3.1
Extraversion	The person is gregarious, assertive, and sociable (as opposed to reserved, timid, and quiet).	The "Big Five" Personality Traits
Agreeableness	The person is cooperative, warm, and agreeable (rather than cold, disagreeable, and antagonistic).	
Conscientiousness	The person is hardworking, organized, and dependable (as opposed to lazy, disorganized, and unreliable).	
Emotional stability	The person is calm, self-confident, and cool (as opposed to insecure, anxious, and depressed).	
Openness to experience	The person is creative, curious, and cultured (rather than practical with narrow interests).	

SOURCES: P. T. Costa and R. R. McCrae, *The NEO-PI Personality Inventory* (Odessa, Fla.: Psychological Assessment Resources, 1992); J. F. Salgado, "The Five Factor Model of Personality and Job Performance in the European Community," *Journal of Applied Psychology* 82 (1997): 30–43.

emotional stability and extraversion are traits of top performers.[14] The Big Five framework has also been applied across cultures. It has held up well among Spanish and Mexican populations.[15] It remains to be seen whether or not the Big Five traits will emerge in studies of cultures that are extremely different from Western cultures.[16]

How would you classify Sir Richard Branson's personality in terms of the Big Five personality characteristics? How has openness to experience helped Branson be successful?

The trait approach has been the subject of considerable criticism. Some theorists argue that simply identifying traits is not enough; instead, personality is dynamic and not completely stable. Further, early trait theorists tended to ignore the influence of situations.[17] Also, the trait theory tends to ignore process—that is, how we get from a trait to a particular outcome.

INTEGRATIVE APPROACH

Recently, researchers have taken a broader, more *integrative approach* to the study of personality.[18] To capture its influence on behavior, personality is described as a composite of the individual's psychological processes. Personality dispositions include emotions, cognitions, attitudes, expectancies, and fantasies.[19] *Dispositions*, in this approach, simply mean the tendencies of individuals to respond to situations in consistent ways. Influenced by both genetics and experiences, dispositions can be modified. The integrative approach focuses on both person (dispositions) and situational variables as combined predictors of behavior.

integrative approach
The broad theory that describes personality as a composite of an individual's psychological processes.

◀◀think critically▶▶

Why should students of organizational behavior care about these theories? How do theories help your understanding of organizational behavior?

core self-evaluation
A set of personality traits reflecting an individual's fundamental evaluation of himself or herself.

locus of control
An individual's generalized belief about internal control (self-control) versus external control (control by the situation or by others).

general self-efficacy
An individual's general belief that he or she is capable of meeting job demands in a wide variety of situations.

■ PERSONALITY CHARACTERISTICS IN ORGANIZATIONS

Managers should learn as much as possible about personality in order to understand their employees. Hundreds of personality characteristics have been identified. We have selected three characteristics because of their particular influence on individual behavior in organizations: core self-evaluations (CSE), self-monitoring, and positive/negative affect. Because these characteristics affect performance at work, managers need to have a working knowledge of them.

CORE SELF-EVALUATIONS

Core self-evaluation (CSE) is a broad set of personality traits that refers to self-concept.[20] It is comprised of locus of control, self-esteem, generalized self-efficacy, and emotional stability. CSE has been found to predict both goal-directed behavior and performance,[21] even in non-U.S. cultures (e.g., Japan).[22] Each characteristic comprising CSE with the exception of emotional stability (as we discussed in the Big Five approach earlier) is addressed next.

LOCUS OF CONTROL

An individual's generalized belief about internal (self) versus external (situation or others) control is called *locus of control*. People who believe they control what happens to them are said to have an internal locus of control, whereas people who believe that circumstances or other people control their fate have an external locus of control.[23] Research on locus of control has strong implications for organizations. Internals (those with an internal locus of control) have been found to have higher job satisfaction and performance,[24] to be more likely to assume managerial positions, and to prefer participative management styles.[25] You can assess your locus of control in Challenge 3.1.

Internals and externals have similar positive reactions to being promoted, which include high job satisfaction, job involvement, and organizational commitment. The difference between the two is that internals continue to be happy long after the promotion, whereas externals' joy over the promotion is short lived. This might occur because externals do not believe their own performance led to the promotion.[26]

Knowing about locus of control can prove valuable to managers. Because internals believe they control what happens to them, they will want to exercise control in their work environment. Allowing internals considerable voice in how work is performed is important. Internals will not react well to being closely supervised. Externals, in contrast, may prefer a more structured work setting, and they may be more reluctant to participate in decision making.

SELF-EFFICACY

General self-efficacy is a person's overall view of himself/herself as being able to perform effectively in a wide variety of situations.[27] Employees with high general self-efficacy have more confidence in their job-related abilities and other personal resources (i.e., energy, influence over others, etc.) that help them function effectively on the job. People with low general self-efficacy often feel ineffective at work and may express doubts about performing a new task well. Previous success or performance is one of the most important determinants of self-efficacy. People who have

CHALLENGE 3.1

What's Your Locus of Control?

Below is a short scale that can give you an idea of your locus of control. For each of the four items, circle either choice a or choice b.

1. a. Becoming a success is a matter of hard work; luck has little or nothing to do with it.
   b. Getting a good job depends mainly on being in the right place at the right time.

2. a. The average citizen can have an influence in government decisions.
   b. This world is run by the few people in power, and there is not much the little guy can do about it.

3. a. As far as world affairs are concerned, most of us are the victims of forces we can neither understand nor control.
   b. By taking an active part in political and social affairs, people can control world events.

4. a. With enough effort, we can wipe out political corruption.
   b. It is difficult for people to have much control over the things politicians do in office.

Scoring Key:

The internal locus of control answers are:
1a, 2a, 3b, 4a

The external locus of control answers are:
1b, 2b, 3a, 4b

Determine which category you circled most frequently using the key to the left. This gives you an approximation of your locus of control.

Sources: T. Adeyemi-Bello, "Validating Rotter's Locus of Control Scale with a Sample of Not-for-Profit Leaders," *Management Research News* 24 (2001): 25–35; J. B. Rotter, "Generalized Expectancies for Internal vs. External Locus of Control of Reinforcement," *Psychological Monographs* 80, whole No. 609 (1966).

positive beliefs about their efficacy for performance are more likely to attempt difficult tasks, to persist in overcoming obstacles, and to experience less anxiety when faced with adversity.[28] People with high self-efficacy also value the ability to provide input, or "voice," at work. Because they are confident in their capability to provide meaningful input, they value the opportunity to participate.[29] High self-efficacy has also been recently related to higher job satisfaction and performance.[30]

There is another form of self-efficacy, called task-specific self-efficacy, which we will cover in Chapter 6. Task-specific self-efficacy is a person's belief that he or she can perform a specific task (for example, "I believe I can do this sales presentation today."). In contrast, general self-efficacy is more broad (for example, "I believe I can perform well in just about any part of the job.").

SELF-ESTEEM

Self-esteem is an individual's general feeling of self-worth. Individuals with high self-esteem have positive feelings about themselves, perceive themselves to have strengths as well as weaknesses, and believe their strengths are more important than their weaknesses.[31] Individuals with low self-esteem view themselves

self-esteem
An individual's general feeling of self-worth.

negatively. They are more strongly affected by what other people think of them, and they compliment individuals who give them positive feedback while cutting down people who give them negative feedback.[32]

Evaluations from other people affect our self-esteem. For example, you might be liked for who you are or you might be liked for your achievements. Being liked for who you are is more stable, and people who have this type of self-esteem are less defensive and more honest with themselves. Being liked for your achievement is more unstable; it waxes and wanes depending on how high your achievements are.[33]

A person's self-esteem affects a host of other attitudes and has important implications for behavior in organizations. People with high self-esteem perform better and are more satisfied with their jobs.[34] When they are involved in a job search, they seek out higher status jobs.[35] A work team made up of individuals with high self-esteem is more likely to be successful than a team with low or average self-esteem.[36]

Very high self-esteem may be too much of a good thing. When people with high self-esteem find themselves in stressful situations, they may brag inappropriately.[37] This may be viewed negatively by others, who see spontaneous boasting as egotistical. Very high self-esteem may also lead to overconfidence and to relationship conflicts with others who may not evaluate this behavior favorably.[38] Individuals with high self-esteem may shift their social identities to protect themselves when they do not live up to some standard. Take two students, Denise and Teresa, for example. If Denise outperforms Teresa on a statistics exam, Teresa may convince herself that Denise is not really a good person to compare against because Denise is an engineering major and Teresa is a physical education major. Teresa's high self-esteem is protecting her from this unfavorable comparison.[39]

Self-esteem may be strongly affected by situations. Success tends to raise self-esteem, whereas failure tends to lower it. Given that high self-esteem is generally a positive characteristic, managers should encourage employees to raise their self-esteem by giving them appropriate challenges and opportunities for success. These three characteristics along with the effects of emotional stability as discussed in the section on the Big Five constitute an important personality trait known as core self-evaluations. CSE is a strong predictor of both job satisfaction and job performance next only to GMA.[40]

SELF-MONITORING

self-monitoring
The extent to which people base their behavior on cues from other people and situations.

A characteristic with great potential for affecting behavior in organizations is *self-monitoring*—the extent to which people base their behavior on cues from other people and situations.[41] High self-monitors pay attention to what is appropriate in particular situations and to the behavior of other people, and they behave accordingly. Low self-monitors, in contrast, are not as vigilant to observe situational cues and act from internal states rather than paying attention to the situation. As a result, the behavior of low self-monitors is consistent across situations. High self-monitors, because their behavior varies with the situation, appear to be more unpredictable and less consistent. You can use Challenge 3.2 to assess your own self-monitoring tendencies.

Research is currently focusing on the effects of self-monitoring in organizations. In one study, the authors tracked the careers of 139 MBAs for five years to see whether high self-monitors were more likely to be promoted, change

CHALLENGE   3.2

Are You a High or Low Self-Monitor?

For the following items, circle T (true) if the statement is characteristic of your behavior. Circle F (false) if the statement does not reflect your behavior.

1. I find it hard to imitate the behavior of other people.   T   F
2. At parties and social gatherings, I do not attempt to do or say things that others will like.   T   F
3. I can only argue for ideas that I already believe.   T   F
4. I can make impromptu speeches even on topics about which I have almost no information. T   F
5. I guess I put on a show to impress or entertain others.   T   F
6. I would probably make a good actor.   T   F
7. In a group of people, I am rarely the center of attention.   T   F
8. In different situations and with different people, I often act like very different persons.   T   F
9. I am not particularly good at making other people like me.   T   F
10. I am not always the person I appear to be.   T   F
11. I would not change my opinions (or the way I do things) in order to please others or win their favor.   T   F
12. I have considered being an entertainer.   T   F
13. I have never been good at games like charades or at improvisational acting.   T   F
14. I have trouble changing my behavior to suit different people and different situations.   T   F
15. At a party, I let others keep the jokes and stories going.   T   F
16. I feel a bit awkward in company and do not show up quite as well as I should.   T   F
17. I can look anyone in the eye and tell a lie with a straight face (if it is for a good cause).   T   F
18. I may deceive people by being friendly when I really dislike them.   T   F

Scoring:

To score this questionnaire, give yourself 1 point for each of the following items that you answered T (true): 4, 5, 6, 8, 10, 12, 17, and 18. Now give yourself 1 point for each of the following items that you answered F (false): 1, 2, 3, 7, 9, 11, 13, 14, 15, and 16. Add both subtotals to find your overall score. If you scored 11 or above, you are probably a *high self-monitor*. If you scored 10 or under, you are probably a *low self-monitor*.

Source: From Mark Snyder, *Public Appearances, Private Realities: The Psychology of Self-Monitoring* (New York: W. H. Freeman. 1987). Used with permission.

employers, or make a job-related geographic move. The results were "yes" to each question. High self-monitors get promoted because they accomplish tasks through meeting the expectations of others and because they seek out central positions in social networks.[42] They are also more likely to use self-promotion to make others aware of their skills and accomplishments.[43] However, the high self-monitor's flexibility may not be suited for every job, and the tendency to move may not fit every organization.[44] Because high self-monitors base their behavior on cues from others and from the situation, they demonstrate higher levels of managerial self-awareness. This means that, as managers, they assess their own workplace behavior accurately.[45] Managers who are high self-monitors are also good at reading their employees' needs and changing the way they interact with employees depending on those needs.[46]

Although research on self-monitoring in organizations is in its early stages, we can speculate that high self-monitors respond more readily to work group norms, organizational culture, and supervisory feedback than do low self-monitors, who adhere more to internal guidelines for behavior ("I am who I am"). In addition, high self-monitors may be enthusiastic participants in the trend toward work teams because of their ability to assume flexible roles.

POSITIVE/NEGATIVE AFFECT

Recently, researchers have explored the effects of persistent mood dispositions at work. Individuals who focus on the positive aspects of themselves, other people, and the world in general are said to have *positive affect*.[47] In contrast, those who accentuate the negative in themselves, others, and the world are said to possess *negative affect* (also referred to as negative affectivity).[48] Positive affect is linked with job satisfaction, which we discuss at length in Chapter 4. Individuals with positive affect are more satisfied with their jobs.[49] In addition, individuals in a positive mood are more likely to help others at work and also engage in more organizational citizenship behaviors (OCBs).[50] Employees with positive affect are absent from work less often.[51] Positive affect has been linked to more life satisfaction and better performance across a variety of life and work domains.[52] Individuals with negative affect report more work stress.[53] Individual affect also influences the work group. Positive individual affect produces positive team affect, and this leads to more cooperation and less conflict within the team.[54]

Positive affect is a definite asset in work settings. Managers can do several things to promote positive affect, including allowing participative decision making and providing pleasant working conditions. We need to know more about inducing positive affect in the workplace.

The characteristics previously described are but a few of the personality characteristics that affect behavior and performance in organizations. Negative affect, for example, affects work stress as you'll see in Chapter 7. Another personality characteristic related to stress is Type A behavior, also presented in Chapter 7. You'll see other personality characteristics woven in throughout the book. Can managers predict the behavior of their employees by knowing their personalities? Not completely. You may recall that the interactional psychology model (Figure 3.1) requires both person and situation variables to predict behavior. Another idea to remember in predicting behavior is the strength of situational influences. Some situations are *strong situations* in that they overwhelm the effects of individual personalities. These situations are interpreted in the same way by different individuals, evoke agreement on the appropriate behavior in the situation, and provide cues to appropriate behavior. A performance appraisal session is an example of a strong situation. Employees know to listen to their boss and to contribute when asked to do so.

positive affect
An individual's tendency to accentuate the positive aspects of himself or herself, other people, and the world in general.

negative affect
An individual's tendency to accentuate the negative aspects of himself or herself, other people, and the world in general.

strong situation
A situation that overwhelms the effects of individual personalities by providing strong cues for appropriate behavior.

A weak situation, in contrast, is one that is open to many interpretations. It provides few cues to appropriate behavior and no obvious rewards for one behavior over another. Thus, individual personalities have a stronger influence in weak situations than in strong situations. An informal meeting without an agenda can be seen as a weak situation.

Organizations present combinations of strong and weak situations; therefore, personality has a stronger effect on behavior in some situations than in others.[55]

❷ APPLICATION OF PERSONALITY THEORY IN ORGANIZATIONS: THE MYERS-BRIGGS TYPE INDICATOR® INSTRUMENT

One approach to applying personality theory in organizations is the Jungian approach and its measurement tool, the MBTI instrument.

Swiss psychiatrist Carl Jung built his work on the notion that people are fundamentally different, but also fundamentally alike. His classic treatise *Psychological Types* proposed that the population was made up of two basic types—Extraverted types and Introverted types.[56] He went on to identify two types of Perceiving (Sensing and Intuition) and two types of Judgment (Thinking and Feeling). Perceiving (how we gather information) and Judging (how we make decisions) represent the basic mental functions that everyone uses.

Jung suggested that human similarities and differences could be understood by combining preferences. We prefer and choose one way of doing things over another. We are not exclusively one way or another; rather, we have a preference for Extraversion or Introversion, just as we have a preference for right-handedness or left-handedness. We may use each hand equally well, but when a ball is thrown at us by surprise, we will reach to catch it with our preferred hand. Jung's type theory argues that no preferences are better than others. Differences are to be understood, celebrated, and appreciated.

During the 1940s, a mother–daughter team became fascinated with individual differences among people and with the work of Carl Jung. Katharine Briggs and her daughter, Isabel Briggs Myers, developed the *Myers-Briggs Type Indicator® instrument* to put Jung's type theory into practical use. The MBTI instrument is used extensively in organizations as a basis for understanding individual differences. More than 3 million people complete the instrument per year in the United States.[57] The MBTI instrument has been used in career counseling, team building, conflict management, and understanding management styles.[58] In Experiential Exercise 3.1 at the end of this chapter, you can assess your own MBTI type. You might find it helpful to do this before reading on.

▦ THE PREFERENCES

There are four scale dichotomies in type theory with two possible choices for each scale. Table 3.2 shows these preferences. The combination of these preferences makes up an individual's psychological type.

5. Discuss Carl Jung's contribution to our understanding of individual differences, and explain how his theory is used in the Myers-Briggs Type Indicator® instrument.

6. Evaluate the importance of the MBTI to managers.

Myers-Briggs Type Indicator (MBTI)® instrument
An instrument developed to measure Carl Jung's theory of individual differences.

EXTRAVERSION	INTROVERSION	THINKING	FEELING
Outgoing	Quiet	Analytical	Subjective
Publicly expressive	Reserved	Clarity	Harmony
Interacting	Concentrating	Head	Heart
Speaks, then thinks	Thinks, then speaks	Justice	Mercy
Gregarious	Reflective	Rules	Circumstances
SENSING	**INTUITION**	**JUDGING**	**PERCEIVING**
Practical	General	Structured	Flexible
Specific	Abstract	Time oriented	Open ended
Feet on the ground	Head in the clouds	Decisive	Exploring
Details	Possibilities	Makes lists/uses them	Makes lists/loses them
Concrete	Theoretical	Organized	Spontaneous

TABLE 3.2

Type Theory Preferences and Descriptions

Extraversion

A preference indicating that an individual is energized by interaction with other people.

Introversion

A preference indicating that an individual is energized by time alone.

Sensing

Gathering information through the five senses.

Intuiting

Gathering information through a "sixth sense" and focusing on what could be rather than what actually exists.

EXTRAVERSION/INTROVERSION

The *Extraversion/Introversion* preference represents where you get your energy. The Extraverted type (E) is energized by interaction with other people. The Introverted type (I) is energized by time alone. Extraverted types typically have a wide social network, whereas Introverted types have a more narrow range of relationships. As articulated by Jung, this preference has nothing to do with social skills. Many Introverted types have excellent social skills but prefer the internal world of ideas, thoughts, and concepts. Extraverted types represent approximately 70 percent of the U.S. population.[59] Our culture rewards Extraverted types and nurtures them. Jung contended that the Extraversion/Introversion preference reflects the most important distinction between individuals.

In work settings, Extraverted types prefer variety, and they do not mind the interruptions of the phone or visits from coworkers. They communicate freely but may say things that they regret later. Introverted types prefer quiet for concentration, and they like to think things through in private. They do not mind working on a project for a long time and are careful with details. Introverted types dislike telephone interruptions, and they may have trouble recalling names and faces.

You may be surprised to learn that one of the most successful CEOs in the history of information technology, Michael Dell, is a confirmed introvert. He is known for his shyness and egoless demeanor. Knowing his personality, along with his strengths and weaknesses, has proved to be a formula for success. Michael Dell is one of the longest-tenured company founders and is now chairman of the Board at Dell.[60]

SENSING/INTUITING

The *Sensing/Intuiting* preference represents perception or how we prefer to gather information. In essence this preference reflects what we pay attention to. The Sensing type (S) pays attention to information gathered through the five senses and to what actually exists. The Intuitive type (N) pays attention to a "sixth sense" and to what could be rather than to what actually exists.[61] Approximately 70 percent of people in the United States are Sensing types.[62]

At work, Sensing types prefer specific answers to questions and can become frustrated with vague instructions. They like jobs that yield tangible results, and they enjoy using established skills more than learning new ones. Intuitive types like solving new problems and are impatient with routine details. They enjoy learning new skills more than actually using them. Intuitive types tend to think about several things at once, and they may be seen by others as absentminded. They like figuring out how things work just for the fun of it.

THINKING/FEELING

The *Thinking/Feeling* preference represents the way we prefer to make decisions. The Thinking type (T) makes decisions in a logical, objective fashion, whereas the Feeling type (F) makes decisions in a personal, value-oriented way. The general U.S. population is divided 50/50 on the Thinking/Feeling type preference, but it is interesting that two-thirds of all males are Thinking types, whereas two-thirds of all females are Feeling types. It is the one preference in type theory that has a strong gender difference. Thinking types tend to analyze decisions, whereas Feeling types sympathize. Thinking types try to be impersonal, whereas Feeling types base their decisions on how the outcome will affect the people involved.

In work settings, Thinking types tend to show less emotion, and they may become uncomfortable with people who do. They are likely to respond more readily to other people's thoughts. They tend to be firm minded and like putting things into a logical framework. Feeling types, in contrast, tend to be more comfortable with emotion in the workplace. They enjoy pleasing people and may enjoy frequent praise and encouragement.

Thinking
Making decisions in a logical, objective fashion.

Feeling
Making decisions in a personal, value-oriented way.

JUDGING/PERCEIVING

The *Judging/Perceiving* dichotomy reflects one's orientation to the outer world. The Judging type (J) loves closure. Judging types prefer to lead a planned, organized life and like making decisions. A person with a preference for Perceiving (P), in contrast, prefers a more flexible and spontaneous life and wants to keep options open. Imagine two people, one with a preference for Judging and the other for Perceiving, going out for dinner. The J asks the P to choose a restaurant, and the P suggests 10 alternatives. The J just wants to decide and get on with it, whereas the P wants to explore all the options.

For Judging types in all arenas of life, and especially at work, they love getting things accomplished and delight in marking off the completed items on their calendars. Perceiving types tend to adopt a wait-and-see attitude and to collect new information rather than draw conclusions. Perceiving types are curious and welcome new information. They may start too many projects and not finish them.

Judging Preference
Preferring closure and completion in making decisions.

Perceiving Preference
Preferring to explore many alternatives and flexibility.

■ THE SIXTEEN TYPES

The preferences combine to form 16 distinct types. For example, let's examine ESTJ. This type has Extraversion, Sensing, Thinking, and Judging preferences. ESTJs see the world as it is (S); make decisions objectively (T); and like structure, schedules, and order (J). Combining these qualities with their preference for interacting with others makes them natural managers. ESTJs are seen by others as dependable, practical, and able to get any job done. They are conscious of the chain of command and see work as a series of goals to be reached by following rules and regulations. They may have little tolerance for disorganization and have a high need for control. Research results from the *MBTI Atlas* show that most of the 7,463 managers studied were ESTJs.[63]

There are no good and bad types, and each type has its own strengths and weaknesses. Type has been found to be related to learning style, teaching style, and choice of occupation. For example, the MBTI types of engineering students at Georgia Tech were studied in order to see who was attracted to engineering and who was likely to leave the major. STs and NTs were more attracted to engineering. Es and Fs were more likely to withdraw from engineering courses.[64] Recent studies have begun to focus on the relationship between type and specific managerial behaviors. The Introverted type (I) and the Feeling type (F), for example, have been shown to be more effective at participative management than their counterparts, the Extraverted type and the Thinking type.[65] Companies like AT&T, ExxonMobil, and Honeywell use the MBTI instrument in their management development programs to help employees understand the different viewpoints of others in the organization. The MBTI instrument can also be used for team building. Hewlett-Packard and Armstrong World Industries use the MBTI instrument to help teams realize that diversity and differences lead to successful performance.

We turn now to another psychological process that forms the basis for individual differences. Perception shapes the way we view the world, and it varies greatly among individuals.

: **7.** Define *social perception* and explain how characteristics of the perceiver, the target, and the situation affect it.

social perception
The process of interpreting information about another person.

🔲 SOCIAL PERCEPTION

Perception involves the way we view the world around us. It adds meaning to information gathered via the five senses of touch, smell, hearing, vision, and taste. Perception is the primary vehicle through which we come to understand ourselves and our surroundings. Companies like Virgin Airlines, led by Richard Branson, rely heavily on consumers' perceptions of their marketing efforts. In this chapter, we focus specifically on one particular type of perception—social perception. *Social perception* is the process of interpreting information about another person. Virtually all management activities rely on perception. In appraising performance, managers use their perceptions of an employee's behavior as a basis for the evaluation.

One work situation that highlights the importance of perception is the selection interview. The consequences of a bad match between an individual and the organization are devastating for both parties, so it is essential that the data gathered be accurate. Typical first interviews are brief, and the candidate is usually one of many seen by an interviewer during a day. How long does it take for the interviewer to reach a decision about a candidate? In the first four to five minutes, the interviewer often makes an accept or reject decision based on his or her perception of the candidate.[66]

Perception is also culturally determined. Based on our cultural backgrounds, we tend to perceive things in certain ways. Read the following sentence:

Finished files are the result of years of scientific study combined with the experience of years.

Now quickly count the number of *F*s in the sentence. Individuals for whom English is their second language see all six *F*s. Most native English speakers report that there are three *F*s. Because of cultural conditioning, *of* is not an important word and is ignored.[67] Culture affects our interpretation of the data we gather, as well as the way we add meaning to it.

Valuing diversity, including cultural diversity, has been recognized as a key to international competitiveness.[68] This challenge and others make social perception skills essential to managerial success.

Richard Branson is an entrepreneur who is adept at managing social perceptions. He admits he is not one to ever pass up an opportunity for publicity. He believes that one core cause of his success is his enthusiasm for managing his relationship with both the media and people. A passionate activist, he recently pledged $3 billion to the fight against global warming. This amount constitutes profits from Virgin for 10 years and is estimated to be half his personal fortune. He is also known for his passion for environmentally friendly fuels, fighting HIV/AIDS, and education. It's the sum of his individual differences that makes Branson a unique leader.

Three major categories of factors influence our perception of another person: characteristics of ourselves, as perceivers; characteristics of the target person we are perceiving; and characteristics of the situation in which the interaction takes place. Figure 3.2 shows a model of social perception.

CHARACTERISTICS OF THE PERCEIVER

Several characteristics of the perceiver can affect social perception. One such characteristic is *familiarity* with the target (the person being perceived). When we are familiar with a person, we have multiple observations on which to base

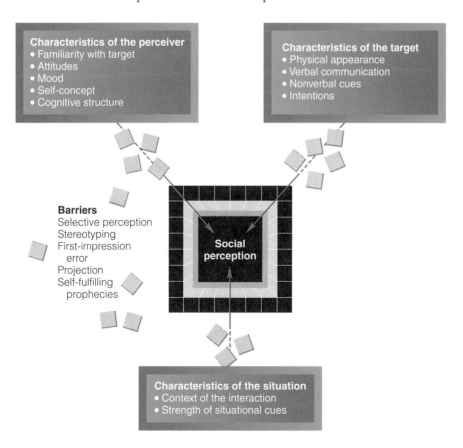

FIGURE 3.2

A Model for Social Perception

our impression of him or her. If the information we have gathered during these observations is accurate, we may have an accurate perception of the other person. Familiarity does not always mean accuracy, however. Sometimes, when we know a person well, we tend to screen out information that is inconsistent with what we believe the person is like. This is a particular danger in performance appraisals where the rater is familiar with the person being rated.

The perceiver's *attitudes* also affect social perception. Suppose you are interviewing candidates for a very important position in your organization—a position that requires negotiating contracts with suppliers, most of whom are male. You may feel that women are not capable of holding their own in tough negotiations. This attitude will doubtless affect your perceptions of the female candidates you interview.

Mood can have a strong influence on the way we perceive someone.[69] We think differently when we are happy than we do when we are depressed. In addition, we remember information that is consistent with our mood state better than information that is inconsistent with our mood state. When in a positive mood, we form more positive impressions of others. When in a negative mood, we tend to evaluate others unfavorably.

Another factor that can affect social perception is the perceiver's *self-concept.* An individual with a positive self-concept tends to notice positive attributes in another person. In contrast, a negative self-concept can lead a perceiver to pick out negative traits in another person. Greater understanding of self allows us to have more accurate perceptions of others.

Cognitive structure, an individual's pattern of thinking, also affects social perception. Some people have a tendency to perceive physical traits, such as height, weight, and appearance, more readily. Others tend to focus more on central traits, or personality dispositions. Cognitive complexity allows a person to perceive multiple characteristics of another person rather than attending to just a few traits.

▌ CHARACTERISTICS OF THE TARGET

Characteristics of the target, who is the person being perceived, influence social perception. *Physical appearance* plays a big role in our perception of others. The perceiver will notice the target's physical features like height, weight, estimated age, race, and gender. Clothing says a great deal about a person. Blue pin-striped suits, for example, are decoded to mean banking or Wall Street. Perceivers tend to notice physical appearance characteristics that contrast with the norm, that are intense, or that are new or unusual.[70] A loud person, one who dresses outlandishly, a very tall person, or a hyperactive child will be noticed because he or she provides a contrast to what is commonly encountered. In addition, people who are novel can attract attention. Newcomers or minorities in the organization are examples of novel individuals.

Physical attractiveness often colors our entire impression of another person. Interviewers rate attractive candidates more favorably, and attractive candidates are awarded higher starting salaries.[71, 72] People who are perceived as physically attractive face stereotypes as well. We will discuss these and other stereotypes later in this chapter.

Verbal communication from targets also affects our perception of them. We listen to the topics they speak about, their voice tone, and their accent and make judgments based on this input.

Nonverbal communication conveys a great deal of information about the target. Eye contact, facial expressions, body movements, and posture all are deciphered by the perceiver in an attempt to form an impression of the target. It is interesting that some nonverbal signals mean very different things in different cultures. The "okay" sign in the United States (forming a circle with the thumb and forefinger) is an insult in South America. Facial expressions, however, seem to have universal meanings. Individuals from different cultures are able to recognize and decipher expressions the same way.[73]

The *intentions* of the target are inferred by the perceiver, who observes the target's behavior. We may see our boss appear in our office doorway and think, "Oh no! She's going to give me more work to do." Or we may perceive that her intention is to congratulate us on a recent success. In any case, the perceiver's interpretation of the target's intentions affects the way the perceiver views the target. Recall our opening discussion of Sir Richard Branson. What is your perception of Richard Branson? How do you think your perceptions are affected by characteristics of you as the perceiver and Branson as the perceptual target?

CHARACTERISTICS OF THE SITUATION

The situation in which the interaction between the perceiver and the target takes place also influences the perceiver's impression of the target. The *social context* of the interaction is a major influence. Meeting a professor in his or her office affects your impression in a certain way that may contrast with the impression you would form had you met the professor in a local restaurant. In Japan, *social context* is very important. Business conversations after working hours or at lunch are taboo. If you try to talk business during these times, you may be perceived as rude.[74]

The *strength of situational cues* also affects social perception. As we discussed earlier in the chapter, strong situations provide strong cues as to appropriate behavior. In these situations, we assume that the individual's behavior can be accounted for by the situation, and that it may not reflect the individual's disposition. This is the *discounting principle* in social perception.[75] For example, you may encounter an automobile salesperson who has a warm and personable manner, asks about your work and hobbies, and seems genuinely interested in your taste in cars. Can you assume that this behavior reflects the salesperson's personality? You probably cannot, because of the influence of the situation. This person is trying to sell you a car, and in this particular situation he or she probably treats all customers in this manner.

discounting principle
The assumption that an individual's behavior is accounted for by the situation.

You can see that characteristics of the perceiver, the target, and the situation all affect social perception. It would be wonderful if all of us had accurate social perception skills. Unfortunately, barriers often prevent us from perceiving another person accurately.

BARRIERS TO SOCIAL PERCEPTION

Several factors lead us to form inaccurate impressions of others. Five of these barriers to social perception are selective perception, stereotyping, first-impression error, projection, and self-fulfilling prophecies.

: 8. Identify five common barriers to social perception.

selective perception
The process of selecting information that supports our individual viewpoints while discounting information that threatens our viewpoints.

stereotype
A generalization about a group of people.

We receive a vast amount of information. *Selective perception* is our tendency to choose information that supports our viewpoints. Individuals often ignore information that makes them feel uncomfortable or threatens their viewpoints.

Stereotypes reduce information about other people to a workable level, and they are efficient for compiling and using information. Stereotypes become even stronger when they are shared with and validated by others.[76] Stereotypes can be accurate; when they are accurate, they can be useful perceptual guidelines. Some of the time, however, stereotypes are inaccurate. They harm individuals when inaccurate impressions of them are inferred and are never tested or changed.[77] An illustration of such discrimination was found in research on hiring decisions conducted by researchers at MIT and the University of Chicago. They found that the callback rates on identical résumés were substantially higher for white-sounding names than for black-sounding names. There was as much discrimination in less skilled jobs (cashier, mailroom worker) as was found in more highly skilled jobs like manager and assistant to the president.[78] In multicultural work teams, members often stereotype foreign coworkers rather than getting to know them before forming an impression. Team members from less developed countries are often assumed to have less knowledge simply because their homeland is economically or technologically less developed.[79] Stereotypes like these can deflate the productivity of the work team, as well as create low morale.

Stereotyping pervades work life. When there is a contrast against a stereotype, the member of the stereotyped group is treated more positively (given more favorable comments or pats on the back). For example, a female softball player may be given more applause for a home run hit than a male teammate. This occurs because some people may stereotype women as less athletic than men, or because they hold female players to a lower standard. Either way, the contrast is still part of stereotyping.[80]

First impressions are lasting impressions, so the saying goes. Individuals place a good deal of importance on first impressions, and for good reason. We tend to remember what we perceive first about a person, and sometimes we are quite reluctant to change our initial impressions.[81] *First-impression error* occurs when we observe a very brief bit of a person's behavior in our first encounter and infer that this behavior reflects what the person is really like. Primacy effects can be particularly dangerous in interviews, given that we form first impressions quickly and that these impressions may be the basis for long-term employment relationships.

What factors do interviewers rely on when forming first impressions? Perceptions of the candidate, such as whether they like the person, whether they trust the person, and whether or not the person seems credible, all influence the interviewer's decision.

Projection, also known as the false-consensus effect, is a cause of inaccurate perceptions of others. It is the misperception of the commonness of our own beliefs, values, and behaviors such that we overestimate the number of others who share these things. Projection occurs most often when you surround yourself with others similar to you.

Self-fulfilling prophecies are also barriers to social perception. Sometimes our expectations affect the way we interact with others such that we get what we wish for. Self-fulfilling prophecy has been studied in many settings, including at sea. The Israeli Defense Forces told one group of naval cadets that they probably

first-impression error
The tendency to form lasting opinions about an individual based on initial perceptions.

projection
Overestimating the number of people who share our own beliefs, values, and behaviors.

self-fulfilling prophecy
The situation in which our expectations about people affect our interaction with them in such a way that our expectations are fulfilled.

wouldn't experience seasickness, and even if they did, it wouldn't affect their performance. The self-fulfilling prophecy worked! These cadets were rated better performers than other groups, and they also had less seasickness. The information improved the cadets' self-efficacy—they believed they could perform well even if they became seasick.[82] Managers can harness the power of the self-fulfilling prophecy to improve productivity in the organization. It appears that high expectations of individuals come true. Can a manager extend these high expectations to an entire group and have similar positive results? The answer is yes. When a manager expects positive things from a group, the group delivers.[83]

■ IMPRESSION MANAGEMENT

Most people want to make favorable impressions on others. This is particularly true in organizations, where individuals compete for jobs, favorable performance evaluations, and salary increases. The process by which individuals try to control the impressions others have of them is called *impression management*. Individuals use several techniques to control others' impressions of them.[84]

Some impression management techniques are self-enhancing. These techniques focus on enhancing others' impressions of the person using the technique. Name-dropping, which involves mentioning an association with important people in the hopes of improving one's image, is often used. Managing one's appearance is another technique for impression management. Individuals dress carefully for interviews because they want to "look the part" in order to get the job. Self-descriptions, or statements about one's characteristics, are used to manage impressions as well.

Another group of impression management techniques is *other-enhancing*. The aim of these techniques is to focus on the individual on whom one is trying to make an impression rather than on one's self. Flattery is a common other-enhancing technique whereby compliments are given to an individual in order to win his or her approval. Favors are also used to gain the approval of others. Agreement with someone's opinion is a technique often used to gain a positive impression. People with disabilities, for example, often use other-enhancing techniques. They may feel that they must take it upon themselves to make others comfortable interacting with them. Impression management techniques are used by individuals with disabilities as a way of dealing with potential avoidance by others.[85]

Are impression management techniques effective? Most research on this topic has focused on employment interviews; the results indicate that candidates who engage in impression management by self-promoting performed better in interviews, were more likely to obtain site visits with potential employers, and were more likely to get hired.[86, 87] In addition, employees who engage in impression management are rated more favorably in performance appraisals than those who do not.[88]

Impression management seems to have an impact on others' impressions. As long as the impressions conveyed are accurate, this process can be beneficial to organizations. If the impressions are found to be false, however, a strongly negative overall impression may result. Furthermore, excessive impression management can lead to the perception that the user is manipulative or insincere.[89] We have discussed the influences on social perception, the potential barriers to perceiving another person, and impression management. Another psychological process that managers should understand is attribution.

impression management
The process by which individuals try to control the impressions others have of them.

◢ ATTRIBUTION IN ORGANIZATIONS

As human beings, we are innately curious. We are not content merely to observe the behavior of others; rather, we want to know *why* they behave the way they do. We also seek to understand and explain our own behavior. *Attribution theory* explains how we pinpoint the causes of our own behavior and that of other people.[90]

attribution theory
A theory that explains how individuals pinpoint the causes of their own behavior and that of others.

The attributions, or inferred causes, we provide for behavior have important implications in organizations. In explaining the causes of our performance, good or bad, we are asked to explain the behavior that was the basis for the performance.

: **9.** Explain the attribution process and how attributions affect managerial behavior.

▮ INTERNAL AND EXTERNAL ATTRIBUTIONS

Attributions can be made to an internal source of responsibility (something within the individual's control) or an external source (something outside the individual's control). Suppose you perform well on an exam in this course. You might say you aced the test because you are smart or because you studied hard. If you attribute your success to ability or effort, you are making an internal attribution.

Alternatively, you might make an external attribution for your performance. You might say it was an easy test (you would attribute your success to degree of task difficulty) or that you had good luck. In this case, you are attributing your performance to sources beyond your control, or external sources. You can see that internal attributions include such causes as ability and effort, whereas external attributions include causes like task difficulty or luck.

Attribution patterns differ among individuals.[91] Achievement-oriented individuals attribute their success to ability and their failures to lack of effort, both internal causes. Failure-oriented individuals attribute their failures to lack of ability, and they may develop feelings of incompetence as a result of their attributional pattern. Evidence indicates that this attributional pattern also leads to depression.[92] Women managers, in contrast to men managers, are less likely to attribute their success to their own ability. This may be because they are adhering to social norms that compel women to be more modest about their accomplishments or because they believe that success has less to do with ability than with hard work.[93]

Attribution theory has many applications in the workplace. The way you explain your own behavior affects your motivation. For example, suppose you must give an important presentation to your executive management group. You believe you have performed well, and your boss tells you that you've done a good job. To what do you attribute your success? If you believe careful preparation and rehearsal led to your success, you're likely to take credit for the performance and to have a sense of self-efficacy about future presentations. If, however, you believe that you were just lucky, you may not be motivated to repeat the performance because you believe you had little influence on the outcome.

One situation in which a lot of attributions are made is the employment interview. Candidates are often asked to explain the causes of previous performance (Why did you perform poorly in math classes?) to interviewers. In addition, candidates often feel they should justify why they should be hired (I work well with people, so I'm looking for a managerial job). Research shows that successful and unsuccessful candidates differ in the way they make attributions for negative outcomes. Successful candidates are less defensive and make internal attributions for negative events. Unsuccessful candidates attribute negative outcomes to things beyond their control (external attributions), which gives interviewers the impression that the candidate failed to learn from the event. In addition, interviewers fear that the individuals would be likely to blame others when something goes wrong in the workplace.[94]

■ ATTRIBUTIONAL BIASES

The attribution process may be affected by two very common errors: the fundamental attribution error and the self-serving bias. The tendency to make attributions to internal causes when focusing on someone else's behavior is known as the *fundamental attribution error*.[95] The other error, *self-serving bias*, occurs when focusing on one's own behavior. Individuals tend to make internal attributions for their own successes and external attributions for their own failures.[96] In other words, when we succeed, we take credit for it; when we fail, we blame the situation on other people.

Both of these biases were illustrated in a study of health care managers who were asked to cite the causes of their employees' poor performance.[97] The managers claimed that internal causes (their employees' lack of effort or lack of ability) were the basis for their employees' poor performance. This is an example of the fundamental attribution error. When the employees were asked to pinpoint the cause of their own performance problems, they blamed a lack of support from the managers (an external cause), which illustrates self-serving bias.

There are cultural differences in these two attribution errors. As described previously, these biases apply to people from the United States. In more fatalistic cultures, such as India's, people tend to believe that fate is responsible for much that happens. People in such cultures tend to emphasize external causes of behavior.[98]

In China, people are taught that hard work is the route to accomplishment. When faced with either a success or a failure, Chinese individuals first introspect about whether they tried hard enough or whether their attitude was correct. In a study of attributions for performance in sports, Chinese athletes attributed both their successes and failures to internal causes. Even when the cause of poor athletic performance was clearly external, such as bad weather, the Chinese participants made internal attributions. In terms of the Chinese culture, this attributional pattern is a reflection of moral values that are used to evaluate behavior. The socialistic value of selfless morality dictates that individual striving must serve collective interests. Mao Ze-dong stressed that external causes function only through internal causes; therefore, the main cause of results lies within oneself. Chinese are taught this from childhood and form a corresponding attributional tendency. In analyzing a cause, they first look to their own effort.[99]

The way individuals interpret the events around them has a strong influence on their behavior. People try to understand the causes of behavior in order to gain predictability and control over future behavior. Managers use attributions in all aspects of their jobs. In evaluating performance and rewarding employees, managers must determine the causes of behavior and a perceived source of responsibility. One tough call managers often make is whether allegations of sexual harassment actually resulted from sexual conduct, and if harassment did occur, what should be done about it. To make such tough calls, managers use attributions.

Attribution theory can explain how performance evaluation judgments can lead to differential rewards. A supervisor attributing an employee's good performance to

10. Evaluate the accuracy of managerial attributions from the standpoint of attribution biases and errors.

fundamental attribution error
The tendency to make attributions to internal causes when focusing on someone else's behavior.

self-serving bias
The tendency to attribute one's own successes to internal causes and one's failures to external causes.

internal causes, such as effort or ability, may give a larger raise than a supervisor attributing the good performance to external causes, such as help from others or good training. Managers are often called on to explain their own actions as well, and in doing so they make attributions about the causes of their own behavior. We continue our discussion of attributions in Chapter 6 in terms of how attributions are used in managing employee performance by presenting Kelley's attribution theory.

◀◀ think critically ▶▶

Suppose a manager makes a misattribution of an employee's poor performance. What are the possible consequences for such a mistake in attribution? Think about the ethical consequences and its effect on employee attitude, morale, and motivation?

MANAGERIAL IMPLICATIONS: USING PERSONALITY, PERCEPTION, AND ATTRIBUTION AT WORK

Managers need to know as much as possible about individual differences in order to understand themselves and those with whom they work. An understanding of personality characteristics can help a manager appreciate differences in employees. With the increased diversity of the workforce, tools like the MBTI can be used to help employees see someone else's point of view. These tools can also help make communication among diverse employees more effective.

Managers use social perception constantly on the job. Knowledge of the forces that affect perception and the barriers to accuracy can help the manager form more accurate impressions of others.

Determining the causes of job performance is a major task for the manager, and attribution theory can be used to explain how managers go about determining causality. In addition, knowledge of the fundamental attribution error and self-serving bias can help a manager guard against these biases in the processes of looking for causes of behavior on the job.

In this chapter, we have explored the psychological processes of personality, perception, and attribution as individual differences. In the next chapter, we will continue our discussion of individual differences in terms of attitudes, values, and ethics.

LOOKING BACK :: NOT YOUR TYPICAL CEO

Richard Branson is not a conventional businessperson —and he never intended to be one. In fact, Sir Richard is about as far removed from the stereotypical CEO as one can possibly imagine. "He continues to be a corporate iconoclast, defying conventional wisdom, pushing the envelope, poking fun at the big guys, saying exactly what he thinks and doing exactly what he wants." Branson has irreverence for authority that he claims to have inherited from both of his parents. He relishes becoming involved in "industries that charge too much (music) or hold consumers hostage (cellular) or treat them badly and bore them to tears (airlines)." His aim is to upset the status quo in these types of industries.

CHAPTER SUMMARY

1. Individual differences are factors that make individuals unique. They include personalities, perceptions, skills and abilities, attitudes, emotions, and ethics.

2. The Big Five personality classification classifies people along five basic personality characteristics.

3. Managers should understand personality because of its effect on behavior. Several characteristics affect behavior in organizations, including core self-evaluations, locus of control, self-esteem, self-monitoring, and positive/negative affect.

4. Personality has a stronger influence in weak situations, where there are few cues to guide behavior.

5. One useful framework for understanding individual differences is type theory, developed by Carl Jung and measured by the Myers-Briggs Type Indicator (MBTI).

6. Social perception is the process of interpreting information about another person. It is influenced by characteristics of the perceiver, the target, and the situation.

7. Barriers to social perception include selective perception, stereotyping, first-impression error, projection, and self-fulfilling prophecies.

8. Impression management techniques such as name-dropping, managing one's appearance, self-descriptions, flattery, favors, and agreement are used by individuals to control others' impressions of them.

9. Attribution is the process of determining the cause of behavior. It is used extensively by managers, especially in evaluating performance.

KEY TERMS

attribution theory (p. 84)
core self-evaluation (CSE) (p. 70)
discounting principle (p. 81)
extraversion (p. 76)
feeling (p. 77)
first-impression error (p. 82)
fundamental attribution error (p. 85)
general self-efficacy (p. 70)
impression management (p. 83)
individual differences (p. 66)
integrative approach (p. 69)

interactional psychology (p. 67)
introversion (p. 76)
intuiting (p. 76)
Judging Preference (p. 77)
locus of control (p. 70)
Myers-Briggs Type Indicator (MBTI)® instrument (p. 75)
negative affect (p. 74)
Perceiving Preference (p. 77)
personality (p. 68)
positive affect (p. 74)
projection (p. 82)

selective perception (p. 82)
self-esteem (p. 71)
self-fulfilling prophecy (p. 82)
self-monitoring (p. 72)
self-serving bias (p. 85)
sensing (p. 76)
social perception (p. 78)
stereotype (p. 82)
strong situation (p. 74)
thinking (p. 77)

REVIEW QUESTIONS

1. What are individual differences, and why should managers understand them?

2. Define *personality* and describe the Big Five personality model.

4. Describe the eight preferences of the Myers-Briggs Type Indicator. How does this instrument measure Carl Jung's ideas?

5. What factors influence social perception? What are the barriers to social perception?

6. Describe the errors that affect the attribution process.

Discussion and Communication QUESTIONS

1. What contributions can high self-monitors make in organizations? Low self-monitors?
2. How can managers improve their perceptual skills?
3. Which has the stronger impact on personality: heredity or environment?
4. How can managers make more accurate attributions?
5. How can managers encourage self-efficacy in employees?
6. How can self-serving bias and the fundamental attribution error be avoided?
7. (*communication question*) You have been asked to develop a training program for interviewers.

An integral part of this training program focuses on helping interviewers develop better social perception skills. Write an outline for this section of the training program. Be sure to address barriers to social perception and ways to avoid these barriers.

8. (*communication question*) Form groups of four to six, then split each group in half. Debate the origins of personality, with one half taking the position that personality is inherited, and the other half taking the position that personality is formed by the environment. Each half should also discuss the implications of its position for managers.

ETHICAL DILEMMA

Alice loves to hire new people. As manager of the Medicare Reimbursement Department of a large hospital, she sees it as a great responsibility to aggressively pursue and hire the best people. She has already experienced the challenges of hiring the wrong person. She knows a bad personality match could undermine the culture she has worked so hard to build. Alice plans to do everything in her power to never repeat the mistake of a bad hire again.

This latest hire, however, is proving to be a bigger challenge than she had expected. The problem is that the position requires a good deal of specialized knowledge. Alice needs someone who knows the current Medicare regulations and who would be able to decipher new ones. The pool of candidates with this knowledge is extremely small. Truthfully, she has interviewed only one person with the skills and knowledge that she needs.

Jana had interviewed two weeks ago. She knew the regulations better than anyone Alice has ever met. Every question Alice asked, Jana answered. What an asset Jana would be to the department. The dilemma is that Jana seems to be extremely extroverted, needing and wanting a lot of social involvement. This job would not offer that opportunity. Even worse, Mike, the main person with whom Jana would be working, is an extreme introvert. He rarely speaks to anyone and prefers that people speak to him as little as possible. Alice can see nothing but problems between these two employees.

Alice does not know what to do. She values Mike a great deal and does not want to do anything to make him unhappy in his job. But she desperately needs someone in this vacant position. She has been depending on everyone to pitch in and cover the workload for weeks now. She knows that has to stop. Yet, is it fair to bring in someone she feels sure would be unhappy in the job and would ultimately quit? She may even end up losing both Jana and Mike. She has no idea what is the right thing to do.

QUESTIONS

1. Who are the stakeholders affected by Alice's decisions?
2. How much importance should Alice place on Mike's needs and wants?
3. Using rule, virtue, right, and justice theories, evaluate Alice's decision alternatives.

EXPERIENTIAL EXERCISES

3.1 MBTI TYPES AND MANAGEMENT STYLES

PART I. This questionnaire will help you determine your preferences. For each item, circle either a or b. If you feel both a and b are true, decide which one is more like you, even if it is only slightly more true.

1. I would rather
   a. Solve a new and complicated problem.
   b. Work on something I have done before.

2. I like to
   a. Work alone in a quiet place.
   b. Be where the action is.

3. I want a boss who
   a. Establishes and applies criteria in decisions.
   b. Considers individual needs and makes exceptions.

4. When I work on a project, I
   a. Like to finish it and get some closure.
   b. Often leave it open for possible changes.

5. When making a decision, the most important considerations are
   a. Rational thoughts, ideas, and data.
   b. People's feelings and values.

6. On a project, I tend to
   a. Think it over and over before deciding how to proceed.
   b. Start working on it right away, thinking about it as I go along.

7. When working on a project, I prefer to
   a. Maintain as much control as possible.
   b. Explore various options.

8. In my work, I prefer to
   a. Work on several projects at a time and learn as much as possible about each one.
   b. Have one project that is challenging and keeps me busy.

9. I often
   a. Make lists and plans whenever I start something and may hate to seriously alter my plans.
   b. Avoid plans and just let things progress as I work on them.

10. When discussing a problem with colleagues, it is easy for me to
    a. See "the big picture."
    b. Grasp the specifics of the situation.

11. When the phone rings in my office or at home, I usually
    a. Consider it an interruption.
    b. Do not mind answering it.

12. Which word describes you better?
    a. Analytical.
    b. Empathetic.

13. When I am working on an assignment, I tend to
    a. Work steadily and consistently.
    b. Work in bursts of energy with "down time" in between.

14. When I listen to someone talk on a subject, I usually try to
    a. Relate it to my own experience and see if it fits.
    b. Assess and analyze the message.

15. When I come up with new ideas, I generally
    a. "Go for it."
    b. Like to contemplate the ideas some more.

16. When working on a project, I prefer to
    a. Narrow the scope so it is clearly defined.
    b. Broaden the scope to include related aspects.

17. When I read something, I usually
    a. Confine my thoughts to what is written there.
    b. Read between the lines and relate the words to other ideas.

18. When I have to make a decision in a hurry, I often
    a. Feel uncomfortable and wish I had more information.
    b. Am able to do so with available data.

19. In a meeting, I tend to
    a. Continue formulating my ideas as I talk about them.
    b. Only speak out after I have carefully thought the issue through.

20. In work, I prefer spending a great deal of time on issues of
    a. Ideas.
    b. People.

21. In meetings, I am most often annoyed with people who
    a. Come up with many sketchy ideas.
    b. Lengthen meetings with many practical details.

22. I am a
    a. Morning person.
    b. Night owl.

23. What is your style in preparing for a meeting?
    a. I am willing to go in and be responsive.
    b. I like to be fully prepared and usually sketch an outline of the meeting.

24. In a meeting, I would prefer for people to
    a. Display a fuller range of emotions.
    b. Be more task oriented.

25. I would rather work for an organization where
    a. My job is intellectually stimulating.
    b. I am committed to its goals and mission.

26. On weekends, I tend to
    a. Plan what I will do.
    b. Just see what happens and decide as I go along.

27. I am more
    a. Outgoing.
    b. Contemplative.

28. I would rather work for a boss who is
    a. Full of new ideas.
    b. Practical.

In items 29–32, choose the word in each pair that appeals to you more:

29. a. Social.
    b. Theoretical.

30. a. Ingenuity.
    b. Practicality.

31. a. Organized.
    b. Adaptable.

32. a. Active.
    b. Concentration.

SCORING KEY

Count one point for each item listed below that you have circled in the inventory.

Score for I	Score for E	Score for S	Score for N	Score for T	Score for F	Score for J	Score for P
2a	2b	1b	1a	3a	3b	4a	4b
6a	6b	10b	10a	5a	5b	7a	7b
11a	11b	13a	13b	12a	12b	8b	8a
15b	15a	16a	16b	14b	14a	9a	9b
19b	19a	17a	17b	20a	20b	18b	18a
22a	22b	21a	21b	24b	24a	23b	23a
27b	27a	28b	28a	25a	25b	26a	26b
32b	32a	30b	30a	29b	29a	31a	31b

Total

Circle the one with more points—I or E.   Circle the one with more points—S or N.   Circle the one with more points—T or F.   Circle the one with more points—J or P.

Your score is
I or E _____   T or F _____
S or N _____   J or P _____

PART II. The purpose of this part of the exercise is to give you experience in understanding some of the individual differences that were proposed by Carl Jung and are measured by the MBTI.

Step 1. Your instructor will assign you to a group.

Step 2. Your group is a team of individuals who want to start a business. You are to develop a mission statement and a name for your business.

Step 3. After you have completed Step 2, analyze the decision process that occurred within the group. How did you decide on your company's name and mission?

Step 4. Your instructor will have each group report to the class the name and mission of the company, and then the decision process used. Your instructor will also give you some additional information about the exercise and provide some interesting insights about your management style.

SOURCE : "MBTI Types and Management Styles" from D. Marcic and P. Nutt, "Personality Inventory," in D. Marcic, ed., *Organizational Behavior: Experiences and Cases* (St. Paul: West, 1989): 9–16. Reprinted by permission.

3.2 STEREOTYPES IN EMPLOYMENT INTERVIEWS

Step 1. Your instructor will give you a transcript that records an applicant's interview for a job as a laborer. Your task is to memorize as much of the interview as possible.

Step 2. Write down everything you can remember about the job candidate.

Step 3. Your instructor will lead you in a discussion.

SOURCE: Adapted from D. A. Sachau and M. Hussang, "How Interviewers' Stereotypes Influence Memory: An Exercise," *Journal of Management Education* 16 (1992): 391–396. Copyright © 1992 by Sage Publications. Reprinted with permission of Sage Publications, Inc.

4

Attitudes, Emotions, and Ethics

LEARNING OBJECTIVES

After reading this chapter, you should be able to do the following:

: 1. Describe attitudes and how they are formed.

: 2. Define *job satisfaction* and *organizational commitment,* and suggest potential tips for managers to help build these two attitudes among their employees.

: 3. Compare how positive and negative attitudes affect work behaviors such as performance, OCB, and WDB.

: 4. Identify the characteristics of the source, target, and message that affect persuasion.

: 5. Discuss the definition and importance of emotions at work.

: 6. Justify the importance of understanding emotional contagion, emotional intelligence, and emotional labor at work.

: 7. Contrast the effects of individual and organizational influences on ethical behavior.

: 8. Discuss how values affect ethical behavior and how generational and cultural differences in values present a challenge for managers.

THINKING AHEAD :: WHOLE FOODS MARKET, INC.

Values Driven

Whole Foods Market, Inc., the world's largest natural and organic foods market, was founded in Austin, Texas, in 1980. For six consecutive years, Whole Foods has earned the distinction of being one of *Fortune*'s Top 100 Companies to Work For. Its motto, "Whole Foods, Whole People, Whole Planet," reflects the company's commitment to customer satisfaction and wellness and employee excellence and happiness. The company was the first grocer in the United States to have its retail operations certified organic. Its customers are focused on healthy living and eating well. By 2006, Whole Foods had 187 stores and well over $3 billion in sales.

The company extends its philosophy to working closely with local farmers, in many cases displaying a minibiography of the farmer near the produce sold in its markets. In addition to foods, the Whole Body Department offers herbal teas, essential oils, books, vitamins and supplements, and yoga products. Whole Foods replaced 10 percent of its electricity with clean wind energy, making it one of the largest private purchasers of wind energy in the nation. It maintains strict environmental policies and gives a minimum of 5 percent of profits each year to community and nonprofit groups. Whole Foods recently made a commitment not to sell live lobsters after evaluating the entire supply chain process. Leadership at Whole Foods felt that selling lobsters was not in synch with the company's commitment to humane treatment and quality of life for animals.

But even Whole Foods experiences controversy. Two animal rights groups, Vegetarians International Voice for Animals (VivaUSA) and People for the Ethical Treatment of Animals (PETA), attacked the company for doing business with farms that abuse ducks. PETA members stormed the podium at Whole Foods' annual shareholder meeting, and company executives walked out. This conflict presented a dilemma: Given its values and image, what would Whole Foods do? We'll continue the story in the Looking Back feature at the end of the chapter.[1,2]

In this chapter, we continue the discussion of individual differences we began in Chapter 3 with personality, perception, and attribution. Persons and situations jointly influence behavior, and individual differences help us to better understand the influence of the person. Our focus now is on three other individual difference factors: attitudes, emotions, and ethics.

ATTITUDES

An *attitude* is a psychological tendency that is expressed by evaluating a particular entity with some degree of favor or disfavor.[3] We respond favorably or unfavorably toward many things: animals, coworkers, our own appearance, politics.

Attitudes are important because of their links to behavior. Attitudes are also an integral part of the world of work. Managers speak of workers who have "bad attitudes" and conduct "attitude adjustment" talks with employees. Often, poor performance attributed to bad attitudes really stems from lack of motivation, minimal feedback, lack of trust in management, or other problems. These are areas that managers must explore. It is important for managers to understand the antecedents to attitudes as well as their consequences. Managers also need to understand the different components of attitudes, how attitudes are formed, the major attitudes that affect work behavior, and how to use persuasion to change attitudes.

1. Describe attitudes and how they are formed.

attitude
A psychological tendency expressed by evaluating an entity with some degree of favor or disfavor.

We generally prefer consistency (consonance) between attitudes and behavior. Anything that disrupts this consistency causes tension (dissonance), which motivates individuals to change either their attitudes or their behavior to return to a state of consistency. The tension produced when there is a conflict between attitudes and behavior is *cognitive dissonance.*[4]

cognitive dissonance
A state of tension that is produced when an individual experiences conflict between attitudes and behavior.

Suppose, for example, a salesperson is required to sell damaged televisions for the full retail price, without revealing the damage to customers. She believes, however, that doing so constitutes unethical behavior. This creates a conflict between her attitude (concealing information from customers is unethical) and her behavior (selling defective TVs without informing customers about the damage).

The salesperson, experiencing the discomfort from dissonance, will try to resolve the conflict. She might change her behavior by refusing to sell the defective TV sets. Alternatively, she might rationalize that the defects are minor and that the customers will not be harmed by not knowing about them. These are attempts by the salesperson to restore equilibrium between her attitudes and behavior, thereby eliminating the tension from cognitive dissonance.

Managers need to understand cognitive dissonance because employees often find themselves in situations in which their attitudes conflict with their behavior. They manage the tension by changing their attitudes or behavior. Employees who display sudden shifts in behavior may be attempting to reduce dissonance. Some employees find the conflicts between strongly held attitudes and required work behavior so uncomfortable that they leave the organization to escape the dissonance.

ATTITUDE FORMATION

Attitudes are learned. Our responses to people and issues evolve over time. Two major influences on attitudes are direct experience and social learning.

Direct experience with an object or person is a powerful influence on attitudes. How do you know that you like biology or dislike math? You have probably formed these attitudes from experience in studying the subjects. Research has shown that attitudes that are derived from direct experience are stronger, held more confidently, and more resistant to change than attitudes formed through indirect experience.[5] One reason attitudes derived from direct experience are so powerful is their availability. This means that the attitudes are easily accessed and are active in our cognitive processes.[6] When attitudes are available, we can call them quickly into consciousness. Attitudes that are not learned from direct experience are not as available, so we do not recall them as easily.

social learning
The process of deriving attitudes from family, peer groups, religious organizations, and culture.

In *social learning*, the family, peer groups, religious organizations, and culture shape an individual's attitudes in an indirect manner.[7] Children learn to adopt certain attitudes by the reinforcement they are given by their parents when they display behaviors that reflect an appropriate attitude. This is evident when very young children express political preferences similar to their parents'. Peer pressure molds attitudes through group acceptance of individuals who express popular attitudes and through sanctions, such as exclusion from the group, placed on individuals who espouse unpopular attitudes.

Substantial social learning occurs through *modeling*, in which individuals acquire attitudes by merely observing others. After overhearing other individuals expressing an opinion or watching them engaging in a behavior that reflects an attitude, the observer adopts the attitude.

For an individual to learn from observing a model, four processes must take place:

1. The learner must focus attention on the model.

2. The learner must retain what was observed from the model. Retention is accomplished in two basic ways. In one, the learner "stamps in" what was observed by forming a verbal code for it. The other way is through symbolic rehearsal, by which the learner forms a mental image of himself or herself behaving like the model.

3. Behavioral reproduction must occur; that is, the learner must practice the behavior.

4. The learner must be motivated to learn from the model.

Culture also plays a definitive role in attitude development. Consider, for example, the contrast in the North American and European attitudes toward vacation and leisure. The typical vacation in the United States is two weeks, and some workers do not use all of their vacation time. In Europe, the norm is longer vacations; and in some countries, *holiday* means everyone taking a month off. The European attitude is that an investment in longer vacations is important to health and performance.

■ ATTITUDES AND BEHAVIOR

If you have a favorable attitude toward participative management, will your management style be participative? As managers, if we know an employee's attitude, to what extent can we predict the person's behavior? These questions illustrate the fundamental issue of attitude–behavior correspondence, that is, the degree to which an attitude predicts behavior.

This correspondence has concerned organizational behaviorists and social psychologists for quite some time. Can attitudes predict behaviors like being absent from work or quitting your job? Some studies suggested that attitudes and behavior are closely linked, while others found no relationship at all or a weak relationship at best. Attention then became focused on when attitudes predict behavior and when they do not. Attitude–behavior correspondence depends on five things: attitude specificity, attitude relevance, the timing of the measurement, personality factors, and social constraints.

Individuals possess both general and specific attitudes. You may favor women's right to reproductive freedom (a general attitude) and prefer pro-choice political candidates (a specific attitude) but not attend pro-choice rallies or send money to Planned Parenthood. That you don't perform these behaviors may make the link between your attitude and behavior on this issue seem rather weak. However, given a choice between a pro-choice and an anti-abortion political candidate, you will probably vote for the pro-choice candidate. In this case, your attitude seems quite predictive of your behavior. The point is that the greater the attitude specificity, the stronger its link to behavior.[8]

Another factor that affects the attitude–behavior link is relevance.[9] Attitudes that address an issue in which we have some self-interest are more relevant for us, and our subsequent behavior is consistent with our expressed attitude. Suppose there is a proposal to raise income taxes for those who earn $150,000 or more. If you are a student, you may not find the issue of great personal relevance. Individuals in that income bracket, however, might find it highly relevant; their attitude toward the issue would be strongly predictive of whether they would vote for the tax increase.

The timing of the measurement also affects attitude–behavior correspondence. The shorter the time between the attitude measurement and the observed behavior, the stronger the relationship. For example, voter preference polls taken close to an election are more accurate than earlier polls.

Personality factors also influence the attitude–behavior link. One personality disposition that affects the consistency between attitudes and behavior is self-monitoring. Recall from Chapter 3 that low self-monitors rely on their internal states when making decisions about behavior, while high self-monitors are more responsive to situational cues. Low self-monitors therefore display greater correspondence between their attitudes and behaviors.[10] High self-monitors may display little correspondence between their attitudes and behavior because they behave according to signals from others and from the environment.

Finally, social constraints affect the relationship between attitudes and behavior.[11] The social context provides information about acceptable attitudes and behaviors.[12, 13] New employees in an organization, for example, are exposed to the attitudes of their work group. Suppose a newcomer from Afghanistan holds a negative attitude toward women in management because in his country the prevailing attitude is that women should not be in positions of power. He sees, however, that his work group members respond positively to their female supervisor. His own behavior may therefore be compliant because of social constraints. This behavior is inconsistent with his attitude and cultural belief system.

■ WORK ATTITUDES

2. Define *job satisfaction* and *organizational commitment,* and suggest potential tips for managers to help build these two attitudes among their employees.

Attitudes at work are important because, directly or indirectly, they affect work behavior. Chief among the things that negatively affect employees' work attitudes are jobs that are very demanding, combined with a lack of control on the part of the employee.[14] A positive psychological climate at work, on the other hand, can lead to positive attitudes and good performance.[15] A study found that when hotel employees offered helpful, concerned service, hotel customers developed a warmer, more positive attitude toward the hotel itself. This attitude resulted in greater customer loyalty, greater likelihood that the customers would stay at the hotel, and even a willingness to pay more for the same service. Customer attitudes were strongly influenced by employee gestures, facial expressions, and words. In this study, customer attitudes were crucial to the success of the firm, and employee behaviors were crucial in forming customer attitudes, meaning firms can "train" their employees to "train" customers to have better attitudes![16]

Although many work attitudes are important, two attitudes in particular have been emphasized. Job satisfaction and organizational commitment are key attitudes of interest to managers and researchers.

JOB SATISFACTION

job satisfaction
A pleasurable or positive emotional state resulting from the appraisal of one's job or job experiences.

Most of us believe that work should be a positive experience. *Job satisfaction* is a pleasurable or positive emotional state resulting from the appraisal of one's job or job experiences.[17] It has been treated both as a general attitude and as satisfaction with five specific dimensions of the job: pay, the work itself, promotion opportunities, supervision, and coworkers.[18] You can assess your own job satisfaction by completing Challenge 4.1.

C H A L L E N G E 4 . 1

Assess Your Job Satisfaction

Think of the job you have now or a job you've had in the past. Indicate how satisfied you are with each aspect of your job below, using the following scale:

1 = Extremely dissatisfied
2 = Dissatisfied
3 = Slightly dissatisfied
4 = Neutral
5 = Slightly satisfied
6 = Satisfied
7 = Extremely satisfied

1. The amount of job security I have.
2. The amount of pay and fringe benefits I receive.
3. The amount of personal growth and development I get in doing my job.
4. The people I talk to and work with on my job.
5. The degree of respect and fair treatment I receive from my boss.
6. The feeling of worthwhile accomplishment I get from doing my job.
7. The chance to get to know other people while on the job.
8. The amount of support and guidance I receive from my supervisor.
9. The degree to which I am fairly paid for what I contribute to this organization.
10. The amount of independent thought and action I can exercise in my job.
11. How secure things look for me in the future in this organization.
12. The chance to help other people while at work.

13. The amount of challenge in my job.
14. The overall quality of the supervision I receive on my work.

Now, compute your scores for the facets of job satisfaction.

Pay satisfaction:
Q2 + Q9 =   Divided by 2:

Security satisfaction:
Q1 + Q11 =   Divided by 2:

Social satisfaction:
Q4 + Q7 + Q12 =   Divided by 3:

Supervisory satisfaction:
Q5 + Q8 + Q14 =   Divided by 3:

Growth satisfaction:
Q3 + Q6 + Q10 + Q13 =   Divided by 4:

Scores on the facets range from 1 to 7. (Scores lower than 4 suggest there is room for change.)

This questionnaire is an abbreviated version of the Job Diagnostic Survey, a widely used tool for assessing individuals' attitudes about their jobs. Compare your scores on each facet to the following norms for a large sample of managers.

Pay satisfaction:	4.6
Security satisfaction:	5.2
Social satisfaction:	5.6
Supervisory satisfaction:	5.2
Growth satisfaction:	5.3

How do your scores compare? Are there actions you can take to improve your job satisfaction?

Source: *Work Redesign* by Hackman/Oldham, © 1980. Reprinted by permission of Pearson Education, Inc., Upper Saddle River, N.J.

An individual may hold different attitudes toward various aspects of the job. For example, an employee may like her job responsibilities but be dissatisfied with the opportunities for promotion. Characteristics of individuals also affect job satisfaction.[19] Those with high negative affectivity are more likely to be dissatisfied with their jobs. Challenging work, valued rewards, opportunities for advancement, competent supervision, and supportive coworkers are dimensions of the job that can lead to satisfaction.

There are several measures of job satisfaction. One of the most widely used measures comes from the Job Descriptive Index (JDI). This index measures the specific facets of satisfaction by asking employees to respond yes, no, or cannot decide to a series of statements describing their jobs. Another popular measure is the Minnesota Satisfaction Questionnaire (MSQ).[20] This survey also asks employees to respond to statements about their jobs, using a five-point scale that ranges from very dissatisfied to very satisfied. Figure 4.1 presents some sample items from each questionnaire.

FIGURE 4.1

Sample Items from Satisfaction Questionnaires

Job Descriptive Index

Think of the work you do at present. How well does each of the following words or phrases describe your work? In the blank beside each word given below, write

____Y____ for "Yes" if it describes your work
____N____ for "No" if it does NOT describe it
____?____ if you cannot decide

WORK ON YOUR PRESENT JOB:

_____ Routine
_____ Satisfying
_____ Good

Think of the majority of the people that you work with now or the people you meet in connection with your work. How well does each of the following words or phrases describe these people? In the blank beside each word, write

____Y____ for "Yes" if it describes the people you work with
____N____ for "No" if it does NOT describe them
____?____ if you cannot decide

COWORKERS (PEOPLE):

_____ Boring
_____ Responsible
_____ Intelligent

Minnesota Satisfaction Questionnaire

1 = Very dissatisfied
2 = Dissatisfied
3 = I can't decide whether I am satisfied or not
4 = Satisfied
5 = Very satisfied

On my present job, this is how I feel about:

_____ The chance to work alone on the job (independence)
_____ My chances for advancement on this job (advancement)
_____ The chance to tell people what to do (authority)
_____ The praise I get for a good job (recognition)
_____ My pay and the amount of work I do (compensation)

SOURCES: The Job Descriptive Index is copyrighted by Bowling Green State University. The complete forms, scoring key, instructions, and norms can be obtained from Dr. Patricia C. Smith, Department of Psychology, Bowling Green State University, Bowling Green, OH 43403. Minnesota Satisfaction Questionnaire from D. J. Weiss, R. V. Davis, G. W. England, and L. H. Lofquist, *Manual for the Minnesota Satisfaction Questionnaire* (University of Minnesota Vocational Psychology Research, 1967).

Managers and employees hold a common belief that happy or "satisfied" employees are more productive at work. Most of us feel more satisfied than usual when we believe that we are performing better than usual.[21] Interestingly, the relationship between job satisfaction and performance is quite a bit more complex than that. Are satisfied workers more productive? Or, are more productive workers more satisfied? The link between satisfaction and performance has been widely explored. One view holds that satisfaction causes good performance. If this were true, then the manager's job would simply be to keep workers happy. Although this may be the case for certain individuals, job satisfaction for most people is one of several causes of good performance.

Another view holds that good performance causes satisfaction. If this were true, managers would need to help employees perform well, and satisfaction would follow. However, some employees who are high performers are not satisfied with their jobs.

The research shows modest support for both views, but no simple, direct relationship between satisfaction and performance has been found.[22] One reason for these results may be the difficulty of demonstrating the attitude–behavior links we described earlier in this chapter. Future studies using specific, relevant attitudes and measuring personality variables and behavioral intentions may be able to demonstrate a link between job satisfaction and performance.

Another reason for the lack of a clear relationship between satisfaction and performance is the intervening role of rewards. Employees who receive valued rewards are more satisfied. In addition, employees who receive rewards that are contingent on performance (the higher the performance, the larger the reward) tend to perform better. Rewards thus influence both satisfaction and performance. The key to influencing both satisfaction and performance through rewards is that the rewards are valued by employees and are tied directly to performance.

Job satisfaction has been shown to be related to many other important personal and organizational outcomes. Job satisfaction is related to *organizational citizenship behavior (OCB)*—behavior that is above and beyond the call of duty. Satisfied employees are more likely to help their coworkers, make positive comments about the company, and refrain from complaining when things at work do not go well.[23] Going beyond the call of duty is especially important to organizations using teams to get work done. Employees depend on extra help from each other to get things accomplished. When massive wildfires swept through California in 2003, most businesses in the San Diego area closed for one or more days as choking black smoke filled the air and thousands of homes were threatened. Aplus.net, an Internet presence provider, chose to remain open; however, due to the danger involved, the company did not require its employees to report to work. Yet, in spite of thick smoke, most of the firm's employees came to work anyway, even though some were unsure if their homes would be waiting for them when they left work that evening.[24] Because of their willingness to go the extra mile, Aplus.net and its customers remained up and running throughout the fires. The firm reported in November that the massive fires had no negative impact on its financial results for the quarter.

Satisfied workers are more likely to want to give something back to the organization because they want to reciprocate their positive experiences.[25] Often, employees may feel that citizenship behaviors are not recognized because

3. Compare how positive and negative attitudes affect work behaviors such as performance, OCB, and WDB.

organizational citizenship behavior Behavior that is above and beyond the call of duty.

they occur outside the confines of normal job responsibilities. Organizational citizenship behaviors do, however, influence performance evaluations. Employees who exhibit behaviors such as helping others, making suggestions for innovations, and developing their skills receive higher performance ratings.[26] And, different parts of an attitude relate to different targets of OCBs. Affect tends to direct OCBs toward other people, while job cognitions direct OCBs toward the organization.[27]

Individuals who identify strongly with the organization are more likely to perform OCBs.[28] High self-monitors, who base their behavior on cues from the situation, are also more likely to perform OCBs.[29] Good deeds, in the form of OCBs, can be contagious. One study found that when a person's close coworkers chose to perform OCBs, that person was more likely to reciprocate. When the norm among other team members was to engage in OCBs, the individual worker was more likely to offer OCBs. The impact of one worker's OCBs can spread throughout an entire department.[30]

Although researchers have had a tough time demonstrating the link between job satisfaction and individual performance, this has not been the case for the link between job satisfaction and organizational performance. Companies with satisfied workers have better performance than companies with dissatisfied workers.[31] This may be due to the more intangible elements of performance, like organizational citizenship behavior, that contribute to organizational effectiveness but aren't necessarily captured by just measuring individual job performance.

Job satisfaction is related to some other important outcomes. People who are dissatisfied with their jobs are absent more frequently. The type of dissatisfaction that most often leads employees to miss work is dissatisfaction with the work itself. In addition, dissatisfied workers are more likely to quit their jobs, and turnover at work can be very costly to organizations. Dissatisfied workers also report more psychological and medical problems than do satisfied employees.[32]

Like all attitudes, job satisfaction is influenced by culture. American workers tend to hold to the "Protestant work ethic," which values work for its own sake and makes it a central part of their lives. Consistent with this basic view, American managers place a high value on outcomes such as autonomy, independence, and achievement. Koreans, in contrast to Americans, generally grow up in a more authoritarian system, which places greater value on family and less value on work for its own sake. Americans place greater value on and find greater job satisfaction through intrinsic job factors, whereas Koreans prefer extrinsic factors.[33]

This finding was echoed in a study comparing job satisfaction across 49 countries. Job characteristics and job satisfaction were more tightly linked in richer countries, more individualistic countries, and smaller power-distance countries. These findings suggest that cultural differences have strong influences on job satisfaction and the factors that produce job satisfaction.[34]

Because organizations face the challenge of operating in the global environment, managers must understand that job satisfaction is significantly affected by culture. Employees from different cultures may have differing expectations of their jobs; thus, there may be no single prescription for increasing the job satisfaction of a multicultural workforce.

Workplace deviance behavior (WDB) is another outcome of attitudes at work, and it consists of counterproductive behavior that violates organizational norms and causes harm to others or the organization.[35] Deviance is garnering attention due to negative events in the business world such as downsizing, technological insecurities, and other challenges being faced by many organizations. Layoffs, for example, may cause employees to develop negative attitudes and to feel anger and hostility for the organization; then some employees indulge in retaliatory behaviors. Even when an employee keeps his/her job, but believes the procedure used to determine the layoff is unfair, workplace deviance such as bad mouthing the employer or revenge against the manager may occur.[36, 37] Unfairness at work is a major cause of deviance, sabotage, and retaliation. Positive attitudes about the work environment lead to lower deviance (Witt et. al, 2002). Preventing and managing WDB is important, because it harms department and organizational performance. You may be surprised at some of the things that constitute workplace deviance. Take Challenge 4.2 to see whether you've engaged in this type of behavior at work.

ORGANIZATIONAL COMMITMENT

The strength of an individual's identification with an organization is known as *organizational commitment.* There are three kinds of organizational commitment: affective, continuance, and normative. *Affective commitment* is an employee's intention to remain in an organization because of a strong desire to do so. It consists of three factors:

> A belief in the goals and values of the organization.

> A willingness to put forth effort on behalf of the organization.

> A desire to remain a member of the organization.[38]

Affective commitment encompasses loyalty, but it is also a deep concern for the organization's welfare.

Continuance commitment is an employee's tendency to remain in an organization because the person cannot afford to leave.[39] Sometimes, employees believe that if they leave, they will lose a great deal of their investments in time, effort, and benefits and that they cannot replace these investments.

Normative commitment is a perceived obligation to remain with the organization. Individuals who experience normative commitment stay with the organization because they feel that they should.[40]

Certain organizational conditions encourage commitment. Participation in decision making and job security are two such conditions. Certain job characteristics also positively affect commitment. These include autonomy, responsibility, and interesting work.[41]

Affective and normative commitments are related to lower rates of absenteeism, higher quality of work, increased productivity, and several different types of performance.[42] Managers should encourage affective commitment because committed individuals expend more task-related effort and are less likely than others to leave the organization.[43]

Managers can increase affective commitment by communicating that they value employees' contributions and that they care about employees' well-being.[44] Affective commitment also increases when the organization and employees share the same values, and when the organization emphasizes values like moral integrity,

workplace deviance behavior
Workplace deviance is defined as any voluntary counterproductive behavior that violates organizational norms and causes some degree of harm to organizational functioning.

organizational commitment
The strength of an individual's identification with an organization.

affective commitment
The type of organizational commitment that is based on an individual's desire to remain in an organization.

continuance commitment
The type of organizational commitment that is based on the fact that an individual cannot afford to leave.

normative commitment
The type of organizational commitment that is based on an individual's perceived obligation to remain with an organization.

CHALLENGE 4.2

Who, Me? Engage in Workplace Deviance Behavior?

Think of the job you have now or a job you've had in the past. Indicate to what extent you engaged in the following behaviors. Use the following scale:

1 Very slightly or not at all
2 A little
3 Moderately
4 Quite a bit
5 Definitely

1. Worked on a personal matter instead of work for your employer
2. Took property from work without permission
3. Spent too much time fantasizing or daydreaming instead of working
4. Made fun of someone at work
5. Falsified a receipt to get reimbursed for more money than you spent on business expenses
6. Said something hurtful to someone at work
7. Took an additional or a longer break than is acceptable at your workplace
8. Repeated a rumor or gossip about your company
9. Made an ethnic, religious, or racial remark or joke at work
10. Came in late to work without permission
11. Littered your work environment
12. Cursed at someone at work
13. Called in sick when you were not
14. Told someone about the lousy place where you work
15. Lost your temper while at work
16. Neglected to follow your boss's instructions
17. Intentionally worked slower than you could have worked
18. Discussed confidential company information with an unauthorized person
19. Left work early without permission
20. Played a mean prank on someone at work
21. Left your work for someone else to finish
22. Acted rudely toward someone at work
23. Repeated a rumor or gossip about your boss or coworkers
24. Made an obscene comment at work
25. Used an illegal drug or consumed alcohol on the job
26. Put little effort into your work
27. Publicly embarrassed someone at work
28. Dragged out work in order to get overtime

Interpreting your score: Total scores can range from 0 to 140, with higher scores showing greater tendencies toward WDB. Remember, even subtle WDB can be costly to the organization.

Source: Copyright 2000 by the American Psychological Association. Adapted with permission. The official citation that should be used in referencing this material is Bennett, R. J., and Robinson, S. L. (2000). Development of a measure of workplace deviance. *Journal of Applied Psychology*, 85, 349–360. No further reproduction or distribution is permitted without written permission from the American Psychological Association.

fairness, creativity, and openness.[45] Negative experiences at work can undoubtedly diminish affective commitment. One such experience is discrimination. Perceived age discrimination, whether for being too old or too young, can dampen affective commitment.[46]

Several researchers have examined organizational commitment in different countries. One study revealed that American workers displayed higher affective commitment than did Korean and Japanese workers.[47] Another study showed that Chinese workers place high value on social relationships at work and that those with stronger interpersonal relationships are more committed to their organizations.[48] The authors suggest that Chinese firms improve employee commitment and retention by organizing activities to help cultivate relationships among employees. This means that expatriate managers should be sensitive to the quality of relationships among their Chinese employees if they want to improve organizational commitment.

Job satisfaction and organizational commitment are two important work attitudes that managers can strive to improve among their employees. And these two attitudes are strongly related. Both affective and normative commitment are related to job satisfaction. Increasing job satisfaction is likely to increase commitment as well. To begin with, managers can use attitude surveys to reveal employees' satisfaction or dissatisfaction with specific facets of their jobs. Then they can take action to make the deficient aspects of the job more satisfying. Work attitudes are also important because they influence business outcomes. Some leaders, like John Mackey of Whole Foods, are not in business just to create wealth for their organizations but also because they care deeply about the societies and the environments in which they operate. Such leaders especially strive to hire people who share these attitudes and can identify with what the organization stands for, which leads to highly satisfied and committed employees.

Job satisfaction and organizational citizenship behavior are linked to customer satisfaction and company profitability.[49]

■ PERSUASION AND ATTITUDE CHANGE

: 4. Identify the characteristics of the source, target, and message that affect persuasion.

To understand how attitudes can change, it is necessary to understand the process of persuasion. The days of command-and-control management, in which executives simply told employees what do to, are long gone. Modern managers must be skilled in the art of persuasion.[50] Through persuasion, one individual (the source) tries to change the attitude of another person (the target). Certain characteristics of the source, target, and message affect the persuasion process. There are also two cognitive routes to persuasion.

SOURCE CHARACTERISTICS

Three major characteristics of the source affect persuasion: expertise, trustworthiness, and attractiveness.[51] A source who is perceived as an expert is particularly persuasive. Trustworthiness is also important. John Mack, head of Credit Suisse First Boston (CSFB), understands the importance of trust. When he came to CSFB, the investment bank was a huge mess, but in a short time, Mack achieved amazing results by persuading his employees to trust him. First, he told CSFB's bankers that their pay packages were excessive and the firm could not afford them. The bankers gave back more than $400 million in cash bonuses. Next, he asked CSFB's executives to give up some of the richest pay packages in the business. Mack was able to convince them to give up amounts that sometimes exceeded $20 million, all so that younger executives could receive bonuses and remain with the firm. And when lawyers discovered an e-mail suggesting a top CSFB employee had covered up wrongdoing from federal regulators, Mack immediately contacted federal regulators to blow the whistle. John Mack's employees trust him because he doesn't just talk about teamwork, integrity, and trust; he demonstrates them in his own career. This trustworthiness allowed him to persuade his employees to help him save the firm.[52] Finally, attractiveness and likability play a role in persuasion. Attractive communicators have long been used in advertising to persuade consumers to buy certain products. As a source of persuasion, managers who are perceived as being experts, who are trustworthy, or who are attractive or likable will have an edge in changing employee attitudes.

TARGET CHARACTERISTICS

Some people are more easily persuaded than others. Individuals with low self-esteem are more likely to change their attitudes in response to persuasion than are individuals with high self-esteem. Individuals who hold very extreme attitudes are more resistant to persuasion, and people who are in a good mood are easier to persuade.[53] Undoubtedly, individuals differ widely in their susceptibility to persuasion. Managers must recognize these differences and realize that their attempts to change attitudes may not receive universal acceptance.

MESSAGE CHARACTERISTICS

Suppose you must implement an unpopular policy at work. You want to persuade your employees that the policy is a positive change. Should you present one side of the issue or both sides? Given that your employees are already negatively inclined toward the policy, you will have more success in changing their attitudes if you present both sides. This shows support for one side of the issue while acknowledging that another side does exist. Moreover, refuting the other side makes it more difficult for the targets to hang on to their negative attitudes.

Messages that are obviously designed to change the target's attitude may be met with considerable negative reaction. In fact, undisguised deliberate attempts at changing attitudes may cause an attitude change in the opposite direction! This is most likely to occur when the target of the persuasive communication feels her or his freedom is threatened.[54] Less threatening approaches are less likely to elicit negative reactions. The emotional tone of the message is also important. Persuasion is more successful when messages are framed with the same emotion as that felt by the receiver.[55]

COGNITIVE ROUTES TO PERSUASION

When are message characteristics more important, and when are other characteristics more important in persuasion? The elaboration likelihood model of persuasion, presented in Figure 4.2, proposes that persuasion occurs over two routes: the central route and the peripheral route.[56] The routes are differentiated by the amount of elaboration, or scrutiny, the target is motivated to give the message.

The *central route* to persuasion involves direct cognitive processing of the message's content. When an issue is personally relevant, the individual is motivated to think carefully about it. The listener may nod his/her head when the argument is strong and shake his/her head if the argument is weak.[57] In the central route, the content of the message is very important. If the arguments presented are logical and convincing, attitude change will follow.

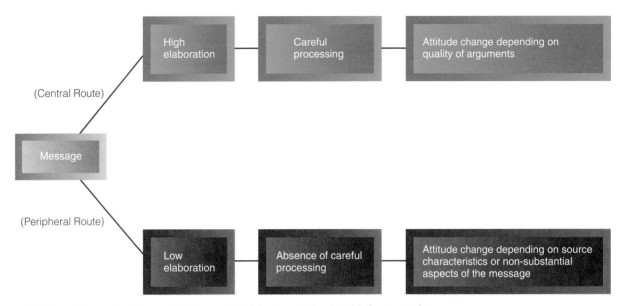

SOURCE: Adapted from R. E. Petty and J. T. Cacioppo, "The Elaboration Likelihood Model of Persuasion," in L. Berkowitz, ed., *Advances in Experimental Social Psychology,* vol. 19 (New York: Academic Press, 1986): 123–205.

FIGURE 4.2

The Elaboration Likelihood Model of Persuasion

In the *peripheral route* to persuasion, the individual is not motivated to pay much attention to the message's content. This is because the message may not be perceived as personally relevant, or the individual may be distracted. Instead, the individual is persuaded by characteristics of the persuader—for example, expertise, trustworthiness, and attractiveness. In addition, the individual may be persuaded by statistics, the number of arguments presented, or the method of presentation—all of which are nonsubstantial aspects of the message.

The elaboration likelihood model shows that the target's level of involvement with the issue is important. That involvement also determines which route to persuasion will be more effective. In some cases, attitude change comes about through both the central and the peripheral routes. To cover all of the bases, managers should structure the content of their messages carefully, develop their own attributes that will help them be more persuasive, and choose a method of presentation that will be attractive to the audience.[58]

We have seen that the process of persuading individuals to change their attitudes is affected by the source, the target, the message, and the route. When all is said and done, however, managers are important catalysts for encouraging attitude change. This is a difficult process. Recently, researchers have proposed that people hold attitudes at two different levels.

▨ EMOTIONS AT WORK

: 5. Discuss the definition and importance of emotions at work.

Traditional management theories did not place a premium on studying the effects of employee emotions at work. This was largely because of the viewpoint that emotions were thought to be "bad" for rational decision making. Ideas about management centered around the stereotypical ideal employee who kept his/her emotions in check and behaved in a totally rational, rather than an emotional,

emotions
Mental states that typically include feelings, physiological changes, and the inclination to act.

manner. Because of recent research, we know that emotions and cognitions are intertwined and that both are normal parts of decision making.

Emotions (e.g., anger, joy, pride, hostility) are short-lived, intense reactions to an event that affect work behaviors.[59] Individuals differ in their capacity to experience both positive emotions (e.g., happiness, pride) and negative emotions (e.g., anger, fear, guilt).[60] Employees have to cope with both positive and negative events at work almost on a daily basis, and these events lead to moods and emotions. When events at work are positive and goals are being met, employees experience positive emotions.[61] Events that threaten or thwart the achievement of goals cause negative emotions, which then threaten job satisfaction and commitment. Positive emotions such as joviality, attention, and interest lead employees to perform more OCBs.[62]

As we discussed earlier, negative emotions lead to workplace deviance. Positive emotions produce better cognitive functioning, physical, psychological health, and coping mechanisms.[63] People who experience positive emotion tend to experience positive emotions repeatedly. And, people who experience positive emotions are more creative.[64] Overall, people who experience positive emotions are more successful across a variety of life domains and report higher life satisfaction. Negative emotions, on the other hand, lead to unhealthy coping behaviors, lower cardiovascular function, and poor physical health.

When organizations and their employees go through change and/or huge losses, the pain caused by such trauma is sometimes not eased by sound reason. Good leaders use emotions like compassion to heal and rebuild employee morale.[65] Some leaders stand by their people with strength and empathy in times of tragedy, yet several organizations in New York refused to give their employees September 12 off in the face of the September 11 terrorist attacks and did not create a comfortable place for their employees to share their mutual grief and trauma. Issues such as this devastating event require caring compassionate leaders who are not afraid to let their emotions show appropriately and also are not disdainful of employees' feelings.

: 6. Justify the importance of understanding emotional contagion, emotional intelligence, and emotional labor at work.

Emotions are pervasive at all times at work. Much of our decision making is driven by emotions. A recent article in the *Harvard Business Review* argues that it is not worthwhile to have company mottos such as "Think not Feel" as IBM used to have. This author points at the work of Antonio Damasio, who is the head of neurology at the University of Iowa. The significant finding of this research is that no decision we make can ever be completely devoid of emotion. Hence, managers can make the best use of emotions by acknowledging them and using them. For example, if you have to fire your best friend at work, this research suggests that it is best for managers to show whatever emotion they might be feeling (e.g., guilt, anger, and regret).[66] There are many applications of emotions in organizations, including emotional contagion, emotional intelligence, and emotional labor.

emotional contagion
A dynamic process through which the emotions of one person are transferred to another either consciously or unconsciously through nonverbal channels.

Emotions must be managed at work because emotions are very infectious. The process by which emotions spread is known as *emotional contagion*. Emotional contagion occurs primarily through nonverbal cues and is affected through the basic human tendency of mimicry. We tend to mimic each other's facial expressions, body language, speech patterns, and vocal tones. Contagion is an important work process because most jobs today require some degree of interpersonal interaction. Examples of such interactions could be dealing with a customer who is angry, a coworker who is fearful of a layoff decision, a leader who displays a high degree of pride in employees' work, and so on. The thing to note is that in many of these instances contagion could occur and as such cause emotions to travel throughout the work group. Positive emotions that travel through a work group through emotional contagion produce cooperation and task performance.[67] The opposite can occur as well. Negative emotions can spread throughout a work group and destroy morale and performance.

◀◀**think critically**▶▶

As a manager, how could you use contagion to improve work group cohesion and performance?

Emotional intelligence is a set of competencies that involve recognizing and managing your own emotions as well as those of other people. Employees who perceive their own and others' emotions accurately can manage such emotions better and form effective social relationships at work. Emotional intelligence, over and above general intelligence, leads to better interview performance and better overall job performance.[68, 69] High EI individuals are better able to cope with negative emotions by buffering them with positive emotions.[70] And, individuals with EI have accurate self-assessments. They see themselves as others see them. In other words, EI is that "extra something" that leads to career success. It helps us understand why even some very intelligent people do not perform well at work—they lack emotional intelligence. EI is particularly important for leaders who must manage the emotions of their employees. We will elaborate on EI and leadership in Chapter 11.

> **emotional intelligence**
> An individual difference that reflects the ability to recognize and manage one's own emotions and those of others.

Emotions were studied extensively by Arie Hochschild who examined the effects of training practices on flight attendants at Delta Air Lines. She documented how a flight attendant who is expected to act cheerful and happy when not experiencing such emotions naturally could lead to health-related problems and psychological distress symptoms. She coined the term *emotional labor* for the process of managing emotions in order to fit the rules of the job. Customer service jobs, like that of a flight attendant, require you to give service with a smile and to reflect positive emotions to customers even when you may not feel like it.[71, 72]

> **emotional labor**
> The act of managing one's emotions in accordance with an organization's display rules.

Emotional labor is important because customers are vigilant about employees' attitudes and emotions and form impressions about the organization based on what they see.[73] Employees who strictly follow the organization's display rules can experience stress, burnout, and emotional exhaustion.[74] Over a period of time, exhaustion and burnout have been shown to relate to anger and aggressive behavior at work. Managers must be able to recognize and manage such employee emotional exhaustion. One factor that might help employees better cope with emotional labor and assist managers in dealing with emotional demands is emotional intelligence.

ETHICAL BEHAVIOR

Ethics is the study of values and moral behavior. *Ethical behavior* is acting in ways consistent with one's personal values and the commonly held values of the organization and society.[75] Interest in ethics at work may be at an all-time high

> **ethical behavior**
> Acting in ways consistent with one's personal values and the commonly held values of the organization and society.

given the surge of white-collar crime and the corporate scandals like that at Enron. The costs of the unethical behavior of Enron executives were huge. Investors and employees were financially ruined, and even taxpayers paid the price of the subsequent government crackdown on corporate fraud.

There is evidence that paying attention to ethical issues pays off for companies. In the early 1990s, James Burke, then the CEO of Johnson & Johnson, put together a list of companies that devoted a great deal of attention to ethics. The group included Johnson & Johnson, Coca-Cola, Gerber, Kodak, 3M, and Pitney Bowes. Over a 40-year period, the market value of these organizations grew at an annual rate of 11.3 percent, as compared to 6.2 percent for the Dow Jones industrials as a whole.[76] Doing the right thing can have a positive effect on an organization's performance.[77]

Ethical behavior in firms can also lead to practical benefits, particularly in attracting new talent. Firms with better reputations are able to attract more applicants, creating a larger pool from which to hire, and evidence suggests that respected firms are able to choose higher-quality applicants.[78]

Failure to handle situations in an ethical manner can cost companies. Employees who are laid off or terminated are very concerned about the quality of treatment they receive. Honestly explaining the reasons for the dismissal and preserving the dignity of the employee will reduce the likelihood that the employee will initiate a claim against the company. One study showed that less than 1 percent of employees who felt the company was being honest filed a claim; more than 17 percent of those who felt the company was being less than honest filed claims.[79]

Unethical behavior by employees can affect individuals, work teams, and even the organization. Organizations thus depend on individuals to act ethically. For this reason, more and more firms are starting to monitor their employees' Internet usage. "LittleBrother" and "SurfControl Web Filter" are just two of several software packages that allow system administrators to easily monitor employee Web usage, flagging visits to specific Web sites by using neural network technology to classify URL content and block Web traffic.

Although some employees have complained that this type of monitoring violates their privacy, the courts have generally disagreed, arguing that employees are using company hardware and software, hence the company is entitled to monitor what employees do with it. In one such case, Michael Smyth was fired from his job with Pillsbury Co. after company employees read inflammatory comments he made in several e-mails to his supervisor. Smyth sued for wrongful termination, claiming that his right to privacy was violated because the firm had told employees their e-mail would remain confidential. Despite these promises, the court ruled that Smyth had no reasonable expectation of privacy while using the firm's equipment; further, it said, Smyth's right to privacy was outweighed by the firm's need to conduct business in a professional manner. Only future court cases will clarify where a firm's effort to monitor potentially unethical behavior actually crosses its own ethical line.[80]

Today's high-intensity business environment makes it more important than ever to have a strong ethics program in place. In a survey of more than 4,000 employees conducted by the Washington, D.C.–based Ethics Resource Center, one-third of the employees said that they had witnessed ethical misconduct in the past year. If that many employees actually saw unethical acts, imagine how many unethical behaviors occurred behind closed doors! The most common unethical deeds witnessed were lying to supervisors (56 percent), lying on reports or falsifying records (41 percent), stealing or theft (35 percent), sexual harassment (35 percent), drug or alcohol abuse (31 percent), and conflicts of interest (31 percent).[81]

◀◀ think critically ▶▶

Whole Foods CEO John Mackey has a blog on his Web site wherein he offers thought-provoking commentaries and replies to critics on current economic, ethical, and philosophical issues. Read one of those blogs at http://www.wholefoodsmarket.com/blogs/jm/ and comment on what you think about his arguments.

One of the toughest challenges managers face is aligning the ideal of ethical behavior with the reality of everyday business practices. Violations of the public's trust are costly. Since Jack in the Box restaurants' *E. coli* crisis, the company has faced image and financial problems. And Firestone Inc., after spending more than a third of a billion dollars replacing allegedly defective tires on Ford sport utility vehicles in 2000, still faces an uncertain future including billions of dollars in lawsuits. Studies show that firms experience lower accounting returns and slow sales growth for as long as five years after being convicted of a corporate illegality.[82]

The ethical issues that individuals face at work are complex. A review of articles appearing in *The Wall Street Journal* during just one week revealed more than 60 articles dealing with ethical issues in business.[83] As Table 4.1 shows, the

TABLE 4.1

Ethical Issues from One Week in *The Wall Street Journal*

1. **Stealing:** Taking things that don't belong to you.
2. **Lying:** Saying things you know aren't true.
3. **Fraud and deceit:** Creating or perpetuating false impressions.
4. **Conflict of interest and influence buying:** Bribes, payoffs, and kickbacks.
5. **Hiding versus divulging information:** Concealing information that another party has a right to know or failing to protect personal or proprietary information.
6. **Cheating:** Taking unfair advantage of a situation.
7. **Personal decadence:** Aiming below excellence in terms of work performance (e.g., careless or sloppy work).
8. **Interpersonal abuse:** Behaviors that are abusive of others (e.g., sexism, racism, emotional abuse).
9. **Organizational abuse:** Organizational practices that abuse members (e.g., inequitable compensation, misuses of power).
10. **Rule violations:** Breaking organizational rules.
11. **Accessory to unethical acts:** Knowing about unethical behavior and failing to report it.
12. **Ethical dilemmas:** Choosing between two equally desirable or undesirable options.

SOURCE: Kluwer Academic Publishers, by J. O. Cherrington and D. J. Cherrington, "A Menu of Moral Issues: One Week in the Life of *The Wall Street Journal*," *Journal of Business Ethics* 11 (1992): 255–265.

themes appearing throughout the articles were distilled into 12 major ethical issues. You can see that few of these issues are clear cut. All of them depend on the specifics of the situation, and their interpretation depends on the characteristics of the individuals examining them. For example, look at issue 2: lying. We all know that "white lies" are told in business. Is this acceptable? The answer to this question varies from person to person. Thus, the perception of what constitutes ethical versus unethical behavior in organizations varies among individuals.

: 7. Contrast the effects of individual and organizational influences on ethical behavior.

Ethical behavior is influenced by two major categories of factors: individual characteristics and organizational factors.[84] Our purpose in this section is to look at the individual influences on ethical behavior. We examine organizational influences throughout the remainder of the book—particularly in Chapter 15, where we focus on creating an organizational culture that reinforces ethical behavior.

◀◀think critically▶▶

Imagine that a coworker engages in behavior you consider unethical, but which is not prohibited by company standards. How would you handle that behavior?

The model that guides our discussion of individual influences on ethical behavior is presented in Figure 4.3. It shows both individual and organizational influences.

Making ethical decisions is part of each manager's job. It has been suggested that ethical decision making requires three qualities of individuals:[85]

1. The competence to identify ethical issues and evaluate the consequences of alternative courses of action.
2. The self-confidence to seek out different opinions about the issue and decide what is right in terms of a particular situation.

FIGURE 4.3

Individual/Organizational Model of Ethical Behavior

3. Toughmindedness—the willingness to make decisions when all that needs to be known cannot be known and when the ethical issue has no established, unambiguous solution.

What are the individual characteristics that lead to these qualities? Our model presents four major individual differences that affect ethical behavior: value systems, locus of control, Machiavellianism, and cognitive moral development.

◀◀ think critically ▶▶

Some people criticize business school graduates for lack of a personal code of ethics. What do you think? Is ethical behavior a function of graduate school education?

🔖 VALUES

One important source of individual differences in ethical behavior is values. We use them to evaluate our own behavior and that of others. As such, they vary widely among individuals. *Values* are enduring beliefs that a specific mode of conduct or end state of existence is personally or socially preferable to an opposite or converse mode of conduct or end state of existence.[86] This definition was proposed by Rokeach, an early scholar of human values. As individuals grow and mature, they learn values, which may change over the life span as an individual develops a sense of self. Cultures, societies, and organizations shape values. Parents and others who are respected by the individual play crucial roles in value development by providing guidance about what is right and wrong. Because values are general beliefs about right and wrong, they form the basis for ethical behavior. For example, Whole Foods is committed to environmentally friendly causes and has created a society for compassionate treatment of animals. CEO John Mackey was recently named one of the top 30 corporate leaders in American businesses. Mackey has set conventional wisdom aside by refusing to compete with Wal-Mart. Instead, he has led Whole Foods through five consecutive years of 21 percent sales gains by strongly adhering to what he believes in and being environmentally and socially responsible. Visit the company's Web site (http://wholefoods.com) to learn more about how being values-driven can lead to success.

▦ INSTRUMENTAL AND TERMINAL VALUES

Rokeach distinguished between two types of values: instrumental and terminal. *Instrumental values* reflect the means to achieving goals; that is, they represent the acceptable behaviors to be used in achieving some end state. Instrumental values identified by Rokeach include ambition, honesty, self-sufficiency, and courage. *Terminal values*, in contrast, represent the goals to be achieved or the end states of existence. Rokeach identified happiness, love, pleasure, self-respect, and freedom among the terminal values. A complete list of instrumental and terminal values is presented in Table 4.2. Terminal and instrumental values work in concert to provide individuals with goals to strive for and acceptable ways to achieve the goals.

8. Discuss how values affect ethical behavior and how generational and cultural differences in values present a challenge for managers.

values
Enduring beliefs that a specific mode of conduct or end state of existence is personally or socially preferable to an opposite or converse mode of conduct or end state of existence.

instrumental values
Values that represent the acceptable behaviors to be used in achieving some end state.

terminal values
Values that represent the goals to be achieved or the end states of existence.

TABLE 4.2
Instrumental and Terminal Values

INSTRUMENTAL VALUES

Honesty	Ambition	Responsibility
Forgiving nature	Open-mindedness	Courage
Helpfulness	Cleanliness	Competence
Self-control	Affection/love	Cheerfulness
Independence	Politeness	Intelligence
Obedience	Rationality	Imagination

TERMINAL VALUES

World peace	Family security	Freedom
Happiness	Self-respect	Wisdom
Equality	Salvation	Prosperity
Achievement	Friendship	National security
Inner peace	Mature love	Social respect
Beauty in art and nature	Pleasure	Exciting, active life

SOURCE: Table adapted with the permission of The Free Press, a Division of Simon & Schuster, Adult Publishing Group, from *The Nature of Human Values* by Milton Rokeach. Copyright © 1973 by The Free Press. Copyright renewed by Sandra Ball-Rokeach. All rights reserved.

This discussion of values is highlighted in our opening case of Whole Foods. The terminal values of Whole Foods include creating a healthy and organic food base for its customers. Its instrumental values are concern for the environment and the farm communities that make its business happen. These instrumental values are shown in acts such as switching to cleaner energy and displaying a biographical sketch of farmers who supply their products.

Americans' rankings of instrumental and terminal values have shown remarkable stability over time.[87] The highest ranked instrumental values were honesty, ambition, responsibility, forgiving nature, open-mindedness, and courage. The highest ranked terminal values were world peace, family security, freedom, happiness, self-respect, and wisdom.

Age also affects values. Baby boomers' values contrast with those of the baby busters, who are beginning to enter the workforce. The baby busters value family life and time off from work and prefer a balance between work and home life. This contrasts with the more driven, work-oriented value system of the boomers. The baby boomers placed a huge emphasis on achievement values. Their successors, Generation X and Generation Y, though, are markedly different from the earlier generation in what they value at work. For example, Generation X values self-reliance, individualism, and balance between family and work life. Generation Y, on the other hand, values freedom in scheduling so much that most are employed only part time. Furthermore, they have a "work to live mindset" rather than the "live to work" philosophy of the baby boomers.[88]

■ WORK VALUES

Work values are important because they affect how individuals behave on their jobs in terms of what is right and wrong.[89] Four work values relevant to individuals are achievement, concern for others, honesty, and fairness.[90] Achievement is a concern for the advancement of one's career. This is shown in such behaviors as working hard and seeking opportunities to develop new skills. Concern for others is shown in caring, compassionate behaviors such as encouraging other employees or helping others work on difficult tasks. These behaviors constitute organizational citizenship, as we discussed earlier. Honesty is providing accurate information and refusing to mislead others for personal gain. Fairness emphasizes impartiality and recognizes different points of view. Individuals can rank-order these values in terms of their importance in their work lives.[91] Although individuals' value systems differ, sharing similar values at work produces positive results. Employees who share their supervisor's values are more satisfied with their jobs and more committed to the organization.[92] Values also have profound effects on the choice of jobs. Traditionally, pay and advancement potential have been the strongest influences on job choice decisions. One study, however, found that three other work values—achievement, concern for others, and fairness—exerted more influence on job choice decisions than did pay and promotion opportunities.[93]

This means that organizations recruiting job candidates should pay careful attention to individuals' values and to the messages that organizations send about company values. A new "name and shame" report published in Australia by RepuTex is designed to embarrass companies that behave unethically. Nineteen groups graded each of Australia's top companies on corporate governance policies, environmental friendliness, and workplace practices. The 500-page report named Westpac, a major bank, as the most ethical firm in Australia. Westpac was the only company in the country's top 100 to receive the AAA rating.[94]

▓ CULTURAL DIFFERENCES IN VALUES

As organizations face the challenges of an increasingly diverse workforce and a global marketplace, it becomes more important than ever for them to understand the influence of culture on values. Doing business in a global marketplace often means that managers encounter a clash of values among different cultures. Take the value of loyalty, for example. In Japan, loyalty means "compassionate overtime." Even though you have no work to do, you should stay late to give moral support to your peers who are working late.[95] In contrast, Koreans value loyalty to the person for whom one works.[96] In the United States, family and other personal loyalties are more highly valued than is loyalty to the company or one's supervisor.

Cultures differ in what they value in terms of an individual's contributions to work. Collectivist cultures such as China and Mexico value a person's contributions to relationships in the work team. In contrast, individualist cultures (the United States, the Netherlands) value a person's contribution to task accomplishment. Both collectivist and individualist cultures value rewards based on individual performance.[97] Iran also represents a collectivist culture. Iranian managers' values, which include little tolerance for ambiguity, high need for structure, and willingness to sacrifice for the good of society, are greatly influenced by Islam. Belonging, harmony, humility, and simplicity are all values promoted by Islam.[98]

Values also affect individuals' views of what constitutes authority. French managers value authority as a right of office and rank. Their behavior reflects this value, as they tend to use power based on their position in the organization. In contrast, managers from the Netherlands and Scandinavia value group inputs to decisions and expect their decisions to be challenged and discussed by employees.[99]

Value differences between cultures must be acknowledged in today's global economy. We may be prone to judging the value systems of others, but we should resist the temptation to do so. Tolerating diversity in values can help us understand other cultures. Value systems of other nations are not necessarily right or wrong—they are merely different. The following suggestions can help managers understand and work with the diverse values that characterize the global environment:[100]

1. Learn more about and recognize the values of other peoples. They view their values and customs as moral, traditional, and practical.

2. Avoid prejudging the business customs of others as immoral or corrupt. Assume they are legitimate unless proved otherwise.

3. Find legitimate ways to operate within others' ethical points of view—do not demand that they operate within your value system.

4. Avoid rationalizing "borderline" actions with excuses such as the following:
   > "This isn't really illegal or immoral."
   > "This is in the organization's best interest."
   > "No one will find out about this."
   > "The organization will back me up on this."

5. Refuse to do business when stakeholder actions violate or compromise laws or fundamental organizational values.

6. Conduct relationships as openly and aboveboard as possible.

■ LOCUS OF CONTROL

Another individual influence on ethical behavior is locus of control. In Chapter 3, we introduced locus of control as a personality variable that affects individual behavior. Recall that individuals with an internal locus of control believe that they control events in their lives and that they are responsible for what happens to them. In contrast, individuals with an external locus of control believe that outside forces such as fate, chance, or other people control what happens to them.[101]

Internals are more likely than externals to take personal responsibility for the consequences of their ethical or unethical behavior. Externals are more apt to believe that external forces caused their ethical or unethical behavior. Research has shown that internals make more ethical decisions than do externals.[102] Internals also are more resistant to social pressure and are less willing to hurt another person, even if ordered to do so by an authority figure.[103]

■ MACHIAVELLIANISM

Machiavellianism
A personality characteristic indicating one's willingness to do whatever it takes to get one's own way.

Another individual difference that affects ethical behavior is Machiavellianism. Niccolò Machiavelli was a sixteenth-century Italian statesman. He wrote *The Prince,* a guide for acquiring and using power.[104] The primary method for achieving power that he suggested was manipulation of others. *Machiavellianism,* then, is a personality characteristic indicating one's willingness to do whatever it takes to get one's own way.

High-Mach individuals behave in accordance with Machiavelli's ideas and use deceit in relationships, have a cynical view of human nature, and have little concern for conventional notions of right and wrong.[105] They are skilled manipulators of other people, relying on their persuasive abilities. Low-Machs, in contrast, value loyalty and relationships. They are less willing to manipulate others for personal gain and are concerned with others' opinions.

High-Machs believe that the desired ends justify any means. Thus, high-Machs are likely to justify their manipulative behavior as ethical.[106] They are emotionally detached from other people and are oriented toward objective aspects of situations. And high-Machs are likelier than low-Machs to engage in behavior that is ethically questionable.[107] Employees can counter Machiavellian individuals by focusing on teamwork instead of on one-on-one relationships where high-Machs have the upper hand. It is also beneficial to make interpersonal agreements public and thus less susceptible to manipulation by high-Machs.

■ COGNITIVE MORAL DEVELOPMENT

An individual's level of *cognitive moral development* also affects ethical behavior. Psychologist Lawrence Kohlberg proposed that as individuals mature, they move through a series of six stages (with three overarching levels) of moral development.[108] With each successive stage, they become less dependent on other people's opinions of right and wrong and less self-centered (acting in one's own interest). At higher levels of moral development, individuals are concerned with broad principles of justice and with their self-chosen ethical principles. Kohlberg's model focuses on the decision-making process and on how individuals justify ethical decisions. His model is a cognitive developmental theory about how people think about what is right and wrong and how the decision-making process changes through interaction with peers and the environment.

cognitive moral development
The process of moving through stages of maturity in terms of making ethical decisions.

Cognitive moral development occurs at three levels, and each level consists of two stages. In Level I, called the premoral level, the person's ethical decisions are based on rewards, punishments, and self-interest. In Level II, the conventional level, the focus is on the expectations of others (parents, peers) or society. In Level III, the principled level, what is "right" is determined by universal values. The individual sees beyond laws, rules, and the expectations of other people. As individuals mature, their moral development passes through these stages in an irreversible sequence. Research suggests that most adults are in Level II, or the conventional level. Individuals at higher stages of development are less likely to cheat,[109] more likely to engage in whistle-blowing,[110] and more likely to make ethical business decisions.[111, 112]

There is evidence to support the idea that men and women view ethics differently. A large-scale review of 66 studies found that women were more likely than men to perceive certain business practices as unethical. There is an age/experience effect for both sexes: Experienced workers are more likely to think lying, bribing, stealing, and colluding are unethical.[113]

Individual differences in values, locus of control, Machiavellianism, and cognitive moral development are important influences on ethical behavior in organizations. Given that these influences vary widely from person to person, how can organizations use this knowledge to increase ethical behavior? One action would be to hire individuals who share the organization's values. Another would be to hire only internals, low-Machs, and individuals at higher stages of cognitive moral development. This strategy obviously presents practical and legal problems.

The best way to use the knowledge of individual differences may be to recognize that they help explain why ethical behavior differs among individuals and to focus managerial efforts on creating a work situation that supports ethical behavior.

Most adults are susceptible to external influences; they do not act as independent ethical agents. Instead, they look to others and to the organization for guidance. Managers can offer such guidance by encouraging ethical behavior through codes of conduct, ethics committees, ethics communication systems, training, norms, modeling, and rewards and punishments, as shown in Figure 4.3. We discuss these areas further in Chapter 15.

⬛ MANAGERIAL IMPLICATIONS: ATTITUDES, EMOTIONS, AND ETHICAL BEHAVIOR

Managers must understand attitudes because of their effects on work behavior. By understanding how attitudes are formed and how they can be changed, managers can shape employee attitudes. Attitudes are learned through observation of other employees and by the way they are reinforced. Job satisfaction and organizational commitment are important attitudes to encourage among employees, and participative management is an excellent tool for doing so.

Emotions are also important because of their influences on employee behaviors. Managers should be trained to perceive emotions in employees and manage them effectively. Managers should watch out for burnout and emotional exhaustion, specifically in service occupations that involve a lot of emotional labor. Such emotion management can help foster organizational citizenship behaviors and prevent workplace deviance in the organization.

Ethical behavior at work is affected by individual and organizational influences. A knowledge of individual differences in value systems, locus of control, Machiavellianism, and cognitive moral development helps managers understand why individuals have diverse views about what constitutes ethical behavior.

This chapter concludes our discussion of individual differences that affect behavior in organizations. Attitudes, values, and ethics combine with personality, perception, and attribution to make individuals unique. Individual uniqueness is a major managerial challenge, and it is one reason there is no single best way to manage people.

LOOKING BACK :: WHOLE FOODS MARKET, INC.

Walking the Talk

CEO John Mackey and his leadership team had a problem. Whole Foods was facing a major campaign by PETA and VivaUSA against the grocer for buying ducks from farmers who engaged in inhumane practices. Pressures were mounting.

Mackey wrote to Lauren Ornelas, VivaUSA's director, and began discussions with her. Following these interactions, Whole Foods pledged to uphold humane standards for animals whose meat will be sold in its stores. It refused to do business with farms that abuse ducks.

Was the decision motivated by profit or political correctness, or was it a value-driven decision in line with Whole Foods' mission? Mackey himself claimed that Whole Foods did not respond to coercion; he reexamined the activists' claims and decided they were right. In fact, the incident caused Mackey himself to change from being a conventional vegetarian to a vegan (abstaining from all foods with animal by-products). Mackey said he could not oppose the argument that eating animals causes pain and suffering to the animals.[114, 115]

CHAPTER SUMMARY

1. Cognitive dissonance is the tension produced by a conflict between attitudes and behavior.

2. Attitudes are formed through direct experience and social learning. Direct experience creates strong attitudes because the attitudes are easily accessed and active in cognitive processes.

3. Attitude–behavior correspondence depends on attitude specificity, attitude relevance, timing of measurement, personality factors, and social constraints.

4. Two important work attitudes are job satisfaction and organizational commitment. There are cultural differences in these attitudes, and both attitudes can be improved by providing employees with opportunities for participation in decision making.

5. Emotions can affect organizational citizenship behaviors and workplace deviance behaviors.

6. Emotions and emotional intelligence have important implications for work behavior.

Emotional labor and emotion contagion are two examples of how emotions manifest themselves in the workplace.

7. A manager's ability to persuade employees to change their attitudes depends on characteristics of the manager (expertise, trustworthiness, and attractiveness), the employees (self-esteem, original attitude, and mood), the message (one-sided versus two-sided), and the route (central versus peripheral).

8. Values are enduring beliefs and are strongly influenced by cultures, societies, and organizations.

9. Instrumental values reflect the means to achieving goals; terminal values represent the goals to be achieved.

10. Ethical behavior is influenced by the individual's value system, locus of control, Machiavellianism, and cognitive moral development.

KEY TERMS

affective commitment (p. 101)
attitude (p. 93)
cognitive dissonance (p. 94)
cognitive moral development (p. 115)
continuance commitment (p. 101)
emotional contagion (p. 106)
emotional intelligence (p. 107)
emotional labor (p. 107)
emotions (p. 106)
ethical behavior (p. 107)
instrumental values (p. 111)
job satisfaction (p. 96)
Machiavellianism (p. 114)
normative commitment (p. 101)
organizational citizenship behavior (p. 99)
organizational commitment (p. 101)
social learning (p. 94)
terminal values (p. 111)
values (p. 111)
workplace deviance behavior (p. 101)

REVIEW QUESTIONS

1. How are attitudes formed?
2. Discuss cultural differences in job satisfaction and organizational commitment.
3. Why are emotions relevant to workplace behavior?
4. What are the major influences on attitude–behavior correspondence? Why do some individuals seem to exhibit behavior that is inconsistent with their attitudes?
5. What should managers know about the persuasion process?
6. Define *values*. Distinguish between instrumental values and terminal values. Are these values generally stable, or do they change over time?

7. What is the relationship between values and ethics?

8. How does locus of control affect ethical behavior?

9. What is Machiavellianism, and how does it relate to ethical behavior?

10. Describe the stages of cognitive moral development. How does this concept affect ethical behavior in organizations?

Discussion and Communication QUESTIONS

1. What jobs do you consider to be most satisfying? Why?

2. How can managers increase their employees' job satisfaction?

3. Suppose you have an employee whose lack of commitment is affecting others in the work group. How would you go about persuading the person to change this attitude?

4. What are the most important influences on an individual's perceptions of ethical behavior? Can organizations change these perceptions? If so, how?

5. How can managers encourage organizational citizenship?

6. *(communication question)* Suppose you are a manager in a customer service organization. Your group includes seven supervisors who report directly to you. Each supervisor manages a team of seven customer service representatives. One of your supervisors, Linda, has complained that Joe, one of her employees, has "an attitude problem." She has requested that Joe be transferred to another team. Write a memo to Linda explaining your position on this problem and what should be done.

7. *(communication question)* Select a company that you admire for its values. Use the resources of your university library to answer two questions. First, what are the company's values? Second, how do employees enact these values? Prepare an oral presentation to present in class.

8. *(communication question)* Think of a time when you have experienced cognitive dissonance. Analyze your experience in terms of the attitude and behavior involved. What did you do to resolve the cognitive dissonance? What other actions could you have taken? Write a brief description of your experience and your responses to the questions.

ETHICAL DILEMMA

Sara, a manager in a large software development company, sits at her desk looking out the window. The challenge before her is to pick a project manager for a major new project just given to her department. She has narrowed down her choice to two employees. Sara's first option is Paula, who is probably the most qualified candidate for this project. No one knows this area of software development better than Paula. She also has extensive knowledge of the client. Paula has one other attribute, which can be a positive or a negative factor: attitude. She is the best at her job and she knows it. She also lets everyone else know it. Because of this, she always gets the top projects. The problem is that Paula cares only about Paula and little else. She is not a team player and does little to contribute to the department as a whole. She can be arrogant and extremely self-centered.

Sara's other option is Mark. Mark is also talented with all the markings of becoming a great project manager if given the chance. In addition to his technical skills, Mark is a great coworker. He is a team player that cares as much about the success of the department as he does about his own personal success. He is well-liked by everyone, especially Sara. As a manager, she always appreciates Mark's willingness to consider the department's needs and not just the work that would lead to personal success.

Sara's predicament needs to be resolved by the end of the day. She knows everyone expects her to again choose Paula to head this project. However, Sara really believes it is time to give Mark a chance. She realizes the fallout for not choosing Paula would be great, but she is really tired of doing what everyone, including Paula, expects her to do within her own department.

QUESTIONS

1. What is Sara's obligation to the client?
2. Does this obligation affect her decision?
3. Using rule, virtue, right, and justice theories, evaluate Sara's decision options.

EXPERIENTIAL EXERCISES

4.1 IS THIS BEHAVIOR ETHICAL?

The purpose of this exercise is to explore your opinions about ethical issues faced in organizations. The class should be divided into 12 groups. Each group will randomly be assigned one of the following issues, which reflect the 12 ethical themes found in *The Wall Street Journal* study shown in Table 4.1.

1. Is it ethical to take office supplies from work for home use? Make personal long-distance calls from the office? Use company time for personal business? Or do these behaviors constitute stealing?
2. If you exaggerate your credentials in an interview, is it lying? Is lying in order to protect a coworker acceptable?
3. If you pretend to be more successful than you are in order to impress your boss, are you being deceitful?
4. How do you differentiate between a bribe and a gift?
5. If there are slight defects in a product you are selling, are you obligated to tell the buyer? If an advertised "sale" price is really the everyday price, should you divulge the information to the customer?
6. Suppose you have a friend who works at the ticket office for the convention center where Shania Twain will be appearing. Is it cheating if you ask the friend to get you tickets so that you won't have to fight the crowd to get them? Is buying merchandise for your family at your company's cost cheating?
7. Is it immoral to do less than your best in terms of work performance? Is it immoral to accept workers' compensation when you are fully capable of working?
8. What behaviors constitute emotional abuse at work? What would you consider an abuse of one's position of power?
9. Are high-stress jobs a breach of ethics? What about transfers that break up families?
10. Are all rule violations equally important? Do employees have an ethical obligation to follow company rules?
11. To what extent are you responsible for the ethical behavior of your coworkers? If you witness unethical behavior and don't report it, are you an accessory?
12. Is it ethical to help one work group at the expense of another group? For instance, suppose one group has excellent performance and you want to reward its members with an afternoon off. The other work group will have to pick up the slack and work harder if you do this. Is this ethical?

Once your group has been assigned its issue, you have two tasks:

1. First, formulate your group's answer to the ethical dilemmas.
2. After you have formulated your group's position, discuss the individual differences that may have contributed to your position. You will want to discuss the individual differences presented in this chapter as well as any others that you feel affected your position on the ethical dilemma.

Your instructor will lead the class in a discussion of how individual differences may have influenced your positions on these ethical dilemmas.

SOURCE: J. O. Cherrington and D. J. Cherrington, "A Menu of Moral Issues: One Week in the Life of *The Wall Street Journal*," *Journal of Business Ethics* 11 (1992): 255–265.

4.2 WHEN EMOTIONS RUN AMOK: ROMANCE AT WORK

Shauna is a new hire at Cerebrum Technologies Inc. Shauna had been married for two years to Gilad, who is a brilliant finance guru and vice president of Finance at Cerebrum. She was hired as she was the best software programmer in the pool and had a pleasing personality. Cerebrum Technologies designs software solutions for clients from a wide variety of industries. As such, being agreeable with clients was a major job attribute in addition to good technological skills. Shauna is young, attractive, gregarious, and definitely an extrovert on the Myers-Briggs scale. Everyone at Cerebrum was very excited about having Shauna as their new hire. Shauna's immediate boss was Joseph (late thirties, two beautiful children and his wife, Lucy works in the accounting department of Cerebrum) who also shared the general perception that she would be good for the business. Shauna was part of a software development team that included Mary (middle aged, happily married with a beautiful boy and girl), Cody (young and happily married) and Dean (older with grandkids whose wife had just passed away).

A few weeks into Shauna's term at Cerebrum, the other employees started to notice that Joseph and Shauna spent an inordinate amount of time together. Shauna had started to dress very provocatively for client interactions and was always in Joseph's office under some pretext or other. The times that she wasn't in his office, Joseph could be found perched on Shauna's desk and they would be making plans for the evening or joking about clients. Furthermore, Mary and Cody had overheard lots of sexual innuendos between Joseph and Shauna. Meanwhile, the other members of the team heard from Shauna that she, her husband Gilad, Joseph, and his wife Lucy dined together at least two nights a week and got together for operas and movie nights. They were a little confused by Shauna's open and almost gloating confessions of how much time she and Joseph spent together both at and outside of work. They also couldn't figure out why Shauna was being so indiscreet in discussing her social life at work.

Mary, Cody, and Dean wondered if their respective spouses were aware that Shauna and Joseph were intimate friends at work. Mary had been a good friend of Lucy (Joseph's wife) for years, and they took Pilates classes together two nights a week. She wondered if she should say something to Lucy, decided it was none of her business, and then felt guilty, as she would want Lucy to tell her if the same situation arose. Cody and Joseph had worked together for several years, and Cody did not know what to make of Joseph's behavior.

DISCUSSION QUESTIONS

1. Discuss the effects of office romances from an emotions standpoint. What does it do for the emotions of those involved and those outside watching it unfold?

2. What can Mary do about her guilt? How would you reconcile your feeling of guilt if you were in her position?

3. What are some tangible effects of Shauna's and Joseph's behavior on the work climate at Cerebrum? How might it affect Mary, Cody, and Dean's performance? Shauna's performance?

4. What are some legal implications of this scenario for Cerebrum? What if any of the other employees filed for sexual harassment as the work atmosphere was sexually charged?

5. Discuss Joseph's and Shauna's behavior from a values standpoint.

6. What are the ethical implications of such behavior for all involved?

7. Imagine the emotions that the work group goes through and discuss effects on job satisfaction and organizational citizenship behavior.

8. Should a person discuss their social life at work? Within the first few weeks? How does it shape social perceptions of your colleagues when you do so?

Motivation at Work

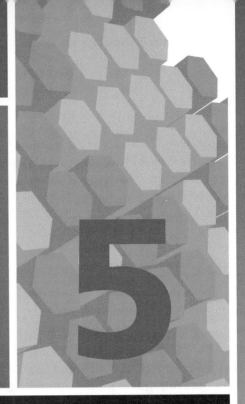

5

LEARNING OBJECTIVES

After reading this chapter, you should be able to do the following:

: 1. Define *motivation*.

: 2. Contrast Theory X and Theory Y with Maslow's needs theory.

: 3. Describe the needs for achievement, power, and affiliation.

: 4. Explain how the two-factor theory influences behavior.

: 5. Describe how equity/inequity and justice/injustice influence motivation and behavior.

: 6. Describe the expectancy theory of motivation.

: 7. Identify cultural differences in motivation.

: 8. Discuss two new ideas in human motivation.

THINKING AHEAD :: PIXAR ANIMATION STUDIOS

In the Beginning . . . Motivated by Basic Needs

Sanjay Patel is a 32-year-old computer animation artist for Pixar, but life has not always been so good. His parents emigrated to the United States from the United Kingdom when he was about five years old. They bought a motel in southern California, which turned out to be very common for Patels. It kind of rhymes: Hotel . . . Motel . . . Patel. In the case of Sanjay's family, it was the Lido Motel off of Route 66. Unfortunately, his mother was schizophrenic, and his parents did not have a lot of resources. In addition, because of his mother's condition, the family was isolated from the Indian community, which was their cultural origin. This created a variety of hardships for Sanjay and left him to spend a lot of time alone in the Lido Motel.

The Lido Motel was not an upscale motel. In fact, they had a lot of short-timers. There was a lot of prostitution. They ended up renting to a lot of marginal characters. The most difficult part was the constant tension that something was going to go wrong at any time. Clearly, this was a challenging environment for Sanjay to grow up in for these

reasons and because there were not many options for him. He grew up watching a lot of television at the motel. However, Sanjay sought a brighter path and found support along the way to go in a much more positive direction. He began to use his imagination and the potential it offered.

Sanjay wanted to produce something that maybe another little Indian kid growing up like him would feel proud of and share with his nonIndian friends. This was a motivation for him. The stereotype is the "Simpson's" icon of Apu, the 7-11 store clerk. Before he finished his journey out of the Lido Motel and into the world of Hollywood, Sanjay would work on every movie produced by Pixar except the original *Toy Story*. Growing up in the Lido Motel gave him the opportunity to rely on his creative impulses and use them to lift himself into an entirely different future reality.

Wow, how did Sanjay do that? In the Looking Back feature at the end of the chapter, we see the path he followed and what else his imagination gave birth to as well.

This is the first of two chapters about motivation, behavior, and performance at work. A comprehensive approach to understanding motivation, behavior, and performance must consider three elements of the work situation—the individual, the job, and the work environment—and how these elements interact.[1] This chapter emphasizes internal and process theories of motivation. It begins with individual need theories of motivation, turns to the two-factor theory of motivation, and finishes by examining two individual–environment interaction or process theories of motivation. The next chapter (Chapter 6) emphasizes external theories of motivation and focuses on factors in the environment to help understand good or bad performance.

: 1. Define *motivation*.

motivation
The process of arousing and sustaining goal-directed behavior.

🎯 MOTIVATION AND WORK BEHAVIOR

Motivation is the process of arousing and sustaining goal-directed behavior. Motivation is one of the more complex topics in organizational behavior. *Motivation* comes from the Latin root word *movere*, which means "to move."

Motivation theories attempt to explain and predict observable behavior. The wide range and variety of motivation theories result from the great diversity of people and the complexity of their behavior in organizations. Motivation theories may be broadly classified into internal, process, and external theories of motivation. Internal theories of motivation give primary consideration to variables within the individual that give rise to motivation and behavior. The hierarchy of needs theory exemplifies the internal theories. Process theories of motivation emphasize the nature of the interaction between the individual and the environment. Expectancy theory exemplifies the process theories. External theories of motivation focus on the elements in the environment, including the consequences of behavior, as the basis for understanding and explaining people's behavior at work. Any single motivation theory explains only a small portion of the variance in human behavior. Therefore, alternative theories have developed over time in an effort to account for the unexplained portions of the variance in behavior.

INTERNAL NEEDS

Philosophers and scholars have theorized for centuries about human needs and motives, especially about what motivates people to work. Early organizational scholars argued that the meaning of work lay not in the work itself but in its deeper potential for contributing to a person's ultimate salvation.[2] Others argued a more complex theory that proposed that much of human motivation was unconscious by nature, and that a person's organizational life was founded on the compulsion to work and the power of love.[3] As we saw in the opening case, Sanjay Patel's desire to succeed was in itself a powerful motivator. During the past century, attention has narrowed to understanding motivation in businesses and other organizations. Among other findings, some research suggests that people's deeper feelings may transcend culture, with most people caring deeply about the same few things.[4]

◀◀ think critically ▶▶

Is it ethical for you to pursue your own needs above others at work? Do you consider the thoughts and feeling of other people at work?

EXTERNAL INCENTIVES

Early organizational theories on external motivation assumed that people were motivated by *self-interest* and economic gain in order to provide for the necessities and conveniences of life. Whether by pay incentives for employees or productivity improvements through increased technology, the emphasis was on reducing the conflict between labor and management and calling for cooperation between the two parties, one that was aimed at enlarging the total profits. There are a number of other factors in the work environment that influence worker performance. Chapter 6 discusses in detail external theories of motivation and factors in the work environment that influence good or bad behavior.

Internal needs and external incentives both play an important role in motivation. Although extrinsic motivation is important, so too is intrinsic motivation, which varies by the individual.[5] Therefore, it is important for managers to consider both internal needs and external incentives when attempting to motivate their employees. Further, managers who are more supportive and less controlling appear to elicit more intrinsic motivation from their employees. In addition to varying by individual, motivation may vary by culture. New research suggests that intrinsic job satisfaction may be stronger in richer countries that provide better government social welfare programs.[6]

self-interest
What is in the best interest and benefit to an individual.

🔲 MASLOW'S NEED HIERARCHY

Abraham Maslow, a psychologist, proposed a need theory of motivation emphasizing psychological and interpersonal needs in addition to physical needs and economic necessity. His theory was based on a need hierarchy later applied through Theory X and Theory Y, two sets of assumptions about people at work.

▮ THE HIERARCHY OF NEEDS

need hierarchy
The theory that behavior is determined by a progression of physical, social, and psychological needs by higher order needs.

The core of Maslow's theory of human motivation is a hierarchy of five need categories.[7] Although he recognized that there were factors other than one's needs (for example, culture) that were determinants of behavior, he focused his theoretical attention on specifying people's internal needs. Maslow labeled the five hierarchical categories as physiological needs, safety and security needs, love (social) needs, esteem needs, and the need for self-actualization. Figure 5.1 shows Maslow's *need hierarchy* and how the needs relate to Douglas McGregor's assumptions about people, which will be discussed next.

Maslow's need theory was tested in research with working populations. For example, one study reported that middle managers and lower-level managers had different perceptions of their need deficiencies and the importance of their needs.[8] One distinguishing feature of Maslow's need hierarchy is the following progression hypothesis. While Sanjay Patel was in the Lido Motel, he had to meet his basic needs for food, clothing, and shelter. Only later would he be able to tap into his upper-level needs. Although some research has challenged the assumption, the theory says that only ungratified needs motivate behavior.[9] Further, it is the lowest level of ungratified needs in the hierarchy that motivates behavior. As one level of need is met, a person progresses to the next higher level of need as a source of motivation. Hence, people progress up the hierarchy as they successively gratify each level of need.

Complete Challenge 5.1 to assess your own self-esteem, which is one dimension of Maslow's esteem needs.

FIGURE 5.1

Maslow's and McGregor's Theories

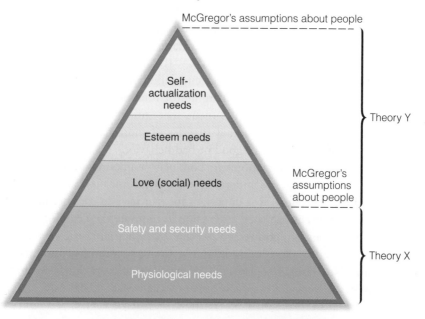

Maslow's Hierarchy of Needs

CHALLENGE 5.1

The Rosenberg Self-Esteem Scale

BELOW IS A LIST OF STATEMENTS DEALING WITH YOUR GENERAL FEELINGS ABOUT YOURSELF. IF YOU **STRONGLY AGREE**, CIRCLE **SA**. IF YOU **AGREE** WITH THE STATEMENT, CIRCLE **A**. IF YOU **DISAGREE**, CIRCLE **D**. IF YOU **STRONGLY DISAGREE**, CIRCLE **SD**.

		1. STRONGLY AGREE	2. AGREE	3. DISAGREE	4. STRONGLY DISAGREE
1.	I feel that I'm a person of worth, at least on an equal plane with others.	SA	A	D	SD
2.	I feel that I have a number of good qualities.	SA	A	D	SD
3.	All in all, I am inclined to feel that I am a failure.**	SA	A	D	SD
4.	I am able to do things as well as most other people.	SA	A	D	SD
5.	I feel I do not have much to be proud of.**	SA	A	D	SD
6.	I take a positive attitude toward myself.	SA	A	D	SD
7.	On the whole, I am satisfied with myself.	SA	A	D	SD
8.	I wish I could have more respect for myself.**	SA	A	D	SD
9.	I certainly feel useless at times.**	SA	A	D	SD
10.	At times I think I am no good at all.**	SA	A	D	SD

- To score the items, assign a value to each of the 10 items as follows:

  For items, 1, 2, 4, 6, 7: Strongly Agree=3, Agree=2, Disagree=1, and Strongly Disagree=0.
  For items 3, 5, 8, 9, 10 (which are reversed in valence, and noted with the asterisks**): Strongly Agree=0, Agree=1, Disagree=2, and Strongly Disagree=3.

Source: Morris Rosenberg, *Society and the Adolescent Self-Image,* revised edition (Middletown, CT: Wesleyan University Press, 1965, 1989): 146. Copyright © The Morris Rosenberg Foundation.

THEORY X AND THEORY Y

2. Contrast Theory X and Theory Y with Maslow's needs theory.

One important organizational implication of the need hierarchy concerns how to manage people at work. Douglas McGregor understood people's motivation using Maslow's need theory. He grouped the physiological and safety needs as "lower order" needs and the social, esteem, and self-actualization needs as "upper order" needs, as shown in Figure 5.1. McGregor proposed two alternative sets of assumptions about people at work based on which set of needs were the motivators.[10] His

TABLE 5.1	THEORY X	THEORY Y
McGregor's Assumptions about People	• People are by nature somewhat lazy and prefer to work as little as possible.	• People become passive or resistant to organizational needs as a result of experiences in organizations.
	• People lack ambition, dislike responsibility, and prefer to be told what to do.	• People are by nature motivated, have the potential to develop, and have the capacity to assume responsibility. Management does not make them so.
	• People are inherently self-centered and indifferent to the company's needs.	• Management has the responsibility to make it possible for people to recognize and develop their own strengths and capacities.
	• People are by nature resistant to change and very much set in their ways.	• The essential task of management is to arrange conditions and methods of work so that people can achieve their own goals best by directing their own efforts toward organizational objectives.
	• People are gullible, not too intelligent, and rather easily misled by unethical leaders.	

SOURCE: Adapted from Douglas McGregor, "The Human Side of Enterprise" (New York: McGraw-Hill, 1960): 132; and Douglas McGregor, "The Human Side of Enterprise" in G. Heil, W. Bennis, and D. C. Stephens (eds.), Douglas McGregor, "Revisited: Managing the Human Side of the Enterprise" (New York: John Wiley, 2000): 130–144.

Theory X
A set of assumptions of how to manage individuals who are motivated by lower order needs.

Theory Y
A set of assumptions of how to manage individuals who are motivated by higher order needs.

Theory X and *Theory Y* assumptions are included in Table 5.1. McGregor saw the responsibility of management as the same under both sets of assumptions. Specifically, "management is responsible for organizing the elements of productive enterprise—money, materials, equipment, people—in the interest of economic ends."[11]

McGregor believed that Theory X assumptions are appropriate for employees motivated by lower order needs. Theory Y assumptions, in contrast, are appropriate for employees motivated by higher order needs. Employee participation programs are one consequence of McGregor's Theory Y assumptions. Therefore, *Fortune 1000* corporations use employee involvement as one motivation strategy for achieving high performance.[12] Whole Foods founder and CEO John Mackey relies on Maslow's hierarchy of needs in leading the company.[13] Specifically, Mackey believes that food is basic to meeting our physiological needs. However, like McGregor, Mackey believes that employee empowerment and teamwork are essential for self-actualization.

Gordon Forward, founding CEO of world-class Chaparral Steel Company, considered the assumptions made about people central to motivation and management.[14] He viewed employees as resources to be developed. Using Maslow's need hierarchy and Theory Y assumptions about people, he cultivated and developed a productive, loyal workforce in TXI's Chaparral Steel unit.

: 3. Describe the needs for achievement, power, and affiliation.

🏛 McCLELLAND'S NEED THEORY

A second major need theory of motivation focuses on personality and learned needs. David McClelland identified three learned or acquired needs, called manifest needs. These manifest needs were the needs for achievement, for power, and for affiliation.

NEED FOR ACHIEVEMENT

The *need for achievement* concerns issues of excellence, competition, challenging goals, persistence, and overcoming difficulties.[15] Individuals with a high need for achievement have three unique characteristics: (1) they set goals that are moderately difficult, yet achievable; (2) they like to receive feedback on their progress toward these goals; and (3) they do not like having external events or other people interfere with their progress toward the goals. Research among achievement-oriented employees found that high skill and challenge were related to more positive mood, task interest, and organizational spontaneity.[16] These findings generalize well across countries with adults who are employed full time.[17] In addition, international differences in the tendency for achievement have been found. Specifically, achievement tendencies are highest for the United States, an individualistic culture, and lowest for Japan and Hungary, collectivistic societies.[18]

need for achievement
A manifest (easily perceived) need that concerns individuals' issues of excellence, competition, challenging goals, persistence, and overcoming difficulties.

NEED FOR POWER

The *need for power* is concerned with making an impact on others, the desire to influence others, the urge to change people or events, and the desire to make a difference in life. People with a high need for power like to control people and events. A high need for power was one distinguishing characteristic of managers rated the "best" in McClelland's research. Specifically, the best managers had a very high need for socialized power, as opposed to personalized power.[19] These managers are concerned for others; have an interest in organizational goals; and have a desire to be useful to the larger group, organization, and society.

While successful managers have the greatest upward velocity in an organization and rise to higher managerial levels more quickly than their contemporaries, they benefit their organizations most if they have a high socialized power need.[20] The need for power is discussed further in Chapter 10, on power and politics.

need for power
A manifest (easily perceived) need that concerns an individual's need to make an impact on others, influence others, change people or events, and make a difference in life.

NEED FOR AFFILIATION

The *need for affiliation* is concerned with establishing and maintaining warm, close, intimate relationships with other people.[21] People with a high need for affiliation are motivated to express their emotions and feelings to others while expecting other people to do the same in return. The relationships they have with others are close and personal, emphasizing friendship and companionship.

Over and above these three needs, Murray's Manifest Needs theory included the need for autonomy, which is the desire for independence and freedom from any constraints. People with a high need for autonomy like to work alone and to control the pace of their work. They dislike bureaucratic rules, regulations, and procedures. The need for relationships is important in each theory. A recent study of 555 nurses in specialized units for mentally deficient patients found that instrumental support on the job contributed positively to the nurses' intrinsic motivation.[22]

need for affiliation
A manifest (easily perceived) need that concerns an individual's need to establish and maintain warm, close, intimate relationships with other people.

HERZBERG'S TWO-FACTOR THEORY

Frederick Herzberg departed from the need theories of motivation and examined the experiences that satisfied or dissatisfied people at work. This motivation theory became known as the two-factor theory.[23] According to the two-factor

4. Explain how the two-factor theory influences behavior.

theory, people have two sets of needs—one related to the avoidance of pain and one related to the desire for psychological growth. Conditions in the work environment would affect one or the other of these needs.

■ MOTIVATION FACTORS

motivation factor
A work condition related to satisfaction of the need for psychological growth.

Work conditions related to satisfaction of the need for psychological growth were labeled *motivation factors*. Job satisfaction is produced by building motivation factors into a job, according to Herzberg, through a process known as job enrichment. Motivation factors lead to positive mental health and challenge people to grow, contribute to the work environment, and invest themselves in the organization. According to the theory and original research, the absence of these factors does not lead to dissatisfaction. Rather, it leads to the lack of satisfaction. The motivation factors are the more important of the two sets of factors, because they directly affect a person's motivational drive to do a good job. When they are absent, the person is demotivated to perform well and achieve excellence. The hygiene factors are a completely distinct set of factors unrelated to the motivation to achieve and do excellent work.

■ HYGIENE FACTORS

hygiene factor
A work condition related to dissatisfaction caused by discomfort or pain.

Work conditions related to dissatisfaction caused by discomfort or pain were labeled *hygiene factors*. Job dissatisfaction occurs when the hygiene factors are either not present or not sufficient. When these hygiene factors are poor or absent, the person complains about "poor supervision," "poor medical benefits," or whatever hygiene factor is poor. Employees experience a deficit and are dissatisfied when the hygiene factors are not present. Excellent hygiene factors result in employees' being *not dissatisfied* and contribute to the absence of complaints about these contextual considerations. Even in the absence of good hygiene factors, employees may still be very motivated to perform their jobs well if the motivation factors are present. Although this may appear to be a paradox, it is not, because the motivation and hygiene factors are independent of each other. Each set of factors related to one aspect of what Herzberg identified as the human being's dual nature regarding the work environment. Thus, motivation factors relate to job satisfaction, and hygiene factors relate to job dissatisfaction,[24] as shown in Figure 5.2. Challenge 5.2 asks you to rank a set of 10 job reward factors in terms of their importance to the average employee, to supervisors, and to you.

■ CRITIQUE OF THE TWO-FACTOR THEORY

One criticism of Herzberg's two-factor theory concerns the classification of the two factors. Data have not shown a clear dichotomization of items onto factors. For example, employees almost equally classify pay as a hygiene factor *and* as a motivation factor. A second criticism is the absence of individual differences. Specifically, age, sex, race, social status, education, or occupational level may influence the classification of factors. A third criticism is that intrinsic job factors, such as the work flow process, may be more important in determining satisfaction or dissatisfaction on the job. Finally, almost all of the supporting data for the theory come from Herzberg and his students. However, independent research found his theory valid in a government research and development environment.[25] Herzberg's two-factor theory has important implications for the design of work, as discussed in Chapter 13.

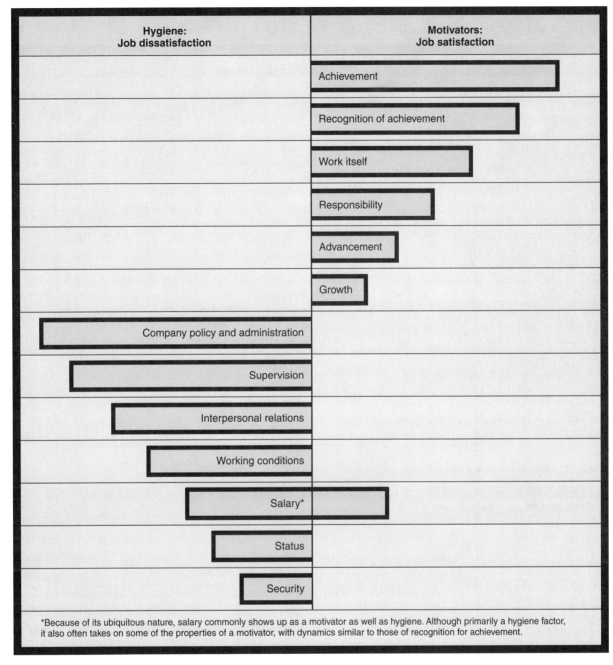

Hygiene: Job dissatisfaction	Motivators: Job satisfaction
	Achievement
	Recognition of achievement
	Work itself
	Responsibility
	Advancement
	Growth
Company policy and administration	
Supervision	
Interpersonal relations	
Working conditions	
Salary*	
Status	
Security	

*Because of its ubiquitous nature, salary commonly shows up as a motivator as well as hygiene. Although primarily a hygiene factor, it also often takes on some of the properties of a motivator, with dynamics similar to those of recognition for achievement.

SOURCE: Reprinted from Frederick Herzberg, *The Managerial Choice: To Be Efficient or to Be Human* (Salt Lake City: Olympus, 1982). Reprinted by permission.

FIGURE 5.2

The Motivation-Hygiene Theory of Motivation

⬛ SOCIAL EXCHANGE AND EQUITY THEORY

Equity theory is a social exchange process theory of motivation that focuses on the individual–environment interaction. In contrast to internal needs theories of motivation, equity theory is concerned with the social processes that influence motivation and behavior. Power and exchange are important considerations in

CHALLENGE   5.2

What's Important to Employees?

There are many possible job rewards that employees may receive. Listed below are 10 possible job reward factors. Rank these factors three times. First, rank them as you think the average employee would rank them. Second, rank them as you think the average employee's supervisor would rank them for the employee. Finally, rank them according to what you consider important.

Your instructor has normative data for 1,000 employees and their supervisors that will help you interpret your results and place the results in the context of Maslow's need hierarchy and Herzberg's two-factor theory of motivation.

Employee	Supervisor	You

1. job security
2. full appreciation of work done
3. promotion and growth in the organization
4. good wages
5. interesting work
6. good working conditions
7. tactful discipline
8. sympathetic help with personal problems
9. personal loyalty to employees
10. a feeling of being in on things

Source: "Crossed Wires on Employee Motivation," *Training and Development* 49 (1995): 59–60. American Society for Training and Development. Reprinted with permission. All rights reserved.

understanding human behavior.[26] In the same vein, Amitai Etzioni developed three categories of exchange relationships that people have with organizations: committed, calculated, and alienated involvements.[27] The implications of these relationships for power are discussed in detail in Chapter 10. Etzioni characterized committed relationships as moral ones of high positive intensity, calculated relationships as ones of low positive or low negative intensity, and alienated relationships as ones of high negative intensity. Committed relationships may characterize a person's involvement with a religious group, and alienated relationships may characterize a person's incarceration in a prison. Social exchange theory may be the best way to understand effort–reward relationships and the sense of fairness at work as seen in a Dutch study.[28] Moral principles in workplace fairness are important because failures in fairness, or unfairness, lead to such things as theft, sabotage, and even violence.[29]

■ DEMANDS AND CONTRIBUTIONS

Calculated involvements are based on the notion of social exchange in which each party in the relationship demands certain things of the other and contributes accordingly to the exchange. Business partnerships and commercial deals are excellent examples of calculated involvements. When they work well and both parties to the exchange benefit, the relationship has a positive orientation. When losses occur or conflicts arise, the relationship has a negative orientation. For example, Canadian steelmaker Dofasco treats employees fairly and equitably, in exchange for which the employees are highly motivated and highly productive. When the company does well, employees prosper, as in 1999 when employees split a record bonus pot of $36 million. In addition, when times are rough, few people . . . if any . . . are laid off. Turnover in Dofasco's primary facility in Hamilton, Ontario, was less than two percent in 2003.[30]

DEMANDS

Each party to the exchange makes demands upon the other. These demands express the expectations that each party has of the other in the relationship. The organization expresses its demands on the individual in the form of goal or mission statements, job expectations, performance objectives, and performance feedback. These are among the primary and formal mechanisms through which people learn about the organization's demands and expectations of them.

The organization is not alone in making demands of the relationship. The individual has needs to be satisfied as well, as we have previously discussed. These needs form the basis for the expectations or demands placed on the organization by the individual. Employee need fulfillment and the feeling of belonging are both important to a healthy exchange and to organizational membership.[31] These needs may be conceptualized from the perspective of Maslow, Herzberg, or McClelland.

CONTRIBUTIONS

Just as each party to the exchange makes demands upon the other, each also has contributions to make to the relationship. These contributions are the basis for satisfying the demands expressed by the other party in the relationship. Employees are able to satisfy organizational demands through a range of contributions, including their skills, abilities, knowledge, energy, professional contacts, and native talents. As people grow and develop over time, they are able to increasingly satisfy the range of demands and expectations placed upon them by the organization.

In a similar fashion, organizations have a range of contributions available to the exchange relationship to meet individual needs. These contributions include salary, benefits, advancement opportunities, security, status, and social affiliation. Some organizations are richer in resources and better able to meet employee needs than other organizations. Thus, one of the concerns that individuals and organizations alike have is whether the relationship is a fair deal or an equitable arrangement for both members of the relationship.

■ ADAMS'S THEORY OF INEQUITY

Blau's and Etzioni's ideas about social process and exchange provide a context for understanding fairness, equity, and inequity in work relationships. Stacy Adams explicitly developed the idea that *inequity* in the social exchange process is an important motivator. Adams's theory of inequity suggests that people are motivated when they find themselves in situations of inequity or unfairness.[32] Inequity occurs when a person receives more, or less, than the person believes is deserved based on effort and/or contribution. Inequity leads to the experience of tension, and tension motivates a person to act in a manner to resolve the inequity.

inequity
The situation in which a person perceives he or she is receiving less than he or she is giving, or is giving less than he or she is receiving.

When does a person know that the situation is inequitable or unfair? Adams suggests that people examine the contribution portion of the exchange relationship just discussed. Specifically, people consider their inputs (their own contributions to the relationship) and their outcomes (the organization's contributions to the relationship). People then calculate an input/outcome ratio, which they compare with that of a generalized or comparison other. Figure 5.3 shows one equity situation and two inequity situations, one negative and one positive. For example, inequity in (b) could occur if the comparison other earned a higher salary, and inequity in (c) could occur if the person had more vacation time, in both cases all else being equal. Although not illustrated in the example, nontangible inputs, like emotional investment, and nontangible outcomes, like job satisfaction, may well enter into a person's equity equation.

Pay inequity has been a particularly thorny issue for women in some professions and companies. Eastman Kodak and other companies have made real progress in addressing this inequity through pay equity.[33] As organizations become increasingly international, it may be difficult to determine pay and benefit equity/inequity across national borders.

◀◀ think critically ▶▶

Assume you know an employee who is being underpaid because the company believes it can save money and the employee will not complain. Is this unethical? Should you tell the employee about the underpayment condition?

■ THE RESOLUTION OF INEQUITY

Once a person establishes the existence of an inequity, a number of strategies can be used to restore equity to the situation. Adams's theory provides seven basic strategies to restore equity for the person: (1) alter the person's outcomes, (2) alter the person's inputs, (3) alter the comparison other's outcomes, (4) alter the comparison other's inputs, (5) change who is used as a comparison other, (6) rationalize the inequity, and (7) leave the organizational situation.

Within each of the first four strategies, a wide variety of tactics can be employed. For example, if an employee has a strategy to increase his or her income by $11,000 per year to restore equity, the tactic might be a meeting between the employee and his or her manager concerning the issue of salary equity. The person would present relevant data on the issue. Another tactic would be for the person to work with the company's compensation specialists. A third tactic would be for the person to bring the matter before an equity committee in the company. A fourth tactic would be for the person to seek advice from the legal department.

The selection of a strategy and a set of tactics is a sensitive issue with possible long-term consequences. In this example, a strategy aimed at reducing the comparison other's outcomes may have the desired short-term effect of restoring equity while having adverse long-term consequences in terms of morale and productivity. Similarly, the choice of legal tactics may result in equity but have the long-term consequence of damaged relationships in the workplace. Therefore, as a person formulates the strategy and tactics to restore equity, the range of consequences of alternative actions must be taken into account. Hence, not all strategies or tactics are equally preferred. The equity theory does not include a hierarchy predicting which inequity reduction strategy a person will or should choose.

Field studies on equity theory suggest that it may help explain important organizational behaviors. For example, one study found that workers who perceived compensation decisions as equitable displayed greater job satisfaction and organizational commitment.[34] In addition, equity theory may play an important role in labor–management relationships with regard to union-negotiated benefits.

■ NEW PERSPECTIVES ON EQUITY THEORY

Since the original formulation of the theory of inequity, now usually referred to as equity theory, a number of revisions have been made in light of new theories and research. One important theoretical revision proposes three types of individuals based on preferences for equity.[35] *Equity sensitives* are those people who prefer equity based on the originally formed theory. Equity sensitivity contributes significantly to variation in free time spent working.[36] *Benevolents* are people who are comfortable with an equity ratio less than that of their comparison other, as exhibited in the Calvinistic heritage of the Dutch.[37] These people may be thought of as givers. *Entitleds* are people who are comfortable with an equity ratio greater than that of their comparison other, as exhibited by some offspring of the affluent who want and expect more.[38] These people may be thought of as takers. Females and minorities have not always been equitably treated in business and commerce.

⚑ JUSTICE AND FAIR TREATMENT AT WORK

The concept of organizational justice has extended Adams's original theory of inequity. In Chapter 2, we introduced the concepts of procedural, distributive, and interactional justice as forms of fair treatment at work according to Jerald Greenberg and others. The basic ideas in justice theories are that employees' perceptions of fair procedures, fair distribution of outcomes, and fairness in interpersonal treatment all influence motivation and behavior. Justice and fairness satisfy the basic human needs to be treated with dignity and respect. Justice and fairness influence people's emotions, their sense of trust and control, and their moral sense

equity sensitive
An individual who prefers an equity ratio equal to that of his or her comparison other.

benevolent
An individual who is comfortable with an equity ratio less than that of his or her comparison other.

entitled
An individual who is comfortable with an equity ratio greater than that of his or her comparison other.

: 5. Describe how equity/inequity and justice/injustice influence motivation and behavior.

of right and wrong. While organizational justice research has a long history,[39] a recent review of the literature on justice perceptions has shown employee perceptions of fairness are linked to their work performance, to organizational citizenship behaviors, and to work attitudes.[40] One justice study suggests that a person's organizational position influences self-imposed performance expectations.[41] Specifically, a two-level move up in an organization with no additional pay creates a higher self-imposed performance expectation than a one-level move up with modest additional pay. Similarly, a two-level move down in an organization with no reduction in pay creates a lower self-imposed performance expectation than a one-level move down with a modest decrease in pay. This suggests that organizational position may be more important than pay in determining the level of a person's performance expectations. Justice and fair treatment at work are positive and important because they create a sense of psychological security, predictability, and stability with regard to procedures, outcomes, and interpersonal relationships. The absence of justice, or injustice, and the absence of fairness, or unfairness, can have unintended and negative consequences.

UNINTENDED CONSEQUENCES OF INJUSTICE AND UNFAIR TREATMENT

When people experience injustice and unfair treatment at work, there can be a variety of unintended, negative consequences. Greenberg has summarized the relationship between organizational justice and stress in the Justice Salience Hierarchy (JSH) shown in Figure 5.4. The highest levels of stress reactions occur when there is distributive injustice, procedural injustice, and interactional injustice while the lowest levels of stress occur when there is distributive, procedural, and interactive

FIGURE 5.4

Summary of Relationship between Organizational Justice and Stress: The Justice Salience Hierarchy (JSH)

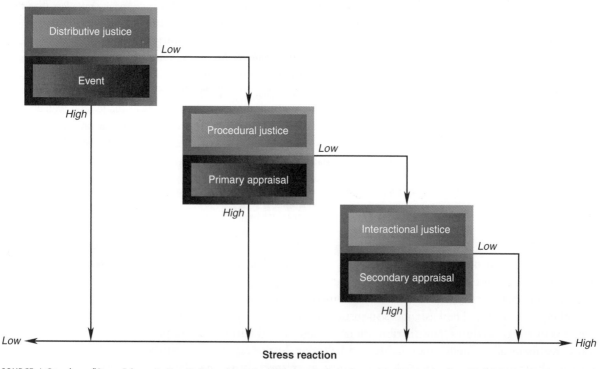

SOURCE: J. Greenberg, "Stress Fairness to Fare No Stress: Managing Workplace Stress by Promoting Organizational Justice," *Organizational Dynamics* 33 (4) (2004): 358. [Figure © 2004, Jerald Greenberg. Reproduced with permission.]

justice. One study found that revenge resulted from the experience of unfair treatment at work.[42] Greenberg himself has linked the experience of unfair treatment to employee theft[43] as well as to insomnia in the case of underpayment inequity.[44] In still another study, injustice has been linked to sabotage behavior on the part of employees.[45] These forms of dysfunctional behavior are among the unintended consequences of injustice and unfair treatment at work. Aggressive reactions or other forms of violent and deviant behavior that do harm to both individuals and the organization are the more extreme forms of dysfunctional behavior. Fortunately, only a small number of individuals respond to such unfairness through dysfunctional behavior.[46] Sanjay Patel was not in that small number even though he experienced the stress and tension of potential wrongdoing that might have occurred at any moment when he was growing up in the Lido Motel. Sanjay chose functional behavior as a response.

■ MANAGERIAL ACTIONS

Managerial actions can make a positive impact on the experience of justice and fairness at work. For example, Greenberg found in his study of insomniac reactions to underpayment inequity mentioned above that supervisory training in interactional justice significantly reduced insomnia for the nurses. Thus, when managers are sensitive to the feelings and emotions of their employees, employees feel appreciated and supported. Interactional justice has stress-relieving benefits because it affords the manager the opportunity to provide social support to employees. Elsewhere, Greenberg suggests that managers can employ just and fair procedures to help bridge the cultural and individual differences in a diverse workplace.[47] When organizational procedures and processes are just, open, transparent, and fair, employees are able to see that different groups or different individuals are treated the same. In one way or another, justice appears to be a universal concern among people across cultures. Managerial training can lead to positive managerial actions with positive benefits for all in the workplace. Managerial training in justice and fair treatment may include explanations of the justice concepts, case studies, directed role-playing exercises, and carefully guided group discussions.[48]

◥ EXPECTANCY THEORY OF MOTIVATION

Whereas equity theory focuses on a social exchange process, Vroom's expectancy theory of motivation focuses on personal perceptions of the performance process. His theory is founded on the basic notions that people desire certain outcomes of behavior and performance, which may be thought of as rewards or consequences of behavior, and that they believe there are relationships between the effort they put forth, the performance they achieve, and the outcomes they receive. Expectancy theory is a cognitive process theory of motivation.

The key constructs in the expectancy theory of motivation are the *valence* of an outcome, *expectancy*, and *instrumentality*.[49] Valence is the value or importance one places on a particular reward. Expectancy is the belief that effort leads to performance (for example, "If I try harder, I can do better"). Instrumentality is the belief that performance is related to rewards (for example, "If I perform better, I

6. Describe the expectancy theory of motivation.

valence
The value or importance one places on a particular reward.

expectancy
The belief that effort leads to performance.

instrumentality
The belief that performance is related to rewards.

FIGURE 5.5

An Expectancy Model for Motivation

"What are my chances of getting the job done if I put forth the necessary effort?"

"What are my chances of getting the rewards I value if I satisfactorily complete the job?"

"What rewards do I value?"

will get more pay"). A model for the expectancy theory notions of effort, performance, and rewards is depicted in Figure 5.5.

Valence, expectancy, and instrumentality are all important to a person's motivation. Expectancy and instrumentality concern a person's beliefs about how effort, performance, and rewards are related. For example, a person may firmly believe that an increase in effort has a direct, positive effect on performance and that a reduced amount of effort results in a commensurate reduction in performance. Another person may have a very different set of beliefs about the effort–performance link. The person might believe that regardless of the amount of additional effort put forth, no improvement in performance is possible. Therefore, the perceived relationship between effort and performance varies from person to person and from activity to activity.

In a similar fashion, people's beliefs about the performance–reward link vary. One person may believe that an improvement in performance has a direct, positive effect on the rewards received, whereas another person may believe that an improvement in performance has no effect on the rewards received. Again, the perceived relationship between performance and rewards varies from person to person and from situation to situation. From a motivation perspective, it is the person's belief about the relationships between these constructs that is important, not the actual nature of the relationship. During volatile times in business, the performance–reward linkage may be confusing.

Expectancy theory has been used by managers and companies to design motivation programs.[50] Sometimes called performance planning and evaluation systems, these motivation programs are designed to enhance a person's belief that effort would lead to better performance and that better performance would lead to merit pay increases and other rewards. Valence and expectancy are particularly important in establishing priorities for people pursuing multiple goals.[51]

A person's motivation increases along with his or her belief that effort leads to performance and that performance leads to rewards, assuming the person wants the rewards. This is the third key idea within the expectancy theory of motivation. It is the idea that the valence, or value, that people place on various rewards varies. One person prefers salary to benefits, whereas another person prefers just the reverse. All people do not place the same value on each reward. Expectancy theory has been used in a wide variety of contexts, including test-taking motivation among students.[52]

■ MOTIVATIONAL PROBLEMS

Within the expectancy theory framework, motivational problems stem from three basic causes. These causes are a disbelief in a relationship between effort and performance, a disbelief in a relationship between performance and rewards, and lack of desire for the rewards offered.

If the motivational problem is related to the person's belief that effort will not result in performance, the solution lies in altering this belief. The person can be shown how an increase in effort, or an alteration in the kind of effort put forth, can be converted into improved performance. For example, the textbook salesperson who does not believe more calls (effort) will result in greater sales (performance) might be shown how to distinguish departments with high-probability sales opportunities from those with low-probability sales opportunities. Hence, more calls (effort) can be converted into greater sales (performance).

If the motivational problem is related to the person's belief that performance will not result in rewards, the solution lies in altering this belief. The person can be shown how an increase in performance or a somewhat altered form of performance will be converted into rewards. For example, the textbook salesperson who does not believe greater sales (performance) will result in overall higher commissions (rewards) might be shown computationally or graphically that a direct relationship does exist. Hence, greater sales (performance) are directly converted into higher commissions (rewards).

If the motivational problem is related to the value the person places on, or the preference the person has for, certain rewards, the solution lies in influencing the value placed on the rewards or altering the rewards themselves. For example, the textbook salesperson may not particularly want higher commissions, given the small incremental gain he would receive at his tax level. In this case, the company might establish a mechanism for sheltering commissions from being taxed or alternative mechanisms for deferred compensation.

Research results on expectancy theory have been mixed.[53] The theory has been shown to predict job satisfaction accurately.[54] However, the theory's complexity makes it difficult to test the full model, and the measures of instrumentality, valence, and expectancy have only weak validity.[55] In addition, measuring the expectancy constructs is time consuming, and the values for each construct change over time for an individual. Finally, a theory assumes the individual is totally rational and acts as a minicomputer, calculating probabilities and values. In reality, the theory may be more complex than people as they typically function.

■ MOTIVATION AND MORAL MATURITY

Expectancy theory would predict that people work to maximize their personal outcomes. This is consistent with Adam Smith's ideas of working for one's own self-interest. Ultimately, Adam Smith and expectancy theories believe that people work to benefit themselves alone. Expectancy theory would not explain altruistic behavior for the benefit of others. For example, expectancy theory does not help to explain the motivation of Sanjay Patel discussed in the opening case. Therefore,

moral maturity
The measure of a person's cognitive moral development.

it may be necessary to consider an individual's *moral maturity* in order to better understand altruistic, fair, and equitable behavior. Moral maturity is the measure of a person's cognitive moral development, which was discussed in Chapter 4. Morally mature people act and behave based on universal ethical principles, whereas morally immature people act and behave based on egocentric motivations.[56]

: 7. Identify cultural differences in motivation.

CULTURAL DIFFERENCES IN MOTIVATION

Most motivation theories in use today have been developed by Americans in the United States and are about Americans.[57] When researchers have examined the universality of these theories, they have found cultural differences, at least with regard to Maslow's, McClelland's, and Herzberg's theories. For example, while self-actualization may be the pinnacle need for Americans in Maslow's need hierarchy, security may be the most important need for people in cultures such as Greece and Japan who have a high need to avoid uncertainty.[58] Although achievement is an important need for Americans, research noted earlier in the chapter suggested that other cultures do not value achievement as much as Americans do.

We saw in the opening vignette about Pixar's Sanjay Patel that culture played a role in contributing to his initial social isolation and his motivation to offer future Indian children another pathway. He always aimed to share that with non-Indian friends, thus bridging the cultural boundaries that often separate people one from another.

The two-factor theory has been tested in other countries as well. Results in New Zealand did not replicate the results found in the United States; supervision and interpersonal relationships were important motivators in New Zealand rather than hygienic factors as in America.[59] Finally, expectancy theory may hold up very nicely in cultures that value individualism but break down in more collectivist cultures that value cooperative efforts. In collectivist cultures, rewards are more closely tied to group and team efforts, thus rendering unnecessary the utility of expectancy theory.

: 8. Discuss two new ideas in human motivation.

◢ NEW IDEAS IN MOTIVATION

While executives like Whole Foods' CEO John Mackey value traditional motivation theories such as Maslow's, others like PepsiCo's CEO Steve Reinemund use new motivational ideas with their employees. New ideas in motivation have emerged in the past decade. One new idea centers on eustress, hope, and vigor. This idea comes from the new discipline of positive organizational scholarship. Another new idea centers on positive energy and full engagement. This idea translates what was learned from high-performance athletes for *Fortune 500* executives and managers, such as those at PepsiCo. Both new ideas concern motivation, behavior, and performance at work.

EUSTRESS, HOPE, AND VIGOR

While stress may be a health risk factor, it can also be a powerful, positive motivator. The positive side of stress concerns its value as a motivational force, as in eustress. *Eustress* is healthy, normal stress.[60] Aligned with eustress in the new discipline of positive organizational scholarship are investing in strengths, finding positive meaning in work, displaying courage and principled action, and drawing on positive emotions at work.[61] This new, positive perspective on organizational life encourages optimism,

eustress
Healthy, normal stress.

hope, and health for people at work. Rather than focusing on the individual's needs, or alternatively on the rewards or punishment metered out in the work environment, this new idea in motivation focuses on the individual's interpretation of events.

Eustress is one manifestation of this broad, positive perspective. People are motivated by eustress when they see opportunities rather than obstacles, when they experience challenges rather than barriers, and when they feel energized rather than frustrated by the daily experiences of organizational life. Thus, eustress is a healthy and positive motivational force for individuals who harness its energy for productive work and organizational contributions.

Closely related to the concept of eustress is the concept of *vigor*.[62] Vigor is a three-dimensional construct. The three dimensions are physical strength, emotional energy, and cognitive aliveness. Physical strength concerns one's feelings about his or her physical ability. Emotional energy is the interpersonal dimension of vigor and concerns one's feelings regarding expressing sympathy, empathy, and other emotions to significant others. Cognitive aliveness concerns one's feelings, flow of thoughts, mental agility, and cognitive alertness. People with high levels of vigor are more energetic and thus able to be more productive, active, and motivated in a wide range of activities.

Vigor
Physical strength, emotional energy, and cognitive aliveness.

■ POSITIVE ENERGY AND FULL ENGAGEMENT

The second new idea in motivation takes lessons learned from professional athletes and applies them in order to develop corporate athletes.[63] Jim Loehr's central tenets are the management of energy rather than time and the strategic use of disengagement to balance the power of full activity engagement.[64] This approach to motivation suggests that individuals do not need to be activated by unmet needs but are already activated by their own physical, emotional, mental, and spiritual energy. A manager's task is to help individuals learn to manage their energy so that they can experience periodic renewal and recovery and thus build positive energy and capacity for work.

A key to positive energy and full engagement is the concept that energy recovery is equally important to, if not more important than, energy expenditure. Individuals may be designed more as sprinters than long-distance runners, putting forth productive energy for short periods and then requiring time for recovery to reenergize. This approach to motivation and work is based on a balanced approach to the human body's potential to build or enhance its capacity, thus enabling the individual to sustain a high level of performance in the face of increasing work demands.

⚑ MANAGERIAL IMPLICATIONS: MANY WAYS TO MOTIVATE PEOPLE

Managers must realize that all motivation theories are not equally good or equally useful. The later motivation theories, such as the equity and expectancy theories, may be more scientifically sound than earlier theories, such as the two-factor theory. Nevertheless, the older theories of motivation have conceptual value, show us the importance of human needs, and provide a basis for the later theories. The individual, internal theories of motivation and the individual–environment interaction process theories uniquely contribute to our overall understanding of human behavior and motivation at work.

Managers cannot assume they understand employees' needs. They should recognize the variety of needs that motivate employee behavior and ask employees for input to better understand their needs. Individual employees differ in their needs, and managers should be sensitive to ethnic, national, gender, and age differences in this regard. Employees with high needs for power must be given opportunities to exercise influence, and employees with high needs for achievement must be allowed to excel at work.

Managers can increase employee motivation by training (increased perceptions of success because of increased ability), coaching (increased confidence), and task assignments (increased perceptions of success because of more experience). Managers should ensure that rewards are contingent on good performance and that valued rewards, such as time off or flexible work schedules, are available. Managers must understand what their employees want.

Finally, managers should be aware that morally mature employees are more likely to be sensitive to inequities at work. At the same time, these employees are less likely to be selfish or self-centered and more likely to be concerned about equity issues for all employees. Morally mature employees will act ethically for the common good of all employees and the organization.

LOOKING BACK :: PIXAR ANIMATION STUDIOS

Motivated to a Different Future . . . The Power of Imagination

Sanjay Patel's pathway out of the Lido Motel was helped very much by a teacher who became a mentor. The teacher at San Bernadino High School made sure that Sanjay entered high school art competitions. She fed him, she gave him some hand-me-down clothes, and she really took care of him. That was a wonderful support and beginning of a new life. Sanjay went from high school to the California Institute of the Arts (CalArts), which was set up by Walt Disney in the 1950s to train his animators. What better place to use your imagination and nurture your creativity than with a whole lot of others motivated in the same creative, imaginative way? His teacher at San Bernardino and CalArts gave Sanjay a great foundation.

Then came the recruitment after his second year at CalArts by Pixar. Sanjay's first reaction was "I don't want to work at Pixar. They use computers." He liked to draw and had not yet been introduced to computer animation. There were only about 200 people working at Pixar when Sanjay was recruited. In his first 10 years at Pixar, the company grew to over 1,000 people working on a whole host of movies and projects. Thus, Pixar truly became his pathway into the future and enabled him to use the gifts and talents that he had nurtured over the years. The power of imagination gave his creativity wings, and Sanjay soared out of the Lido Motel and into the Hollywood scene. Imagination and creativity are hard to contain, and Sanjay did not stop at Pixar.

While continuing to pursue his path at Pixar, Sanjay continued his hand-drawn animations and creative work. His first book is *The Little Book of Hindu Deities*. Drawing on his Indian cultural roots and his father's daily worship, rituals, and prayer session, he created something of beauty and substance. While the little book is designed to be attractive and appealing, like candy, from the outside, there is something more substantive on the inside. Like Sanjay himself, the book is a product of the West, yet it has roots in the East. The power of his imagination continues. Sanjay is working on his next book already, and this one draws on his love of drawing; it is to be a book of hand-drawn animation.[65]

CHAPTER SUMMARY

1. Early economic theories of motivation emphasized extrinsic incentives as the basis for motivation and technology as a force multiplier.
2. Maslow's hierarchy of needs theory of motivation was the basis for McGregor's Theory X and Theory Y assumptions about people at work.
3. According to McClelland, the needs for achievement, power, and affiliation are learned needs that differ among diverse cultures.
4. The two-factor theory found that the presence of motivation factors led to job satisfaction,

and the presence of hygiene factors prevented job dissatisfaction.
5. New ideas in motivation emphasize eustress, hope, positive energy, and full engagement.
6. Social exchange theory holds that people form calculated working relationships and expect fair, equitable, ethical treatment.
7. Expectancy theory says that effort is the basis for motivation and that people want their effort to lead to performance and rewards.
8. Theories of motivation are culturally bound, and differences occur among nations.

KEY TERMS

benevolent (p. 133)
entitled (p. 133)
equity sensitive (p. 133)
eustress (p. 138)
expectancy (p. 135)
hygiene factor (p. 128)
inequity (p. 131)

instrumentality (p. 135)
moral maturity (p. 138)
motivation (p. 122)
motivation factor (p. 128)
need for achievement (p. 127)
need for affiliation (p. 127)
need for power (p. 127)

need hierarchy (p. 124)
self-interest (p. 123)
Theory X (p. 126)
Theory Y (p. 126)
valence (p. 135)
vigor (p. 139)

REVIEW QUESTIONS

1. How can knowledge of motivation theories help managers?
2. What are the five categories of motivational needs described by Maslow? Give an example of how each can be satisfied.
3. What are the Theory X and Theory Y assumptions about people at work? How do they relate to the hierarchy of needs?
4. What three manifest needs does McClelland identify?
5. How do hygiene and motivational factors differ? What are the implications of the two-factor theory for managers?

6. Describe how equity/inequity, justice/injustice influence motivation and behavior.
7. How is inequity determined by a person in an organization? How can inequity be resolved if it exists?
8. What are the key concepts in the expectancy theory of motivation?
9. Describe new ideas that managers can use to motivate employees.

Discussion and Communication QUESTIONS

1. What do you think are the most important motivational needs for the majority of people? Do you think your needs differ from those of most people?

2. At what level in Maslow's hierarchy of needs are you living? Are you basically satisfied at this level?

3. Assume you are leaving your current job to look for employment elsewhere. What will you look for that you do not have now? If you do not have a job, assume you will be looking for one soon. What are the most important factors that you will seek?

4. If you were being inequitably paid in your job, which strategy do you think would be the most helpful to you in resolving the inequity? What tactics would you consider using?

5. Do you believe you can do a better job of working or do a better job of studying than you are currently doing? Do you think you would get more pay and benefits or better grades if you did a better job? Do you care about the rewards (or grades) in your organization (or university)?

6. What important experiences have contributed to your moral and ethical development? Are you working to further your own moral maturity at this time?

7. (*communication question*) Prepare a memo describing the two employees you work with who most closely operate according to Theory X and Theory Y assumptions about human nature. Be as specific and detailed in your description as you can, using quotes and/or observational examples.

8. (*communication question*) Develop an oral presentation about the most current management practices in employee motivation. Find out what at least four different companies are doing in this area. Be prepared to compare these practices with the theory and research in the chapter.

9. (*communication question*) Interview a manager and prepare a memo summarizing the relative importance that manager places on the needs for achievement, power, and affiliation. Include (1) whether these needs have changed over time and (2) what job aspects satisfy these needs.

ETHICAL DILEMMA

Mitch heard the alarm blaring. "It couldn't be 5:00 A.M. already," he thought. He sat on the edge of the bed wondering how he had gotten himself into this mess. Mitch graduated from a good school with a bachelor's degree in management and a good GPA. He had dreams of a great job and a wonderful life. Instead, he found himself working 60 or more hours per week and feeling constantly pressured to work more.

Mitch started working at Acme, an electronics retailer, right out of college. At the time, the company recruiter had painted a picture of great opportunity for the "right" people. Acme wanted employees who had a high need for achievement and a desire to attain positions of power and authority. It sounded perfect for Mitch. He knew he was executive material. The problem was that the company hired only people who were willing to go the extra mile.

Now, two years later, Mitch realized that the company was using his own personal needs against him.

When he was hired by Acme, Mitch was told that the average workweek would be 50 hours. It was not the cushy job he had envisioned, but if it led to the advancement the company alluded to, it was well worth it. Although he was not required to go beyond the stated 50 hours, Mitch had never worked less than 60 hours and often approached 70. From day one, the company had pushed for full commitment. "The only way to advance is to prove yourself and your commitment to the company," was heard more than once. It was the mantra to every unit manager in the organization. Mitch was beginning to believe that the whole process had been a game. Acme hired employees who were highly motivated to achieve and then used that internal motivation against them to get as much productivity from them as possible. The company caused managers to burn out and simply hired new ones when they left. Mitch had never before felt so deceived and used.

QUESTIONS

1. Did Acme mislead Mitch and the other managers?

2. Does Acme have an obligation to its shareholders to maximize productivity and profitability?

3. Using rule, virtue, right, and justice theories, evaluate Acme's hiring practices.

EXPERIENTIAL EXERCISES

5.1 WHAT DO YOU NEED FROM WORK?

This exercise provides an opportunity to discuss your basic needs and those of other students in your class. Refer back to Challenge 5.2, What's Important to Employees?, and look over your ranking of the 10 possible job reward factors. Think about basic needs you may have that are possibly work related and yet would not be satisfied by one or another of these 10 job reward factors.

Step 1. The class will form into groups of approximately six members each. Each group elects a spokesperson and answers the following questions. The group should spend at least five minutes on the first question and make sure each member of the group makes a contribution. The second question will probably take longer for your group to answer, up to 15 minutes. The spokesperson should be ready to share the group's answers.

a. *What important basic needs do you have that are not addressed by one or another of these 10 job reward factors?* Members should focus on the whole range of needs discussed in the different need theories of motivation covered in Chapter 5. Develop a list of the basic needs overlooked by these 10 factors.

b. *What is important to members of your group?* Rank-order all job reward factors (the original 10 and any new ones your group came up with in Step 1) in terms of their importance for your group. If group members disagree about the rankings, take time to discuss the differences among group members. Work for consensus and also note points of disagreement.

Step 2. Each group will share the results of its answers to the questions in Step 1. Cross-team questions and discussion follow.

Step 3. If your instructor has not already shared the normative data for 1,000 employees and their supervisors mentioned in Challenge 5.2, the instructor may do that at this time.

Step 4 (Optional). Your instructor may ask you to discuss the similarities and differences in your group's rankings with the employee and supervisory normative rankings. If he or she does, spend some time addressing two questions.

a. *What underlying reasons do you think may account for the differences that exist?*

b. *How have the needs of employees and supervisors changed over the past 20 years? Are they likely to change in the future?*

5.2 WHAT TO DO?

According to Stacy Adams, the experience of inequity or social injustice is a motivating force for human behavior. This exercise provides you and your group with a brief scenario of an inequity at work. Your task is to consider feasible actions for redress of this inequity.

John and Mary are full professors in the same medical school department of a large private university. As a private institution, neither the school nor the university makes the salaries and benefits of its faculty a matter of public record. Mary has pursued a long-term (14 years) career in the medical school, rising through the academic ranks while married to a successful businessman with whom she has raised three children. Her research and teaching contributions have been broad ranging and award winning. John joined the medical school within the last three years and was recruited for his leading-edge contribution to a novel line of research on a new procedure. Mary thought he was probably attracted with a comprehensive compensation package, yet she had no details until an administrative assistant gave her some information about salary and benefits a month ago. Mary learned that John's base contract salary is 16 percent higher than hers ($250,000 versus $215,000), that he was awarded an incentive pay component for the commercialization of his new procedure, and that he was given an annual discretionary travel budget of $35,000 and a membership in an exclusive private club. Mary is in a quandary about what to do. Given pressures from the board of trustees to hold down costs associated with public and private pressure to keep tuition increases low, Mary wonders how to begin to close this $70,000 inequity gap.

Step 1. Working in groups of six, discuss the equity issues in this medical school department situation using the text material on social exchange and equity theory. Do the outcome differences here appear to be gender based, age based, performance based, or marital status based? Do you need more information? If so, what additional information do you need?

Step 2. Consider each of the seven strategies for the resolution of inequity as portrayed in this situation. Which ones are feasible to pursue based on what you know? Which ones are not feasible? Why? What are the likely consequences of each strategy or course of action? What would you advise Mary to do?

Step 3. Once your group has identified feasible resolution strategies, choose the best strategy. Next, develop a specific plan of action for Mary to follow in attempting to resolve the inequity so that she can achieve the experience and reality of fair treatment at work.

Step 4 (Optional). Your group may be asked to share its preferred strategy for this situation and your rationale for the strategy.

Learning and Performance Management

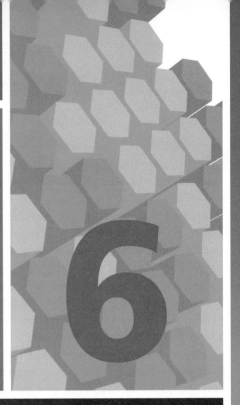

6

LEARNING OBJECTIVES

After reading this chapter, you should be able to do the following:

: 1. Define *learning*.

: 2. Distinguish between classical and operant conditioning.

: 3. Explain ways in which reinforcement, punishment, and extinction can be used to alter behavior.

: 4. Define *goal setting* and identify its three purposes.

: 5. Evaluate the effectiveness of 360-degree feedback as a performance appraisal tool.

: 6. Discuss the advantages and disadvantages of individual and team-oriented reward systems.

: 7. Describe the three-step process that managers can use to correct poor performance.

THINKING AHEAD :: VIRGIN GROUP, LTD.

People, Power, and Performance

Sir Richard Branson grew up in the 1960s, a product of the democratizing ideals of that period.[1] While leading Virgin Group more than 25 years later, he has not given up either his ideals that all people should be treated with respect or his great belief in people power. He has built his business on the premise that people—both customers and employees—come first. Actually, he likes to refer to Virgin employees as belonging to a large extended family. This may be a difficult posture to take in a publicly traded company, but it is quite feasible in a private company like Virgin Group. Everyone in the company continues to call Branson by his first name, and he still eschews the trappings of status and power, as he has from the very start. He may have been well ahead of his time when he focused on persons and not just behavior. As in many families, rewards are shared.

Two examples of Branson's personal approach are reflected in how a British Airways (BA) libel settlement was handled and how Virgin Atlantic responded during the recessionary period of the early 1990s brought on by Operations Desert Shield and Desert Storm. In the first case, Branson used a classic touch by sharing the £610,000 settlement from the libel suit against BA. The money was divided equally among all Virgin staff, each receiving £166. This was known as the "BA Bonus." The message was that they had all conquered BA together. In the second case, when the airline business was depressed by the Gulf War, the company managed not to lay off staff, and there was a common sharing of the pain with everyone suffering a little less.

While many companies are in the midst of flattening out, dismantling their hierarchies, and eliminating outward signs of executive privilege, Virgin has never gone to these places in building its successful business model. Many companies also put into place formalized performance management systems that focus on observable and measurable behaviors, but Virgin is a counterpoint in its personal and familial ways of treating employees. Branson considers keeping faith with his employees to be extremely important. This does not mean that no one at Virgin loses his or her job or that no one is ever fired. Employees are fired occasionally, and the company is always interested in avoiding redundancies for its own benefit. However, the employee who believes that he or she was unjustly fired can appeal directly to the chairman. Branson has been known to intervene personally if he thinks the appeal is justified.

How does Virgin approach performance management within its legal team? Read the Looking Back feature at the end of this chapter.

This is the second of two chapters addressing motivation and behavior. Chapter 5 emphasized internal and process theories of motivation. This chapter focuses on external theories of motivation and factors in the work environment that influence good and bad performance. The first section addresses learning theory and the use of reinforcement, punishment, and extinction at work. It also touches on Bandura's social learning theory and Jung's personality approach to learning. The second section presents theory, research, and practice related to goal setting in organizations. The third section addresses the definition and measurement of performance. The fourth section is concerned with rewarding performance. The fifth and concluding section addresses how to correct poor performance.

☙ LEARNING IN ORGANIZATIONS

Learning is a change in behavior acquired through experience. Learning may begin with the cognitive activity of developing knowledge about a subject, which then leads to a change in behavior. Alternatively, the behaviorist approach to learning assumes that observable behavior is a function of its consequences. According to the behaviorists, learning has its basis in classical and operant conditioning. Learning helps guide and direct motivated behavior.

CLASSICAL CONDITIONING

Classical conditioning is the process of modifying behavior so that a conditioned stimulus is paired with an unconditioned stimulus and elicits an unconditioned response. It is largely the result of the research on animals (primarily dogs) by the Russian physiologist Ivan Pavlov.[2] Classical conditioning builds on the natural consequence of an unconditioned response to an unconditioned stimulus. In dogs, this might be the natural production of saliva (unconditioned response) in response to the presentation of meat (unconditioned stimulus). Classical conditioning may occur in a similar fashion in humans.[3] For example, a person working at a computer terminal may get lower back tension (unconditioned response) as a result of poor posture (unconditioned stimulus). If the person becomes aware of that tension only when the manager enters the work area (conditioned stimulus), then the person may develop a conditioned response (lower back tension) to the appearance of the manager. Although this example is logical, classical conditioning has real limitations in its applicability to human behavior in organizations—for at least three reasons. First, humans are more complex than dogs and less amenable to simple cause-and-effect conditioning. Second, the behavioral environments in organizations are complex and not very amenable to single stimulus–response manipulations. Third, complex human decision making makes it possible to override simple conditioning.

OPERANT CONDITIONING

Operant conditioning is the process of modifying behavior through the use of positive or negative consequences following specific behaviors. It is based on the notion that behavior is a function of its consequences,[4] which may be either positive or negative. The consequences of behavior are used to influence, or shape, behavior through three strategies: reinforcement, punishment, and extinction. Organizational behavior modification (O.B. Mod.) is a form of operant conditioning used successfully in a variety of organizations to shape behavior by Luthans and his colleagues.[5] The three types of consequences used in O.B. Mod. to influence behavior are financial reinforcement, nonfinancial reinforcement, and social reinforcement. A major review of the research on the influence of O.B. Mod. in organizations found that it had significant and positive influence on task performance in both manufacturing and service organizations, but that the effects were most powerful in manufacturing organizations.[6] Recent research showed that money-based (financial) reinforcement improved performance more than routine pay for performance, social recognition, and performance feedback.[7]

---

1. Define *learning.*

learning
A change in behavior acquired through experience.

2. Distinguish between classical and operant conditioning.

classical conditioning
Modifying behavior so that a conditioned stimulus is paired with an unconditioned stimulus and elicits an unconditioned response.

operant conditioning
Modifying behavior through the use of positive or negative consequences following specific behaviors.

: 3. Explain ways in which reinforcement, punishment, and extinction can be used to alter behavior.

◼ THE STRATEGIES OF REINFORCEMENT, PUNISHMENT, AND EXTINCTION

Reinforcement is used to enhance desirable behavior, and punishment and extinction are used to diminish undesirable behavior. The application of reinforcement theory is central to the design and administration of organizational reward systems. Well-designed reward systems help attract and retain the very best employees. Strategic rewards help motivate behavior, actions, and accomplishments, which advance the organization toward specific business goals.[8] Strategic rewards go beyond cash to include training and educational opportunities, stock options, and recognition awards such as travel. Strategic rewards are important positive consequences of people's work behavior.

positive consequences
Results of a behavior that a person finds attractive or pleasurable.

negative consequences
Results of a behavior that a person finds unattractive or aversive.

Reinforcement and punishment are administered through the management of positive and negative consequences of behavior. *Positive consequences* are the results of a person's behavior that the person finds attractive or pleasurable. They might include a pay increase, a bonus, a promotion, a transfer to a more desirable geographic location, or praise from a supervisor. *Negative consequences* are the results of a person's behavior that the person finds unattractive or aversive. They might include disciplinary action, an undesirable transfer, a demotion, or harsh criticism from a supervisor. Positive and negative consequences must be defined for the person receiving them. Therefore, individual, gender, and cultural differences may be important in their classification.

The use of positive and negative consequences following a specific behavior either reinforces or punishes that behavior.[9] Thorndike's law of effect states that behaviors followed by positive consequences are more likely to recur and behaviors followed by negative consequences are less likely to recur.[10] Figure 6.1 shows how

◀◀think critically▶▶

Suppose your company announced that it would pay bonuses to employees who met a certain performance standard. The company did not realize, however, that with hard work, many employees would be able to reach the standard and that the bonuses would cost the company much more than expected. Is it fair to lower the bonus rate? Is it fair to increase the performance standard for bonuses after the fact?

FIGURE 6.1

Reinforcement and Punishment Strategies

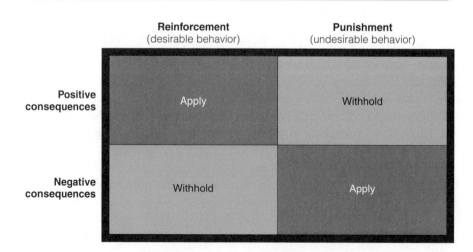

	Reinforcement (desirable behavior)	Punishment (undesirable behavior)
Positive consequences	Apply	Withhold
Negative consequences	Withhold	Apply

positive and negative consequences may be applied or withheld in the strategies of reinforcement and punishment.

REINFORCEMENT

Reinforcement is the attempt to develop or strengthen desirable behavior by either bestowing positive consequences or withholding negative consequences. Positive reinforcement results from the application of a positive consequence following a desirable behavior. Bonuses paid at the end of successful business years are an example of positive reinforcement. Marriott International provides positive reinforcement by honoring 10 to 20 employees each year with its J. Willard Marriott Award of Excellence. Each awardee receives a medallion engraved with the words that express the basic values of the company: dedication, achievement, character, ideals, effort, and perseverance.

Negative reinforcement results from withholding a negative consequence when a desirable behavior occurs. For example, a manager who reduces an employee's pay (negative consequence) if the employee comes to work late (undesirable behavior) and refrains from doing so when the employee is on time (desirable behavior) has negatively reinforced the employee's on-time behavior. The employee avoids the negative consequence (a reduction in pay) by exhibiting the desirable behavior (being on time to work).

reinforcement
The attempt to develop or strengthen desirable behavior by either bestowing positive consequences or withholding negative consequences.

PUNISHMENT

Punishment is the attempt to eliminate or weaken undesirable behavior. It is used in two ways. One way to punish a person is to apply a negative consequence following an undesirable behavior. For example, a professional athlete who is excessively offensive to an official (undesirable behavior) may be ejected from a game (negative consequence). The other way to punish a person is to withhold a positive consequence following an undesirable behavior. For example, a salesperson who makes few visits to companies (undesirable behavior) and whose sales are well below the quota (undesirable behavior) is likely to receive a very small commission check (positive consequence) at the end of the month.

One problem with punishment is that it may have unintended results. Because punishment is discomforting to the individual being punished, the experience of punishment may result in negative psychological, emotional, performance, or behavioral consequences. For example, the person being punished may become angry, hostile, depressed, or despondent. From an organizational standpoint, this result becomes important when the punished person translates negative emotional and psychological responses into negative actions. By keeping faith with employees, organizations like Virgin and leaders like Branson build trusting relationships and reduce the risks of these unintended consequences.

Threat of punishment may also elicit fear. Instead of using fear and coercion to motivate employees, companies should use a performance management system that emphasizes positive relationships, a strategy that Southwest Airlines uses.[11]

punishment
The attempt to eliminate or weaken undesirable behavior by either bestowing negative consequences or withholding positive consequences.

EXTINCTION

An alternative to punishing undesirable behavior is *extinction*—the attempt to weaken a behavior by attaching no consequences (either positive or negative) to it. It is equivalent to ignoring the behavior. The rationale for using extinction is that

extinction
The attempt to weaken a behavior by attaching no consequences to it.

a behavior not followed by any consequence is weakened. Some patience and time may be needed for extinction to be effective, however.

Extinction may be practiced, for example, by not responding (no consequence) to the sarcasm (behavior) of a colleague. Extinction may be most effective when used in conjunction with the positive reinforcement of desirable behaviors. Therefore, in the example, the best approach might be to compliment the sarcastic colleague for constructive comments (reinforcing desirable behavior) while ignoring sarcastic comments (extinguishing undesirable behavior).

Extinction is not always the best strategy, however. In cases of dangerous behavior, punishment might be preferable to deliver a swift, clear lesson. It might also be preferable in cases of seriously undesirable behavior, such as employee embezzlement and other illegal or unethical behavior.

■ BANDURA'S SOCIAL LEARNING THEORY

A social learning theory proposed by Albert Bandura is an alternative and complement to the behavioristic approaches of Pavlov and Skinner.[12] Bandura believes learning occurs through the observation of other people and the modeling of their behavior. Executives might teach their subordinates a wide range of behaviors, such as leader–follower interactions and stress management, by exhibiting these behaviors. Since employees look to their supervisors for acceptable norms of behavior, they are likely to pattern their own responses on the supervisor's.

task-specific self-efficacy

An individual's beliefs and expectancies about his or her ability to perform a specific task effectively.

Central to Bandura's social learning theory is the notion of *task-specific self-efficacy*, an individual's beliefs and expectancies about his or her ability to perform a specific task effectively. (Generalized self-efficacy was discussed in Chapter 3.) Individuals with high self-efficacy believe that they have the ability to get things done, that they are capable of putting forth the effort to accomplish the task, and that they can overcome any obstacles to their success. Self-efficacy is higher in a learning context than in a performance context, especially for individuals with a high learning orientation.[13] There are four sources of task-specific self-efficacy: prior experiences, behavior models (witnessing the success of others), persuasion from other people, and assessment of current physical and emotional capabilities.[14] Believing in one's own capability to get something done is an important facilitator of success. There is strong evidence that self-efficacy leads to high performance on a wide variety of physical and mental tasks.[15] High self-efficacy has also led to success with job interviews. Researchers found that self-efficacy determined success in interviews over and above other variables such as personality and background.[16]

Alexander Stajkovic and Fred Luthans draw on Bandura's ideas of self-efficacy and social learning in expanding their original work in behavioral management and O.B. Mod. into a more comprehensive framework for performance management.[17] Bandura saw the power of social reinforcement, recognizing that financial and material rewards often occur following or in conjunction with the approval of others, whereas undesirable experiences often follow social disapproval. Thus, self-efficacy and social reinforcement can be powerful influences over behavior and performance at work. A comprehensive review of 114 studies found that self-efficacy is positively and strongly related to work performance, especially for tasks that are not too complex.[18] Stajkovic and Luthans suggest that managers and supervisors can be confident that employees with high self-efficacy are going to perform well. The challenge managers face is how to select and develop employees so that they achieve high self-efficacy.

Managers can help employees develop self-efficacy. The strongest way for an employee to develop self-efficacy is to succeed at a challenging task. Managers can help by providing job challenges, coaching and counseling for improved performance, and rewarding employees' achievements. Empowerment, or sharing power with employees, can be accomplished by interventions that help employees increase their self-esteem and self-efficacy. Given the increasing diversity of the workforce, managers may want to target their efforts toward women and minorities in particular. Research has indicated that women and minorities tend to have lower than average self-efficacy.[19]

GOAL SETTING AT WORK

Goal setting is the process of establishing desired results that guide and direct behavior. Goal-setting theory is based on laboratory studies, field research experiments, and comparative investigations by Edwin Locke, Gary Latham, John M. Ivancevich, and others.[20] Goals help crystallize the sense of purpose and mission that is essential to success at work. Priorities, purpose, and goals are important sources of motivation for people at work, often leading to collective achievement, even in difficult times.

GOAL-SETTING THEORY

Goal setting theory may be one of the most practical and useful theories of motivation and work performance.[21,22] The heart of goal-setting theory is the strong, positive relationship between goal difficulty and task performance. This positive, linear relationship between goal level and task performance is captured in Figure 6.2. Following this original conceptualization and rather straightforward statement of the theory, subsequent research has led to a variety of additions and modifications. Specifically, goal commitment, effective performance

: **4.** Define *goal setting* and identify its three purposes.

goal setting
The process of establishing desired results that guide and direct behavior.

FIGURE 6.2

Goal Level and Task Performance

FIGURE 6.3

Goal-Setting Theory

feedback, and required skills and abilities moderate this relationship, as shown in Figure 6.3. Without commitment to the goals, employees may simply give up in the face of the challenge which difficult goals present. Certainly, giving up leads to lower task performance. Effective performance feedback can moderate this relationship as well, enabling an employee to overcome obstacles to achieving difficult goals. Finally, an individual's skills and abilities can moderate the relationship because employees with requisite skills and abilities, when faced with difficult goals, are more likely to persevere.[23, 24]

Emerging research suggests that there may be a role for emotion in future formulations of goal-setting theory. For example, positive affect has been found to lead to higher effort, self-reported persistence, motivation, and task performance.[25] Interestingly, another study found that negative moods foster creativity because negative moods typically signify problems with the current situation and lead an individual to expend more effort as well as think through decisions in a more vigilant manner.[26] However, much more research is required before we have a clear understanding of the role of emotion and affective variables in goal-setting theory, motivation, and task performance. Referring back to Figure 6.3 we see that characteristics of effective goals are another moderator of the goal difficulty to task performance relationship. These characteristics help to fulfill the promise of goal-setting theory and enhance its validity.[27] We therefore turn now to a discussion of the four key characteristics of effective goals as listed in the figure.

■ CHARACTERISTICS OF EFFECTIVE GOALS

Various organizations define the characteristics of effective goals differently. Commonly accepted characteristics of effective goals are specific, measurable, time bound, and prioritized. Specific goals enhance the positive affect of difficult goals by serving to cue or focus the person's attention on exactly what is to be accomplished and to arouse the person to peak performance. Challenge 6.1 gives you an opportunity to evaluate your goals along five dimensions. Employees may experience undue pressure and resort to unethical behavior to achieve

C H A L L E N G E

6.1

Task–Goal Attribute Questionnaire

Listed below is a set of statements that may or may not describe the job or school objectives toward which you are presently working. Please read each statement carefully and rate each on a scale from 1 (agree completely) to 7 (disagree completely) to describe your level of agreement or disagreement with the statement. *Please answer all questions.*

____ 1. I am allowed a high degree of influence in the determination of my work/school objectives.

____ 2. I should not have too much difficulty in reaching my work/school objectives; they appear to be fairly easy.

____ 3. I receive a considerable amount of feedback concerning my quantity of output on the job/in school.

____ 4. Most of my coworkers and peers try to outperform one another on their assigned work/school goals.

____ 5. My work/school objectives are very clear and specific; I know exactly what my job/assignment is.

____ 6. My work/school objectives will require a great deal of effort from me to complete them.

____ 7. I really have little voice in the formulation of my work/school objectives.

____ 8. I am provided with a great deal of feedback and guidance on the quality of my work.

____ 9. I think my work/school objectives are ambiguous and unclear.

____ 10. It will take a high degree of skill and know-how on my part to attain fully my work/school objectives.

____ 11. The setting of my work/school goals is pretty much under my own control.

____ 12. My boss/instructors seldom let(s) me know how well I am doing on my work toward my work/school objectives.

____ 13. A very competitive atmosphere exists among my peers and me with regard to attaining our respective work/school goals; we all want to do better than anyone else in attaining our goals.

____ 14. I understand fully which of my work/school objectives are more important than others; I have a clear sense of priorities on these goals.

____ 15. My work/school objectives are quite difficult to attain.

____ 16. My supervisor/instructors usually ask(s) for my opinions and thoughts when determining my work/school objectives.

Scoring:

Place your response (1 through 7) in the space provided. For questions 7, 12, 9, and 2, subtract your response from 8 to determine your adjusted score. For each scale (e.g., participation in goal setting), add the responses and divide by the number of questions in the scale.

(continued)

Participation in Goal Setting:
Question 1 _____
Question 7 (8 − _____) = _____
Question 11 _____
Question 16 _____
Total divided by 4 = ══════

Feedback on Goal Effort:
Question 3 _____
Question 8 _____
Question 12 (8 − _____) = _____
Total divided by 3 = ══════

Peer Competition:
Question 4 _____
Question 13 _____
Total divided by 2 = ══════

Goal Specificity:
Question 5 _____
Question 9 (8 − _____) = _____
Question 14 _____
Total divided by 3 = ══════

Goal Difficulty:
Question 2 (8 − _____) = _____
Question 6 _____
Question 10 _____
Question 15 _____
Total divided by 4 = ══════

Interpreting your average scale scores:
6 or 7 are very high on this task–goal attribute.
4 is a moderate level on this task–goal attribute.
1 or 2 is very low on this task–goal attribute.

Source: Republished with permission of Academy of Management, P.O. Box 3020, Briar Cliff Manor, NY 10510-8020, adapted from R. M. Steers, "Factors Affecting Job Attitudes in a Goal-Setting Environment," *Academy of Management Journal* 19 (1976): 9; permission conveyed through Copyright Clearance Center, Inc.

ambitious goals when not given the knowledge or tools to accomplish them.[28] Measurable, quantitative goals are useful as a basis for feedback about goal progress. Qualitative goals, like improving customer relationships, are also valuable.[29] Time-bound goals enhance measurability. The time limit may be implicit in the goal, or it may need to be made explicit. The priority ordering of goals allows for effective decision making about resource allocation.[30] As time, energy, or other resources become available, a person can move down the list of goals in descending order.

◀◀think critically▶▶

Suppose a team of behavioral scientists was asked to enhance the motivation of management personnel to put their "mom and pop" competitors out of business. Is this request ethical? Is it socially desirable? Should the team accept the assignment? Explain.

More traditionally, goal setting serves one or more of three functions. First, it can increase work motivation and task performance.[31] Second, it can reduce the role stress that is associated with conflicting or confusing expectations.[32] Third, it can improve the accuracy and validity of performance evaluation.[33]

▊ INCREASING WORK MOTIVATION AND TASK PERFORMANCE

Goals are often used to increase employee effort and motivation, which in turn improve task performance. The higher the goal, the better the performance; that is, people work harder to reach difficult goals. The positive relationship between goal difficulty and task performance is depicted in Figure 6.3. Three important behavioral aspects of enhancing performance motivation through goal setting are employee participation, supervisory commitment, and useful performance feedback. Employee participation in goal setting leads to goal acceptance by employees. Special attention has been given to factors that influence commitment to difficult goals, such as participation in the process of setting the difficult goals.[34] Supervisory goal commitment is a reflection of the organization's commitment to goal setting. Organizational commitment is a prerequisite for successful goal-setting programs, such as management by objectives (MBO) programs.[35] (MBO is discussed in more detail later in the chapter.) The supervisor plays a second important role by providing employees with interim performance feedback on progress toward goals. Performance feedback is most useful when the goals are specific, and specific goals improve performance most when interim feedback is given.[36] When done correctly, negative performance feedback can lead to performance improvement.[37]

▊ REDUCING ROLE STRESS, CONFLICT, AND AMBIGUITY

A second function of goal setting is to reduce the role stress associated with conflicting and confusing expectations. This is done by clarifying the task–role expectations communicated to employees. Supervisors, coworkers, and employees are all important sources of task-related information. A 14-month evaluation of goal setting found that role stress was reduced through goal setting.[38] The improved role clarity resulting from goal setting may be attributable to improved communication between managers and employees. An early study of the MBO goal-setting program at Ford Motor Company found an initial 25 percent lack of agreement between managers and their bosses concerning the definition of the managers' jobs. Through effective goal-setting activities, this lack of agreement was reduced to about 5 percent.[39] At FedEx, managers are encouraged to include communication-related targets in their annual MBO goal-setting process.[40] Within Virgin Group, as we saw at the beginning of the chapter, there is more of a family culture with less formalized and more personal relationships.

▊ IMPROVING PERFORMANCE EVALUATION

The third major function of goal setting is improving the accuracy and validity of performance evaluation. One of the best methods of doing so is to use *management by objectives (MBO)*.[41] According to Peter Drucker, who originated the concept, the objectives-setting process begins with the employee writing an "employee's letter" to the manager. The letter explains the employee's general understanding of the scope of the manager's job; outlines the scope of the employee's own job; and sets out specific objectives to be pursued. After discussion and negotiation, the manager and the employee finalize these into a performance plan. Drucker considers MBO a participative, interactive process.

management by objectives (MBO)
A goal-setting program based on interaction and negotiation between employees and managers.

This does not mean that goal setting begins at the bottom of the organization. It means that goal setting is applicable to all employees, with lower-level organizational members and professional staff having a clear influence over the goal-setting process.[42] (The performance aspect of goal setting is discussed in the next section of the chapter.)

The two central ingredients in goal-setting programs are planning and evaluation. The planning component consists of organizational and individual goal setting. Organizational goal setting is an essential prerequisite to individual goal setting; the two must be closely linked for the success of both.[43] In planning, discretionary control is usually given to individuals and departments to develop operational and tactical plans to support the corporate objectives. The emphasis is on formulating a clear, consistent, measurable, and ordered set of goals to articulate *what* to do. It is also assumed that operational support planning helps determine *how* to do it. The concept of intention is used to encompass both the goal (*what*) and the set of pathways that lead to goal attainment (*how*), thus recognizing the importance of both what and how.[44]

The evaluation component consists of interim reviews of goal progress, conducted by managers and employees, and formal performance evaluation. The reviews are mid-term assessments designed to help employees take self-corrective action. They are not designed as final or formal performance evaluations. The formal performance evaluation occurs at the close of a reporting period, usually once a year. To be effective, performance reviews need to be tailored to the business, capture what goes on in the business, and be easily changed when the business changes.[45]

Goal-setting programs are most easily implemented in stable, predictable industrial settings. Although most programs allow for some flexibility and change, they are less useful in organizations where high levels of unpredictability exist. Finally, individual, gender, and cultural differences do not appear to threaten the success of goal-setting programs.[46] Thus, goal-setting programs may be widely applied and effective in a diverse workforce.

PERFORMANCE: A KEY CONSTRUCT

Goal setting is designed to improve work performance, an important organizational behavior directly related to the production of goods or the delivery of services. Performance is most often thought of as task accomplishment, the term *task* coming from Taylor's early notion of a worker's required activity.[47] Some early management research found performance standards and differential piece-rate pay to be key ingredients in achieving high levels of performance, while other early research found stress helpful in improving performance up to an optimum point.[48] Hence, outcomes and effort are both important for good performance. This section focuses on task-oriented performance.

Predicting job performance has been a concern for over 100 years. Early theories around the time of World War I focused on the importance of intelligence and general mental ability, the latter being highly predictive of job knowledge in military jobs.[49] As important to predicting job performance is defining job performance.

◾ PERFORMANCE MANAGEMENT

Performance management is a process of defining, measuring, appraising, providing feedback on, and improving performance.[50] The skill of defining performance in behavioral terms is an essential first step in the performance management process. Once defined, performance can be measured and assessed. This information about performance can then be fed back to the individual and used as a basis for setting goals and establishing plans for improving performance. Positive performance behaviors should be rewarded, and poor performance behaviors should be corrected. This section of the chapter focuses on defining, measuring, appraising, and providing feedback on performance. The last two sections of the chapter focus on rewarding, correcting, and improving performance.

◾ DEFINING PERFORMANCE

Performance must be clearly defined and understood by the employees who are expected to perform well at work. Performance in most lines of work is multidimensional. For example, a sales executive's performance may require administrative and financial skills along with the interpersonal skills needed to motivate a sales force. Or a medical doctor's performance may demand the positive interpersonal skills of a bedside manner to complement the necessary technical diagnostic and treatment skills for enhancing the healing process. Each specific job in an organization requires the definition of skills and behaviors essential to excellent performance. Defining performance is a prerequisite to measuring and evaluating performance on the job.

Although different jobs require different skills and behaviors, organizational citizenship behavior (OCB) is one dimension of individual performance that spans many jobs. OCB was defined in Chapter 4 as behavior that is above and beyond the call of duty. OCB involves individual discretionary behavior that promotes the organization and is not explicitly rewarded; it includes helping behavior, sportsmanship, and civic virtue. According to supervisors, OCB is enhanced most through employee involvement programs aimed at engaging employees in the work organization rather than through employee involvement in employment decisions in nonunion operations.[51] OCB emphasizes collective performance in contrast to individual performance or achievement. OCB is just one of a number of performance dimensions to consider when defining performance for a specific job within an organization.

Performance appraisal is the evaluation of a person's performance once it is well defined. Accurate appraisals help supervisors fulfill their dual roles as evaluators and coaches. As a coach, a supervisor is responsible for encouraging employee growth and development. As an evaluator, a supervisor is responsible for making judgments that influence employees' roles in the organization. Although procedural justice is often thought of as a unidimensional construct, recent research shows that in the performance appraisal content it can be conceptualized as two dimensional.[52]

Cross-cultural research has found that North American, Asian, and Latin American managers' perceptions of their employees' motivation are different and that their perceptions affect their appraisals of employee performance.[53]

performance management
A process of defining, measuring, appraising, providing feedback on, and improving performance.

performance appraisal
The evaluation of a person's performance.

The major purposes of performance appraisals are to give employees feedback on performance, to identify the employees' developmental needs, to make promotion and reward decisions, to make demotion and termination decisions, and to develop information about the organization's selection and placement decisions. For example, a review of 57,775 performance appraisals found higher ratings on appraisals done for administrative reasons and lower ratings on appraisals done for research or for employee development.[54]

■ MEASURING PERFORMANCE

Ideally, actual performance and measured performance are the same. Practically, this is seldom the case. Measuring operational performance is easier than measuring managerial performance because of the availability of quantifiable data. Measuring production performance is easier than measuring research and development performance because of the reliability of the measures. Recent research has focused on measuring motivation for task performance and has found that wording and context may influence the validity of direct self-reports.[55]

Performance appraisal systems are intended to improve the accuracy of measured performance and increase its agreement with actual performance. The extent of agreement is called the true assessment. There can be performance measurement problems that contribute to inaccuracy. Three key problems are deficiency, unreliability, and invalidity. Deficiency occurs when the evaluator overlooks important aspects of a person's actual performance. Unreliability occurs when poor-quality performance measures are used. Invalidity occurs when there is an inaccurate definition of the expected job performance.

Early performance appraisal systems were often quite biased. Even contemporary executive appraisals have a dark side, arousing managers' and executives' defenses. Addressing emotions and defenses is important to making appraisal sessions developmental.[56] Some performance review systems lead to forced rankings of employees, which may be controversial.

Performance-monitoring systems using modern electronic technology are sometimes used to measure the performance of vehicle operators, computer technicians, and customer service representatives. For example, such systems might record the rate of keystrokes or the total number of keystrokes for a computer technician. The people subject to this type of monitoring are in some cases unaware that their performance is being measured. What is appropriate performance monitoring? What constitutes inappropriate electronic spying on the employee? Are people entitled to know when their performance is being measured? The ethics of monitoring performance may differ by culture. The United States and Sweden, for example, respect individual freedom more than Japan and China do. The overriding issue, however, is how far organizations should go in using modern technology to measure human performance.

Goal setting and MBO are results-oriented methods of performance appraisal that do not necessarily rely on modern technology. Like performance-monitoring systems, they shift the emphasis from subjective, judgmental performance dimensions to observable, verifiable results. Goals established in the planning phase of goal setting become the standard against which to measure subsequent performance. However, rigid adherence to a results-oriented approach may risk overlooking performance opportunities.

Enterprise Rent-a-Car uses metrics to measure performance. Managers are rewarded by how well their customers judge their branch's performance. The company uses a quantitative metric called the Enterprise Service Quality Index (EQI) that shows the percentage of customers who rate the branch 5 of 5, indicating complete satisfaction. The manager and employees benefit when the branch achieves or exceeds the company's average EQI.

■ PERFORMANCE FEEDBACK: A COMMUNICATION CHALLENGE

Once clearly defined and accurate performance measures are developed, there is still the challenge of performance feedback. Feedback sessions are among the more stressful events for supervisors and employees. Early research at General Electric found that employees responded constructively to positive feedback and were defensive over half the time in response to critical or negative feedback. Typical responses to negative feedback included shifting responsibility for the shortcoming or behavior, denying it outright, or providing a wide range of excuses for it.[57] Employees may find it difficult to give feedback to managers, especially if it is criticism. However, research shows that managers need trusted advisors who give them honest performance feedback.[58]

Both parties to a performance feedback session should try to make it a constructive learning experience, since positive and negative performance feedback has long-term implications for the employee's performance and for the working relationship. American Airlines follows three guidelines in providing evaluative feedback so that the experience is constructive for supervisor and employee alike.[59] First, refer to specific, verbatim statements and specific, observable behaviors displayed by the person receiving the feedback. This is especially relevant when giving feedback to minority employees. For example, whites may positively bias feedback given to black employees in an effort to not appear bigoted.[60] So being specific enhances the acceptance of the feedback while reducing the chances of denial. Second, focus on changeable behaviors, as opposed to intrinsic or personality-based attributes. People are often more defensive about who they are than about what they do. Third, plan and organize for the session ahead of time. Be sure to notify the person who will receive the feedback. Both the leader and the follower should be ready.

In addition to these ideas, many companies recommend beginning coaching and counseling sessions with something positive. The intent is to reduce defensiveness and enhance useful communication. There is almost always at least one positive element to emphasize. Once the session is under way and rapport is established, then the evaluator can introduce more difficult and negative material. Because people are not perfect, there is always an opportunity for them to learn and to grow through performance feedback sessions. Critical feedback is the basis for improvement and is essential to a performance feedback session. Specific feedback is beneficial for initial performance but discourages exploration and undermines the learning needed for later, more independent performance.[61]

: 5. Evaluate the effectiveness of 360-degree feedback as a performance appraisal tool.

360-degree feedback
A process of self-evaluation and evaluations by a manager, peers, direct reports, and possibly customers.

◼ 360-DEGREE FEEDBACK

Many organizations use *360-degree feedback* as a tactic to improve the accuracy of performance appraisals because it is based on multiple sources of information. When self-evaluations are included in this process, there is evidence that the evaluation interviews can be more satisfying, more constructive, and less defensive.[62] One of the criticisms of self-evaluations is their low level of agreement with supervisory evaluations.[63] However, high levels of agreement may not necessarily be desirable if the intent of the evaluation is to provide a full picture of the person's performance. This is a strength of the 360-degree feedback method, which provides a well-rounded view of performance from superiors, peers, followers, and customers.[64]

An example of a 360-degree feedback evaluation occurred in a large military organization for a midlevel civilian executive. The midlevel executive behaved very differently in dealing with superiors, peers, and followers. With superiors, he was positive, compliant, and deferential. With peers, he was largely indifferent, often ignoring them. With followers, he was tough and demanding, bordering on cruel and abusive. Without each of these perspectives, the executive's performance would not have been accurately assessed. When the executive received feedback, he was then able to see the inconsistency in his behavior.

Two recommendations have been made to improve the effectiveness of the 360-degree feedback method. The first one is to add a systematic coaching component to the 360-degree feedback.[65] By focusing on enhanced self-awareness and behavioral management, this feedback-coaching model can enhance performance as well as satisfaction and commitment, and reduce intent to turnover. The second one is that the performance feedback component of the 360-degree appraisal be separated from the management development component.[66] The feedback component should emphasize quantitative feedback and performance measures, while the management development component should emphasize qualitative feedback and competencies for development. Recent research indicates that employees who work in environments with high levels of informal supervisor and coworker feedback perceive less organizational politics.[67]

◼ DEVELOPING PEOPLE AND ENHANCING CAREERS

A key function of a good performance appraisal system is to develop people and enhance careers. Developmentally, performance appraisals should emphasize individual growth needs and future performance. If the supervisor is to coach and develop employees effectively, there must be mutual trust. The supervisor must be vulnerable and open to challenge from the subordinate while maintaining a position of responsibility for what is in the subordinate's best interests.[68] The supervisor must also be a skilled, empathetic listener who encourages the employee to talk about hopes and aspirations.[69]

The employee must be able to take active responsibility for future development and growth. This might mean challenging the supervisor's ideas about future development as well as expressing individual preferences and goals. Passive, compliant employees are unable to accept responsibility for themselves or to achieve full emotional development. Individual responsibility is a key characteristic of the culture of the Chaparral Steel Company (part of TXI). The company joke is that the company manages by "adultry" (pun intended). Chaparral Steel treats people like adults and expects adult behavior from them.

KEY CHARACTERISTICS OF AN EFFECTIVE APPRAISAL SYSTEM

An effective performance appraisal system has five key characteristics: validity, reliability, responsiveness, flexibility, and equitability. Its validity comes from capturing multiple dimensions of a person's job performance. Its reliability comes from capturing evaluations from multiple sources and at different times over the course of the evaluation period. Its responsiveness allows the person being evaluated some input into the final outcome. Its flexibility leaves it open to modification based on new information, such as federal requirements. Its equitability results in fair evaluations against established performance criteria, regardless of individual differences.

REWARDING PERFORMANCE

One function of a performance appraisal system is to provide input for reward decisions. If an organization wants good performance, then it must reward good performance. If it does not want bad performance, then it must not reward bad performance. If companies talk "teamwork," "values," and "customer focus," then they need to reward behaviors related to these ideas. Although this idea is conceptually simple, it can become very complicated in practice. Reward decisions are among the most difficult and complicated decisions made in organizations, and among the most important decisions. When leaders confront decisions about pay every day, they should know that it is a myth that people work for money.[70] While pay and rewards for performance have value, so too do trust, fun, and meaningful work. As we saw in the beginning of the chapter, Sir Richard Branson shares rewards with Virgin Group employees in a fashion similar to many families.

A KEY ORGANIZATIONAL DECISION PROCESS

Reward and punishment decisions in organizations affect many people throughout the system, not just the persons being rewarded or punished. Reward allocation involves sequential decisions about which people to reward, how to reward them, and when to reward them. Taken together, these decisions shape the behavior of everyone in the organization, because of the vicarious learning that occurs as people watch what happens to others, especially when new programs or initiatives are implemented. People carefully watch what happens to peers who make mistakes or have problems with the new system; then they gauge their own behavior accordingly.

INDIVIDUAL VERSUS TEAM REWARD SYSTEMS

One of the distinguishing characteristics of Americans is the value they place on individualism. Systems that reward individuals are common in organizations in the United States. One of the strengths of these systems is that they foster autonomous and independent behavior that may lead to creativity, to novel solutions to old problems, and to distinctive contributions to the organization. Individual

6. Discuss the advantages and disadvantages of individual and team-oriented reward systems.

reward systems directly affect individual behavior and may encourage competitive striving within a work team. Although motivation and reward techniques in the United States are individually focused, they are often group focused outside the United States.[71]

Too much competition within a work environment, however, may be dysfunctional. At the Western Company of North America (now part of BJ Services Company), individual success in the MBO program was tied too tightly to rewards, and individual managers became divisively competitive. For example, some managers took last-minute interdepartmental financial actions in a quarter to meet their objectives, but by doing so, they caused other managers to miss their objectives. These actions raise ethical questions about how far individual managers should go in serving their own self-interest at the expense of their peers.

Team reward systems solve the problems caused by individual competitive behavior. These systems emphasize cooperation, joint efforts, and the sharing of information, knowledge, and expertise. The Japanese and Chinese cultures, with their collectivist orientations, place greater emphasis than Americans on the individual as an element of the team, not a member apart from the team. Digital Equipment Corporation (now part of Hewlett-Packard) used a partnership approach to performance appraisals. Self-managed work group members participated in their own appraisal process. Such an approach emphasizes teamwork and responsibility.

Some organizations have experimented with individual and group alternative reward systems.[72] At the individual level, these include skill-based and pay-for-knowledge systems. Each emphasizes skills or knowledge possessed by an employee over and above the requirements for the basic job. At the group level, gain-sharing plans emphasize collective cost reduction and allow workers to share in the gains achieved by reducing production or other operating costs. In such plans, everyone shares equally in the collective gain. Avnet, Inc., found that collective profit sharing improved performance.

The notion of entitlement at work is counterproductive when taken to the extreme because it counteracts the power of earning.[73] People who believe they are entitled to rewards regardless of their behavior or performance are not motivated to behave constructively. Merit raises in some organizations, for example, have come to be viewed as entitlements, thus reducing their positive value in the organizational reward system. People believe they have a right to be taken care of by someone, whether that is the organization or a specific person. Entitlement engenders passive, irresponsible behavior, whereas earning engenders active, responsible, adult behavior. If rewards depend on performance, then people must perform responsibly to receive them. The power of earning rests on a direct link between performance and rewards.

: 7. Describe the three-step process that managers can use to correct poor performance.

◪ CORRECTING POOR PERFORMANCE

Often a complicated, difficult challenge for supervisors, correcting poor performance is a three-step process. First, the cause or primary responsibility for the poor performance must be identified. Second, if the primary responsibility is a person's, then the source of the personal problem must be determined. Third, a plan of action to correct the poor performance must be developed.

CHALLENGE 6.2

Correcting Poor Performance

At one time or another, each of us has had a poor performance of some kind. It may have been a poor test result in school, a poor presentation at work, or a poor performance in an athletic event. Think of a poor performance event that you have experienced and work through the following three steps.

Step 1. Briefly describe the specific event in some detail. Include why you label it a poor performance (bad score? someone else's evaluation?).

Step 2. Analyze the Poor Performance

a. List all the possible contributing causes to the poor performance. Be specific, such as the room was too hot, you did not get enough sleep, you were not told how to perform the task, etc. You might ask other people for possible ideas, too.

1. _____
2. _____
3. _____
4. _____
5. _____
6. _____
7. _____

b. Is there a primary cause for the poor performance? What is it?

Step 3. Plan to Correct the Poor Performance

Develop a step-by-step plan of action that specifies what you can change or do differently to improve your performance the next time you have an opportunity. Include seeking help if it is needed. Once your plan is developed, look for an opportunity to execute it.

Challenge 6.2 gives you an opportunity to examine a poor performance you have experienced.

Poor performance may result from a variety of causes, the more important being poorly designed work systems, poor selection processes, inadequate training and skills development, lack of personal motivation, and personal problems intruding on the work environment. Not all poor performance is self-motivated; some is induced by the work system. Therefore, a good diagnosis should precede corrective action. For example, it may be that an employee is subject to a work design or selection system that does not allow the person to exhibit good performance. To avoid such a problem, Loop Customer Management Ltd. involved employees to help change its performance management system to fit its new work design.[74] Identifying the cause of the poor performance comes first and should be done in communication with the employee. If the problem is with the system and the supervisor can fix it, then everyone wins as a result.

If the poor performance is not attributable to work design or organizational process problems, then attention should be focused on the employee. At least three possible causes of poor performance can be attributed to the employee. The problem may lie in (1) some aspect of the person's relationship to the organization or supervisor, (2) some area of the employee's personal life, or (3) a training or developmental deficiency. In the latter two cases, poor performance may be treated as a symptom as opposed to a motivated consequence. In such cases, identifying financial problems, family difficulties, or health disorders may enable the supervisor to help the employee solve problems before they become too extensive. Employee assistance programs (EAPs) can be helpful to employees managing personal problems and are discussed in Chapter 7 in relation to managing stress.

Poor performance may also be motivated by an employee's displaced anger or conflict with the organization or supervisor. In such cases, the employee may or may not be aware of the internal reactions causing the problem. In either event, sabotage, work slowdowns, work stoppages, and similar forms of poor performance may result from such motivated behavior. The supervisor may attribute the cause of the problem to the employee, and the employee may attribute it to the supervisor or organization. To solve motivated performance problems requires treating the poor performance as a symptom with a deeper cause. Resolving the underlying anger or conflict results in the disappearance of the symptom (poor performance).

■ PERFORMANCE AND KELLEY'S ATTRIBUTION THEORY

According to attribution theory, managers make attributions (inferences) concerning employees' behavior and performance.[75] The attributions may not always be accurate. For example, an executive with Capital Cities Corporation/ABC (now part of the Disney Company) who had a very positive relationship with his boss was not held responsible for profit problems in his district. The boss attributed the problem to the economy instead. Supervisors and employees who share perceptions and attitudes, as in the Capital Cities situation, tend to evaluate each other highly.[76] Supervisors and employees who do not share perceptions and attitudes are more likely to blame each other for performance problems. Further, unless specific information about team member contributions is provided, a work group's success is more likely attributed to men than to women.[77]

Harold Kelley's attribution theory aims to help us explain the behavior of other people. He also extended attribution theory by trying to identify the antecedents of internal and external attributions. Kelley proposed that individuals make attributions based on information gathered in the form of three informational cues: consensus, distinctiveness, and consistency.[78, 79] We observe an individual's behavior and then seek out information in the form of these three cues. *Consensus* is the extent to which peers in the same situation behave the same way. *Distinctiveness* is the degree to which the person behaves the same way in other situations. *Consistency* refers to the frequency of a particular behavior over time.

We form attributions based on whether these cues are low or high. Figure 6.4 shows how the combination of these cues helps us form internal or external attributions. Suppose you have received several complaints from customers regarding one of your customer service representatives, John. You have not received complaints about your other service representatives (low consensus). Upon reviewing John's records, you note that he also received customer complaints during his previous job as a sales clerk (low distinctiveness). The complaints have been coming in steadily for about three months (high consistency). In this case, you would most likely make an internal attribution and conclude that the complaints must stem from John's behavior. The combination of low consensus, low distinctiveness, and high consistency leads to internal attributions.

consensus
An informational cue indicating the extent to which peers in the same situation behave in a similar fashion.

distinctiveness
An informational cue indicating the degree to which an individual behaves the same way in other situations.

consistency
An informational cue indicating the frequency of behavior over time.

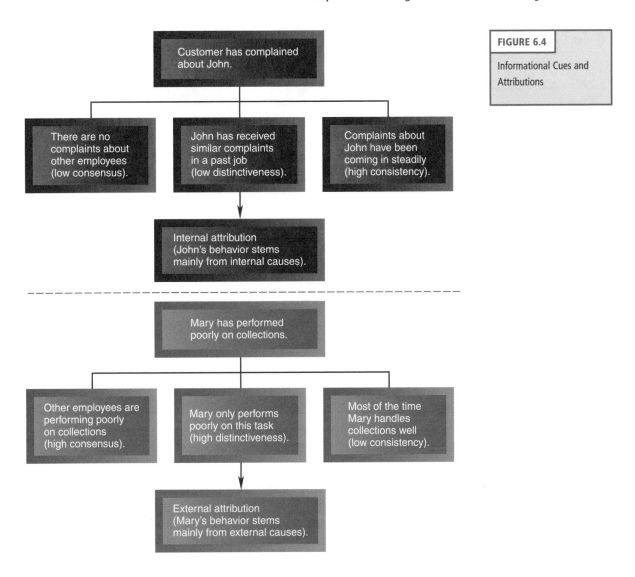

Other combinations of these cues, however, produce external attributions. High consensus, high distinctiveness, and low consistency, for example, produce external attributions. Suppose one of your employees, Mary, is performing poorly on collecting overdue accounts. You find that the behavior is widespread within your work team (high consensus) and that Mary is performing poorly only on this aspect of the job (high distinctiveness), and that most of the time she handles this aspect of the job well (low consistency). You will probably decide that something about the work situation caused the poor performance—perhaps work overload or an unfair deadline.

Consensus, distinctiveness, and consistency are the cues used to determine whether the cause of behavior is internal or external. The process of determining the cause of a behavior may not be simple and clear cut, however, because of some biases that occur in forming attributions.

Figure 6.5 presents an attribution model that specifically addresses how supervisors respond to poor performance. A supervisor who observes poor performance seeks cues about the employee's behavior in the three forms discussed above: consensus, consistency, and distinctiveness.

FIGURE 6.5

Attribution Model

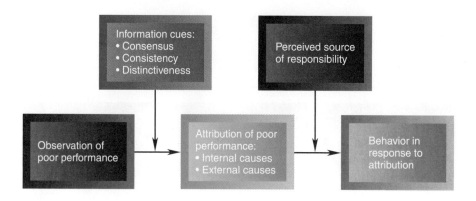

On the basis of this information, the supervisor makes either an internal (personal) attribution or an external (situational) attribution. Internal attributions might include low effort, lack of commitment, or lack of ability. External attributions are outside the employee's control and might include equipment failure or unrealistic goals. The supervisor then determines the source of responsibility for the performance problem and tries to correct the problem.

Supervisors may choose from a wide range of responses. They can, for example, express personal concern, reprimand the employee, or provide training. Supervisors who attribute the cause of poor performance to a person (an internal cause) will respond more harshly than supervisors who attribute the cause to the work situation (an external cause). Supervisors should try not to make either of the two common attribution errors discussed in Chapter 3: the fundamental attribution error and the self-serving bias.

■ COACHING, COUNSELING, AND MENTORING

Supervisors have important coaching, counseling, and mentoring responsibilities to their subordinates. Supervisors and coworkers have been found to be more effective in mentoring functions than assigned, formal mentors from higher up in the organizational hierarchy.[80] Success in the mentoring relationship also hinges on the presence of openness and trust.[81] This relationship may be one where performance-based deficiencies are addressed or one where personal problems that diminish employee performance, such as depression, are addressed.[82] In either case, the supervisors can play a helpful role in employee problem-solving activities without accepting responsibility for the employees' problems. One important form of help is to refer the employee to trained professionals.

mentoring

A work relationship that encourages development and career enhancement for people moving through the career cycle.

Coaching and counseling are among the career and psychosocial functions of a mentoring relationship.[83] *Mentoring* is a work relationship that encourages development and career enhancement for people moving through the career cycle. Mentor relationships typically go through four phases: initiation, cultivation, separation, and redefinition. For protégés, mentoring offers a number of career benefits.[84] The relationship can significantly enhance the early development of a newcomer and the mid-career development of an experienced employee. One study found that good performance by newcomers resulted in leaders giving more delegation.[85] Career development can be enhanced through peer relationships as an alternative to traditional mentoring relationships.[86] Executive coaching is increasingly being used as a way of outsourcing the business mentoring functions.[87] Informational, collegial, and special peers aid the individual's development through information sharing, career strategizing, job-related feedback, emotional support, and friendship. Finally, Behavior Modeling Training (BMT) is a training approach that can assist with employee coaching and counseling activities.[88] Describing employees with appropriate behaviors and modeling effective behaviors are two components of BMT.

⚐ MANAGERIAL IMPLICATIONS: PERFORMANCE MANAGEMENT IS A KEY TASK

People in organizations learn from the consequences of their actions. Therefore, managers must exercise care in applying positive and negative consequences to ensure that they are connected to the behaviors the managers intend to reward or punish. Managers should also be judicious in the use of punishment and should consider extinction coupled with positive reinforcement as an alternative to punishment for shaping employee behavior. The strategic use of training and educational opportunities, stock options, and recognition awards is instrumental to successful organizational reward systems. Managers can serve as positive role models for employees' vicarious learning about ethical behavior and high-quality performance.

Goal-setting activities may be valuable to managers in bringing out the best performance from employees. Managers can use challenging, specific goals for this purpose and must be prepared to provide employees with timely, useful feedback on goal progress so that employees will know how they are doing. Goal-setting activities that are misused may create dysfunctional competition in an organization and lead to lower performance.

Good performance management systems are a valuable tool for providing employees with clear feedback on their actions. Managers who rely on valid and reliable performance measures may use them in employee development and to correct poor performance. Managers who use high-technology performance monitoring systems must remember that employees are humans, not machines. Managers are responsible for creating a positive learning atmosphere in performance feedback sessions, and employees are responsible for learning from these sessions. 360-degree feedback is especially effective when combined with coaching.

Finally, managers can use rewards as one of the most powerful positive consequences for shaping employee behavior. If rewards are to improve performance, managers must make a clear connection between specific performance and the rewards. Employees should be expected to earn the rewards they receive; they should expect rewards to be related to performance quality and skill development.

LOOKING BACK :: VIRGIN GROUP, LTD.

Performance through Collaboration, Not Dictation

Performance management emphasizes behaviors, gives careful attention to evaluation and feedback, and is concerned with performance improvement, often through goal setting. While this approach is successful and appropriate in a variety of work contexts, it is not universally used. As we saw in the opening Thinking Ahead, Sir Richard Branson's Virgin Group, Ltd. is a counterpoint organization that does not always follow the conventional wisdom, conventional approach, or traditional pathway to business success and achievement. This is true for Virgin's legal team, which is not a muscular, in-house one. Helena Samaha is Virgin's legal director who works in the group's London headquarters.[89] Rather than a large in-house legal staff, Samaha oversees Virgin's relationship with external lawyers who do about £10 million in legal work annually. In addition, she does Virgin's legal work on new ventures.

Across the entire company, there are only 14 in-house lawyers, some housed in the group's companies such as Virgin Atlantic, Virgin Trains, its hot-air balloon company, or its myriad of other smaller companies. In her words, Samaha does not dictate behavior to the lawyers or executives in these groups. Rather, she uses and encourages a collaborative style of relationship that fits Virgin's entrepreneurial culture, not the combative, antagonistic style stereotypical of the legal profession and courtroom dramas. In this view, she does not evaluate the performance of Virgin's lawyers within the companies but rather leaves that to the executives who are actually managing the companies. This approach opens up a way of macro-managing Virgin's legal work rather than micro-managing the behavior of its lawyers.

Samaha's management style does not mean she's disengaged from performance evaluations and performance management. On the contrary, she conducts a full review of Virgin's external legal panel annually. Because it outsources 80 percent of its legal work to external lawyers, Virgin must keep these lawyers motivated and performing well for the company. Samaha achieves this by annual evaluations of the external legal panel. Annual reviews give her the flexibility to retain legal firms who perform well, such as Allen & Overy, while letting others, such as Hammonds, drop off retainer. In addition, she looks carefully at the possibility of renegotiating fees with the external lawyers. This activity is all aimed at enhancing both motivation and performance among the external lawyers because of the contingent rewards offered. While Virgin Group has kept its in-house legal team minimal, it has stayed on top of its legal work through a motivated panel of external lawyers who are managed well by the company and who give it flexibility in meeting its legal needs.

CHAPTER SUMMARY

1. Learning is a change in behavior acquired through experience.

2. The operant conditioning approach to learning states that behavior is a function of positive and negative consequences.

3. Reinforcement is used to develop desirable behavior; punishment and extinction are used to decrease undesirable behavior.

4. Bandura's social learning theory suggests that task-specific self-efficacy is important to effective learning.

5. Goal setting improves work motivation and task performance, reduces role stress, and improves the accuracy and validity of performance appraisal.

6. Performance management and 360-degree feedback can lead to improved performance.

7. Making accurate attributions about the behavior of others is an essential prerequisite to correcting poor performance.

8. High-quality performance should be rewarded and poor performance should be corrected.

9. Mentoring is a relationship for encouraging development and career enhancement for people moving through the career cycle.

K E Y   T E R M S

classical conditioning (p. 147)
consensus (p. 164)
consistency (p. 164)
distinctiveness (p. 164)
extinction (p. 149)
goal setting (p. 151)
learning (p. 147)

management by objectives (MBO) (p. 155)
mentoring (p. 166)
negative consequences (p. 148)
operant conditioning (p. 147)
performance appraisal (p. 157)
performance management (p. 157)

positive consequences (p. 148)
punishment (p. 149)
reinforcement (p. 149)
task-specific self-efficacy (p. 150)
360-degree feedback (p. 160)

R E V I E W   Q U E S T I O N S

1. Define the terms *learning, reinforcement, punishment,* and *extinction.*

2. What are positive and negative consequences in shaping behavior? How should they be managed? Explain the value of extinction as a strategy.

3. How can task-specific self-efficacy be enhanced? What are the differences in the way introverted and extroverted and intuitive and sensing people learn?

4. What are the five characteristics of well-developed goals? Why is feedback on goal progress important?

5. What are the purposes of conducting performance appraisals? What are the benefits of 360-degree feedback?

6. What are the two possible attributions of poor performance? What are the implications of each?

7. How can managers and supervisors best provide useful performance feedback?

8. How do mentors and peers help people develop and enhance their careers?

Discussion and Communication Q U E S T I O N S

1. Which learning approach—the behavioral approach or Bandura's social learning theory—do you find more appropriate for people?

2. Given your personality type, how do you learn best? Do you miss learning some things because of how they are taught?

3. What goals do you set for yourself at work? In your personal life? Will you know if you achieve them?

4. If a conflict occurred between your self-evaluation and the evaluation given to you by your supervisor or instructor, how would you respond? What, specifically, would you do? What have you learned from your supervisor or instructor during the last reporting period?

5. What rewards are most important to you? How hard are you willing to work to receive them?

6. *(communication question)* Prepare a memo detailing the consequences of behavior in your

work or university environment (e.g., grades, awards, suspensions, and scholarships). Include in your memo your classification of these consequences as positive or negative. Should your organization or university change the way it applies these consequences?

7. *(communication question)* Develop an oral presentation about the most current management practices in employee rewards and performance management. Find out what at least four different companies are doing in this area. Be prepared to discuss their fit with the text materials.

8. *(communication question)* Interview a manager or supervisor who is responsible for completing performance appraisals on people at work. Ask the manager which aspects of performance appraisal and the performance appraisal interview process are most difficult and how he or she manages these difficulties.

ETHICAL DILEMMA

Donna Hermann shuffled the papers on her desk. She was very surprised by what she read. On her desk sat the annual evaluations of Julie Stringer, an employee in Donna's department. Both worked for Telecom Solutions, a large call center in the Midwest where it was the policy to do 360-degree annual evaluation on all employees. Each individual was evaluated by his or her supervisor, peers, and subordinates if the person was in a management position. As Julie's supervisor, Donna was looking at the evaluations completed by three of Julie's peers and three of her subordinates.

Julie's peers' opinion of her performance closely matched Donna's. Working at Telecom was intense and the managers had worked hard to create an environment where they supported each other. They felt that Julie was not supporting this environment. She never got in anyone's way but she never pitched in to help either. Julie came to Telecom every day to work, nothing else. She never cared to make friends or to be a part of the team. Donna felt this was not good for the morale of her department and had hoped this annual evaluation would help her start the process of replacing Julie. However, the problem was Julie's employees loved her. Quite frankly, Donna

had never seen such glowing reviews by anyone's subordinates. Obviously, Julie was not remote with her team. One of Julie's highest ratings from her team was her willingness to pitch in at any time for any reason. This was a very different perception from the management team.

Donna had no personal problem with Julie; she was concerned about her entire department. Since Julie joined the company, things had not been the same. However, was it more important for Julie's peers to be happy or her employees? Her group was always productive. Also, was it fair to punish someone for coming to the office to work? But, was it right to let Julie's behaviors to continue chipping away at the culture that Donna and the other managers had worked so hard to achieve?

QUESTIONS

1. What is Donna's primary responsibility?
2. Does Donna have a greater responsibility to her direct reports or to those who are one level down?
3. Using rule, virtue, right, and justice theories, evaluate Donna's decision regarding Julie.

EXPERIENTIAL EXERCISES

6.1 POSITIVE AND NEGATIVE REINFORCEMENT

Purpose: To examine the effects of positive and negative reinforcement on behavior change.

1. Two or three volunteers are selected to receive reinforcement from the class while performing a particular task. The volunteers leave the room.
2. The instructor identifies an object for the student volunteers to locate when they return to the room. (The object should be unobtrusive but clearly visible to the class. Some that have worked well are a small triangular piece of paper that was left behind when a notice was torn off a classroom bulletin board, a smudge on the chalkboard, and a chip in the plaster of a classroom wall.)
3. The instructor specifies the reinforcement contingencies that will be in effect when the volunteers return to the room. For negative

reinforcement, students should hiss, boo, and throw things (although you should not throw anything harmful) when the first volunteer is moving away from the object; cheer and applaud when the second volunteer is getting closer to the object; and if a third volunteer is used, use both negative and positive reinforcement.

4. The instructor should assign a student to keep a record of the time it takes each of the volunteers to locate the object.
5. Volunteer number 1 is brought back into the room and is instructed: "Your task is to locate and touch a particular object in the room, and the class has agreed to help you. You may begin."
6. Volunteer number 1 continues to look for the object until it is found while the class assists by giving negative reinforcement.

7. Volunteer number 2 is brought back into the room and is instructed: "Your task is to locate and touch a particular object in the room, and the class has agreed to help you. You may begin."

8. Volunteer number 2 continues to look for the object until it is found while the class assists by giving positive reinforcement.

9. Volunteer number 3 is brought back into the room and is instructed: "Your task is to locate and touch a particular object in the room, and the class has agreed to help you. You may begin."

10. Volunteer number 3 continues to look for the object until it is found while the class assists by giving both positive and negative reinforcement.

11. In a class discussion, answer the following questions:

    a. How did the behavior of the volunteers differ when different kinds of reinforcement (positive, negative, or both) were used?

    b. What were the emotional reactions of the volunteers to the different kinds of reinforcement?

    c. Which type of reinforcement—positive or negative—is most common in organizations? What effect do you think this has on motivation and productivity?

6.2 CORRECTING POOR PERFORMANCE

This exercise provides an opportunity for you to engage in a performance diagnosis role-play as either the assistant director of the Academic Computing Service Center or as a member of a university committee appointed by the president of the university at the request of the center director. The instructor will divide the class into groups of five or six students and either ask the group to select who is to be the assistant director or assign one group member to be the assistant director.

Performance diagnosis, especially where some poor performance exists, requires making attributions and determining causal factors as well as formulating a plan of action to correct any poor performance.

Step 1. (5 minutes) Once the class is formed into groups, the instructor provides the assistant director with a copy of the role description and each university committee member with a copy of the role context information. Group members are to read through the materials provided.

Step 2. (15 minutes) The university committee is to call in the assistant director of the Academic Computing Service Center for a performance diagnostic interview. This is an information-gathering interview, not an appraisal session. The purpose is to gather information for the center director.

Step 3. (15 minutes) The university committee is to agree on a statement that reflects their understanding of the assistant director's poor performance and to include a specification of the causes. Based on this problem statement, the committee is to formulate a plan of action to correct the poor performance. The assistant director is to do the same, again ending with a plan of action.

Step 4. (10–15 minutes, optional) The instructor may ask the groups to share the results of their work in Step 3 of the role-play exercise.

PART 3

Interpersonal Processes and Behavior

Communication

7

LEARNING OBJECTIVES

After reading this chapter, you should be able to do the following:

: 1. Discuss the significance of the communicator, the receiver, perceptual screens, and the message in interpersonal communication.

: 2. Describe five communication skills that effective supervisors possess.

: 3. Explain five communication barriers and gateways through them.

: 4. Distinguish between defensive and nondefensive communication.

: 5. Explain positive, healthy communication.

: 6. Describe how managers can use new technologies to communicate effectively.

173

THINKING AHEAD :: Cisco Systems

Behind the Firewall

The very latest in information technology is a central aspect of the overall communications strategy within an organization. E-mails have become the quintessential paradox in many organizations as these electronic communications flood employees' mailboxes. Managers may well receive hundreds of e-mail communications each day, depending upon their industry and functional position within the company. The flood of e-mails comes both from within an organization and from external customers or other constituents. SPAM screening devices installed by many companies can be helpful in reviewing and sorting this communications flow, but there is always the risk that these SPAM screens may put important messages in the electronic recycle bin, erroneously. Thus, building an effective and functional firewall for internal organizational communications that does not kill important inbound messages from external customers is a real system design challenge.

Inside the corporate walls, however, Cisco Systems aims for a win–win strategy with its intranet such that the fun and business elements of using this electronic communications device are blended into a seamless package. That is, Cisco's intranet aims to be effective and fun at the same time. Cisco has worked to achieve this combined objective by positioning its intranet in the context of its overall communications strategy as an organization. A primary focus for Cisco was on ways to make the intranet helpful to employees in managing e-mails. One of the nice features within Cisco's intranet enables e-mails on related subjects to be presented in a Web interface with checkboxes to speed the replies. For example, one natural grouping of e-mails for a Cisco manager might be grouping e-mails from all employees requesting vacation time.

The Cisco intranet also supports a great deal of personalization of content access and delivery, and the company has found the benefits of this to be considerable. However, the ultimate focus of a successful intranet must be on the content, regardless of all the other features that may make it fun or entertaining. If employees cannot find the information they need in their e-mails and other electronic communications, or if they cannot trust the information to be both correct and current, then all the other entertaining and fun features serve to only highlight the deficiencies of the company's intranet. The fun features are the attention-getters in the communications, but employees know that the message content must be sound, dependable, reliable, and substantive. That is where the real heart of any high-quality communication is, electronic or otherwise. So, Cisco's intranet does satisfy the company's internal customers. But how well does Cisco take care of communication with external customers in its supply chain?[1]

---

communication
The evoking of a shared or common meaning in another person.

interpersonal communication
Communication between two or more people in an organization.

Communication is the evoking of a shared or common meaning in another person. *Interpersonal communication* is communication that occurs between two or more people in an organization. Reading, listening, managing and interpreting information, and serving clients are among the interpersonal communication skills identified by the Department of Labor as being necessary for successful functioning in the workplace.[2] Interpersonal communication is the key to social support for preventive stress management.[3] Interpersonal communication is central to health and well-being.

This chapter addresses the interpersonal and technological dimensions of communication in organizations. The first section presents an interpersonal communication model and a reflective listening technique intended to improve communication. The next section of the chapter addresses the five communication skills that characterize effective supervisors. The third section examines five barriers to effective communication and gives suggestions for overcoming them. The fourth section compares defensive and nondefensive communication. The fifth section discusses kinds of nonverbal communication. The sixth section describes positive, healthy communication. The final section gives an overview of the latest technologies for information management in organizations.

INTERPERSONAL COMMUNICATION

Interpersonal communication is important in building and sustaining human relationships at work. Interpersonal communication cannot be replaced by the advances in information technology and data management that have taken place during the past several decades. The model in this section of the chapter provides a basis for understanding the key elements of interpersonal communication. These elements are the communicator, the receiver, the perceptual screens, and the message. Reflective listening is a valuable tool for improving interpersonal communication.

AN INTERPERSONAL COMMUNICATION MODEL

Figure 7.1 presents an interpersonal communication model as a basis for the discussion of communication. The model has four basic elements: the communicator, the receiver, perceptual screens, and the message. The *communicator* is the person originating the message. The *receiver* is the person receiving the message. The receiver must interpret and understand the message. *Perceptual screens* are the windows through which we interact with people in the world. The communicator's and the receiver's perceptual screens influence the quality, accuracy, and clarity of the message. The screens influence whether the message sent and the message received are the same or whether distortion occurs in the message. Perceptual screens are composed of the personal factors each person brings to interpersonal communication, such as age, gender, values, beliefs, past experiences, cultural influences, and individual needs. The extent to which these screens are open or closed significantly influences both the sent and received messages.

The *message* contains the thoughts and feelings that the communicator intends to evoke in the receiver. The message has two primary components. The thought or conceptual component of the message (its content) is contained in the words, ideas, symbols, and concepts chosen to relay the message. The feeling or emotional

1. Discuss the significance of the communicator, the receiver, perceptual screens, and the message in interpersonal communication.

communicator
The person originating a message.

receiver
The person receiving a message.

perceptual screen
A window through which we interact with people that influences the quality, accuracy, and clarity of the communication.

message
The thoughts and feelings that the communicator is attempting to elicit in the receiver.

FIGURE 7.1
A Basic Interpersonal Communication Model

feedback

Information fed back that completes two-way communication.

language

The words, their pronunciation, and the methods of combining them used and understood by a group of people.

data

Uninterpreted and unanalyzed facts.

information

Data that have been interpreted, analyzed, and have meaning to some user.

richness

The ability of a medium or channel to elicit or evoke meaning in the receiver.

reflective listening

A skill intended to help the receiver and communicator clearly and fully understand the message sent.

component of the message (its affect) is contained in the intensity, force, demeanor, and sometimes the gestures of the communicator. This component of the message adds the emotional overtones, such as joy or anger, fear, or pain, to the conceptual component. This addition often enriches and clarifies the message. The feeling component gives the message its full meaning. At Cisco, the personalization features of their intranet help keep employees' "feelings" in this new electronic medium.

Feedback may or may not be activated in the model. Feedback occurs when the receiver provides the communicator with a response to the message. More broadly, feedback occurs when information is fed back that completes two-way communication. For example, Intuit Corporation has established a direct feedback mechanism from its customers to its employees which has paid off positively.[4]

The *language* of the message is increasingly important because of the multinational nature of many organizations. Language is the words, their pronunciation, and the methods of combining them used by a community of people. Language will be addressed as a possible barrier to communication. For example, special language barriers arise for non-Japanese-speaking Americans who work with Japanese workers and for non-Spanish-speaking Canadians who work with Spanish-speaking workers.

Data are the uninterpreted, unanalyzed elements of a message. *Information* is data with meaning to some person who has interpreted or analyzed them. Messages are conveyed through a medium, such as a telephone or face-to-face discussion. Messages differ in *richness*, the ability of the medium to convey the meaning.[5] Table 7.1 compares different media with regard to data capacity and information richness. Attributes of communication media affect how influence-seeking behavior is generated and perceived in organizations.[6]

REFLECTIVE LISTENING

Reflective listening is the skill of carefully listening to another person and repeating back to the speaker the heard message to correct any inaccuracies or misunderstandings. This kind of listening emphasizes the role of the receiver or audience in interpersonal communication. Managers use it to understand other

TABLE 7.1

Communication Media: Information Richness and Data Capacity

MEDIUM	INFORMATION RICHNESS	DATA CAPACITY
Face-to-face discussion	Highest	Lowest
Telephone	High	Low
Electronic mail	Moderate	Moderate
Individualized letter	Moderate	Moderate
Personalized note or memo	Moderate	Moderate
Formal written report	Low	High
Flyer or bulletin	Low	High
Formal numeric report	Lowest	Highest

SOURCE: Created by E. A. Gerloff from "Information Richness: A New Approach to Managerial Behavior and Organizational Design" by Richard L. Daft and R. H. Lengel in *Research in Organizational Behavior* 6 (1984): 191–233. Reprinted by permission of JAI Press Inc.

people and help them solve problems at work.[7] Reflective listening enables the listener to understand the communicator's meaning, reduce perceptual distortions, and overcome interpersonal barriers that lead to communication failures. Reflective listening ensures that the meanings of the sent and received messages are the same. Reflecting back the message helps the communicator clarify and sharpen the intended meaning. It is especially useful in problem solving. Reflective listening can be learned in a short time with positive effects on behaviors and emotions in corporate settings.[8]

Reflective listening can be characterized as personal, feeling oriented, and responsive.[9] First, reflective listening emphasizes the personal elements of the communication process, not the impersonal or abstract elements of the message. The reflective listener demonstrates empathy and concern for the communicator as a person, not an inanimate object. Second, reflective listening emphasizes the feelings communicated in the message. Thoughts and ideas are often the primary focus of a receiver's response, but that is not the case in reflective listening. The receiver should pay special attention to the feeling component of the message. Third, reflective listening emphasizes responding to the communicator, not leading the communicator. Receivers should distinguish their own feelings and thoughts from those of the speaker so as not to confuse the two. The focus must be on the speaker's feelings and thoughts in order to respond to them. A good reflective listener does not lead the speaker according to the listener's own thoughts and feelings.

Four levels of verbal response by the receiver are part of active reflective listening: affirming contact, paraphrasing expressed thoughts and feelings, clarifying implicit thoughts and feelings, and reflecting "core" feelings not fully expressed. Nonverbal behaviors also are useful in reflective listening. Specifically, silence and eye contact are responses that enhance reflective listening.

Each reflective response is illustrated through the case of a software engineer and her supervisor. The engineer has just discovered a major problem, which is not yet fully defined, in a large information system she is building for a very difficult customer.

AFFIRMING CONTACT

The receiver affirms contact with the communicator by using simple statements such as "I see," "Uh-huh," and "Yes, I understand." The purpose of an affirmation response is to communicate attentiveness, not necessarily agreement. In the case of the software engineer, the supervisor might most appropriately use several affirming statements as the engineer begins to talk through the problem. Affirming contact is especially reassuring to a speaker in the early stages of expressing thoughts and feelings about a problem, especially when there may be some associated anxiety or discomfort. As the problem is more fully explored and expressed, it is increasingly useful for the receiver to use additional reflective responses.

PARAPHRASING THE EXPRESSED

After an appropriate time, the receiver might paraphrase the expressed thoughts and feelings of the speaker. Paraphrasing is useful because it reflects back to the speaker the thoughts and feelings as the receiver heard them. This verbal response enables the receiver to build greater empathy, openness, and acceptance into the relationship while ensuring the accuracy of the communication process.

In the case of the software engineer, the supervisor may find paraphrasing the engineer's expressed thoughts and feelings particularly useful for both of them in developing a clearer understanding of the system problem. For example, the supervisor might say, "I hear you saying that you are very upset about this problem and that you are not yet clear about what is causing it." It is difficult to solve a problem until it is clearly understood.

CLARIFYING THE IMPLICIT

People often communicate implicit thoughts and feelings about a problem in addition to their explicitly expressed thoughts and feelings. Implicit thoughts and feelings are not clearly or fully expressed. The receiver may or may not assume that the implicit thoughts and feelings are within the awareness of the speaker. For example, the software engineer may be anxious about how to talk with a difficult customer concerning the system problem. This may be implicit in her discussion with her supervisor because of the previous discussions about this customer. If her anxiety feelings are not expressed, the supervisor may want to clarify them. For example, the supervisor might say, "I hear that you are feeling very upset about the problem and may be worried about the customer's reaction when you inform him." This would help the engineer shift the focus of her attention from the main problem, which is in the software, to the important and related issue of discussing the matter with the customer.

REFLECTING "CORE" FEELINGS

Next, the receiver should go beyond the explicit or implicit thoughts and feelings that the speaker is expressing. The receiver, in reflecting the core feelings that the speaker may be experiencing, is reaching beyond the immediate awareness level of the speaker. "Core" feelings are the deepest and most important ones from the speaker's perspective. For example, if the software engineer had not been aware of any anxiety in her relationship with the difficult customer, her supervisor's ability to sense the tension and bring it to the engineer's awareness would exemplify reflecting core feelings.

The receiver runs a risk of overreaching in reflecting core feelings if a secure, empathetic relationship with the speaker does not already exist or if strongly repressed feelings are reflected back. Even if the receiver is correct, the speaker may not want those feelings brought to awareness. In fact, researchers analyzing the hit TV series, "The Apprentice" found that women candidates received more criticism for losing emotional control than men candidates.[10] Therefore, it is important to exercise caution and care in reflecting core feelings to a speaker.

SILENCE

Long, extended periods of silence may cause discomfort and be a sign or source of embarrassment, but silence can help both speaker and listener in reflective listening. From the speaker's perspective, silence may be useful in moments of thought or confusion about how to express difficult ideas or feelings. The software engineer may need some patient, silent response as she thinks through what to say next. Listeners can use brief periods of silence to sort out their own thoughts and feelings from those of the speaker. Reflective listening focuses only on the latter. In the case of the software engineer's supervisor, any personal, angry feelings toward the difficult customer should not intrude on the engineer's immediate problem. Silence provides time to identify and isolate the listener's personal responses and exclude them from the dialogue.

EYE CONTACT

Eye contact is a nonverbal behavior that may help open up a relationship and improve communication between two people. The absence of any direct eye contact during an exchange tends to close communication. Cultural and individual differences influence what constitutes appropriate eye contact. For example, some cultures, such as in India, place restrictions on direct eye contact initiated by women or children. Too much direct eye contact, regardless of the individual or culture, has an intimidating effect.

Moderate direct eye contact, therefore, communicates openness and affirmation without causing either speaker or listener to feel intimidated. Periodic aversion of the eyes allows for a sense of privacy and control, even in intense interpersonal communication.

ONE-WAY VERSUS TWO-WAY COMMUNICATION

Reflective listening encourages two-way communication. *Two-way communication* is an interactive form of communication in which there is an exchange of thoughts, feelings, or both and through which shared meaning often occurs. Problem solving and decision making are often examples of two-way communication. *One-way communication* occurs when a person sends a message to another person and no feedback, questions, or interaction follow. Giving instructions or giving directions are examples of one-way communication. One-way communication occurs whenever a person sends a one-directional message to a receiver with no reflective listening or feedback in the communication.

One-way communication is faster, although how much faster depends on the amount and complexity of information communicated and the medium chosen. Even though it is faster, one-way communication is often less accurate than two-way communication. This is especially true for complex tasks where clarifications and iterations may be required for task completion. Where time and accuracy are both important to the successful completion of a task, such as in combat or emergency situations, extensive training prior to execution enhances accuracy and efficiency of execution without two-way communication.[11] Fire fighters and military combat personnel engage extensively in such training to minimize the need for communication during emergencies. These highly trained professionals rely on fast, abbreviated, one-way communication as a shorthand for more complex information. However, this communication only works within the range of situations for which the professionals are specifically trained. New research suggests that organizational culture and values play an important role in employees knowing what to do, especially in crisis situations.[12]

It is difficult to draw general conclusions about people's satisfaction with one-way versus two-way communication. For example, communicators with a stronger need for feedback or who are not uncomfortable with conflicting or confusing questions may find two-way communication more satisfying. In contrast, receivers who believe that a message is very straightforward may be satisfied with one-way communication and dissatisfied with two-way communication because of its lengthy, drawn-out nature.

two-way communication
A form of communication in which the communicator and receiver interact.

one-way communication
Communication in which a person sends a message to another person and no feedback, questions, or interaction follow.

: 2. Describe five communication skills that effective supervisors possess.

FIVE KEYS TO EFFECTIVE SUPERVISORY COMMUNICATION

Interpersonal communication, especially between managers and employees, is a critical foundation for effective performance in organizations, as well as for health and well-being as seen later in the chapter. Language and power are intertwined in the communication that occurs between managers and their employees.[13] One large study of managers in a variety of jobs and industries found that managers with the most effective work units engaged in routine communication within their units, whereas the managers with the highest promotion rates engaged in networking activities with superiors.[14] Another study of male and female banking managers suggested that higher performing managers are better and less apprehensive communicators than lower performing managers.[15] Oral communication (voice) and cooperative behaviors are important contextual performance skills that have positive effects on the psychosocial quality of the work environment.[16]

A review of the research on manager–employee communication identified five communication skills that distinguish "good" from "bad" supervisors.[17] These skills include being expressive speakers, empathetic listeners, persuasive leaders, sensitive people, and informative managers. Some supervisors are good and effective without possessing each of these skills, and some organizations value one or another skill over the others. Thus, dyadic relationships are at the core of much organization-based communication.[18]

EXPRESSIVE SPEAKERS

Better supervisors express their thoughts, ideas, and feelings and speak up in meetings. They are comfortable expressing themselves. They tend toward extroversion. Supervisors who are not talkative or who tend toward introversion may at times leave their employees wondering what their supervisors are thinking or how they feel about certain issues. Supervisors who speak out let the people they work with know where they stand, what they believe, and how they feel.

EMPATHETIC LISTENERS

In addition to being expressive speakers, the better supervisors are willing, empathetic listeners. They use reflective listening skills; they are patient with, and responsive to, problems that employees, peers, and others bring to them about their work. They respond to and engage the concerns of other people. For example, the president of a health care company estimated that he spent 70 percent of his interpersonal time at work listening to others.[19] He listens empathetically to personal and work dilemmas without taking responsibility for others' problems. Empathetic listeners are able to hear the feelings and emotional dimensions of the messages people send them, as well as the content of the ideas and issues. Better supervisors are approachable and willing to listen to suggestions and complaints. Challenge 7.1 gives you an opportunity to evaluate how active a listener you are.

PERSUASIVE LEADERS (AND SOME EXCEPTIONS)

Better supervisors are persuasive leaders rather than directive, autocratic ones. All supervisors and managers must exercise power and influence in organizations if they are to ensure performance and achieve results. These better supervisors are

<table>
</table>

CHALLENGE 7.1

Are You an Active Listener?

Reflective listening is a skill that you can practice and learn. Here are 10 tips to help you become a better listener.

1. Stop talking. You cannot listen if your mouth is moving.
2. Put the speaker at ease. Break the ice to help the speaker relax. Smile!
3. Show the speaker you want to listen. Put away your work. Do not look at your watch. Maintain good eye contact.
4. Remove distractions. Close your door. Do not answer the telephone.
5. Empathize with the speaker. Put yourself in the speaker's shoes.
6. Be patient. Not everyone delivers messages at the same pace.
7. Hold your temper. Do not fly off the handle.
8. Go easy on criticism. Criticizing the speaker can stifle communication.
9. Ask questions. Paraphrase and clarify the speaker's message.
10. Stop talking. By this stage, you are probably very tempted to start talking, but do not. Be sure the speaker has finished.

Think of the last time you had a difficult communication with someone at work or school. Evaluate yourself in that situation against each of the 10 items. Which one(s) do you need to improve on the most?

distinguished by their use of persuasive communication when influencing others. Specifically, they encourage others to achieve results instead of telling others what to do. They are not highly directive or manipulative in their influence attempts. Patience may be a virtue in this context because the sleeper effect, or delayed influence, may be active in some situations.[20]

The exceptions to this pattern of communication occur in emergency or high-risk situations, such as life-threatening traumas in medical emergency rooms or in oil rig firefighting. In these cases, the supervisor must be directive and assertive.

SENSITIVE TO FEELINGS

Better supervisors are also sensitive to the feelings, self-image, and psychological defenses of their employees. Although the supervisor is capable of giving criticism and negative feedback to employees, he or she does it confidentially and constructively. Care is taken to avoid giving critical feedback or reprimanding employees in public. Those settings are reserved for the praise of employees' accomplishments, honors, and achievements. In this manner, the better supervisors are sensitive to the self-esteem of others. They work to enhance that self-esteem as appropriate to the person's real talents, abilities, and achievements.

■ INFORMATIVE MANAGERS

Finally, better supervisors keep those who work for them well informed and are skilled at appropriately and selectively disseminating information. This role involves receiving large volumes of information, through a wide range of written and verbal communication media and then filtering through the information before distributing it appropriately. The failure to filter and disseminate information selectively to employees can lead to either information overload for the employees or a lack of sufficient information for performance and task accomplishment. As we saw in the opening case, Cisco's intranet helps employees filter and group e-mails so that they do not become totally overloaded with electronic information. Better supervisors favor giving advance notice of organizational changes and explaining the rationale for organizational policies.

A person may become a good supervisor even in the absence of one of these communication skills. For example, a person with special talents in planning and organizing or in decision making may compensate for a shortcoming in expressiveness or sensitivity. Further, when supervisors and employees engage in overt behaviors of communication and forward planning, they have a greater number of agreements about the employee's performance and behavior.[21] Overall, interpersonal communication is a key foundation for human relationships.

3. Explain five communication barriers and gateways through them.

barriers to communication
Aspects of the communication content and context that can impair effective communication in a workplace.

gateways to communication
Pathways through barriers to communication and antidotes to communication problems.

❷ BARRIERS AND GATEWAYS TO COMMUNICATION

Barriers to communication are factors that block or significantly distort successful communication. About 20 percent of communication problems that cause organizational conflicts and drain profitability can be prevented or solved by communication policy guidelines.[22] *Gateways to communication* are pathways that serve as antidotes to the problems caused by communication barriers. Communication barriers may be temporary and can be overcome. Awareness and recognition are the first steps in formulating ways to overcome the barriers. Five communication barriers are virtual work, emotions, gender differences, cultural diversity, and language. The discussion of each concludes with one or two ways to overcome the barrier.

■ VIRTUAL WORK

The increase in virtual work-from-home offices and remote locations can pose a barrier to communication. In addition to the problems of reduced cues and information richness in the communication process that result from virtual work, there are interpersonal social risks as well. These include social isolation and loneliness.[23] Telephones and electronic mail may help bridge the physical gap. We address a variety of new technologies in the closing section of the chapter. Although telephones and technology can be helpful, they are not as information rich as face-to-face communication (see Table 7.1).

Periodic face-to-face interactions are one antidote to the physical separation associated with virtual work, because the communication is much richer as a result of nonverbal cues. Information rich communication is helpful in reducing confusion, conflict, or misunderstandings. Another communication gateway in the context of virtual work is regularly scheduled meetings for people who are organizationally interrelated. Finally, professional associations such as Rotary Clubs can provide supplemental social contact for those engaged in virtual work.

◀◀**think critically**▶▶

Suppose that a company has many employees who telecommute on a regular basis. They are consistently good performers and exceed all performance goals. However, the company does not promote telecommuters at the same rate as employees who work from the office because the company believes telecommuters are not as committed to their jobs. Should this be allowed? Explain.

▦ EMOTIONS

Some emotions can pose barriers to successful communication, causing people to go either to silence or to violence, even if that is verbal violence. One key framework identifies eight primary emotions as joy, accepted, aware, anger, sadness, rejected, surprised, and fearful. Strong, intense emotions can leave people unable to verbally express themselves clearly and coherently. This is especially true when intense emotion hijacks higher-level brain functions through which thoughts and ideas are articulated and expressed. Intense emotion can also place the receiver in a defensive posture.

One of the gateways in a time of intense emotion is a strategic pause that allows time for the emotion to pass and enables the speaker to regain composure. A second gateway is to vent, express, or discharge intense emotions in channels or places that are safe and nonthreatening. In addition, strong, passionate emotions may be capitalized on to inspire others to action, thus serving a positive value for the person and others in the work environment. Finally, emotional competencies in self-awareness and self-management as well as other-awareness and other-management are positive gateways to communication.[24]

▦ GENDER DIFFERENCES

Communication barriers can be explained in part by differences in conversational styles between men and women. Men tend to use language that may seem boastful or even arrogant, while women tend to use language that takes people's feelings into account, being careful not to appear boastful. Some research suggests that these differences in conversational styles between men and women begin at childhood. Boys will play outside in large, hierarchically structured groups and use language of status and independence. On the other hand, girls will play in small groups or in pairs and use language of connection and intimacy.[25] In adulthood, the socialization of boys and girls becomes a form of cross-cultural communication in male–female conversation.

An important gateway through the gender barrier to communication is developing an awareness of gender-specific differences in conversational style. These differences can enrich organizational communication and empower professional relationships.[26] A second gateway is to recognize conversational styles as conventions of communication, not to be taken literally. When ways of speaking are interpreted literally, miscommunication often occurs. However, when everyone is familiar with these conventions, communication with members of the opposite sex can work well.[27]

CULTURAL DIVERSITY

Cultural values and patterns of behavior can be very confusing barriers to communication. Important international differences in work-related values exist among people in the United States, Germany, the United Kingdom, Japan, and other nations.[28] These value differences have implications for motivation, leadership, and teamwork in work organizations.[29] Habitual patterns of interaction within a culture often substitute for communication. Outsiders working in a culture foreign to them often find these habitual patterns confusing and at times bizarre. For example, the German culture places greater value on authority and hierarchical differences. It is therefore more difficult for German workers to engage in direct, open communication with their supervisors than it is for U.S. workers.[30] The overuse of cultural stereotypes can be confusing and misleading in cross-cultural communication. It is important to remember that there are important and significant individual differences within every culture.

One gateway through cultural diversity is increasing awareness and sensitivity. In addition, companies can provide seminars for expatriate managers as part of their training for overseas assignments. A second gateway is developing or acquiring a guide, map, or beacon for understanding and interacting with members of other cultures. One approach to doing this is to describe a nation in terms of a suitable and complex metaphor.[31] For example, Irish conversations, the Spanish bullfight, and American football are consensually derived metaphors that can enable those outside the culture to understand members within the culture.

LANGUAGE

Language is a central element in communication. It may pose a barrier if its use obscures meaning and distorts intent. Although English is the international language of aviation, it is not the international language of business. Where the native languages of supervisors and employees differ, the risk of barriers to communication exists. For example, "yes" in American English does not have the same meaning as "yes" in Indian English. When Indians say "yes," they typically mean "I'll try" or "I'll make an honest effort," not "It's almost certain to happen and if not, I'll take personal responsibility."[32] Less obvious, subtle distinctions in dialects within the same language may cause confusion and misunderstanding. For example, the word *lift* means an elevator in Great Britain and a ride in the United States. Technical terminology may be a language barrier across disciplines and professional boundaries. Acronyms and technical terms may be very useful shorthand for those inside of a profession or discipline while confusing those outside the profession.[33]

Communication gateways include the use of simple, direct, declarative language. Speak in brief sentences and use terms or words you have heard from your audience. As much as possible, speak in the language of the listener. Do not use jargon or technical language except with those who clearly understand it. Communication is complete when the speaker and listener understand the same message and meaning.

⬛ DEFENSIVE AND NONDEFENSIVE COMMUNICATION

Defensive communication in organizations also can create barriers between people, whereas nondefensive communication helps open up relationships.[34] *Defensive communication* includes both aggressive, attacking, angry communication and passive, withdrawing communication. Organizations are increasingly engaged in courtroom battles and media exchanges, which are especially fertile settings for defensive communication. Defensive communication in organizations leads to a wide range of problems, including injured feelings, communication breakdowns, alienation in working relationships, destructive and retaliatory behaviors, nonproductive efforts, and problem-solving failures. When such problems arise in organizations, everyone is prone to blame everyone else for what is not working.[35] The defensive responses of counterattack or sheepish withdrawal derail communication. Such responses tend to lend heat, not light, to the communication.

Nondefensive communication, in contrast, provides a basis for asserting and defending oneself when attacked, without being defensive. There are appropriate ways to defend oneself against aggression, attack, or abuse. *Nondefensive communication* is an assertive, direct, powerful form of communication that restores order, balance, and effectiveness in working relationships.

▣ DEFENSIVE COMMUNICATION AT WORK

Defensive communication often elicits defensive communication in response. The two basic patterns of defensiveness are dominant defensiveness and subordinate defensiveness. One must be able to recognize various forms of defensive communication before learning to engage in constructive, nondefensive communication. Challenge 7.2 helps you examine your defensive communication. Complete it before reading the following text material.

SUBORDINATE DEFENSIVENESS

Subordinate defensiveness is characterized by passive, submissive, withdrawing behavior. The psychological attitude of the subordinately defensive person is "You are right, and I am wrong." People with low self-esteem may be prone to this form of defensive behavior, as well as people at lower organizational levels.

DOMINANT DEFENSIVENESS

Dominant defensiveness is characterized by active, aggressive, attacking behavior. It is offensive in nature: "The best defense is a good offense." The psychological attitude of the dominantly defensive person is "I am right, and you are wrong." People who compensate for low self-esteem may exhibit this pattern of behavior, as well as people who are in higher-level positions within the organizational hierarchy.

▣ DEFENSIVE TACTICS

Unfortunately, defensive tactics are all too common in work organizations. Eight major defensive tactics are summarized in Table 7.2. They might be best understood in the context of a work situation: Joe is in the process of completing a critical report for his boss, and the report's deadline is drawing near. Mary, one of Joe's peers at work, is to provide him with some input for the report, and the

4. Distinguish between defensive and nondefensive communication.

defensive communication
Communication that can be aggressive, attacking, and angry, or passive and withdrawing.

nondefensive communication
Communication that is assertive, direct, and powerful.

C H A L L E N G E   7 . 2

What Kind of a Defender Are You?

Not all of our communication is defensive, but each of us has a tendency to engage in either subordinate or dominant defensiveness. The following table presents 12 sets of choices that will help you see whether you tend to be more subordinate or dominant when you communicate defensively.

Complete the questionnaire by allocating 10 points between the two alternatives in each of the 12 rows. For example, if you never ask permission when it is not needed, but you do give or deny permission frequently, you may give yourself 0 and 10 points, respectively, in the third row. However, if you do each of these behaviors about equally, though at different times, you may want to give yourself 5 points for each alternative.

Add your total points for each column. Whichever number is larger identifies your defensive style.

Subordinate Defensiveness

_____ Explain, prove, justify your actions, ideas, or feelings more than is required for results wanted.

_____ Ask why things are done the way they are, when you really want to change them. *Why don't they . . . ?*

_____ Ask permissions when not needed. *Is it okay with you if . . . ?*

_____ Give away decisions, ideas, or power when it would be appropriate to claim them as your own. *Don't you think that . . . ?*

_____ Apologize, feel inadequate, say *I'm sorry* when you're not.

_____ Submit or withdraw when it's not in your best interest. *Whatever you say . . .*

_____ Lose your cool, lash out, cry where it's inappropriate (turning your anger toward yourself).

_____ Go blank, click off, be at a loss for words just when you want to have a ready response. *I should've said . . .* (afterwards)

_____ Use coping humor, hostile jocularity, or put yourself down when "buying time" or honest feedback would get better results. *Why don't you lay off?*

_____ Use self-deprecating adjectives and reactive verbs. *I'm just a . . . I'm just doing what I was told.*

_____ Use the general *you* and *they* when *I* and personal names would state the situation more clearly. *They really hassle you here.*

_____ Smile to cover up feelings or put yourself down since you don't know what else to do and it's *nice*.

_____ TOTAL Subordinate Points

Dominant Defensiveness

_____ Prove that you're right. *I told you so. Now see, that proves my point.*

_____ Give patient explanations but few answers. *It's always been done this way. We tried that before, but . . .*

_____ Give or deny permission. *Oh, I couldn't let you do that.*

_____ Make decisions or take power as your natural right. *The best way to do it is . . . Don't argue, just do as I say.*

_____ Prod people to get the job done. *Don't just stand there . . .*

_____ Take over a situation or decision even when it's delegated; get arbitrary. *My mind is made up.*

_____ Lose your cool, yell, pound the desk where it's inappropriate (turning your anger toward others).

_____ Shift responsibility for something you should have taken care of yourself. *You've always done it before. What're you all of a sudden upset for now?*

_____ Use coping humor, baiting, teasing, hostile jocularity, mimicry to keep other people off balance so you don't have to deal with them. *What's the matter, can't you take it?*

_____ Impress others with how many important people you know. *The other night at Bigname's party when I was talking to . . .*

_____ Don't listen: interpret. Catch the idea of what they're saying, then list rebuttals or redefine their point. *Now what you really mean is . . .*

_____ Use verbal dominance, if necessary, to make your point. Don't let anyone interrupt what you have to say.

_____ TOTAL Dominant Points

TABLE 7.2

Defensive Tactics

DEFENSIVE TACTIC	SPEAKER	WORK EXAMPLE
Power play	The boss	"Finish this report by month's end or lose your promotion."
Put-down	The boss	"A capable manager would already be done with this report."
Labeling	The boss	"You must be a slow learner. Your report is still not done?"
Raising doubts	The boss	"How can I trust you, Joe, if you can't finish an easy report?"
Misleading information	Joe	"Mary has not gone over with me the information I need from her for the report." (She left him a copy.)
Scapegoating	Joe	"Mary did not give me her input until just today."
Hostile jokes	Joe	"You can't be serious! The report isn't that important."
Deception	Joe	"I gave it to the secretary. Did she lose it?"

department secretary is to prepare a final copy of the report. Each work example in the table is related to this situation.

Until defensiveness and defensive tactics are recognized for what they are, it is difficult either to change them or to respond to them in nondefensive ways. Defensive tactics are how defensive communication is acted out. In many cases, such tactics raise ethical dilemmas and issues for those involved. For example, is it ethical to raise doubts about another person's values, beliefs, or sexuality? At what point does simple defensiveness become unethical behavior?

NONVERBAL COMMUNICATION

Most of the meaning in a message (an estimated 65 to 90 percent) is conveyed through nonverbal communication.[36] *Nonverbal communication* includes all elements of communication, such as gestures and the use of space, that do not involve words or do not involve language.[37] The four basic kinds of nonverbal communication are proxemics, kinesics, facial and eye behavior, and paralanguage. They are important topics for managers attempting to understand the types and meanings of nonverbal signals from employees. Nonverbal communication is influenced by both psychological and physiological processes.[38]

Some scholars consider this area of communication to be less scientifically rigorous than other areas of communication. In any case, the interpretation of nonverbal communication is specific to the context of the interaction and the actors. That is, nonverbal cues only give meaning in the context of the situation and the interaction of the actors. For example, some federal and state judges attempt to curb nonverbal communication in the courtroom. The judges' primary concern is that nonverbal behavior may unfairly influence jurors' decisions. It is also important to note that nonverbal behavior is culturally bound. Gestures, facial expressions, and body locations have different meanings in different cultures. The

nonverbal communication
All elements of communication that do not involve words.

FIGURE 7.2

Zones of Territorial Space
in U.S. Culture

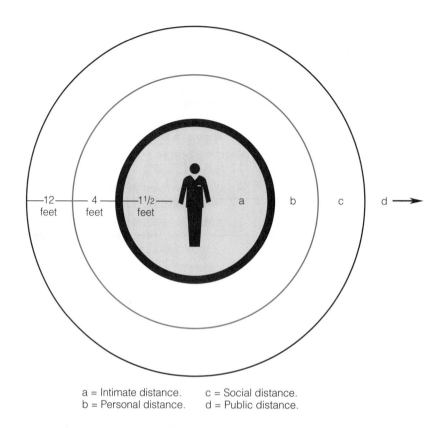

a = Intimate distance.   c = Social distance.
b = Personal distance.   d = Public distance.

globalization of business means managers should be sensitive to the nonverbal customs of other cultures in which they do business.

▉ PROXEMICS

The study of an individual's perception and use of space, including territorial space, is called *proxemics*.[39] *Territorial space* refers to bands of space extending outward from the body. These bands constitute comfort zones. In each comfort zone, different cultures prefer different types of interaction with others. Figure 7.2 presents four zones of territorial space based on U.S. culture.

The first zone, intimate space, extends outward from the body to about 1½ feet. In this zone, we interact with spouses, significant others, family members, and others with whom we have an intimate relationship. The next zone, the personal distance zone, extends from 1½ feet outward to 4 feet. Friends typically interact within this distance. The third zone, the social distance zone, spans the distance from 4 to 12 feet. We prefer that business associates and acquaintances interact with us in this zone. The final zone is the public distance zone, extending 12 feet from the body outward. Most of us prefer that strangers stay at least 12 feet from us, and we become uncomfortable when they move closer.

Territorial space varies greatly across cultures. People often become uncomfortable when operating in territorial spaces different from those in which they are familiar. Edward Hall, a leading proxemics researcher, says Americans working in the Middle East tend to back away to a comfortable conversation distance when interacting with Arabs. Because Arabs' comfortable conversation distance is closer than that of Americans, Arabs perceive Americans as cold and aloof. One Arab wondered, "What's the matter? Does he find me somehow offensive?"[40] Personal space tends to be larger in cultures with cool climates, such as the United States, Great Britain, and northern Europe, and smaller in cultures with warm climates, such as southern Europe, the Caribbean, India, or South America.[41]

Our relationships shape our use of territorial space. For example, we hold hands with, or put an arm around, significant others to pull them into intimate space. Conversely, the use of territorial space can shape people's interactions. A four-foot-wide business desk pushes business interactions into the social distance zone. An exception occurred for one SBC manager who met with her seven first-line supervisors around her desk. Being elbow to elbow placed the supervisors in one another's intimate and personal space. They appeared to act more like friends and frequently talked about their children, favorite television shows, and other personal concerns. When the manager moved the staff meeting to a larger room and the spaces around each supervisor were in the social distance zone, the personal exchanges ceased, and they acted more like business associates again.

Seating dynamics, another aspect of proxemics, is the art of seating people in certain positions according to the person's purpose in communication. Figure 7.3 depicts some common seating dynamics. To encourage cooperation, you should seat the other party beside you, facing the same direction. To facilitate direct and open communication, seat the other party across a corner of your desk from you or in another place where you will be at right angles. This allows for more honest disclosure. To take a competitive stand with someone, position the person directly across from you. Suppose you hold a meeting around a conference table, and two of the attendees are disrupting your meeting. Where should you seat them? If you place one on each side of yourself, it should stifle the disruptions (unless one is so bold as to lean in front of you to keep chatting).

▓ KINESICS

Kinesics is the study of body movements, including posture.[42] Like proxemics, kinesics is culturally bound; there is no single universal gesture. For example, the U.S. hand signal for "okay" is an insult in other countries. With this in mind, we can

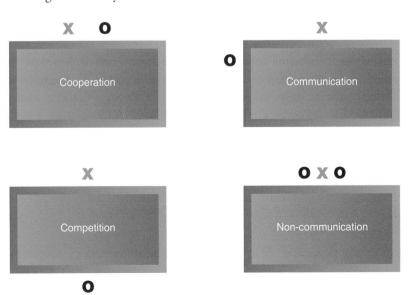

FIGURE 7.3
Seating Dynamics

interpret some common U.S. gestures. Rubbing one's hands together or exhibiting a sharp intake of breath indicates anticipation. Stress is indicated by a closed hand position (that is, tight fists), hand wringing, or rubbing the temples. Nervousness may be exhibited through drumming fingers, pacing, or jingling coins in the pocket. Perhaps most fun to watch is preening behavior, seen most often in couples on a first date. Preening communicates "I want to look good for you" to the other party and consists of smoothing skirts, straightening the tie, or arranging the hair. No discussion of gestures would be complete without mention of insult gestures—some learned at an early age, much to the anxiety of parents. Sticking out one's tongue and waving fingers with one's thumbs in the ears is a childhood insult gesture.

▉ FACIAL AND EYE BEHAVIOR

The face is a rich source of nonverbal communication. Facial expression and eye behavior are used to add cues for the receiver. The face may give unintended clues to emotions the sender is trying to hide. Dynamic facial actions and expressions in a person's appearance are key clues of truthfulness, especially in deception situations.[43]

Although smiles have universal meaning, frowns, raised eyebrows, and wrinkled foreheads must all be interpreted in conjunction with the actors, the situation, and the culture. One study of Japanese and U.S. students illustrates the point. The students were shown a stress-inducing film, and their facial expressions were videotaped. When alone, the students had almost identical expressions. However, the Japanese students masked their facial expressions of unpleasant feelings much better than did the American students when another person was present.[44]

As mentioned earlier, eye contact can enhance reflective listening and, along with smiling, is one good way of displaying positive emotion.[45] However, eye contact must be understood in a cultural context. A direct gaze indicates honesty, truthfulness, and forthrightness in the United States. This may not be true in other cultures. For example, Barbara Walters was uncomfortable interviewing Muammar al-Qaddafi in Libya because he did not look directly at her. However, in Libya, it is a serious offense to look directly at a woman.[46] In Asian cultures, it is considered good behavior to bow the head in deference to a superior rather than to look in the supervisor's eyes.

▉ PARALANGUAGE

Paralanguage consists of variations in speech, such as pitch, loudness, tempo, tone, duration, laughing, and crying.[47] People make attributions about the sender by deciphering paralanguage cues. A high-pitched, breathy voice in a female may contribute to the stereotype of the "dumb blonde." Rapid, loud speech may be taken as a sign of nervousness or anger. Interruptions such as "mmm" and "ah-hah" may be used to speed up the speaker so that the receiver can get in a few words. Clucking of the tongue or the "tsk-tsk" sound is used to shame someone. All these cues relate to how something is said.

▉ HOW ACCURATELY DO WE DECODE NONVERBAL CUES?

Peoples' confidence in their ability to decode nonverbal communication is greater than their accuracy in doing so. Judges with several years' experience in interviewing were asked in one study to watch videotapes of job applicants and to rate the applicants' social skills and motivation levels.[48] The judges were fairly accurate about the social skills, but not about motivation. The judges relied on smiling, gesturing, and speaking as cues to motivation, yet none of these cues are motivation indicators. Thus, incorrectly interpreting nonverbal codes leads to inaccuracy.

Studies of deception emphasize how to use nonverbal cues to interpret whether someone is lying. In one simulation study, customers were asked to detect whether or not automobile salespeople were lying. The customers' ability to detect lies in this study was no better than chance. Does this suggest that salespeople are skilled deceivers who control nonverbal behaviors to prevent detection?[49]

Paul Ekman, a psychologist who has trained judges, Secret Service agents, and polygraphers to detect lies, says that the best way to detect lies is to look for inconsistencies in the nonverbal cues. Rapidly shifting facial expressions and discrepancies between the person's words and body, voice, or facial expressions are some clues.[50]

Nonverbal communication is important for managers because of its impact on the meaning of the message. However, a manager must consider the total message and all media of communication. A message can only be given meaning in context, and cues are easy to misinterpret. Table 7.3 presents common nonverbal behaviors exhibited by managers and how employees may interpret them. Nonverbal cues can give others the wrong signal.

TABLE 7.3

Common Nonverbal Cues from Manager to Employee

NONVERBAL COMMUNICATION	SIGNAL RECEIVED	REACTION FROM RECEIVER
Manager looks away when talking to the employee.	Divided attention.	My supervisor is too busy to listen to my problem or simply does not care.
Manager fails to acknowledge greeting from fellow employee.	Unfriendliness.	This person is unapproachable.
Manager glares ominously (i.e., gives the evil eye).	Anger.	Reciprocal anger, fear, or avoidance, depending on who is sending the signal in the organization.
Manager rolls the eyes.	Not taking person seriously.	This person thinks he or she is smarter or better than I am.
Manager sighs deeply.	Disgust or displeasure.	My opinions do not count. I must be stupid or boring to this person.
Manager uses heavy breathing (sometimes accompanied by hand waving).	Anger or heavy stress.	Avoid this person at all costs.
Manager does not maintain eye contact when communicating.	Suspicion or uncertainty.	What does this person have to hide?
Manager crosses arms and leans away.	Apathy or closed-mindedness.	This person already has made up his or her mind; my opinions are not important.
Manager peers over glasses.	Skepticism or distrust.	He or she does not believe what I am saying.
Manager continues to read a report when employee is speaking.	Lack of interest.	My opinions are not important enough to get the supervisor's undivided attention.

SOURCE: From "Steps to Better Listening" by C. Hamilton and B. H. Kleiner. Copyright © February 1987. Reprinted with permission, *Personnel Journal*. All rights reserved.

communicative disease
The absence of heartfelt communication in human relationships leading to loneliness and social isolation.

◢ POSITIVE, HEALTHY COMMUNICATION

The absence of heartfelt communication in human relationships leads to loneliness and social isolation and has been labeled *communicative disease* by James Lynch.[51] Communicative disease has adverse effects on the heart and cardiovascular system and can ultimately lead to premature death. According to Lynch, heartfelt communication is a healing dialogue and central antidote for communicative disease. Positive, healthy communication is central to health and well-being. While communication may often be thought of as a cognitive activity of the head, Lynch suggests that the heart may be more important in the communications process.

Positive, healthy communication is one important aspect of working together when the term "working together" is taken for its intrapersonal meaning as well as its interpersonal meaning.[52] The balance between head and heart is achieved when a person displays positive emotional competence and is able to have a healthy internal conversation between his or her thoughts and feelings, ideas, and emotions. In addition, working together occurs when there are cooperative work behaviors between people based upon positive, healthy, and open communication that is based on trust and truthfulness. Honest competition within the workplace is not inconsistent with this notion of working together; forthright, well-managed, honest competition can bring out the best in all those involved.

Positive, healthy communication is at the core of personal integrity as displayed by healthy executives.[53] Former President Ronald Reagan was a great communicator who displayed strong ethical character, personal integrity, and simplicity in his communication. He exemplified communication from the heart in the sense that his messages came from his core values, beliefs, and aspirations for himself and others. His optimism shone through from the core of his person, displaying a continuing positive attitude that drew even his opponents to like him. Communication from core values and beliefs is communication anchored in personal integrity and ethical character.

Personal integrity in positive, healthy communication is achieved through emotional competence and the head-to-heart dialogue mentioned earlier. In addition to the public self, as is familiar in the case of Ronald Reagan, all executives have a private self. Karol Wasylyshyn has shown that one dimension of coaching star executives is to enhance their emotional competence and capacity to talk through challenging issues, both personally and professionally.[54] Quick and Macik-Frey focus on the private-self aspect of positive, healthy communication in developing their model of executive coaching through deep interpersonal communication.[55] Their executive coaching model relies on what Lynch might call a healing dialogue between executive and coach. However, their model of deep interpersonal communication is one that can enhance positive, healthy communication in a wider range of human relationships.

◢ COMMUNICATING THROUGH NEW TECHNOLOGIES

New technologies are an essential feature of modern management. Many organizations around the world are now plugging into the Internet, an electronic and computer-based technology that allows for the easy transfer of information and data across continents. For example, FedEx's Insight is a web-based communication advance that lets customers check on the status of inbound shipments while the company's PowerPad allows couriers to send and receive near-real-time information and updates from a wireless network.[56]

Managers in today's business world have access to more communication tools than ever before. All of these new technologies are, surprisingly, having relatively little impact on work culture. In addition, security concerns since 9/11 have complicated wireless access. An understanding of the use of these new technologies influences effective, successful communication. In addition, it is important to understand how these new technologies affect others' communication and behavior. Finally, information technology can encourage or discourage moral dialogue, and moral conversations are central to addressing ethical issues at work.[57]

Computer-mediated communication was once used only by technical specialists but now influences virtually all managers' behavior in the work environment. Informational databases are becoming more commonplace. These databases provide a tremendous amount of information with the push of a button. Another example is found in many university libraries where books and journals are available through electronic card catalogs. Companies like Cisco Systems, as we saw at the beginning of the chapter, can find success by incorporating an intranet into their overall communication strategies.

Electronic mail (e-mail) represents another technology; users can leave messages via the computer to be accessed at any time by the receiver. This eliminates the time delay of regular mail and allows for immediate reply. Research comparing e-mail versus face-to-face communication on choices individuals make found that the effects vary with the nature of the decisions and may depend on the complexity and content of what needs to be communicated.[58] Thus, e-mail has strengths and advantages in communication as well as limitations with which to exercise caution. Unfortunately, some people feel much less inhibited when using e-mail and end up sending caustic messages they would never consider saying in person.

Cell phones and personal digital assistants (PDAs) are perhaps the most widely used communication mode, permitting communication while away from the office and on the commute to and from work. They are used extensively in sales jobs involving travel. Not all reactions to these devices are positive. For example, one oil producer did not want his thinking time while driving disturbed by a cell phone. The use of cell phones and other communications devices while driving is also risky, with some estimates suggesting that using a cell phone while driving is as risky as driving while under the influence of alcohol. For this reason, some states have outlawed the use of cell phones while driving a motor vehicle.

Voice mail and facsimile (fax) systems are also widely used communication modes, especially in sales jobs where people are away from the office. Voice behavior influences the quality of the work environment. This has implications for the quality of voice mail as well. Some voice mail systems allow the user to retrieve messages from remote locations. Timely retrieval of messages is important. One manager in the office furniture industry had a problem with her voice mail when first learning to use it. She would forget to check it until late in the day. Employees with problems early in the day felt frustrated with her slow response time. When using voice mail, it is important to remember that the receiver may not retrieve the messages in a timely manner. Urgent messages must be delivered directly.

Facsimile (fax) machine systems allow the immediate transmission of documents. This medium allows the sender to communicate facts, graphs, and illustrations very rapidly. Fax machines are used in cars, as well as offices and remote locations.

◀◀ think critically ▶▶

Should you leave confidential messages on a voice mail system in someone's office because you assume that only that person will listen to the voice mail? Can you be confident about the security of a company e-mail system?

■ HOW DO COMMUNICATION TECHNOLOGIES AFFECT BEHAVIOR?

Information communication technology (ICT)

The various new technologies, such as electronic mail, voice mail, teleconferencing, and wireless access, which are used for interpersonal communication.

Information communication technology (ICT) provides faster, more immediate access to information than was available in the past. It provides instant exchange of information in minutes or seconds across geographic boundaries and time zones. Schedules and office hours become irrelevant. The normal considerations of time and distance become less important in the exchange. Hence, these technologies have important influences on people's behavior.

One aspect of computer-mediated communication is its impersonal nature. As a result, there is a risk of flaming or making rude or obscene outbursts by computer.[59] Interpersonal skills like tact and graciousness diminish, and managers are more blunt when using electronic media. People who are quiet and polite when face to face may become impolite and uninhibited when they communicate electronically.[60] Another risk is that of information overload, which is particularly great with the new communication technologies. Not only is information available more quickly, the sheer volume of information at the manager's fingertips also is staggering.

Another effect of the new technologies is the absence of nonverbal cues we rely on to decipher a message. Gesturing, touching, facial expressions, and eye contact are not available, so the emotional element of the message is difficult to access. In addition, clues to power, such as organizational position and departmental membership, may not be available, so the social context of the exchange is altered.

Communication via technologies also changes group interaction. It tends to equalize participation, because group members participate more equally, and charismatic or higher status members may have less power.[61] Decisions via computer interaction take longer to reach consensus than in face-to-face groups. In addition, computer-mediated groups are more uninhibited, and there is less influence from any one dominant person. Thus, social and organizational barriers come down in computer-mediated groups.

A paradox created by the new, modern communication technology lies in the danger it may pose for managers. The danger is that managers cannot get away from the office as much as in the past, because they are more accessible to coworkers, subordinates, and the boss via telecommunications. Interactions are no longer confined to the 8:00 to 5:00 work hours. In addition, the use of new technologies encourages polyphasic activity (that is, doing more than one thing at a time). Managers can simultaneously make phone calls, send computer messages, and work on memos. Polyphasic activity has its advantages in terms of getting more done—but only up to a point. Paying attention to more than one task at a time may increase errors and reduce effectiveness.

Finally, the new technologies may make people less patient with face-to-face communication. The speed advantage of the electronic media may translate into an expectation of greater speed in all forms of communication. However, individuals may miss the social interaction with others and may find their social needs unmet. Communicating via computer means an absence of small talk; people tend to get to the point right away.

With many of these technologies, the potential for immediate feedback is reduced, and the exchange can become one-way. Managers can use the new technologies more effectively by keeping the following hints in mind:

1. Strive for completeness in your message.
2. Build in opportunities for feedback.
3. Do not assume you will get an immediate response.
4. Ask yourself if the communication is really necessary.
5. "Disconnect" yourself from the technology at regular intervals.
6. Provide opportunities for social interaction at work.

◢ MANAGERIAL IMPLICATIONS: COMMUNICATE WITH STRENGTH AND CLARITY

Interpersonal communication is important for the quality of working relationships in organizations. Managers who are sensitive and responsive in communicating with employees encourage the development of trusting, loyal relationships. Managers and employees alike benefit from secure working relations. Managers who are directive, dictatorial, or overbearing with employees, in contrast, are likely to find such behavior counterproductive, especially in periods of change.

Encouraging feedback and practicing reflective listening skills at work can open up communication channels in the work environment. Open communication benefits decision-making processes, because managers are better informed and more likely to base decisions on complete information. Open communication encourages nondefensive relationships, as opposed to defensive relationships, among people at work. Defensive relationships create problems because of the use of tactics that create conflict and division among people.

Managers benefit from sensitivity to employees' nonverbal behavior and territorial space, recognizing that understanding individual and cultural diversity is important in interpreting a person's nonverbal behavior. Seeking verbal clarification on nonverbal cues improves the accuracy of the communication and helps build trusting relationships. In addition, managers benefit from communicating honestly and openly, displaying a healthy balance between head and heart.

Managers may complement good interpersonal contact with the appropriate use of new information technology. New information technologies' high data capacity is an advantage in a global workplace. The high information richness of interpersonal contacts is an advantage in a culturally diverse workforce. Therefore, managers benefit from both interpersonal and technological media by treating them as complementary modes of communication, not as substitutes for each other.

LOOKING BACK :: Cisco Systems

Cisco Came, It Surveyed, and It Improved

While Cisco System's intranet focuses on employees as internal communications customers, communication pathways to its external customers are important to Cisco as well. The company is well aware of the current mantra in a very competitive global market concerning delighting these customers to ensure that they *remain* customers. Customers! Customers! Customers! Yes, customers are important to both manufacturing and service companies. In addition, for manufacturing companies, the beginning of the supply chain can be just as important. For this reason, Cisco recognized the importance of starting well in its supply chain by having excellent interaction and communication with its strategic supplier partners. The company found that it needed honest information about whether it was causing "undue pain" for any of its suppliers because its goal was to have a virtual, closed-loop supply chain that worked and worked well.

This concern for suppliers was in the context of Cisco's larger operational framework of three- to five-year goals, an approach that was a huge cultural shift for the company. These goals are communicated as specific milestones and outcomes that allow the company to fulfill its larger mission and vision concept. We know the power of goal setting in transforming performance in a positive way. However, goals cannot transform performance if they are not communicated or not understood. Once goals are set and communicated, then strategies must be developed that support the goals and enable the fulfillment of the vision. That is where the supply chain comes in for a manufacturing company and where strategic supply partners become critical to achieving milestones and desired outcomes. At Cisco, the communication interaction may demand change.

In the case of suppliers, Cisco developed targeted surveys through which it could communicate with its supply partners and receive feedback on performance. In one situation, a survey returned from one supplier gave low scores in communication and spurred internal discussion about how to improve. The supplier's specific need was for executive representation and two-way communication during supplier performance reviews. Once Cisco understood what the need was, the company developed an action plan to get its executives more involved in quarterly supplier performance reviews. Going one step further, the company developed a new executive sponsorship program in which one contact is designated to facilitate communications with strategic suppliers. Thus, Cisco works a dynamic process of communicating with its suppliers to ensure that all goes well at the start of its virtual and essential supply chain.[62]

CHAPTER SUMMARY

1. The perceptual screens of communicators and listeners either help clarify or distort a message that is sent and received. Age, gender, and culture influence the sent and received messages.

2. Reflective listening involves affirming contact, paraphrasing what is expressed, clarifying the implicit, reflecting "core" feelings, and using appropriate nonverbal behavior to enhance communication.

3. The best supervisors talk easily with diverse groups of people, listen empathetically, are generally persuasive and not directive, are sensitive to a person's self-esteem, and are communication minded.

4. Virtual work, emotions, gender differences, cultural diversity, and language are potential communication barriers that can be overcome.

5. Active or passive defensive communication destroys interpersonal relationships, whereas assertive, nondefensive communication leads to clarity.

6. Nonverbal communication includes the use of territorial space, seating arrangements, facial gestures, eye contact, and paralanguage.

Nonverbal communication varies by nation and culture around the world.

7. Communicative disease is the absence of heartfelt communication in human relationships and can lead to loneliness and social isolation.

8. Information communication technology (ICT) includes electronic mail, voice mail, and cell phones. High-tech innovations require high-touch responses.

KEY TERMS

barriers to communication (p. 182)

communication (p.174)

communicative disease (p.192)

communicator (p. 175)

data (p. 176)

defensive communication (p. 185)

feedback (p. 176)

gateways to communication (p. 182)

information (p. 176)

Information communication technology (ICT) (p. 194)

interpersonal communication (p. 174)

language (p. 176)

message (p. 175)

nondefensive communication (p. 185)

nonverbal communication (p. 187)

one-way communication (p. 179)

perceptual screen (p. 175)

receiver (p. 175)

reflective listening (p. 176)

richness (p. 176)

two-way communication (p. 179)

REVIEW QUESTIONS

1. What different components of a person's perceptual screens may distort communication?

2. What are the three defining features of reflective listening?

3. What are the four levels of verbal response in reflective listening?

4. Compare one-way communication and two-way communication.

5. What are the five communication skills of effective supervisors and managers?

6. Describe dominant and subordinate defensive communication. Describe nondefensive communication.

7. What four kinds of nonverbal communication are important in interpersonal relationships?

8. What are helpful nonverbal behaviors in the communication process? Unhelpful behaviors?

9. What is communicative disease?

10. Describe at least five new communication technologies in terms of data richness.

Discussion and Communication QUESTIONS

1. Who is the best communicator you know? Why do you consider that person to be so?

2. Who is the best listener you have ever known? Describe what that person does that makes him or her so good at listening.

3. What methods have you found most helpful in overcoming barriers to communication that are physical? That are status-based? That are cultural? That are linguistic?

4. Who makes you the most defensive when you talk with that person? What does the person do that makes you so defensive or uncomfortable?

5. With whom are you the most comfortable and nondefensive in conversation? What does the person do that makes you so comfortable or nondefensive?

6. What nonverbal behaviors do you find most helpful in others when you are attempting to talk with them? When you try to listen to them?

7. (*communication question*) Identify a person at work or at the university who is difficult to talk to and arrange an interview in which you practice good reflective listening skills. Ask the person questions about a topic in which you think he or she is interested. Pay particular attention to being patient, calm, and nonreactive. After the interview, summarize what you learned.

8. (*communication question*) Go to the library and read about communication problems and barriers. Write a memo categorizing the problems and barriers you find in the current

literature (last five years). What changes do organizations or people need to make to solve these problems?

9. (*communication question*) Develop a role-playing activity for class that demonstrates defensive (dominant or subordinate) and nondefensive communication. Write brief role descriptions that classmates can act out.

10. (*communication question*) Read everything you can find in the library about a new communication technology. Write a two-page memo summarizing what you have learned and the conclusions you draw about the new technology's advantages and disadvantages.

ETHICAL DILEMMA

Pat Williams sat at her desk listening to the conversation in the next cubical. She didn't want to listen, but it was impossible to miss. The discussion was between Jake Timmons, a coworker and their supervisor, Mark Andersen. They were in a heated discussion about one of the company's biggest clients, Patel Manufacturing.

An executive from Patel had contacted Mark to tell him that Jake had not been giving them the attention such a large client deserved. He claimed that Jake did not return phone calls and often missed appointments. Mark was furious about the situation and was demanding an explanation. Jake tried to explain that he was doing everything he could to effectively manage the account, but the breakdown was on the other end. John, his contact at Patel, was the problem. He rarely responded to any of Jake's calls or e-mail. Jake had thought about reporting him but didn't want to get him in trouble with his manager.

Mark seemed not to hear a word Jake was saying. He simply continued to accuse Jake of endangering their most important customer. As Pat listened to

this conversation, she considered whether or not she should get involved. It was obvious that Mark was not listening to anything Jake said. She had overheard Jake on several occasions trying to reach John without success. She could testify to that. But, she had worked with John herself and had never experienced any problems. Also, she had only Jake's word for just how bad things were. She really didn't know Jake very well, and what if he was really slacking on his end and using John as an excuse? She didn't want to add to the disparaging comments about John if they weren't true. But she also didn't think it was fair that Mark was not giving any credit to what Jake was trying to explain. She didn't want to get Mark angry at her but felt she needed to support Jake in some way.

QUESTIONS

1. Does Pat have a duty to support Jake?
2. Does she have a responsibility to John?
3. Evaluate Pat's decision using rule, virtue, rights, and justice theory.

EXPERIENTIAL EXERCISES

7.1 COMMUNICATE, LISTEN, UNDERSTAND

The following exercise gives you an opportunity to work within a three-person group to do a communication skill-building exercise. You can learn to apply some of the reflective listening and two-way

communication materials from the early sections of the chapter, as well as some of the lessons on managing difficult communication in a nondefensive manner.

Step 1. The class is formed into three-person groups, and each group designates its members "A," "B," and

"C." There will be three 5- to 7-minute conversations among the group members: first, between A and B; second, between B and C; third, between C and A. During each conversation, the nonparticipating group member is to observe and make notes about two communicating group members.

Step 2. Your instructor will give you a list of controversial topics and ask A to pick a topic. A is then asked to discuss her or his position on this topic, with the rationale for the position, with B. B is to practice reflective listening and engage in listening checks periodically by paraphrasing what he or she understands to be A's position. C should observe whether B is practicing good listening skills or becoming defensive. C should also observe whether A is becoming dominantly defensive in the communication. This should be a two-way communication.

Step 3. Repeat Step 2 with B as communicator, C as listener, and A as observer.

Step 4. Repeat Step 2 with C as communicator, A as listener, and B as observer.

Step 5. After your instructor has had all groups complete Steps 1 through 4, your three-person group should answer the following questions:

a. *Did either the listener or the communicator become visibly (or internally) angry or upset during the discussion?*

b. *What were the biggest challenges for the listeners in the controversial communication? For the communicator?*

c. *What are the most important skill improvements (e.g., better eye contact or more patience) the listener and communicator could have made to improve the quality of understanding achieved through the communication process?*

7.2 PREPARING FOR AN EMPLOYMENT-SELECTION INTERVIEW

The purpose of this exercise is to help you develop guidelines for an employment-selection interview. Employment-selection interviews are one of the more important settings in which supervisors and job candidates use applied communication skills. There is always the potential for defensiveness and

confusion as well as lack of complete information exchange in this interview. This exercise allows you to think through ways to maximize the value of an employment-selection interview, whether you are the supervisor or the candidate, so that it is a productive experience based on effective applied communication.

Your instructor will divide your class into groups of students. Each group should work through Steps 1 and 2 of the exercise.

Step 1. *Guidelines for the Supervisor*

Develop a set of guidelines for the supervisor in preparing for and then conducting an employment-selection interview. Consider the following questions in developing your guidelines:

a. What should the supervisor do before the interview?

b. How should the supervisor act and behave during the interview?

c. What should the supervisor do after the interview?

Step 2. *Guidelines for the Employee*

Develop another set of guidelines for the employee in preparing for and then being involved in an employment-selection interview. Consider the following questions in developing your guidelines:

a. What should the employee do before the interview?

b. How should the employee act and behave during the interview?

c. What should the employee do after the interview?

Once each group has developed the two sets of guidelines, the instructor will lead the class in a general discussion in which groups share and compare their guidelines. Consider the following questions during this discussion:

1. What similarities are there among the groups for each set of guidelines?

2. What unique or different guidelines have some of the groups developed?

3. What are essential guidelines for conducting an employment-selection interview?

8

Work Teams and Groups

LEARNING OBJECTIVES

After reading this chapter, you should be able to do the following:

: 1. Define *group* and *work team*.

: 2. Discuss four important aspects of group behavior.

: 3. Describe group formation, the four stages of a group's development, and the characteristics of a mature group.

: 4. Explain the role of task and maintenance functions in groups and teams.

: 5. Discuss diversity and creativity in teams.

THINKING AHEAD :: WHOLE FOODS MARKET, INC.

Team Member Excellence and Happiness

Whole Foods Market's motto "Whole Foods, Whole People, Whole Planet" emphasizes its dedication to its retail customers and employees. The company says that there is no place for the "us-versus-them" thinking that permeates some organizations. Employees at Whole Foods are referred to as *team members*, whether they are retail team members or "behind the scene" team members. The company strives to build positive and healthy relationships among all team members. Its goal is to achieve unity of vision and to build trust among team members in the organization while supporting a balanced life for each team member. The best way to achieve these aims, goals, and outcomes is to encourage participation and involvement at all levels of the business. Whole Foods does this by having a collective, team-oriented focus in much of its organizational life.

Whole Foods encourages teamwork in the organization along a number of dimensions. Self-directed teams meet regularly to discuss issues, solve problems, and appreciate each other's contributions to the business. Communication throughout the company is increased through team member forums and team member advisory groups. In addition, communication is enhanced through open-book, open-door, and open-people practices that build relationships and trust among team members. Team

member incentive programs, such as labor gainsharing, emphasize team-oriented behaviors as opposed to individual effort and achievement. The company's stock options and stock purchase plan further highlight this collective emphasis. These policies and practices aim to help each team member reach his or her full potential.

Despite the best efforts at teamwork in some organizations, an us-versus-them mentality does materialize. Whole Foods is the nation's largest non-union food retailer after Wal-Mart. Some unions would love to organize the large Whole Foods workforce, just as they would like to do in the case of Wal-Mart. Whole Foods' CEO John Mackey knows that this can happen when management does not listen to employees. When employees are not heard, they have a tendency to turn to unions for the sympathetic ear not available within the organization. While some managers and executives may not pay enough attention to employees throughout their organizations, others truly do care about their employees' attitudes, concerns, and feelings. In either case, employees who feel neglected, unheard, unappreciated, or in the more extreme cases, mistreated are highly likely to turn to unions to have their needs met.[1] Will the spirit of teamwork be strong enough at Whole Foods to fend off efforts by some employees to unionize?

Northrop Grumman was able to achieve teamwork among employees, customers, and partners through knowledge sharing in integrated product teams.[2] Not all teams and groups work face to face. In today's information age, advanced computer and telecommunications technologies enable organizations to be more flexible through the use of virtual teams.[3] Virtual teams also address new workforce demographics, enabling companies to access expertise and the best employees who may be located anywhere in the world. Whether a traditional group or a virtual team, groups and teams continue to play a vital role in organizational behavior and performance at work.

A *group* is two or more people having common interests, objectives, and continuing interaction. Table 8.1 summarizes the characteristics of a well-functioning,

1. Define *group* and *work team*.

group
Two or more people with common interests, objectives, and continuing interaction.

TABLE 8.1

Characteristics of a Well-Functioning, Effective Group

- The atmosphere tends to be relaxed, comfortable, and informal.
- The group's task is well understood and accepted by the members.
- The members listen well to one another; most members participate in a good deal of task-relevant discussion.
- People express both their feelings and their ideas.
- Conflict and disagreement are present and centered around ideas or methods, not personalities or people.
- The group is aware and conscious of its own operation and function.
- Decisions are usually based on consensus, not majority vote.
- When actions are decided, clear assignments are made and accepted by members of the group.

work team
A group of people with complementary skills who are committed to a common mission, performance goals, and approach for which they hold themselves mutually accountable.

effective group.[4] A **work team** is a group of people with complementary skills who are committed to a common mission, performance goals, and approach for which they hold themselves mutually accountable.[5] All work teams are groups, but not all groups are work teams. Groups emphasize individual leadership, individual accountability, and individual work products. Work teams emphasize shared leadership, mutual accountability, and collective work products.

2. Discuss four important aspects of group behavior.

⚎ GROUP BEHAVIOR

Group behavior has been a subject of interest in social psychology for a long time, and many different aspects of group behavior have been studied over the years. We now look at four topics relevant to groups functioning in organizations: norms of behavior, group cohesion, social loafing, and loss of individuality. Group behavior topics related to decision making, such as polarization and groupthink, are addressed in Chapter 9.

▮ NORMS OF BEHAVIOR

norms of behavior
The standards that a work group uses to evaluate the behavior of its members.

The standards that a work group uses to evaluate the behavior of its members are its **norms of behavior**. These norms may be written or unwritten, verbalized or not verbalized, implicit or explicit. As long as individual members of the group understand the norms, the norms can be effective in influencing behavior. Norms may specify what members of a group should do (such as a specified dress code for men and for women), or they may specify what members of a group should not do (such as executives not behaving arrogantly with employees).

Norms may exist in any aspect of work group life. They may evolve informally or unconsciously within a group, or they may arise in response to challenges, such as the norm of disciplined behavior by firefighters in responding to a three-alarm fire to protect the group.[6] Performance norms are among the most important group norms from the organization's perspective. For example, cooperative standards within teams lead to members working for mutual benefit, which in turn facilitate team performance.[7] We discuss performance standards further in a later section of this chapter. Organizational culture and corporate codes of ethics, such as Johnson & Johnson's credo (see Chapter 2), reflect behavioral norms expected within work groups. Finally, norms that create awareness of emotions and help regulate emotions are critical to groups' effectiveness.[8]

GROUP COHESION

The "interpersonal glue" that makes the members of a group stick together is *group cohesion*. Group cohesion can enhance job satisfaction for members and improve organizational productivity.[9] Highly cohesive groups are able to control and manage their membership better than work groups low in cohesion. In one study of 381 banking teams in Hong Kong and the United States, increased job complexity and task autonomy led to increased group cohesiveness, which translated into better performance.[10] In addition to performance, highly cohesive groups are strongly motivated to maintain good, close relationships among the members. We examine group cohesion in further detail, along with factors leading to high levels of group cohesion, when discussing the common characteristics of well-developed groups.

group cohesion
The "interpersonal glue" that makes members of a group stick together.

SOCIAL LOAFING

Social loafing occurs when one or more group members rely on the efforts of other group members and fail to contribute their own time, effort, thoughts, or other resources to a group.[11] This may create a real drag on the group's efforts and achievements. Some scholars argue that, from the individual's standpoint, social loafing, or free riding, is rational behavior in response to an experience of inequity or when individual efforts are hard to observe. However, it shortchanges the group, which loses potentially valuable resources possessed by individual members.[12]

A number of methods for countering social loafing exist, such as having identifiable individual contributions to the group product and member self-evaluation systems. For example, if each group member is responsible for a specific input to the group, a member's failure to contribute will be noticed by everyone. If members must formally evaluate their contributions to the group, they are less likely to loaf.

social loafing
The failure of a group member to contribute personal time, effort, thoughts, or other resources to the group.

◀◀**think critically**▶▶

Assume that someone in your work group is engaged in social loafing. What should you do? Is this person acting in an unethical manner?

LOSS OF INDIVIDUALITY

Social loafing may be detrimental to group achievement, but it does not have the potentially explosive effects of *loss of individuality*. Loss of individuality, or deindividuation, is a social process in which individual group members lose self-awareness and its accompanying sense of accountability, inhibition, and responsibility for individual behavior.[13]

When individuality is lost, people may engage in morally reprehensible acts and even violent behavior as committed members of their group or organization. For example, loss of individuality was one of several contributing factors in the violent and aggressive acts that led to the riot that destroyed sections of Los Angeles following the Rodney King verdict in the early 1990s. Loss of individuality is not always negative or destructive, however. The loosening of normal ego control

loss of individuality
A social process in which individual group members lose self-awareness and its accompanying sense of accountability, inhibition, and responsibility for individual behavior.

mechanisms in the individual may lead to prosocial behavior and heroic acts in dangerous situations.[14] A group that successfully develops into a mature group may not encounter problems with loss of individuality.

: 3. Describe group formation, the four stages of a group's development, and the characteristics of a mature group.

GROUP FORMATION AND DEVELOPMENT

After its formation, a group goes through predictable stages of development. If successful, it emerges as a mature group. One logical group development model proposes four stages following the group's formation.[15] These stages are mutual acceptance, decision making, motivation and commitment, and control and sanctions. To become a mature group, each of the stages in development must be successfully negotiated.

According to this group development model, a group addresses three issues: interpersonal issues, task issues, and authority issues.[16] The interpersonal issues include matters of trust, personal comfort, and security. The task issues include the mission or purpose of the group, the methods the group employs, and the outcomes expected of the group. The authority issues include decisions about who is in charge, how power and influence are managed, and who has the right to tell whom to do what. This section addresses group formation, each stage of group development, and the characteristics of a mature group.

GROUP FORMATION

Formal and informal groups form in organizations for different reasons. Formal groups are sometimes called official or assigned groups, and informal groups may be called unofficial or emergent groups. Formal groups gather to perform various tasks and include an executive and staff, standing committees of the board of directors, project task forces, and temporary committees. An example of a formal group was the task force that General Motor's Mike DiGiovanni put together to build the highly successful H2. He picked outspoken networkers, not those on top of the seniority lists, who then formed a very innovative, unconventional, and productive team.[17]

Diversity is an important consideration in the formation of groups. For example, Monsanto Agricultural Company, now simply Monsanto Company, created a task force titled Valuing Diversity to address subtle discrimination resulting from workforce diversity.[18] The original task force was titled Eliminating Subtle Discrimination (ESD) and was composed of 15 women, minorities, and white males. Subtle discrimination might include the use of gender- or culture-specific language. Monsanto and the task force's intent was to build on individual differences—whether in terms of gender, race, or culture—in developing a dominant heterogeneous culture. Diversity can enhance group performance. One study of gender diversity among U.S. workers found that men and women in gender-balanced groups had higher job satisfaction than those in homogeneous groups.[19]

Ethnic diversity has characterized many industrial work groups in the United States since the 1800s. This was especially true during the early years of the 1900s, when waves of immigrant workers arrived from Germany, Yugoslavia, Italy, Poland, Scotland, the Scandinavian countries, and many other nations. Organizations were challenged to blend these culturally and linguistically diverse peoples into effective work groups.

In addition to ethnic, gender, and cultural diversity, there is interpersonal diversity. Chaparral Steel Company (part of Texas Industries) has a team of officers who achieved compatibility through interpersonal diversity. Successful interpersonal relationships are the basis of group effort, a key foundation for business success. In the case of the Chaparral Steel officers, they differed in their needs for inclusion in activities, control of people and events, and interpersonal affection from others. Though diverse in their interpersonal needs, the officers as a group found strength through balance and complementarity.

Informal groups evolve in the work setting to gratify a variety of member needs not met by formal groups. For example, organizational members' inclusion and affection needs might be satisfied through informal athletic or interest groups. Athletic teams representing a department, unit, or company may achieve semiofficial status, such as the AT&T National Running Team that uses the corporate logo on its race shirts.

■ STAGES OF GROUP DEVELOPMENT

All groups, formal and informal, go through stages of development from forming interpersonal relationships among the members to becoming a mature and productive unit. Mature groups are able to work through the necessary interpersonal, task, and authority issues to achieve at high levels. Demographic diversity and group fault lines (i.e., potential breaking points in a group) are two potential predictors of the sense-making process, subgroup formation patterns, and nature of group conflict at various stages of group development.[20] Hence, group development through these stages may not always be smooth.

In addition to the Bennis and Shepard group development model, we want to look at two other group development models. These two well-known models are Tuckman's and Gersick's. Each of these models looks at the evolution of behavior in teams, and Tuckman's model also focuses on leadership.

THE FIVE-STAGE MODEL

Bruce Tuckman's model of group development proposes that team behavior progresses through five stages: forming, storming, norming, performing, and adjourning.[21] This may be especially true when people enter groups as factions in the form of twosomes or even threesomes. This often takes place during corporate mergers. The larger the demographic differences between the groups prior to the merger, the more likely that the combined group will experience increased emotional conflict, task conflict, and behavioral disintegration.[22] These stages and the emphasis on relationships and leadership styles in each are shown in Figure 8.1.

> **FIGURE 8.1**
>
> Tuckman's Five-Stage Model of Group Development

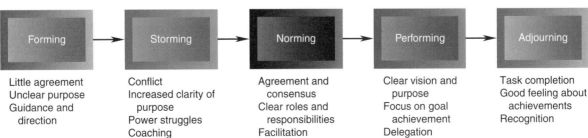

Forming	Storming	Norming	Performing	Adjourning
Little agreement Unclear purpose Guidance and direction	Conflict Increased clarity of purpose Power struggles Coaching	Agreement and consensus Clear roles and responsibilities Facilitation	Clear vision and purpose Focus on goal achievement Delegation	Task completion Good feeling about achievements Recognition

Dependence on guidance and direction is the defining characteristic in the *forming* stage. Team members are unclear about individual roles and responsibilities and tend to rely heavily on the leader to answer questions about the team's purpose, objectives, and external relationships. Moving from this stage requires that team members feel they are part of the team.

Team members compete for position in the *storming* stage. As the name suggests, this is a stage of considerable conflict as power struggles, cliques, and factions within the group begin to form. Clarity of purpose increases, but uncertainties still exist. This is also the stage when members assess one another with regard to trustworthiness, emotional comfort, and evaluative acceptance. For the Valuing Diversity task force at Monsanto, trust was one of the early issues to be worked through. A coaching style by the leader is key during this stage of group development as team members may challenge him or her.

Agreement and consensus are characteristic of team members in the *norming* stage. It is in this stage that roles and responsibilities become clear and accepted with big decisions being made by group agreement. The focus turns from interpersonal relations to decision-making activities related to the group's task accomplishment. Small decisions may be delegated to individuals or small teams within the group. The group addresses authority questions like these: Who is responsible for what aspects of the group's work? Does the group need one primary leader and spokesperson? Wallace Supply Company, an industrial distributor of pipes, valves, and fittings, has found employee teams particularly valuable in this aspect of work life.[23] Leadership is facilitative with some leadership responsibilities being shared by the team.

As a team moves into the *performing* stage, it becomes more strategically aware and clear about its mission and purpose. In this stage of development, the group has successfully worked through the necessary interpersonal, task, and authority issues and can stand on its own two feet with little interference from the leader. Primarily, the team makes decisions, and disagreements are resolved positively with necessary changes to structure and processes attended to by the team. A mature group is able to control its members through the judicious application of specific positive and negative sanctions based on the evaluation of specific member behaviors. Recent research shows that evaluation biases stemming from liking someone operate in face-to-face groups but not in electronic groups, such as virtual teams.[24] Members at this stage do not need to be instructed but may ask for assistance from the leader with personal or interpersonal development. The team requires a leader who delegates and oversees.

The final stage of group development is the *adjourning* stage. When the task is completed, everyone on the team can move on to new and different things. Team members have a sense of accomplishment and feel good knowing that their purpose is fulfilled. The leader's role is primarily one of recognition of the group's achievements. Unless the group is a task force or other informal team, most groups in organizations remain at the performing stage and do not disband as the adjourning stage suggests.

PUNCTUATED EQUILIBRIUM MODEL

Though it is still highly cited in team and group research, Tuckman's "forming–storming–norming–performing–adjourning" model may be unrealistic from an organizational perspective. In fact, research has shown that many teams experience relational conflicts at different times and in different contexts. Connie

Gersick proposes that groups do not necessarily progress linearly from one step to another in a predetermined sequence but alternate between periods of inertia with little visible progress toward goal achievement *punctuated* by bursts of energy as work groups develop. It is in these periods of energy where the majority of a group's work is accomplished.[25] For example, a task force given nine months to complete a task may use the first four months to choose its norms, explore contextual issues, and determine how it will communicate.

■ CHARACTERISTICS OF A MATURE GROUP

The description of a well-functioning, effective group in Table 8.1 characterizes a mature group. Such a group has four distinguishing characteristics: a clear purpose and mission, well-understood norms and standards of conduct, a high level of group cohesion, and a flexible status structure.

PURPOSE AND MISSION

The purpose and mission may be assigned to a group (as in the previous example of the team to build the H2) or emerge from within the group (as in the case of the AT&T National Running Team). Even in the case of an assigned mission, the group may reexamine, modify, revise, or question the mission. It may also embrace the mission as stated. The importance of mission is exemplified in IBM's Process Quality Management, which requires that a process team of not more than 12 people develop a clear understanding of mission as the first step in the process.[26] The IBM approach demands that all members agree to go in the same direction. The mission statement is converted into a specific agenda, clear goals, and a set of critical success factors. Stating the purpose and mission in the form of specific goals enhances productivity over and above any performance benefits achieved through individual goal setting.[27]

BEHAVIORAL NORMS

Behavioral norms, which evolve over a period of time, are well-understood standards of behavior within a group.[28] They are benchmarks against which team members are evaluated and judged by other team members. Some behavioral norms become written rules, such as an attendance policy or an ethical code for a team. Other norms remain informal, such as expressing positive appreciation toward team members as illustrated in the Whole Foods opening case. Behavioral norms also evolve around performance and productivity.[29] Productivity norms even influence the performance of sports teams.[30] The group's productivity norm may or may not be consistent with, and supportive of, the organization's productivity standards. A high-performance team sets productivity standards above organizational expectations with the intent to excel. Average teams set productivity standards based on, and consistent with, organizational expectations. Noncompliant or counterproductive teams may set productivity standards below organizational expectations with the intent of damaging the organization or creating change.

GROUP COHESION

Group cohesion was earlier described as the interpersonal attraction binding group members together. It enables a group to exercise effective control over its members in relation to its behavioral norms and standards. Goal conflict in a group, unpleasant experiences, and domination of a subgroup are among the threats to a

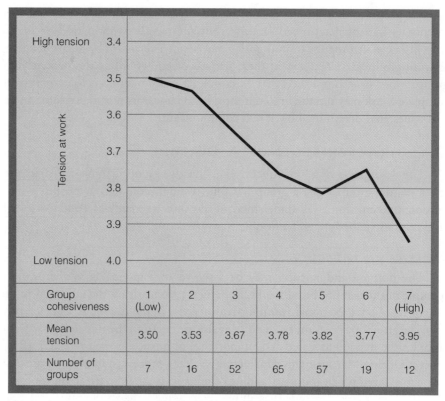

FIGURE 8.2

Cohesiveness and Work-Related Tension*

Group cohesiveness	1 (Low)	2	3	4	5	6	7 (High)
Mean tension	3.50	3.53	3.67	3.78	3.82	3.77	3.95
Number of groups	7	16	52	65	57	19	12

Note: Product-moment correlation is .28, and critical ratio is 4.20; p is less than .001.

*The measure of tension at work is based on group mean response to the question "Does your work ever make you feel 'jumpy' or nervous?" A low numerical score represents relatively high tension.

SOURCE: From S. E. Seashore, *Group Cohesiveness in the Industrial Work Group*, 1954. Research conducted by Stanley E. Seashore at the Institute for Social Research, University of Michigan. Reprinted by permission.

group's cohesion. Groups with low levels of cohesion have greater difficulty exercising control over their members and enforcing their standards of behavior. A classic study of cohesiveness in 238 industrial work groups found cohesion to be an important factor influencing anxiety, tension, and productivity within the groups.[31] Specifically, work-related tension and anxiety were lower in teams high in cohesion, and they were higher in teams low in cohesion, as depicted in Figure 8.2. This suggests that cohesion has a calming effect on team members, at least concerning work-related tension and anxiety. In addition, actual productivity was found to vary significantly less in highly cohesive teams, making these teams much more predictable with regard to their productivity. The actual productivity levels were primarily determined by the productivity norms within each work group. That is, highly cohesive groups with high production standards are very productive. Similarly, highly cohesive groups with low productivity standards are unproductive. Member satisfaction, commitment, and communication are better in highly cohesive groups. Groupthink may be a problem in highly cohesive groups and is discussed in Chapter 9. New research found that groups that had more surface-level diversity were more persistent and confident at voicing dissenting perspectives.[32] Challenge 8.1 includes the three group cohesion questions from Seashore's research project. Complete Challenge 8.1 to determine the level of cohesion in a group of which you are a member.

CHALLENGE   8.1

How Cohesive Is Your Group?

Think about a group of which you are a member. Answer each of the following questions in relation to this group by circling the number next to the alternative that most reflects your feelings.

1. Do you feel that you are really a part of your group?
   5—Really a part of the group.
   4—Included in most ways.
   3—Included in some ways, but not in others.
   2—Do not feel I really belong.
   1—Do not work with any one group of people.

2. If you had a chance to do the same activities in another group, for the same pay if it is a work group, how would you feel about moving?
   1—Would want very much to move.
   2—Would rather move than stay where I am.
   3—Would make no difference to me.
   4—Would rather stay where I am than move.
   5—Would want very much to stay where I am.

3. How does your group compare with other groups that you are familiar with on each of the following points?
   - The way people get along together.
     5—Better than most.
     3—About the same as most.
     1—Not as good as most.
   - The way people stick together.
     5—Better than most.
     3—About the same as most.
     1—Not as good as most.
   - The way people help one another on the job.
     5—Better than most.
     3—About the same as most.
     1—Not as good as most.

Add up your circled responses. If you have a number of 20 or above, you view your group as highly cohesive. If you have a number between 10 and 19, you view your group's cohesion as average. If you have a number of 7 or less, you view your group as very low in cohesion.

Source: From S. E. Seashore, *Group Cohesiveness in the Industrial Work Group,* University of Michigan, 1954. Reprinted by permission.

Group cohesion is influenced by a number of factors, most notably time, size, the prestige of the team, external pressure, and internal competition. Group cohesion evolves gradually over time through a group's normal development. Smaller groups—those of five or seven members, for example—are more cohesive than those of more than 25, although cohesion does not decline much with size after 40 or more members. Prestige or social status also influences a group's cohesion, with more prestigious groups, such as the U.S. Air Force Thunderbirds or the U.S. Navy Blue Angels, being highly cohesive. However, even groups of very low prestige may be highly cohesive in how they stick together. Finally, external pressure and internal competition influence group cohesion. Although the mechanics' union, pilots, and other internal constituencies at Eastern Airlines had various differences of opinion, they all pulled together in a cohesive fashion in resisting Frank Lorenzo when he came in to reshape the airline before its demise. Whereas external pressures tend to enhance cohesion, internal competition usually decreases cohesion within a team. One study found that company-imposed work pressure disrupted group cohesion by increasing internal competition and reducing cooperative interpersonal activity.[33]

STATUS STRUCTURE

status structure
The set of authority and task relations among a group's members.

Status structure is the set of authority and task relations among a group's members. The status structure may be hierarchical or egalitarian (i.e., democratic), depending on the group. Successful resolution of the authority issue within a team results in a well-understood status structure of leader–follower relationships. Where leadership problems arise, it is important to find solutions and build team leader effectiveness.[34] Whereas groups tend to have one leader, teams tend to share leadership. For example, one person may be the team's task master who sets the agenda, initiates much of the work activity, and ensures that the team meets its deadlines. Another team member may take a leadership role in maintaining effective interpersonal relationships in the group. Hence, shared leadership is very feasible in teams. An effective status structure results in role interrelatedness among group members.

Diversity in a group is healthy, and members may contribute to the collective effort through one of four basic styles.[35] These are the contributor, the collaborator, the communicator, and the challenger. The contributor is data driven, supplies necessary information, and adheres to high performance standards. The collaborator sees the big picture and is able to keep a constant focus on the mission and urge other members to join efforts for mission accomplishment. The communicator listens well, facilitates the group's process, and humanizes the collective effort. The challenger is the devil's advocate who questions everything from the group's mission, purpose, and methods to its ethics. Members may exhibit one or more of these four basic styles over a period of time. In addition, an effective group must have an integrator.[36] This can be especially important in cross-functional teams, where different perspectives carry the seeds of conflict. However, cross-functional teams are not necessarily a problem. Effectively managing cross-functional teams of artists, designers, printers, and financial experts enabled Hallmark Cards to cut its new-product development time in half.[37]

Emergent leadership in groups was studied among 62 men and 60 women.[38] Groups performed tasks not classified as either masculine or feminine, that is, "sex-neutral" tasks. Men and women both emerged as leaders, and neither gender had significantly more emergent leaders. However, group members who described themselves in masculine terms were significantly more likely to emerge as leaders than group members who described themselves in feminine, androgynous (both masculine and feminine), or undifferentiated (neither masculine nor feminine) terms. Hence, gender stereotypes may play a role in emergent leadership.

4. Explain the role of task and maintenance functions in groups and teams.

psychological intimacy
Emotional and psychological closeness to other team or group members.

integrated involvement
Closeness achieved through tasks and activities.

■ TASK AND MAINTENANCE FUNCTIONS

An effective group or team carries out various task functions to perform its work successfully and various maintenance functions to ensure member satisfaction and a sense of team spirit.[39] Task and maintenance functions help groups and teams achieve *psychological intimacy* and *integrated involvement*, both of which are social benefits of successful group and team membership and are important contributors to their overall health. Teams that successfully fulfill these functions afford their members the potential for psychological intimacy and integrated involvement. Table 8.2 presents nine task and nine maintenance functions in teams or groups.

TASK FUNCTIONS	MAINTENANCE FUNCTIONS
Initiating activities	Supporting others
Seeking information	Following others' leads
Giving information	Gatekeeping communication
Elaborating concepts	Setting standards
Coordinating activities	Expressing member feelings
Summarizing ideas	Testing group decisions
Testing ideas	Consensus testing
Evaluating effectiveness	Harmonizing conflict
Diagnosing problems	Reducing tension

TABLE 8.2

Task and Maintenance Functions in Teams or Groups

Task functions are those activities directly related to the effective completion of the team's work. For example, the task of initiating activity involves suggesting ideas, defining problems, and proposing approaches and/or solutions to problems. As we saw in the opening case, one of the key tasks of work teams at Whole Foods is to solve problems. The task of seeking information involves asking for ideas, suggestions, information, or facts. Effective teams have members who fulfill various task functions as they are required.

Some task functions are more important at one time in the life of a group, and other functions are more important at other times. For example, during the engineering test periods for new technologies, the engineering team needs members who focus on testing the practical applications of suggestions and those who diagnose problems and suggest solutions.

The effective use of task functions leads to the success of the group, and the failure to use them may lead to disaster. For example, the successful initiation and coordination of an emergency room (ER) team's activities by the senior resident saved the life of a knife wound victim.[40] The victim was stabbed one-quarter inch below the heart, and the ER team acted quickly to stem the bleeding, begin intravenous fluids, and monitor the victim's vital signs.

Maintenance functions are those activities essential to the effective, satisfying interpersonal relationships within a group or team. For example, following another group member's lead may be as important as leading others. Communication gatekeepers within a group ensure balanced contributions from all members. Because task activities build tension into teams and groups working together, tension-reduction activities are important to drain off negative or destructive feelings. For example, in a study of 25 work groups over a five-year period, humor and joking behavior were found to enhance the social relationships in the groups.[41] The researchers concluded that performance improvements in the 25 groups indirectly resulted from improved relationships attributable to the humor and joking behaviors. Maintenance functions enhance togetherness, cooperation, and teamwork, enabling members to achieve psychological intimacy while furthering the success of the team. Jody Grant's supportive attitude and comfortable demeanor as chairman and CEO of Texas Capital Bancshares enabled him to build a vibrant bank in the aftermath of the great Texas banking crash. Grant was respected for his expertise *and* his ability to build relationships.

task function
An activity directly related to the effective completion of a team's work.

maintenance function
An activity essential to effective, satisfying interpersonal relationships within a team or group.

◢ WORK TEAMS IN ORGANIZATIONS

Work teams are task-oriented groups, though in some organizations the term *team* has a negative connotation for unions and union members. Work teams make important and valuable contributions to the organization and are important to members need satisfaction. For example, an idea to implement a simple change in packaging from a work team at Glenair, a UK-based aerospace and defense contractor, saved the company 25 minutes of packaging time per unit. Additionally, a job that used to take one worker half an hour to complete was reduced to only five minutes, freeing the worker to perform other work in the factory.[42]

Several kinds of work teams exist. One classification scheme uses a sports analogy. Some teams work like baseball teams with set responsibilities, other teams work like football teams through coordinated action, and still other teams work like doubles tennis teams with primary yet flexible responsibilities. In addition, crews are a distinct type of work teams that can be studied using the concept of "crewness."[43] Although each type of team may have a useful role in the organization, the individual expert should not be overlooked.[44] That is, at the right time and in the right context, individual members must be allowed to shine. A relatively new form of team is called an action-learning team (ALT). These types of teams are typically found in telecom companies where team members are charged with developing special capabilities to close process gaps or generate new processes where none existed.[45]

▪ WHY WORK TEAMS?

Teams are very useful in performing work that is complicated, complex, interrelated, and/or more voluminous than one person can handle. Harold Geneen, while chairman of ITT, said, "If I had enough arms and legs and time, I'd do it all myself." Obviously, people working in organizations cannot do everything because of the limitations of arms, legs, time, expertise, knowledge, and other resources. Individual limitations are overcome and problems are solved through teamwork and collaboration. World-class U.S. corporations, such as Motorola Inc., are increasingly deploying work teams in their global affiliates to meet the competition and gain an advantage.[46] Motorola's "Be Cool" team in the Philippines has a family atmosphere and may even begin a meeting with a prayer, yet is committed to improving individual and team performance.

teamwork
Joint action by a team of people in which individual interests are subordinated to team unity.

Teams make important contributions to organizations in work areas that lend themselves to teamwork. *Teamwork* is a core value at Hewlett-Packard. Complex, interdependent work tasks and activities that require collaboration particularly lend themselves to teamwork. A study of 92 teams in a U.S. Air Force officer training program found that team members with a greater mastery of teamwork concepts were better at solving team-level tasks and were more effective overall.[47] Teams are appropriate where knowledge, talent, skills, and abilities are dispersed across organizational members and require integrated effort for task accomplishment. The recent emphasis on team-oriented work environments is based on empowerment with collaboration, not on power and competition. Larry Hirschhorn labels this "the new team environment" founded on a significantly more empowered workforce in the industrial sectors of the American economy. This new team environment is compared with the old work environment in Table 8.3. The spirit of teamwork can also improve worker satisfaction particularly if they have a common purpose. One example of this is the employees at the World Wildlife

NEW TEAM ENVIRONMENT	OLD WORK ENVIRONMENT
Person comes up with initiatives.	Person follows orders.
Team has considerable authority to chart its own steps.	Team depends on the manager to chart its course.
Members form a team because people learn to collaborate in the face of their emerging right to think for themselves. People both rock the boat and work together.	Members were a team because people conformed to direction set by the manager. No one rocked the boat.
People cooperate by using their thoughts and feelings. They link up through direct talk.	People cooperated by suppressing their thoughts and feelings. They wanted to get along.

TABLE 8.3

A Comparison of the New Team Environment versus the Old Work Environment

SOURCE: Larry Hirschhorn, *Managing in the New Team Environment* (Englewood Cliffs, NJ: Prentice Hall, 1991), 13.

Fund (WWF).[48] While the IT team members at WWF bonded particularly well, it was not because they did specific team-building activities like whitewater rafting. Rather, it was because of their unity and a common purpose in their work.

That teams are necessary is a driving principle of total quality efforts in organizations. Total quality efforts often require the formation of teams—especially cross-functional teams composed of people from different functions, such as manufacturing and design, who are responsible for specific organizational processes. Former Eastman Kodak CEO George Fisher believed in the importance of participation and cooperation as foundations for teamwork and a total quality program. In a study of 40 machine crews in a northeastern U.S. paper mill, organizational citizenship behaviors, specifically helping behavior and sportsmanship, contributed significantly to the quantity and quality of work group performance.[49]

■ WORK TEAM STRUCTURE AND WORK TEAM PROCESS

Work team effectiveness in the new team environment requires attention by management to both work team structure and work team process.[50] The primary structural issues for work teams are goals and objectives, operating guidelines, performance measures, and the specification of roles. A work team's goals and objectives specify what must be achieved, while the operating guidelines set the organizational boundaries and decision-making limits within which the team must function. The goal-setting process was discussed in Chapter 6 and has applicability for work teams, too. In addition to these two structural elements, the work team needs to know what performance measures are being used to assess its task accomplishment. For example, a medical emergency team's performance measures might include the success rate in saving critically injured patients and the average number of hours a patient is in the emergency room before being transferred to a hospital bed. Finally, work team structure requires a clearly specified set of roles for the executives and managers who oversee the work of the team, for the work team leaders who exercise influence over team members, and for team members. These role specifications should include information about required role behaviors, such as decision making and task performance, as well as restrictions or limits on role behaviors, such as the limitations on managerial interventions in work team activities and decision making. Expectations as well as experience may be especially important for newcomer role performance in work teams.[51]

Work team process is the second important dimension of effectiveness. Two of the important process issues in work teams are the managing of cooperative behaviors and the managing of competitive behaviors. Both sets of behaviors are helpful in task accomplishment, and they should be viewed as complementary sets of behaviors. Cooperative teamwork skills include open communication, trust, personal integrity, positive interdependence, and mutual support. On the other hand, positive competitive teamwork skills include the ability to enjoy competition, play fair, be a good winner or loser; to have access to information for monitoring where the team and members are in the competition; and not to overgeneralize or exaggerate the results of any specific competition. In a study of reward structures in 75 four-member teams, competitive rewards enhanced speed of performance, while cooperative rewards enhanced accuracy of performance.[52]

Work team process issues have become more complex in the global workplace with teams composed of members from many cultures and backgrounds. This is enhanced by the presence of virtual work teams operating on the global landscape. Our discussions of diversity earlier in the text have particular relevance to multicultural work teams. In addition to the process issues of cooperation, competition, and diversity, two other process issues are related to topics we discuss elsewhere in the text. These are team decision making, which is discussed in Chapter 9; and conflict management and resolution, which are discussed in Chapter 12.

◀◀ think critically ▶▶

Suppose a team leader makes a mistake at your place of work that damages some property but does not hurt anyone. Assuming the employee was empowered to act, should the team leader be punished for the unfortunate consequences of the action? Would your answer differ depending on whether the team leader had been properly trained and given a set of guidelines for action before being made a team leader?

5. Discuss diversity and creativity in teams.

🔲 DIVERSITY AND CREATIVITY IN TEAMS

Diversity and creativity are important, emerging issues in the study of teams and teamwork. Recent research in diversity has focused on the issue of dissimilarity and its effect within the team itself. This is often studied based on social identity theory and self-categorization theory. Creativity concerns new and/or dissimilar ideas or ways of doing things within teams. Novelty and innovation are creativity's companions. While creativity is developed in some detail in Chapter 9, we treat it briefly here in the context of teams.

▮ DISSIMILARITY

We defined diversity in Chapter 1 in terms of individual differences. Recent relational demography research finds that demographic dissimilarity influences employees' absenteeism, commitment, turnover intentions, beliefs, work group relationships, self-esteem, and organizational citizenship behavior (OCB).[53] Thus, dissimilarity may have positive or negative effects in teams and on team members. While value dissimilarity may be positively related to task and relationship conflict, it is negatively related to team involvement.[54] This highlights the importance of managing dissimilarity in teams, being open to diversity, and turning conflicts over ideas into positive outcomes.

Functional background is one way to look at dissimilarity in teams. One study of 262 professionals in 37 cross-functional teams found that promoting functional background social identification helped individuals perform better as team members.[55] Another study of multifunctional management teams in a *Fortune* 100 company found that functional background predicted team involvement.[56] Finally, in a slightly different study of 129 members on 20 multidisciplinary project teams, informational dissimilarity had no adverse effects when there was member task and goal congruence.[57] Where there was incongruence, dissimilarity adversely affected team identification and OCBs.

CREATIVITY

Creativity is often thought of in an individual context rather than a team context. However, there is such a thing as team creativity. In a study of 54 research and development teams, one study found that team creativity scores would be explained by aggregation processes across both people and time.[58] The investigators concluded that it is important to consider aggregation across time as well as aggregation across individuals when one is attempting to understand team creativity.

Some think that the deck is stacked against teams as agents of creativity. Leigh Thompson thinks differently and suggests that team creativity and divergent thinking can be enhanced through greater diversity in teams, brainwriting, training facilitators, membership change in teams, electronic brainstorming, and building a playground.[59] These practices can overcome social loafing, conformity, and downward norm setting in teams and organizations. Team members might exercise care in timing the insertion of their novel ideas into the team process so as to maximize the positive impact and benefits.[60] Challenge 8.2 provides you an opportunity to assess the creativity in your team.

CHALLENGE **8.2**

Creativity in Teams

Think back to a time when you were a member of an especially creative team. This might have been at work or at school.

1. What was it about the makeup of the team that made it so creative?

2. What member behaviors, including yours, helped or hindered the creative process?

3. What did you learn about teamwork and creativity in this team?

⚑ MANAGERIAL IMPLICATIONS: TEAMWORK FOR PRODUCTIVITY AND QUALITY

Work groups and teams are important vehicles through which organizations achieve high-quality performance. The current emphasis on the new team environment, shown in Table 8.3, places unique demands on managers, teams, and individuals in leading, working, and managing. Managing these demands requires an understanding of individual diversity and the interrelationships of individuals, teams, and managers, as depicted in the triangle in Figure 8.3. Expectations associated with these three key organizational roles for people at work are different. The first role is as an individual, empowered employee. The second is as an active member of one or more teams. The third is the role of manager or formal supervisor. Earlier in the chapter, we discussed the foundations for teamwork, empowerment, and working in the new team environment. Individual empowerment must be balanced with collaborative teamwork.

The manager in the triangle is responsible for creating a receptive organizational environment for work groups and teams. This requires that the manager achieve a balance between setting limits (so that individuals and teams do not go too far afield) and removing barriers (so that empowered individuals and self-managed teams can accomplish their work). In addition, the manager should establish a flexible charter for each team. Once the charter is established, the manager continues to be available to the team as a coaching resource, as necessary. The manager establishes criteria for evaluating the performance effectiveness of the team, as well as the individuals, being supervised. In an optimum environment, this involves useful and timely performance feedback to teams that carries a sense of equity and fairness with it. The manager's responsibilities are different from the team leader's.

Effective team leaders may guide a work group or share leadership responsibility with their teams, especially self-managed teams. Team leaders

FIGURE 8.3

The Triangle for Managing in the New Team Environment

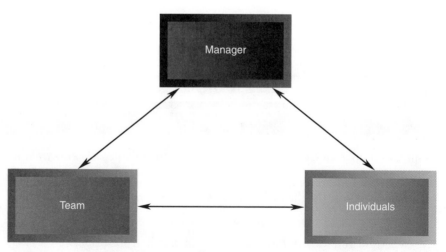

SOURCE: Larry Hirschhorn, *Managing in the New Team Environment* (Englewood Cliffs, NJ: Prentice Hall, 1991), 14. Copyright © 2002 by Larry Hirschhorn. Reprinted by permission of the author.

are active team members with responsibility for nurturing the development and performance of the team.[61] They require skills different from those of the manager. Whereas the manager establishes the environment in which teams flourish, the team leader teaches, listens, solves problems, manages conflict, and enhances the dynamics of team functioning to ensure the team's success. It is the team leader's task to bring the team to maturity; help the team work through interpersonal, task, and authority issues; and be skilled in nurturing a cohesive, effective team. A team leader requires the hands-on skills of direct involvement and full membership in the team. Flexibility, delegation, and collaboration are characteristics of healthy teams and team leaders. Increasing globalization requires team leaders to be skilled at forging teamwork among diverse individuals, whereas managers must be skilled at forging collaboration among diverse groups.

LOOKING BACK :: WHOLE FOODS MARKET, INC.

Empowerment, Trust, and Open Communication

Whole Foods uses no preservatives in its foods and keeps natural products at the center of its business model. John Mackey wants the same in Whole Foods' employees—natural and with no preservatives. In this vein, he believes in empowering his employees through open communication and trust. Open communication and trust are founded on the sharing and exchange of influence and power. These principles assume the existence of a common purpose and a common interest for all concerned. The greatest benefits of teamwork come when team members operate out of common interest and not self-interest. In an ideal world, and in a healthy organization, the common interest of all and the self-interest of the individual are joined as one. In a healthy, team-based organization, empowered employees act in the best interests of all concerned!

Whole Foods has no unions, and John Mackey is opposed to unionization because of the risks its poses for the spirit of teamwork in the company. Unions may have a place in some organizations, but the potential exists for union leadership to become a self-interested power center in conflict with the interests of management. Debbie Rasmussen was fired by Whole Foods for breaking the rules and store policy in the Madison, Wisconsin, store. Rasmussen claims she was fired for pro-union activism. Regardless of who is right and who is not in this conflict, teamwork is damaged. However, management cannot go too far either. Whole Foods has put a ceiling on executive pay such that no executive can earn cash pay more than 14 times what its average employee makes. Balancing employee and executive interests is important.

Companies often get the type of union that management deserves whenever the unionization process first occurs. In a healthy organization with open communication and trust, management is able to hear employee concerns and/or grievances in such a way that they become addressed for a win–win outcome. John Mackey clearly understood this and recognized that Whole Foods may have neglected its team members over a several-year period. He also recognized that the concern for team members could be put back in balance. One example of how the company did that was by allowing employees to vote on benefit plans to choose how much money individuals might allocate for everything from health care to tuition reimbursement. Organizations that give employees voice, such as this example at Whole Foods, are able to preclude the need for a union in the first place. When management addresses employee concerns and employees support management direction and plans, then the organization truly is operating within the spirit and the practice of teamwork.[62]

C H A P T E R   S U M M A R Y

1. Groups are often composed of diverse people at work. Teams in organizations are a key to enhance quality and achieve success.

2. Important aspects of group behavior include norms of behavior, group cohesion, social loafing, and loss of individuality.

3. Once a group forms, it generally goes through five stages of development. If successful, the group can function independently, with little interference from its leader.

4. Effective teams and groups carry out various task and maintenance functions to ensure member satisfaction and a sense of team spirit.

Success at fulfilling these functions affords team members the potential for psychological intimacy and integrated involvement.

5. Functional and value dissimilarity may have positive or negative effects on teams. Managing dissimilarity in teams and being open to diversity is highly important for promoting creativity.

6. Managing in the new team environment places new demands on managers, teams, and individuals. Managers must create a supportive and flexible environment for collaborative teams and empowered individuals. Team leaders must nurture the team's development.

K E Y   T E R M S

group (p. 201)
group cohesion (p. 203)
integrated involvement (p. 210)
loss of individuality (p. 203)

maintenance function (p. 211)
norms of behavior (p. 202)
psychological intimacy (p. 210)
social loafing (p. 203)

status structure (p. 210)
task function (p. 211)
teamwork (p. 212)
work team (p. 202)

R E V I E W   Q U E S T I O N S

1. What is a group? A work team?

2. Explain four aspects of group behavior. How can each aspect help or hinder the group's functioning?

3. Describe what happens in each stage of a group's development according to Tuckman's five-stage model. What are the leadership requirements in each stage?

4. Describe the four characteristics of mature groups.

5. Why are work teams important to organizations today? How and why are work teams formed?

6. Describe at least five task and five maintenance functions that effective work teams must perform.

7. Discuss diversity and creativity in teams.

8. What are the benefits and potential drawbacks of self-managed teams?

9. What is the role of the manager in the new team environment? What is the role of the team leader?

Discussion and Communication Q U E S T I O N S

1. Which was the most effective group (or team) of which you have been a member? What made that group (or team) so effective?

2. Have you ever experienced peer pressure to act more in accordance with the behavioral norms of a group? Have you ever engaged in a little

social loafing? Have you ever lost your head and been caught up in a group's destructive actions?

3. Name a company that successfully uses teamwork and empowerment. What has that company done that makes it so successful at teamwork and empowerment? Has its team approach made a difference in its performance? How?

4. Name a person you think is a particularly good team member. What makes this person a good team member? Name a person who is a problem as a team member. What makes this person a problem?

5. Think about your current work environment. Does your work environment use self-managed teams? What are the barriers to teamwork and empowerment in that environment? What elements of the environment enhance or encourage teamwork and empowerment? (If you do not work, discuss this question with a friend who does.)

6. (*communication question*) Prepare a memo describing your observations about work teams and groups in your workplace or your university. Where have you observed teams or groups to be most effective? Why? What changes might be made at work or in the university to make teams more effective?

7. (*communication question*) Develop an oral presentation about what the most important norms of behavior should be in an academic community and workplace. Be specific. Discuss how these norms should be established and reinforced.

8. (*communication question*) Interview an employee or manager about what he or she believes contributes to cohesiveness in work groups and teams. Ask the person what the conclusions are based on. Be prepared to discuss what you have learned in class.

E T H I C A L   D I L E M M A

Greg Towns and Michele Brown sat chatting. Michele had come to Greg's office to discuss the first meeting of the strategic planning team. Michele had found out only last week that she would be the team leader for this very important project. Recently, upper management had discovered that many of their employees didn't feel that their needs, desires, or capabilities were being considered in the formation of company goals. In response, the president had requested that a team of employees be formed to provide employee input for the new plan.

This would be Michele's first time in a leadership position. She was excited, especially since she had been handpicked by the president. She had come to Greg's office to ask for his support in the meetings. Michele did not have confidence in her leadership skills and wanted to know that she could count on someone to back her. Greg confidently assured Michele that she could count on him.

Everyone was excited as the meeting began. They were all happy to be working for a company that cared enough about its employees to create this committee. Michele began the meeting by reminding everyone why they were called together. She felt this was their time to shine for management.

People began offering suggestions. Michele dismissed the first two as too broad. The third she called juvenile. The room fell silent. Michele was surprised by the silence and asked if everyone was out of suggestions. Allen Jamison finally spoke up. He told Michele that no one wanted to make suggestions if she was just going to shoot down every idea. Michele denied that she was discounting the others' ideas. She just wanted to be sure that they sent management their very best suggestions. Michele looked to Greg, waiting for the promised support.

Greg felt trapped. He agreed with Allen. Michele's behavior did not encourage input. She was acting like a dictator, not a team leader. He had promised to support her, but he never dreamt that she would act this way. Supporting her behavior went against his beliefs. But he had promised.

QUESTIONS

1. How would Greg's promise to support Michele still hold given Michele's behavior?

2. Evaluate Greg's decision using rule, virtue, rights, and justice theory.

E X P E R I E N T I A L   E X E R C I S E S

8.1 TOWER BUILDING: A GROUP DYNAMICS ACTIVITY

This exercise gives you an opportunity to study group dynamics in a task-oriented situation. Each group must bring materials to class for building a tower. All materials must fit in a box no greater than eight cubic feet (i.e., 2 ft. × 2 ft. × 2 ft. or 1 ft. × 2 ft. × 4 ft.).

Step 1. Each group is assigned a meeting place and a workplace. One or two observers should be assigned in each group. The instructor may assign a manager to each group.

Step 2. Each group plans for the building of the paper tower (no physical construction is allowed during this planning period). Towers will be judged on the basis of height, stability, beauty, and meaning. (Another option is to have the groups do the planning outside of class and come prepared to build the tower.)

Step 3. Each group constructs its tower.

Step 4. Groups inspect other towers, and all individuals rate towers other than their own. See the evaluation sheet at the right. Each group turns in its point totals (i.e., someone in the group adds up each person's total for all groups rated) to the instructor, and the instructor announces the winner.

Step 5. Group dynamics analysis. Observers report observations to their own groups, and each group analyzes the group dynamics that occurred during the planning and building of the tower.

Step 6. Groups report on major issues in group dynamics that arose during the tower planning and building. Complete the tower building aftermath questionnaire as homework if requested by your instructor.

CRITERIA	GROUPS							
	1	2	3	4	5	6	7	8
Height								
Stability/Strength								
Beauty								
Meaning/Significance								
TOTALS								

Rate each criterion on a scale of 1–10, with 1 being lowest or poorest, and 10 being highest or best.

SOURCE: Andrew D. Szilagyi and Marc J. Wallace, *Organizational Behavior and Performance*, 5/e, © 1997. Adapted by permission of Pearson Education, Inc., Upper Saddle River, NJ.

8.2 DESIGN A TEAM

The following exercise gives you an opportunity to design a team. Working in a six-person group, address the individual characteristics, team composition, and norms for an effective group whose task is to make recommendations on improving customer relations. The president of a small clothing manufacturer is concerned that his customers are not satisfied enough with the company's responsiveness, product quality, and returned-orders process. He has asked your group to put together a team to address these problems.

Step 1. The class will form into groups of approximately six members each. Each group elects a spokesperson and answers the following questions. The group should spend an equal amount of time on each question.

a. *What characteristics should the individual members of the task team possess?*

Members may consider professional competence, skills, department, and/or personality and behavioral characteristics in the group's discussion.

b. *What should the composition of the task team be?* Once your group has addressed individual characteristics, consider the overall composition of the task team. Have special and/or unique competencies, knowledge, skills, and abilities been considered in your deliberations?

c. *What norms of behavior do you think the task team should adopt?* A team's norms of behavior may evolve, or they may be consciously discussed and agreed upon. Take the latter approach.

Step 2. Each group will share the results of its answers to the questions in Step 1. Cross-team questions and discussion follow.

Decision Making by Individuals and Groups

LEARNING OBJECTIVES

After reading this chapter, you should be able to do the following:

: **1.** Explain the assumptions of bounded rationality.

: **2.** Describe and evaluate the role of intuition and creativity in decision making.

: **3.** Critique your own level of creativity and list ways of improving it.

: **4.** Compare and contrast the advantages and disadvantages of group decision making.

: **5.** Discuss the symptoms of groupthink and ways to prevent it.

: **6.** Evaluate the strengths and weaknesses of several group decision-making techniques.

: **7.** Explain the emerging role of virtual decision making in organizations.

: **8.** Utilize an "ethics check" for examining managerial decisions.

THINKING AHEAD :: DISNEY-PIXAR ANIMATION STUDIOS

The Fairy Tale Success of Pixar

Pixar is now owned by Disney and is a household name synonymous with family entertainment at its finest. Pixar extends from a solid platform of computer-generated special effects with roots in the 1970s revolution in computer graphics. While Disney had its fingers everywhere—in radio, television, and theme parks—Pixar had released only seven features since its 1995 debut with *Toy Story* until 2006. At the same time, Disney was struggling to compete with Pixar's creative genius. The only films that were truly successful were the ones that Disney distributed for Pixar. Finally, Disney made a strategic decision in 2006 by acquiring Pixar, thus combining the creative firepower and financial horsepower of two animation giants. Like most acquisitions, this story has its twists and turns. For example, Pixar laid out certain conditions prior to signing the deal. For example, Pixar insisted that all of its primary directors and creative executives were to join the newly formed Disney-Pixar. It would also get to keep the Pixar culture and brand name alive by retaining its original offices and Pixar University. Every movie released thereafter would be from "Disney-Pixar."

One might wonder how a small animation powerhouse such as Pixar can get to be such an invaluable asset for Disney. The success of Pixar can be traced at least in part to the extraordinary management style of one person at Pixar: Ed Catmull. He is now president of the combined Disney-Pixar Animation Studios. His ascent to the presidency and the work he leads is in some ways an unlikely story. As with most healthy children, Ed had a dream growing up. His dream was to be a Disney animator. Unfortunately, he was confronted with the reality of his limited drawing abilities. During Ed's childhood, animation was done by gifted artists who drew Mickey Mouse, Donald Duck, Minnie Mouse, and Goofy. These animators were the cornerstones for the whole fantasy and dream world that Walt Disney imagined and then created. Fortunately for Ed Catmull, animation did not remain trapped in a time warp, and his own career redirection became a detour that ultimately led him back to the fulfillment of his dream. Ed Catmull is known as the driving force behind Pixar's astounding success as he revolutionized the animation business model (as encapsulated by Disney) by refusing to micromanage and encouraging participative decision making from everyone: the janitor to the creative directors.[1]

⬛ THE DECISION-MAKING PROCESS

programmed decision
A simple, routine matter for which a manager has an established decision rule.

nonprogrammed decision
A new, complex decision that requires a creative solution.

Decision making is a critical activity in the lives of managers. The decisions a manager faces can range from very simple, routine matters for which the manager has an established decision rule (*programmed decisions*) to new and complex decisions that require creative solutions (*nonprogrammed decisions*).[2] Scheduling lunch hours for one's work group is a programmed decision. The manager performs the decision activity on a daily basis, using an established procedure with the same clear goal in mind. In contrast, decisions like buying out another company are nonprogrammed. The decision to acquire a company is unique and unstructured and requires considerable judgment. For example, Disney's acquisition of Pixar is a nonprogrammed decision requiring considerable processing of unique and novel information. Regardless of the type of decision made, it is helpful to understand as much as possible about how individuals and groups make decisions.

Decision making is a process involving a series of steps, as shown in Figure 9.1. The first step is recognition of the problem; that is, the manager realizes that a decision must be made. Identification of the real problem is important; otherwise, the manager may be reacting to symptoms and firefighting rather than dealing with the root cause of the problem. Next, a manager must identify the objective of the decision. In other words, the manager must determine what is to be accomplished by the decision.

The third step in the decision-making process is gathering information relevant to the problem. The manager must pull together sufficient information about why the problem occurred. This involves conducting a thorough diagnosis of the situation and going on a fact-finding mission.

The fourth step is listing and evaluating alternative courses of action. During this step, a thorough "what-if" analysis should also be conducted to determine the various factors that could influence the outcome. It is important to generate a wide range of options and creative solutions in order to be able to move on to the fifth step.

Next, the manager selects the alternative that best meets the decision objective. If the problem has been diagnosed correctly and sufficient alternatives have been identified, this step is much easier.

Finally, the solution is implemented. The situation must then be monitored to see whether the decision met its objective. Consistent monitoring and periodic feedback are essential parts of the follow-up process.

Decision making can be stressful. Managers must make decisions with significant risk and uncertainty, and often without full information. They must trust and rely on others in arriving at their decisions, but they are ultimately responsible. Sometimes the decisions are painful and involve exiting businesses, firing people, and admitting wrong. Blue Man Group has a history of making effective decisions. Their theatrical productions are a creative combination of comedy, music, and multi-media in a type of entertainment that is totally unique. They have grown wildly famous and successful by making sound business choices, even though none of the founders has any formal training in music, acting, or business. The group turned down offers to sell credit cards, soft drinks, breath mints, and paint, all of course related to the color blue. With each new opportunity, the three founders use the same evaluation. "Okay, that's all good and well, that's a nice thought—but is it Blue Man?" They also have achieved what a lot of businesses want to do but never complete: a detailed 132-page operating manual. The founders make decisions by unanimous agreement.[3]

FIGURE 9.1

The Decision-Making Process

🔲 MODELS OF DECISION MAKING

The success of any organization depends on managers' abilities to make *effective decisions*. An effective decision is timely, is acceptable to the individuals affected by it, and meets the desired objective.[4] This section describes three models of decision making: the rational model, the bounded rationality model, and the garbage can model.

effective decision
A timely decision that meets a desired objective and is acceptable to those individuals affected by it.

RATIONAL MODEL

rationality
A logical, step-by-step approach to decision making, with a thorough analysis of alternatives and their consequences.

Rationality refers to a logical, step-by-step approach to decision making, with a thorough analysis of alternatives and their consequences. The rational model of decision making comes from classic economic theory and contends that the decision maker is completely rational in his or her approach. The rational model has the following important assumptions:

1. The outcome will be completely rational.

2. The decision maker has a consistent system of preferences, which is used to choose the best alternative.

3. The decision maker is aware of all the possible alternatives.

4. The decision maker can calculate the probability of success for each alternative.[5]

In the rational model, the decision maker strives to optimize, that is, to select the best possible alternative.

Given the assumptions of the rational model, it is unrealistic. There are time constraints and limits to human knowledge and information-processing capabilities. In addition, a manager's preferences and needs change often. The rational model is thus an ideal that managers strive for in making decisions. It captures the way a decision should be made but does not reflect the reality of managerial decision making.[6]

1. Explain the assumptions of bounded rationality.

BOUNDED RATIONALITY MODEL

Recognizing the deficiencies of the rational model, Herbert Simon suggested that there are limits on how rational a decision maker can actually be. His decision theory, the bounded rationality model, earned a Nobel Prize in 1978.

Simon's model, also referred to as the "administrative man" theory, rests on the idea that there are constraints that force a decision maker to be less than completely rational. The bounded rationality model has four assumptions:

1. Managers select the first alternative that is satisfactory.

2. Managers recognize that their conception of the world is simple.

3. Managers are comfortable making decisions without determining all the alternatives.

4. Managers make decisions by rules of thumb or heuristics.

bounded rationality
A theory that suggests that there are limits to how rational a decision maker can actually be.

satisfice
To select the first alternative that is "good enough," because the costs in time and effort are too great to optimize.

heuristics
Shortcuts in decision making that save mental activity.

Bounded rationality assumes that managers *satisfice*; that is, they select the first alternative that is "good enough," because the costs of optimizing in terms of time and effort are too great.[7] Further, the theory assumes that managers develop shortcuts, called *heuristics*, to make decisions in order to save mental activity. Heuristics are rules of thumb that allow managers to make decisions based on what has worked in past experiences.

Does the bounded rationality model more realistically portray the managerial decision process? Research indicates that it does.[8] One of the reasons managers face limits to their rationality is that they must make decisions under risk and time pressure. The situation they find themselves in is highly uncertain, and the probability of success is not known.

◼ GARBAGE CAN MODEL

Sometimes the decision-making process in organizations appears to be haphazard and unpredictable. In the *garbage can model*, decisions are random and unsystematic.[9] Figure 9.2 depicts the garbage can model. In this model, the organization is a garbage can in which problems, solutions, participants, and choice opportunities are floating around randomly. If the four factors happen to connect, a decision is made.[10] The quality of the decision depends on timing. The right participants must find the right solution to the right problem at the right time.

The garbage can model illustrates the idea that not all organizational decisions are made in a step-by-step, systematic fashion. Especially under conditions of high uncertainty, the decision process may be chaotic. Some decisions appear to happen out of sheer luck.

On the high-speed playing field of today's businesses, managers must make critical decisions quickly, with incomplete information, and must also involve employees in the process.

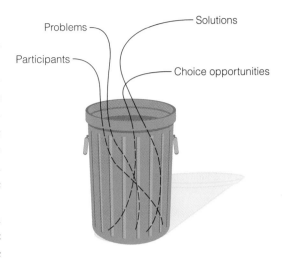

Problems — Solutions
Participants — Choice opportunities

FIGURE 9.2

The Garbage Can Model

SOURCE: From M. D. Cohen, J. G. March, and J. P. Olsen, "A Garbage Can Model of Organizational Choice," *Administrative Science Quarterly* 17 (March 1972): 1–25. Reprinted by permission of the Administrative Science Quarterly.

◀◀ **think critically** ▶▶

Research Disney's acquisition of Pixar and evaluate it from the standpoint of decision-making models. Was it similar to the rational, bounded rationality, or garbage can model? Why?

▣ DECISION MAKING AND RISK

Many decisions involve some element of risk. For managers, hiring decisions, promotions, delegation, acquisitions and mergers, overseas expansions, new product development, and other decisions make risk a part of the job.

◼ RISK AND THE MANAGER

Individuals differ in terms of their willingness to take risks. Some people experience *risk aversion*. They choose options that entail fewer risks, preferring familiarity and certainty. Other individuals are risk takers; that is, they accept greater potential for loss in decisions, tolerate greater uncertainty, and in general are more likely to make risky decisions. Risk takers are also more likely to take the lead in group discussions.[11]

Research indicates that women are more averse to risk taking than men and that older, more experienced managers are more risk averse than younger managers. There is also some evidence that successful managers take more risks than unsuccessful managers.[12] However, the tendency to take risks or avoid them is only part of behavior toward risk. Risk taking is influenced not only by an individual's tendency but also by organizational factors. In commercial banks, loan decisions that require the assessment of risk are made every day.

Upper-level managers face a tough task in managing risk-taking behavior. By discouraging lower-level managers from taking risks, they may stifle creativity and

garbage can model
A theory that contends that decisions in organizations are random and unsystematic.

risk aversion
The tendency to choose options that entail fewer risks and less uncertainty.

innovation. If upper-level managers are going to encourage risk taking, however, they must allow employees to fail without fear of punishment. One way to accomplish this is to consider failure "enlightened trial and error."[13] The key is establishing a consistent attitude toward risk within the organization.

ESCALATION OF COMMITMENT

escalation of commitment
The tendency to continue to support a failing course of action.

Continuing to support a failing course of action is known as *escalation of commitment*.[14] In situations characterized by escalation of commitment, individuals who make decisions that turn out to be poor choices tend to hold fast to those choices, even when substantial costs are incurred.[15] An example of escalation is the price wars that often occur between airlines. The airlines reduce their prices in response to competitors until at a certain stage, both airlines are in a "no-win" situation. Yet they continue to compete despite the heavy losses they are incurring. The desire to win is a motivation to continue to escalate, and each airline continues to reduce prices (lose money) based on the belief that the other airline will pull out of the price war. Another example of escalation of commitment is NASA's enormous International Space Station. Originally estimated to cost $8 billion, the Space Station has been redesigned five times and remains unfinished. As of 2003, its estimated cost topped $30 billion, and some pundits speculate that the total bill may reach $100 billion for what physicist Robert Park describes as "the biggest technological blunder in history." Despite the station's drain on virtually every other NASA program, it remains a focal point of NASA's work and continues to consume vast resources.[16]

Why does escalation of commitment occur? One explanation is offered by cognitive dissonance theory, as we discussed in Chapter 4. This theory assumes that humans dislike inconsistency, and that when there is inconsistency among their attitudes or inconsistency between their attitudes and behavior, they strive to reduce the dissonance.[17]

Other reasons why people may hang on to a losing course of action are optimism and control. Some people are overly optimistic and overestimate the likelihood that positive things will happen to them. Other people operate under an illusion of control—that they have special skills to control the future that other people don't have.[18] In addition, sunk costs may encourage escalation. Individuals think, "Well, I've already invested this much . . . what's a few dollars more?" And the closer a project is to completion, the more likely escalation is to occur.[19]

Hanging on to a poor decision can be costly to organizations. While most U.S. airlines (including United, American, and TWA) originally placed orders for the prestigious Mach 2 Concorde airliner during the 1960s, all U.S. orders for the plane were eventually cancelled, leaving only British Airways and Air France as customers. While these two firms doggedly held onto their marginally profitable Concorde operations for almost three decades, a crash in 2000 led to closer scrutiny of the aging fleet, which was eventually retired in 2003. Industry insiders estimate that every customer who took the Concorde rather than a 747 cost British Airways more than $1,200 in profits.[20] Organizations can deal with escalation of commitment in several ways. One is to split the responsibility for decisions about projects. One individual can make the initial decision, and another individual can make subsequent decisions on the project. Companies have also tried to eliminate escalation of commitment by closely monitoring decision makers.[21] Another suggestion is to provide individuals with a graceful exit from poor decisions so that their images are not threatened. One way of accomplishing this is to reward people who admit to poor decisions before escalating their commitment to them. A study also suggested that having groups, rather than individuals, make an initial investment decision would reduce escalation. Support has been found for this idea. Participants in group decision making may experience a diffusion of responsibility for the failed decision rather than feeling personally responsible; thus, they can pull out of a bad decision without threatening their image.[22]

We have seen that there are limits to how rational a manager can be in making decisions. Most managerial decisions involve considerable risk, and individuals react differently to risk situations.

◀◀think critically▶▶

Recall one instance from work or school when you held on to a decision even though you realized it was wrong. How would you change your course of action based upon the preceding discussion of escalation of commitment?

INDIVIDUAL INFLUENCES ON DECISION MAKING

Many individual differences affect a manager's decision making. Other personality characteristics, attitudes, and values, along with all of the individual differences variables that were discussed in Chapters 3 and 4, have implications for managerial decision making. Managers must use both their logic and their creativity to make effective decisions. Most of us are more comfortable using either logic or creativity, and we show that preference in everyday decision making. Challenge 9.1 is an activity that will tell you which process, logic or creativity, is your preferred one. Take Challenge 9.1 now, and then read on to interpret your score.

Brain hemispheric dominance is related to students' choices of college majors. Left-brained students gravitate toward business, engineering, and sciences, whereas right-brained students are attracted to education, nursing, communication, and literature.[23]

Our brains have two lateral halves (Figure 9.3). The right side is the center for creative functions, while the left side is the center for logic, detail, and planning. There are advantages to both kinds of thinking, so the ideal situation is to be "brain-lateralized" or to be able to use either logic or creativity or both, depending on the situation. There are ways to develop the side of the brain you are not accustomed to using. To develop your right side, or creative side, you can ask "what-if" questions, engage in play, and follow your intuition. To develop the left side, you can set goals for completing tasks and work to attain these goals. For managers, it is important to see the big picture, craft a vision, and plan strategically—all of which require right-brain skills. It is equally important to be able to understand day-to-day operations and flow chart work processes, which are left-hemisphere brain skills.

Two particular individual influences that can enhance decision-making effectiveness will be highlighted next: intuition and creativity.

2. Describe and evaluate the role of intuition and creativity in decision making.

CHALLENGE 9.1

Which Side of Your Brain Do You Favor?

There are no "right" or "wrong" answers to this questionnaire. It is more of a self-assessment than a test. Do not read the questions more than once. Don't overanalyze. Merely circle "A" or "B" to indicate which answer is more typical of you.

1. Typically, when I have a problem to solve,
   A I make a list of possible solutions, prioritize them, and then select the best answer.
   B I "let it sit" for a while or talk it over with someone before I attempt to reach a solution.

2. When I sit with my hands clasped in my lap (FOLD YOUR HANDS THAT WAY RIGHT NOW BEFORE GOING ON, THEN LOOK AT YOUR HANDS), the thumb that is on top is
   A my right thumb.
   B my left thumb.

3. I have hunches
   A sometimes, but do not place much faith in them.
   B frequently and I usually follow them.

4. If I am at a meeting or lecture, I tend to take extensive notes.
   A True
   B False

5. I am well-organized, have a system for doing things, have a place for everything and everything in its place, and can assimilate information quickly and logically.
   A True
   B False

6. I am good with numbers.
   A True
   B False

7. Finding words in a dictionary or looking up names in a telephone book is something I can do easily and quickly.
   A True
   B False

8. If I want to remember directions or other information,
   A I make notes.
   B I visualize the information.

9. I express myself well verbally.
   A True
   B False

10. To learn dance steps or athletic moves,
    A I try to understand the sequence of the steps and repeat them mentally.
    B I don't think about it; I just try to get the feel of the game or the music.

Interpretation:

> Four, five, or six "A" answers indicate lateralization—an ability to use either hemisphere easily and to solve problems according to their nature rather than according to a favored manner.

> One, two, or three "A" answers indicate right-hemisphere dominance; corresponding traits include inventiveness, creativity, innovation, risk taking, whimsy, and an ability to see the "big picture."

> Seven, eight, or nine "A" answers indicate a left-hemisphere dominance—a tendency toward attention to detail, the use of logic, and traits of thoroughness and accuracy.

Source: "Which Side of the Brain Do You Favor?" from *Quality Driven Designs.* Copyright 1992 Pfeiffer/Jossey-Bass. Reprinted by permission of Jossey-Bass, Inc., a subsidiary of John Wiley & Sons, Inc.

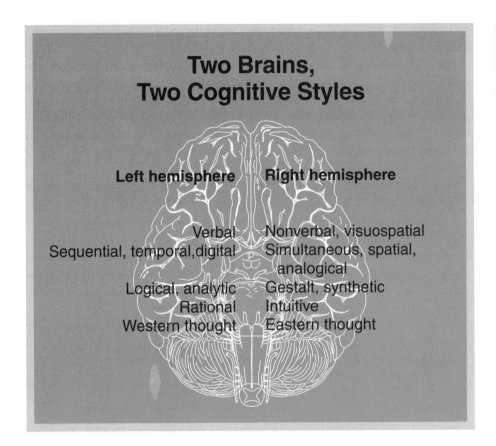

FIGURE 9.3

Functions of the Left and Right Brain Hemispheres

SOURCES: Created based on ideas from *Left Brain, Right Brain* by Springer and Deutsch, p. 272. © 1993 by Sally P. Springer and Georg Deutsch (New York: W. H. Freeman and Company, 1993). DILBERT reprinted by permission of United Feature Syndicate, Inc.

■ THE ROLE OF INTUITION

There is evidence that managers use their *intuition* to make decisions.[24] Henry Mintzberg, in his work on managerial roles, found that in many cases managers do not appear to use a systematic, step-by-step approach to decision making. Rather, Mintzberg argued, managers make judgments based on "hunches."[25] Daniel Isenberg studied the way senior managers make decisions and found that intuition was used extensively, especially as a mechanism to evaluate decisions made more rationally.[26] Robert Beck studied the way managers at BankAmerica (now Bank of America) made decisions about the future direction of the company following the deregulation of the banking industry. Beck described their use of intuition as an antidote

intuition
A fast, positive force in decision making that is utilized at a level below consciousness and involves learned patterns of information.

to "analysis paralysis," or the tendency to analyze decisions rather than developing innovative solutions.[27]

Dr. Gary Klein, a renowned cognitive psychologist, has written a book on the power of intuition. Dr. Klein and his colleagues insist that skilled decision makers rely on patterns of learned information in making quick and efficient decisions. In a series of studies conducted with the U.S. Navy, firefighters, and the U.S. Army, they found that decision makers normally relied on intuition in unfamiliar, challenging situations. These decisions were superior to those made after careful evaluation of information and potential alternatives.[28]

Just what is intuition? In the Myers-Briggs Type Indicator we discussed in Chapter 3, intuiting (N) is one preference used to gather data. This is only one way that the concept of intuition has been applied to managerial decision making, and it is perhaps the most widely researched form of the concept of intuition. There are, however, many definitions of *intuition* in the managerial literature. Chester Barnard, one of the early influential management researchers, argued that intuition's main attributes were speed and the inability of the decision maker to determine how the decision was made.[29] Other researchers have contended that intuition occurs at an unconscious level and that this is why the decision maker cannot verbalize how the decision was made.[30]

Intuition has been variously described as follows:

> The ability to know or recognize quickly and readily the possibilities of a situation.[31]

> Smooth automatic performance of learned behavior sequences.[32]

> Simple analyses frozen into habit and into the capacity for rapid response through recognition.[33]

These definitions share some common assumptions. First, there seems to be a notion that intuition is fast. Second, intuition is utilized at a level below consciousness. Third, there seems to be agreement that intuition involves learned patterns of information. Fourth, intuition appears to be a positive force in decision making.

The use of intuition may lead to more ethical decisions. Intuition allows an individual to take on another's role with ease, and role taking is a fundamental part of developing moral reasoning. You may recall from Chapter 4 the role of cognitive moral development in ethical decision making. One study found a strong link between cognitive moral development and intuition. The development of new perspectives through intuition leads to higher moral growth, and thus to more ethical decisions.[34]

One question that arises is whether managers can be taught to use their intuition. Weston Agor, who has conducted workshops on developing intuitive skills in managers, has attained positive results in organizations such as the city of Phoenix and entertainment powerhouse Walt Disney Enterprises. After giving intuition tests to more than 10,000 executives, he has concluded that in most cases, higher management positions are held by individuals with higher levels of intuition. Just as the brain needs both hemispheres to work, Agor cautions that organizations need both analytical and intuitive minds to function at their peak. Consider Grant Tinker, former head of NBC. "Sometimes the boss has to go by his gut, hold his nose, and jump," Tinker writes in *Tinker in Television*. Lee Iaccoca, in his autobiography, spends pages extolling intuition: "To a certain extent, I've always operated by gut feeling."[35] Agor suggests relaxation techniques, using images to guide the mind, and taking creative pauses before making a decision.[36] A review of the research on intuition suggests that although intuition itself cannot be taught, managers can be trained to rely more fully on the promptings of their intuition.[37] Intuition is an elusive concept, and one with many definitions. There is an interesting paradox regarding intuition. Some researchers view "rational" methods as preferable to intuition, yet satisfaction with a rational decision is usually determined by how the decision feels intuitively.[38] Intuition appears to have a positive effect on managerial decision making, but it is not without controversy. Some writers argue that intuition has its place and that instincts should be trusted, but not as a substitute for reason. With new technologies, managers can analyze a lot more information in a lot less time, making the rational method less time consuming than it once was.[39]

■ CREATIVITY AT WORK

Creativity is a process influenced by individual and organizational factors that results in the production of novel and useful ideas, products, or both.[40] The social and technological changes that organizations face require creative decisions.[41] Managers of the future need to develop special competencies to deal with the turbulence of change, and one of these important competencies is the ability to promote creativity in organizations.[42]

Creativity is a process that is at least in part unconscious. The four stages of the creative process are preparation, incubation, illumination, and verification.[43] Preparation means seeking out new experiences and opportunities to learn, because creativity grows from a base of knowledge. Travel and educational opportunities of all kinds open the individual's mind. Incubation is a process of reflective thought and is often conducted subconsciously. During incubation, the individual engages in other pursuits while the mind considers the problem and works on it. Illumination occurs when the individual senses an insight for solving the problem. Finally, verification is conducted to determine if the solution or idea is valid. This is accomplished by thinking through the implications of the decision, presenting the idea to another person, or trying out the decision. Momentary quieting of the brain through relaxation can also increase "coherence" or the ability of different parts of the brain to work together.[44, 45] Both individual and organizational influences affect the creative process.

INDIVIDUAL INFLUENCES

Several individual variables are related to creativity. One group of factors involves the cognitive processes that creative individuals tend to use. One cognitive process is divergent thinking, meaning the individual's ability to generate several potential solutions to a problem.[46] In addition, associational abilities and the use of imagery are associated with creativity.[47] Unconscious processes such as dreams are also essential cognitive processes related to creative thinking.[48]

Personality factors have also been related to creativity in studies of individuals from several different occupations. These characteristics include intellectual and artistic values, breadth of interests, high energy, concern with achievement, independence of judgment, intuition, self-confidence, and a creative self-image.[49]

: **3.** Critique your own level of creativity and list ways of improving it.

creativity
A process influenced by individual and organizational factors that results in the production of novel and useful ideas, products, or both.

Tolerance of ambiguity, intrinsic motivation, risk taking, and a desire for recognition are also associated with creativity.

◄◄ **think critically** ►►

Which of the Big Five personality factors discussed in Chapter 3 should be associated with creativity? Why?

There is also evidence that people who are in a good mood are more creative.[50] Positive affect is related to creativity in work teams because being in a positive mood allows team members to explore new ways of thinking.[51] Positive emotions enhance creativity by broadening one's cognitive patterns and resources. For example, repeated experiences of love, interest, courage, and gratitude cause one to discard old theories and automatic ways of doing things. Instead, these positive emotions initiate thoughts and actions that are novel and unscripted.[52,53] Moreover, it is a cyclical process, because creative thoughts and incidents lead to more positive affect. You might say that thinking positively makes us more creative, and being more creative makes us think positively.[54] In tasks involving considerable cognitive demands though, it has been found that people in negative moods perform better. When an individual experiences negative moods or emotions, it is a signal to the individual that all is not well, which leads to more attention and vigilance in cognitive activity. Positive moods signal that all is well with the status quo, and this can lead to decreased performance on some decision-making tasks involving complex mental activity.[55,56]

ORGANIZATIONAL INFLUENCES

The organizational environment in which people work can either support creativity or impede creative efforts. Creativity killers include focusing on how work is going to be evaluated, being closely monitored while you are working, and competing with other people in win–lose situations. In contrast, creativity facilitators include feelings of autonomy, being part of a team with diverse skills, and having creative supervisors and coworkers.[57] High-quality, supportive relationships with supervisors are related to creativity.[58] Flexible organizational structures and participative decision making have also been associated with creativity. An organization can also present impediments to creativity. These barriers include internal political problems, harsh criticism of new ideas, destructive internal competition, and avoidance of risk.[59] The physical environment can also hamper creativity. Companies like Oticon, a Danish hearing-aid manufacturer, and Ethicon Endo-Surgery, a division of Johnson & Johnson, use open-plan offices that eliminate office walls and cubicles so that employees interact more frequently. When people mix, ideas mix as well.[60]

Studies of the role of organizational rewards in encouraging creativity have mixed results. Some studies have shown that monetary incentives improve creative performance, whereas others have found that material rewards do not influence innovative activity.[61] Still other studies have indicated that explicitly contracting to obtain a reward led to lower levels of creativity when compared with contracting for no reward, being presented with just the task, or being presented with the task and receiving the reward later.[62] Organizations can therefore enhance individuals' creative decision making by providing a supportive environment, participative decision making, and a flexible structure. Pixar encourages its employees to be creative by providing unique working spaces and encouraging nontraditional workplace behavior (e.g., riding around on razor scooters and wearing Hawaiian shirts to work).

◀◀ **think critically** ▶▶

Is it all fun and games at Pixar Studios? Why does Pixar invest in fun activities? Would you like to work for a company like Pixar?

INDIVIDUAL/ORGANIZATION FIT

Research has indicated that creative performance is highest when there is a match, or fit, between the individual and organizational influences on creativity. For example, when individuals who desire to be creative are matched with an organization that values creative ideas, the result is more creative performance.[63]

A common mistaken assumption regarding creativity is that either you have it or you do not. Research refutes this myth and has shown that individuals can be trained to be more creative.[64] The Disney Institute features a wide range of programs offered to companies, and one of their best-sellers is creativity training.

Part of creativity training involves learning to open up mental locks that keep us from generating creative alternatives to a decision or problem. The following are some mental locks that diminish creativity:

> Searching for the "right" answer.
> Trying to be logical.
> Following the rules.
> Avoiding ambiguity.
> Striving for practicality.
> Being afraid to look foolish.
> Avoiding problems outside our own expertise.
> Fearing failure.
> Believing we are not really creative.
> Not making play a part of work.[65]

Note that many of these mental locks stem from values within organizations. Organizations can facilitate creative decision making in many ways. Rewarding creativity, allowing employees to fail, making work more fun, and providing creativity training are a few suggestions. Also, companies can encourage creativity by exposing employees to new ideas. This can be done in several ways, including job rotation, which moves employees through different jobs and gives them exposure to different information, projects, and teams. Employees can also be assigned to work with groups outside the company, such as suppliers or consultants. Finally, managers can encourage employees to surround themselves with stimuli that they have found to enhance their creative processes. These may be music, artwork, books, or anything else that encourages creative thinking.[66]

We have seen that both individual and organizational factors can produce creativity. Creativity can also mean finding problems as well as fixing them. Recently, four different types of creativity have been proposed, based on the source of the trigger (internal or external) and the source of the problem (presented versus discovered). Responsive creativity means responding to a problem that is presented to you by others because it is part of your job. Expected creativity is discovering problems because you are expected to by the organization. Contributory creativity is responding to problems presented to you because you want to be creative. Proactive creativity is discovering problems because you want to be creative.[67]

3M consistently ranks among the top ten in *Fortune*'s annual list of most admired corporations. It earned this reputation through innovation: More than one-quarter of 3M's sales are from products less than four years old. Post-It Notes, for example, were created by a worker who wanted little adhesive papers to mark hymns for church services. He thought of another worker who had perfected a light adhesive, and the two spent their "free time" developing Post-It Notes. 3M has continued its tradition of innovation with Post-It Flags, Pop-Up Tape Strips, and Nexcare Ease-Off Bandages.

Leaders can play key roles in modeling creative behavior. Sir Richard Branson, founder and chairman of U.K.-based Virgin Group, Ltd., believes that if you do not use your employees' creative potential, you are doomed to failure. At Virgin Group, the culture encourages risk taking and rewards innovation. Rules and regulations are not its thing, nor is analyzing ideas to death. Branson says an employee can have an idea in the morning and implement it in the afternoon.[68]

Creativity is a global concern. Poland, for example, is undergoing a major shift from a centrally planned economy and monoparty rule to a market economy and Western-style democracy. One of the major concerns for Polish managers is creativity. Finding ingenious solutions and having the ability to think creatively can be a question of life or death for Polish organizations, which are making the transition to a faster pace of learning and change.[69]

Both intuition and creativity are important influences on managerial decision making. Both concepts require additional research so that managers can better understand how to use intuition and creativity, as well as how to encourage their employees to use them to make more effective decisions.

⬡ PARTICIPATION IN DECISION MAKING

Effective management of people can improve a company's economic performance. Firms that capitalize on this fact share several common practices. Chief among them is participation of employees in decision making.[70] Many companies do this through highly empowered self-managed teams like the ones we discussed in Chapter 8. Even in situations where formal teams are not feasible, decision authority can be handed down to front-line employees who have the knowledge and skills to make a difference. At Hampton Inn hotels, for example, guest services personnel are empowered to do whatever is necessary to make guests happy—without consulting their superiors.

■ THE EFFECTS OF PARTICIPATION

Participative decision making occurs when individuals who are affected by decisions influence the making of those decisions. Participation buffers employees from the negative experiences of organizational politics.[71] In addition, participative management has been found to increase employee creativity, job satisfaction, and productivity.[72]

GE Capital believes in participation. Each year it holds dreaming sessions, and employees from all levels of the company attend strategy and budget meetings to discuss where the company is heading. As a result, young employees came up with many e-commerce ideas that were highly successful.[73]

As our economy becomes increasingly based on knowledge work, and as new technologies make it easier for decentralized decision makers to connect, participative decision making will undoubtedly increase.[74] Consider the city and county of San Francisco, a combined city/county government organization. When the city and county of San Francisco needed to adopt a single messaging system to meet the needs of more than 20,000 users, it faced a huge challenge in getting all the users to provide input into the decision. Technology helped craft a system that balanced the needs of all the groups involved, and IT planners developed a 28-page spreadsheet to pull together the needs and desires of all 60 departments into a focused decision matrix. Within two years, 90 percent of the users had agreed on and moved to a single system, reducing costs and complexity.[75]

participative decision making
Decision making in which individuals who are affected by decisions influence the making of those decisions.

◗ THE GROUP DECISION-MAKING PROCESS

Managers use groups to make decisions for several reasons. One is *synergy*, which occurs when group members stimulate new solutions to problems through the process of mutual influence and encouragement within the group. Another reason for using a group is to gain commitment to a decision. Groups also bring more knowledge and experience to the problem-solving situation.

Group decisions can sometimes be predicted by comparing the views of the initial group members with the final group decision. These simple relationships are known as *social decision schemes.* One social decision scheme is the majority-wins rule, in which the group supports whatever position is taken by the majority of its members. Another scheme, the truth-wins rule, predicts that the correct decision will emerge as an increasing number of members realize its appropriateness. The two-thirds-majority rule means that the decision favored by two-thirds or more of the members is supported. Finally, the first-shift rule states that members support a decision represented by the first shift in opinion shown by a member.

Research indicates that these social decision schemes can predict a group decision as much as 80 percent of the time.[76] Current research is aimed at discovering which rules are used in particular types of tasks. For example, studies indicate that the majority-wins rule is used most often in judgment tasks (that is, when the decision is a matter of preference or opinion), whereas the truth-wins rule predicts decisions best when the task is an intellective one (that is, when the decision has a correct answer).[77]

synergy
A positive force that occurs in groups when group members stimulate new solutions to problems through the process of mutual influence and encouragement within the group.

social decision schemes
Simple rules used to determine final group decisions.

▪ ADVANTAGES AND DISADVANTAGES OF GROUP DECISION MAKING

Both advantages and disadvantages are associated with group decision making. The advantages include (1) more knowledge and information through the pooling of group member resources; (2) increased acceptance of, and commitment to, the decision, because the members had a voice in it; and (3) greater understanding of the decision, because members were involved in the various stages of the decision process. The disadvantages of group decision making include (1) pressure within the group to conform and fit in; (2) domination of the group by one forceful member or a dominant clique, who may ramrod the decision; and (3) the amount of time required, because a group makes decisions more slowly than an individual.[78]

Given these advantages and disadvantages, should an individual or a group make a decision? Substantial empirical research indicates that whether a group or an individual should be used depends on the type of task involved. For judgment tasks requiring an estimate or a prediction, groups are usually superior to individuals because of the breadth of experience that multiple individuals bring to the problem.[79] On tasks that have a correct solution, other studies have indicated that the most competent individual outperforms the group.[80] This finding has been called into question, however. Much of the previous research on groups was conducted in the laboratory, where group members interacted only for short periods of time. Researchers wanted to know how a longer experience in the group would affect decisions. Their study showed that groups who worked together for longer periods of time outperformed the most competent member 70 percent of the time. As groups gained experience, the best members became less important to the group's success.[81] This study demonstrated that experience in the group is an important variable to consider when evaluating the individual versus group decision-making question.

Research is just beginning on the role of trust and trustworthiness in team decision making. One study was conducted for six weeks on student teams that were involved in designing an information systems project. The teams' trust of each other and risk taking actions were cyclical. When teams saw the other team as trustworthy, they took a risk; then the other team, based on their perception of the first team's trustworthiness, decided whether or not to take a risk, and so on. The study showed that the trust process works between teams much the same as it does between individuals.[82]

Given the emphasis on teams in the workplace, many managers believe that groups produce better decisions than do individuals, yet the evidence is mixed. It is evident that more research needs to be conducted in organizational settings to help answer this question.

Two potential liabilities are found in group decision making: groupthink and group polarization. These problems are discussed in the following sections.

groupthink
A deterioration of mental efficiency, reality testing, and moral judgment resulting from pressures within the group.

▪ GROUPTHINK

One liability of a cohesive group is its tendency to develop *groupthink*, a dysfunctional process. Irving Janis, the originator of the groupthink concept, describes groupthink as "a deterioration of mental efficiency, reality testing, and moral judgment" resulting from pressures within the group.[83]

Certain conditions favor the development of groupthink. One of the conditions is high cohesiveness. Cohesive groups tend to favor solidarity because members identify strongly with the group.[84] High-ranking teams that make decisions without outside help are especially prone to groupthink because they are likely to have shared mental models; that is, they are more likely to think alike.[85] And homogeneous groups (ones with little to no diversity among members) are more likely to suffer from groupthink.[86] Two other conditions that encourage groupthink are having to make a highly consequential decision and time constraints.[87] A highly consequential decision is one that will have a great impact on the group members and on outside parties. When group members feel that they have a limited time in which to make a decision, they may rush through the process. These antecedents cause members to prefer concurrence in decisions and to fail to evaluate one another's suggestions critically. A group suffering from groupthink shows recognizable symptoms. Table 9.1 presents these symptoms and makes suggestions on how to avoid groupthink.

◀◀think critically▶▶

How could groupthink affect ethical decision making?

An incident cited as a prime example of groupthink is the 1986 *Challenger* disaster, in which the space shuttle exploded and killed all seven crew members. A presidential commission concluded that flawed decision making was the primary cause of the accident. Sadly, organizations often struggle to learn from their mistakes. In 2003, the shuttle *Columbia* exploded over Texas upon reentering the earth's atmosphere, killing all seven crew members. Within days of the *Columbia* disaster, questions began to surface about the decision-making process that led flight engineers to assume that damage caused to the shuttle upon take-off was minor and to continue the mission. The subsequent investigation of the disaster led observers to note that NASA's decision-making process appears just as flawed today as it was in 1986, exhibiting all the classic symptoms of groupthink. The final accident report blamed the NASA culture that downplayed risk and suppressed dissent for the decision.[88, 89]

Consequences of groupthink include an incomplete survey of alternatives, failure to evaluate the risks of the preferred course of action, biased information processing, and a failure to work out contingency plans. The overall result of groupthink is defective decision making. This was evident in the *Challenger* situation. The group considered only two alternatives: launch or no launch. They failed to consider the risks of their decision to launch the shuttle, and they did not develop any contingency plans.

Table 9.1 presents Janis's guidelines for avoiding groupthink. Many of these suggestions center around the notion of ensuring that decisions are evaluated completely, with opportunities for discussion from all group members. This strategy helps encourage members to evaluate one another's ideas critically.

Janis has used the groupthink framework to conduct historical analyses of several political and military fiascoes, including the Bay of Pigs invasion, the Vietnam War, and Watergate. One review of the decision situation in the *Challenger* incident proposed that two variables, time and leadership style, are important to

TABLE 9.1
Symptoms of Groupthink and How to Prevent It

SYMPTOMS OF GROUPTHINK

- *Illusions of invulnerability.* Group members feel that they are above criticism. This symptom leads to excessive optimism and risk taking.
- *Illusions of group morality.* Group members feel they are moral in their actions and therefore above reproach. This symptom leads the group to ignore the ethical implications of their decisions.
- *Illusions of unanimity.* Group members believe there is unanimous agreement on the decisions. Silence is misconstrued as consent.
- *Rationalization.* Group members concoct explanations for their decisions to make them appear rational and correct. The results are that other alternatives are not considered, and there is an unwillingness to reconsider the group's assumptions.
- *Stereotyping the enemy.* Competitors are stereotyped as evil or stupid. This leads the group to underestimate its opposition.
- *Self-censorship.* Members do not express their doubts or concerns about the course of action. This prevents critical analysis of the decisions.
- *Peer pressure.* Any members who express doubts or concerns are pressured by other group members who question their loyalty.
- *Mindguards.* Some members take it upon themselves to protect the group from negative feedback. Group members are thus shielded from information that might lead them to question their actions.

GUIDELINES FOR PREVENTING GROUPTHINK

- Ask each group member to assume the role of the critical evaluator who actively voices objections or doubts.
- Have the leader avoid stating his or her position on the issue prior to the group decision.
- Create several groups that work on the decision simultaneously.
- Bring in outside experts to evaluate the group process.
- Appoint a devil's advocate to question the group's course of action consistently.
- Evaluate the competition carefully, posing as many different motivations and intentions as possible.
- Once consensus is reached, encourage the group to rethink its position by reexamining the alternatives.

SOURCE: Irving L. Janis, *Groupthink: Psychological Studies of Policy Decisions and Fiascoes,* Second Edition (New York: Houghton Mifflin, 1982), 174–175. Copyright © 1982 by Houghton Mifflin Company. Used with permission.

include.[90] When a decision must be made quickly, there is more potential for groupthink. Leadership style can either promote groupthink (if the leader makes his or her opinion known up front) or avoid groupthink (if the leader encourages open and frank discussion).

There are few empirical studies of groupthink, and most of these involved students in a laboratory setting. More applied research may be seen in the future, however, as a questionnaire has been developed to measure the constructs associated with groupthink.[91] Janis's work on groupthink has led to several interdisciplinary efforts at understanding policy decisions.[92] The work underscores the need to examine multiple explanations for failed decisions.

GROUP POLARIZATION

Another group phenomenon was discovered by a graduate student. His study showed that groups made riskier decisions; in fact, the group and each individual accepted greater levels of risk following a group discussion of the issue. Subsequent studies uncovered another shift—toward caution. Thus, group discussion produced shifts both toward more risky positions and toward more cautious positions.[93] Further research revealed that individual group member attitudes simply became more extreme following group discussion. Individuals who were initially against an issue became more radically opposed, and individuals who were in favor of the issue became more strongly supportive following discussion. These shifts came to be known as *group polarization.*[94]

The tendency toward polarization has important implications for group decision making. Groups whose initial views lean a certain way can be expected to adopt more extreme views following interaction.

Several ideas have been proposed to explain why group polarization occurs. One explanation is the social comparison approach. Prior to group discussion, individuals believe they hold better views than the other members. During group discussion, they see that their views are not so far from average, so they shift to more extreme positions.[95] A second explanation is the persuasive arguments view. It contends that group discussion reinforces the initial views of the members, so they take a more extreme position.[96] Both explanations are supported by research. It may be that both processes, along with others, cause the group to develop more polarized attitudes.

Group polarization leads groups to adopt extreme attitudes. In some cases, this can be disastrous. For instance, if individuals are leaning toward a dangerous decision, they are likely to support it more strongly following discussion. Both groupthink and group polarization are potential liabilities of group decision making, but several techniques can be used to help prevent or control these two liabilities.

group polarization
The tendency for group discussion to produce shifts toward more extreme attitudes among members.

TECHNIQUES FOR GROUP DECISION MAKING

Once a manager has determined that a group decision approach should be used, he or she can determine the technique that is best suited to the decision situation. Five techniques will be briefly summarized: brainstorming, nominal group technique, Delphi technique, devil's advocacy, and dialectical inquiry.

6. Evaluate the strengths and weaknesses of several group decision-making techniques.

BRAINSTORMING

Brainstorming is a good technique for generating alternatives. The idea behind *brainstorming* is to generate as many ideas as possible, suspending evaluation until all of the ideas have been suggested. Participants are encouraged to build upon the suggestions of others, and imagination is emphasized. One company that benefits from brainstorming is Toyota. Despite its success with the baby-boomer generation, Toyota's executives realized that they were failing to connect with younger buyers who viewed the firm as stodgy. In response, Toyota assembled a group of

brainstorming
A technique for generating as many ideas as possible on a given subject, while suspending evaluation until all the ideas have been suggested.

younger employees to brainstorm new products for this market. The result was the Toyota Scion, an entirely new line of boxy crossover vehicles aimed at the younger set.[97,98,99] Evidence suggests, however, that group brainstorming is less effective than a comparable number of individuals working alone. In groups, participants engage in discussions that can make them lose their focus.[100]

One recent trend is the use of electronic brainstorming instead of verbal brainstorming in groups. Electronic brainstorming overcomes two common problems that can produce group brainstorming failure: production blocking and evaluation apprehension. In verbal brainstorming, individuals are exposed to the inputs of others. While listening to others, individuals are distracted from their own ideas.[101] This is referred to as production blocking. When ideas are recorded electronically, participants are freed from hearing the interruptions of others; thus, production blocking is reduced. Some individuals suffer from evaluation apprehension in brainstorming groups. They fear that others might respond negatively to their ideas. In electronic brainstorming, input is anonymous, so evaluation apprehension is reduced. Studies indicate that anonymous electronic brainstorming groups outperform face-to-face brainstorming groups in the number of ideas generated.[102]

NOMINAL GROUP TECHNIQUE

nominal group technique (NGT)
A structured approach to group decision making that focuses on generating alternatives and choosing one.

A structured approach to decision making that focuses on generating alternatives and choosing one is called *nominal group technique (NGT)*. NGT involves the following discrete steps:

1. Individuals silently list their ideas.
2. Ideas are written on a chart one at a time until all ideas are listed.
3. Discussion is permitted but only to clarify the ideas. No criticism is allowed.
4. A written vote is taken.

NGT is a good technique to use in a situation where group members fear criticism from others.[103]

DELPHI TECHNIQUE

Delphi technique
Gathering the judgments of experts for use in decision making.

The *Delphi technique*, which originated at the Rand Corporation, involves gathering the judgments of experts for use in decision making. Experts at remote locations respond to a questionnaire. A coordinator summarizes the responses to the questionnaire, and the summary is sent back to the experts. The experts then rate the various alternatives generated, and the coordinator tabulates the results. The Delphi technique is valuable in its ability to generate a number of independent judgments without the requirement of a face-to-face meeting.[104]

DEVIL'S ADVOCACY

devil's advocacy
A technique for preventing groupthink in which a group or an individual is given the role of critic during decision making.

In the *devil's advocacy* decision method, a group or an individual is given the role of critic. This devil's advocate has the task of coming up with the potential problems of a proposed decision. This helps organizations avoid costly mistakes in decision making by identifying potential pitfalls in advance.[105] As we discussed in Chapter 8, a devil's advocate who challenges the CEO and top management team can help sustain the vitality and performance of the upper echelon.

▮ DIALECTICAL INQUIRY

Dialectical inquiry is essentially a debate between two opposing sets of recommendations. Although it sets up a conflict, it is a constructive approach, because it brings out the benefits and limitations of both sets of ideas.[106] When using this technique, it is important to guard against a win–lose attitude and to concentrate on reaching the most effective solution for all concerned. Research has shown that the way a decision is framed (that is, win–win versus win–lose) is very important. A decision's outcome could be viewed as a gain or a loss, depending on the way the decision is framed.[107]

dialectical inquiry
A debate between two opposing sets of recommendations.

⬛ DIVERSITY AND CULTURE IN DECISION MAKING

Styles of decision making vary greatly among cultures. Many of the dimensions proposed by Hofstede that were presented in Chapter 2 affect decision making. Uncertainty avoidance, for example, can affect the way people view decisions. In the United States, a culture with low uncertainty avoidance, decisions are seen as opportunities for change. In contrast, cultures such as those of Indonesia and Malaysia attempt to accept situations as they are rather than to change them.[108] Power distance also affects decision making. In more hierarchical cultures, such as India, top-level managers make decisions. In countries with low power distance, lower-level employees make many decisions. The Swedish culture exemplifies this type.

The individualist/collectivist dimension has implications for decision making. Japan, with its collectivist emphasis, favors group decisions. The United States has a more difficult time with group decisions because it is an individualistic culture. Time orientation affects the frame of reference of the decision. In China, with its long-term view, decisions are made with the future in mind. In the United States, many decisions are made considering only the short term.

The masculine/feminine dimension can be compared to the Jungian thinking/feeling preferences for decision making. Masculine cultures, as in many Latin American countries, value quick, assertive decisions. Feminine cultures, as in many Scandinavian countries, value decisions that reflect concern for others.

Managers should learn as much as possible about the decision processes in other cultures. NAFTA, for example, has eliminated many barriers to trade with Mexico. In Mexican organizations, decision-making authority is centralized, autocratic, and retained in small groups of top managers. As a consequence, Mexican employees are reluctant to participate in decision making and often wait to be told what to do rather than take a risk. Significant differences exist amongst Hispanic work-related ethics and non-Hispanic work-related ethics as well. These differences need to be managed effectively by managers to help individuals make decisions that are aligned with organizational values and ethics.[109] In addition, joint ventures with family-owned *grupos* (large groups of businesses) can be challenging. It may be difficult to identify the critical decision maker in the family and to determine how much decision-making authority is held by the grupo's family board.[110] Mexican managers may be more likely to engage in escalation of commitment or continue to invest in a losing venture. However, because lower-level managers in Mexico have control over smaller amounts of resources, they tend to invest in smaller increments than do U.S. managers.[111]

Recent research examining the effects of cultural diversity on decision making has found that when individuals in a group are racially dissimilar, they engage in more open information sharing, encourage dissenting perspectives, and arrive at better decisions than racially similar groups.[112] Other kinds of diversity such as functional background have been studied as well. Top management teams whose members come from a variety of functional backgrounds (for example, marketing, accounting, information systems) engage in greater debate in decision making than top management teams in which the members come from similar backgrounds. This diversity results in better financial performance for the firm.[113]

: 7. Explain the emerging role of virtual decision making in organizations.

▨ DECISION MAKING IN THE VIRTUAL WORKPLACE

Managers today are working in flexible organizations—so flexible in fact that many workplaces are unconstrained by geography, time, and organizational boundaries. Virtual teams are emerging as a new form of working arrangement. Virtual teams are groups of geographically dispersed coworkers who work together using a combination of telecommunications and information technologies to accomplish a task. Virtual teams seldom meet face to face, and membership often shifts according to the project at hand.

How are decisions made in virtual teams? These teams require advanced technologies for communication and decision making. Many technologies aid virtual teams in decision making: desktop videoconferencing systems (DVCS), group decision support systems (GDSS), Internet/intranet systems, expert systems, and agent-based modeling.[114]

Desktop videoconferencing systems are the major technologies that form the basis for other virtual team technologies. DVCS recreate the face-to-face interactions of teams and go one step beyond by supporting more complex levels of communication among virtual team members. Small cameras on top of computer monitors provide video feeds, and voice transmissions are made possible through earpieces and microphones. High-speed data connections are used for communication. All team members can be connected, and outside experts can even be added. A local group can connect with up to 15 different individuals or groups. Users can simultaneously work on documents, analyze data, or map out ideas.

Managers use decision support systems (DSS) as tools to enhance their ability to make complex decisions. DSS are computer and communication systems that process incoming data and synthesize pertinent information for managers to use. Another tool for decision making focuses on helping groups make decisions. A group decision support system (GDSS) uses computer support and communication facilities to support group decision-making processes in either face-to-face meetings or dispersed meetings. The GDSS has been shown to affect conflict management within a group by depersonalizing the issue and by forcing the group to discuss its conflict management process.[115] Team decisions often improve by using a GDSS because members share information more fully when they use a GDSS.[116]

GDSS make real-time decision making possible in the virtual team. They are ideal systems for brainstorming, focus groups, and group decisions. By using support tools within the GDSS, users can turn off their individual identities and interact with anonymity, and poll participants and assemble statistical information relevant to the decision being made. GDSS are thus the sophisticated software that makes collaboration possible in virtual teams.

Internal internets, or intranets, are adaptations of Internet technologies for use within a company. For virtual teams, the Internet and intranets can be rich communication and decision-making resources. These tools allow virtual teams to archive text, visual, audio, and data files for use in decision making. They permit virtual teams to inform other organization members about the team's progress and enable the team to monitor other projects within the organization.

By using DVCS, GDSS, and Internet/intranet technologies, virtual teams can capitalize on a rich communications environment for decision making. It is difficult, however, to duplicate the face-to-face environment. The effectiveness of a virtual team's decision making depends on its members' ability to use the tools that are available. Collaborative systems can enhance virtual teams' decision quality if they are used well.[117]

Artificial intelligence is used to develop an expert system, which is a programmed decision tool. The system is set up using decision rules, and the effectiveness of the expert system is highly dependent on its design. Because expert systems are sources of knowledge and experience and not just passive software, the organization must decide who is responsible for the decisions made by expert systems. Organizations must therefore be concerned about the liability for using the recommendations of expert systems.

Agent Based Modeling (ABM) is an agent-based simulation, in which a computer creates thousands, even millions, of individual actors known as agents. Each of these virtual agents makes virtual decisions, thus providing an estimate of how each decision type might affect outcomes.[118]

Several organizations have adopted agent-based modeling to evaluate potential consequences of important decisions. For example, when Macy's was considering a major remodeling of its store space, it enlisted the services of PricewaterhouseCoopers to develop an ABM system that virtually modeled the changes in floor plans and consumers' responses to these changes. This simulation helped Macy's experiment with differing layout plans in cyberspace thus predicting consumer behavior before it risked costly changes in the real world. You can see that for organizations like Macy's, ABM is a software simulation that can be very useful in making complex, nonroutine decisions involving some degree of uncertainty.

Decision making in the virtual workplace is characterized by the use of sophisticated technologies to assist in decision making. Some of these technologies, like videoconferencing, DSS, and GDSS, simply assist humans in making the decision. Others, like expert systems and some forms of agent-based modeling, play a greater role in making the decision. Regardless of the degree to which they play a role, all of these technologies make decision making in today's virtual workplace easier.

⬛ ETHICAL ISSUES IN DECISION MAKING

: 8. Utilize an "ethics check" for examining managerial decisions.

One criterion that should be applied to decision making is the ethical implications of the decision. Ethical decision making in organizations is influenced by many factors, including individual differences and organizational rewards and punishments.

Kenneth Blanchard and Norman Vincent Peale proposed an "ethics check" for decision makers in their book *The Power of Ethical Management.*[119] They contend that the decision maker should ponder the following three questions:

1. Is it legal? (Will I be violating the law or company policy?)

2. Is it balanced? (Is it fair to all concerned in the short term and long term? Does it promote win–win relationships?)

3. How will it make me feel about myself? (Will it make me proud of my actions? How will I feel when others become aware of the decision?)

> **◀◀ think critically ▶▶**
>
> Using the "ethics check," evaluate the decision to launch the *Challenger*. How could knowledge of ethical decision making have aided the individuals who made this decision?

General Dynamics, a major defense contractor that builds weapons ranging from submarines to fighter jets, faced charges of defrauding the government out of more than $2 billion on the Los Angeles class submarine project. While the company ultimately admitted no guilt, the scandal cost Admiral Hyman Rickover his career. And audiotapes of the firm's CEO and CFO discussing their plans to "screw the Navy," combined with revelations that a company vice president billed the Navy for the cost of kenneling his dog while he was out of town, started a long downhill slide which ultimately cost the two executives their jobs and cost General Dynamics its reputation.[120]

In summary, all decisions, whether made by individuals or by groups, must be evaluated for their ethics. Organizations should reinforce ethical decision making among employees by encouraging and rewarding it. Socialization processes should convey to newcomers the ethical standards of behavior in the organization. Groups should use devil's advocates and dialectical methods to reduce the potential for groupthink and the unethical decisions that may result. Effective and ethical decisions are not mutually exclusive.

◼ MANAGERIAL IMPLICATIONS: DECISION MAKING IS A CRITICAL ACTIVITY

Decision making is important at all levels of every organization. At times, managers may have the luxury of optimizing (selecting the best alternative), but more often they are forced to satisfice (select the alternative that is good enough). And, at times, the decision process can even seem unpredictable and random.

Individuals differ in their preferences for risk, as well as in their styles of gathering information and making judgments. Understanding individual differences can help managers maximize strengths in employee decision styles and build teams that capitalize on strengths. Creativity is one such strength. It can be encouraged by providing employees with a supportive environment that nourishes innovative ideas. Creativity training has been used in some organizations with positive results.

Some decisions are best made by individuals and some by teams or groups. The task of the manager is to diagnose the situation and implement the appropriate level of participation. To do this effectively, managers should know the advantages and disadvantages of various group decision-making techniques and should minimize the potential for groupthink. Finally, decisions made by individuals or groups should be analyzed to see whether they are ethical.

LOOKING BACK :: DISNEY-PIXAR ANIMATION STUDIOS

Good Decisions: Happy Endings

Embedding a culture of innovation in a fantasy industry can be a challenge in itself. When asked about whether he was concerned that others were stealing his ideas early on, Walt Disney responded by saying that he could create ideas faster than others could steal them. Disney planned to stay ahead of the curve. By its decision to acquire Pixar, one could argue that it is staying ahead of the curve. Disney-Pixar recognizes that as soon as you are successful, competitors jump on the bandwagon. And, imitators can do a great job of replicating cutting-edge creations. Disney-Pixar's distinctive competence lies in its creation of a variety of original software programs and wealth of technical wizardry combined with financial strength and market access. Prior to the acquisition, Pixar was the only major studio working exclusively in computer-generated animation. Pixar's program can model surface textures, such as metal, cloth, or hair, and create lighting effects, such as bright sunlight or flickering candlelight. The studio's RenderMan program captures all the data and helps artists create the final images. RenderMan won an Academy Award for technical achievement. More than bells and whistles, Pixar has distinctive competence in the good stories that emerge from its movie scripts; that is the foundation of its business.[121,122] And its recent synergy with Disney is touted as one of the happiest endings in animation history.

C H A P T E R   S U M M A R Y

1. Bounded rationality assumes that there are limits to how rational managers can be.

2. The garbage can model shows that under high uncertainty, decision making in organizations can be an unsystematic process.

3. Intuition and creativity are positive influences on decision making and should be encouraged in organizations.

4. Techniques such as brainstorming, nominal group technique, Delphi technique, devil's advocacy, and dialectical inquiry can help managers reap the benefits of group methods while limiting the possibilities of groupthink and group polarization.

5. Technology has aided managerial and group decision making through the use of several techniques such as DVCS, DSS, GDSS, ABM, and expert systems.

6. Managers should carefully weigh the ethical issues surrounding decisions and encourage ethical decision making throughout the organization.

K E Y   T E R M S

bounded rationality (p. 224)

brainstorming (p. 239)

creativity (p. 231)

Delphi technique (p. 240)

devil's advocacy (p. 240)

dialectical inquiry (p. 241)

effective decision (p. 223)

escalation of commitment (p. 226)

garbage can model (p. 225)

group polarization (p. 239)

groupthink (p. 236)

heuristics (p. 224)

intuition (p. 229)

nominal group technique (NGT) (p. 240)

nonprogrammed decision (p. 222)

participative decision making (p. 235)

programmed decision (p. 222)

rationality (p. 224)

risk aversion (p. 225)

satisfice (p. 224)

social decision schemes (p. 235)

synergy (p. 235)

R E V I E W   Q U E S T I O N S

1. Compare the garbage can model with the bounded rationality model. Compare the usefulness of these models in today's organizations.

2. What are the individual and organizational influences on creativity?

3. Describe the advantages and disadvantages of group decision making.

4. Describe the symptoms of groupthink, and identify actions that can be taken to prevent it.

5. What technologies can be used to improve decision making in the virtual workplace?

Discussion and Communication   Q U E S T I O N S

1. Why is identification of the real problem the first and most important step in the decision-making process? How does attribution theory explain mistakes that can be made as managers and employees work together to explain why the problem occurred?

2. How can organizations effectively manage both risk taking and escalation of commitment in the decision-making behavior of employees?

3. How can organizations encourage creative decision making?

4. What are some organizations that use expert systems? Group decision support systems? How will these two technologies affect managerial decision making?

5. *(communication question)* Form a team of four persons. Find two examples of recent decisions

made in organizations: one that you consider a good decision, and one that you consider a bad decision. Two members should work on the good decision, and two on the bad decision. Each pair should write a brief description of the decision. Then write a summary of what went right, what went wrong, and what could be done to improve the decision process. Compare and contrast your two examples in a presentation to the class.

6. *(communication question)* Reflect on your own experiences in groups with groupthink. Describe the situation in which you encountered groupthink, the symptoms that were present, and the outcome. What remedies for groupthink would you prescribe? Summarize your answers in a memo to your instructor.

ETHICAL DILEMMA

Slowly the managers of Beckman Services began arriving. An unexpected meeting had been called for 8:30 this morning and not everyone anticipated the news they were about to hear. Beckman was a financial services company that sold its services to individuals and companies. Since the terrorist attacks on 9/11, Beckman had been experiencing financial difficulties. In order to boost sales, an incentive plan had been rolled out last December which management hoped would solve the problem. The plan challenged the sales force to increase sales by 15 percent. A daunting task, but the generous incentives made the challenge well worth the endeavor.

The meeting began and CEO Frank May opened by welcoming everyone to "one of the most difficult meetings he has ever had to call." Frank explained that although the incentive plan seemed to be working very well, the company's cash reserves were not as strong as they had hoped and delivering the promised bonuses would be more difficult than they had anticipated. He realized this was not going to be a popular decision, but Frank felt sure the salespeople would understand.

Richard Johnson, VP of Human Resources, sat quietly in the meeting. He could not believe what was happening. It was now early November and the salespeople had been working hard for the last 10 months. He knew many of the salespeople well, and they were counting on the promised bonuses. What message would the company be sending if it canceled this program at the last minute? He also knew he should say something, but disagreeing with Frank was never a good idea, especially when everyone else seemed to agree with the plan. Richard looked up and realized that the meeting was coming to an end. To challenge Frank in front of the team could be the end of his career at Beckman. But it couldn't be possible that everyone really agreed with Frank, could they? "Any questions or concerns about proceeding?" Frank asked. Richard needed to make a decision and make it fast.

QUESTIONS

1. Who are the stakeholders in Beckman Services, and what is Frank May's responsibility to them?
2. To whom does Richard Johnson have a responsibility?
3. Evaluate Richard Johnson's decision using rule, virtue, right, and justice theories.

EXPERIENTIAL EXERCISES

9.1 MAKING A LAYOFF DECISION

Purpose
In this exercise, you will examine how to weigh a set of facts and make a difficult personnel decision about laying off valued employees during a time of financial hardship. You will also examine your own values and criteria used in the decision-making process.

The Problem
Walker Space Institute (WSI) is a medium-sized firm located in Connecticut. The firm essentially has been a subcontractor on many large space contracts that have been acquired by firms like Alliant Techsystems and others.

With the cutback in many of the National Aeronautics and Space Administration programs, Walker has an excess of employees. Stuart Tartaro, the head of one of the sections, has been told by his superior that he must reduce his section of engineers from nine to six. He is looking at the following summaries of their vitae and pondering how he will make this decision:

1. *Roger Allison*, age 26, married, two children. Allison has been with WSI for a year and a half. He is a very good engineer, with a degree from Rensselaer Polytech. He has held two prior jobs and lost both of them because of cutbacks in the space program. He moved to Connecticut from California to take this job. Allison is well liked by his coworkers.

2. *Dave Jones*, age 24, single. Jones is an African-American, and the company looked hard to get him because of affirmative action pressure. He is not very popular with his coworkers. Because he has been employed less than a year, not too much is known about his work. On his one evaluation (which was average), Jones accused his supervisor of bias against African-Americans. He is a graduate of the Detroit Institute of Technology.

3. *William Foster*, age 53, married, three children. Foster is a graduate of "the school of hard knocks." After serving in the Vietnam War, he started to go to school but dropped out because of high family expenses. Foster has worked at the company for 20 years. His ratings were excellent for 15 years. The last five years they have been average. Foster feels his supervisor grades him down because he does not "have sheepskins covering his office walls."

4. *Donald Boyer*, age 32, married, no children. Boyer is well liked by his coworkers. He has been at WSI five years, and he has a B.S. and M.S. in engineering from Purdue University. Boyer's ratings have been mixed. Some supervisors rated him high and some average. Boyer's wife is an M.D.

5. *Ann Shuster*, age 29, single. Shuster is a real worker, but a loner. She has a B.S. in engineering from the University of California. She is working on her M.S. at night, always trying to improve her technical skills. Her performance ratings have been above average for the three years she has been at WSI.

6. *Sherman Soltis*, age 37, divorced, two children. He has a B.S. in engineering from Ohio State University. Soltis is very active in community affairs: Scouts, Little League, and United Way. He is a friend of the vice president through church work. His ratings have been average, although some recent ones indicate that he is out of date. He is well liked and has been employed at WSI for 14 years.

7. *Warren Fortuna*, age 44, married, five children. He has a B.S. in engineering from Georgia Tech. Fortuna headed this section at one time. He worked so hard that he had a heart attack. Under doctor's orders, he resigned from the supervisory position. Since then, he has done good work, though because of his health, he is a bit slower than the others. Now and then he must spend extra time on a project because he did get out of date during the eight years he headed the section. His performance evaluations for the last two years have been above average. He has been employed at WSI for 14 years.

8. *Robert Treharne*, age 47, single. He began an engineering degree at MIT but had to drop out for financial reasons. He tries hard to stay current by regular reading of engineering journals and taking all the short courses the company and nearby colleges offer. His performance evaluations have varied, but they tend to be average to slightly above average. He is a loner, and Tartaro thinks this has negatively affected Treharne's performance evaluations. He has been employed at WSI 16 years.

9. *Sandra Rosen*, age 22, single. She has a B.S. in engineering technology from the Rochester Institute of Technology. Rosen has been employed less than a year. She is enthusiastic, a very good worker, and well liked by her coworkers. She is well regarded by Tartaro.

Tartaro does not quite know what to do. He sees the good points of each of his section members. Most have been good employees. They all can pretty much do one another's work. No one has special training.

He is fearful that the section will hear about the downsizing and morale will drop. Work would fall off. He does not even want to talk to his wife about it, in case she would let something slip. Tartaro has come to you, Edmund Graves, personnel manager at WSI, for some guidelines on this decision—legal, moral, and best personnel practice.

Assignment
You are Edmund Graves. Write a report with your recommendations for termination and a careful analysis of the criteria for the decision. You should also carefully explain to Tartaro how you would go about the terminations and what you would consider reasonable termination pay. You should also advise him about the pension implications of this decision. Generally, fifteen years' service entitles you to at least partial pension.

SOURCE: William F. Glueck, *Personnel: A Diagnostic Approach*, rev. ed. (Dallas: Business Publications Inc., 1982), 24–26. Reprinted by permission of McGraw-Hill Irwin.

9.2 DILEMMA AT 29,000 FEET

Purpose
Making ethical decisions often requires taking decisive actions in ambiguous situations. Making these decisions entails not just weighing options and making rational choices but making choices between competing but equally important demands. Managers must not only take action, but they also must provide compelling reasons that make their choices rationally accountable to others. This exercise requires you to think through an ethical situation, take an action, and create a convincing justification for your action. The exercise is designed to encourage critical thinking about complex problems and to encourage thinking about how you might resolve a dilemma outside your area of expertise.

The Problem

Imagine you are the sole leader of a mountain-climbing expedition and have successfully led a group of three climbers to the mountain summit. However, on your descent, trouble sets in as a fierce storm engulfs the mountain and makes progression down nearly impossible. One climber collapses from exhaustion at 24,000 feet and cannot continue down the mountain. The two stronger climbers insist on continuing down without you because they know if they stay too long at high altitude death is certain. No one has ever survived overnight on the mountain. A rescue attempt is impossible because helicopters cannot reach you above 18,000 feet.

As the leader, you are faced with a difficult choice: abandon your teammate and descend alone or stay with your dying teammate and face almost certain death. On one hand, you might stay with your dying teammate in hopes that the storm might clear and a rescue party will be sent. However, you know that if you stay both of you will most likely die. On the other hand, you are still strong and may be able to make it down to safety, abandoning your teammate to die alone on the mountain.

Assignment

Your assignment is to make an argument for one of the actions: staying with your teammate or descending alone. The technical aspects of mountain climbing are not important, nor is it good enough to state that you would not get in this situation in the first place! What is important is that you provide a well-reasoned argument for your action. A good argument might address the following points:

1. A discussion of the pros and cons of each action: staying with your teammate or descending alone.

2. A discussion of the underlying values and assumptions of each action. For example, staying with the teammate implies that you have a particular obligation as the leader of a team; descending alone suggests that you may place a higher value on your own life.

3. A discussion of your own values and viewpoints on the topic. In other words, take a stand and

justify your position. How, for example, might you justify to the family of the abandoned climber your decision to descend alone? How might you justify to your own family your decision to stay with the ailing climber?

4. What prior experience, knowledge, or beliefs lead you to your conclusion?

5. How might this situation be similar to or different from the dilemmas faced in more typical organizations? For example, do leaders need to take actions that require them to make similar difficult decisions? Have you experienced any similar dilemmas that had no easy answer in the workplace, and how did you resolve them?

Final Thoughts

Remember, there is no right or wrong answer to this case. The point is to consider and make clear your own ethical choices by evaluating all relevant information, evaluating the underlying assumptions of each, and creating a clear and convincing argument for action. A quote by philosopher Martha Craven Nussbaum might act as a starting point for your study. She writes,

> Both alternatives make a serious claim on your practical attention. You might sense that no matter how you choose, you will be left with some regret that you did not do the other thing. Sometimes you may be clear about which is the better choice and yet feel pain over the frustration of the other significant concerns. It is extremely important to realize that the problem is not just one difficult decision but that conflicts arise when the final decision itself is perfectly obvious.

Good luck in your decision!

SOURCE: D. C. Kayes, "Dilemma at 29,000 Feet: An Exercise in Ethical Decision Making Based on the 1996 Mt. Everest Climbing Disaster," *Journal of Management Education* 26 (2002): 307–321. Reprinted by permission of Sage Publications.

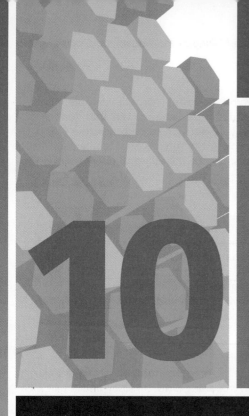

10

Power and Politics

LEARNING OBJECTIVES

After reading this chapter, you should be able to do the following:

: 1. Distinguish among power, influence, and authority.

: 2. Compare interpersonal and intergroup sources of power.

: 3. Understand the ethical use of power.

: 4. Define organizational politics and understand the role of political skill and major influence tactics.

: 5. Develop a plan for managing employee–boss relationships.

: 6. Discuss how managers can empower others.

THINKING AHEAD :: CISCO SYSTEMS

The Highs and Lows of Power

John Chambers, CEO of Cisco, has known both the highs and the lows that often accompany power. From his humble roots in West Virginia, Chambers, though mildly dyslexic, graduated second in his high school class. Throughout most of the 1990s, Cisco was at the top of the world, and John Chambers was clearly at the top of Cisco. Sales tripled in his first three years at the helm. From a relatively small maker of switching equipment, Cisco grew to power the Internet bubble, at one time boasting that its equipment handled 75 percent of all Internet traffic. As the Internet grew, Cisco grew even faster, and at its amazing peak in March 2000, Cisco briefly became the most valuable company on the planet, worth more than half a trillion dollars. John Chambers was named *Chief Executive*'s 2000 CEO of the Year, and he and Cisco were truly powerful.

The peak of power was short-lived. Almost exactly one year later, the Internet bubble had burst, and Chambers sat with top managers finalizing plans to lay off almost 20 percent of the firm's employees. Along the way, more than 3,000 resellers and 800 suppliers were eliminated, and the firm wrote off more than $2 billion in inventory. Shortly after the layoffs, major customers including AT&T called a meeting to deliver a chilling message: Cisco's telecom software was too buggy, and unless the firm provided an immediate fix, they would take their business elsewhere.

The year 2001 ended with a net loss of $1 billion and Cisco's stock price languishing. Chambers, previously touted as a business icon in the same league as Bill Gates or Alfred P. Sloan, and who had once enjoyed serving ice cream to his employees on Fridays, found himself forced to hire bodyguards to travel with him in the face of threats from disgruntled former employees. From prince to pariah, John Chambers had experienced both the highs and the lows of corporate power. Only time would reveal the next chapter in his story.[1,2,3,4]

⬛ THE CONCEPT OF POWER

Power is the ability to influence someone else. As an exchange relationship, it occurs in transactions between an agent and a target. The agent is the person using the power, and the target is the recipient of the attempt to use power.[5]

Because power is an ability, individuals can learn to use it effectively. *Influence* is the process of affecting the thoughts, behavior, and feelings of another person. *Authority* is the right to influence another person.[6] It is important to understand the subtle differences among these terms. For instance, a manager may have authority but no power. She may have the right, by virtue of her position as boss, to tell someone what to do. But she may not have the skill or ability to influence other people.

In a relationship between the agent and the target, there are many influence attempts that the target considers legitimate. Working 40 hours per week, greeting customers, solving problems, and collecting bills are actions that, when requested by the manager, are considered legitimate by a customer service representative. Requests such as these fall within the employee's *zone of indifference*—the range in which attempts to influence the employee are perceived as legitimate and are acted on without a great deal of thought.[7] The employee accepts that the manager has the authority to request such behaviors and complies with the requests. Some requests, however, fall outside the zone of indifference, so the manager must work to enlarge the employee's zone of indifference. Enlarging the zone is accomplished with power (an ability) rather than with authority (a right).

: 1. Distinguish among power, influence, and authority.

power
The ability to influence another person.

influence
The process of affecting the thoughts, behavior, and feelings of another person.

authority
The right to influence another person.

zone of indifference
The range in which attempts to influence a person will be perceived as legitimate and will be acted on without a great deal of thought.

Suppose the manager asks the employee to purchase a birthday gift for the manager's wife or to overcharge a customer for a service call. The employee may think that the manager has no right to ask these things. These requests fall outside the zone of indifference; they're viewed as extraordinary, and the manager has to operate from outside the authority base to induce the employee to fulfill them. In some cases, no power base is enough to induce the employee to comply, especially if the behaviors requested by the manager are considered unethical by the employee.

Failures to understand power and politics can be costly in terms of your career. In the wake of the attacks on September 11, 2001, American Airlines CEO, Donald Carty managed to wrest over a billion dollars from unions in terms of concessions to keep American from having to file for bankruptcy. Unfortunately, on the same day the agreement was announced, more news was made. It was disclosed that special pension trust funding and huge retention bonuses were given to American Airlines executives, including Carty—despite the fact that union workers had agreed to the steep pay cuts. Carty spent the next three and a half weeks apologizing, even giving the money back, before falling on his sword. He may have lost his job because he lost the trust of his American Airlines employees. This example illustrates that managers must learn as much as possible about power and politics to be able to use them effectively and to manage the inevitable political behavior in organizations.[8,9]

: 2. Compare interpersonal and intergroup sources of power.

⚑ FORMS AND SOURCES OF POWER IN ORGANIZATIONS

Individuals have many forms of power to use in their work settings. Some of them are interpersonal—used in interactions with others. One of the earliest and most influential theories of power comes from French and Raven, who tried to determine the sources of power managers use to influence other people.

▪ INTERPERSONAL FORMS OF POWER

French and Raven identified five forms of interpersonal power that managers use. They are reward, coercive, legitimate, referent, and expert power.[10]

reward power
Power based on an agent's ability to control rewards that a target wants.

Reward power is power based on the agent's ability to control rewards that a target wants. For example, managers control the rewards of salary increases, bonuses, and promotions. Reward power can lead to better performance, but only as long as the employee sees a clear and strong link between performance and rewards. To use reward power effectively, then, the manager should be explicit about the behavior being rewarded and should make the connection clear between the behavior and the reward.

coercive power
Power that is based on an agent's ability to cause an unpleasant experience for a target.

Coercive power is power that is based on the agent's ability to cause the target to have an unpleasant experience. To coerce someone into doing something means to force the person to do it, often with threats of punishment. Managers using coercive power may verbally abuse employees or withhold support from them.

legitimate power
Power that is based on position and mutual agreement; agent and target agree that the agent has the right to influence the target.

Legitimate power, which is similar to authority, is power that is based on position and mutual agreement. The agent and target agree that the agent has the right to influence the target. It doesn't matter that a manager thinks he has the right to influence his employees; for legitimate power to be effective, the employees must also believe the manager has the right to tell them what to do. In Native American societies, the chieftain has legitimate power; tribe members believe in his right to influence the decisions in their lives.

Referent power is an elusive power that is based on interpersonal attraction. The agent has referent power over the target because the target identifies with or wants to be like the agent. Charismatic individuals are often thought to have referent power. Interestingly, the agent need not be superior to the target in any way. People who use referent power well are most often individualistic and respected by the target.

Expert power is the power that exists when the agent has specialized knowledge or skills that the target needs. For expert power to work, three conditions must be in place. First, the target must trust that the expertise given is accurate. Second, the knowledge involved must be relevant and useful to the target. Third, the target's perception of the agent as an expert is crucial. Using easy-to-understand language signals the target that the expert has an appreciation for real-world concerns and increases the target's trust in the expert.[11]

Which type of interpersonal power is most effective? Research has focused on this question since French and Raven introduced their five forms of power. Some of the results are surprising. Reward power and coercive power have similar effects.[12] Both lead to compliance. That is, employees will do what the manager asks them to, at least temporarily, if the manager offers a reward or threatens them with punishment. Reliance on these sources of power is dangerous, however, because it may require the manager to be physically present and watchful in order to apply rewards or punishment when the behavior occurs. Constant surveillance creates an uncomfortable situation for managers and employees and eventually results in a dependency relationship. Employees will not work unless the manager is present.

Legitimate power also leads to compliance. When told "Do this because I'm your boss," most employees will comply. However, the use of legitimate power has not been linked to organizational effectiveness or to employee satisfaction.[13] In organizations where managers rely heavily on legitimate power, organizational goals are not necessarily met.

Referent power is linked with organizational effectiveness. It is the most dangerous power, however, because it can be too extensive and intensive in altering the behavior of others. Charismatic leaders need an accompanying sense of responsibility for others. Christopher Reeve's referent power made him a powerful spokesperson for research on spinal injuries and stem cell research.

Expert power has been called the power of the future.[14] Of the five forms of power, it has the strongest relationship with performance and satisfaction. It is through expert power that vital skills, abilities, and knowledge are passed on within the organization. Employees internalize what they observe and learn from managers they perceive to be experts.

The results on the effectiveness of these five forms of power pose a challenge in organizations. The least effective power bases—legitimate, reward, and coercive—are the ones most likely to be used by managers.[15] Managers inherit these power bases as part of the position when they take a supervisory job. In contrast, the most effective power bases—referent and expert—are ones that must be developed and strengthened through interpersonal relationships with employees.

referent power
An elusive power that is based on interpersonal attraction.

expert power
The power that exists when an agent has specialized knowledge or skills that the target needs.

: 3. Understand the ethical use of power.

■ USING POWER ETHICALLY

Managers can work at developing all five of these forms of power for future use. The key to using them well is using them ethically, as Table 10.1 shows. Coercive power, for example, requires careful administration if it is to be used in an ethical manner. Employees should be informed of the rules in advance, and any punishment should be used consistently, uniformly, and privately. The key to

TABLE 10.1

Guidelines for the Ethical Use of Power

FORM OF POWER	GUIDELINES FOR USE
Reward power	Verify compliance.
	Make feasible, reasonable requests.
	Make only ethical requests.
	Offer rewards desired by subordinates.
	Offer only credible rewards.
Coercive power	Inform subordinates of rules and penalties.
	Warn before punishing.
	Administer punishment consistently and uniformly.
	Understand the situation before acting.
	Maintain credibility.
	Fit punishment to the infraction.
	Punish in private.
Legitimate power	Be cordial and polite.
	Be confident.
	Be clear and follow up to verify understanding.
	Make sure request is appropriate.
	Explain reasons for request.
	Follow proper channels.
	Exercise power consistently.
	Enforce compliance.
	Be sensitive to subordinates' concerns.
Referent power	Treat subordinates fairly.
	Defend subordinates' interests.
	Be sensitive to subordinates' needs and feelings.
	Select subordinates similar to oneself.
	Engage in role modeling.
Expert power	Maintain credibility.
	Act confident and decisive.
	Keep informed.
	Recognize employee concerns.
	Avoid threatening subordinates' self-esteem.

SOURCE: *Leadership in Organizations,* 5th ed. by Gary A. Yukl. Copyright © 1981, 144–152. Adapted by permission of Pearson Education, Inc., Upper Saddle River, NJ.

using all five types of interpersonal power ethically is to be sensitive to employees' concerns and to communicate well.

To French and Raven's five power sources, we can add a source that is very important in today's organizations. *Information power* is access to and control over important information. Consider, for example, the CEO's administrative assistant. He or she has information about the CEO's schedule that people need if they are going to get in to see the CEO. Central to the idea of information power is the person's position in the communication networks in the organization, both formal and informal. Also important is the idea of framing, which is the "spin" that managers put on information. Managers not only pass information on to subordinates; they interpret this information and influence the subordinates' perceptions of it. Information power occurs not only in the downward direction; it may also flow upward from subordinates to managers. In manufacturing plants, database operators often control information about plant metrics and shipping performance that is vital to managerial decision making. Information power can also flow laterally. Salespersons convey information from the outside environment (their customers) that is essential for marketing efforts.

information power
Access to and control over important information.

Determining whether a power-related behavior is ethical is complex. Another way to look at the ethics surrounding the use of power is to ask three questions that show the criteria for examining power-related behaviors:[16]

1. *Does the behavior produce a good outcome for people both inside and outside the organization?* This question represents the criterion of *utilitarian outcomes*. The behavior should result in the greatest good for the greatest number of people. If the power-related behavior serves only the individual's self-interest and fails to help the organization reach its goals, it is considered unethical. A salesperson might be tempted to discount a product deeply in order to make a sale that would win a contest. Doing so would be in her self-interest but would not benefit the organization.

2. *Does the behavior respect the rights of all parties?* This question emphasizes the criterion of *individual rights*. Free speech, privacy, and due process are individual rights that are to be respected, and power-related behaviors that violate these rights are considered unethical.

3. *Does the behavior treat all parties equitably and fairly?* This question represents the criterion of *distributive justice*. Power-related behavior that treats one party arbitrarily or benefits one party at the expense of another is unethical. Granting a day of vacation to one employee in a busy week in which coworkers must struggle to cover for him might be considered unethical.

◀◀ think critically ▶▶

Evaluate American Airlines CEO Donald Carty's agreement with the union in terms of these three questions. Do you think the outcome might have been different if Carty had used these criteria?

To be considered ethical, power-related behavior must meet all three criteria. If the behavior fails to meet the criteria, then alternative actions should be considered. Unfortunately, most power-related behaviors are not easy to analyze. Conflicts may exist among the criteria; for example, a behavior may maximize the greatest good for the greatest number of people but may not treat all parties equitably. Individual rights may need to be sacrificed for the good of the organization. A CEO may need to be removed from power for the organization to be saved. Still, these criteria can be used on a case-by-case basis to sort through the complex ethical issues surrounding the use of power.

■ INTERGROUP SOURCES OF POWER

Groups or teams within an organization can also use power from several sources. One source of intergroup power is control of *critical resources*.[17] When one group controls an important resource that another group desires, the first group holds power. Controlling resources needed by another group allows the power-holding group to influence the actions of the less powerful group. This process can continue in an upward spiral. Groups seen as powerful tend to be given more resources from top management.[18]

Groups also have power to the extent that they control *strategic contingencies*— activities that other groups depend on in order to complete their tasks.[19] The dean's office, for example, may control the number of faculty positions to be filled in each department of a college. The departmental hiring plans are thus contingent on approval from the dean's office. In this case, the dean's office controls the strategic contingency of faculty hiring, and thus has power.

Three factors can give a group control over a strategic contingency.[20] One is the *ability to cope with uncertainty*. If one group can help another group deal with uncertainty, it has power. One organizational group that has gained power in recent years is the legal department. Faced with increasing government regulations and fears of litigation, many other departments seek guidance from the legal department.

Another factor that can give a group control power is a *high degree of centrality* within the organization. If a group's functioning is important to the organization's success, it has high centrality. The sales force in a computer firm, for example, has power because of its immediate effect on the firm's operations and because other groups (accounting and servicing groups, for example) depend on its activities.

The third factor that can give a group power is *nonsubstitutability*—the extent to which a group performs a function that is indispensable to an organization. A team of computer specialists may be powerful because of its expertise with a system. It may have specialized experience that another team cannot provide.

The strategic contingencies model thus shows that groups hold power over other groups when they can reduce uncertainty, when their functioning is central to the organization's success, and when the group's activities are difficult to replace.[21] The key to all three of these factors, as you can see, is dependency. When one group controls something that another group needs, it creates a dependent relationship—and gives one group power over the other.

■ POLITICAL BEHAVIOR IN ORGANIZATIONS

Like power, the term politics in organizations may conjure up a few negative images. However, *organizational politics* is not necessarily negative; it is the use of power and influence in organizations. Because organizations are arenas

strategic contingencies
Activities that other groups depend on in order to complete their tasks.

: 4. Define organizational politics and understand the role of political skill and major influence tactics.

organizational politics
The use of power and influence in organizations.

in which people have competing interests, effective managers must reconcile competing interests. Organizational politics are central to managing. As people try to acquire power and expand their power base, they use various tactics and strategies. Some are sanctioned (acceptable to the organization); others are not. *Political behavior* refers to actions not officially sanctioned by an organization that are taken to influence others in order to meet one's personal goals.[22] Sometimes personal goals are aligned with team or organizational goals, and they can be achieved in support of others' interests. But other times personal goals and the interests of others collide, and individuals pursue politics at the expense of others' interests.[23]

Politics is a controversial topic among managers. Some managers take a favorable view of political behavior; others see it as detrimental to the organization. Some workers who perceive their workplace as highly political actually find the use of political tactics more satisfying and report greater job satisfaction when they engage in political behavior. Some people may therefore thrive in political environments, while others may find office politics distasteful and stressful.[24]

Most people are also amazingly good at recognizing political behavior at all levels of the firm. Employees are not only keenly aware of political behavior at their level but can also spot political behavior at both their supervisor's level and the topmost levels of the organization.[25]

Many organizational conditions encourage political activity. Among them are unclear goals, autocratic decision making, ambiguous lines of authority, scarce resources, and uncertainty.[26] Even supposedly objective activities may involve politics. One such activity is the performance appraisal process. A study of 60 executives who had extensive experience in employee evaluation indicated that political considerations were nearly always part of the performance appraisal process.[27]

Individuals who use power in organizations are organizational politicians. Challenge 10.1 shows the personal characteristics of effective organizational politicians and can help you assess your own political potential.

The effects of political behavior in organizations can be quite negative when the political behavior is strategically undertaken to maximize self-interest. If people within the organization are competitively pursuing selfish ends, they're unlikely to be attentive to the concerns of others. The workplace can seem less helpful, more threatening, and more unpredictable. People focus on their own concerns rather than on organizational goals. If employees view the organization's political climate as extreme, they experience more anxiety, tension, fatigue, and burnout. They are also dissatisfied with their jobs and are more likely to leave.[28] Not all political behavior is destructive. Constructive political behavior is selfless, rather than selfish, in nature. Constructive organizational politicians see the difference between ethical and unethical behavior, understand that relationships drive the political process, and use power with a sense of responsibility.[29]

■ INFLUENCE TACTICS

Influence is the process of affecting the thoughts, behavior, or feelings of another person. That other person could be the boss (upward influence), an employee

political behavior
Actions not officially sanctioned by an organization that are taken to influence others in order to meet one's personal goals.

CHALLENGE   10.1

Evaluate Your Political Potential

Examine the following table and answer the questions that follow it:

Personal Characteristics of Effective Political Actors

Personal Characteristic	Behavioral Example
Articulate	• Must be able to clearly communicate ideas.
Sensitive	• Must be sensitive to other individuals, situations, and opportunities.
Socially adept	• Must understand the social norms of the organization and behave so as to be perceived by influential others as "fitting in well."
Competent	• Must have the necessary skills and qualifications.
Popular	• Must be liked or admired by others in the organization.
Extraverted	• Must be interested in what happens outside of him or her.
Self-confident	• Must have confidence in his or her abilities.
Aggressive	• Must be self-assertive and forceful.
Ambitious	• Must be eager to attain success.
Devious	• Must be willing to use any tactic to get his or her way.
"Organization man or woman"	• Must emphasize the well-being of the organization.
Highly intelligent	• Must be able to use his or her knowledge to solve problems.
Logical	• Must be capable of reasoning.

1. Which characteristics do you possess? Which do you need to work on? Ask a friend which characteristics you possess.

2. On the basis of the table, are you an effective political actor? Explain.

3. Can we assume that all of these characteristics are worth having?

Source: Table 2. *Personal Characteristics of Effective Political Actors Organizational Politics: Tactics and Characteristics of Its Actors,* Allen, Robert W., Dan L. Madison, Lyman W. Porter, Patricia A. Renwick, and Bronston T. Mayes, Vol. 22, No. 1 (Fall 1979): 77–83.

(downward influence), or a coworker (lateral influence). There are eight basic types of influence tactics. They are listed and described in Table 10.2.[30]

Research has shown that the four tactics used most frequently are consultation, rational persuasion, inspirational appeals, and ingratiation. Upward appeals and coalition tactics are used moderately. Exchange tactics are used least often. Cisco has managed to pull itself out of the corporate meltdown scenario described in the Thinking Ahead feature by adopting considerable lateral influence strategies. It has teamed up with Microsoft on some applications such as security issues and IBM on others by developing products and services to protect client computing from worms and viruses.

TACTICS	DESCRIPTION	EXAMPLES
Pressure	The person uses demands, threats, or intimidation to convince you to comply with a request or to support a proposal.	If you don't do this, you're fired. You have until 5:00 to change your mind, or I'm going without you.
Upward appeals	The person seeks to persuade you that the request is approved by higher management or appeals to higher management for assistance in gaining your compliance with the request.	I'm reporting you to my boss. My boss supports this idea.
Exchange	The person makes an explicit or implicit promise that you will receive rewards or tangible benefits if you comply with a request or support a proposal or reminds you of a prior favor to be reciprocated.	You owe me a favor. I'll take you to lunch if you'll support me on this.
Coalition	The person seeks the aid of others to persuade you to do something or uses the support of others as an argument for you to agree also.	All the other supervisors agree with me. I'll ask you in front of the whole committee.
Ingratiation	The person seeks to get you in a good mood or to think favorably of him or her before asking you to do something.	Only you can do this job right. I can always count on you, so I have another request.
Rational persuasion	The person uses logical arguments and factual evidence to persuade you that a proposal or request is viable and likely to result in the attainment of task objectives.	This new procedure will save us $150,000 in overhead. It makes sense to hire John; he has the most experience.
Inspirational appeals	The person makes an emotional request or proposal that arouses enthusiasm by appealing to your values and ideals or by increasing your confidence that you can do it.	Being environmentally conscious is the right thing. Getting that account will be tough, but I know you can do it.
Consultation	The person seeks your participation in making a decision or planning how to implement a proposed policy, strategy, or change.	This new attendance plan is controversial. How can we make it more acceptable? What do you think we can do to make our workers less fearful of the new robots on the production line?

SOURCE: Copyright 1990 by the American Psychological Association. Adapted with permission. The official citation that should be used in referencing this material is Yukl, G., and Falbe, C. M. (1990). "Influence Tactics and Objectives in Upward, Downward, and Lateral Influence Attempts," *Journal of Applied Psychology* 75: 132–140. No further reproduction or distribution is permitted without written permission from the American Psychological Association.

TABLE 10.2

Influence Tactics Used in Organizations

◀◀**think critically**▶▶

What are the most common types of influence tactics you encounter at work and in school? Which are most effective? Are these influence tactics also ethical?

Influence tactics are used for impression management, which was described in Chapter 3. In impression management, individuals use influence tactics to control others' impressions of them. One way in which people engage in impression management is through image building. Another way is to use impression management to get support for important initiatives or projects.

Ingratiation is an example of one tactic often used for impression management. Ingratiation can take many forms, including flattery, opinion conformity, and subservient behavior.[31] Exchange is another influence tactic that may be used for impression management. Offering to do favors for someone in an effort to create a favorable impression is an exchange tactic.

Which influence tactics are most effective? It depends on the target of the influence attempt and the objective. Individuals use different tactics for different purposes, and they use different tactics for different people. Influence attempts with subordinates, for example, usually involve assigning tasks or changing behavior. With peers, the objective is often to request help. With superiors, influence attempts are often made to request approval, resources, political support, or personal benefits. Rational persuasion and coalition tactics are used most often to get support from peers and superiors to change company policy. Consultation and inspirational appeals are particularly effective for gaining support and resources for a new project.[32] Cisco incorporated Corporate Citizenship Councils made up of functional leaders from all its business units. The purpose of the councils is to address issues that are important to all of Cisco's stakeholders: employees, customers, investors, governments, and communities it operates in. Such a strategy is a consultation strategy that is used to help align Cisco's stakeholder concerns with organizational objectives. Overall, the most effective tactic in terms of achieving objectives is rational persuasion. Pressure is the least effective tactic.

Influence tactics are often used on bosses in order to get the boss to evaluate the employee more favorably or to give the employee a promotion. Two tactics—rational persuasion and ingratiation—appear to work effectively. Employees who use these tactics receive higher performance evaluations than other employees who don't use rational persuasion and ingratiation.[33] When supervisors believe an employee's motive for doing favors for the boss is simply to be a good citizen, they are likely to reward that employee. However, when the motive is seen as brownnosing (ingratiation), supervisors respond negatively.[34] And, as it becomes more obvious that the employee has something to gain by impressing the boss, the likelihood that ingratiation will succeed decreases.

Still, a well-disguised ingratiation is hard to resist. Attempts that are not obvious usually succeed in increasing the target's liking for the ingratiator.[35] Most people have trouble remaining neutral when someone flatters them or agrees with them. However, witnesses to the ingratiation are more likely to question the motive behind the flattery or agreement. Observers are more skeptical than the recipients of the ingratiation.

There is evidence that men and women view politics and influence attempts differently. Men tend to view political behavior more favorably than do women. When both men and women witness political behavior, they view it more positively if the agent is of their gender and the target is of the opposite gender.[36] Women executives often view politics with distaste and expect to be recognized and promoted only on the merit of their work. A lack of awareness of organizational politics is a barrier that holds women back in terms of moving into senior executive ranks.[37] Women may have fewer opportunities to develop political skills because of a lack of mentors and role models and because they are often excluded from informal networks.[38]

Different cultures prefer different influence tactics at work. One study found that American managers dealing with a tardy employee tended to rely on pressure tactics such as "If you don't start reporting on time for work, I will have no choice but to start docking your pay." In contrast, Japanese managers relied on influence tactics that either appealed to the employee's sense of duty ("It is your duty as a responsible employee of this company to begin work on time.") or emphasized a consultative approach ("Is there anything I can do to help you overcome the problems that are preventing you from coming to work on time?").[39]

It is important to note that influence tactics do have some positive effects. When investors form coalitions and put pressure on firms to increase their research and development efforts, it works.[40] However, some influence tactics, including pressure, coalition building, and exchange, can have strong ethical implications. There is a fine line between being an impression manager and being seen as a manipulator.

How can a manager use influence tactics well? First, a manager can develop and maintain open lines of communication in all directions: upward, downward, and lateral. Then, the manager can treat the targets of influence attempts—whether managers, employees, or peers—with basic respect. Finally, the manager can understand that influence relationships are reciprocal—they are two-way relationships. As long as the influence attempts are directed toward organizational goals, the process of influence can be advantageous to all involved.

POLITICAL SKILL

Researchers at Florida State University have generated an impressive body of research on *political skill*.[41] They argue that political skill is a distinct interpersonal attribute that is important for managerial success and should be considered in hiring and promotion decisions. They found that a leader's political skill has a positive effect on team performance, trust for the leader, and support for the leader.[42,43] Furthermore, political skill was found to buffer the negative effects of stressors such as role conflict in work settings. This set of research findings points at the importance of developing political skill for managerial success.[44] So what exactly is political skill? It is the ability to get things done through positive interpersonal relationships outside the formal organization. Politically skilled individuals have the ability to accurately understand others and use this knowledge to influence others in order to meet personal or organizational goals. Political skill is made up of four key dimensions: social astuteness, interpersonal influence, networking ability, and sincerity. Social astuteness refers to accurate perception and evaluation of social situations. Socially astute individuals manage social situations in ways that present them in the most favorable light. Interpersonal influence refers to a subtle and influential personal style that is effective in getting things done. Individuals with interpersonal influence are very flexible in adapting their behavior to differing targets of influence or differing contexts in order to achieve their goals. Networking ability is an individual's capacity to develop and retain diverse and extensive social networks. People who have networking ability are effective in building successful alliances and coalitions, thus making them skilled at negotiation and conflict resolution. Sincerity refers to an individual's ability to portray forthrightness and authenticity in all of their dealings. Individuals who can appear sincere inspire more confidence and trust, which makes them very successful in influencing other people.[45] These four dimensions of political skill can be taught. Several organizations now offer training to help develop their employees' political skill. For example, the Center for Creative Leadership investigated why top executives fail. They found that the most potent cause of failure is lack of social effectiveness.[46] High self-monitors and politically savvy individuals score higher on an index of political skill, as do individuals who are emotionally intelligent. Challenge 10.2 helps you assess your political skill.

political skill
The ability to get things done through favorable interpersonal relationships outside of formally prescribed organizational mechanisms.

CHALLENGE

10.2

Rate Your Political Skills

Using the following seven-point scale, please place the number on the blank before each item that best describes how much you agree with each statement about yourself.

           1 = *Strongly disagree*
           2 = *Disagree*
           3 = *Slightly disagree*
           4 = *Neutral*
           5 = *Slightly agree*
           6 = *Agree*
           7 = *Strongly agree*

1. _____ I spend a lot of time and effort at work networking with others.

2. _____ I am able to make most people feel comfortable and at ease around me.

3. _____ I am able to communicate easily and effectively with others.

4. _____ It is easy for me to develop good rapport with most people.

5. _____ I understand people very well.

6. _____ I am good at building relationships with influential people at work.

7. _____ I am particularly good at sensing the motivations and hidden agendas of others.

8. _____ When communicating with others, I try to be genuine in what I say and do.

9. _____ I have developed a large network of colleagues and associates at work who I can call on for support when I really need to get things done.

10. _____ At work, I know a lot of important people and am well connected.

11. _____ I spend a lot of time at work developing connections with others.

12. _____ I am good at getting people to like me.

13. _____ It is important that people believe I am sincere in what I say and do.

14. _____ I try to show a genuine interest in other people.

15. _____ I am good at using my connections and network to make things happen at work.

16. _____ I have good intuition or savvy about how to present myself to others.

17. _____ I always seem to instinctively know the right things to say or do to influence others.

18. _____ I pay close attention to people's facial expressions.

The higher your total score, the better are your political skills.

◀◀think critically▶▶

How might people misuse political skill? Recall some instances of such politically skilled individuals that you have encountered either at work or in school.

MANAGING POLITICAL BEHAVIOR IN ORGANIZATIONS

Politics cannot and should not be eliminated from organizations. Managers can, however, take a proactive stance and manage the political behavior that inevitably occurs.[47]

Open communication is one key to managing political behavior. Uncertainty tends to increase political behavior, and communication that reduces the uncertainty is important. One form of communication that will help is to clarify the sanctioned and nonsanctioned political behaviors in the organization. For example, you may want to encourage social power as opposed to personal power.[48]

Another key is to clarify expectations regarding performance. This can be accomplished through the use of clear, quantifiable goals and through the establishment of a clear connection between goal accomplishment and rewards.[49]

Participative management is yet another key. Often, people engage in political behavior when they feel excluded from decision-making processes in the organization. By including them, you will encourage positive input and eliminate behind-the-scenes maneuvering.

Encouraging cooperation among work groups is another strategy for managing political behavior. Managers can instill a unity of purpose among work teams by rewarding cooperative behavior and by implementing activities that emphasize the integration of team efforts toward common goals.[50]

Managing scarce resources well is also important. An obvious solution to the problem of scarce resources is to increase the resource pool, but few managers have this luxury. Clarifying the resource allocation process and making the connection between performance and resources explicit can help discourage dysfunctional political behavior.

Providing a supportive organizational climate is another way to manage political behavior effectively. A supportive climate allows employees to discuss controversial issues promptly and openly. This prevents the issue from festering and potentially causing friction among employees.[51]

Managing political behavior at work is important. The perception of dysfunctional political behavior can lead to dissatisfaction.[52] When employees perceive that there are dominant interest groups or cliques at work, they are less satisfied with pay and promotions. When they believe that the organization's reward practices are influenced by who you know rather than how well you perform, they are less satisfied.[53] In addition, when employees believe that their coworkers are exhibiting increased political behavior, they are less satisfied with their coworkers. Open communication, clear expectations about performance and rewards, participative decision-making practices, work group cooperation, effective management of scarce resources, and a supportive organizational climate can help managers prevent the negative consequences of political behavior.

MANAGING UP: MANAGING THE BOSS

5. Develop a plan for managing employee–boss relationships.

One of the least discussed aspects of power and politics is the relationship between you and your boss. This is a crucial relationship, because your boss is your most important link with the rest of the organization.[54] The employee–boss

TABLE 10.3

Managing Your Relationship with Your Boss

MAKE SURE YOU UNDERSTAND YOUR BOSS AND HER CONTEXT, INCLUDING:

Her goals and objectives.

The pressures on her.

Her strengths, weaknesses, and blind spots.

Her preferred work style.

ASSESS YOURSELF AND YOUR NEEDS, INCLUDING:

Your own strengths and weaknesses.

Your personal style.

Your predisposition toward dependence on authority figures.

DEVELOP AND MAINTAIN A RELATIONSHIP THAT:

Fits both your needs and styles.

Is characterized by mutual expectations.

Keeps your boss informed.

Is based on dependability and honesty.

Selectively uses your boss's time and resources.

SOURCE: Reprinted by permission of Harvard Business Review. From "Managing Your Boss," by J. J. Gabarro and J. P. Kotter (May–June 1993): 155. Copyright © 1993 by the Harvard Business School Publishing Corporation; all rights reserved.

relationship is one of mutual dependence; you depend on your boss to give you performance feedback, provide resources, and supply critical information. She depends on you for performance, information, and support. Because it's a mutual relationship, you should take an active role in managing it. Too often, the management of this relationship is left to the boss; but if the relationship doesn't meet your needs, chances are you haven't taken the responsibility to manage it proactively.

Table 10.3 shows the basic steps to take in managing your relationship with your boss. The first step is to try to understand as much as you can about your boss. What are the person's goals and objectives? What kind of pressures does the person face in the job? Many individuals naively expect the boss to be perfect and are disappointed when they find that this is not the case. What are the boss's strengths, weaknesses, and blind spots? Because this is an emotionally charged relationship, it is difficult to be objective; but this is a critical step in forging an effective working relationship. What is the boss's preferred work style? Does the person prefer everything in writing or hate detail? Does the boss prefer that you make appointments, or is dropping in at the boss's office acceptable? The point is to gather as much information about your boss as you can and to try to put yourself in that person's shoes.

The second step in managing this important relationship is to assess yourself and your own needs in much the same way that you analyzed your boss's. What are your strengths, weaknesses, and blind spots? What is your work style? How do you normally relate to authority figures? Some of us have tendencies toward counterdependence; that is, we rebel against the boss as an authority and view the boss as a hindrance to our performance. Or, in contrast, we might take an overdependent stance, passively accepting the employee–boss relationship and treating the boss as an all-wise, protective parent. What is your tendency? Knowing how you react to authority figures can help you understand your interactions with your boss.

Once you have done a careful self-analysis and tried to understand your boss, the next step is to work to develop an effective relationship. Both parties' needs and styles must be accommodated. A fundraiser for a large volunteer organization related a story about a new boss, describing him as cold, aloof, unorganized, and inept. She made repeated attempts to meet with him and clarify expectations, and his usual reply was that he didn't have the time. Frustrated, she almost looked for a new job. "I just can't reach him!" was her refrain. Then she stepped back to consider her boss's and her own styles. Being an intuitive-feeling type of person, she prefers constant feedback and reinforcement from others. Her boss, an intuitive-thinker, works comfortably without feedback from others and has a tendency to fail to praise or reward others. She sat down with him and cautiously discussed the differences in their needs. This discussion became the basis for working out a comfortable relationship. "I still don't like him, but I understand him better," she said.

Another aspect of managing the relationship involves working out mutual expectations. One key activity is to develop a plan for work objectives and have the boss agree to it.[55] It is important to do things right, but it is also important to do the right things. Neither party to the relationship is a mind reader, and clarifying the goals is a crucial step.

Keeping the boss informed is also a priority. No one likes to be caught off guard, and there are several ways to keep the boss informed. Give the boss a weekly to-do list as a reminder of the progress towards goals. When you read something pertaining to your work, clip it out for the boss. Most busy executives appreciate being given materials they don't have time to find for themselves. Give the boss interim reports, and let the boss know if the work schedule is slipping. Don't wait until it's too late to take action.

The employee–boss relationship must be based on dependability and honesty. This means giving and receiving positive and negative feedback. Most of us are reluctant to give any feedback to the boss, but positive feedback is welcomed at the top. Negative feedback, while tougher to initiate, can clear the air. If given in a problem-solving format, it can even bring about a closer relationship.[56]

Finally, remember that the boss is on the same team as you are. The golden rule is to make the boss look good, because you expect the boss to do the same for you.

🔲 SHARING POWER: EMPOWERMENT

Another positive strategy for managing political behavior is *empowerment*—sharing power within an organization. As modern organizations grow flatter, eliminating layers of management, empowerment becomes more and more important. Jay Conger defines *empowerment* as "creating conditions for heightened motivation

6. Discuss how managers can empower others.

empowerment
Sharing power within an organization.

through the development of a strong sense of personal self-efficacy."[57] This means sharing power in such a way that individuals learn to believe in their ability to do the job. The driving idea of empowerment is that the individuals closest to the work and to the customers should make the decisions and that this makes the best use of employees' skills and talents. You can empower yourself by developing your sense of self-efficacy.

Four dimensions comprise the essence of empowerment: meaning, competence, self-determination, and impact.[58] *Meaning* is a fit between the work role and the employee's values and beliefs. It is the engine of empowerment through which employees become energized about their jobs. If employees' hearts are not in their work, they cannot feel empowered. *Competence* is the belief that one has the ability to do the job well. Without competence, employees will feel inadequate and lack a sense of empowerment. *Self-determination* is having control over the way one does his or her work. Employees who feel they're just following orders from the boss cannot feel empowered. *Impact* is the belief that one's job makes a difference within the organization. Without a sense of contributing to a goal, employees cannot feel empowered.

Employees need to experience all four of the empowerment dimensions in order to feel truly empowered. Only then will organizations reap the hoped-for rewards from empowerment efforts. The rewards sought are increased effectiveness, higher job satisfaction, and less stress.

◀◀ think critically ▶▶

Imagine that you are the CEO of an organization. You have just empowered lower-level employees who do not believe they are competent and their jobs have any impact. What might happen to individual and organizational outcomes over a period of one, six, and twelve months?

Empowerment is easy to advocate but difficult to put into practice. Conger offers some guidelines on how leaders can empower others.

First, managers should express confidence in employees and set high performance expectations. Second, managers should create opportunities for employees to participate in decision making. This means participation in the forms of both voice and choice. Employees should not just be asked to contribute their opinions about any issue; they should also have a vote in the decision that is made. Third, managers should remove bureaucratic constraints that stifle autonomy. Often, companies have antiquated rules and policies that prevent employees from managing themselves. Fourth, managers should set inspirational or meaningful goals. When individuals feel they "own" a goal, they are more willing to take personal responsibility for it.

The empowerment process also carries with it a risk of failure. When you delegate responsibility and authority, you must be prepared to allow employees to fail; and failure is not something most managers tolerate well. At Merck, some say the CEO Ray Gilmartin empowered scientists too much and that their failures cost Merck its profitability and reputation as one of *Fortune's* Most Admired Companies. One example of this empowerment involved a diabetes drug that early research showed caused tumors in mice. Scientists argued that despite early studies showing the drug wasn't viable, research should continue, and it did . . . until the drug was finally axed, costing the company considerably in terms of time and money.[59]

☝ MANAGERIAL IMPLICATIONS: USING POWER EFFECTIVELY

Sydney Finkelstein, a professor at Dartmouth University, spends his time studying why executives fail. Interestingly, most of these failures involve the misuse of power and organizational politics. Here are several reasons why executives fail:

> *They see themselves and their companies as dominating their environments.* While confidence is helpful, the perception that a company is without peer is a recipe for failure. On a more personal level, CEOs who come to see themselves as uniquely gifted in comparison to their competitors and coworkers are generally ripe for a fall.

> *They think they have all the answers.* While decisive leadership and vision often lead to the executive suite, an unwillingness to admit ignorance or seek others' input is a recipe for disaster. A reluctance to empower others leads to failure.

> *They ruthlessly eliminate anyone who isn't 100 percent behind them.* Business history is replete with leaders who culled the ranks of those who were willing to voice different opinions, only to find themselves blundering down the road to disaster without anyone to yell "Stop!"

> *They stubbornly rely on what worked for them in the past.* Like most of us, business leaders tend to fall back on what has worked before. Unfortunately, yesterday's solution is rarely an ideal fit for today's challenge, and successes of the past may well inhibit success in the future.

> *They have no clear boundaries between their personal interests and corporate interests.* As a top leader invests more time and effort in a firm, it's easy for him or her to become convinced that the firm is simply a reflection of his or her own enormous ego. Ironically, leaders who fail to make this distinction tend to be far less careful about spending corporate resources, leading to often embarrassing revelations of executive excess at employee and stockholder expense.[60]

While Finkelstein is quick to point out that corporate executives are, almost without exception, amazingly bright and talented individuals, they also tend to succumb to the same temptations as lesser mortals. Given the extreme power they wield, their failures tend to be much more visible, painful, and far reaching than most. Corporate executives need accountability to help them avoid these blunders.

In addition to learning from failure, there is research on how to use power successfully. John Kotter argues that managers therefore need to develop power strategies to operate effectively.[61] Kotter offers some guidelines for managing dependence on others and for using power successfully:

> *Use power in ethical ways.* People make certain assumptions about the use of power. One way of using the various forms of power ethically is by applying the criteria of utilitarian outcomes, individual rights, and distributive justice.

> *Understand and use all of the various types of power and influence.* Successful managers diagnose the situation, understand the people involved, and choose a compatible influence method.

> *Seek jobs that allow you to develop your power skills.* Recognize that managerial positions are dependent ones, and look for positions that allow you to focus on a critical issue or problem.

> *Use power tempered by maturity and self-control.* Power for its own sake should not be a goal, nor should power be used for self-aggrandizement.

> *Accept that influencing people is an important part of the management job.* Power means getting things accomplished; it is not a dirty word. Acquiring and using power well is a key to managerial success.

You can use these guidelines to enhance your own power skills. Mastering the power and politics within an organization takes respect and patience. When all people are empowered, the total amount of power within the organization will increase.

LOOKING BACK :: Cisco Systems

Powering Up

Coworkers who endured the Cisco layoffs of 2001 recall how devastated John Chambers was by the difficult decision; as one put it, the normally optimistic Chambers was somber for a full year following the cuts. Others note that Cisco's dark years noticeably aged the CEO, putting a full decade of lines on his congenial face in only three years.

Amazingly, out of the rubble of the dot.com bust, a handful of firms have emerged stronger than ever; perhaps not surprisingly, John Chambers and Cisco appear to be among the survivors. Chambers' reputation was scorched in 2001 when he refused to lower his projections of Cisco's performance; even when he finally scaled back profit projections, he was still proven harshly wrong. And the firm's reputation for being obsessively customer focused was also called into question, as its clients began to pound the firm's products. Furthermore, many of its former suppliers were alienated, as two-thirds of them were eliminated and others were forced to offer discounts and longer warranty periods. And in perhaps his toughest sell to date, Chambers tried to tame the firm's freewheeling culture by requiring executives to provide regular reports on productivity and adding new procedures to bring some organization to the firm's chaotic ordering process. Perhaps most impressively, Chambers tied top execu-

tives' bonuses to teamwork, with 30 percent of their bonuses based on how well they collaborated with others in the firm. The result? Despite flat revenues, earnings for 2003 almost doubled those of 2002. Since then, Cisco seems to have not looked back. It was awarded the Presidential Corporate Leadership award in 2003 and acquired several smaller firms throughout 2004 and 2005.[62] Chambers also took on the task of personally repairing customer relations, calling several telecom executives to apologize for his arrogance. The result? Orders rose 20 percent over the previous year. And in perhaps the most telling sign of his persistence, Chambers himself appears to have regained his optimism about the firm's future, albeit now tempered with a dose of hard-earned wisdom. In retrospect, Chambers was late to react, but he made the tough decisions, regardless of how they might be perceived. His appropriate use of power, along with his ability to learn from mistakes, are the reasons Cisco is still in business today when many of its former dot.com rivals no longer exist. Most importantly, in contrast with all the anger that former employees of John Chambers reported in 2002, today, Cisco boasts very high job satisfaction levels: 85 percent of its employees report being completely satisfied with their jobs and Cisco.

CHAPTER SUMMARY

1. Power is the ability to influence others. Influence is the process of affecting the thoughts, behavior, and feelings of others. Authority is the right to influence others.

2. French and Raven's five forms of interpersonal power are reward, coercive, legitimate, referent, and expert power. Information power is another form of interpersonal power.

3. The key to using all of these types of power well is to use them ethically.

4. Intergroup power sources include control of critical resources and strategic contingencies.

5. Organizational politics is an inevitable feature of work life. Political behavior consists of actions not officially sanctioned that are taken to influence others in order to meet personal goals. Managers should take a proactive role in managing politics.

6. The ability to get things done through favorable interpersonal relationships outside of formally prescribed organizational mechanisms is known as political skill.

7. The employee–boss relationship is an important political relationship. Employees can use their skills to develop more effective working relationships with their bosses.

8. Empowerment is a positive strategy for sharing power throughout the organization.

KEY TERMS

authority (p. 251)
coercive power (p. 252)
empowerment (p. 265)
expert power (p. 253)
influence (p. 251)

information power (p. 255)
legitimate power (p. 252)
organizational politics (p. 256)
political behavior (p. 257)
political skill (p. 261)

power (p. 251)
referent power (p. 253)
reward power (p. 252)
strategic contingencies (p. 256)
zone of indifference (p. 251)

REVIEW QUESTIONS

1. What are the five types of power according to French and Raven? What are the effects of these types of power? What is information power?

2. What are the intergroup sources of power?

3. How do organizations encourage political activity?

4. Which influence tactics are most effective?

5. What are some of the characteristics of an effective relationship between you and your boss?

6. What are some ways to empower people at work?

Discussion and Communication QUESTIONS

1. Who is the most powerful person you know personally? What is it that makes that person so powerful?

2. Why is it hard to determine if power has been used ethically?

3. How does attribution theory explain the reactions supervisors can have to influence tactics? How can managers prevent the negative consequences of political behavior?

4. Are people in your work environment empowered? How could they become more empowered?

5. Chapter 2 discussed power distance as a dimension of cultural differences. How would empowerment efforts be different in a country with high power distance?

6. *(communication question)* Think of a person you admire. Write a newspaper feature analyzing the person's use of power in terms of the ideas presented in the chapter.

ETHICAL DILEMMA

James Allen, a manager for a large retail department store, sat at his desk remembering how this whole thing began. He had called a meeting of his team in early June in which he had laid out his plan to increase productivity over the next six months. Between back to school and the holidays, July through December was always a busy time in retail, but this year needed to be exceptional. Just weeks before that meeting, James had been informed that the store manager was retiring and his successor would be appointed from within the organization. Specifically, the manager whose department was the most productive and efficient through the end of the year would be named the new general manager.

It was now October, and the evaluation period was half over. James felt confident that things were going well in his department. His concern at the moment was Tom Sharp's department. One of Tom's employees had confided that Tom was promising favors to his employees who helped him gain this promotion. Once promoted, he would be in a position to give raises or even promote those who had helped him advance. To help Tom accomplish his goals, the department employees were willing to do just about anything, even work overtime off the clock to reduce labor costs.

James knew that these practices were wrong and against the company's mission and policies. His concern was how to handle it. He felt confident that his department would be the best, so Tom's unethical practices would not affect the outcome. And if he were the new general manager, he could handle the problem then. However, was it right to let these behaviors continue for another three months? Was James sending the wrong signal to his own employees by keeping quiet? Was it enough to say that fair and just practices win in the end? If he did blow the whistle, would the people he would soon supervise think badly of him for being a snitch? James really wanted to do the right thing, but he just was not sure what that was.

QUESTIONS

1. Who are the stakeholders that would be affected by James's decision?

2. Does James have a responsibility to come forward with this information?

3. Using rule, virtue, right, and justice theories, evaluate James's decision options.

EXPERIENTIAL EXERCISES

10.1 SOCIAL POWER ROLE-PLAYS

1. Divide the class into five groups of equal size, each of which is assigned one of the French and Raven types of power.

2. Read the following paragraph and prepare an influence plan using the type of power that has been assigned to your group. When you have finished your planning, select one member to play the role of instructor. Then choose from

your own or another group a "student" who is to be the recipient of the "instructor's" efforts.

You are an instructor in a college class and have become aware that a potentially good student has been repeatedly absent from class and sometimes is unprepared when he is there. He seems to be satisfied with the grade he is getting, but you would like to see him attend regularly, be better prepared, and thus do better in the class. You even feel that the student might get really turned on to pursuing a career in this field, which is an exciting one for you. You are respected and liked by your students, and it irritates you that this person treats your dedicated teaching with such a cavalier attitude. You want to influence the student to start attending regularly.

3. Role-playing.
   a. Each group role-plays its influence plan.
   b. During the role-playing, members in other groups should think of themselves as the student being influenced. Fill out the following "Reaction to Influence Questionnaire" for each role-playing episode, including your own.

4. Tabulate the results of the questionnaire within your group. For each role-playing effort, determine how many people thought the power used was reward, coercive, and so on; then add up each member's score for item 2, then for items 3, 4, and 5.

5. Group discussion.
   a. As a class, discuss which influence strategy is the most effective in compliance, long-lasting effect, acceptable attitude, and enhanced relationships.
   b. What are the likely side effects of each type of influence strategy?

REACTION TO INFLUENCE QUESTIONNAIRE

Role-Play #1

1. Type of power used (mark one):

   Reward—Ability to influence because of potential reward.
   Coercive—Ability to influence because of capacity to coerce or punish.
   Legitimate—Stems from formal position in organization.
   Referent—Comes from admiration and liking.
   Expert—Comes from superior knowledge or ability to get things done.

ROLE-PLAYS

1	2	3	4	5

Think of yourself on the receiving end of the influence attempt just described and record your own reaction with an "X" in the appropriate box.

2. As a result of this influence attempt, I will . . .
   definitely not comply   definitely comply
   1 2 3 4 5

3. Any change that does come about will be . . .
   temporary   long-lasting
   1 2 3 4 5

4. My own personal reaction is . . .
   resistant   accepting
   1 2 3 4 5

5. As a result of this influence attempt, my relationship with the instructor will probably be . . .
   worse   better
   1 2 3 4 5

ROLE-PLAYS

1	2	3	4	5

SOURCE: Gib Akin, *Exchange* 3, No. 4 (1978): 38–39. Reprinted by permission of Gib Akin, McIntire School of Commerce, University of Virginia.

10.2 A SIMPLE – BUT POWERFUL – POWER SIMULATION

PART A—SIMULATION

1. **Divide groups**

   Students turn in a dollar bill to the teacher and are divided into three groups based on criteria given by the instructor, assigned to their workplaces, and instructed to read the rules and tasks that follow. The money is divided into thirds: two-thirds is given to the top group, one-third is given to the middle group, and none is given to the bottom group.

2. **Conduct simulation**

   Groups go to their assigned workplaces and complete their tasks.

Rules:

a. Members of the top group are free to enter the space of either of the other groups and to communicate whatever they wish, whenever they wish. Members of the middle group may enter the space of the lower group when they wish but must request permission to enter the top group's space (which the top group can refuse). Members of the lower group may not disturb the top group in any way unless specifically invited by the top group. The lower group does have the right to knock on the door of the middle group and request permission to communicate with them (which can be refused).

b. The members of the top group have the authority to make any change in the rules they wish, at any time, with or without notice.

Tasks:

Top Group: To be responsible for the overall effectiveness and learning from the simulation, and to decide how to use its money.

Middle Group: To assist the top group in providing for the overall welfare of the organization, and to decide how to use its money.

Bottom Group: To identify its resources and to decide how best to provide for learning and the overall effectiveness of the organization.

PART B—DEBRIEF

1. **Representative Discussion**

   Each of the three groups chooses two representatives to go to the front of the class and discuss the following questions with the instructor:

   a. What can we learn about power from this experience? Does it remind us of events we have seen in other organizations?

   b. What did each of us learn individually? How did we think about what power is? Were we satisfied with the amount of power we had? How did we try to exercise or gain more power?

2. **Class Discussion**

   a. What occurred within and between the three groups?

   b. What were the in-group/out-group dynamics?

   c. How did trust and mistrust figure into the simulation?

   d. What does this exercise say about structural injustice?

   e. What were some differences between being in the top group and being in the bottom one?

SOURCE: Lee Bolman and Terrence E. Deal, "A Simple—But Powerful—Power Simulation," *Exchange*, Vol. 4, No. 3 (1979): 38–42.

Leadership and Followership

LEARNING OBJECTIVES

After reading this chapter, you should be able to do the following:

: 1. Define *leadership* and *followership.*

: 2. Discuss the differences between leadership and management and between leaders and managers.

: 3. Evaluate the effectiveness of autocratic, democratic, and laissez-faire leadership styles.

: 4. Explain initiating structure and consideration, leader behaviors, and the Leadership Grid.

: 5. Evaluate the usefulness of Fiedler's contingency theory of leadership.

: 6. Compare and contrast the path–goal theory, leader-member exchange, and the Situational Leadership® model.

: 7. Distinguish among transformational, charismatic, and authentic leaders.

: 8. Discuss the characteristics of effective and dynamic followers.

THINKING AHEAD :: VIRGIN GROUP, LTD.

Richard Branson—Not Your Average Leader

Sir Richard Branson, head of Virgin Group, Ltd., is a lot like other corporate CEOs . . . and yet nothing like them at all. Like many corporate leaders, he starts his day early, often at 4:30 A.M. But unlike most of them, he typically begins it lying in a hammock in his swim trunks, thinking through the business of the day, and jotting notes or writing letters in a small black book. Like many other CEOs, Branson is comfortable discussing technology, having been invited to speak at a recent Microsoft conference; unlike most of them, he never uses a computer, preferring to jot down e-mail messages, which he then dictates to his administrative assistant. For urgent reminders, he simply writes a note on the back of his hand.

Branson's eccentricities extend to other parts of his life. He sports a costly Breitling watch, a gift from its maker, which includes an emergency transmitter to summon a rescue helicopter; alas, the watch shows the incorrect time, since the pin to change the time is next to the pin for summoning help, and

Branson can never remember which is which. More than once, he has been caught without cash for a cab fare or lunch, although his net worth is estimated to be more than $3.2 billion.[1] His preferred briefcase is an athletic duffle bag.

Branson's unique personal style influences every aspect of his companies, which have succeeded in a diverse array of markets from bridal gowns to airlines. In each case, Richard Branson's peculiar perspective on life has helped shape the company's unique and creative business strategies and the way it competes against more traditional firms.[2] Recently, Sir Branson scaled new heights in Britain's "stiff upper lip" culture by setting up a nonprofit blood bank to store umbilical cord blood samples to be used in stem cell research. This move is seen by many as a risky one as stem research has garnered a lot of attention not only for the infinite promise it offers in helping treat diseases such as Alzheimer's and Parkinson's but also over its moral validity.[3]

1. Define *leadership* and *followership*.

leadership
The process of guiding and directing the behavior of people in the work environment.

formal leadership
Officially sanctioned leadership based on the authority of a formal position.

informal leadership
Unofficial leadership accorded to a person by other members of the organization.

followership
The process of being guided and directed by a leader in the work environment.

Leadership in organizations is the process of guiding and directing the behavior of people in the work environment. The first section of the chapter distinguishes leadership from management. *Formal leadership* occurs when an organization officially bestows on a leader the authority to guide and direct others in the organization. *Informal leadership* occurs when a person is unofficially accorded power by others in the organization and uses influence to guide and direct their behavior. Leadership is among the most researched topics in organizational behavior and one of the least understood social processes in organizations.

Leadership has a long, rich history in organizational behavior. In this chapter, we explore many of the theories and ideas that have emerged along the way in that history. To begin, we examine the differences between leaders and managers. Next, we explore the earliest theories of leadership, the trait theories, which try to identify a set of traits that leaders have in common. Following the trait theories, behavioral theories were developed, proposing that leader behaviors, not traits, are what counts. Contingency theories followed soon after. These theories argue that appropriate leader behavior depends on the situation and the followers. Next, we present some exciting contemporary theories of leadership, known as the inspirational theories of leadership, followed by the "hot" and exciting new issues that are arising in leadership. We end by discussing *followership* and providing you with some guidelines for using this leadership knowledge.

LEADERSHIP AND MANAGEMENT

John Kotter suggests that leadership and management are two distinct, yet complementary systems of action in organizations.[4] Specifically, he believes that effective leadership produces useful change in organizations and that good management controls complexity in the organization and its environment. Fred Smith, who founded Federal Express (FedEx) in 1971, has been producing constant change since the company's start. FedEx began with primarily high-dollar medical and technology shipments. The company recently bought Kinko's to extend its reach from the back office to the front.[5] Bill Gates has successfully controlled complexity—Microsoft has grown exponentially from early times when his company's sole product was DOS. Healthy organizations need both effective leadership and good management.

For Kotter, the management process involves (1) planning and budgeting, (2) organizing and staffing, and (3) controlling and problem solving. The management process reduces uncertainty and stabilizes an organization. Alfred P. Sloan's integration and stabilization of General Motors after its early growth years are an example of good management.

In contrast, the leadership process involves (1) setting a direction for the organization; (2) aligning people with that direction through communication; and (3) motivating people to action, partly through empowerment and partly through basic need gratification. The leadership process creates uncertainty and change in an organization. Donald Peterson's championing of a quality revolution at Ford Motor Company is an example of effective leadership.

An advocate for stability and the status quo, Abraham Zaleznik proposes that leaders have distinct personalities that stand in contrast to the personalities of a manager.[6] Zaleznik suggests that both leaders and managers make a valuable contribution to an organization and that each one's contribution is different. Whereas *leaders* agitate for change and new approaches, *managers* advocate stability and the status quo. Sir Branson is a leader who constantly strives for change by acquiring new business divisions and adopting unorthodox business moves. For example, cabin crews of rival airline British Airways (BA) went on strike and BA had to cancel several flights. Sir Branson made a bold move by announcing free first class train tickets on Virgin Trains for anyone with a BA ticket for the days when flights were cancelled! This move caused BA much embarrassment among its customer base, and it rushed to make several accommodations for passengers who were affected by the cancellations.[7] There is a dynamic tension between leaders and managers that makes it difficult for each to understand the other. Leaders and managers differ along four separate dimensions of personality: attitudes toward goals, conceptions of work, relationships with other people, and sense of self. The differences between these two personality types are summarized in Table 11.1. Zaleznik's distinction between leaders and managers is similar to the distinction made between transactional and transformational leaders, or between leadership and supervision. Transactional leaders use formal rewards and punishment to engage in deal making and contractual obligations, which you will read about later in this chapter.

It has been proposed that some people are strategic leaders who embody both the stability of managers and the visionary abilities of leaders. Thus, strategic

2. Discuss the differences between leadership and management and between leaders and managers.

leader
An advocate for change and new approaches to problems.

manager
An advocate for stability and the status quo.

TABLE 11.1			
Leaders and Managers			

PERSONALITY DIMENSION	MANAGER	LEADER
Attitudes toward goals	Has an impersonal, passive, functional attitude; believes goals arise out of necessity and reality	Has a personal and active attitude; believes goals arise from desire and imagination
Conceptions of work	Views work as an enabling process that combines people, ideas, and things; seeks moderate risk through coordination and balance	Looks for fresh approaches to old problems; seeks high-risk positions, especially with high payoffs
Relationships with others	Avoids solitary work activity, preferring to work with others; avoids close, intense relationships; avoids conflict	Is comfortable in solitary work activity; encourages close, intense working relationships; is not conflict averse
Sense of self	Is once born; makes a straightforward life adjustment; accepts life as it is	Is twice born; engages in a struggle for a sense of order in life; questions life

SOURCE: Reprinted by permission of *Harvard Business Review*. From "Managers and Leaders: Are They Different?" by A. Zaleznik (January 2004). Copyright © 2004 by the Harvard Business School Publishing Corporation; all rights reserved.

leaders combine the best of both worlds in a synergistic way. The unprecedented success of both Coca-Cola and Microsoft suggests that their leaders, the late Robert Goizueta (of Coke) and Bill Gates, were strategic leaders.[8]

3. Evaluate the effectiveness of autocratic, democratic, and laissez-faire leadership styles.

EARLY TRAIT THEORIES

The first studies of leadership attempted to identify what physical attributes, personality characteristics, and abilities distinguished leaders from other members of a group.[9] The physical attributes considered have been height, weight, physique, energy, health, appearance, and even age. With regard to leader abilities, attention has been devoted to such constructs as social skills, intelligence, scholarship, speech fluency, cooperativeness, and insight. In this area, there is some evidence that leaders are more intelligent, verbal, and cooperative and have a higher level of scholarship than the average group member. This line of research yielded some interesting findings. However, very few valid generalizations emerged from this line of inquiry. The trait theories have had very limited success in being able to identify the universal, distinguishing attributes of leaders.

4. Explain initiating structure and consideration, leader behaviors, and the Leadership Grid.

BEHAVIORAL THEORIES

Behavioral theories emerged as a response to the deficiencies of the trait theories. Trait theories told us what leaders were like, but didn't address how leaders behaved. Three theories are the foundations of many modern leadership theories: the Lewin, Lippitt, and White studies; the Ohio State studies; and the Michigan studies.

The earliest research on leadership style, conducted by Kurt Lewin and his students, identified three basic styles: autocratic, democratic, and laissez-faire.[10] Leaders with an *autocratic* style use rules and regulations to run the work environment. The leader with a *democratic style* is collaborative, responsive, and interactive in relationships and emphasizes rules and regulations less than the autocratic leader. The leader with a *laissez-faire style* abdicates the authority and responsibility of the position, and this style often results in chaos. The second major behavioral leadership perspective stemmed from the leadership research program at The Ohio State University. This research with pilots and their aircrews identified two major classes of leader behaviors known as initiating structure and consideration.[11,12] *Initiating structure* is leader behavior aimed at defining and organizing work relationships and roles, as well as establishing clear patterns of organization, communication, and ways of getting things done. *Consideration* is leader behavior aimed at nurturing friendly, warm working relationships, as well as encouraging mutual trust and interpersonal respect within the work unit. These two leader behaviors are independent of each other. That is, a leader may be high on both, low on both, or high on one while low on the other. The Ohio State studies were intended to describe leader behavior, not to evaluate or judge behavior.[13]

Another approach to the study of leadership, developed at the University of Michigan, suggests that the leader's style has very important implications for the emotional atmosphere of the work environment and, therefore, for the followers who work under that leader. Two styles of leadership were identified: employee oriented and production oriented.[14] A production-oriented style leads to a work environment characterized by constant influence attempts on the part of the leader, either through direct, close supervision or through the use of many written and unwritten rules and regulations for behavior. The focus is clearly on getting work done. In comparison, an employee-oriented leadership style leads to a work environment that focuses on relationships. The leader exhibits less direct or less close supervision and establishes fewer written or unwritten rules and regulations for behavior. Employee-oriented leaders display concern for people and their needs. These three groups of studies (the Lewin, Lippitt, and White studies; Ohio State studies; and Michigan studies) taken together form the building blocks of many recent leadership theories. What the studies have in common is that two basic leadership styles were identified, with one focusing on tasks (autocratic, production oriented, initiating structure) and one focusing on people (democratic, employee oriented, consideration). Use Challenge 11.1 to assess your supervisor's task- versus people-oriented styles.

■ THE LEADERSHIP GRID: A CONTEMPORARY EXTENSION

Robert Blake and Jane Mouton's *Leadership Grid*, originally called the Managerial Grid, was developed with a focus on attitudes.[15] The two underlying dimensions of the grid are labeled Concern for Results and Concern for People. These two attitudinal dimensions are independent of each other and in different combinations form various leadership styles. Blake and Mouton originally identified five

autocratic style
A style of leadership in which the leader uses strong, directive, controlling actions to enforce the rules, regulations, activities, and relationships in the work environment.

democratic style
A style of leadership in which the leader takes collaborative, responsive, interactive actions with followers concerning the work and work environment.

laissez-faire style
A style of leadership in which the leader fails to accept the responsibilities of the position.

initiating structure
Leader behavior aimed at defining and organizing work relationships and roles, as well as establishing clear patterns of organization, communication, and ways of getting things done.

consideration
Leader behavior aimed at nurturing friendly, warm working relationships, as well as encouraging mutual trust and interpersonal respect within the work unit.

Leadership Grid
An approach to understanding a leader's or manager's concern for results (production) and concern for people.

CHALLENGE   11.1

How Does Your Supervisor Lead?

Answer the following 16 questions concerning your supervisor's (or professor's) leadership behaviors using the seven-point Likert scale. Then complete the summary to examine your supervisor's behaviors.

		Not at All					Very Much	
1. Is your superior strict about observing regulations?		1	2	3	4	5	6	7
2. To what extent does your superior give you instructions and orders?		1	2	3	4	5	6	7
3. Is your superior strict about the amount of work you do?		1	2	3	4	5	6	7
4. Does your superior urge you to complete your work by the time he or she has specified?		1	2	3	4	5	6	7
5. Does your superior try to make you work to your maximum capacity?		1	2	3	4	5	6	7
6. When you do an inadequate job, does your superior focus on the inadequate way the job was done instead of on your personality?		1	2	3	4	5	6	7
7. Does your superior ask you for reports about the progress of your work?		1	2	3	4	5	6	7
8. Does your superior work out precise plans for goal achievement each month?		1	2	3	4	5	6	7
9. Can you talk freely with your superior about your work?		1	2	3	4	5	6	7
10. Generally, does your superior support you?		1	2	3	4	5	6	7
11. Is your superior concerned about your personal problems?		1	2	3	4	5	6	7
12. Do you think your superior trusts you?		1	2	3	4	5	6	7
13. Does your superior give you recognition when you do your job well?		1	2	3	4	5	6	7
14. When a problem arises in your workplace, does your superior ask your opinion about how to solve it?		1	2	3	4	5	6	7
15. Is your superior concerned about your future benefits like promotions and pay raises?		1	2	3	4	5	6	7
16. Does your superior treat you fairly?		1	2	3	4	5	6	7

Add up your answers to Questions 1 through 8. This total indicates your supervisor's performance orientation:

Task orientation = _____

Add up your answers to Questions 9 through 16. This total indicates your supervisor's maintenance orientation:

People orientation = _____

A score above 40 is high, and a score below 20 is low.

Source: Reprinted from "The Performance-Maintenance Theory of Leadership: Review of a Japanese Research Program" by J. Misumi and M. F. Peterson, published in *Administrative Science Quarterly* 30 (1985): 207. By permission of Administrative Science Quarterly © 1985.

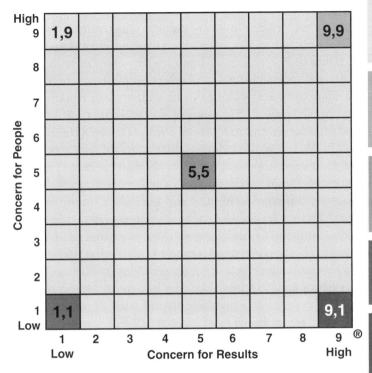

1,9 Country Club Management:
Thoughtful attention to the needs of the people for satisfying relationships leads to a comfortable, friendly organization atmosphere and work tempo.

9,9 Team Management:
Work accomplishment is from committed people; interdependence through a "common stake" in organization purpose leads to relationships of trust and respect.

5,5 Middle-of-the-Road Management:
Adequate organization performance is possible through balancing the necessity to get work out while maintaining morale of people at a satisfactory level.

1,1 Impoverished Management:
Exertion of minimum effort to get required work done is appropriate to sustain organization membership.

9,1 Authority-Compliance Management:
Efficiency in operations results from arranging conditions of work in such a way that human elements interfere to a minimum degree.

Opportunistic Management

In Opportunisitic Management, people adapt and shift to any grid style needed to gain the maximum advantage. Performance occurs according to a system of selfish gain. Effort is given only for an advantage for personal gain.

9+9: Paternalism/Maternalism Management:
Reward and approval are bestowed to people in return for loyalty and obedience; failure to comply leads to punishment.

SOURCE: "The Leadership Grid®" figure, Paternalism Figure and Opportunism from *Leadership Dilemmas—Grid Solutions,* by Robert R. Blake and Anne Adams McCanse (Formerly the Managerial Grid by Robert R. Blake and Jane S. Mouton). Houston: Gulf Publishing Company (Grid Figure: p. 29; Paternalism Figure: p. 30; Opportunism Figure: p. 31). Copyright 1991 by Blake and Mouton, and Scientific Methods, Inc. Reproduced by permission of the owners.

FIGURE 11.1
The Leadership Grid

distinct managerial styles, and further development of the grid has led to the seven distinct leadership styles shown in Figure 11.1.

The *organization man manager (5,5)* is a middle-of-the-road leader who has a medium concern for people and production. This leader attempts to balance a concern for both people and production without a commitment to either.

organization man manager (5,5)
A middle-of-the-road leader.

authority-compliance manager (9,1)
A leader who emphasizes efficient production.

country club manager (1,9)
A leader who creates a happy, comfortable work environment.

team manager (9,9)
A leader who builds a highly productive team of committed people.

impoverished manager (1,1)
A leader who exerts just enough effort to get by.

paternalistic "father knows best" manager (9 + 9)
A leader who promises reward and threatens punishment.

opportunistic "what's in it for me" manager (Opp)
A leader whose style aims to maximize self-benefit.

The *authority-compliance manager (9,1)* has great concern for production and little concern for people. This leader desires tight control in order to get tasks done efficiently and considers creativity and human relations unnecessary. Authority-compliance managers may become so focused on running an efficient organization that they actually use tactics such as bullying. Some authority-compliance managers may intimidate, verbally and mentally attack, and otherwise mistreat subordinates. This form of abuse is quite common, with one in six U.S. workers reporting that they have been bullied by a manager.[16] The *country club manager (1,9)* has great concern for people and little concern for production, attempts to avoid conflict, and seeks to be well liked. This leader's goal is to keep people happy through good interpersonal relations, which are more important to him or her than the task. (This style is not a sound human relations approach but rather a soft Theory X approach.)

The *team manager (9,9)* is considered ideal and has great concern for both people and production. This leader works to motivate employees to reach their highest levels of accomplishment, is flexible, responsive to change, and understands the need for change. The *impoverished manager (1,1)* is often referred to as a laissez-faire leader. This leader has little concern for people or production, avoids taking sides, and stays out of conflicts; he or she does just enough to get by. Two new leadership styles have been added to these five original leadership styles within the grid. The *paternalistic "father knows best" manager (9 + 9)* promises reward for compliance and threatens punishment for noncompliance. The *opportunistic "what's in it for me" manager (Opp)* uses the style that he or she feels will return him or her the greatest self-benefits.

The Leadership Grid is distinguished from the original Ohio State research in two important ways. First, it has attitudinal overtones that are not present in the original research. Whereas the Ohio State researchers aimed to describe leader behavior, the grid addresses both the behavior and the attitude of the leader. Second, the Ohio State approach is fundamentally descriptive and nonevaluative, whereas the grid is normative and prescriptive. Specifically, the grid evaluates the team manager (9,9) as the very best style of managerial behavior. This is the basis on which the grid has been used for team building and leadership training in an organization's development. As an organizational development method, the grid aims to transform the leader in the organization to lead in the "one best way," which according to the grid is the team approach. The team style is one that combines optimal concern for people with optimal concern for results.

◀◀ think critically ▶▶

What are the major limitations of the trait and behavioral approaches to leadership?

CONTINGENCY THEORIES

Contingency theories involve the belief that leadership style must be appropriate for the particular situation. By their nature, contingency theories are "if–then" theories: If the situation is _____, then the appropriate leadership behavior is _____. We examine four such theories, including Fiedler's contingency theory, path–goal theory, normative decision theory, and situational leadership theory.

FIEDLER'S CONTINGENCY THEORY

Fiedler's contingency theory of leadership proposes that the fit between the leader's need structure and the favorableness of the leader's situation determine the team's effectiveness in work accomplishment. This theory assumes that leaders are either task oriented or relationship oriented, depending upon how the leaders obtain their primary need gratification.[17] Task-oriented leaders are primarily gratified by accomplishing tasks and getting work done. Relationship-oriented leaders are primarily gratified by developing good, comfortable interpersonal relationships. Accordingly, the effectiveness of both types of leaders depends on the favorableness of their situation. The theory classifies the favorableness of the leader's situation according to the leader's position power, the structure of the team's task, and the quality of the leader–follower relationships.

5. Evaluate the usefulness of Fiedler's contingency theory of leadership.

THE LEAST PREFERRED COWORKER

Fiedler classifies leaders using the Least Preferred Coworker (LPC) Scale.[18] The LPC Scale is a projective technique through which a leader is asked to think about the person with whom he or she can work least well (the *least preferred coworker*, or *LPC*).

The leader is asked to describe this least preferred coworker using sixteen eight-point bipolar adjective sets. Two of these bipolar adjective sets follow (the leader marks the blank most descriptive of the least preferred coworker):

> Efficient : : : : : : : : : Inefficient
> Cheerful : : : : : : : : : Gloomy

Leaders who describe their least preferred coworker in positive terms (that is, pleasant, efficient, cheerful, and so on) are classified as high LPC, or relationship-oriented, leaders. Those who describe their least preferred coworker in negative terms (that is, unpleasant, inefficient, gloomy, and so on) are classified as low LPC, or task-oriented, leaders.

The LPC score is a controversial element in contingency theory.[19] The LPC score has been critiqued conceptually and methodologically because it is a projective technique with low measurement reliability.

least preferred coworker (LPC)
The person a leader has least preferred to work with over his or her career.

SITUATIONAL FAVORABLENESS

The leader's situation has three dimensions: task structure, position power, and leader–member relations. Based on these three dimensions, the situation is either favorable or unfavorable for the leader. *Task structure* refers to the number and clarity of rules, regulations, and procedures for getting the work done. *Position power* refers to the leader's legitimate authority to evaluate and reward performance, punish errors, and demote group members.

The quality of *leader–member relations* is measured by the Group-Atmosphere Scale, composed of nine eight-point bipolar adjective sets. Two of these bipolar adjective sets follow:

> Friendly : : : : : : : : : Unfriendly
> Accepting : : : : : : : : : Rejecting

A favorable leadership situation is one with a structured task for the work group, strong position power for the leader, and good leader–member relations.

task structure
The degree of clarity, or ambiguity, in the work activities assigned to the group.

position power
The authority associated with the leader's formal position in the organization.

leader–member relations
The quality of interpersonal relationships among a leader and the group members.

In contrast, an unfavorable leadership situation is one with an unstructured task, weak position power for the leader, and moderately poor leader–member relations. Between these two extremes, the leadership situation has varying degrees of moderate favorableness for the leader.

LEADERSHIP EFFECTIVENESS

The contingency theory suggests that low and high LPC leaders are each effective if placed in the right situation.[20] Specifically, low LPC (task-oriented) leaders are most effective in either very favorable or very unfavorable leadership situations. In contrast, high LPC (relationship-oriented) leaders are most effective in situations of intermediate favorableness. Figure 11.2 shows the nature of these relationships and suggests that leadership effectiveness is determined by the degree of fit between the leader and the situation. Recent research has shown that relationship-oriented leaders encourage team learning and innovativeness, which helps products get to market faster. This means that most relationship-oriented leaders perform well in leading new product development teams. In short, the right team leader can help get creative new products out the door faster, while a mismatch between the leader and the situation can have the opposite effect.[21]

FIGURE 11.2

Leadership Effectiveness in the Contingency Theory

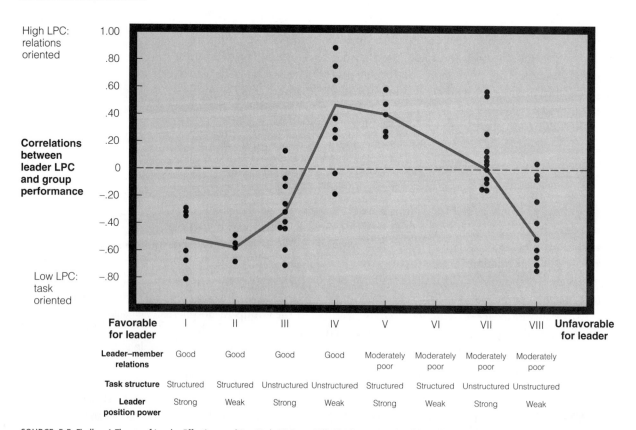

SOURCE: F. E. Fiedler, *A Theory of Leader Effectiveness* (New York: McGraw-Hill, 1964). Reprinted with permission of the author.

What, then, is to be done if there is a misfit? That is, what happens when a low LPC leader is in a moderately favorable situation or when a high LPC leader is in a highly favorable or highly unfavorable situation? It is unlikely that the leader can be changed, according to the theory, because the leader's need structure is an enduring trait that is hard to change. Fiedler recommends that the leader's situation be changed to fit the leader's style.[22] A moderately favorable situation would be reengineered to be more favorable and therefore more suitable for the low LPC leader. A highly favorable or highly unfavorable situation would be changed to one that is moderately favorable and more suitable for the high LPC leader.

Fiedler's theory makes an important contribution in drawing our attention to the leader's situation.

▪ PATH–GOAL THEORY

Robert House developed a path–goal theory of leader effectiveness based on an expectancy theory of motivation.[23] From the perspective of path–goal theory, the basic role of the leader is to clear the follower's path to the goal. The leader uses the most appropriate of four leader behavior styles to help followers clarify the paths that lead them to work and personal goals. The key concepts in the theory are shown in Figure 11.3.

A leader selects from the four leader behavior styles, shown in Figure 11.3, the one that is most helpful to followers at a given time. The directive style is used when the leader must give specific guidance about work tasks, schedule work, and let followers know what is expected. The supportive style is used when the leader needs to express concern for followers' well-being and social status. The participative style is used when the leader must engage in joint decision-making activities with followers. The achievement-oriented style is used when the leader must set challenging goals for followers and show strong confidence in those followers.

In selecting the appropriate leader behavior style, the leader must consider both the followers and the work environment. A few characteristics are included in Figure 11.3. Let us look at two examples. In Example 1, the followers are inexperienced and working on an ambiguous, unstructured task. The leader in this situation might best use a directive style. In Example 2, the followers are highly trained professionals, and the task is a difficult, yet achievable one. The leader

: 6. Compare and contrast the path–goal theory, leader–member exchange, and the Situational Leadership® model.

FIGURE 11.3

The Path–Goal Theory of Leadership

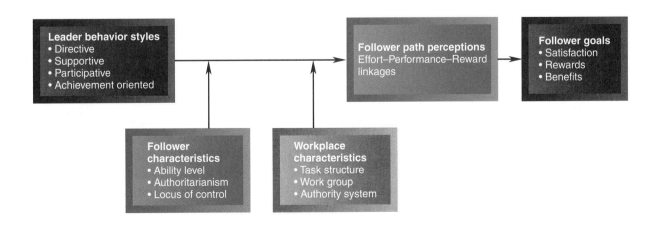

in this situation might best use an achievement-oriented style. The leader always chooses the leader behavior style that helps followers achieve their goals.

The path–goal theory assumes that leaders adapt their behavior and style to fit the characteristics of the followers and the environment in which they work. Actual tests of the path–goal theory and its propositions provide conflicting evidence.[24] The path–goal theory does have intuitive appeal and reinforces the idea that the appropriate leadership style depends on both the work situation and the followers. Research is focusing on which style works best in specific situations. For example, in small organizations, leaders who used visionary, transactional, and empowering behaviors, while avoiding autocratic behaviors, were most successful.[25]

▪ LEADER–MEMBER EXCHANGE

leader-member exchange theory (LMX)

A theory that recognizes that leaders form two groups of followers, an in-group and an out-group.

Leader–member exchange theory, or *LMX*, recognizes that leaders may form different relationships with followers. The basic idea behind LMX is that leaders form two groups, in-groups and out-groups, of followers. In-group members tend to be similar to the leader and given greater responsibilities, more rewards, and more attention. They work within the leader's inner circle of communication. As a result, in-group members are more satisfied, have lower turnover, and have higher organizational commitment. In contrast, out-group members are outside the circle and receive less attention and fewer rewards. They are managed by formal rules and policies.[26]

Research on LMX is supportive. In-group members are more likely to engage in organizational citizenship behavior, while out-group members are more likely to retaliate against the organization.[27] And, the type of stress varies by the group to which a subordinate belongs. In-group members' stress comes from the additional responsibilities placed on them by the leader, whereas out-group members' stress comes from being left out of the communication network.[28] One surprising finding is that more frequent communication with the boss may either help or hurt a worker's performance ratings, depending on whether the worker is in the in-group or the out-group. Among the in-group, more frequent communication generally leads to higher performance ratings, while members of the out-group who communicate more often with the superior tend to receive lower performance ratings. Perhaps the out-group members get to talk to the boss only when something has gone wrong![29]

▪ THE SITUATIONAL LEADERSHIP® MODEL

The Situational Leadership® model, developed by Paul Hersey and Kenneth Blanchard, suggests that the leader's behavior should be adjusted to the maturity level of the followers.[30] The model employs two dimensions of leader behavior as used in the Ohio State studies; one dimension is task oriented, and the other is relationship oriented. Follower maturity is categorized into four levels, as shown in Figure 11.4. Follower readiness is determined by the follower's ability and willingness to complete a specific task. Readiness can therefore be low or high depending on the particular task. In addition, readiness varies within a single person according to the task. One person may be willing and able to satisfy simple requests from customers (high readiness) but less able or willing to give highly technical advice to customers (low readiness). It is important that the leader be able to evaluate the readiness level of each follower for each task. The four styles

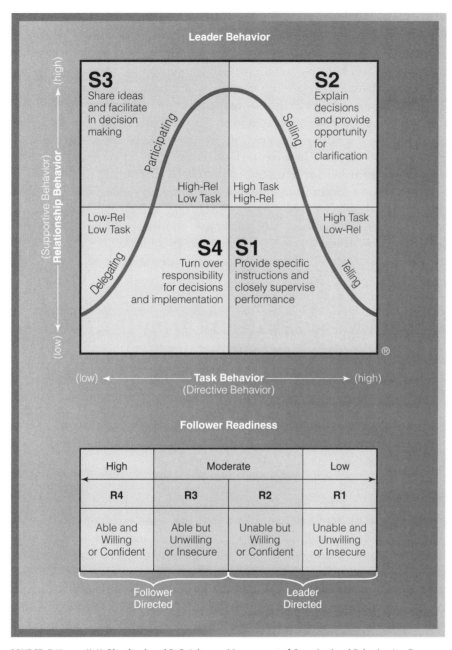

SOURCE: P. Hersey, K. H. Blanchard, and D. E. Johnson, *Management of Organizational Behavior: Leading Human Resources*, 8th ed. (Upper Saddle River, N.J.: Pearson Education, Inc., 2001): 182. Copyright © 2001, Center for Leadership Studies, Escondido, CA. Used with permission.

of leader behavior associated with the four readiness levels are depicted in the figure as well.

According to the Situational Leadership® model, a leader should use a telling style (S1) when a follower is unable and unwilling to do a certain task. This style involves providing instructions and closely monitoring performance. As such, the telling style involves considerable task behavior and low relationship behavior. When a follower is unable but willing and confident to do a task, the leader can use the selling style (S2) in which there is high task behavior and high relationship behavior. In this case, the leader explains decisions and provides opportunities for the employee to seek clarification or help. Sometimes a follower will be able to complete a task but may seem unwilling or insecure about doing so. In these cases, a participating style (S3) is warranted, which involves high relationship but low task behavior. The leader in this case encourages the follower to participate in decision making. Finally, for tasks in which a follower is able and willing, the leader is able to use a delegating style (S4), characterized by low task behavior and low relationship behavior. In this case, follower readiness is high, and low levels of leader involvement (task or relationship) are needed.

One key limitation of the Situational Leadership® model is the absence of central hypotheses that could be tested, which would make it a more valid, reliable theory of leadership.[31] However, the theory has intuitive appeal and is widely used for training and development in corporations. In addition, the theory focuses attention on follower maturity as an important determinant of the leadership process.

🔖 THE EMERGENCE OF INSPIRATIONAL LEADERSHIP THEORIES

Leadership is an exciting area of organizational behavior, one in which new research is constantly emerging. Three new developments are important to understand. These are transformational leadership, charismatic leadership, and authentic leadership.

: 7. Distinguish among transformational, charismatic, and authentic leaders.

transformational leaders
Leaders who inspire followers to transcend their self-interests and achieve exceptional performance.

▪ TRANSFORMATIONAL LEADERSHIP

As we indicated earlier in the chapter, transactional leaders are those who use rewards and punishment to strike deals with followers and shape their behavior. In contrast, transformational leaders inspire and excite followers to high levels of performance.[32] They rely on their personal attributes instead of their official position to manage followers. There is some evidence that *transformational leadership* can be learned.[33] Transformational leadership consists of the following four subdimensions: charisma, individualized consideration, inspirational motivation, and intellectual stimulation. We describe charisma in detail below. Individualized consideration refers to how much the leader displays concern for each follower's individual needs and acts as a coach or a mentor. Inspirational motivation is the extent to which the leader is able to articulate a vision that is appealing to followers.[34] An extensive research study shows that transformational leadership predicts several criteria such as follower job satisfaction, leader effectiveness ratings, group or organizational performance, and follower motivation.[35]

▪ CHARISMATIC LEADERSHIP

Steve Jobs, the pioneer behind the Macintosh computer and the growing music download market, has an uncanny ability to create a vision and convince others to become part of it. This was evidenced by Apple's continual overall success despite its major blunders in the desktop computer wars. Jobs' unique ability is so powerful that Apple employees coined a term in the 1980s for it, the *reality-distortion field*. This expression is used to describe the persuasive ability and peculiar charisma of managers like Steve Jobs. This reality-distortion field allows Jobs to convince even skeptics that his plans are worth supporting, no matter how unworkable they may appear. Those close to these managers become passionately committed to possibly insane projects, without regard to the practicality of their implementation or competitive forces in the marketplace.[36]

Charismatic leadership results when a leader uses the force of personal abilities and talents to have profound and extraordinary effects on followers.[37] Some scholars see transformational leadership and charismatic leadership as very similar, but others believe they are different. *Charisma* is a Greek word meaning "gift"; the charismatic leader's unique and powerful gifts are the source of the leader's great influence with followers.[38] In fact, followers often view the charismatic leader as one who possesses superhuman, or even mystical, qualities.[39] Charismatic leaders rely heavily on referent power, discussed in Chapter 10, and charismatic leadership is especially effective in times of uncertainty.[40] Charismatic leadership falls to those who are chosen (are born with the "gift" of charisma) or who cultivate that gift. Some say charismatic leaders are born, and others say they are taught.

Charismatic leadership carries with it not only great potential for high levels of achievement and performance on the part of followers but also shadowy risks of destructive courses of action that might harm followers or other people. Several researchers have attempted to demystify charismatic leadership and distinguish its two faces.[41] The ugly face of charisma is revealed in the personalized power motivations of Adolf Hitler in Nazi Germany and David Koresh of the Branch Davidian cult in Waco, Texas. Both men led their followers into struggle, conflict, and death. The brighter face of charisma is revealed in the socialized power motivations of U.S. President Franklin D. Roosevelt. Former presidents Bill Clinton and Ronald Reagan, while worlds apart in terms of their political beliefs, were actually quite similar in their use of personal charisma to inspire followers and motivate them to pursue the leader's vision. In each case, followers perceived the leader as imbued with a unique vision for America and unique abilities to lead the country there.

charismatic leadership
A leader's use of personal abilities and talents in order to have profound and extraordinary effects on followers.

▌ AUTHENTIC LEADERSHIP

Recently, a new form of leadership has started to garner attention thanks to the ethical scandals rocking the business environment. In response to concerns about the potential negative side of inspirational forms of leadership, a group of researchers from the Gallup Institute and University of Nebraska advocated what is now known as *authentic leadership*.[42] Authentic leadership is a multidimensional construct that includes transformational, charismatic, or transactional leadership as the situation might demand. However, authentic leadership differs from the other kinds in that such authentic leaders have a conscious and well-developed sense of values. They act in ways that are consistent with their value systems. Thus, authentic leaders have a highly evolved sense of moral right and wrong. Their life experiences (labeled "moments that matter") are believed to lead to such authentic leadership development and to allow authentic leaders to be their true selves.[43]

authentic leader
A leader who is guided by explicit values that emphasize collective interest, enabling them to operate at high levels of moral integrity.

Authentic leaders arouse and motivate followers to higher levels of performance by building a workforce characterized by high levels of hope, optimism, resiliency, and self-efficacy.[44] Followers also experience more positive emotions and trust leadership as a result of transparency and a collective caring climate engendered by the leader. Does it seem a bit too Utopian? University of Nebraska researchers argue that this is the kind of leadership embodied by Gandhi, Nelson Mandela, and others like them throughout history. Empirical research in this domain is just emerging, and only time and solid management research will tell if this approach can yield results for organizational leadership. One recent development in the identification of authentic leaders stems from the emotions arena. Scholars have started to argue that emotions act as checks and balances that not only keep the ugly side of charisma in check but also provide certain cues to followers. For example, a leader who espouses benevolence (as a value) and does not display compassion (an emotion) might not be very authentic in followers' eyes.[45] Similarly, a leader who displays compassion when announcing a layoff was seen by followers as more morally worthy and held in higher regard.[46]

EMERGING ISSUES IN LEADERSHIP

Along with the recent developments in theory, some exciting issues have emerged of which leaders must be aware. These include emotional intelligence, trust, and gender and leadership.

EMOTIONAL INTELLIGENCE

It has been suggested that effective leaders possess emotional intelligence, which is the ability to recognize and manage emotion in oneself and in others. In fact, some researchers argue that emotional intelligence is more important for effective leadership than either IQ or technical skills.[47] Emotional intelligence is made up of several competencies, including self-awareness, empathy, adaptability, and self-confidence. While most people gain emotional intelligence as they age, not everyone starts with an equal amount. Fortunately, emotional intelligence can be learned. With honest feedback from coworkers and ongoing guidance, almost any leader can improve emotional intelligence, and with it, the ability to lead in times of adversity.[48]

Emotional intelligence affects the way leaders make decisions. Under high stress, leaders with higher emotional intelligence tend to keep their cool and make better decisions, while leaders with low emotional intelligence make poor decisions and lose their effectivness.[49]

Joe Torre, manager of the New York Yankees, gets the most out of his team, makes his boss happy, and delivers wins. He is a model of emotional intelligence: compassionate, calm under stress, and a great motivator. He advocates "managing against the cycle," which means staying calm when situations are tough, but turning up the heat on players when things are going well.[50]

TRUST

Trust is an essential element in leadership. Trust is the willingness to be vulnerable to the actions of another.[51] This means that followers believe that their leader will act with the followers' welfare in mind. Trustworthiness is also one of the competencies in emotional intelligence. Trust among top management team members facilitates strategy implementation; that means that if team members trust each other, they have a better chance of getting "buy-in" from employees on the direction of the company.[52] And if employees trust their leaders, they will buy in more readily.

Leading virtual teams requires trust, because face-to-face interaction that is the hallmark of leadership is not possible. Leaders must not only come to trust their subordinates, but they must also express that trust. Research has shown that workers who believe their boss trusts them (called "felt trustworthiness") enjoy their work more, are more productive, and are more likely to "go the extra mile" at work and perform organizational citizenship behaviors.[53]

Effective leaders also understand both *who* to trust and *how* to trust. At one extreme, leaders often trust a close circle of advisors, listening only to them and gradually cutting themselves off from dissenting opinions. At the opposite extreme, lone-wolf leaders may trust nobody, leading to preventable mistakes. Wise leaders carefully evaluate both the competence and the position of those they trust, seeking out a variety of opinions and input.[54]

▮ GENDER AND LEADERSHIP

An important emergent leadership question is this: Do women and men lead differently? Historical stereotypes persist, and people characterize successful managers as having more male-oriented attributes than female-oriented attributes.[55] Although legitimate gender differences may exist, the same leadership traits may be interpreted differently in a man and a woman because of stereotypes. The real issue should be leader behaviors that are not bound by gender stereotypes.

Early evidence shows that women tend to use a more people-oriented style that is inclusive and empowering. Women managers excel in positions that demand strong interpersonal skills.[56] More and more women are assuming positions of leadership in organizations. Donna Dubinsky, founder and CEO of palmOne, cofounded Palm and Handspring, and is known as the mother of the handheld computer. She wants to change the world such that PDAs outsell PCs. Interestingly, much of what we know about leadership is based on studies that were conducted on men. We need to know more about the ways women lead.

> ◀◀ **think critically** ▶▶
>
> What kinds of gender stereotypes exist for leadership roles? Do you think the United States will ever have a female president? Explain.

▮ FOLLOWERSHIP

In contrast to leadership, the topic of followership has not been extensively researched. Much of the leadership literature suggests that leader and follower roles are highly differentiated. The traditional view casts followers as passive, whereas a more contemporary view casts the follower role as an active one with potential for leadership.[57] The follower role has alternatively been cast as one of self-leadership in which the follower assumes responsibility for influencing his or her own performance.[58] This approach emphasizes the follower's individual responsibility and self-control. Self-led followers perform naturally motivating tasks and do work that must be done but that is not naturally motivating. Self-leadership enables followers to be disciplined and effective, essential first steps if one is to become a leader. Organizational programs such as empowerment and self-managed work teams may be used to further activate the follower role.[59]

: 8. Discuss the characteristics of effective and dynamic followers.

■ TYPES OF FOLLOWERS

Contemporary work environments are ones in which followers recognize their interdependence with leaders and learn to challenge them while at the same time respecting the leaders' authority.[60] Effective followers are active, responsible, and autonomous in their behavior and critical in their thinking without being insubordinate or disrespectful. Effective followers and four other types of followers are identified based on two dimensions: (1) activity versus passivity and (2) independent, critical thinking versus dependent, uncritical thinking.[61] Figure 11.5 shows these follower types.

Alienated followers think independently and critically, yet are very passive in their behavior. As a result, they become psychologically and emotionally distanced from their leaders. Alienated followers are potentially disruptive and a threat to the health of the organization. Sheep are followers who do not think independently or critically and are passive in their behavior. They simply do as they are told by

FIGURE 11.5

Five Types of Followers

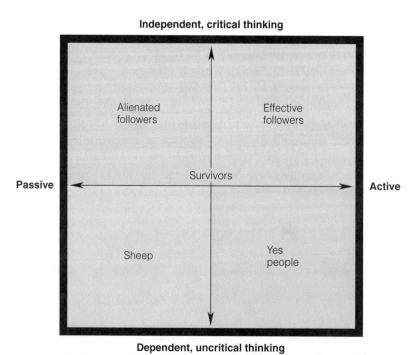

SOURCE: Reprinted by permission of *Harvard Business Review.* From "In Praise of Followers" by R. E. Kelley (November–December 1988): 145. Copyright © 1988 by Harvard Business School Publishing Corporation; all rights reserved.

their leaders. Yes people are followers who also do not think independently or critically, yet are very active in their behavior. They uncritically reinforce the thinking and ideas of their leaders with enthusiasm, never questioning or challenging the wisdom of the leaders' ideas and proposals. Yes people are the most dangerous to a leader because they are the most likely to give a false positive reaction and give no warning of potential pitfalls. Survivors are the least disruptive and the lowest risk followers in an organization. They perpetually sample the wind, and their motto is "better safe than sorry."

Effective followers are the most valuable to a leader and an organization because of their active contributions. Effective followers share four essential qualities. First, they practice self-management and self-responsibility. A leader can delegate to an effective follower without anxiety about the outcome. Second, they are committed to both the organization and a purpose, principle, or person outside themselves. Effective followers are not self-centered or self-aggrandizing. Third, effective followers invest in their own competence and professionalism and focus their energy for maximum impact. Effective followers look for challenges and ways in which to add to their talents or abilities. Fourth, they are courageous, honest, and credible. Challenge 11.2 gives you an opportunity to consider your effectiveness as a follower.

Effective followers might be thought of as self-leaders who do not require close supervision.[62] The notion of self-leadership, or superleadership, blurs the distinction between leaders and followers. Caring leaders are able to develop dynamic followers.

■ THE DYNAMIC FOLLOWER

The traditional stereotype of the follower or employee is of someone in a powerless, dependent role rather than in a potent, active, significant role. The latter, in which the follower is dynamic, is a more contemporary, healthy role.[63] The *dynamic follower* is a responsible steward of his or her job, is effective in managing the relationship with the boss, and practices responsible self-management.

The dynamic follower becomes a trusted adviser to the boss by keeping the supervisor well informed and building trust and dependability into the relationship. He or she is open to constructive criticism and solicits performance feedback. The dynamic follower shares needs and is responsible. It takes time and patience to nurture a good relationship between a follower and a supervisor. Once this relationship has been developed, it is a valuable resource for both.

dynamic follower
A follower who is a responsible steward of his or her job, is effective in managing the relationship with the boss, and practices self-management.

▨ CULTURAL DIFFERENCES IN LEADERSHIP

The situational approaches to leadership would lead to the conclusion that a leader must factor in culture as an important situational variable when exercising influence and authority. Thus, global leaders should expect to be flexible enough to alter their approaches when crossing national boundaries and working with people from foreign cultures.[64]

We are beginning to learn more about how perspectives on effective leadership vary across cultures. You might assume that most Europeans view leadership

CHALLENGE

11.2

Are You an Effective Follower?

To determine whether you are an effective follower, read the text section on "Types of Followers," and work through the following four steps. Answer each question in the four steps yes or no.

Step 1. Self-Management and Self-Responsibility

_____ Do you take the initiative at work?

_____ Do you challenge the system at work when appropriate?

_____ Do you ask questions when you need more information?

_____ Do you successfully bring your projects to completion?

Step 2. Commitment beyond Yourself

_____ Are you committed to your boss's and company's success?

_____ Is there a higher purpose in life that you value deeply?

_____ Is there a principle(s) that you will not compromise?

_____ Is there a person at work or elsewhere you admire greatly?

Step 3. Self-Development

_____ Do you attend a professional development class annually?

_____ Do you have a program of self-study or structured learning?

_____ Do you take at least one class each semester in the year?

_____ Have you identified new skills to learn for your job?

Step 4. Courage and Honesty

_____ Have you disagreed with your boss twice this year?

_____ Have you taken two unpopular positions at work this year?

_____ Have you given critical feedback to someone, kindly?

_____ Have you taken one risk at work to do a better job?

Scoring:

Count the number of "yes" answers in Steps 1 through 4: _____

If you have 10 to 16 "yes" answers, this would suggest that you are an effective follower. If you have 7 or fewer "yes" answers, this may suggest that you fall into one of the other four categories of followers.

People who are self-reliant may also be effective followers, and effective followers may also be self-reliant. If you are an effective follower, were you also self-reliant in Challenge 7.2? If you were not self-reliant in Challenge 7.2, did you fall into a category other than the effective follower category?

in the same way. Research tells us instead that there are many differences among European countries. In Nordic countries like Finland, leaders who are direct and close to subordinates are viewed positively, while in Turkey, Poland, and Russia this is not the case. And leaders who give subordinates autonomy are viewed more positively in Germany and Austria than in the Czech Republic and Portugal.[65] There are even differences between the American view of transformational leadership and that found in the United Kingdom. The U.K. approach to transformational leadership is much closer to what we in the United States refer to as servant leadership. It involves more connectedness between leaders and followers and more vulnerability on the part of the leader.[66]

To be effective, leaders must understand other cultures. U.S. executives often perceive specific global regions as being made up of relatively homogenous individuals. For example, some U.S. leaders think that most of Latin America is populated with people of similar values and beliefs. But a recent study of more than 1,000 small business owners in the region demonstrated that despite similarities, these business leaders are quite diverse in terms of their individual goals. Mexican and Brazilian leaders had values that were very different from leaders in other countries in the region. This means that we cannot stereotype people from Latin America as being totally similar.[67]

Whereas most American workers follow traditional Protestant work values, workers from other countries base their work values on very different sets of beliefs, drawing in some cases from multiple philosophies. China, for instance, draws from not one but three perspectives, as Buddhism, Taoism, and Confucianism harmonize to create work values such as trust, hierarchy, loyalty, and networks.[68]

⬡ MANAGERIAL IMPLICATIONS: LEADERSHIP GUIDELINES

Leadership is a key to influencing organizational behavior and achieving organizational effectiveness. When artifacts are eliminated, studies of leadership succession show a moderately strong leader influence on organizational performance.[69] With this said, it is important to recognize that other factors also influence organizational performance. These include environmental factors (such as general economic conditions) and technological factors (such as efficiency).

Corporate leaders play a central role in setting the ethical tone and moral values for their organizations. While many corporate leaders talk about ethics, many never have to actually risk the firm's fortune on an ethical decision. In 1976, when James Burke, head of Johnson & Johnson, challenged his management team to reaffirm the company's historic commitment to ethical behavior, he had no idea he would be asked to demonstrate that commitment in action. But six years later, when poisoned packages of Tylenol appeared on store shelves, Burke did not hesitate to act on what he had pledged. The company pulled the product from the shelves at a cost of $100 million. It also offered a reward and revamped the product's packaging. In the end, Tylenol recovered and is once again the leading pain medication in the United States. Jim Burke was recently recognized by *Fortune* as one of the 10 greatest CEOs of all time, and Johnson & Johnson continues to be rated one of the best companies for which to work.[70]

Five useful guidelines appear to emerge from the extensive leadership research of the past 60 years:

> First, leaders and organizations should appreciate the unique attributes, predispositions, and talents of each leader. No two leaders are the same, and there is value in this diversity.

> Second, although there appears to be no single best style of leadership, there are organizational preferences in terms of style. Leaders should be chosen who challenge the organizational culture, when necessary, without destroying it.

> Third, participative, considerate leader behaviors that demonstrate a concern for people appear to enhance the health and well-being of followers in the work environment. This does not imply, however, that a leader must ignore the team's work tasks.

> Fourth, different leadership situations call for different leadership talents and behaviors. This may result in different individuals taking the leader role, depending on the specific situation in which the team finds itself.

> Fifth, good leaders are likely to be good followers. Although there are distinctions between their social roles, the attributes and behaviors of leaders and followers may not be as distinct as is sometimes thought.

LOOKING BACK :: VIRGIN GROUP, LTD.

Leadership Advice from Richard Branson

Even an unconventional leader like Sir Richard Branson is sometimes asked to break it all down to a few rules. Here are the basic principles he practices and preaches:

1. *Follow your passions.* Love to fly? Start an airline. Hire drop-dead-gorgeous flight attendants and an onboard masseuse. Enter a hot-air balloon race. It'll get you some ink, and it's fun.

2. *Keep it simple.* Running your life out of a black book and a gym bag means you know where everything is. It also means you stay focused on what's important.

3. *Get the best people to help you.* If you don't like math, hire some bean counters. If you're an optimist, hire some realists. Make sure you do enough outrageous stuff that their lives never get boring. Treat them to nice vacations.

4. *Recreate yourself.* Kids buying less music from your stores? Start a cell phone business. Variety wards off boredom—and it could save your hide.

5. *Play.* Play practical jokes on your CEOs. Play tennis with your kids. Wear your bathing suit all day long.[71]

CHAPTER SUMMARY

1. Leadership is the process of guiding and directing the behavior of followers in organizations. Followership is the process of being guided and directed by a leader. Leaders and followers are companions in these processes.

2. A leader creates meaningful change in organizations, whereas a manager controls

complexity. Inspirational leaders have a profound impact on their followers.

3. Autocratic leaders create high pressure for followers, whereas democratic leaders create healthier environments for followers.

4. The five styles in the Leadership Grid are organization man manager, authority-obedience

manager, country club manager, team manager, and impoverished manager.

5. According to Fiedler's contingency theory, task-oriented leaders are most effective in highly favorable or highly unfavorable leadership situations, and relationship-oriented leaders are most effective in moderately favorable leadership situations.

6. The path–goal theory, leader–member exchange, and Situational Leadership® model say that a leader should adjust his or her behav-

ior to the situation and should appreciate diversity among followers.

7. There are many developments in leadership. Emerging issues include emotional intelligence, trust, and gender differences in leadership.

8. Effective, dynamic followers are competent and active in their work, assertive, independent thinkers, sensitive to their bosses' needs and demands, and responsible self-managers. Caring leadership and dynamic followership go together.

KEY TERMS

authentic leadership (p. 287)

authority-compliance manager (9,1) (p. 280)

autocratic style (p. 277)

charismatic leadership (p. 287)

consideration (p. 277)

country club manager (1,9) (p. 280)

democratic style (p. 277)

dynamic follower (p. 291)

followership (p. 274)

formal leadership (p. 274)

impoverished manager (1,1) (p. 280)

informal leadership (p. 274)

initiating structure (p. 277)

laissez-faire style (p. 277)

leader (p. 275)

leader–member exchange theory (LMX) (p. 284)

leader–member relations (p. 281)

leadership (p. 274)

Leadership Grid (p. 277)

least preferred coworker (LPC) (p. 281)

manager (p. 275)

opportunistic "what's in it for me" manager (Opp) (p. 280)

organization man manager (5,5) (p. 279)

paternalistic "father knows best" manager (9 + 9) (p. 280)

position power (p. 281)

task structure (p. 281)

team manager (9,9) (p. 280)

transformational leadership (p. 286)

REVIEW QUESTIONS

1. Define *leadership* and *followership*. Distinguish between formal leadership and informal leadership.

2. Discuss transformational, charismatic, and authentic leadership. Would you expect these styles of leadership to exist in all cultures? Differ across cultures?

3. Describe the differences between autocratic and democratic work environments. How do they differ from a laissez-faire workplace?

4. Define *initiating structure* and *consideration* as leader behaviors.

5. Describe the middle-of-the-road manager, authority-compliance manager, country club manager, team manager, and impoverished manager.

6. How does the LPC scale measure leadership style? What are the three dimensions of the leader's situation?

7. Compare House's path–goal theory of leadership with the Situational Leadership® model.

8. Describe alienated followers, sheep, yes people, survivors, and effective followers.

Discussion and Communication QUESTIONS

1. Do you (or would you want to) work in an autocratic, democratic, or laissez-faire work environment? What might be the advantages of each work environment? The disadvantages?

2. Is your supervisor or professor someone who is high in concern for production? High in concern for people? What is his or her Leadership Grid style?

3. Discuss the similarities and differences between effective leadership and dynamic followership. Are you dynamic?

4. Describe the relationship you have with your supervisor or professor. What is the best part of the relationship? The worst part? What could you do to make the relationship better?

5. *(communication question)* Who is the leader you admire the most? Write a description of this person's characteristics and attributes that you admire. Note any aspects of this leader's behavior that you find less than wholly admirable.

6. *(communication question)* Refresh yourself on the distinction between leaders (also called transformational leaders) and managers (also called transactional leaders) in the text. Then read about four contemporary business leaders. Prepare a brief summary of each and classify them as leaders or managers.

7. *(communication question)* Interview a supervisor or manager about the best follower the supervisor or manager has worked with. Ask questions about the characteristics and behaviors that made this person such a good follower. Note in particular how this follower responds to change. Be prepared to present your interview results in class.

ETHICAL DILEMMA

Sam Bennett has been president of Chateau Bank for the past 35 years. Next to his family, running the bank has been the focus of his life. When Sam took over as president, the bank was small and poorly run. Today, there are 50 branch offices across three counties, an accomplishment in which Sam takes great pride. Now Sam is almost 70 and is ready to retire. He has been preparing for this event for some time. Grooming his replacement is very important and something he has been working on for years.

For several years, Chris Hollister has been the heir apparent. Chris had caught Sam's eye when he first joined the bank. Sam has watched with great interest as Chris rose through the ranks. As Chris began moving into the upper echelons, Sam made it well known that Chris was his choice to succeed him as president. The problem Sam now faces is that Chateau is not the same bank. It has, and rightly so, become a bank of the 21st century. Computers run everything. But Chris is from the old school. He understands computers well enough, but to move this company into the future, it needs someone who understands that technology is the catalyst to do that.

Dana Heart might just be that person. Dana joined the company at the management level just 12 years ago, straight from graduate school. She grew up in the technology era and knows how to use technology to her and the bank's advantage. Dana is not only good at what she does, but she also has a vision for the future. Sam likes Dana, but how can he turn his back on Chris?

Should his loyalty be with the man he has been grooming for so long or with the growth needs of the organization? Sam is sure that Chris could get the job done, but Dana would move the company forward.

QUESTIONS

1. Does Sam have an obligation to appoint Chris as the next president?

2. Evaluate each of Sam's alternatives, choosing Chris or Dana, using rule, virtue, right, and justice theories.

EXPERIENTIAL EXERCISES

11.1 NATIONAL CULTURE AND LEADERSHIP

Effective leadership often varies by national culture, as Hofstede's research has shown. This exercise gives you the opportunity to examine your own and your group's leadership orientation compared to norms from 10 countries, including the United States.

Exercise Schedule

1. Preparation (before class)
Complete the 29-item questionnaire.

2. Individual and Group Scoring
Your instructor will lead you through the scoring of the questionnaire, both individually and as a group.

3. Comparison of Effective Leadership Patterns by Nation
Your instructor leads a discussion on Hofstede's value system and presents the culture dimension scores for the 10 countries.

In the questionnaire below, indicate the extent to which you agree or disagree with each statement. For example, if you strongly agree with a particular statement, circle the 5 next to the statement.

1 = strongly disagree
2 = disagree
3 = neither agree nor disagree
4 = agree
5 = strongly agree

QUESTIONNAIRE

	STRONGLY DISAGREE			STRONGLY AGREE
1. It is important to have job instructions spelled out in detail so that employees always know what they are expected to do.	1 2	3	4	5
2. Managers expect employees to closely follow instructions and procedures.	1 2	3	4	5
3. Rules and regulations are important because they inform employees what the organization expects of them.	1 2	3	4	5
4. Standard operating procedures are helpful to employees on the job.	1 2	3	4	5
5. Instructions for operations are important for employees on the job.	1 2	3	4	5
6. Group welfare is more important than individual rewards.	1 2	3	4	5
7. Group success is more important than individual success.	1 2	3	4	5
8. Being accepted by the members of your work group is very important.	1 2	3	4	5
9. Employees should pursue their own goals only after considering the welfare of the group.	1 2	3	4	5
10. Managers should encourage group loyalty even if individual goals suffer.	1 2	3	4	5
11. Individuals may be expected to give up their goals in order to benefit group success.	1 2	3	4	5
12. Managers should make most decisions without consulting subordinates.	1 2	3	4	5
13. Managers should frequently use authority and power when dealing with subordinates.	1 2	3	4	5
14. Managers should seldom ask for the opinions of employees.	1 2	3	4	5
15. Managers should avoid off-the-job social contacts with employees.	1 2	3	4	5

	STRONGLY DISAGREE				STRONGLY AGREE
16. Employees should not disagree with management decisions.	1	2	3	4	5
17. Managers should not delegate important tasks to employees.	1	2	3	4	5
18. Managers should help employees with their family problems.	1	2	3	4	5
19. Managers should see to it that employees are adequately clothed and fed.	1	2	3	4	5
20. A manager should help employees solve their personal problems.	1	2	3	4	5
21. Management should see that all employees receive health care.	1	2	3	4	5
22. Management should see that children of employees have an adequate education.	1	2	3	4	5
23. Management should provide legal assistance for employees who get into trouble with the law.	1	2	3	4	5
24. Managers should take care of their employees as they would their children.	1	2	3	4	5
25. Meetings are usually run more effectively when they are chaired by a man.	1	2	3	4	5
26. It is more important for men to have a professional career than it is for women to have a professional career.	1	2	3	4	5
27. Men usually solve problems with logical analysis; women usually solve problems with intuition.	1	2	3	4	5
28. Solving organizational problems usually requires an active, forcible approach, which is typical of men.	1	2	3	4	5
29. It is preferable to have a man, rather than a woman, in a high-level position.	1	2	3	4	5

SOURCES: By Peter Dorfman, *Advances in International Comparative Management*, Vol. 3 (1988): 127–150. Reprinted by permission of JAI Press Inc. D. Marcic and S. M. Puffer, "Dimensions of National Culture and Effective Leadership Patterns: Hofstede Revisited," *Management International* (Minneapolis/St. Paul: West Publishing, 1994): 10–15. All rights reserved. May not be reproduced without written permission of the publisher.

11.2 LEADERSHIP AND INFLUENCE

To get a better idea of what your leadership style is and how productive it would be, fill out the following questionnaire. If you are currently a manager or have been a manager, answer the questions considering "members" to be your employees. If you have never been a manager, think of situations when you were a leader in an organization and consider "members" to be people working for you.

Response choices for each item:

A = always   B = often   C = occasionally
D = seldom   E = never

A B C D E

1. I would act as the spokesperson of the group.
2. I would allow the members complete freedom in their work.
3. I would encourage overtime work.
4. I would permit the members to use their own judgment in solving problems.
5. I would encourage the use of uniform procedures.
6. I would needle members for greater effort.
7. I would stress being ahead of competing groups.
8. I would let the members do their work the way they think best.
9. I would speak as the representative of the group.
10. I would be able to tolerate postponement and uncertainty.
11. I would try out my ideas in the group.
12. I would turn the members loose on a job, and let them go on it.
13. I would work hard for a promotion.
14. I would get swamped by details.
15. I would speak for the group when visitors are present.
16. I would be reluctant to allow the members any freedom of action.
17. I would keep the work moving at a rapid pace.

A B C D E

18. I would let some members have authority that I should keep.
19. I would settle conflicts when they occur in the group.
20. I would allow the group a high degree of initiative.
21. I would represent the group at outside meetings.
22. I would be willing to make changes.
23. I would decide what will be done and how it will be done.
24. I would trust the members to exercise good judgment.
25. I would push for increased production.
26. I would refuse to explain my actions.
27. Things usually turn out as I predict.
28. I would permit the group to set its own pace.
29. I would assign group members to particular tasks.
30. I would act without consulting the group.
31. I would ask the members of the group to work harder.
32. I would schedule the work to be done.
33. I would persuade others that my ideas are to their advantage.
34. I would urge the group to beat its previous record.
35. I would ask that group members follow standard rules and regulations.

SCORING

People oriented: Place a check mark by the number if you answered either A or B to any of these questions:

Question #	2 ___	10 ___	22 ___
	4 ___	12 ___	24 ___
	6 ___	18 ___	28 ___
	8 ___	20 ___	

Place a check mark by the number if you answered either D or E to any of these questions:

14 ___ 16 ___ 26 ___ 30 ___

Count your check marks to get your total people-oriented score. ___

Task oriented: Place a check mark by the number if you answered either A or B to any of these questions:

3 ___	7 ___	11 ___	13 ___
17 ___	25 ___	29 ___	31 ___
34 ___			

Place a check mark by the number if you answered C or D to any of these questions:

1 ___	5 ___	9 ___	15 ___
19 ___	21 ___	23 ___	27 ___
32 ___	33 ___	35 ___	

Count your check marks to get your total task-oriented score. ___

RANGE	RANGE		
People 0–7;	Task 0–10	You are not involved enough in either the task or the people.	Uninvolved
People 0–7;	Task 10–20	You tend to be autocratic, a whip-snapper. You get the job done, but at a high emotional cost.	Task-oriented
People 8–15;	Task 0–10	People are happy in their work, but sometimes at the expense of productivity.	People-oriented
People 8–15;	Task 10–20	People enjoy working for you and are productive. They naturally expend energy because they get positive reinforcement for doing a good job.	Balanced

As a leader, most people tend to be more task-oriented or more people-oriented. Task-orientation is concerned with getting the job done, while people-orientation focuses on group interactions and the needs of individual workers.

Effective leaders, however, are able to use both styles, depending on the situation. There may be times when a rush job demands great attention placed on task completion. During a time of low morale, though, sensitivity to workers' problems would be more appropriate. The best managers are able to balance both task and people concerns. Therefore, a high score on both would show this balance. Ultimately, you will gain respect, admiration, and productivity from your workers.

EXERCISE SCHEDULE

1. Preparation (before class)
Complete and score inventory.

2. Group discussion
The class should form four groups based on the scores on the Leadership Style Inventory. Each group will be given a separate task.

Uninvolved: Devise strategies for developing task- and people-oriented styles.

Task-oriented: How can you develop a more people-oriented style? What problems might occur if you do not do so?

People-oriented: How can you develop a more task-oriented style? What problems might occur if you do not do so?

Balanced: Do you see any potential problems with your style? Are you a fully developed leader?

SOURCE: From Thomas Sergiovanni, Richard Metzcus, and Larry Burden, "Toward a Particularistic Approach to Leadership Style: Some Findings," *American Educational Research Journal*, Vol. 6 (1), (January 1969). Copyright 1969 The American Educational Research Association. Reprinted with permission of AERA.

Conflict and Negotiation

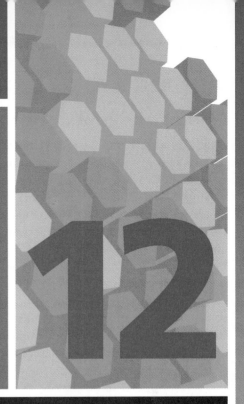

12

LEARNING OBJECTIVES

After reading this chapter, you should be able to do the following:

: **1.** Diagnose functional versus dysfunctional conflict.

: **2.** Identify the causes of conflict in organizations.

: **3.** Identify the different forms of conflict.

: **4.** Understand the defense mechanisms that individuals exhibit when they engage in interpersonal conflict.

: **5.** Understand and avoid ineffective techniques for managing conflict.

: **6.** Describe and apply effective techniques for managing conflict.

: **7.** Define and apply five styles of conflict management and diagnose your own preferred style.

301

THINKING AHEAD :: Whole Foods Market, Inc.

Conflict within One of the "Best Companies"

Only a relative handful of companies ever make *Fortune*'s list of "100 Best Companies to Work For." At Austin, Texas-based Whole Foods Market, Inc., making the esteemed list has become something of an annual tradition. In fact, the company's place on the 2007 list marked its tenth consecutive appearance there. Whole Foods is one of only 18 firms in the country to have made the list in every single year since the list first began.

What makes Whole Foods such a great place to work? Employees cite perks like solid health care for both full- and part-time employees, generous stock options for nonexecutives, and a profit-sharing plan that boosts employee earnings when the firm prospers. John Mackey, the firm's presi-

dent, says this has been his plan since day one: to empower his people as a means to achieve business success. When it comes to keeping employees happy, Whole Foods appears to have the recipe for success down.

Yet, Whole Foods is not immune to conflict. If Whole Foods is such a perfect place to work, why did workers at the Madison, Wisconsin, store vote to organize a labor union? And if Whole Foods is committed to empowering its workers, why did the company quickly announce that it would not recognize its workers' legally organized union? And is it just coincidence that shortly after the organizing drive, two of the organizers were fired? Is Whole Foods really a great place to work or not?[1]

THE NATURE OF CONFLICTS IN ORGANIZATIONS

conflict

Any situation in which incompatible goals, attitudes, emotions, or behaviors lead to disagreement or opposition between two or more parties.

All of us have experienced conflict of various types, yet we probably fail to recognize the variety of conflicts that occur in organizations. *Conflict* is defined as any situation in which incompatible goals, attitudes, emotions, or behaviors lead to disagreement or opposition between two or more parties.[2]

Today's organizations may face greater potential for conflict than ever before in history. The marketplace, with its increasing competition and globalization, magnifies differences among people in terms of personality, values, attitudes, perceptions, languages, cultures, and national backgrounds.[3] With the increasing diversity of the workforce, furthermore, comes the potential for incompatibility and conflict.

IMPORTANCE OF CONFLICT MANAGEMENT SKILLS FOR THE MANAGER

Estimates show that managers spend about 21 percent of their time dealing with conflict.[4] That is the equivalent of one day every week. And conflict management skills are a major predictor of managerial success.[5] Emotional intelligence (EI) relates to the ability to manage conflict. It is the power to control one's emotions and perceive emotions in others, adapt to change, and manage adversity. Conflict management skills may be more a reflection of EI than of IQ. People who lack emotional intelligence, especially empathy or the ability to see life from another person's perspective, are more likely to be causes of conflict than managers of conflict.[6] EI seems to be valid across cultures. It is common among successful people not only in North America, but also in Nigeria, India, Argentina, and France.

POSITIVE CONSEQUENCES	NEGATIVE CONSEQUENCES
• Leads to new ideas • Stimulates creativity • Motivates change • Promotes organizational vitality • Helps individuals and groups establish identities • Serves as a safety valve to indicate problems	• Diverts energy from work • Threatens psychological well-being • Wastes resources • Creates a negative climate • Breaks down group cohesion • Can increase hostility and aggressive behaviors

TABLE 12.1

Consequences of Conflict

■ FUNCTIONAL VERSUS DYSFUNCTIONAL CONFLICT

1. Diagnose functional versus dysfunctional conflict.

Not all conflict is bad. In fact, some types of conflict encourage new solutions to problems and enhance creativity in the organization. In these cases, managers will want to encourage the conflicts. Thus, the key to conflict management is to stimulate functional conflict and prevent or resolve dysfunctional conflict. The difficulty, however, is distinguishing between dysfunctional and functional conflicts. The consequences of conflict can be positive or negative, as shown in Table 12.1.

Functional conflict is a healthy, constructive disagreement between two or more people. Functional conflict can produce new ideas, learning, and growth among individuals. When individuals engage in constructive conflict, they develop a better awareness of themselves and others. In addition, functional conflict can improve working relationships; when two parties work through their disagreements, they feel they have accomplished something together. By releasing tensions and solving problems in working together, morale is improved.[7] Functional conflict can lead to innovation and positive change for the organization.[8] Because it tends to encourage creativity among individuals, this positive form of conflict can translate into increased productivity.[9] A key to recognizing functional conflict is that it is often cognitive in origin; that is, it arises from someone challenging old policies or thinking of new ways to approach problems.

Dysfunctional conflict is an unhealthy, destructive disagreement between two or more people. Its danger is that it takes the focus away from the work to be done and places the focus on the conflict itself and the parties involved. Excessive conflict drains energy that could be used more productively. A key to recognizing a dysfunctional conflict is that its origin is often emotional or behavioral. Disagreements that involve personalized anger and resentment directed at specific individuals rather than specific ideas are dysfunctional.[10] Individuals involved in dysfunctional conflict tend to act before thinking, and they often rely on threats, deception, and verbal abuse to communicate. In dysfunctional conflict, the losses to both parties may exceed any potential gain from the conflict. Diagnosing conflict as good or bad is not easy. The manager must look at the issue, the context of the conflict, and the parties involved. The following questions can be used to diagnose the nature of the conflict a manager faces:

> Are the parties approaching the conflict from a hostile standpoint?

> Is the outcome likely to be a negative one for the organization?

functional conflict
A healthy, constructive disagreement between two or more people.

dysfunctional conflict
An unhealthy, destructive disagreement between two or more people.

> Do the potential losses of the parties exceed any potential gains?

> Is energy being diverted from goal accomplishment?

If the majority of the answers to these questions are yes, then the conflict is probably dysfunctional. Once the manager has diagnosed the type of conflict, he or she can either work to resolve it (if it is dysfunctional) or to stimulate it (if it is functional).

It is easy to make mistakes in diagnosing conflicts. Sometimes task conflict, which is functional, can be misattributed as being personal, and dysfunctional conflict can follow. Developing trust within the work group can keep this misattribution from occurring.[11] A study of group effectiveness found that American decision-making groups made up of friends were able to more openly engage in disagreement than groups made up of strangers, allowing the friends' groups to make more effective decisions. When group members (friends) felt comfortable and trusting enough to express conflicting opinions, optimal performance resulted. But similar groups made up of Chinese friends and strangers exhibited both high levels of conflict *and* low levels of performance, suggesting that open disagreement in these groups was not helpful. This finding should serve as a cautionary tale for managers trying to apply one country's management style and techniques in another cultural setting.[12]

One occasion when managers should work to stimulate conflict is when they suspect their group is suffering from groupthink, discussed in Chapter 9.[13] When a group fails to consider alternative solutions and becomes stagnant in its thinking, it might benefit from healthy disagreements. Teams exhibiting symptoms of groupthink should be encouraged to consider creative problem solving and should appoint a devil's advocate to point out opposing perspectives. These actions can help stimulate constructive conflict in a group.

: 2. Identify the causes of conflict in organizations.

◼ CAUSES OF CONFLICT IN ORGANIZATIONS

Conflict is pervasive in organizations. To manage it effectively, managers should understand the many sources of conflict. They can be classified into two broad categories: structural factors, which stem from the nature of the organization and the way in which work is organized, and personal factors, which arise from differences among individuals. Figure 12.1 summarizes the causes of conflict within each category.

FIGURE 12.1

Causes of Conflict in Organizations

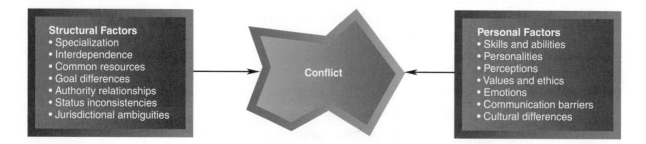

Structural Factors
• Specialization
• Interdependence
• Common resources
• Goal differences
• Authority relationships
• Status inconsistencies
• Jurisdictional ambiguities

Conflict

Personal Factors
• Skills and abilities
• Personalities
• Perceptions
• Values and ethics
• Emotions
• Communication barriers
• Cultural differences

◼ STRUCTURAL FACTORS

The causes of conflict related to the organization's structure include specialization, interdependence, common resources, goal differences, authority relationships, status inconsistencies, and jurisdictional ambiguities.

SPECIALIZATION

When jobs are highly specialized, employees become experts at certain tasks. For example, one software company has one specialist for databases, one for statistical packages, and another for expert systems. Highly specialized jobs can lead to conflict, because people have little awareness of the tasks that others perform.

A classic conflict of specialization may occur between salespeople and engineers. Engineers are technical specialists responsible for product design and quality. Salespeople are marketing experts and liaisons with customers. Salespeople are often accused of making delivery promises to customers that engineers cannot keep because the sales force lacks the technical knowledge necessary to develop realistic delivery deadlines.

INTERDEPENDENCE

Work that is interdependent requires groups or individuals to depend on one another to accomplish goals.[14] Depending on other people to get work done is fine when the process works smoothly. When there is a problem, however, it becomes very easy to blame the other party, and conflict escalates. In a garment manufacturing plant, for example, when the fabric cutters get behind in their work, the workers who sew the garments are delayed as well. Considerable frustration may result when the workers at the sewing machines feel their efforts are being blocked by the cutters' slow pace, and their pay is affected because they are paid piece-rate.

COMMON RESOURCES

Any time multiple parties must share resources, there is potential for conflict.[15] This potential is enhanced when the shared resources become scarce. For example, managers often share secretarial support. Not uncommonly, one secretary supports ten or more managers, each of whom believes his or her work is most important. This puts pressure on the secretary and leads to potential conflicts in prioritizing and scheduling work.

GOAL DIFFERENCES

When work groups have different goals, these goals may be incompatible. For example, in one cable television company, the salesperson's goal was to sell as many new installations as possible. This created problems for the service department, because its goal was timely installations. With increasing sales, the service department's workload became backed up, and orders were delayed. Often, these types of conflicts occur because individuals do not have knowledge of another department's objectives.

AUTHORITY RELATIONSHIPS

A traditional boss–employee relationship is hierarchical in nature with a boss who is superior to the employee. For many employees, such a relationship is not a comfortable one, because another individual has the right to tell them what to do. Some people resent authority more than others, and obviously this creates conflicts. In addition, some bosses are more autocratic than others; this compounds the potential for conflict in the relationship. As organizations move toward the team approach and empowerment, there should be less potential for conflict from authority relationships.

STATUS INCONSISTENCIES

Some organizations have a strong status difference between management and nonmanagement workers. Managers may enjoy privileges—such as flexible schedules, reserved parking spaces, and longer lunch hours—that are not available to nonmanagement employees. This may result in resentment and conflict.

JURISDICTIONAL AMBIGUITIES

Have you ever telephoned a company with a problem and had your call transferred through several different people and departments? This situation illustrates *jurisdictional ambiguity*—that is, unclear lines of responsibility within an organization.[16] The classic situation here involves the hardware/software dilemma. You call the company that made your computer, and they inform you that the problem is caused by the software. You call the software division, and they tell you it's the hardware . . . you get the idea.

The factors just discussed are structural in that they arise from the ways in which work is organized. Other conflicts come from differences among individuals.

jurisdictional ambiguity
The presence of unclear lines of responsibility within an organization.

▇ PERSONAL FACTORS

The causes of conflict that arise from individual differences include skills and abilities, personalities, perceptions, values and ethics, emotions, communication barriers, and cultural differences.

SKILLS AND ABILITIES

The workforce is composed of individuals with varying levels of skills and ability. Diversity in skills and abilities may be positive for the organization, but it also holds potential for conflict, especially when jobs are interdependent. Experienced, competent workers may find it difficult to work alongside new and unskilled recruits. Workers can become resentful when their new boss, fresh from college, knows a lot about managing people but is unfamiliar with the technology with which they are working.

PERSONALITIES

Individuals do not leave their personalities at the doorstep when they enter the workplace. Personality conflicts are realities in organizations. To expect that you will like all of your coworkers may be a naive expectation, as would be the expectation that they will all like you.

One personality trait that many people find difficult to deal with is abrasiveness.[17] An abrasive person ignores the interpersonal aspects of work and the feelings of colleagues. Abrasive individuals are often achievement oriented and hardworking, but their perfectionist, critical style often leaves others feeling unimportant. This style creates stress and strain for those around the abrasive person.[18] Can Bill Gates be abrasive?

◀◀**think critically**▶▶

How can managers handle personality conflicts?

PERCEPTIONS

Differences in perception can also lead to conflict. For example, managers and workers may not have a shared perception of what motivates people. In this case, the reward system can create conflicts if managers provide what they think employees want rather than what employees really want.

VALUES AND ETHICS

Differences in values and ethics can be sources of disagreement. Older workers, for example, value company loyalty and probably would not take a sick day when they were not really ill. Younger workers, valuing mobility, like the concept of "mental health days," or calling in sick to get away from work. This may not be true for all workers, but it illustrates that differences in values can lead to conflict.

Most people have their own sets of values and ethics. The extent to which they apply these ethics in the workplace varies. Some people have strong desires for approval from others and will work to meet others' ethical standards. Some people are relatively unconcerned about approval from others and strongly apply their own ethical standards. Still others operate seemingly without regard to ethics or values.[19] When conflicts about values or ethics do arise, heated disagreement is common because of the personal nature of the differences.

EMOTIONS

The emotions of others can be a source of conflict in the workplace. Problems at home often spill over into the work arena, and the related moods can be hard for others to deal with.

Conflict by its nature is an emotional interaction,[20] and the emotions of the parties involved in conflict play a pivotal role in how they perceive the negotiation and respond to one another. In fact, emotions are now considered critical elements of any negotiation that must be included in any examination of the process and how it unfolds.[21]

One important research finding has been that emotion can play a problematic role in negotiations. In particular, when negotiators begin to act based on emotions rather than on cognitions, they become much more likely to reach an impasse.[22]

COMMUNICATION BARRIERS

Communication barriers such as physical separation and language can create distortions in messages, and these can lead to conflict. Another communication barrier is value judgment, in which a listener assigns a worth to a message before it is received. For example, suppose a team member is a chronic complainer. When this individual enters the manager's office, the manager is likely to devalue the message before it is even delivered. Conflict can then emerge.

CULTURAL DIFFERENCES

Although cultural differences are assets in organizations, sometimes they can be seen as sources of conflict. Often, these conflicts stem from a lack of understanding of another culture. In one MBA class, for example, Indian students were horrified when American students challenged the professor. Meanwhile, the American students thought the students from India were too passive. Subsequent discussions revealed that professors in India expected to be treated deferentially and with great respect. While students might challenge an idea vigorously, they would rarely challenge the professor. Diversity training that emphasizes education on cultural differences can make great strides in preventing misunderstandings.

▣ GLOBALIZATION AND CONFLICT

Large transnational corporations employ many different ethnic and cultural groups. In these multiethnic corporations, the widely differing cultures represent vast differences among individuals, so the potential for conflict increases.[23] As indicated in Chapter 2, Hofstede has identified five dimensions along which cultural differences may emerge: individualism/collectivism, power distance, uncertainty avoidance, masculinity/femininity, and long-term/short-term orientation.[24] These cultural differences have many implications for conflict management in organizations.

Individualism means that people believe that their individual interests take priority over society's interests. Collectivism, in contrast, means that people put the good of the group first. For example, the United States is a highly individualistic culture, whereas Japan is a very collectivist culture. The individualism/collectivism dimension of cultural differences strongly influences conflict management behavior. People from collectivist cultures tend to display a more cooperative approach to managing conflict.[25]

Hofstede's second dimension of cultural differences is power distance. In cultures with high power distance, individuals accept that people in organizations have varying levels of power. In contrast, in cultures with low power distance, individuals do not automatically respect those in positions of authority. For example, the United States is a country of low power distance, whereas Brazil is a country with a high power distance. Differences in power distance can lead to conflict. Imagine a U.S. employee managed by a Brazilian supervisor who expects deferential behavior. The supervisor would expect automatic respect based on legitimate power. When this respect is not given, conflict would arise.

Uncertainty avoidance also varies by culture. In the United States, employees can tolerate high levels of uncertainty, whereas employees in Israel tend to prefer certainty in their work settings. A U.S.-based multinational firm might run into conflicts operating in Israel. Suppose such a firm is installing a new technology. Its expatriate workers from the United States would tolerate the uncertainty of the technological transition better than would their Israeli coworkers, and this might lead to conflicts among the employees.

Masculinity versus femininity illustrates the contrast between preferences for assertiveness and material goods versus preferences for human capital and quality of life. The United States is a masculine society, whereas Sweden is considered a feminine society. Adjustment to the assertive interpersonal style of U.S. workers may be difficult for Swedish coworkers.

Conflicts can also arise between cultures that vary in their time orientation of values. China, for example, has a long-term orientation; the Chinese prefer values that focus on the future, such as saving and persistence. The United States and Russia, in contrast, have short-term orientations. These cultures emphasize values in the past and present, such as respect for tradition and fulfillment of social obligations. Conflicts can arise when managers fail to understand the nature of differences in values.

An organization whose workforce consists of multiple ethnicities and cultures holds potential for many types of conflict because of the sheer volume of individual differences among workers. The key to managing conflict in a multicultural workforce is understanding cultural differences and appreciating their value.

✌ FORMS OF CONFLICT IN ORGANIZATIONS

: 3. Identify the different forms of conflict.

Conflict can take on any of several different forms in an organization, including interorganizational, intergroup, intragroup, interpersonal, and intrapersonal conflicts. It is important to note that the prefix *inter* means "between," whereas the prefix *intra* means "within."

▮ INTERORGANIZATIONAL CONFLICT

Conflict that occurs between two or more organizations is called *interorganizational conflict.* Competition can heighten interorganizational conflict. Corporate takeovers, mergers, and acquisitions can also produce interorganizational conflict. What about the interorganizational conflict between Major League Baseball's players' union and management, which is sometimes characterized as a battle between millionaires and multimillionaires (not sure which is which)? The players regularly go on strike to extract more of the profits from management, while management cries that it is not making a dime.

Conflicts among organizations abound. Some of these conflicts can be functional, as when firms improve the quality of their products and services in the spirit of healthy competition. Other interorganizational conflicts can have dysfunctional results.

interorganizational conflict
Conflict that occurs between two or more organizations.

▮ INTERGROUP CONFLICT

When conflict occurs between groups or teams, it is known as *intergroup conflict.* Conflict between groups can have positive effects within each group, such as increased group cohesiveness, increased focus on tasks, and increased loyalty to the group. There are, however, negative consequences as well. Groups in conflict tend to develop an "us against them" mentality whereby each sees the other team as the enemy, becomes more hostile, and decreases its communication with the other group. Groups are even more competitive and less cooperative than individuals. The inevitable outcome is that one group gains and the other group loses.[26]

Competition between groups must be managed carefully so that it does not escalate into dysfunctional conflict. Research has shown that when groups compete for a goal that only one group can achieve, negative consequences like territoriality, aggression, and prejudice toward the other group can result.[27] Managers

intergroup conflict
Conflict that occurs between groups or teams in an organization.

should encourage and reward cooperative behaviors across groups. Some effective ways of doing this include modifying performance appraisals to include assessing intergroup behavior and using an external supervisor's evaluation of intergroup behavior. Group members will be more likely to help other groups when they know that the other group's supervisor will be evaluating their behavior, and that they will be rewarded for cooperation.[28] In addition, managers should encourage social interactions across groups so that trust can be developed. Trust allows individuals to exchange ideas and resources with members of other groups and results in innovation when members of different groups cooperate.[29] Conflict often results when older employees fear that younger new-hires may take over their jobs. Social interaction can help reduce these perceived threats, creating trust and reducing the intergroup conflict in the process.[30]

■ INTRAGROUP CONFLICT

intragroup conflict
Conflict that occurs within groups or teams.

Conflict that occurs within groups or teams is called *intragroup conflict*. Some conflict within a group is functional. It can help the group avoid groupthink, as we discussed in Chapter 9.

Even the newest teams, virtual teams, are not immune to conflict. The nuances and subtleties of face-to-face communication are often lacking in these teams, and misunderstandings can result. To avoid dysfunctional conflicts, virtual teams should make sure their tasks fit their methods of interacting. Complex strategic decisions may require face-to-face meetings rather than e-mails or threaded discussions. Face-to-face and telephone interactions early on can eliminate later conflicts and allow virtual teams to move on to use electronic communication because trust has been developed.[31]

Teams can experience many types of conflict. Using Challenge 12.1, you can assess the types of conflict in a team you belong to, as well as design ways to manage those conflicts.

■ INTERPERSONAL CONFLICT

interpersonal conflict
Conflict that occurs between two or more individuals.

Conflict between two or more people is *interpersonal conflict*. Conflict between people can arise from many individual differences, including personalities, attitudes, values, perceptions, and the other differences we discussed in Chapters 3 and 4. Later in this chapter, we look at defense mechanisms that individuals exhibit in interpersonal conflict and at ways to cope with difficult people.

■ INTRAPERSONAL CONFLICT

intrapersonal conflict
Conflict that occurs within an individual.

When conflict occurs within an individual, it is called *intrapersonal conflict*. There are several types of intrapersonal conflict, including interrole (conflicting demands in multiple roles that the same individual has), intrarole (conflict within a single role), and person–role conflicts (clashing of values and role demands). Intrapersonal conflicts can have positive consequences. Often, professional responsibilities clash with deeply held values. A budget shortfall may force you to lay off a loyal, hardworking employee. Your daughter may have a piano recital on the same day your largest client is scheduled to be in town visiting the office. In such conflicts, we often have to choose between right and right; that is, there's no correct response. These may be thought of as *defining moments* that challenge us

CHALLENGE 12.1

Assess Your Team's Conflict

Think of a team you're a member of or one you were part of in the past. Answer the following eight questions regarding that team.

1. How much emotional tension was there in your team?

   No tension   Lots of tension
   1   2   3   4   5

2. How much conflict of ideas was there in your team?

   No idea conflict   Lots of idea conflict
   1   2   3   4   5

3. How often did people get angry while working in your team?

   Never   Often
   1   2   3   4   5

4. How different were your views on the content of your project?

   Very similar views   Very different views
   1   2   3   4   5

5. How much were personality clashes evident in your team?

   No clashes evident   Personality clashes very evident
   1   2   3   4   5

6. How much did you talk through disagreements about your team projects?

   Never talked through disagreements   Always talked through disagreements
   1   2   3   4   5

7. How much interpersonal friction was there in your team?

   No friction   Lots of friction
   1   2   3   4   5

8. How much disagreement was there about task procedure in your team?

   No disagreement about procedure   Lots of disagreement about procedure
   1   2   3   4   5

Total for items 2, 4, 6, and 8 = _____ indicating task conflict.

Total for items 1, 3, 5, and 7 = _____ indicating relationship conflict.

- Did your team experience higher relationship or task conflict?
- What actions can you take to better manage task conflict? Relationship conflict?
- Was there an absence of both, or either, types of conflict in your team? What does this indicate?

Source: Adapted from K. Jehn, "A Multimethod Examination of the Benefits and Detriments of Intragroup Conflict," *Administrative Science Quarterly* 40 (1995): 256–282.

to choose between two or more things in which we believe.[32] Character is formed in defining moments because they cause us to shape our identities. They help us crystallize our values and serve as opportunities for personal growth.

INTRAPERSONAL CONFLICT

Intrapersonal conflict can be managed with careful self-analysis and diagnosis of the situation. Three actions in particular can help prevent or resolve intrapersonal conflicts.

First, when seeking a new job, you should find out as much as possible about the values of the organization.[33] Many person–role conflicts center around differences between the organization's values and the individual's values. Research has shown that when there is a good fit between the values of the individual and the organization, the individual is more satisfied and committed and is less likely to leave the organization.[34]

Second, to manage intrarole or interrole conflicts, role analysis is a good tool.[35] In role analysis, the individual asks the various role senders what they expect of him or her. The outcomes are clearer work roles and the reduction of conflict and ambiguity.[36] Role analysis is a simple tool that clarifies the expectations of both parties in a relationship and reduces the potential for conflict within a role or between roles.

Third, political skills can help buffer the negative effects of stress that stem from role conflicts. Effective politicians, as we discussed in Chapter 10, can negotiate role expectations when conflicts occur. All these forms of conflict can be managed. An understanding of the many forms is a first step. The next section focuses more extensively on interpersonal conflict because of its pervasiveness in organizations.

◀◀ think critically ▶▶

Can managers handle intrapersonal conflict that their subordinates might be experiencing? If so, how?

▣ INTERPERSONAL CONFLICT

When a conflict occurs between two or more people, it is known as interpersonal conflict. To manage interpersonal conflict, it is helpful to understand defense mechanisms exhibited by individuals and ways to cope with difficult people.

▣ DEFENSE MECHANISMS

: 4. Understand the defense mechanisms that individuals exhibit when they engage in interpersonal conflict.

When individuals are involved in conflict with another human being, frustration often results.[37] Conflicts can often arise within the context of a performance appraisal session. Most people do not react well to negative feedback, as was illustrated in a classic study.[38] In this study, when employees were given criticism about their work, over 50 percent of their responses were defensive.

When individuals are frustrated, as they often are in interpersonal conflict, they respond by exhibiting defense mechanisms.[39] Defense mechanisms are common reactions to the frustration that accompanies conflict. Table 12.2 describes several defense mechanisms seen in organizations.

Aggressive mechanisms, such as fixation, displacement, and negativism, are aimed at attacking the source of the conflict. In *fixation*, an individual fixates on the conflict, or keeps up a dysfunctional behavior that obviously will not solve the conflict. An example of fixation occurred in a university, where a faculty member became embroiled in a battle with the dean because the faculty member felt he had not received a large enough salary increase. He persisted in writing angry letters to the dean, whose hands were tied because of a low budget allocation to the college.

fixation

An aggressive mechanism in which an individual keeps up a dysfunctional behavior that obviously will not solve the conflict.

DEFENSE MECHANISM	PSYCHOLOGICAL PROCESS
Aggressive Mechanisms	
• Fixation	Person maintains a persistent, nonadjustive reaction even though all the cues indicate the behavior will not cope with the problem.
• Displacement	Individual redirects pent-up emotions toward persons, ideas, or objects other than the primary source of the emotion.
• Negativism	Person uses active or passive resistance, operating unconsciously.
Compromise Mechanisms	
• Compensation	Individual devotes himself or herself to a pursuit with increased vigor to make up for some feeling of real or imagined inadequacy.
• Identification	Individual enhances own self-esteem by patterning behavior after another's, frequently also internalizing the values and beliefs of the other person; also vicariously shares the glories or suffering in the disappointments of other individuals or groups.
• Rationalization	Person justifies inconsistent or undesirable behavior, beliefs, statements, and motivations by providing acceptable explanations for them.
Withdrawal Mechanisms	
• Flight or withdrawal	Through either physical or psychological means, person leaves the field in which frustration, anxiety, or conflict is experienced.
• Conversion	Emotional conflicts are expressed in muscular, sensory, or bodily symptoms of disability, malfunctioning, or pain.
• Fantasy	Person daydreams or uses other forms of imaginative activity to obtain an escape from reality and obtain imagined satisfactions.

TABLE 12.2

Common Defense Mechanisms

SOURCE: Timothy W. Costello and Sheldon S. Zalkind, adapted table from "Psychology in Administration: A Research Orientation" from *Journal of Conflict Resolution* III (1959): 148–149. Reprinted by permission of Sage Publications, Inc.

Displacement means directing anger toward someone who is not the source of the conflict. For example, a manager may respond harshly to an employee after a telephone confrontation with an angry customer. Another aggressive defense mechanism is *negativism*, which is active or passive resistance. Negativism is illustrated by a manager who, when appointed to a committee on which she did not want to serve, made negative comments throughout the meeting.

Compromise mechanisms, such as compensation, identification, and rationalization, are used by individuals to make the best of a conflict situation. *Compensation* occurs when an individual tries to make up for an inadequacy by putting increased energy into another activity. Compensation can be seen when a person makes up

displacement
An aggressive mechanism in which an individual directs his or her anger toward someone who is not the source of the conflict.

negativism
An aggressive mechanism in which a person responds with pessimism to any attempt at solving a problem.

compensation
A compromise mechanism in which an individual attempts to make up for a negative situation by devoting himself or herself to another pursuit with increased vigor.

identification

A compromise mechanism whereby an individual patterns his or her behavior after another's.

rationalization

A compromise mechanism characterized by trying to justify one's behavior by constructing bogus reasons for it.

flight/withdrawal

A withdrawal mechanism that entails physically escaping a conflict (flight) or psychologically escaping (withdrawal).

conversion

A withdrawal mechanism in which emotional conflicts are expressed in physical symptoms.

fantasy

A withdrawal mechanism that provides an escape from a conflict through daydreaming.

for a bad relationship at home by spending more time at the office. *Identification* occurs when one individual patterns his or her behavior after another's. One supervisor at a construction firm, not wanting to acknowledge consciously that she was not likely to be promoted, mimicked the behavior of her boss, even going so far as to buy a car just like the boss's. *Rationalization* is trying to justify one's behavior by constructing bogus reasons for it. Employees may rationalize unethical behavior like padding their expense accounts because "everyone else does it."

Withdrawal mechanisms are exhibited when frustrated individuals try to flee from a conflict using either physical or psychological means. Flight, conversion, and fantasy are examples of withdrawal mechanisms. Physically escaping a conflict is *flight*. When an employee takes a day off after a blowup with the boss is an example. *Withdrawal* may take the form of emotionally leaving a conflict, such as exhibiting an "I don't care anymore" attitude. *Conversion* is a process whereby emotional conflicts become expressed in physical symptoms. Most of us have experienced the conversion reaction of a headache following an emotional exchange with another person. *Fantasy* is an escape by daydreaming. In the Internet age, fantasy as an escape mechanism has found new meaning. A study conducted by International Data Corporation (IDC) showed that 30 to 40 percent of all Internet surfing at work is non–work-related and that more than 70 percent of companies have had sex sites accessed from their networks, suggesting that employees' minds aren't always focused on their jobs.[40]

When employees exhibit withdrawal mechanisms, they often fake it by pretending to agree with their bosses or coworkers in order to avoid facing an immediate conflict. Many employees fake it because the firm informally rewards agreement and punishes dissent. The long-term consequence of withdrawal and faking it is emotional distress for the employee.[41]

Knowledge of these defense mechanisms can be extremely beneficial to a manager. By understanding the ways in which people typically react to interpersonal conflict, managers can be prepared for employees' reactions and help them uncover their feelings about a conflict.

◼ CONFLICT MANAGEMENT STRATEGIES AND TECHNIQUES

The overall approach (or strategy) you use in a conflict is important in determining whether the conflict will have a positive or negative outcome.

These overall strategies are competitive versus cooperative strategies. Table 12.3 depicts the two strategies and four different conflict scenarios. The competitive

TABLE 12.3

Win–Lose Versus Win–Win Strategies

STRATEGY	DEPARTMENT A	DEPARTMENT B	ORGANIZATION
Competitive	Lose	Lose	Lose
	Lose	Win	Lose
	Win	Lose	Lose
Cooperative	Win–	Win–	Win

strategy is founded on assumptions of win–lose and entails dishonest communication, mistrust, and a rigid position from both parties.[42] The cooperative strategy is founded on different assumptions: the potential for win–win outcomes, honest communication, trust, openness to risk and vulnerability, and the notion that the whole may be greater than the sum of the parts.

To illustrate the importance of the overall strategy, consider the case of two groups competing for scarce resources. Suppose budget cuts have to be made at an insurance company. The claims manager argues that the sales training staff should be cut, because agents are fully trained. The sales training manager argues that claims personnel should be cut, because the company is processing fewer claims. This could turn into a dysfunctional brawl, with both sides refusing to give ground. This would constitute a win–lose, lose–win, or lose–lose scenario. Personnel cuts could be made in only one department, or in both departments. In all three cases, with the competitive approach the organization winds up in a losing position.

Even in such intense conflicts as those over scarce resources, a win–win strategy can lead to an overall win for the organization. In fact, conflicts over scarce resources can be productive if the parties have cooperative goals—a strategy that seeks a winning solution for both parties. To achieve a win–win outcome, the conflict must be approached with open-minded discussion of opposing views. Through open-minded discussion, both parties integrate views and create new solutions that facilitate productivity and strengthen their relationship; the result is feelings of unity rather than separation.[43]

In the example of the conflict between the claims manager and sales training manager, open-minded discussion might reveal that there are ways to achieve budget cuts without cutting personnel. Sales support might surrender part of its travel budget, and claims might cut out overtime. This represents a win–win situation for the company. The budget has been reduced, and relationships between the two departments have been preserved. Both parties have given up something (note the "Win–" in Table 12.3), but the conflict has been resolved with a positive outcome.

You can see the importance of the broad strategy used to approach a conflict. We now move from broad strategies to more specific techniques.

■ INEFFECTIVE TECHNIQUES

There are many specific techniques for dealing with conflict. Before turning to techniques that work, it should be recognized that some actions commonly taken in organizations to deal with conflict are not effective.[44]

Nonaction is doing nothing in hopes that the conflict will disappear. Generally, this is not a good technique, because most conflicts do not go away, and the individuals involved in the conflict react with frustration.

Secrecy, or trying to keep a conflict out of view of most people, only creates suspicion. An example is an organizational policy of pay secrecy. In some organizations, discussion of salary is grounds for dismissal. When this is the case, employees suspect that the company has something to hide. Secrecy may result in secret political activity by employees who hope to uncover the secret![45]

Administrative orbiting is delaying action on a conflict by buying time, usually by telling the individuals involved that the problem is being worked on or that the boss is still thinking about the issue. Like nonaction, this technique leads to frustration and resentment.

: 5. Understand and avoid ineffective techniques for managing conflict.

nonaction
Doing nothing in hopes that a conflict will disappear.

secrecy
Attempting to hide a conflict or an issue that has the potential to create conflict.

administrative orbiting
Delaying action on a conflict by buying time.

due process nonaction
A procedure set up to address conflicts that is so costly, time consuming, or personally risky that no one will use it.

Due process nonaction is a procedure set up to address conflicts that is so costly, time consuming, or personally risky that no one will use it. Some companies' sexual harassment policies are examples of this technique. To file a sexual harassment complaint, detailed paperwork is required, the accuser must go through appropriate channels, and the accuser risks being branded a troublemaker. Thus, the company has a procedure for handling complaints (due process), but no one uses it (nonaction).

character assassination
An attempt to label or discredit an opponent.

Character assassination is an attempt to label or discredit an opponent. Character assassination can backfire and make the individual who uses it appear dishonest and cruel. It often leads to name-calling and accusations by both parties, and both parties end up losers in the eyes of those who witness the conflict.

: 6. Describe and apply effective techniques for managing conflict.

■ EFFECTIVE TECHNIQUES

Fortunately, there are effective conflict management techniques. These include appealing to superordinate goals, expanding resources, changing personnel, changing structure, and confronting and negotiating.

SUPERORDINATE GOALS

superordinate goal
An organizational goal that is more important to both parties in a conflict than their individual or group goals.

An organizational goal that is more important to both parties in a conflict than their individual or group goals is a *superordinate goal.*[46] Superordinate goals cannot be achieved by an individual or by one group alone. The achievement of these goals requires cooperation by both parties.

One effective technique for resolving conflict is to appeal to a superordinate goal—in effect, to focus the parties on a larger issue on which they both agree. This helps them realize their similarities rather than their differences.

In the conflict between service representatives and cable television installers that was discussed earlier, appealing to a superordinate goal would be an effective technique for resolving the conflict. Both departments can agree that superior customer service is a goal worthy of pursuit and that this goal cannot be achieved unless cables are installed properly and in a timely manner, and customer complaints are handled effectively. Quality service requires that both departments cooperate to achieve the goal.

EXPANDING RESOURCES

One conflict resolution technique is so simple that it may be overlooked. If the conflict's source is common or scarce resources, providing more resources may be a solution. Of course, managers working with tight budgets may not have the luxury of obtaining additional resources. Nevertheless, it is a technique to be considered. In the example earlier in this chapter, one solution to the conflict among managers over secretarial support would be to hire more secretaries.

CHANGING PERSONNEL

In some cases, long-running severe conflict may be traced to a specific individual. For example, managers with lower levels of emotional intelligence have been demonstrated to have more negative work attitudes, to exhibit less altruistic behavior, and to produce more negative work outcomes. A chronically disgruntled manager who exhibits low EI may not only frustrate his employees but also impede his department's performance. In such cases, transferring or firing an individual may be the best solution, but only after due process.[47]

CHANGING STRUCTURE

Another way to resolve a conflict is to change the structure of the organization. One way of accomplishing this is to create an integrator role. An integrator is a liaison between groups with very different interests. In severe conflicts, it may be best that the integrator be a neutral third party.[48] Creating the integrator role is a way of opening dialogue between groups that have difficulty communicating.

Using cross-functional teams is another way of changing the organization's structure to manage conflict. In the old methods of designing new products in organizations, many departments had to contribute, and delays resulted from difficulties in coordinating the activities of the various departments. Using a cross-functional team made up of members from different departments improves coordination and reduces delays by allowing many activities to be performed at the same time rather than sequentially.[49] The team approach allows members from different departments to work together and reduces the potential for conflict. In teamwork, it is helpful to break up a big task so that it becomes a collection of smaller, less complex tasks, and to have smaller teams work on the smaller tasks. This helps to reduce conflict, and organizations can potentially improve the performance of the overall team by improving the outcomes in each subteam.[50]

CONFRONTING AND NEGOTIATING

Some conflicts require confrontation and negotiation between the parties. Both these strategies require skill on the part of the negotiator and careful planning before engaging in negotiations. The process of negotiating involves an open discussion of problem solutions, and the outcome often is an exchange in which both parties work toward a mutually beneficial solution.

Negotiation is a joint process of finding a mutually acceptable solution to a complex conflict. Negotiating is a useful strategy under the following conditions:

> There are two or more parties. Negotiation is primarily an interpersonal or intergroup process.
> There is a conflict of interest between the parties such that what one party wants is not what the other party wants.
> The parties are willing to negotiate because each believes it can use its influence to obtain a better outcome than by simply taking the side of the other party.
> The parties prefer to work together rather than to fight openly, give in, break off contact, or take the dispute to a higher authority.

There are two major negotiating approaches: distributive bargaining and integrative negotiation.[51] *Distributive bargaining* is an approach in which the goals of one party are in direct conflict with the goals of the other party. Resources are limited, and each party wants to maximize its share of the resources (get its part of the pie). It is a competitive or win–lose approach to negotiations. Sometimes distributive bargaining causes negotiators to focus so much on their differences that they ignore their common ground. In these cases, distributive bargaining can become counterproductive. The reality is, however, that some situations

distributive bargaining
A negotiation approach in which the goals of the parties are in conflict, and each party seeks to maximize its resources.

are distributive in nature, particularly when the parties are interdependent. If a negotiator wants to maximize the value of a single deal and is not worried about maintaining a good relationship with the other party, distributive bargaining may be an option.

integrative negotiation

A negotiation approach that focuses on the merits of the issues and seeks a win–win solution.

In contrast, *integrative negotiation* is an approach in which the parties' goals are not seen as mutually exclusive and in which the focus is on making it possible for both sides to achieve their objectives. Integrative negotiation focuses on the merits of the issues and is a win–win approach. (How can we make the pie bigger?) For integrative negotiation to be successful, certain preconditions must be present. These include having a common goal, faith in one's own problem-solving abilities, a belief in the validity of the other party's position, motivation to work together, mutual trust, and clear communication.[52]

Cultural differences in negotiation must be acknowledged. Japanese negotiators, for example, when working with American negotiators, tend to see their power as coming from their role (buyer versus seller). Americans, in contrast, view their power as their ability to walk away from the negotiations.[53] Neither culture understands the other very well, and the negotiations can resemble a dance in which one person is waltzing and the other doing a samba. The collectivism–individualism dimension (discussed in Chapter 2) has a great bearing on negotiations. Americans, with their individualism, negotiate from a position of self-interest; Japanese focus on the good of the group. Cross-cultural negotiations can be more effective if you learn as much about other cultures as possible.

Gender may also play a role in negotiation. There appears to be no evidence that men are better negotiators that women or vice versa. The differences lie in how negotiators are treated. Women are blatantly discriminated against in terms of the offers made to them in negotiations.[54] Gender stereotypes also affect the negotiating process. Women may be seen as accommodating, conciliatory, and emotional (negatives in negotiations) and men may be seen as assertive, powerful, and convincing (positive for negotiations) in accordance with traditional stereotypes. Sometimes, when women feel they're being stereotyped, they exhibit stereotype reactance, which is a tendency to display behavior inconsistent with (or opposite of) the stereotype. This means they become more assertive and convincing. Alternatively, men may choke when they're expected to fulfill the stereotype, fearing that they might not be able to live up to the stereotype.

One way to help men and women avoid stereotyping each other is to promote shared, positive identities between the negotiators. This means recognizing similarities between the two parties; for example, recognizing each other as highly successful professionals. This results in more cooperation because of shared and equal status, as opposed to more competition because of gender stereotypes.[55]

: 7. Define and apply five styles of conflict management and diagnose your own preferred style.

CONFLICT MANAGEMENT STYLES

Managers have at their disposal a variety of conflict management styles: avoiding, accommodating, competing, compromising, and collaborating. One way of classifying styles of conflict management is to examine the styles' assertiveness (the extent to which you want your goals met) and cooperativeness (the extent to which you want to see the other party's concerns met).[56] Figure 12.2 graphs the five

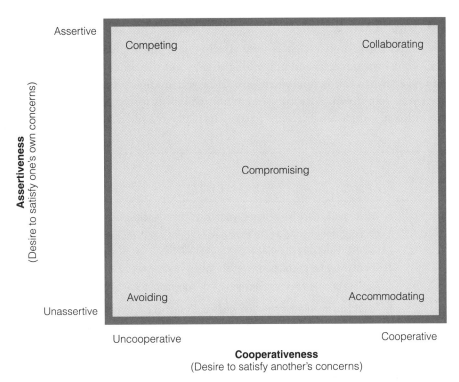

SOURCE: K. W. Thomas, "Conflict and Conflict Management," in M. D. Dunnette, *Handbook of Industrial and Organizational Psychology* (Chicago: Rand McNally, 1976): 900. Used with permission of M. D. Dunnette.

conflict management styles using these two dimensions. Table 12.4 lists appropriate situations for using each conflict management style.

▨ AVOIDING

Avoiding is a style low on both assertiveness and cooperativeness. Avoiding is a deliberate decision to take no action on a conflict or to stay out of a conflict situation. Some relationship conflicts, such as those involving political norms and personal tastes, may distract team members from their tasks and avoiding may be an appropriate strategy.[57] When the parties are angry and need time to cool down, it may be best to use avoidance. There is a potential danger in using an avoiding style too often, however. Research shows that overuse of this style results in negative evaluations from others in the workplace.[58]

▨ ACCOMMODATING

A style in which you are concerned that the other party's goals be met but relatively unconcerned with getting your own way is called accommodating. It is cooperative but unassertive. Appropriate situations for accommodating include times when you find you are wrong, when you want to let the other party have his or her way so that that individual will owe you similar treatment later, or when the relationship is important. Overreliance on accommodating has its dangers. Managers who constantly defer to others may find that others lose respect for them. In addition, accommodating managers may become frustrated because their own needs are never met, and they may lose self-esteem.[59]

■ COMPETING

Competing is a style that is very assertive and uncooperative. You want to satisfy your own interests and are willing to do so at the other party's expense. In an emergency or in situations where you know you are right, it may be appropriate to put your foot down. For example, environmentalists forced Shell Oil Company (part of Royal Dutch/Shell Group) to scrap its plans to build a refinery in Delaware

TABLE 12.4

Uses of Five Styles of Conflict Management

CONFLICT-HANDLING STYLE	APPROPRIATE SITUATION
Competing	1. When quick, decisive action is vital (e.g., emergencies). 2. On important issues where unpopular actions need implementing (e.g., cost cutting, enforcing unpopular rules, discipline). 3. On issues vital to company welfare when you know you are right. 4. Against people who take advantage of noncompetitive behavior.
Collaborating	1. To find an integrative solution when both sets of concerns are too important to be compromised. 2. When your objective is to learn. 3. To merge insights from people with different perspectives. 4. To gain commitment by incorporating concerns into a consensus. 5. To work through feelings that have interfered with a relationship.
Compromising	1. When goals are important but not worth the effort or potential disruption of more assertive modes. 2. When opponents with equal power are committed to mutually exclusive goals. 3. To achieve temporary settlements to complex issues. 4. To arrive at expedient solutions under time pressure. 5. As a backup when collaboration or competition is unsuccessful.
Avoiding	1. When an issue is trivial or more important issues are pressing. 2. When you perceive no chance of satisfying your concerns. 3. When potential disruption outweighs the benefits of resolution. 4. To let people cool down and regain perspective. 5. When gathering information supersedes immediate decision. 6. When others can resolve the conflict more effectively. 7. When issues seem tangential or symptomatic of other issues.
Accommodating	1. When you find you are wrong—to allow a better position to be heard, to learn, and to show your reasonableness. 2. When issues are more important to others than to yourself—to satisfy others and maintain cooperation. 3. To build social credits for later issues. 4. To minimize loss when you are outmatched and losing. 5. When harmony and stability are especially important. 6. To allow employees to develop by learning from mistakes.

SOURCE: Republished with permission of *Academy of Management,* from K. W. Thomas, "Toward Multidimensional Values in Teaching: The Example of Conflict Behaviors," *Academy of Management Review* 2 (July 1977): 309–325; permission conveyed through Copyright Clearance Center, Inc.

after a bitter "To Hell with Shell" campaign.[60] Relying solely on competing strategies is dangerous, though. Managers who do so may become reluctant to admit when they are wrong and may find themselves surrounded by people who are afraid to disagree with them.

▓ COMPROMISING

The compromising style is intermediate in both assertiveness and cooperativeness, because each party must give up something to reach a solution to the conflict. Compromises are often made in the final hours of union–management negotiations, when time is of the essence. Compromise may be an effective backup style when efforts toward collaboration are not successful.[61]

It is important to recognize that compromises are not optimal solutions. Compromise means partially surrendering one's position for the sake of coming to terms. Often, when people compromise, they inflate their demands to begin with. The solutions reached may only be temporary, and often compromises do nothing to improve relationships between the parties in the conflict.

▓ COLLABORATING

A win–win style that is high on both assertiveness and cooperativeness is known as collaborating. Working toward collaborating involves an open and thorough discussion of the conflict and arriving at a solution that is satisfactory to both parties. Situations where collaboration may be effective include times when both parties need to be committed to a final solution or when a combination of different perspectives can be formed into a solution. Collaborating requires open, trusting behavior and sharing information for the benefit of both parties. Long term, it leads to improved relationships and effective performance.[62]

Research on the five styles of conflict management indicates that although most managers favor a certain style, they have the capacity to change styles as the situation demands.[63] A study of project managers found that managers who used a combination of competing and avoiding styles were seen as ineffective by the engineers who worked on their project teams.[64] In another study of conflicts between R&D project managers and technical staff, competing and avoiding styles resulted in more frequent conflict and lower performance, whereas the collaborating style resulted in less frequent conflict and better performance.[65] Use Challenge 12.2 to assess your dominant conflict management style.

Cultural differences also influence the use of different styles of conflict management. For example, one study compared Turkish and Jordanian managers with U.S. managers. All three groups preferred the collaborating style. Turkish managers also reported frequent use of the competing style, whereas Jordanian and U.S. managers reported that it was one of their least used styles.[66]

The human resources manager of one U.S. telecommunications company's office in Singapore engaged a consultant to investigate the conflict in the office.[67] Twenty-two expatriates from the United States and Canada and 38 Singaporeans worked in the office. The consultant used the Thomas model (Figure 12.2) and distributed questionnaires to all managers to determine their conflict management styles. The results were not surprising: The expatriate managers preferred the competing, collaborating, and compromising styles, while the Asians preferred the avoiding and accommodating styles.

CHALLENGE 12.2

What Is Your Conflict-Handling Style?

Instructions:

For each of the 15 items, indicate how often you rely on that tactic by circling the appropriate number.

		Rarely				Always

1. I argue my case with my coworkers to show the merits of my position. 1—2—3—4—5
2. I negotiate with my coworkers so that a compromise can be reached. 1—2—3—4—5
3. I try to satisfy the expectations of my coworkers. 1—2—3—4—5
4. I try to investigate an issue with my coworkers to find a solution acceptable to us. 1—2—3—4—5
5. I am firm in pursuing my side of the issue. 1—2—3—4—5
6. I attempt to avoid being "put on the spot" and try to keep my conflict with my coworkers to myself. 1—2—3—4—5
7. I hold on to my solution to a problem. 1—2—3—4—5
8. I use "give and take" so that a compromise can be made. 1—2—3—4—5
9. I exchange accurate information with my coworkers to solve a problem together. 1—2—3—4—5
10. I avoid open discussion of my differences with my coworkers. 1—2—3—4—5
11. I accommodate the wishes of my coworkers. 1—2—3—4—5
12. I try to bring all our concerns out in the open so that the issues can be resolved in the best possible way. 1—2—3—4—5
13. I propose a middle ground for breaking deadlocks. 1—2—3—4—5
14. I go along with the suggestions of my coworkers. 1—2—3—4—5
15. I try to keep my disagreements with my coworkers to myself in order to avoid hard feelings. 1—2—3—4—5

Scoring Key:

Collaborating		Accommodating		Competing		Avoiding		Compromising	
Item	Score	Item	Score	Item	Score	Item	Score	Item	Score
4. ___		3. ___		1. ___		6. ___		2. ___	
9. ___		11. ___		5. ___		10. ___		8. ___	
12. ___		14. ___		7. ___		15. ___		13. ___	
Total = ___		Total = ___		Total = ___		Total = ___		Total = ___	

Your primary conflict-handling style is: _____   Your backup conflict-handling style is: _____
  (The category with the highest total.)   (The category with the second highest total.)

Source: Reprinted with permission of Academy of Management, PO Box 3020, Briar Cliff Manor, NY 10510-8020. *A Measure of Styles of Handling Interpersonal Conflict* (Adaptation), M. A. Rahim, *Academy of Management Journal*, June 1983. Reproduced by permission of the publisher via Copyright Clearance Center, Inc.

Workshops were conducted within the firm to develop an understanding of the differences and how they negatively affected the firm. The Asians interpreted the results as reflecting the tendency of Americans to "shout first and ask questions later." They felt that the Americans had an arrogant attitude and could not handle having their ideas rejected. The Asians attributed their own styles to their cultural background. The Americans attributed the results to the stereotypical view of Asians as unassertive and timid, and they viewed their own results as reflecting their desire to "get things out in the open."

The process opened a dialogue between the two groups, who began to work on the idea of harmony through conflict. They began to discard the traditional stereotypes in favor of shared meanings and mutual understanding.

It is important to remember that preventing and resolving dysfunctional conflict is only half the task of effective conflict management. Stimulating functional conflict is the other half.

🔲 MANAGERIAL IMPLICATIONS: CREATING A CONFLICT-POSITIVE ORGANIZATION

Dean Tjosvold argues that well-managed conflict adds to an organization's innovation and productivity.[68] He discusses procedures for making conflict positive. Too many organizations take a win–lose, competitive approach to conflict or avoid conflict altogether. These two approaches view conflict as negative. A positive view of conflict, in contrast, leads to win–win solutions. Four interrelated steps are involved in creating a conflict-positive organization:

1. *Value diversity and confront differences.* Differences should be seen as opportunities for innovation, and diversity should be celebrated. Open and honest confrontations bring out differences, and they are essential for positive conflict.

2. *Seek mutual benefits and unite behind cooperative goals.* Conflicts have to be managed together. Through conflict, individuals learn how much they depend on one another. Even when employees share goals, they may differ on how to accomplish the goals. The important point is that they are moving toward the same objectives. Joint rewards should be given to the whole team for cooperative behavior.

3. *Empower employees to feel confident and skillful.* People must be made to feel that they control their conflicts and that they can deal with their differences productively. When they do so, they should be recognized.

4. *Take stock to reward success and learn from mistakes.* Employees should be encouraged to appreciate one another's strengths and weaknesses and to talk directly about them. They should celebrate their conflict management successes and work out plans for ways they can improve in the future.

Tjosvold believes that a conflict-positive organization has competitive advantages for the future.

A complimentary perspective comes from Peter J. Frost, who proposed that over time, organizational practices like poor conflict management can "poison" the organization as well as those who work within it. He describes how compassionate leaders can help reduce the effects of organizational toxins on their coworkers and how these toxin handlers should be rewarded for this crucial role in maintaining organizational health. Frost's position echoes Tjosvold's, as he calls for firms to become emotionally healthy workplaces for the good of their employees as well as for the good of their stockholders.[69]

Finally, don't overlook the importance of high emotional intelligence in the work of a good conflict manager. The ability to influence your own and others' emotions is not just a practical tool, but it can also serve as an important tactical asset, making you a better negotiator in a variety of situations and helping reduce conflict and increase productivity in your organization.[70]

LOOKING BACK :: WHOLE FOODS MARKET, INC.

There Are No Easy Answers

Whole Foods, in response to suggestions from throughout the company, took the unprecedented step of allowing its employees to vote on benefits such as health care and purchase discounts at company stores. In what the company terms an example of democracy in action, Whole Foods' employees were allowed the type of input that is typically reserved for unionized employees. Further, the firm plans to repeat the vote in future years, making it, at least at first glance, one of the most responsive employers around.

But questions still remain about Whole Foods and the way it treats its workers. Company founder and libertarian John Mackey bundles labor unions (which he has compared to "herpes") with other outsiders, such as organized crime, who might try to interfere with his firm's operations. Some Web sites condemn his actions as union busting, while others call for Whole Foods' workers throughout the country to organize.[71]

Is John Mackey's anti-union position consistent with Whole Foods' stated values of helping its people grow and prosper, or is it simply a way to keep wages low and profits up? Who holds the high ground in this long-running battle? Expect to see further encounters between Whole Foods and organized labor in the future. And, unless things change radically, expect to see Whole Foods back on *Fortune*'s list of "100 Best Companies to Work For" again next year, despite the conflict.

CHAPTER SUMMARY

1. Conflict management skills are keys to management success. The manager's task is to stimulate functional conflict and prevent or resolve dysfunctional conflict.

2. Structural causes of conflict include specialization, interdependence, common resources, goal differences, authority relationships, status inconsistencies, and jurisdictional ambiguities.

3. Personal factors that lead to conflict include differences in skills and abilities, personalities, perceptions, or values and ethics; emotions; communication barriers; and cultural differences. The increasing diversity of the workforce and globalization of business have potential to increase conflict arising from these differences.

4. The levels of conflict include interorganizational, intergroup, interpersonal, and intrapersonal.

5. Individuals engaged in interpersonal conflict often display aggressive, compromise, or withdrawal defense mechanisms.

6. Ineffective techniques for managing conflict include nonaction, secrecy, administrative orbiting, due process nonaction, and character assassination.
7. Effective techniques for managing conflict include appealing to superordinate goals, expanding resources, changing personnel, changing structure, and confronting and negotiating.
8. In negotiating, managers can use a variety of conflict management styles, including avoiding, accommodating, competing, compromising, and collaborating.
9. Managers should strive to create a conflict-positive organization—one that values diversity, empowers employees, and seeks win–win solutions to conflicts.

KEY TERMS

administrative orbiting (p. 315)
character assassination (p. 316)
compensation (p. 313)
conflict (p. 302)
conversion (p. 314)
displacement (p. 313)
distributive bargaining (p. 317)
due process nonaction (p. 316)
dysfunctional conflict (p. 303)

fantasy (p. 314)
fixation (p. 312)
flight/withdrawal (p. 314)
functional conflict (p. 303)
identification (p. 314)
integrative negotiation (p. 318)
intergroup conflict (p. 309)
interorganizational conflict (p. 309)

interpersonal conflict (p. 310)
intragroup conflict (p. 310)
intrapersonal conflict (p. 310)
jurisdictional ambiguity (p. 306)
negativism (p. 313)
nonaction (p. 315)
rationalization (p. 314)
secrecy (p. 315)
superordinate goal (p. 316)

REVIEW QUESTIONS

1. Discuss the differences between functional and dysfunctional conflict. Why should a manager understand conflict?
2. Identify the structural and personal factors that contribute to conflict.
3. Discuss the four major forms of conflict in organizations.
4. What defense mechanisms do people use in interpersonal conflict?
5. What are the most effective techniques for managing conflict at work? What are some ineffective techniques?
6. Identify and discuss five styles of conflict management.

Discussion and Communication QUESTIONS

1. What causes you the most conflict at work or school?
2. Identify the different intragroup, interrole, intrarole, and person–role conflicts that you experience.
3. Which defense mechanism do you see people exhibiting most frequently? Why do you think this is the case? How can you manage this type of reaction to a conflict?
4. Are you comfortable with your preferred conflict management style? Would you consider modifying it?
5. *(communication question)* Think of a person with whom you have had a recent conflict. Write a letter to this person, attempting to resolve the conflict. Use the concepts from the chapter to accomplish your objective. Be sure to address whether the conflict is functional or dysfunctional, what styles each party has used, effective strategies for resolving the conflict, and ineffective strategies that should be avoided.

ETHICAL DILEMMA

Scott Davis sat at his desk anxiously waiting for the next few minutes to pass. It was almost time for the meeting he had scheduled between Debra Cronin and Ken Brown. Scott knew this meeting would be challenging for everyone. Debra and Ken had been at odds for quite some time. The problems started soon after Ken joined the company. At first, Scott thought the conflict was healthy and would bring some much needed change to the department. Scott soon learned that the disputes between Debra and Ken were more personal than professional.

Debra had been with the company for seven years. Scott had no complaints about her performance. She was a hard worker that got the job done. Unfortunately, Debra was also the source of a lot of conflict in the department. She always felt she knew the best way to do everything and freely shared that opinion with everyone, whether they wanted it or not. Scott has spent many hours listening to employees' complaints about Debra's insistence on showing them the "proper" way to do their jobs. Debra's interference had caused a fair amount of discontent in the department, but Scott never felt it was enough to consider termination. The meeting today may well change that opinion.

Ken Brown was new to the company. He had joined Scott's department just four months ago. He was young with a lot of fresh, new ideas. Scott liked everything about Ken and thought he would be great for the department and the company. But just like those before him, Ken found working with Debra difficult. She was set in her ways and was not going to change. Worse, she was undermining the other employees' interest in changing. Scott felt that he had done everything he could to resolve the conflict between the two, without success. He felt sure that today's meeting would end with one person leaving the company. His decision was which one: Debra, the long-time employee, or Ken, the newcomer, with the vision for the future?

QUESTIONS

1. Does Scott have a greater responsibility to Debra than to Ken?

2. To whom does Scott owe the greatest responsibility?

3. Evaluate Scott's decision alternatives using rule, virtue, rights, and justice theories.

EXPERIENTIAL EXERCISES

12.1 CONFLICTS OVER UNETHICAL BEHAVIOR

Many conflicts in work organizations arise over differences in beliefs concerning what constitutes ethical versus unethical behavior. The following questionnaire provides a list of behaviors that you or your coworkers might engage in when working for a company. Go over each item, and circle the number that best indicates the frequency with which you personally would (or do, if you work now) engage in that behavior. Then put an X over the number you think represents how often your coworkers would (or do) engage in that behavior. Finally, put a check mark beside the item (in the "Needs Control" column) if you believe that management should control that behavior.

	AT EVERY OPPOR-TUNITY	OFTEN	ABOUT HALF THE TIME	SELDOM	NEVER	NEEDS CONTROL
1. Passing blame for errors to an innocent coworker.	5	4	3	2	1	____
2. Divulging confidential information.	5	4	3	2	1	____
3. Falsifying time/quality/quantity reports.	5	4	3	2	1	____

	AT EVERY OPPORTUNITY	OFTEN	ABOUT HALF THE TIME	SELDOM	NEVER	NEEDS CONTROL
4. Claiming credit for someone else's work.	5	4	3	2	1	_____
5. Padding an expense account by over 10 percent.	5	4	3	2	1	_____
6. Pilfering company materials and supplies.	5	4	3	2	1	_____
7. Accepting gifts/favors in exchange for preferential treatment.	5	4	3	2	1	_____
8. Giving gifts/favors in exchange for preferential treatment.	5	4	3	2	1	_____
9. Padding an expense account by up to 10 percent.	5	4	3	2	1	_____
10. Authorizing a subordinate to violate company rules.	5	4	3	2	1	_____
11. Calling in sick to take a day off.	5	4	3	2	1	_____
12. Concealing one's errors.	5	4	3	2	1	_____
13. Taking longer than necessary to do a job.	5	4	3	2	1	_____
14. Using company services for personal use.	5	4	3	2	1	_____
15. Doing personal business on company time.	5	4	3	2	1	_____
16. Taking extra personal time (lunch hour, breaks, early departure, and so forth).	5	4	3	2	1	_____
17. Not reporting others' violations of company policies and rules.	5	4	3	2	1	_____
18. Overlooking a superior's violation of policy to prove loyalty to the boss.	5	4	3	2	1	_____

DISCUSSION QUESTIONS

1. Would (do) your coworkers seem to engage in these behaviors more often than you would (do)? Why do you have this perception?

2. Which behaviors tend to be most frequent?

3. How are the most frequent behaviors different from the behaviors engaged in less frequently?

4. What are the most important items for managers to control? How should managers control these behaviors?

5. Select a particular behavior from the list. Have two people debate whether the behavior is ethical or not.

6. What types of conflicts could emerge if the behaviors in the list occurred frequently?

SOURCE: From *Managerial Experience,* 3e by Jauch L. © 1983. Reprinted with permission of South-Western, a division of Thomson Learning: http://www.thomsonlearning.com. Fax 800-730-2215.

12.2 THE WORLD BANK GAME: AN INTERGROUP NEGOTIATION

The purposes of this exercise are to learn about conflict and trust between groups and to practice negotiation skills. In the course of the exercise, money will be won or lost. Your team's objective is to win as much money as it can. Your team will be paired with another team, and both teams will receive identical instructions. After reading these instructions, each team will have 10 minutes to plan its strategy.

Each team is assumed to have contributed $50 million to the World Bank. Teams may have to pay more or may receive money from the World Bank, depending on the outcome.

Each team will receive 20 cards. These cards are the weapons. Each card has a marked side (*X*) and an unmarked side. The marked side signifies that the weapon is armed; the unmarked side signifies that the weapon is unarmed.

At the beginning, each team will place 10 of its 20 weapons in their armed position (marked side up) and the remaining 10 in their unarmed position (marked side down). The weapons will remain in the team's possession and out of sight of the other team at all times.

The game will consist of *rounds* and *moves.* Each round will be composed of seven moves by each team. There will be two or more rounds in the game, depending on the time available. Payoffs will be determined and recorded after each round. The rules are as follows:

1. A move consists of turning two, one, or none of the team's weapons from armed to unarmed status, or vice versa.

2. Each team has one and a half minutes for each move. There is a 30-second period between each move. At the end of the one and a half minutes, the team must have turned two, one, or none of its weapons from armed to unarmed

status or from unarmed to armed status. If the team fails to move in the allotted time, no change can be made in weapon status until the next move.

3. The two-minute length of the period between the beginning of one move and the beginning of the next is unalterable.

Finances:
The funds each team has contributed to the World Bank are to be allocated in the following manner: $30 million will be returned to each team to be used as the team's treasury during the course of the game, and $20 million will be retained for the operation of the World Bank.

Payoffs:
1. If there is an attack:

   a. Each team may announce an attack on the other team by notifying the banker during the 30 seconds following any minute-and-a-half period used to decide upon the move (including the seventh, or final, decision period in any round). The choice of each team during the decision period just ended counts as a move. An attack may not be made during negotiations.

   b. If there is an attack by one or both teams, two things happen: (1) the round ends, and (2) the World Bank assesses a penalty of $2.5 million on each team.

   c. The team with the greater number of armed weapons wins $1.5 million for each armed weapon it has over and above the number of armed weapons of the other team. These funds are paid directly from the treasury of the losing team to the treasury of the winning team. The banker will manage the transfer of funds.

2. If there is no attack:

At the end of each round (seven moves), each team's treasury will receive from the World Bank $1 million for each of its weapons that is at that point unarmed; and each team's treasury will pay to the World Bank $1 million for each of its weapons remaining armed.

Negotiations:
Between moves, each team will have the opportunity to communicate with the other team through its negotiations. Either team may call for negotiations by notifying the banker during any of the 30-second

periods between decisions. A team is free to accept or reject any invitation to negotiate.

Negotiators from both teams are required to meet after the third and sixth moves (after the 30-second period following the move, if there is no attack).

Negotiations can last no longer than three minutes. When the two negotiators return to their teams, the minute-and-a-half decision period for the next move will begin once again.

Negotiators are bound only by (a) the three-minute time limit for negotiations and (b) their required appearance after the third and sixth moves. They are always free to say whatever is necessary to benefit themselves or their teams. The teams are not bound by agreements made by their negotiators, even when those agreements are made in good faith.

Special Roles:
Each team has 10 minutes to organize itself and plan team strategy. During this period, before the first round begins, each team must choose persons to fill the following roles:

- A *negotiator*—activities stated above.
- A *representative*—to communicate the team's decisions to the banker.
- A *recorder*—to record the moves of the team and to keep a running balance of the team's treasury.
- A *treasurer*—to execute all financial transactions with the banker.

The instructor will serve as the banker for the World Bank and will signal the beginning of each of the rounds.

At the end of the game, each participant should complete the following questionnaire, which assesses reactions to the World Bank Game.

World Bank Questionnaire:
1. To what extent are you satisfied with your team's strategy?

Highly dissatisfied   1 2 3 4 5 6 7   Highly satisfied

2. To what extent do you believe the other team is trustworthy?

Highly untrustworthy   1 2 3 4 5 6 7   Highly trustworthy

3. To what extent are you satisfied with the performance of your negotiator?

Highly dissatisfied   1 2 3 4 5 6 7   Highly satisfied

4. To what extent was there a consensus on your team regarding its moves?

Very little   1 2 3 4 5 6 7   A great deal

5. To what extent do you trust the other members of your team?

Very little   1 2 3 4 5 6 7   A great deal

6. Select one word that describes how you feel about your team: _____.

7. Select one word that describes how you feel about the other team: _____.

Negotiators only:
How did you see the other team's negotiator?

Phony and insincere   1 2 3 4 5 6 7   Authentic and sincere

At the end of the game, the class will reconvene and discuss team members' responses to the World Bank Questionnaire. In addition, the following questions are to be addressed:

1. What was each team's strategy for winning? What strategy was most effective?

2. Contrast the outcomes in terms of win–win solutions to conflict versus win–lose solutions.

SOURCE: Adapted by permission from N. H. Berkowitz and H. A. Hornstein, "World Bank: An Intergroup Negotiation," in J. W. Pfeiffer and J. E. Jones, eds., *The 1975 Handbook for Group Facilitators* (San Diego: Pfeiffer): 58–62. Copyright © 1975 Pfeiffer/Jossey-Bass. This material is used by permission of John Wiley & Sons, Inc.

(continued)

WORLD BANK RECORD SHEET

	Round One		Round Two		Round Three		Round Four	
	Armed	Unarmed	Armed	Unarmed	Armed	Unarmed	Armed	Unarmed
Move	10	10	10	10	10	10	10	10
1								
2								
3								
Required Negotiation 4								
5								
6								
Required Negotiation 7								

Funds in Team Treasury	$30 million				
Funds of Other Treasury	$30 million				
Funds in World Bank	$40 million				

PART 4

Organizational Processes and Structure

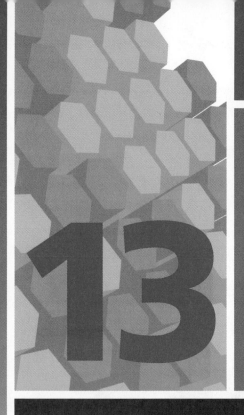

13

Job Design and Redesign

LEARNING OBJECTIVES

After reading this chapter, you should be able to do the following:

: 1. Define the term *job* in an organizational context and contrast job with *work*.

: 2. Discuss the benefits and drawbacks of the four traditional approaches to job design.

: 3. Describe the Job Characteristics Model and the five core job characteristics.

: 4. Compare the social information-processing (SIP) model with traditional job design approaches.

: 5. Explain ergonomics and the interdisciplinary framework for the design of work.

: 6. Compare and contrast Japanese, German, and Scandinavian approaches to work.

: 7. Discuss three contemporary issues in the design of work.

THINKING AHEAD :: PIXAR ANIMATION STUDIOS

Playing at Pixar

The work environment at Pixar has been described as "semicontrolled chaos," which is guided by the Pixar philosophy that good work and performance come from creative people bouncing ideas off each other. Common areas like the cafeteria, mailroom, and even the restrooms encourage people from different departments to meet and trade ideas. Hence, common functions facilitate the bouncing. The imagination of the artists, writers, animators, and programmers who work at Pixar is evident in their office décor. One row of offices is noted for its varied roofing materials. One is topped with a thatch tiki-room design, the next in Spanish tile, and a third in suburban shingles with a satellite dish. Hanging from the ceiling is the large Canadian flag that flew from a pole at Pixar's front entrance in honor of Glenn McQueen, an animator who died of cancer in 2002.

All this happens in the context of a two-story, 220,000-square-foot building of brick, steel beams, and filtered glass set on a 16-acre campus of rolling green that includes an outdoor amphitheater and half a soccer field. The studio resembles a community college rather than a business. This contextual design was not as intended. The original plan called for having a separate building for those who worked on the story lines, another one for those who worked on animation, a third for those whose work was technology, and so on. This is actually how a "regular" movie studio would have its work done. While this approach to work appears logical and rational and gets people to focus narrowly on their type of work (e.g., animation) that contributes to the whole, there is also a definite downside to the approach.

The downside is reflected in a story. Disney animators, Frank Thomas and Ollie Johnston, recollected what Walt Disney did for them after their success with *Snow White and the Seven Dwarfs.* Disney had a set built for them that was to be the utopian animation studio. Every person had an office, and each wing of the building was separated so that every office would have natural light. This design served to separate and isolate people so that no one knew what was going on. There was no real interaction. Based on this story, Pixar scrapped the multibuilding plan. Pixar's CEO Steve Jobs wanted to go even further than one building; he wanted one bathroom to create a "bathroom effect" where people would interact and be creative.[1] Will the creativity and imagination of Pixar's artists, writers, animators, and programmers be enough to take them "to infinity and beyond"?

A *job* is defined as an employee's specific work and task activities in an organization. A job is not the same as an organizational position or a career. *Organizational position* identifies a job in relation to other parts of the organization; career refers to a sequence of job experiences over time.

This chapter focuses on job design and redesign as elements of the organization's structure. Jobs help people define their work and become integrated into the organization. The first section in the chapter examines the meaning of work in organizations. The second major section addresses four traditional approaches to job design developed between the late 1800s and the 1970s. The third major section examines four alternative approaches to job design developed over the past couple of decades. The final section addresses emerging issues in job design.

:: **1.** Define the term *job* in an organizational context, and contrast job with *work.*

job
A set of specified work and task activities that engage an individual in an organization.

WORK IN ORGANIZATIONS

Work is effortful, productive activity resulting in a product or a service. Work is one important reason why organizations exist. A job is composed of a set of specific tasks, each of which is an assigned piece of work to be done in a specific time period.

work
Mental or physical activity that has productive results.

Work is an especially important human endeavor because it has a powerful effect in binding a person to reality. Through work, people become securely attached to reality and securely connected in human relationships. However, work may also overshadow one's personal life. This is an emerging concern in the United Kingdom, as is evidenced by work life surveys conducted by Croner Consulting with its employees.[2]

Work has different meanings for different people. For all people, work is organized into jobs, and jobs fit into the larger structure of an organization. The structure of jobs is the concern of this chapter, and the structure of the organization is the concern of the next chapter. Both chapters emphasize organizations as sets of task and authority relationships through which people get work done.

◼ JOBS IN ORGANIZATIONS

Task and authority relationships define an organization's structure. Jobs are the basic building blocks of this task–authority structure and are considered the microstructural element to which employees most directly relate. Jobs are usually designed to complement and support other jobs in the organization. Isolated jobs are rare, although one was identified at Coastal Corporation during the early 1970s. Shortly after Oscar Wyatt moved the company from Corpus Christi, Texas, to Houston, Coastal developed organizational charts and job descriptions because the company had grown so large. In the process of charting the organization's structure, it was discovered that the beloved corporate economist reported to no one. Everyone assumed he worked for someone else. Such peculiarities are rare, however.

Jobs in organizations are interdependent and designed to make a contribution to the organization's overall mission and goals. For salespeople to be successful, the production people must be effective. For production people to be effective, the material department must be effective. These interdependencies require careful planning and design so that all of the "pieces of work" fit together into a whole. For example, an envelope salesperson who wants to take an order for one million envelopes from John Hancock Financial Services must coordinate with the production department to establish an achievable delivery date. The failure to incorporate this interdependence into his planning could create conflict and doom the company to failure in meeting John Hancock's expectations. The central concerns of this chapter are designing work and structuring jobs to prevent such problems and to ensure employee well-being. Inflexible jobs that are rigidly structured have an adverse effect and lead to stressed-out employees.

Chapter 14 addresses the larger issues in the design of organizations. In particular, it examines the competing processes of differentiation and integration in organizations. Differentiation is the process of subdividing and departmentalizing the work of an organization. Jobs result from differentiation, which is necessary because no one can do it all (contrary to the famous statement made by Harold Geneen, former chairman of ITT: "If I had enough arms and legs and time, I'd do it all myself"). Even small organizations must divide work so that each person is able to accomplish a manageable piece of the whole. At the same time the organization divides up the work, it must also integrate those pieces back into a whole. Integration is the process of connecting jobs and departments into a coordinated, cohesive whole. For example, if the envelope salesperson had coordinated with the production manager before finalizing the order with John Hancock, the company could have met the customer's expectations, and integration would have occurred.

🖋 TRADITIONAL APPROACHES TO JOB DESIGN

: **2.** Discuss the benefits and drawbacks of the four traditional approaches to job design.

Failure to differentiate, integrate, or both may result in badly designed jobs, which in turn cause a variety of performance problems in organizations. Good job design helps avoid these problems, improves productivity, and enhances employee well-being. Four approaches to job design that were developed during the twentieth century are scientific management, job enlargement/job rotation, job enrichment, and the job characteristics theory. Each approach offers unique benefits to the organization, the employee, or both, but each also has limitations and drawbacks. Furthermore, an unthinking reliance on a traditional approach can be a serious problem in any company. The later job design approaches were developed to overcome the limitations of traditional job design approaches. For example, job enlargement was intended to overcome the problem of boredom associated with scientific management's narrowly defined approach to jobs.

▨ SCIENTIFIC MANAGEMENT

Scientific management, an approach to work design first advocated by Frederick Taylor, emphasized work simplification. *Work simplification* is the standardization and the narrow, explicit specification of task activities for workers.[3] Jobs designed through scientific management have a limited number of tasks, and each task is scientifically specified so that the worker is not required to think or deliberate. According to Taylor, the role of management and the industrial engineer is to calibrate and define each task carefully. The role of the worker is to execute the task. The elements of scientific management, such as time and motion studies, differential piece-rate systems of pay, and the scientific selection of workers, all focus on the efficient use of labor to the economic benefit of the corporation. Employees who are satisfied with various aspects of repetitive work may like scientifically designed jobs.

work simplification
Standardization and the narrow, explicit specification of task activities for workers.

Two arguments supported the efficient and standardized job design approach of scientific management in the early days of the American Industrial Revolution. The first argument was that work simplification allowed workers of diverse ethnic and skill backgrounds to work together in a systematic way. This was important during the first great period of globalization in the late 1800s during which Germans, Scots, Hungarians, Poles, and other immigrants came to work in America.[4] Taylor's unique approach to work standardization allowed diverse individuals to be blended into a functional workforce.

The second argument for scientific management was that work simplification led to production efficiency in the organization and, therefore, to higher profits. This economic argument for work simplification tended to treat labor as a means of production and dehumanized it. This is a problem in some modern service jobs, such as flipping hamburgers.

A fundamental limitation of scientific management is that it undervalues the human capacity for thought and ingenuity. Jobs designed through scientific management use only a portion of a person's capabilities. This underutilization makes work boring, monotonous, and understimulating. The failure to fully utilize the workers' capacity in a constructive fashion may cause a variety of work problems. Contemporary approaches to enhancing motivation through pay and compensation work to overcome these problems through modern job designs that retain talent and reduce turnover.[5]

■ JOB ENLARGEMENT/JOB ROTATION

job enlargement
A method of job design that increases the number of activities in a job to overcome the boredom of overspecialized work.

job rotation
A variation of job enlargement in which workers are exposed to a variety of specialized jobs over time.

Job enlargement is a traditional approach to overcome the limitations of over-specialized work, such as boredom.[6] *Job enlargement* is a method of job design that increases the number of tasks in a job. *Job rotation*, a variation of job enlargement, exposes a worker to a variety of specialized job tasks over time. The reasoning behind these approaches to the problems of overspecialization is as follows. First, the core problem with overspecialized work was believed to be lack of variety. That is, jobs designed by scientific management were too narrow and limited in the number of tasks and activities assigned to each worker. Second, a lack of variety led to understimulation and underutilization of the worker. Third, the worker would be more stimulated and better utilized by increasing the variety in the job. Variety could be increased by increasing the number of activities or by rotating the worker through different jobs. For example, job enlargement for a lathe operator in a steel plant might include selecting the steel pieces to be turned and performing all of the maintenance work on the lathe. As an example of job rotation, an employee at a small bank might take new accounts one day, serve as a cashier another day, and process loan applications on a third day.

One of the first studies of the problem of repetitive work was conducted at IBM after World War II. The company implemented a job enlargement program during the war and evaluated the effort after six years.[7] The two most important results were a significant increase in product quality and a reduction in idle time, both for people and for machines. Less obvious and measurable are the benefits of job enlargement to IBM through enhanced worker status and improved manager–worker communication. IBM concluded that job enlargement countered the problems of work specialization. A contemporary study in a Swedish electronics assembly plant used physiological measures of muscle tension.[8] Job enlargement had a positive effect on mechanical exposure variability.

A later study examined the effects of mass production jobs on assembly-line workers in the automotive industry.[9] Mass production jobs have six characteristics: mechanically controlled work pace, repetitiveness, minimum skill requirements, predetermined tools and techniques, minute division of the production process, and a requirement for surface mental attention, rather than thoughtful concentration. The researchers conducted 180 private interviews with assembly-line workers and found generally positive attitudes toward pay, security, and supervision. They concluded that job enlargement and job rotation would improve other job aspects, such as repetition and a mechanical work pace.

cross-training
A variation of job enlargement in which workers are trained in different specialized tasks or activities.

Job rotation and *cross-training* programs are variations of job enlargement. Pharmaceutical company Eli Lilly has found that job rotation can be a proactive means for enhancing work experiences for career development and can have tangible benefits for employees in the form of salary increases and promotions.[10] In cross-training, workers are trained in different specialized tasks or activities. All three kinds of programs horizontally enlarge jobs; that is, the number and variety of an employee's tasks and activities are increased. Graphic Controls Corporation (now a subsidiary of Tyco International) used cross-training to develop a flexible workforce that enabled the company to maintain high levels of production.[11]

■ JOB ENRICHMENT

Whereas job enlargement increases the number of job activities through horizontal loading, job enrichment increases the amount of job responsibility through vertical loading. Both approaches to job design are intended, in part, to increase job satisfaction for employees. A study to test whether job satisfaction results from characteristics of the job or of the person found that an interactionist approach is most accurate and that job redesign can contribute to increased job satisfaction for some employees. Another two-year study found that intrinsic job satisfaction and job perceptions are reciprocally related to each other.[12]

Job enrichment is a job design or redesign method aimed at increasing the motivational factors in a job. Job enrichment builds on Herzberg's two-factor theory of motivation, which distinguished between motivational and hygiene factors for people at work. Whereas job enlargement recommends increasing and varying the number of activities a person does, job enrichment recommends increasing the recognition, responsibility, and opportunity for achievement. For example, enlarging the lathe operator's job means adding maintenance activities, and enriching the job means having the operator meet with customers who buy the products.

job enrichment
Designing or redesigning jobs by incorporating motivational factors into them.

Herzberg believes that only certain jobs should be enriched and that the first step is to select the jobs appropriate for job enrichment.[13] He recognizes that some people prefer simple jobs. Once jobs are selected for enrichment, management should brainstorm about possible changes, revise the list to include only specific changes related to motivational factors, and screen out generalities and suggestions that would simply increase activities or numbers of tasks. Those whose jobs are to be enriched should not participate in this process because of a conflict of interest. Two key problems can arise in the implementation of job enrichment. First, an initial drop in performance can be expected as workers accommodate to the change. Second, first-line supervisors may experience some anxiety or hostility as a result of employees' increased responsibility.

A seven-year implementation study of job enrichment at AT&T found the approach beneficial.[14] Job enrichment required a big change in management style, and AT&T found that it could not ignore hygiene factors in the work environment just because it was enriching existing jobs. Although the AT&T experience with job enrichment was positive, a critical review of job enrichment did not find that to be the case generally.[15] One problem with job enrichment as a strategy for work design is that it is based on an oversimplified motivational theory. Another problem is the lack of consideration for individual differences among employees. Job enrichment, like scientific management's work specialization and job enlargement/job rotation, is a universal approach to the design of work and thus does not differentiate among individuals.

◀◀think critically▶▶

Suppose, as a manager, you were given the directive to redesign all the jobs in your company to increase the level of autonomy for its workers. One of your employees notifies you that, for cultural reasons, he does not feel comfortable with this aspect of the job redesign and requests that his job be exempt from the change. What would you do?

: **3.** Describe the Job Characteristics Model and the five core job characteristics.

Job Characteristics Model
A framework for understanding person–job fit through the interaction of core job dimensions with critical psychological states within a person.

Job Diagnostic Survey (JDS)
The survey instrument designed to measure the elements in the Job Characteristics Model.

■ JOB CHARACTERISTICS THEORY

The job characteristics theory, which was initiated during the mid-1960s, is a traditional approach to the design of work that makes a significant departure from the three earlier approaches. It emphasizes the interaction between the individual and specific attributes of the job; therefore, it is a person–job fit model rather than a universal job design model. It originated in a research study of 470 workers in 47 different jobs across 11 industries.[16] The study measured and classified relevant task characteristics for these 47 jobs and found four core job characteristics: job variety, autonomy, responsibility, and interpersonal interaction. The study also found that core job characteristics did not affect all workers in the same way. A worker's values, religious beliefs, and ethnic background influenced how the worker responded to the job. Specifically, workers with rural values and strong religious beliefs preferred jobs high in core characteristics, and workers with urban values and weaker religious beliefs preferred jobs low in core characteristics.

Richard Hackman and his colleagues modified the original model by including three critical psychological states of the individual and refining the measurement of core job characteristics. The result is the *Job Characteristics Model* shown in Figure 13.1.[17] The *Job Diagnostic Survey (JDS)* was developed to diagnose jobs by measuring the five core job characteristics and three critical psychological states shown in the model. The core job characteristics stimulate the critical psychological states in the manner shown in Figure 13.1. This results in varying personal and work outcomes, as identified in the figure.

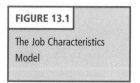

FIGURE 13.1

The Job Characteristics Model

SOURCE: J. R. Hackman and G. R. Oldham, "The Relationship among Core Job Dimensions, the Critical Psychological States, and On-the-Job Outcomes," *The Job Diagnostic Survey: An Instrument for the Diagnosis of Jobs and the Evaluation of Job Redesign Projects*, 1974. Reprinted by permission of Greg R. Oldham.

The five core job characteristics are defined as follows:

1. *Skill variety.* The degree to which a job includes different activities and involves the use of multiple skills and talents of the employee.
2. *Task identity.* The degree to which the job requires completion of a whole and identifiable piece of work—that is, doing a job from beginning to end with a tangible outcome.
3. *Task significance.* The degree to which the job has a substantial impact on the lives or work of other people, whether in the immediate organization or in the external environment.
4. *Autonomy.* The degree to which the job provides the employee with substantial freedom, independence, and discretion in scheduling the work and in determining the procedures to be used in carrying it out.
5. *Feedback from the job itself.* The degree to which carrying out the work activities results in the employee's obtaining direct and clear information about the effectiveness of his or her performance.

Hackman and his colleagues say that the five core job characteristics interact to determine an overall Motivating Potential Score (MPS) for a specific job. The MPS indicates a job's potential for motivating incumbents. An individual's MPS is determined by the following equation:

$$\text{MPS} = \frac{\left[\begin{array}{c}\text{Skill}\\\text{variety}\end{array}\right] + \left[\begin{array}{c}\text{Task}\\\text{identity}\end{array}\right] + \left[\begin{array}{c}\text{Task}\\\text{significance}\end{array}\right]}{3} \times [\text{Autonomy}] \times [\text{Feedback}]$$

Challenge 13.1 enables you to answer five questions from the JDS short form to get an idea about the motivating potential of your present job or any job you have held.

The Job Characteristics Model includes *growth need strength* (the desire to grow and fully develop one's abilities) as a moderator. People with a high growth need strength respond favorably to jobs with high MPSs, and individuals with low growth need strength respond less favorably to such jobs. The job characteristics theory further suggests that core job dimensions stimulate three critical psychological states according to the relationships specified in the model. These critical psychological states are defined as follows:

1. *Experienced meaningfulness of the work,* or the degree to which the employee experiences the job as one that is generally meaningful, valuable, and worthwhile.
2. *Experienced responsibility for work outcomes,* or the degree to which the employee feels personally accountable and responsible for the results of the work he or she does.
3. *Knowledge of results,* or the degree to which the employee knows and understands, on a continuous basis, how effectively he or she is performing the job.

In one early study, Hackman and Oldham administered the JDS to 658 employees working on 62 different jobs in seven business organizations.[18] The JDS was useful for job redesign efforts through one or more of five implementing

Diagnosing Your Job

This questionnaire challenges you to examine the motivating potential in your job. If you are not currently working, complete the questionnaire for any job you have ever held for which you want to examine the motivating potential. For each of the following five questions, circle the number of the most accurate description of the job. Be as objective as you can in describing the job by answering these questions.

1. How much *autonomy* is there in the job? That is, to what extent does the job permit a person to decide *on his or her own* how to go about doing the work?

    1   2   3   4   5   6   7

    Very little; the job gives a person almost no personal say about how and when the work is done.

    Moderate autonomy; many things are standardized and not under the control of the person, but he or she can make some decisions about the work.

    Very much; the job gives the person almost complete responsibility for deciding how and when the work is done.

2. To what extent does the job involve doing a *"whole"* and *identifiable piece of work?* That is, is the job a complete piece of work that has an obvious beginning and end? Or is it a small part of the overall piece of work, which is finished by other people or by automatic machines?

    1   2   3   4   5   6   7

    The job is only a tiny part in the overall piece of work; the results of the person's activities cannot be seen in the final product or service.

    The job is a moderate-sized "chunk" of the overall piece of work; the person's own contribution can be seen in the final outcome.

    The job involves doing the whole piece of work, from start to finish; the results of the person's activities are easily seen in the final product or service.

3. How much *variety* is there in the job? That is, to what extent does the job require a person to do many different things at work, using a variety of his or her skills and talents?

    1   2   3   4   5   6   7

    Very little; the job requires the person to do the same routine things over and over again.

    Moderate variety.

    Very much; the job requires the person to do many different things, using a number of different skills and talents.

4. In general, how *significant* or *important* is the job? That is, are the results of the person's work likely to affect significantly the lives or well-being of other people?

    1   2   3   4   5   6   7

    Not at all significant; the outcome of the work is *not* likely to affect anyone in any important way.

    Moderately significant.

    Highly significant; the outcome of the work can affect other people in very important ways.

(continued)

5. To what extent *does doing the job itself* provide the person with information about his or her work performance? That is, does the actual work itself provide clues about how well the person is doing—aside from any feedback coworkers or supervisors may provide?

1	2	3	4	5	6	7

Very little; the job itself is set up so a person could work forever without finding out how well he or she is doing.

Moderately; sometimes doing the job provides feedback to the person; sometimes it does not.

Very much; the job is set up so that a person gets almost constant feedback as he or she works about how well he or she is doing.

To score your questionnaire, place your responses to Questions 3, 2, 4, 1, and 5, respectively, in the blank spaces in the following equation:

$$\text{Motivating Potential Score (MPS)} = \frac{[\quad]_{Q\#3} + [\quad]_{Q\#2} + [\quad]_{Q\#4}}{3} \times [\quad]_{Q\#1} \times [\quad]_{Q\#5} = \underline{\quad}.$$

If the MPS for the job you rated is between

> 200 and 343, it is high in motivating potential.

> 120 and 199, it is moderate in motivating potential.

> 0 and 119, it is low in motivating potential.

Source: J. R. Hackman and G. R. Oldham, "The Job Diagnostic Survey: An Instrument for the Diagnosis of Jobs and the Evaluation of Job Redesign Projects," *Technical Report No.* 4, 1974, 2–3 of the Short Form. Reprinted by permission of Greg R. Oldham..

concepts: (1) combining tasks into larger jobs, (2) forming natural work teams to increase task identity and task significance, (3) establishing relationships with customers, (4) loading jobs vertically with more responsibility, and/or (5) opening feedback channels for the job incumbent. For example, if an automotive mechanic received little feedback on the quality of repair work performed, one redesign strategy would be to solicit customer feedback one month after each repair.

A more recent sequence of two studies conducted in Egypt aimed to disaggregate work autonomy, one important component in job design theory.[19] Study 1 included 534 employees in two Egyptian organizations. Study 2 involved 120 managers in four organzations. The results indicated that separate work method, work schedule, and work criteria autonomy were three separate facets of work autonomy.

In another international study, the Job Characteristics Model was tested in a sample of 57 jobs from 37 organizations in Hong Kong.[20] Job incumbents and their supervisors both completed questionnaires about the incumbents' jobs.[21] The supervisory version asked the supervisor to rate the employee's job. The study supported the model in general. However, task significance was not a reliable core job dimension in Hong Kong, which suggests either national differences in the measurement of important job dimensions or cultural biases about work. This result also suggests that value differences may exist between American and Asian people with regard to jobs.

An alternative to the Job Characteristics Model is the Job Characteristics Inventory (JCI) developed by Henry Sims and Andrew Szilagyi.[22] The JCI primarily measures core job characteristics. It is not as comprehensive as the JDS because it does not incorporate critical psychological states, personal and work outcomes, or employee needs. The JCI does give some consideration to structural and individual variables that affect the relationship between core job characteristics and the individual.[23] One comparative analysis of the two models found similarities in the measures and in the models' predictions.[24] The comparative analysis also found two differences. First, the variety scales in the two models appear to have different effects on performance. Second, the autonomy scales in the two models appear to have different effects on employee satisfaction. Overall, the two models together support the usefulness of a person–job fit approach to the design of work over the earlier, universal theories.

◼ ENGAGEMENT

engagement

The expression of oneself as one performs in work or other roles.

Psychological conditions related to job design features are a particular concern of the Job Characteristics Model.[25] One study of over 200 managers and employees in a midwestern insurance company found that meaningfulness, safety, and availability were three important psychological conditions that affected employees' *engagement* in their jobs and work roles. Engagement at work is important for its positive individual and organizational outcomes. Engagement is the harnessing of organizational members to their work roles. When engaged, people employ and express themselves physically, cognitively, and emotionally as they perform their jobs and their work roles. As an example, Gallup's Q was used to improve engagement for a clinical nutrition group at St. Mary's/Duluth Clinic Health System.[26]

Full engagement requires the strategic management of one's energy in response to the environment.[27] Being fully engaged in one's work role and job can be highly appropriate and yet demand energy, time, and effort. To achieve balance and afford opportunity for recovery, there is a commensurate need to strategically and appropriately disengage from one's job and work role on a periodic basis. The effective management of energy in response to one's job and work role leads to both high performance and personal renewal. Thus, while the design of work is important, the human spirit's response to job characteristics and work design features is equally important.

◤ ALTERNATIVE APPROACHES TO JOB DESIGN

Because each of the traditional job design approaches has limitations, several alternative approaches to job design have emerged over the past couple of decades. This section examines four of these alternatives that are in the process of being tried and tested. First, it examines the social information-processing model. Second, it reviews ergonomics and the interdisciplinary framework of

Michael Campion and Paul Thayer. Their framework builds on the traditional job design approaches. Third, this section examines the international perspectives of the Japanese, Germans, and Scandinavians. Finally, it focuses on the health and well-being aspects of work design. Healthy work enables individuals to adapt, function well, and balance work with private life activities.[28] An emerging fifth approach to the design of work through teams and autonomous work groups was addressed in Chapter 8.

SOCIAL INFORMATION PROCESSING

The traditional approaches to the design of work emphasize objective core job characteristics. In contrast, the *social information-processing (SIP) model* emphasizes the interpersonal aspects of work design. Specifically, the SIP model says that what others tell us about our jobs is important.[29] The SIP model has four basic premises about the work environment.[30] First, other people provide cues we use to understand the work environment. Second, other people help us judge what is important in our jobs. Third, other people tell us how they see our jobs. Fourth, other people's positive and negative feedback helps us understand our feelings about our jobs.

People's perceptions and reactions to their jobs are shaped by information from other people in the work environment.[31] In other words, what others believe about a person's job may be important to understanding the person's perceptions of, and reactions to, the job. This does not mean that objective job characteristics are unimportant; rather, it means that others can modify the way these characteristics affect us. For example, one study of task complexity found that the objective complexity of a task must be distinguished from the subjective task complexity experienced by the employee.[32] While objective task complexity may be a motivator, the presence of others in the work environment, social interaction, or even daydreaming may be important additional sources of motivation. The SIP model makes an important contribution to the design of work by emphasizing the importance of other people and the social context of work. In some cases, these aspects of the work environment may be more important than objective core job characteristics. For example, the subjective feedback of other people about how difficult a particular task is may be more important to a person's motivation to perform than an objective probability estimate of the task's difficulty.

ERGONOMICS AND AN INTERDISCIPLINARY FRAMEWORK

Michael Campion and Paul Thayer use *ergonomics* based on engineering, biology, and psychology to develop an interdisciplinary framework for the design of work. Actually, they say that four approaches—the mechanistic, motivational, biological, and perceptual/motor approaches—are necessary because no one approach can solve all performance problems caused by poorly designed jobs. Each approach has its benefits as well as its limitations. One ergonomics study found that workstation redesign resulted in lower levels of upper body pain along with other positive outcomes.[33]

The interdisciplinary framework allows the job designer or manager to consider tradeoffs and alternatives among the approaches based on desired outcomes.

4. Compare the social information-processing (SIP) model with traditional job design approaches.

social information-processing (SIP) model
A model that suggests that the important job factors depend in part on what others tell a person about the job.

5. Explain ergonomics and the interdisciplinary framework for the design of work.

ergonomics
The science of adapting work and working conditions to the employee or worker.

If a manager finds poor performance a problem, for example, the manager should analyze the job to ensure a design aimed at improving performance. The interdisciplinary framework is important because badly designed jobs cause far more performance problems than managers realize.[34]

Table 13.1 summarizes the positive and negative outcomes of each job design approach. The mechanistic and motivational approaches to job design are very similar to scientific management's work simplification and to the Job Characteristics Model, respectively. Because these were discussed earlier in the chapter, they are not further elaborated here.

The biological approach to job design emphasizes the person's interaction with physical aspects of the work environment and is concerned with the amount of physical exertion, such as lifting and muscular effort, required by the position. For example, an analysis of medical claims at TXI's Chaparral Steel Company identified lower back problems as the most common physical problem experienced by steel workers and managers alike. As a result, the company instituted an education and exercise program under expert guidance to improve care of the lower back. Program graduates received back cushions for their chairs with "Chaparral Steel Company" embossed on them. Herman Miller designed an office chair to support the lower back and other parts of the human body.[35] The chair was tested in several offices including that of the director of human resources for Valero Energy Corporation prior to large-scale production. Lower back problems associated with improper lifting may be costly, but they are not fatal. Campion describes

TABLE 13.1

Summary of Outcomes from Various Job Design Approaches

JOB DESIGN APPROACH (DISCIPLINE)	POSITIVE OUTCOMES	NEGATIVE OUTCOMES
Mechanistic Approach (mechanical engineering)	Decreased training time Higher personnel utilization levels Lower likelihood of error Less chance of mental overload Lower stress levels	Lower job satisfaction Lower motivation Higher absenteeism
Motivational Approach (industrial psychology)	Higher job satisfaction Higher motivation Greater job involvement Higher job performance Lower absenteeism	Increased training time Lower personnel utilization levels Greater chance of errors Greater chance of mental overload and stress
Biological Approach (biology)	Less physical effort Less physical fatigue Fewer health complaints Fewer medical incidents Lower absenteeism Higher job satisfaction	Higher financial costs because of changes in equipment or job environment
Perceptual Motor Approach (experimental psychology)	Lower likelihood of error Lower likelihood of accidents Less chance of mental stress Decreased training time Higher personnel utilization levels	Lower job satisfaction Lower motivation

SOURCE: Reprinted from *Organizational Dynamics*, Winter/1987 Copyright © 1987, with permission from Elsevier Science.

the potentially catastrophic problem that occurred at Three Mile Island, when nuclear materials contaminated the surrounding area and threatened disaster. Campion concluded that poor design of the control room operator's job caused the problem.

The perceptual/motor approach to job design also emphasizes the person's interaction with physical aspects of the work environment and is based on engineering that considers human factors such as strength or coordination, ergonomics, and experimental psychology. It places an important emphasis on human interaction with computers, information, and other operational systems. This approach addresses how people mentally process information acquired from the physical work environment through perceptual and motor skills. The approach emphasizes perception and fine motor skills, as opposed to the gross motor skills and muscle strength emphasized in the mechanistic approach. The perceptual/motor approach is more likely to be relevant to operational and technical work, such as keyboard operations and data entry jobs, which may tax a person's concentration and attention, than to managerial, administrative, and custodial jobs, which are less likely to strain concentration and attention.

One study using the interdisciplinary framework to improve jobs evaluated 377 clerical, 80 managerial, and 90 analytical positions.[36] The jobs were improved by combining tasks and adding ancillary duties. The improved jobs provided greater motivation for the incumbents and were better from a perceptual/motor standpoint. The jobs were poorly designed from a mechanical engineering standpoint, however, and they were unaffected from a biological standpoint. Again, the interdisciplinary framework considers tradeoffs and alternatives when evaluating job redesign efforts.

▩ INTERNATIONAL PERSPECTIVES ON THE DESIGN OF WORK

: 6. Compare and contrast Japanese, German, and Scandinavian approaches to work.

Each nation or ethnic group has a unique way of understanding and designing work.[37] As organizations become more global and international, an appreciation of the perspectives of other nations is increasingly important. The Japanese, Germans, and Scandinavians in particular have distinctive perspectives on the design and organization of work.[38] Each country's perspective is forged within its unique cultural and economic system, and each is distinct from the approaches used in North America.

THE JAPANESE APPROACH

The Japanese began harnessing their productive energies during the 1950s by drawing on the product quality ideas of W. Edwards Deming.[39] In addition, the central government became actively involved in the economic resurgence of Japan, and it encouraged companies to conquer industries rather than to maximize profits.[40] Such an industrial policy, which built on the Japanese cultural ethic of collectivism, has implications for how work is done. Whereas Frederick Taylor and his successors in the United States emphasized the job of an individual worker, the Japanese work system emphasizes the strategic level and encourages collective and cooperative working arrangements.[41] While the Japanese emphasize performance, accountability, and other- or self-directedness in defining work, Americans emphasize the positive affect, personal identity, and social benefits of work.

lean production
Using committed employees with ever-expanding responsibilities to achieve zero waste, 100 percent good product, delivered on time, every time.

sociotechnical systems (STS)
Giving equal attention to technical and social considerations in job design.

The Japanese success with lean production has drawn the attention of managers. *Lean production* methods are similar to the production concept of *sociotechnical systems (STS)*, although there are some differences.[42] In particular, STS gives greater emphasis to teamwork and self-managed and autonomous work groups, to the ongoing nature of the design process, and to human values in the work process. The approaches are similar, however, in that both differ from Taylor's scientific management and both emphasize job variety, feedback to work groups and teams, support of human resources, and control of production variance close to the point of origin. One three-year evaluation of lean teams, assembly lines, and workflow formalization as lean production practices was conducted in Australia.[43] Employees in all lean production groups were negatively affected, and the assembly line employees the worst.

THE GERMAN APPROACH

The German approach to work has been shaped by Germany's unique educational system, cultural values, and economic system. The Germans are a highly educated and well-organized people. For example, their educational system has a multitrack design with technical and university alternatives. The German economic system puts a strong emphasis on free enterprise, private property rights, and management–labor cooperation. A comparison of voluntary and mandated management–labor cooperation in Germany found that productivity was superior under voluntary cooperation.[44] The Germans value hierarchy and authority relationships and, as a result, are generally disciplined.[45] Germany's workers are highly unionized, and their discipline and efficiency have enabled Germany to be highly productive while its workers labor substantially fewer hours than do Americans.

technocentric
Placing technology and engineering at the center of job design decisions.

anthropocentric
Placing human considerations at the center of job design decisions.

The traditional German approach to work design was *technocentric*, an approach that placed technology and engineering at the center of job design decisions. Recently, German industrial engineers have moved to a more *anthropocentric* approach, which places human considerations at the center of job design decisions. The former approach uses a natural scientific process in the design of work, whereas the latter relies on a more humanistic process, as shown in Figure 13.2. In the anthropocentric approach, work is evaluated using the criteria of practicability and worker satisfaction at the individual level and the criteria of endurability and acceptability at the group level. Figure 13.2 also identifies problem areas and disciplines concerned with each aspect of the work design.

THE SCANDINAVIAN APPROACH

The Scandinavian cultural values and economic system stand in contrast to the German system. The social democratic tradition in Scandinavia has emphasized social concern rather than industrial efficiency. The Scandinavians place great emphasis on a work design model that encourages a high degree of worker control and good social support systems for workers.[46] Lennart Levi believes that circumstantial and inferential scientific evidence provides a sufficiently strong basis for legislative and policy actions for redesigns aimed at enhancing worker well-being. An example of such an action for promoting good working environments and occupational health was Swedish Government Bill 1976/77:149, which stated, "Work should be safe both physically and mentally *but also* provide opportunities for involvement, job satisfaction, and personal development." In

Scientific approaches of labor sciences	Levels of evaluation of human work	Problem areas and assignment to disciplines
View from natural science	Practicability	Technical, anthropometric, and psychophysical problems (ergonomics)
	Endurability	Technical, physiological, and medical problems (ergonomics and occupational health)
Primarily oriented to individuals / Primarily oriented to groups	Acceptability	Economical and sociological problems (occupational psychology and sociology, personnel management)
View from cultural studies	Satisfaction	Sociopsychological and economic problems (occupational psychology and sociology, personnel management)

FIGURE 13.2

Hierarchical Model of Criteria for the Evaluation of Human Work

SOURCE: H. Luczak, "'Good Work' Design: An Ergonomic, Industrial Engineering Perspective," in J. C. Quick, L. R. Murphy, and J. J. Hurrell, eds., *Stress and Well-Being at Work* (Washington, D.C.).

1991, the Swedish Parliament set up the Swedish Working Life Fund to fund research, intervention programs, and demonstration projects in work design. For example, a study of Stockholm police on shift schedules found that going from a daily, counterclockwise rotation to a clockwise rotation was more compatible with human biology and resulted in improved sleep, less fatigue, lower systolic blood pressure, and lower blood levels of triglycerides and glucose.[47] Hence, the work redesign improved the police officers' health.

CONTEMPORARY ISSUES IN THE DESIGN OF WORK

7. Discuss three contemporary issues in the design of work.

A number of contemporary issues related to specific aspects of the design of work have an effect on increasing numbers of employees. Rather than addressing job design or worker well-being in a comprehensive way, these issues address one or another aspects of a job. The issues include telecommuting, alternative work patterns, and technostress. Telecommuting and alternative work patterns such as job sharing can increase flexibility for employees. Companies use these and other approaches to the design of work as ways to manage a growing business while contributing to a healthy organizational environment and a better balance of work and family life for employees. Challenge 13.2 provides you with an opportunity to evaluate how psychologically healthy your own work environment is.

TELECOMMUTING

Telecommuting, as noted in Chapter 2, is when employees work at home or in other locations geographically separate from their company's main location.

CHALLENGE   13.2

Is Your Work Environment a Healthy One?

To determine whether your work environment is a healthy one, complete the following four steps. Answer each question in the five steps "yes" or "no."

Step 1. Control and Influence

_____ Do you have influence over the pace of your work?

_____ Are system response times neither too fast nor too slow?

_____ Do you have a say in your work assignments and goals?

_____ Is there an opportunity for you to comment on your performance appraisal?

Step 2. Information and Uncertainty

_____ Do you receive timely information to complete your work?

_____ Do you receive complete information for your work assignments?

_____ Is there adequate planning for changes that affect you at work?

_____ Do you have access to all the information you need at work?

Step 3. Conflict at Work

_____ Does the company apply policies clearly and consistently?

_____ Are job descriptions and task assignments clear and unambiguous?

_____ Are there adequate policies and procedures for the resolution of conflicts?

_____ Is your work environment an open, participative one?

Step 4. Job Scope and Task Design

_____ Is there adequate variety in your work activities and/or assignments?

_____ Do you receive timely, constructive feedback on your work?

_____ Is your work important to the overall mission of the company?

_____ Do you work on more than one small piece of a big project?

Scoring:

Count the number of "yes" answers in Steps 1 through 4: _____

If you have 10 to 16 "yes" answers, this suggests that your work environment is a psychologically healthy one.

If you have 7 or fewer "yes" answers, this may suggest that your work environment is not as psychologically healthy as it could be.

Telecommuting may entail working in a combination of home, satellite office, and main office locations. This flexible arrangement is designed to achieve a better fit between the needs of the individual employee and the organization's task demands. Cisco Systems manager Christian Renaud moved from California and began telecommuting from Johnston, Iowa, when he and his wife began their family.

Telecommuting has been around since the 1970s but was slower to catch on than some expected.[48] This was due to the inherent paradoxes associated with telecommuting.[49] Actually, with a greater emphasis on managing the work rather than the worker, managers can enhance control, effectively decentralize, and even encourage teamwork through telecommuting. A number of companies, such as AT&T in Phoenix and Bell Atlantic (now part of Verizon Communications), have programs in telecommuting for a wide range of employees. These flexible arrangements help some companies respond to changing demographics and a shrinking labor pool. The Travelers Group (now part of Citigroup) was one of the first companies to try telecommuting and was considered an industry leader in telecommuting. Because of its confidence in its employees, Travelers reaped rewards from telecommuting, including higher productivity, reduced absenteeism, expanded opportunities for workers with disabilities, and an increased ability to attract and retain talent.[50]

Pacific Bell (now part of SBC Communications) tried telecommuting on a large scale.[51] In 1990, Pacific Bell had 1,500 managers who telecommuted. For example, an employee might work at home four days a week as an information systems designer and spend one day a week at the main office location in meetings, work exchanges, and coordination with others. Of 3,000 Pacific Bell managers responding to a mail survey, 87 percent said telecommuting would reduce employee stress, 70 percent said it would increase job satisfaction while reducing absenteeism, and 64 percent said it would increase productivity.

Telecommuting is neither a cure-all nor a universally feasible alternative. Many telecommuters feel a sense of social isolation. Furthermore, not all forms of work are amenable to telecommuting. For example, firefighters and police officers must be at their duty stations to be successful in their work. Employees for whom telecommuting is not a viable option within a company may feel jealous of those able to telecommute. In addition, telecommuting may have the potential to create the sweatshops of the twenty-first century.

ALTERNATIVE WORK PATTERNS

Job sharing is an alternative work pattern in which more than one person occupies a single job. Job sharing may be an alternative to telecommuting for addressing demographic and labor pool concerns. Job sharing is found throughout a wide range of managerial and professional jobs, as well as in production and service jobs. It is not common among senior executives.

job sharing
An alternative work pattern in which more than one person occupies a single job.

The *four-day workweek* is a second type of alternative work schedule. Information systems personnel at the United Services Automobile Association (USAA) in San Antonio, Texas, work four 10-hour days and enjoy a three-day weekend. This arrangement provides the benefit of more time for those who want to balance work and family life through weekend travel. However, the longer workdays may be a drawback for employees with many family or social activities on weekday evenings. Hence, the four-day workweek has both benefits and limitations.

Flextime is a third alternative work pattern. Flextime, in which employees can set their own daily work schedules, has been applied in numerous ways in work organizations and can lead to reduced absenteeism. Companies in highly concentrated urban areas, like Houston, Los Angeles, and New York City, may allow employees to set their own daily work schedules as long as they start their eight hours at any 30-minute interval from 6:00 A.M. to 9:00 A.M. This arrangement is designed to ease traffic and commuting pressures. It also is somewhat responsive to individual biorhythms, allowing early risers to go to work early and nighthawks to

flextime
An alternative work pattern that enables employees to set their own daily work schedules.

work late. Typically, 9:00 A.M. to 3:00 P.M. is the required core working time for everyone in the company. Even in companies without formal flextime programs, flextime may be an individual option arranged between supervisor and subordinate. For example, a first-line supervisor who wants to complete a college degree may negotiate a work schedule accommodating both job requirements and course schedules at the university. Flextime options may be more likely for high performers who assure their bosses that work quality and productivity will not suffer.[52] On the cautionary side, one study found that a woman on a flexible work schedule was perceived to have less job–career dedication and less advancement motivation, though no less ability.[53]

◀◀think critically▶▶

Assume that a company has many older, mature workers. Rather than retrain them in new technologies, the company decides to replace the older workers with younger ones. Should the company be allowed to do this? Does the company have any moral or ethical obligations to the older workers? Explain.

■ TECHNOLOGY AT WORK

New technologies and electronic commerce are here to stay and are changing the face of work environments, dramatically in some cases. Many government jobs expect to change, and even disappear, with the advent of e-government using Internet technology. As forces for change, new technologies are a double-edged sword that can be used to improve job performance or to create stress. On the positive side, modern technologies are helping to revolutionize the way jobs are designed and the way work gets done. The ***virtual office*** is a mobile platform of computer, telecommunication, and information technology and services that allows mobile workforce members to conduct business virtually anywhere, anytime, globally. While virtual offices have benefits, they may also lead to a lack of social connection or to technostress.

Technostress is stress caused by new and advancing technologies in the workplace, most often information technologies.[54] For example, the widespread use of electronic bulletin boards as a forum for rumors of layoffs may cause feelings of uncertainty and anxiety (technostress). However, the same electronic bulletin boards can be an important source of information and thus reduce uncertainty for workers.

New information technologies enable organizations to monitor employee work performance, even when the employee is not aware of the monitoring.[55] These new technologies also allow organizations to tie pay to performance because performance is electronically monitored.[56] Three guidelines can help make electronic workplace monitoring, especially of performance, less distressful. First, workers should participate in the introduction of the monitoring system. Second, performance standards should be seen as fair. Third, performance records should be used to improve performance, not to punish the performer. In the extreme, new technologies that allow for virtual work in remote locations take employees beyond such monitoring.[57]

virtual office
A mobile platform of computer, telecommunication, and information technology and services.

technostress
The stress caused by new and advancing technologies in the workplace.

⬢ MANAGERIAL IMPLICATIONS: THE CHANGING NATURE OF WORK

Work is an important aspect of a healthy life. The two central needs in human nature are to engage in productive work and to form healthy relationships with others. Work means different things to different ethnic and national groups. Therefore, job design efforts must be sensitive to cultural values and beliefs.

In crafting work tasks and assignments, managers should make an effort to fit the jobs to the people who are doing them. There are no universally accepted ways to design work, and early efforts to find them have been replaced by a number of alternatives. Early approaches to job design were valuable for manufacturing and administrative jobs of the mid-1900s. Now, however, the changing nature of work in the United States and the Americans with Disabilities Act (ADA) challenge managers to find new ways to define work and design jobs.

The distinguishing feature of job design in the foreseeable future is flexibility. Dramatic global, economic, and organizational changes dictate that managers be flexible in the design of work in their organizations. Jobs must be designed to fit the larger organizational structures discussed in Chapter 14. Organizations must ask, does the job support the organization's mission? Employees must ask, does the job meet my short- and long-term needs?

Technology is one of the distinguishing features of the modern workplace. Advances in information, mechanical, and computer technology are transforming work into a highly scientific endeavor demanding employees who are highly educated, knowledgeable workers. American workers can expect these technological advances to continue during their lifetimes and should expect to meet the challenge through continuous skill development and enhancement.

LOOKING BACK :: Pixar Animation Studios

Pixar—To Infinity and Beyond

When callers reach the main number at Pixar, they hear an enthusiastic phone message that is unlike the kind of "corporate-speak" that most U.S. businesses present to the public. The phone greeting reflects Pixar's philosophy of not taking itself too seriously. Take the "bathroom effect" mentioned in the opening Thinking Ahead. CEO Steve Jobs had an interesting idea of installing one bathroom for the whole building. However, 700 people is a lot of traffic. So, the studios placed eight restrooms on two floors in the central atrium. This concentration of four men's rooms and four women's rooms still serves the purpose of creating interactions between people from all over the building. This arrangement exemplifies the entire culture of not taking anything or anyone too seriously, except maybe for the work.

The studios' creative types are engaged in the time-consuming and expensive process of animation. When Pixar started in 1985, it took eight hours to render one frame of computer animation. That frame of computer animation played in 1/24th of a second—quicker than a heartbeat. Twenty years later, it still takes eight hours to create one frame of computer animation because the artwork in each frame is far more complex. Technology has been infused into the world of animation in a big way. The brain of Pixar's computers is a collection of some 300 machines, each with eight processors that collectively can perform 400 billion computations per second. There is a serious leveraging of human talent with advanced technology to produce leading-edge computer animations. While the computers are powerful, the animators are still in charge.

The animators and creative types at Pixar are excited about the possibilities of taking the technology even further, to the next level. However, an organization needs more than creativity and technology to stay afloat. With its split from Disney, Pixar faces some economic uncertainty as it works to craft a new business model that factors Disney out of, rather than into, the picture. The risk for Pixar is that the studios may become overly cautious, accountant driven, and bureaucratic. Reenter John Lasseter whose formal job is executive vice president and whose real position is the studios' longtime creative leader. Lasseter's humor and imagination keep the creative juices flowing. As he wanders around visiting Pixar's creative types, he may play with most of the toys in the office—and there are plenty of toys. He wants to know the story behind this toy or that toy. If he occasionally stays too long, that is OK. In the long run, Lasseter's job is to keep Pixar very much alive and vital and take it "to infinity and beyond"![58]

CHAPTER SUMMARY

1. Different countries have different preferences for one or more of six distinct patterns of defining work.

2. Scientific management, job enlargement/job rotation, job enrichment, and the job characteristics theory are traditional American approaches to the design of work and the management of workforce diversity.

3. The social information-processing (SIP) model suggests that information from others and the social context are important in a job.

4. Ergonomics and the interdisciplinary framework draw on engineering, psychology, and biology in considering the advantages and disadvantages of job and work design efforts.

5. The cultural values and social organizations in Japan, Germany, and Scandinavia lead to unique approaches to the design of work.

6. Telecommuting, alternative work patterns, and technostress are emerging issues in the design of work and the use of information technology.

KEY TERMS

anthropocentric (p. 346)
cross-training (p. 336)
engagement (p. 342)
ergonomics (p. 343)
flextime (p. 349)
job (p. 333)
Job Characteristics Model (p. 338)

Job Diagnostic Survey (JDS) (p. 338)
job enlargement (p. 336)
job enrichment (p. 337)
job rotation (p. 336)
job sharing (p. 349)
lean production (p. 346)
social information-processing (SIP) model (p. 343)

sociotechnical systems (STS) (p. 346)
technocentric (p. 346)
technostress (p. 350)
virtual office (p. 350)
work (p. 333)
work simplification (p. 335)

REVIEW QUESTIONS

1. Define a job in its organizational context.

2. Describe six patterns of working that have been studied in different countries.

3. Describe four traditional approaches to the design of work in America.

4. Identify and define the five core job dimensions and the three critical psychological states in the Job Characteristics Model.

5. What are the salient features of the social information-processing (SIP) model of job design?

6. List the positive and negative outcomes of the four job design approaches considered by the interdisciplinary framework.

7. How do the Japanese, German, and Scandinavian approaches to work differ from one another and from the American approach?

8. What are three emerging issues in jobs and the design of work?

Discussion and Communication QUESTIONS

1. Is there ever one best way to design a particular job?

2. What should managers learn from the traditional approaches to the design of work used in the United States?

3. It is possible for American companies to apply approaches to the design of work that were developed in other countries?

4. What is the most important emerging issue in the design of work?

5. *(communication question)* Read about new approaches to jobs, such as job sharing. Prepare a memo comparing what you have learned from your reading with one or more approaches to job design discussed in the chapter. What changes in approaches to jobs and job design do you notice from this comparison?

6. *(communication question)* Interview an employee in your organization or another organization and develop an oral presentation about how the job the employee is doing could be enriched. Make sure you ask questions about all aspects of the employee's work (e.g., what specific tasks are done and with whom the employee interacts on the job).

7. *(communication question)* Based on the materials in the chapter, prepare a memo detailing the advantages and disadvantages of flextime job arrangements. In a second part of the memo, identify the specific conditions and characteristics required for a successful flextime program. Would you like to work under a flextime arrangement?

ETHICAL DILEMMA

Bill Rider is the manager for the medical records department of a large university-based hospital. He loves his job, but there are times when it really stretches his tolerance. He has been dealing with one such challenge for the last several weeks. Bill is trying to hire someone for a key position in his department. The hospital is in a large city that usually offers a great applicant pool from which to fill openings. But this position has always been different. It is a very demanding job and one that is often extremely stressful. Bill has tried everything he knows to restructure the position, but it remains one of the most difficult jobs in his department.

The position has been open for two months now, and the pressure to hire someone is increasing. Bill has interviewed many people. Only one person stands out in Bill's mind: Elizabeth Murry. She is smart and has plenty of medical records experience. She would be perfect for the job except for Bill's concerns about putting her in such a stressful position.

During the interview process, Bill and Elizabeth had chatted about her life as a single mom. Bill had respected Elizabeth's honesty. He also recognized how badly she needs this job. The position comes with a generous pay raise and a much shorter commute. Both things would allow Elizabeth to provide better for her children.

Bill's concern is that Elizabeth does not realize just how demanding this job could be. He also realizes that Elizabeth does not fully understand the dynamics of the job. Bill had not lied, but he had not been completely honest either. He is afraid she will not accept the position if she really understands what she is getting into. No job is perfect, but this one has some real flaws. Bill is unsure what to do. He could be honest and chance losing Elizabeth, or he could just be quiet and hope Elizabeth is willing to live with the negatives of the position.

QUESTIONS

1. Where does Bill's primary responsibility lie?

2. Will his responsibilities to his employer be met if he hires Elizabeth under these conditions?

3. Evaluate Bill's decision using rule, virtue, rights, and justice theories.

EXPERIENTIAL EXERCISES

13.1 CHAOS AND THE MANAGER'S JOB

Managers' jobs are increasingly chaotic as a result of high rates of change, uncertainty, and turbulence. Some managers thrive on change and chaos, but others have a difficult time responding to high rates of change and uncertainty in a positive manner. This questionnaire gives you an opportunity to evaluate how you would react to a manager's job that is rather chaotic.

Exercise Schedule

1. Preparation (preclass)
   Complete the questionnaire.

2. Individual Scoring
   Give yourself 4 points for each A, 3 points for each B, 2 points for each C, 1 point for each D, and 0 points for each E. Compute the total, divide by 24, and round to one decimal place.

3. Group Discussion
   Your instructor may have you discuss your scores in groups of six students. The higher your score, the more you respond positively to change and chaos; the lower your score, the more difficulty you would have responding to this manager's job in a positive manner. In addition, answer the following questions:

   a. If you could redesign this manager's job, what are the two or three aspects of the job that you would change first?

   b. What are the two or three aspects of the job that you would feel no need to change?

SOURCE: "Chaos and the Manager's Job" in D. Marcic, "Option B. Quality and the New Management Paradigm," *Organizational Behavior: Experiences and Cases,* 4th ed. (Minneapolis/St. Paul: West Publishing, 1995): 296–297. Reprinted by permission.

A Manager's Job

Listed below are some statements a 37-year-old manager made about his job at a large and successful corporation. If your job had these characteristics, how would you react to them? After each statement are five letters, A–E. Circle the letter that best describes how you would react according to the following scale:

A. I would enjoy this very much; it's completely acceptable.

B. This would be enjoyable and acceptable most of the time.

C. I'd have no reaction one way or another, or it would be about equally enjoyable and unpleasant.

D. This feature would be somewhat unpleasant for me.

E. This feature would be very unpleasant for me.

1. I regularly spend 30–40 percent of my time in meetings.   A B C D E

2. A year and a half ago, my job did not exist, and I have been essentially inventing it as I go along.   A B C D E

3. The responsibilities I either assume or am assigned consistently exceed the authority I have for discharging them.   A B C D E

4. At any given moment in my job, I average about a dozen phone calls to be returned.   A B C D E

5. There seems to be very little relation in my job between the quality of my performance and my actual pay and fringe benefits.   A B C D E

6. I need about two weeks of management training a year to stay current in my job.   A B C D E

7. Because we have very effective equal employment opportunity in my company and because it is thoroughly multinational, my job consistently brings me into close contact at a professional level with people of many races, ethnic groups, and nationalities and of both sexes.   A B C D E

8. There is no objective way to measure my effectiveness.   A B C D E

9. I report to three different bosses for different aspects of my job, and each has an equal say in my performance appraisal.   A B C D E

10. On average, about a third of my time is spent dealing with unexpected emergencies that force all scheduled work to be postponed.   A B C D E

11. When I need to meet with the people who report to me, it takes my secretary most of a day to find a time when we are all available, and even then I have yet to have a meeting where everyone is present for the entire meeting. A B C D E

12. The college degree I earned in preparation for this type of work is now obsolete, and I probably should return for another degree. A B C D E

13. My job requires that I absorb about 100–200 pages a week of technical material. A B C D E

14. I am out of town overnight at least one night a week. A B C D E

15. My department is so interdependent with several other departments in the company that all distinctions about which department is responsible for which tasks are quite arbitrary. A B C D E

16. I will probably get a promotion in about a year to a job in another division that has most of these same characteristics. A B C D E

17. During the period of my employment here, either the entire company or the division I worked in has been reorganized every year or so. A B C D E

18. While I face several possible promotions, I have no real career path. A B C D E

19. While there are several possible promotions I can see ahead of me, I think I have no realistic chance of getting to the top levels of the company. A B C D E

20. While I have many ideas about how to make things work better, I have no direct influence on either the business policies or the personnel policies that govern my division. A B C D E

21. My company has recently put in an "assessment center" where I and other managers must go through an extensive battery of psychological tests to assess our potential. A B C D E

22. My company is a defendant in an antitrust suit, and if the case comes to trial, I will probably have to testify about some decisions that were made a few years ago. A B C D E

23. Advanced computer and other electronic office technology is continually being introduced into my division, necessitating constant learning on my part. A B C D E

24. The computer terminal and screen I have in my office can be monitored in my boss's office without my knowledge. A B C D E

SOURCE: "A Manager's Job" by Peter B. Vaill in *Managing as a Performing Art: New Ideas for a World of Chaotic Change*, 1989. Reprinted by permission of Jossey-Bass Inc., Publishers.

13.2 A JOB REDESIGN EFFORT

This activity will help you consider ways in which work can be redesigned to improve its impact on people and its benefit to the organization. Consider the following case:

Eddie is a quality control inspector for an automotive assembly line. His job is to inspect the body, interior, and engine of cars as they roll off the assembly line. Eddie's responsibility is to identify quality problems that either hinder the functioning of these parts of the car or noticeably mar the car's appearance. He is to report the problem so that it can be corrected. Sometimes late in the day, especially on Thursdays and Fridays, Eddie lets assembly problems slip past him. In addition, Eddie's back feels sore at the end of the day, and sometimes he is very stiff in the morning. There are times when he is not sure whether he is seeing a serious problem or just a glitch.

As a five-person team, your job is to evaluate two alternative approaches to redesigning Eddie's job using theories presented in the chapter. Answer the following questions as a team. Your team should be prepared to present its recommendations to the class as a whole.

DISCUSSION QUESTIONS

Your instructor will lead a class discussion of each of the following questions:

1. For this particular job, which are the two best models to use in a redesign effort? Why?

2. Does your team need any additional information before it begins to redesign Eddie's job? If so, what information do you need?

3. Using the two models you chose in Question 1, what would your team specifically recommend to redesign Eddie's job?

14

Organizational Design and Structure

LEARNING OBJECTIVES

After reading this chapter, you should be able to do the following:

: 1. Distinguish between *differentiation* and *integration* as organizational design processes.

: 2. Identify six basic design dimensions of an organization.

: 3. Briefly describe five structural configurations for organizations and how coordination is achieved with each.

: 4. Describe four contextual variables for an organization and their effect on organizational structure.

: 5. Describe the forces reshaping organizations.

: 6. Discuss emerging organizational structures.

: 7. Identify two cautions about the effect of organizational structures on people.

BASIS FOR DIFFERENCE	MARKETING	ENGINEERING
Goal orientation	Sales volume	Design
Time orientation	Long run	Medium run
Interpersonal orientation	People oriented	Task oriented
Structure	Less formal	More formal

TABLE 14.1

Differentiation between Marketing and Engineering

Horizontal, vertical, and spatial differentiation indicate the amount of width, height, and breadth an organizational structure needs. Just because an organization is highly differentiated along one of these dimensions does not mean it must be highly differentiated along the others. The university environment, for example, is generally characterized by great horizontal differentiation but relatively little vertical and spatial differentiation. This is quite different from a company such as Coca-Cola that is characterized by a great deal of all three types of differentiation. The more structurally differentiated an organization is, the more complex it is.[6]

Complexity refers to the number of activities, subunits, or subsystems within the organization. Lawrence and Lorsch suggest that an organization's complexity should mirror the complexity of its environment. As the complexity of an organization increases, its need for mechanisms to link and coordinate the differentiated parts also increases. If these links do not exist, the departments or differentiated parts of the organization can lose sight of the organization's larger mission, and the organization runs the risk of chaos. Designing and building linkage and coordination mechanisms is known as *integration*.

◾ INTEGRATION

Integration is the process of coordinating the different parts of an organization to achieve unity among individuals and groups in various jobs, departments, and divisions in the accomplishment of organizational goals and tasks.[7] Integration helps keep the organization in a state of dynamic equilibrium, a condition in which all the parts of the organization are interrelated and balanced, both vertically and horizontally. Vertical linkages are used to integrate activities up and down the organizational chain of command. A variety of structural devices can be used to achieve vertical linkage. These include hierarchical referral, rules and procedures, plans and schedules, positions added to the structure of the organization, and management information systems.[8] Horizontal integration mechanisms provide the communication and coordination that are necessary for links across jobs and departments in the organization. The need for horizontal integration mechanisms increases as the complexity of the organization increases. The horizontal linkages are built into the design of the organization by including liaison roles, task forces, integrator positions, and teams. The use of these linkage mechanisms varies from organization to organization, as well as within areas of the same organization. In general, the flatter the organization, the more necessary are horizontal integration mechanisms.

integration
The process of coordinating the different parts of an organization.

⚑ BASIC DESIGN DIMENSIONS

Differentiation, then, is the process of dividing work in the organization, and integration is the process of coordinating work in the organization. From a structural perspective, every manager and organization looks for the best combination of differentiation and integration for accomplishing the goals of the organization. There are many ways to approach this process. One way is to establish a desired level of each structural dimension on a high to low continuum and then develop a structure that meets the desired configuration. These structural dimensions include the following:[9]

formalization

The degree to which the organization has official rules, regulations, and procedures.

centralization

The degree to which decisions are made at the top of the organization.

specialization

The degree to which jobs are narrowly defined and depend on unique expertise.

standardization

The degree to which work activities are accomplished in a routine fashion.

complexity

The degree to which many different types of activities occur in the organization.

hierarchy of authority

The degree of vertical differentiation across levels of management.

1. *Formalization:* The degree to which an employee's role is defined by formal documentation (procedures, job descriptions, manuals, and regulations).
2. *Centralization:* The extent to which decision-making authority has been delegated to lower levels of an organization. An organization is centralized if the decisions are made at the top of the organization and decentralized if decision making is pushed down to lower levels in the organization.
3. *Specialization:* The degree to which organizational tasks are subdivided into separate jobs. The division of labor and the degree to which formal job descriptions spell out job requirements indicate the level of specialization in the organization.
4. *Standardization:* The extent to which work activities are described and performed routinely in the same way. Highly standardized organizations have little variation in the defining of jobs.
5. *Complexity:* The number of activities within the organization and the amount of differentiation needed within the organization.
6. *Hierarchy of authority:* The degree of vertical differentiation through reporting relationships and the span of control within the structure of the organization.

An organization that is high on formalization, centralization, specialization, standardization, and complexity and has a tall hierarchy of authority is said to be highly bureaucratic. Bureaucracies are not in and of themselves bad; however, they are often tainted by abuse and red tape. The Royal Bank of Canada redesigned its mortgage process to be more decentralized, thus avoiding potential bottlenecks while waiting to receive information from another location.[10]

An organization that is on the opposite end of each of these continua is very flexible and loose. Control is very hard to implement and maintain in such an organization, but at certain times such an organization is appropriate. The research and development departments in many organizations are often more flexible than other departments in order to stimulate creativity. An important organizational variable, which is not included in the structural dimensions, is trust.

Another approach to the process of accomplishing organizational goals is to describe what is and is not important to the success of the organization rather than worry about specific characteristics. Henry Mintzberg feels that the following questions can guide managers in designing formal structures that fit each organization's unique set of circumstances:[11]

1. How many tasks should a given position in the organization contain, and how specialized should each task be?

2. How standardized should the work content of each position be?

3. What skills, abilities, knowledge, and training should be required for each position?

4. What should be the basis for the grouping of positions within the organization into units, departments, divisions, and so on?

5. How large should each unit be, and what should the span of control be (that is, how many individuals should report to each manager)?

6. How much standardization should be required in the output of each position?

7. What mechanisms should be established to help individuals in different positions and units adjust to the needs of other individuals?

8. How centralized or decentralized should decision-making power be in the chain of authority? Should most of the decisions be made at the top of the organization (centralized) or lower down in the chain of authority (decentralized)?

The manager who can answer these questions has a good understanding of how the organization should implement the basic structural dimensions. These basic design dimensions act in combination with one another and are not entirely independent characteristics of an organization. Challenge 14.1 gives you (or a friend) an opportunity to consider how decentralized your company is.

FIVE STRUCTURAL CONFIGURATIONS

Differentiation, integration, and the basic design dimensions combine to yield various structural configurations. Very early organization structures were often either based on product or function. The matrix organization structure crossed these two ways of organizing.[12] Mintzberg moved beyond these early approaches and proposed five structural configurations: the simple structure, the machine bureaucracy, the professional bureaucracy, the divisionalized form, and the adhocracy.[13] Table 14.2 summarizes the prime coordinating mechanism, the key part of the organization, and the type of decentralization for each of these structural configurations. The five basic parts of the organization, for Mintzberg, are the

3. Briefly describe five structural configurations for organizations and how coordination is achieved with each.

TABLE 14.2

Five Structural Configurations of Organizations

STRUCTURAL CONFIGURATION	PRIME COORDINATING MECHANISM	KEY PART OF ORGANIZATION	TYPE OF DECENTRALIZATION
Simple structure	Direct supervision	Upper echelon	Centralization
Machine bureaucracy	Standardization of work processes	Technical staff	Limited horizontal decentralization
Professional bureaucracy	Standardization of skills	Operating level	Vertical and horizontal decentralization
Divisionalized form	Standardization of outputs	Middle level	Limited vertical decentralization
Adhocracy	Mutual adjustment	Support staff	Selective decentralization

SOURCE: From H. Mintzberg, *The Structuring of Organizations,* © 1979, 20. Reprinted by permission of Pearson Education, Inc., Upper Saddle River, N.J.

CHALLENGE 14.1

How Decentralized Is Your Company?

Decentralization is one of the key design dimensions in an organization. It is closely related to several behavioral dimensions of an organization, such as leadership style, degree of participative decision making, and the nature of power and politics within the organization.

The following questionnaire allows you to get an idea about how decentralized your organization is. (If you do not have a job, have a friend who does work complete the questionnaire to see how decentralized his or her organization is.) Which level in your organization has the authority to make each of the following 11 decisions? Answer the questionnaire by circling one of the following:

0 = The board of directors makes the decision.
1 = The CEO makes the decision.
2 = The division/functional manager makes the decision.
3 = A subdepartment head makes the decision.
4 = The first-level supervisor makes the decision.
5 = Operators on the shop floor make the decision.

Decision Concerning:		Circle Appropriate Level					
a. The number of workers required.		0	1	2	3	4	5
b. Whether to employ a worker.		0	1	2	3	4	5
c. Internal labor disputes.		0	1	2	3	4	5
d. Overtime worked at shop level.		0	1	2	3	4	5
e. Delivery dates and order priority.		0	1	2	3	4	5
f. Production planning.		0	1	2	3	4	5
g. Dismissal of a worker.		0	1	2	3	4	5
h. Methods of personnel selection.		0	1	2	3	4	5
i. Method of work to be used.		0	1	2	3	4	5
j. Machinery or equipment to be used.		0	1	2	3	4	5
k. Allocation of work among workers.		0	1	2	3	4	5

Scoring

Add up all your circled numbers.
Total = _____.
The higher your number (for example, 45 or more), the more decentralized your organization. The lower your number (for example, 25 or less), the more centralized your organization.

Source: Reprinted from "Psychological and Traditional Determinants of Structure" by D. Miller and C. Droge, published in *Administrative Science Quarterly* 31 (1986): 558. Reprinted by permission of the *Administrative Science Quarterly* © 1986.

upper echelon or strategic apex; the middle level; the operating core, where work is accomplished; the technostructure; and the support staff. Figure 14.1 depicts these five basic parts with a small strategic apex, connected by a flaring middle line to a large, flat operating core. Each configuration affects people in the organization somewhat differently. As we saw in the case of Cisco Systems at the beginning

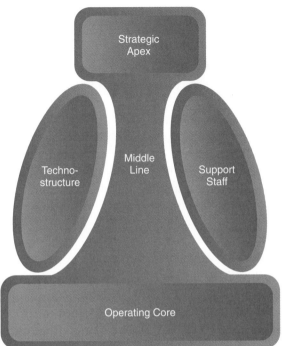

SOURCE: From H. Mintzberg, *The Structuring of Organizations,* © 1979, 20. Reprinted by permission of Pearson Education, Inc., Upper Saddle River, N.J.

of the chapter, this is not necessarily the one best form of organization structure and examining how the industry context, organization structure, and people fit together is important.

■ SIMPLE STRUCTURE

The *simple structure* is an organization with little technical and support staff, strong centralization of decision making in the upper echelon, and a minimal middle level. This structure has a minimum of vertical differentiation of authority and minimal formalization. It achieves coordination through direct supervision, often by the chief executive in the upper echelon. An example of a simple structure is a small, independent landscape practice in which one or two landscape architects supervise the vast majority of work with no middle-level managers. Even an organization with as few as 30 people can become dysfunctional as a simple structure after an extended period.

simple structure
A centralized form of organization that emphasizes the upper echelon and direct supervision.

■ MACHINE BUREAUCRACY

The *machine bureaucracy* is an organization with a well-defined technical and support staff differentiated from the line operations of the organization, limited horizontal decentralization of decision making, and a well-defined hierarchy of authority. The technical staff is powerful in a machine bureaucracy. There is strong formalization through policies, procedures, rules, and regulations. Coordination is achieved through the standardization of work processes. An example of a machine bureaucracy is an automobile assembly plant with routinized operating tasks. The strength of the machine bureaucracy is efficiency of operation in stable, unchanging

machine bureaucracy
A moderately decentralized form of organization that emphasizes the technical staff and standardization of work processes.

environments. The weakness of the machine bureaucracy is its slow responsiveness to external changes and to individual employee preferences and ideas.

■ PROFESSIONAL BUREAUCRACY

professional bureaucracy

A decentralized form of organization that emphasizes the operating core and standardization of skills.

The *professional bureaucracy* emphasizes the expertise of the professionals in the operating core of the organization. The technical and support staffs serve the professionals. There is both vertical and horizontal differentiation in the professional bureaucracy. Coordination is achieved through the standardization of the professionals' skills. Examples of professional bureaucracies are hospitals and universities. The doctors, nurses, and professors are given wide latitude to pursue their work based on professional training and indoctrination through professional training programs. Large accounting firms may fall into the category of professional bureaucracies.

■ DIVISIONALIZED FORM

divisionalized form

A moderately decentralized form of organization that emphasizes the middle level and standardization of outputs.

The *divisionalized form* is a loosely coupled, composite structural configuration.[14] It is a configuration composed of divisions, each of which may have its own structural configuration. Each division is designed to respond to the market in which it operates. There is vertical decentralization from the upper echelon to the middle of the organization, and the middle level of management is the key part of the organization. This form of organization may have one division that is a machine bureaucracy, one that is an adhocracy, and one that is a simple structure. An example of this form of organization is Valero Energy Corporation, headquartered in San Antonio, Texas, with oil refining operations throughout the country. The divisionalized organization uses standardization of outputs as its coordinating mechanism.

■ ADHOCRACY

adhocracy

A selectively decentralized form of organization that emphasizes the support staff and mutual adjustment among people.

The *adhocracy* is a highly open and decentralized, rather than highly structured, configuration with minimal formalization and order. It is designed to fuse interdisciplinary experts into smoothly functioning ad hoc project teams. Liaison devices are the primary mechanism for integrating the project teams through a process of mutual adjustment. There is a high degree of horizontal specialization based on formal training and expertise. Selective decentralization of the project teams occurs within the adhocracy. An example of this form of organization is the National Aeronautics and Space Administration (NASA), which is composed of many talented experts who work in small teams on a wide range of projects related to America's space agenda. New high-technology businesses also often select an adhocracy design. Paradoxically, though, some new high-tech ventures choose bureaucratic design strategies as antidotes for the uncertainty, anxiety, and stress of their typically turbulent operating environments.

◳ CONTEXTUAL VARIABLES

The basic design dimensions and the resulting structural configurations play out in the context of the organization's internal and external environments. Four contextual variables influence the success of an organization's design: size, technology, environment, and strategy and goals. These variables provide a manager with key considerations for the right organizational design, although they do not determine the structure. The amount of change in the contextual variables throughout the life of the organization influences the amount of change needed in the basic dimensions of the organization's structure.[15] For example, competitive pressures in many industries have led to outsourcing, labeled one of the greatest shifts in organization structure in a century.[16]

◄◄think critically►►

> Should legal limits be set to prevent large companies from engaging in very competitive behavior to drive small companies out of business?

▌ SIZE

The total number of employees is the appropriate definition of size when discussing the design of organizational structure. This is logical, because people and their interactions are the building blocks of structure. Other measures, such as net assets, production rates, and total sales, are usually highly correlated with the total number of employees but may not reflect the actual number of interpersonal relationships that are necessary to effectively structure an organization.

Electronic Data Systems (EDS) began as an entrepreneurial venture of H. Ross Perot and had grown into an internationally prominent provider of information technology services when it was bought by General Motors Corporation (GM) in the early 1980s. Nearly half of EDS's revenues came from GM at the time of the buyout. The early culture of EDS placed a premium on technical competence, high achievement drive, an entrepreneurial attitude, and a maverick spirit. EDS continued to grow and change. In 1996, it was spun off by GM and became an autonomous company once again.[17] However, following the spin-off, the company struggled to find a clear focus and identity and lost two chairmen (Les Aberthal and Dick Brown) in the process.

Although there is some argument over the degree of influence that size has on organizational structure, there is no argument that it does influence design options. In one study, Meyer found size of the organization to be the most important of all variables considered in influencing the organization's structure and design, whereas other researchers argue that the decision to expand the organization's business causes an increase in size as the structure is adjusted to accommodate the planned growth.[18] Downsizing is a planned strategy to reduce the size of an organization, and is often accompanied by related restructuring and revitalization activities.[19]

How much influence size exerts on the organization's structure is not as important as the relationship between size and the design dimensions of structure. In other words, when exploring structural alternatives, what should the manager know about designing structures for large and small organizations?

Table 14.3 illustrates the relationships among each of the design dimensions and organizational size. Formalization, specialization, and standardization all tend to be greater in larger organizations because they are necessary to control activities within the organization. For example, larger organizations are more likely to use

4. Describe four contextual variables for an organization and their effect on organizational structure.

TABLE 14.3		

BASIC DESIGN DIMENSIONS	SMALL ORGANIZATIONS	LARGE ORGANIZATIONS
Formalization	Less	More
Centralization	High	Low
Specialization	Low	High
Standardization	Low	High
Complexity	Low	High
Hierarchy of authority	Flat	Tall

TABLE 14.3

Relationship between Organizational Size and Basic Design Dimensions

documentation, rules, written policies and procedures, and detailed job descriptions than to rely on personal observation by the manager. The more relationships that have to be managed by the structure, the more formalized and standardized the processes need to be. McDonald's has several volumes that describe how to make all its products, how to greet customers, how to maintain the facilities, and so on. This level of standardization, formalization, and specialization helps McDonald's maintain the same quality of product no matter where a restaurant is located. In contrast, at a small, locally owned café, your hamburger and french fries may taste a little different every time you visit. This is evidence of a lack of standardization.

Formalization and specialization also help a large organization decentralize decision making. Because of the complexity and number of decisions in a large organization, formalization and specialization are used to set parameters for decision making at lower levels. Can you imagine the chaos if the president of the United States, commander-in-chief of all U.S. military forces, had to make operational-level decisions in the war on terrorism? By decentralizing decision making, the larger organization adds horizontal and vertical complexity, but not necessarily spatial complexity. However, it is more common for a large organization to have more geographic dispersion.

Another dimension of design, hierarchy of authority, is related to complexity. As size increases, complexity increases; thus, more levels are added to the hierarchy of authority. This keeps the span of control from getting too large. However, there is a balancing force, because formalization and specialization are added. The more formalized, standardized, and specialized the roles within the organization, the wider the span of control can be.

Although some have argued that the future belongs to small, agile organizations, others argue that size continues to be an advantage. To take advantage of size, organizations must become centerless corporations with a global core.[20] These concepts are pioneered by Booz Allen Hamilton based on its worldwide technology and management consulting. The global core provides strategic leadership, helps distribute and provide access to the company's capabilities and knowledge, creates the corporate identity, ensures access to low cost capital, and exerts control over the enterprise as a whole.

■ TECHNOLOGY

An organization's technology is an important contextual variable in determining the organization's structure, as noted in Chapter 2.[21] Technology is defined as the tools, techniques, and actions used by an organization to transform inputs into outputs.[22] The inputs of the organization include human resources, machines, materials, information, and money. The outputs are the products and services that the organization offers to the external environment. Determining the relationship between technology and structure is complicated, because different departments may employ very different technologies. As organizations become larger, there is greater variation in technologies across units in the organization. Joan Woodward, Charles Perrow, and James Thompson have developed ways to understand traditional organizational technologies. More work is needed to better understand the contemporary engineering, research and development, and knowledge-based technologies of the information age. In 2001, we saw that Cisco aimed to use 11 key technology areas as the basis for transitioning its overall organization structure from three lines of business to 11 key technology groups.

Woodward introduced one of the best-known classification schemes for technology, identifying three types: unit, mass, or process production. Unit technology is small-batch manufacturing technology and, sometimes, made-to-order production. Examples include Smith & Wesson's arms manufacture and the manufacture of fine furniture. Mass technology is large-batch manufacturing technology. Examples include American automotive assembly lines and latex glove production. Process production is continuous-production processes. Examples include oil refining and beer making. Woodward classified unit technology as the least complex, mass technology as more complex, and process technology as the most complex. The more complex the organization's technology, the more complex the administrative component or structure of the organization needs to be.

Perrow proposed an alternative to Woodward's scheme based on two variables: task variability and problem analyzability. Task variability considers the number of exceptions encountered in doing the tasks within a job. Problem analyzability examines the types of search procedures followed to find ways to respond to task exceptions. For example, for some exceptions encountered while doing a task, the appropriate response is easy to find. If you are driving down a street and see a sign that says, "Detour—Bridge Out," it is very easy to respond to the task variability. When Thomas Edison was designing the first electric light bulb, however, the problem analyzability was very high for his task.

Perrow went on further to identify the four key aspects of structure that could be modified to the technology. These structural elements are (1) the amount of discretion that an individual can exercise to complete a task, (2) the power of groups to control the unit's goals and strategies, (3) the level of interdependence among groups, and (4) the extent to which organizational units coordinate work using either feedback or planning. Figure 14.2 summarizes Perrow's findings about types of technology and basic design dimensions.[23]

Thompson offered yet another view of technology and its relationship to organizational design. This view is based on the concept of *technological interdependence* (i.e., the degree of interrelatedness of the organization's various technological elements) and the pattern of an organization's work flows. Thompson's research suggests that greater technological interdependence leads to greater organizational complexity and that the problems of this greater complexity may be offset by decentralized decision making.[24]

technological interdependence
The degree of interrelatedness of the organization's various technological elements.

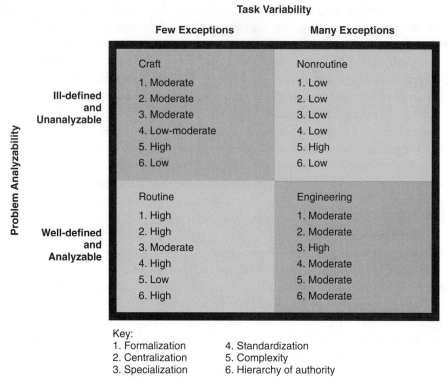

Task Variability

		Few Exceptions	Many Exceptions
Problem Analyzability	**Ill-defined and Unanalyzable**	Craft 1. Moderate 2. Moderate 3. Moderate 4. Low-moderate 5. High 6. Low	Nonroutine 1. Low 2. Low 3. Low 4. Low 5. High 6. Low
	Well-defined and Analyzable	Routine 1. High 2. High 3. Moderate 4. High 5. Low 6. High	Engineering 1. Moderate 2. Moderate 3. High 4. Moderate 5. Moderate 6. Moderate

Key:
1. Formalization
2. Centralization
3. Specialization
4. Standardization
5. Complexity
6. Hierarchy of authority

SOURCE: Built from C. Perrow, "A Framework for the Comparative Analysis of Organizations," *American Sociological Review* (April 1967): 194–208.

The research of these three early scholars on the influence of technology on organizational design can be combined into one integrating concept—routineness in the process of changing inputs into outputs in an organization. This routineness has a very strong relationship with organizational structure. The more routine and repetitive the tasks of the organization, the higher the degree of formalization that is possible; the more centralized, specialized, and standardized the organization can be; and the more hierarchical levels with wider spans of control that are possible.

Since the work of Woodward, Perrow, and Thompson, however, an important caveat to the discussion of technology has emerged: The advance of information technology has influenced how organizations transform inputs into outputs. The introduction of computer-integrated networks, CAD/CAM systems, and computer-integrated manufacturing has broadened the span of control, flattened the organizational hierarchy, decentralized decision making, and lowered the amount of specialization and standardization.[25] Advances in information technology have allowed for other advances in manufacturing, such as mass customization. Hewlett-Packard has found a key to mass customization in postponing the task of differentiating a product for a specific customer until the latest possible time.[26]

Further, the emergence of new digital technologies along with the globalization of the economy are major forces for change. These two forces affect all organizations throughout the economy, ushering in a new economy that has four characteristics. Stanley M. Davis describes these as (1) *any time*—customers can get their goods and services 24/7; (2) *any place*—customers can order from anywhere if they have Internet access; (3) *no matter*—intangibles are adding value to products, such as through digital photography; and (4) *mass customization*—technology and information allow for rapid, responsive customization of products.[27] Thus, digital technology and economic change have resulted in downsizing and restructuring activities in the private sector.

▌ ENVIRONMENT

The third contextual variable for organizational design is *environment*. The environment of an organization is most easily defined as anything outside the boundaries of that organization. Different aspects of the environment have varying degrees of influence on the organization's structure. In one study of 318 CEOs between 1996 and 2000, strategic decision speed was found to moderate the relationship between the environment and the organization structure and performance.[28] For example, in response to the 9/11 terrorist attack on the World Trade Center, President George W. Bush acted swiftly to restructure the U.S. federal government and create the Department of Homeland Security. The general environment includes all conditions that may have an impact on the organization. These conditions could include economic factors, political considerations, ecological changes, sociocultural demands, and governmental regulation.

environment
Anything outside the boundaries of an organization.

TASK ENVIRONMENT

When aspects of the general environment become more focused in areas of direct interest to the organization, those aspects become part of the *task environment*, or specific environment. The task environment is that part of the environment that is directly relevant to the organization. Typically, this level of environment includes stakeholders such as unions, customers, suppliers, competitors, government regulatory agencies, and trade associations.

task environment
The elements of an organization's environment that are related to its goal attainment.

The domain of the organization refers to the area the organization claims for itself with respect to how it fits into its relevant environments. The domain is particularly important because it is defined by the organization, and it influences how the organization perceives and acts within its environments.[29] For example, Wal-Mart and Neiman Marcus both sell clothing apparel, but their domains are very different.

The organization's perceptions of its environment and the actual environment may not be the same. The environment that the manager perceives is the environment to which the organization responds and for which it organizes.[30] Therefore, two organizations may be in relatively the same environment from an objective standpoint, but if the managers perceive differences, the organizations may enact very different structures to deal with this same environment.

ENVIRONMENTAL UNCERTAINTY

The perception of *environmental uncertainty* or the perception of the lack of environmental uncertainty is how the contextual variable of environment most influences organizational design. Some organizations have relatively static environments with little uncertainty, whereas others are so dynamic that no one is sure what tomorrow may bring. Binney & Smith, for example, has made relatively the same product for more than 50 years with very few changes in the product design or packaging. The environment for its Crayola products is relatively static. In fact, customers rebelled when the company tried to get rid of some old colors and add

environmental uncertainty
The amount and rate of change in the organization's environment.

BASIC DESIGN DIMENSIONS	MECHANISTIC	ORGANIC
Formalization	High	Low
Centralization	High	Low
Specialization	High	Low
Standardization	High	Low
Complexity	Low	High
Hierarchy of authority	Strong, tall	Weak, flat

mechanistic structure

An organizational design
that emphasizes struc-
tured activities, specialized tasks, and centralized
decision making.

organic structure

An organizational design
that emphasizes team-
work, open communica-
tion, and decentralized
decision making.

new ones. In contrast, in the last two decades, competitors in the airline industry
have encountered deregulation, mergers, bankruptcies, safety changes, changes in
cost and price structures, changes in customer and employee demographics, and
changes in global competition. The uncertainty of the environment of the major
airlines has been relatively high during this period.

The amount of uncertainty in the environment influences the structural dimensions. Burns and Stalker labeled two structural extremes that are appropriate
for the extremes of environmental uncertainty—*mechanistic structure* and *organic
structure*.[31] Table 14.4 compares the structural dimensions of these two extremes.
The mechanistic and organic structures are opposite ends of a continuum of organizational design possibilities. One study of 68 organizations found that mechanistic
versus organic structures moderated organizational justice processes and perceptions.[32] Although the general premise of environmental uncertainty and structural
dimensions has been upheld by research, the organization must make adjustments
for the realities of its perceived environment when designing its structure.[33]

The question for those trying to design organizational structures is how to
determine environmental uncertainty. Dess and Beard defined three dimensions
of environment that should be measured in assessing the degree of uncertainty:
capacity, volatility, and complexity.[34] The capacity of the environment reflects the
abundance or scarcity of resources. If resources abound, the environment supports
expansion, mistakes, or both. In contrast, in times of scarcity, the environment
demands survival of the fittest. Volatility is the degree of instability. The airline
industry is in a volatile environment. This makes it difficult for managers to know
what needs to be done. The complexity of the environment refers to the differences
and variability among environmental elements.

If the organization's environment is uncertain, dynamic, and complex and
resources are scarce, the manager needs an organic structure that is better able to
adapt to its environment. Such a structure allows the manager to monitor the environment from a number of internal perspectives, thus helping the organization
to maintain flexibility in responding to environmental changes.[35]

■ STRATEGY AND GOALS

The fourth contextual variable that influences how the design dimensions of
structure should be enacted is the strategies and goals of the organization. Strategies and goals provide legitimacy to the organization, as well as employee direction,

STRATEGIC DIMENSION	PREDICTED STRUCTURAL CHARACTERISTICS
Innovation—to understand and manage new processes and technologies	Low formalization Decentralization Flat hierarchy
Market differentiation—to specialize in customer preferences	Moderate to high complexity Moderate to high formalization Moderate centralization
Cost control—to produce standardized products efficiently	High formalization High centralization High standardization Low complexity

TABLE 14.5

Miller's Integrative Framework of Structural and Strategic Dimensions

SOURCE: D. Miller, "The Structural and Environmental Correlates of Business Strategy," *Strategic Management Journal* 8 (1987): 55–76. Copyright © John Wiley & Sons Limited. Reproduced with permission.

decision guidelines, and criteria for performance.[36] In addition, strategies and goals help the organization fit into its environment.

As more understanding of the contextual influence of strategies and goals has developed, several strategic dimensions that influence structure have been defined. One of these definitions was put forth by Danny Miller.[37] His framework for these strategic dimensions and their implications for organizational structure are shown in Table 14.5.

For example, when Apple Computer introduced personal computers to the market, its strategies were very innovative. The structure of the organization was relatively flat and informal. Apple had Friday afternoon beer and popcorn discussion sessions, and eccentric behavior was easily accepted. As the personal computer market became more competitive, however, the structure of Apple changed to help it differentiate its products and control costs. The innovative strategies and structures devised by Steve Jobs, one of Apple's founders, were no longer appropriate. The board of directors recruited John Scully, a marketing expert from PepsiCo, to help Apple better compete in the market it had created. In 1996 and 1997, Apple reinvented itself again and brought back Jobs to try to restore its innovative edge. Since his return, Apple has become a major player in the digital music market with its introduction of the iPod, selling over 200,000 units in one quarter.

Limitations exist, however, on how much strategies and goals influence structure. Because the structure of the organization includes the formal information-processing channels in the organization, it stands to reason that the need to change strategies may not be communicated throughout the organization. In such a case, the organization's structure influences its strategic choice.

The inefficiency of the structure to perceive environmental changes may even lead to organizational failure. In the airline industry, several carriers failed to adjust quickly enough to deregulation and the highly competitive marketplace. Only

TABLE 14.6

Examples of How Structure Affects the Strategic Decision Process

FORMALIZATION

As the level of formalization increases, so does the probability of the following:

1. The strategic decision process will become reactive to crisis rather than proactive through opportunities.
2. Strategic moves will be incremental and precise.
3. Differentiation in the organization will not be balanced with integrative mechanisms.
4. Only environmental crises that are in areas monitored by the formal organizational systems will be acted upon.

CENTRALIZATION

As the level of centralization increases, so does the probability of the following:

1. The strategic decision process will be initiated by only a few dominant individuals.
2. The decision process will be goal-oriented and rational.
3. The strategic process will be constrained by the limitations of top managers.

COMPLEXITY

As the level of complexity increases, so does the probability of the following:

1. The strategic decision process will become more politicized.
2. The organization will find it more difficult to recognize environmental opportunities and threats.
3. The constraints on good decision processes will be multiplied by the limitations of each individual within the organization.

SOURCE: Republished with permission of Academy of Management, PO Box 3020, Briar Cliff Manor, NY 10510-8020. "The Strategic Decision Process and Organizational Structure" (Table), J. Fredrickson, *Academy of Management Review* (1986): 284. Reproduced by permission of the publisher via Copyright Clearance Center, Inc.

those airlines that were generally viewed as lean structures with good information-processing systems have flourished in the turbulent years since deregulation. Examples of how different design dimensions can affect the strategic decision process are listed in Table 14.6.

The four contextual variables—size, technology, environment, and strategy and goals—combine to influence the design process. However, the existing structure of the organization influences how the organization interprets and reacts to information about each of the variables. Each of the contextual variables has management researchers who claim that it is the most important variable in determining the best structural design. Because of the difficulty in studying the interactions of the four contextual dimensions and the complexity of organizational structures, the argument about which variable is most important continues.

What is apparent is that there must be some level of fit between the structure and the contextual dimensions of the organization. The better the fit, the more likely the organization will achieve its short-run goals. In addition, the better the fit, the more likely the organization will process information and design appropriate organizational roles for long-term prosperity, as indicated in Figure 14.3.

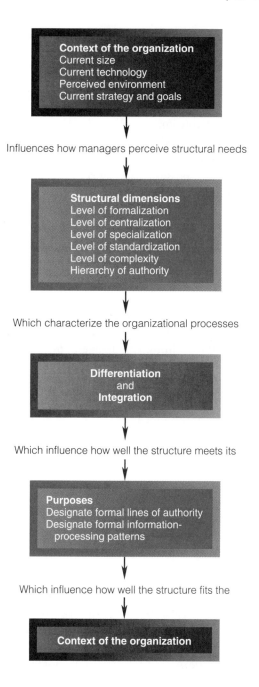

FIGURE 14.3

The Relationship among Key Organizational Design Elements

FORCES RESHAPING ORGANIZATIONS

5. Explain the forces reshaping organizations.

Managers and researchers traditionally examine organizational design and structure within the framework of basic design dimensions and contextual variables. Several forces reshaping organizations are causing managers to go beyond the traditional frameworks and to examine ways to make organizations more responsive to customer needs. Some of these forces include shorter life cycles within the organization, globalization, and rapid changes in information technology. These forces together increase the demands on process capabilities within the organization and emerging organizational structures. To successfully retain their health and vitality, organizations must function as open systems, as discussed in Chapter 1, that are responsive to their task environment.[38]

LIFE CYCLES IN ORGANIZATIONS

organizational life cycle
The differing stages of an organization's life from birth to death.

Organizations are dynamic entities. As such, they ebb and flow through different stages. Usually, researchers think of these stages as *organizational life cycles.* The total organization has a life cycle that begins at birth, moves through growth and maturity to decline, and possibly experiences revival.[39]

Organizational subunits may have very similar life cycles. Because of changes in technology and product design, many organizational subunits, especially those that are product based, are experiencing shorter life cycles. Hence, the subunits that compose the organization are changing more rapidly than in the past. These shorter life cycles enable the organization to respond quickly to external demands and changes.

When a new organization or subunit is born, the structure is organic and informal. If the organization or subunit is successful, it grows and matures. This usually leads to formalization, specialization, standardization, complexity, and a more mechanistic structure. If the environment changes, however, the organization must be able to respond. A mechanistic structure is not able to respond to a dynamic environment as well as an organic one. If the organization or subunit does respond, it becomes more organic and revives; if not, it declines and possibly dies.

Shorter life cycles put more pressure on the organization to be both flexible and efficient at the same time. Further, as flexible organizations use design to their competitive advantage, discrete organizational life cycles may give way to a kaleidoscope of continuously emerging, efficiency-seeking organizational designs.[40] The manager's challenge in this context becomes one of creating congruency among various organizational design dimensions to fit continuously changing markets and locations.

GLOBALIZATION

Another force that is reshaping organizations is the process of globalization. In other words, organizations operate worldwide rather than in just one country or region. Global corporations can become pitted against sovereign nations when rules and laws conflict across national borders. Globalization makes spatial differentiation even more of a reality for organizations. Besides the obvious geographic differences, there may be deep cultural and value system differences. This adds another type of complexity to the structural design process and necessitates the creation of integrating mechanisms so that people are able to understand and interpret one another, as well as coordinate with one another.

The choice of structure for managing an international business is generally based on choices concerning the following three factors:

1. *The level of vertical differentiation.* A hierarchy of authority must be created that clarifies the responsibilities of both domestic and foreign managers.
2. *The level of horizontal differentiation.* Foreign and domestic operations should be grouped in such a way that the company effectively serves the needs of all customers.

3. *The degree of formalization, specialization, standardization, and centralization.* The global structure must allow decisions to be made in the most appropriate area of the organization. However, controls must be in place that reflect the strategies and goals of the parent firm.[41]

CHANGES IN INFORMATION-PROCESSING TECHNOLOGIES

Many of the changes in information-processing technologies have allowed organizations to move into new product and market areas more quickly. However, just as shorter life cycles and globalization have caused new concerns for designing organizational structures, so has the increased availability of advanced information-processing technologies.

Organizational structures are already feeling the impact of advanced information-processing technologies. More integration and coordination are evident, because managers worldwide can be connected through computerized networks. The basic design dimensions have also been affected as follows:

1. The hierarchy of authority has been flattened.

2. The basis of centralization has been changed. Now managers can use technology to acquire more information and make more decisions, or they can use technology to push information and decision making lower in the hierarchy and thus decrease centralization.

3. Less specialization and standardization are needed, because people using advanced information-processing technologies have more sophisticated jobs that require a broader understanding of how the organization gets work done.[42]

Advances in information processing are leading to knowledge-based organizations, the outlines of which are now only seen dimly. Some of the hallmarks of these new organizational forms are virtual enterprising, dynamic teaming, and knowledge networking.[43] This fifth generation of management thought and practice leads to cocreation of products and services. Future organizations may well be defined by networks of overlapping teams.

DEMANDS ON ORGANIZATIONAL PROCESSES

Because of the forces reshaping organizations, managers find themselves trying to meet what seem to be conflicting goals: an efficiency orientation that results in on-time delivery *and* a quality orientation that results in customized, high-quality goods or services.[44] Traditionally, managers have seen efficiency and customization as conflicting demands.

To meet these conflicting demands, organizations need to become "dynamically stable."[45] To do so, an organization must have managers who see their roles as architects who clearly understand the "how" of the organizing process. Managers must combine long-term thinking with flexible and quick responses that help improve process and know-how. The organizational structure must help define, at least to some degree, roles for managers who hope to successfully address the conflicting demands of dynamic stability. Challenge 14.2 allows you to examine the ways managers in your organization currently operate on the job.

Chapter 14 *Organizational Design and Structure*

CHALLENGE 14.2

Managers of Today and the Future

Are the roles for managers in your organization more oriented toward today or toward the future? (If you do not work, think of an organization where you have worked or talk with a friend about managerial roles in his or her organization.)

Step 1. Reread Table 14.7 and check which orientation (today or future) predominates in your organization for each of the following seven characteristics:

	Today	Future
1. Boss–employee relationships.	————	————
2. Getting work accomplished.	————	————
3. Messenger versus problem solver.	————	————
4. Basis for task accomplishment.	————	————
5. Narrow versus broad functional focus.	————	————
6. Adherence to channels of authority.	————	————
7. Controlling versus coaching subordinates.	————	————

Step 2. Examine the degree of consistency across all seven characteristics. Could the organization make one or two structural changes to achieve a better alignment of the manager's role with today or with the future?

Step 3. Identify one manager in your organization who fits very well into the organization's ideal manager's role. What does this manager do that creates a good person–role fit?

Step 4. Identify one manager in your organization who does not fit very well into the organization's ideal manager's role. What does this manager do that creates a poor person–role fit?

The differences between the structural roles of managers today and managers of the future are illustrated in Table 14.7.

6. Discuss emerging organizational structures.

■ EMERGING ORGANIZATIONAL STRUCTURES

The demands on managers and on process capabilities place demands on structures. The emphasis in organizations is shifting to organizing around processes. This process orientation emerges from the combination of three streams of applied organizational design: high-performance, self-managed teams; managing processes rather than functions; and the evolution of information technology. Information technology and advanced communication systems have led to internetworking. In a study of 469 firms, deeply internetworked firms were found to be more focused and specialized, less hierarchical, and more engaged in external partnering.[46] Three emerging organizational structures associated with these changes are network organizations, virtual organizations, and the circle organization.

Network organizations are weblike structures that contract some or all of their operating functions to other organizations and then coordinate their activities through managers and other employees at their headquarters. Information technology

TABLE 14.7

Structural Roles of Managers Today versus Managers of the Future

ROLES OF MANAGERS TODAY

1. Strictly adhering to boss–employee relationships.
2. Getting things done by giving orders.
3. Carrying messages up and down the hierarchy.
4. Performing a prescribed set of tasks according to a job description.
5. Having a narrow functional focus.
6. Going through channels, one by one by one.
7. Controlling subordinates.

ROLES OF FUTURE MANAGERS

1. Having hierarchical relationships subordinated to functional and peer relationships.
2. Getting things done by negotiating.
3. Solving problems and making decisions.
4. Creating the job by developing entrepreneurial projects.
5. Having broad cross-functional collaboration.
6. Emphasizing speed and flexibility.
7. Coaching their workers.

SOURCE: Adapted from Thomas R. Horton and Peter C. Reid, "What Fate for Middle Managers?," *Management Review* 80, no. 1 (January 1991): 22–23.

is the basis for building the weblike structure of the network organization and business unit managers that are essential to the success of these systems. This type of organization has arisen in the age of electronic commerce and brought into practice transaction cost economics, interorganizational collaborations, and strategic alliances. Network organizations can be global in scope.[47]

Virtual organizations are temporary network organizations consisting of independent enterprises. Many dot.coms were virtual organizations designed to come together swiftly to exploit an apparent market opportunity. They may function much like a theatrical troupe that comes together for a "performance."[48] Trust can be a challenge for virtual organizations because it is a complex phenomenon involving ethics, morals, emotions, values, and natural attitudes. However, trust and trustworthiness are important connective issues in virtual environments. Three key ingredients for the development of trust in virtual organizations are technology that can communicate emotion; a sharing of values, vision, and organizational identity; and a high standard of ethics.[49]

The circle organization is a third emerging structure crafted by Harley-Davidson in its drive to achieve teamwork without teams.[50] The company evolved the circle form of organization shown in Figure 14.4. The three organizational parts are those that (1) create demand, (2) produce product, and (3) provide support. As the figure indicates, these three parts are linked by the leadership and strategy council (LSC). The circle organization is a more open system and an

FIGURE 14.4

Harley-Davidson's Circle Organization

organic structure for customer responsiveness. One innovation in this organizational scheme is the "circle coach," who possesses acute communication, listening, and influencing skills so as to be highly respected by circle members and the company's president.

: **7.** Identify two cautions about the effect of organizational structures on people.

◼ CAUTIONARY NOTES ABOUT STRUCTURE

This chapter has identified the purposes of structure, the processes of organizational design, and the dimensions and contexts that must be considered in structure. In addition, it has looked at forces and trends in organizational design. Two cautionary notes are important for the student of organizational behavior. First, an organizational structure may be weak or deficient. In general, if the structure is out of alignment with its contextual variables, one or more of the following four symptoms appears. First, decision making is delayed because the hierarchy is overloaded and too much information is being funneled through one or two channels. Second, decision making lacks quality because information linkages are not providing the correct information to the right person in the right format. Third, the organization does not respond innovatively to a changing environment, especially when coordinated effort is lacking across departments. Fourth, a great deal of conflict is evident when departments are working against one another rather than working for the strategies and goals of the organization as a whole; the structure is often at fault.

The second caution is that the personality of the chief executive may adversely affect the structure of the organization.[51] Managers' personal, cognitive biases and political ideologies affect their good judgment and decision making.[52] Five dysfunctional combinations of personality and organization have been identified: the paranoid, the depressive, the dramatic, the compulsive, and the schizoid.[53] Each of these personality–organization constellations can create problems for the people who work in the organization. For example, in a paranoid constellation, people are suspicious of each other, and distrust in working relationships may interfere with effective communication and task accomplishment. For another example, in a depressive constellation, people feel depressed and inhibited in their work activities, which can lead to low levels of productivity and task accomplishment. Healthy, productive organizations are open and responsive to their industry context, thus enabling changes in both organizational structures and executive leadership to fit changing conditions. This is what we saw in the Thinking Ahead feature with Cisco Systems and will see again in the Looking Back feature.

◀◀**think critically**▶▶

Suppose an employee complains about organizational design problems and suggests a solution. The organization is redesigned accordingly, but the employee's department is eliminated. Is it ethical for the company to terminate the employee? Should companies always make room for people who have beneficial ideas for the organization?

⚑ MANAGERIAL IMPLICATIONS: FITTING PEOPLE AND STRUCTURES TOGETHER

Organizations are complex social systems composed of numerous interrelated components. They can be complicated to understand. Managers who design, develop, and improve organizations must have a mastery of the basic concepts related to the anatomy and processes of organizational functioning. It is essential for executives at the top to have a clear concept of how the organization can be differentiated and then integrated into a cohesive whole.

People can work better in organizations if they understand how their jobs and departments relate to other jobs and teams in the organization. An understanding of the whole organization enables people to better relate their contribution to the overall mission of the organization and to compensate for structural deficiencies that may exist in the organization.

Different structural configurations place unique demands on the people who work within them. The diversity of people in work organizations suggests that some people are better suited for a simple structure, others are better suited to a professional bureaucracy, and still others are most productive in an adhocracy. Organizational structures are not independent of the people who work within them. This is especially true for organizations operating in a global work environment.

Managers must pay attention to the technology of the organization's work, the amount of change occurring in the organization's environment, and the regulatory pressures created by governmental agencies as the managers design effective organizations and subunits to meet emerging international demands and a diverse, multicultural workforce.

LOOKING BACK :: CISCO SYSTEMS

It's Not Just about the Money ... It's about the People

Large organizations sometimes lose sight of the people with a developing preoccupation with money, profits, and stock price. While no successful business enterprise can ignore these important considerations, neither can they ignore the people. When Cisco Systems went through its 2001 organizational structure transition, it did so in part precisely because of one important group of people—its customers. CEO John Chambers said at the time that the company was evolving its business structure consistent with customer feedback. He said that the company's number one priority had always been customer satisfaction and believed that the new technology group structure allowed Cisco to get closer to the customer. While customers were important, so too were the field sales people very important. Cisco arguably had the best field sales organization in the industry.

Organizational size does not necessarily crowd people out. Cisco Systems ranked number 11 overall on *Fortune*'s 2007 Best Companies to Work For list, up from number 25 in 2006 and number 27 in 2005.[54] Thus, the company is consistently at the top of the list over time, with a 2007 rank of number 5 among large companies. Among the things that make the company so great to work for is the engagement of CEO John Chambers. He stays in touch with the staff, meets with groups of new hires to welcome them soon after they start, and hosts monthly breakfast meetings with workers who are encouraged to ask him tough questions. That is open communication in the context of a large organization.

In 2006, Cisco has grown to a U.S. $28.5 billion business with nearly 50,000 employees both within and outside the United States. The company is also a diverse one. Among its employees, 42 percent are minorities and 24 percent are women. While the company receives over 75,000 applicants annually, there is a voluntary turnover rate of 4 percent and an annualized job growth rate of 8 percent. The most common salaried job is that of software engineer, paying over $130,000 annually. The most common hourly job is that of sales administrator, paying over $55,000 annually. All this suggests that large companies can still be people-friendly companies with dual foci on technology and diversity, on people and profits, and on business as well as the human side of the enterprise.

CHAPTER SUMMARY

1. Three basic types of differentiation occur in organizations: horizontal, vertical, and spatial.

2. The greater the complexity of an organization because of its degree of differentiation, the greater the need for integration.

3. Formalization, centralization, specialization, standardization, complexity, and hierarchy of authority are the six basic design dimensions in an organization.

4. Simple structure, machine bureaucracy, professional bureaucracy, divisionalized form, and adhocracy are five structural configurations of an organization.

5. The contextual variables important to organizational design are size, technology, environment, and strategy and goals.

6. Life cycles, globalization, and demands on process capabilities are forces reshaping organizations today.

7. Network organizations, virtual organizations, and the circle organization are emerging organizational structures.

8. Organizational structures may be inherently weak, or chief executives may create personality–organization constellations that adversely affect employees.

KEY TERMS

adhocracy (p. 364)

centralization (p. 360)

complexity (p. 360)

contextual variables (p. 358)

differentiation (p. 358)

divisionalized form (p. 364)

environment (p. 369)

environmental uncertainty (p. 369)

formalization (p. 360)

hierarchy of authority (p. 360)

integration (p. 359)

machine bureaucracy (p. 363)

mechanistic structure (p. 370)

organic structure (p. 370)

organizational design (p. 357)

organizational life cycle (p. 374)

organizational structure (p. 357)

professional bureaucracy (p. 364)

simple structure (p. 363)

specialization (p. 360)

standardization (p. 360)

task environment (p. 369)

technological interdependence (p. 367)

REVIEW QUESTIONS

1. Define the processes of differentiation and integration.

2. Describe the six basic dimensions of organizational design.

3. Discuss five structural configurations from the chapter.

4. Discuss the effects of the four contextual variables on the basic design dimensions.

5. Identify forces that are reshaping organizations today.

6. Discuss the nature of emerging organizational structures.

7. List five unhealthy personality–organization combinations.

Discussion and Communication Q U E S T I O N S

1. How would you describe the organization you work for (or your college) on each of the basic design dimensions? For example, is it a very formal organization or an informal organization?

2. Do the size, technology, and mission of your organization directly affect you? How?

3. Who are your organization's competitors? What changes do you see in information technology where you work?

4. Does your company show any one or more of the four symptoms of structural deficiency discussed at the end of the chapter?

5. *(communication question)* Write a memo classifying and describing the structural configuration of your university based on the five choices in Table 14.2. Do you need more information than you have to be comfortable with your classification and description? Where could you get the information?

6. *(communication question)* Interview an administrator in your college or university about possible changes in size (Will the college or university get bigger? Smaller?) and technology (Is the college or university making a significant investment in information technology?). What effects does the administrator anticipate from these changes? Be prepared to present your results orally to the class.

E T H I C A L   D I L E M M A

Kate Brown was a human resources manager for Summit Maintenance, a national commercial janitorial service company. She worked hard to represent the employees' best interest to management. Kate worked at one of Summit's regional headquarters. She had four regional human resources representatives that worked in the field to cover her region. Like many large, older companies, Summit was very bureaucratic with several levels of managers. Kate directly reported to the regional human resources vice president, but she also reported to the general manager for her regional office.

At the moment, Kate was feeling the burden of reporting to two different people. She had just left a meeting with Terry Beck, the general manager. Terry had explained that he wanted to make some small changes in the way they interpreted some of the company policies. Terry understood that these policies had been created for a lot of good reasons but were not really appropriate for the more rural area their region covered. He went on to explain that he wasn't asking Kate to break the rules, just enforce them differently and more effectively for their employees.

After listening to Terry, Kate had to agree that his ideas would work much better in their area. The policies Terry was most concerned with were some of the safety policies that were developed for people working in large high-rise buildings or in high crime areas. Their employees worked in neither. They mostly worked in small, rural family businesses. The need to follow policies regarding terrorist attacks or escaping a high-rise fire seemed extremely remote. Yet day after day, employees were forced to carry extra equipment or go through extra procedures to ensure their safety against these dangers. Money, time, and space were wasted following policies that would probably never affect them.

Kate's only concern was her primary supervisor, Vernon Miller, the regional vice president. He would never go for this idea. He was a stickler for rules whether they made sense or not. Kate knew her first duty was to the HR executive, but she saw the value in easing the safety policies for their employees.

QUESTIONS

1. Does Kate have the right to interpret the policies the way she believes to be best?

2. Evaluate Kate's decision using rule, virtue, rights, and justice theories.

E X P E R I E N T I A L   E X E R C I S E S

14.1 WORDS-IN-SENTENCES COMPANY

Purpose: To design an organization for a particular task and carry through to production; to compare design elements with effectiveness.

Group Size: Any number of groups of 6 to 14 persons.

Time Required: 50 to 90 minutes.

Related Topics: Dynamics within groups and work motivation.

BACKGROUND

You are a small company that manufactures words and then packages them in meaningful English-language sentences. Market research has established that sentences of at least three words but not more than six words are in demand. Therefore, packaging, distribution, and sales should be set up for three- to six-word sentences.

The "words-in-sentences" (WIS) industry is highly competitive; several new firms have recently entered what appears to be an expanding market. Since raw materials, technology, and pricing are all standard for the industry, your ability to compete depends on two factors: (1) volume and (2) quality.

YOUR TASK

Your group must design and participate in running a WIS company. You should design your organization to be as efficient as possible during each 10-minute production run. After the first production run, you will have an opportunity to reorganize your company if you want.

RAW MATERIALS

For each production, you will be given a "raw material word or phrase." The letters found in the word or phrase serve as raw materials available to produce new words in sentences. For example, if the raw material word is "organization," you could produce the words and sentence: "Nat ran to a zoo."

PRODUCTION STANDARDS

Several rules must be followed in producing "words-in-sentences." If these rules are not followed, your output will not meet production specifications and will not pass quality-control inspection.

1. The same letter may appear only as often in a manufactured word as it appears in the raw material word or phrase; for example, "organization" has two o's. Thus, "zoo" is legitimate, but not "zoonosis." It has too many o's and s's.

2. Raw material letters can be used again in different manufactured words.

3. A manufactured word may be used only once in a sentence and in only one sentence during a production run; if a word—for example, "a"—is used once in a sentence, it is out of stock.

4. A new word may not be made by adding "s" to form the plural of an already manufactured word.

5. A word is defined by its spelling, not its meaning.

6. Nonsense words or nonsense sentences are unacceptable.

7. All words must be in the English language.

8. Names and places are acceptable.

9. Slang is not acceptable.

MEASURING PERFORMANCE

The output of your WIS company is measured by the total number of acceptable words that are packaged in sentences. The sentences must be legible, listed on no more than two sheets of paper, and handed to the Quality Control Review Board at the completion of each production run.

DELIVERY

Delivery must be made to the Quality Control Review Board 30 seconds after the end of each production run, or else all points are lost.

QUALITY CONTROL

If any word in a sentence does not meet the standards set forth above, all the words in the sentence will be rejected. The Quality Control Review Board (composed of one member from each company) is the final arbiter of acceptability. In the event of a tie on the Review Board, a coin toss will determine the outcome.

EXERCISE SCHEDULE	Unit Time	Total Time
1. Form groups, organizations, and assign workplaces Groups should have between 6 and 14 members (if there are more than 11 or 12 persons in a group, assign one or two observers). Each group is a company.	2–5 min.	2–5 min.
2. Read "Background" Ask the instructor about any points that need clarification.	5 min.	10 min.
3. Design organizations Design your organizations using as many members as you see fit to produce your "words-in-sentences." You may want to consider the following: a. What is your objective? b. What technology would work here? c. What type of division of labor is effective? Assign one member of your group to serve on the Quality Review Board. This person may also take part in production runs.	7–15 min.	14–25 min.
4. Production Run #1 The instructor will hand each WIS company a sheet with a raw material word or phrase. When the instructor announces "Begin production," you are to manufacture as many words as possible and package them in sentences for delivery to the Quality Control Review Board. You will have 10 minutes. When the instructor announces "Stop production," you will have 30 seconds to deliver your output to the Quality Control Review Board. Output received after 30 seconds does not meet the delivery schedule and will not be counted.	7–10 min.	21–35 min.
5. Quality Review Board meets, evaluates output While that is going on, groups discuss what happened during the previous production run.	5–10 min.	26–45 min.
6. Companies evaluate performance and type of organization Groups may choose to restructure and reorganize for the next production run.	5–10 min.	31–55 min.
7. Production Run #2 (same as Production Run #1)	7–10 min.	38–65 min.
8. Quality Review Board meets Quality Review Board evaluates output while groups draw their organization charts (for Runs #1 and #2) on the board.	5–10 min.	43–75 min.
9. Class discussion Instructor leads discussion of exercise as a whole. Discuss the following questions: a. What were the companies' scores for Runs #1 and #2? b. What type of structure did the "winning" company have? Did it reorganize for Run #2? c. What type of task was there? Technology? Environment? d. What would Joan Woodward, Henry Mintzberg, Frederick Taylor, Lawrence and Lorsch, or Burns and Stalker say about WIS company organization?	7–15 min.	50–90 min.

SOURCE: "Words-in-Sentences Company" in Dorothy Marcic, *Organizational Behavior: Experiences and Cases,* 4th ed. (St. Paul: West, 1995), 303–305. Reprinted by permission.

14.2 DESIGN AND BUILD A CASTLE

This exercise is intended to give your group an opportunity to design an organization and produce a product.

Your group is one of three product-development teams working within the research and development division of the GTM (General Turret and Moat) Corporation. GTM has decided to enter new markets by expanding the product line to include fully designed and produced castles, rather than selling components to other companies, as it has in the past.

Each of the three teams has been asked to design a castle for the company to produce and sell. Given its limited resources, the company cannot put more than one design on the market. Therefore, the company will have to decide which of the three designs it will use and will discard the other two designs.

Your task is to develop and design a castle. You will have 45 minutes to produce a finished product. At the end of this period, several typical consumers, picked by scientific sampling techniques, will judge which is the best design. Before the consumers make their choice, each group will have one to two minutes to make a sales presentation.

Step 1. Each group is designated either 1, 2, or 3. The instructor will provide group members a memorandum appropriate for their group. One (or two for larger groups) observer is selected for each group. Observers read their materials.

Step 2. Groups design their organization in order to complete their goal.

Step 3. Each group designs its own castle and draws it on newsprint.

Step 4. "Typical consumers" (may be observers) tour building locations and hear sales pitches. Judges caucus to determine winner.

Step 5. Groups meet again and write up their central goal statement. They also write the organization chart on newsprint with the goal written beneath. These are posted around the room.

Step 6. Instructor leads a class discussion on how the different memos affected organization design. Which design seemed most effective for this task?

NOTE: Your instructor may allow more time and actually have you *build* the castles.

SOURCE: "Design and Build a Castle," from Dorothy Marcic and Richard C. Housley, *Organizational Behavior: Experiences and Cases* (St. Paul: West, 1989), 221–225. Reprinted by permission.

Organizational Culture

15

LEARNING OBJECTIVES

After reading this chapter, you should be able to do the following:

: 1. Describe organizational culture.

: 2. Critically evaluate the roles of the three levels of culture.

: 3. Evaluate the four functions of culture within an organization.

: 4. Explain the relationship between organizational culture and performance.

: 5. Contrast the characteristics of adaptive and nonadaptive cultures.

: 6. Describe five ways leaders reinforce organizational culture.

: 7. Describe the three stages of organizational socialization and the ways culture is communicated in each step.

: 8. Explain actions managers can take to change organizational culture.

THINKING AHEAD :: WHOLE FOODS MARKET, INC.

A Culture of Democratic Capitalism

"Whole Foods Market's culture was founded on shared fate, fairness in the workplace, open communication and team member excellence and happiness."[1] Such descriptions of one of the most revolutionary experiments in the American business model—Whole Foods Market, Inc.—abound. Everyone at Whole Foods, right from founder and CEO John Mackey down to individual team members (what employees are known as), refers to the culture of shared values that embodies the success of Whole Foods. This organic retailing giant was founded in Austin, Texas, in 1980 and has rapidly become one of the fastest growing and consistently successful businesses in America. Throughout its short history, the culture at Whole Foods has been driven by the highest quality standards, sustainable agriculture, empowerment and continuous development of team members, and a commitment to the planet. All this might sound a little too touchy-feely to critics of Whole Foods, who have long held that such ideals have no place in the cutthroat world of the grocery business.

Yet Whole Foods has managed to remain profitable ever since its inception and has consistently ranked in *Fortune*'s 100 Best Companies to Work For in America since 1998. Of particular note in this regard is the company's commitment to its employees encapsulated in its mission statement as a commitment to team member excellence. This is brought about by empowerment, self-responsibility for all successes and failures, self-directed teams, open and timely information sharing, incremental progress, and collective fate. This last value is particularly interesting because it suggests that every team member is responsible for the collective fate of the company as a whole; hence, team members have a say in the important decisions made in the company.[2]

THE KEY ROLE OF ORGANIZATIONAL CULTURE

The concept of organizational culture has its roots in cultural anthropology. Just as there are cultures in larger human society, there seem to be cultures within organizations. These cultures are similar to societal cultures. They are shared, communicated through symbols, and passed down from generation to generation of employees.

The concept of cultures in organizations was alluded to as early as the Hawthorne studies, which described work group culture. The topic came into its own during the early 1970s, when managers and researchers alike began to search for keys to survival for organizations in a competitive and turbulent environment. Then, in the early 1980s, several books on corporate culture were published, including Deal and Kennedy's *Corporate Cultures*,[3] Ouchi's *Theory Z*,[4] and Peters and Waterman's *In Search of Excellence*.[5] These books found wide audiences, and research began in earnest on the elusive topic of organizational cultures. Executives indicated that these cultures were real and could be managed.[6]

: **1.** Describe organizational culture.

CULTURE AND ITS LEVELS

Many definitions of ***organizational culture*** have been proposed. Most of them agree that there are several levels of culture and that these levels differ in terms of their visibility and their ability to be changed. The definition adopted in this

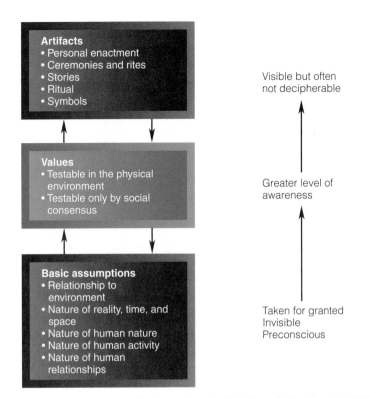

SOURCE: From Edgar H. Schein, *Organizational Culture and Leadership: A Dynamic View.* Copyright © 1985 Jossey-Bass Inc. Reprinted by permission of Jossey-Bass, Inc., a subsidiary of John Wiley & Sons, Inc.

FIGURE 15.1

Levels of Organizational Culture

chapter is that *organizational (corporate) culture* is a pattern of basic assumptions that are considered valid and that are taught to new members as the way to perceive, think, and feel in the organization.[7]

Edgar Schein, in his comprehensive book on organizational culture and leadership, suggests that organizational culture has three levels. His view of culture is presented in Figure 15.1. The levels range from visible artifacts and creations to testable values to invisible and even preconscious basic assumptions. To achieve a complete understanding of an organization's culture, all three levels must be studied.

▨ ARTIFACTS

Symbols of culture in the physical and social work environment are called *artifacts*. They are the most visible and accessible level of culture. The key to understanding culture through artifacts lies in figuring out what they mean. Artifacts are also the most frequently studied manifestation of organizational culture, perhaps because of their accessibility. Among the artifacts of culture are personal enactment, ceremonies and rites, stories, rituals, and symbols.[8]

The corporate culture of Google, for example, is apparent in the offices of Google Headquarters located in Mountain View, California. The lobby is replete with lava lamps, pianos, and live searches on the Google search engine from around the world. The hallways house bikes and exercise machines, while office spaces are laid-back, featuring couches and occupied by dogs who go with their owners to work.[9]

organizational (corporate) culture
A pattern of basic assumptions that are considered valid and that are taught to new members as the way to perceive, think, and feel in the organization.

2. Critically evaluate the roles of the three levels of culture.

artifacts
Symbols of culture in the physical and social work environment.

PERSONAL ENACTMENT

Culture can be understood, in part, through an examination of the behavior of organization members. Personal enactment is behavior that reflects the organization's values. In particular, personal enactment by the top managers provides insight into these values. Steve Irby is the founder and CEO of Stillwater Designs, the company that created Kicker audio speakers. He values good relationships and believes that people are the most important part of his company. Irby builds trust with his employees by sharing the financial results of the business each month. The employees know that if monthly sales are higher than the sales in the same month of the previous year, Irby will hold a cookout for the employees on the following Friday. Irby and the general manager always do the cooking. Eskimo Joe's, a Stillwater, Oklahoma, restaurant chain and one of the largest t-shirt sellers in the United States, could probably have become a national franchise years ago. But founder Stan Clark, who began as co-owner of the once tiny bar, says his intent is to become better, not bigger.[10]

Modeled behavior is a powerful learning tool for employees, as Bandura's social learning theory demonstrated.[11] As we saw in Chapter 5, individuals learn vicariously by observing others' behavior and patterning their own behavior similarly. Culture can be an important leadership tool. Managerial behavior can clarify what is important and coordinate the work of employees, in effect negating the need for close supervision.[12]

CEREMONIES AND RITES

Relatively elaborate sets of activities that are enacted time and again on important occasions are known as organizational ceremonies and rites.[13] These occasions provide opportunities to reward and recognize employees whose behavior is congruent with the values of the company. Ceremonies and rites send a message that individuals who both espouse and exhibit corporate values are heroes to be admired.

The ceremonies also bond organization members together. Southwestern Bell (now part of SBC Communications) emphasized the importance of management training to the company. Training classes were kicked off by a high-ranking executive (a rite of renewal), and completion of the classes was signaled by a graduation ceremony (a rite of passage). Six kinds of rites in organizations have been identified:[14]

1. *Rites of passage* show that an individual's status has changed. Retirement dinners are an example.

2. *Rites of enhancement* reinforce the achievement of individuals. An example is the awarding of certificates to sales contest winners.

3. *Rites of renewal* emphasize change in the organization and commitment to learning and growth. An example is the opening of a new corporate training center.

4. *Rites of integration* unite diverse groups or teams within the organization and renew commitment to the larger organization. Company functions such as annual picnics fall into this category.

5. *Rites of conflict reduction* focus on dealing with conflicts or disagreements that arise naturally in organizations. Examples are grievance hearings and the negotiation of union contracts.

6. *Rites of degradation* are used by some organizations to visibly punish persons who fail to adhere to values and norms of behavior. Some CEOs, for example, are replaced quite publicly for unethical conduct or for failure to achieve organizational goals. In some Japanese organizations, employees who perform poorly are given ribbons of shame as punishment.

Wal-Mart's annual meeting is an important cultural ceremony. Almost 20,000 shareholders, associates (the company's preferred term for employees), and analysts attend the Wal-Mart annual meeting. Celebrities such as Nolan Ryan, Trisha Yearwood, and Amy Grant are featured. Although the meeting doesn't begin until 10 A.M., people start arriving at 7 A.M. for the extravaganza held for the benefit of the associates. Because it is the primary vehicle for perpetuating Wal-Mart's culture, videos of the meeting are played in Wal-Mart stores to motivate associates who are unable to attend.

The annual meeting is like a big family reunion. Patriotism is a common theme. The associates hear stories and watch videos about Wal-Mart's "Buy American" program, which has rescued jobs in small towns and created new ones. Associates who go the "extra mile" for customers are recognized and rewarded. One associate delivered a Sega Genesis on his own time on Christmas Eve, and another group of employees replaced presents for a family whose home was burglarized. Each example points to the generosity and compassion of Wal-Mart associates.[15]

STORIES

Some researchers have argued that the most effective way to reinforce organizational values is through stories.[16] As they are told and retold, stories give meaning and identity to organizations and are especially helpful in orienting new employees. Part of the strength of organizational stories is that the listeners are left to draw their own conclusions—a powerful communication tool.[17]

Some corporate stories even transcend cultural and political boundaries. Visit the Web site of Wal-Mart China, and you will read the true story of Jeff, a pharmacist in Harrison, Arkansas, a small town deep in the Ozarks. When Jeff received an early morning weekend call telling him that a diabetic patient needed insulin, he quickly opened his pharmacy and filled the prescription.[18] While Arkansas and Beijing are worlds apart, stories such as this one help transfer Wal-Mart's corporate "personality" to its new Asian associates.

Research by Joanne Martin and her colleagues has indicated that certain themes appear in stories across different types of organizations:[19]

1. *Stories about the boss.* These stories may reflect whether the boss is "human" or how the boss reacts to mistakes.

2. *Stories about getting fired.* Events leading to employee firings are recounted.

3. *Stories about how the company deals with employees who have to relocate.* These stories relate to the company's actions toward employees who have to move—whether the company is helpful and takes family and other personal concerns into account.

4. *Stories about whether lower-level employees can rise to the top.* Often, these stories describe a person who started out at the bottom and eventually became the CEO.

5. *Stories about how the company deals with crisis situations.* The example of the client crisis at IBM shows how the company overcomes obstacles.

6. *Stories about how status considerations work when rules are broken.* When Tom Watson, Sr., was CEO of IBM, he was once confronted by a security guard because he was not wearing an ID badge.

These are the themes that can emerge when stories are passed down. The information from these stories serves to guide the behavior of organization members.

To be effective cultural tools, stories must be credible. You can't tell a story about your flat corporate hierarchy and then have reserved parking spaces for managers. Stories that aren't backed by reality can lead to cynicism and mistrust.

Effective stories, however, can reinforce culture and create renewed energy. Lucasfilm is the home of director and producer George Lucas and the birthplace of such blockbusters as *Star Wars* and *Forrest Gump*. Stories of the company's legendary accomplishments are used to reinforce the creative culture and to rally the troops. When Gail Currey, former head of the company's digital division, found her 300 designers were grumbling, she reminded them of how they did *Gump* when everyone else said it was impossible and what a hit the film was. The geniuses would then head back to their computers to add to the company's success.[20]

RITUALS

Everyday organizational practices that are repeated over and over are rituals. They are usually unwritten, but they send a clear message about "the way we do things around here." While some companies insist that people address each other by their titles (Mr., Mrs., Ms., Miss) and surnames to reinforce a professional image, others prefer that employees operate on a first-name basis—from the top manager on down. Hewlett-Packard values open communication, so its employees address one another by first names only.

In the fast-paced world of automotive manufacturing, the endless grind of the assembly line makes it tough for workers at most factories to imagine the person who will actually drive the car they are building. But at Saturn's Tennessee assembly plant, each car travels down the assembly line with the customer's name attached to it. And upon delivery, the customer is handed the keys and photographed by the dealer in a small ceremony commemorating the event. Not surprisingly, Saturn owners are among the most loyal in the industry.[21]

As everyday practices, rituals reinforce the organizational culture. Insiders who commonly practice the rituals may be unaware of their subtle influence, but outsiders recognize it easily.

SYMBOLS

Symbols communicate organizational culture by unspoken messages. Southwest Airlines has used symbols in several ways. During its early years, the airline emphasized its customer service value by using the heart symbol (the "love" airline) and love bites (peanuts). More recently, the airline has taken on the theme of fun. Flight attendants wear casual sports clothes in corporate colors. Low fares are "fun fares," and weekend getaways are "fun packs." Some aircraft are painted to resemble Shamu the whale, underscoring the fun image. At Krispy Kreme, customers look for the famous "Hot Doughnuts Now" sign.

Symbols are representative of organizational identity and membership to employees. Nike's trademark "swoosh" is proudly tattooed above the ankles of some Nike employees. Apple Computer employees readily identify themselves as "Apple People." Symbols are used to build solidarity in the organizational culture.[22]

Personal enactment, rites and ceremonies, stories, rituals, and symbols serve to reinforce the values that are the next level of culture.

◀◀ **think critically** ▶▶

Think about an organization where you have worked or are currently working. Analyze the role of artifacts, stories, rituals, and symbols in this organization.

■ VALUES

Values are the second, and deeper, level of culture. They reflect a person's underlying beliefs of what should be or should not be. Values are often consciously articulated, both in conversation and in a company's mission statement or annual report. However, there may be a difference between a company's *espoused values* (what the members say they value) and its *enacted values* (values reflected in the way the members actually behave).[23] Values also may be reflected in the behavior of individuals, which is an artifact of culture.

A firm's values and how it promotes and publicizes those values can also affect how workers feel about their jobs and themselves. A study of 180 managers looked at their employers' effectiveness in communicating concern for employees' welfare. Managers in organizations that consistently communicated concern for workers' well-being and that focused on treating employees fairly reported feeling better about themselves and their role in the organization.[24] The lesson? *Treat* employees like valuable team members, and they are more likely to *feel* like valuable team members.

Values underlie the adaptable and innovative culture at Levi Strauss. As guides for behavior, they are reinforced in the aspirations statement and in the reward system of the organization. Workforce diversity is valued at Levi Strauss. A former strong supporter of the Boy Scouts of America, the company discontinued its funding after the Scouts were shown to discriminate on the basis of sexual orientation. Mary Gross, a Levi Strauss spokesperson, expressed the company's position on valuing diversity: "One of the family values of this company is treating people who are different from you the same as you'd like to be treated. Tolerance is a pretty important family value."[25]

Some organizational cultures are characterized by values that support healthy lifestyle behaviors. When the workplace culture values worker health and psychological needs, there is enhanced potential for high performance and improved well-being.[26] Clif Bar, the energy bar maker, even has a 22-foot rock climbing wall in its corporate office.

When Harley-Davidson hires new customer service employees, they had better be ready to do more than just answer telephones. Working at Harley-Davidson is not just a job, it's about an entire subculture that revolves around Harleys. New employees are immersed in this culture, typically through working at a Harley owners' rally and taking demonstration rides. Over time, most employees become Harley riders or owners, which helps them provide better service to other Harley lovers.[27]

espoused values
What members of an organization say they value.

enacted values
Values reflected in the way individuals actually behave.

Charles S. Schwab Corporation, a financial services firm, is a model of a values-driven business. Its core organizational values are as follows:

> Be fair, empathetic, and responsive in serving our clients.

> Respect and reinforce our fellow employees and the power of teamwork.

> Strive relentlessly to innovate what we do and how we do it.

> Always earn and be worthy of our clients' trust.[28]

ASSUMPTIONS

assumptions

Deeply held beliefs that guide behavior and tell members of an organization how to perceive and think about things.

Assumptions are the deeply held beliefs that guide behavior and tell members of an organization how to perceive and think about things. As the deepest and most fundamental level of an organization's culture, according to Edgar Schein, they are the essence of culture. They are so strongly held that a member behaving in any fashion that would violate them would be unthinkable. Another characteristic of assumptions is that they are often unconscious. Organization members may not be aware of their assumptions and may be reluctant or unable to discuss them or change them.

While unconscious assumptions often guide a firm's actions and decisions, some companies are quite explicit in their assumptions about employees. Earthlink, an Internet service provider, includes several of these assumptions on its Web site. The firm assumes that people who are treated with respect will respond by giving their best. It also assumes that because life is about more than work, that its employees will have fun. And the firm sees competition as a normal, even healthy part of work, due in part to its assumption that competition helps individuals, teams, and firms raise their level of performance. Earthlink is so confident of these assumptions, it encourages visitors who believe it is not living up to these values to "call us on it."[29]

Now that you understand Schein's three levels of culture, you can use Challenge 15.1 to assess a culture you'd like to learn more about.

CHALLENGE 15.1

Analyzing the Three Levels of Culture

Select an organization you respect. Analyze its culture using the following dimensions:

The artifacts of _____'s culture are as follows:

Personal enactment:

Rites and ceremonies:

Stories:

Rituals:

Symbols:

The values embedded in _____'s culture are as follows:

The assumptions of _____'s culture are as follows:

1. On what information did you base your analysis?

2. How complete is your view of this organization's culture?

◢ FUNCTIONS AND EFFECTS OF ORGANIZATIONAL CULTURE

: 3. Evaluate the four functions of culture within an organization.

In an organization, culture serves four basic functions. First, culture provides a sense of identity to members and increases their commitment to the organization.[30] When employees internalize the values of the company, they find their work intrinsically rewarding and identify with their fellow workers. Motivation is enhanced, and employees are more committed.[31]

Second, culture is a sense-making device for organization members. It provides a way for employees to interpret the meaning of organizational events.[32] Leaders can use organizational symbols like corporate logos as sense-making devices to help employees understand the changing nature of their organizational identity. This is specifically so in an environment that is constantly changing.[33] Sometimes symbols can remain the same to ensure that some things stay constant despite changing conditions; other times symbols may have to change to reflect the new culture in the organization.

Third, culture reinforces the values in the organization. The culture at SSM Health Care emphasizes patient care and continuous improvement. The St. Louis-based company, which owns and manages 21 acute care hospitals in four states, values compassionate, holistic, high-quality care. SSM was the first health care organization ever to win the Baldrige Quality Award.

Finally, culture serves as a control mechanism for shaping behavior. Norms that guide behavior are part of culture. If the norm the company wants to promote is teamwork, then its culture must reinforce that norm. The company's culture must be characterized by open communication, cooperation between teams, and integration of teams.[34] Culture can also be used as a powerful tool to discourage dysfunctional and deviant behaviors in organizations. Norms can send clear messages that certain behaviors are unacceptable.[35]

The effects of organizational culture are hotly debated by organizational behaviorists and researchers. It seems that managers attest strongly to the positive effects of culture in organizations, but it is difficult to quantify these effects. John Kotter and James Heskett have reviewed three theories about the relationship between organizational culture and performance and the evidence that either supports or refutes these theories.[36] The three are the strong culture perspective, the fit perspective, and the adaptation perspective.

▮ THE STRONG CULTURE PERSPECTIVE

The strong culture perspective states that organizations with "strong" cultures perform better than other organizations.[37] A *strong culture* is an organizational culture with a consensus on the values that drive the company and with an intensity that is recognizable even to outsiders. Thus, a strong culture is deeply held and widely shared. It also is highly resistant to change. One example of a strong culture is IBM's. Its culture is one we are all familiar with: conservative, with a loyal workforce and an emphasis on customer service.

strong culture
An organizational culture with a consensus on the values that drive the company and with an intensity that is recognizable even to outsiders.

: 4. Explain the relationship between organizational culture and performance.

Strong cultures are thought to facilitate performance for three reasons. First, these cultures are characterized by goal alignment; that is, all employees share common goals. Second, strong cultures create a high level of motivation because of the values shared by the members. Third, strong cultures provide control without the oppressive effects of a bureaucracy.

To test the strong culture hypothesis, Kotter and Heskett selected 207 firms from a wide variety of industries. They used a questionnaire to calculate a culture strength index for each firm, and they correlated that index with the firm's economic performance over a 12-year period. They concluded that strong cultures were associated with positive long-term economic performance, but only modestly.

There are also two perplexing questions about the strong culture perspectives. First, what can be said about evidence showing that strong economic performance can create strong cultures, rather than the reverse? Second, what if the strong culture leads the firm down the wrong path? Sears, for example, is an organization with a strong culture, but in the 1980s, it focused inward, ignoring competition and consumer preferences and damaging its performance. Changing Sears' strong but stodgy culture has been a tough task, with financial performance only recently showing an upward trend.[38]

THE FIT PERSPECTIVE

The "fit" perspective argues that a culture is good only if it fits the industry or the firm's strategy. For example, a culture that values a traditional hierarchical structure and stability would not work well in the computer manufacturing industry, which demands fast response and a lean, flat organization. Three particular characteristics of an industry may affect culture: the competitive environment, customer requirements, and societal expectations.[39] In the computer industry, firms face a highly competitive environment, customers who require highly reliable products, and a society that expects state-of-the-art technology and high-quality service.

A study of 12 large U.S. firms indicated that cultures consistent with industry conditions help managers make better decisions. It also indicated that cultures need not change as long as the industry doesn't change. If the industry does change, however, many cultures change too slowly to avoid negative effects on firms' performance.[40]

The fit perspective is useful in explaining short-term performance but not long-term performance. It also indicates that it is difficult to change culture quickly, especially if the culture is widely shared and deeply held. But it doesn't explain how firms can adapt to environmental change.

THE ADAPTATION PERSPECTIVE

adaptive culture
An organizational culture that encourages confidence and risk taking among employees, has leadership that produces change, and focuses on the changing needs of customers.

The third theory about culture and performance is the adaptation perspective. Its theme is that only cultures that help organizations adapt to environmental change are associated with excellent performance. An *adaptive culture* is a culture that encourages confidence and risk taking among employees,[41] has leadership that produces change,[42] and focuses on the changing needs of customers.[43] 3M is a company with an adaptive culture in that it encourages new product ideas from all levels within the company.

To test the adaptation perspective, Kotter and Heskett interviewed industry analysts about the cultures of 22 firms. The contrast between adaptive cultures and nonadaptive cultures was striking. The results of the study are summarized in Table 15.1.

5. Contrast the characteristics of adaptive and non-adaptive cultures.

Adaptive cultures facilitate change to meet the needs of three groups of constituents: stockholders, customers, and employees. Nonadaptive cultures are

	ADAPTIVE ORGANIZATIONAL CULTURES	NONADAPTIVE ORGANIZATIONAL CULTURES
Core values	Most managers care deeply about customers, stockholders, and employees. They also strongly value people and processes that can create useful change (e.g., leadership up and down the management hierarchy).	Most managers care mainly about themselves, their immediate work group, or some product (or technology) associated with that work group. They value the orderly and risk-reducing management process much more highly than leadership initiatives.
Common behavior	Managers pay close attention to all their constituencies, especially customers, and initiate change when needed to serve their legitimate interests, even if that entails taking some risks.	Managers tend to behave somewhat insularly, politically, and bureaucratically. As a result, they do not change their strategies quickly to adjust to or take advantage of changes in their business environments.

TABLE 15.1

Adaptive Versus Nonadaptive Organizational Cultures

characterized by cautious management that tries to protect its own interests. Adaptive firms showed significantly better long-term economic performance in Kotter and Heskett's study. One contrast that can be made is between Hewlett-Packard (HP), a high performer, and Xerox, a lower performer. The industry analysts viewed HP as valuing excellent leadership more than Xerox did and as valuing all three key constituencies more than Xerox did. Economic performance from 1977 through 1988 supported this difference: HP's index of annual net income growth was 40.2, as compared to Xerox's 13.1. Kotter and Heskett concluded that the cultures that promote long-term performance are the most adaptive. Given that high-performing cultures are adaptive ones, it is important to know how managers can develop adaptive cultures. In the next section, we will examine the leader's role in managing organizational culture.

◪ THE LEADER'S ROLE IN SHAPING AND REINFORCING CULTURE

According to Edgar Schein, leaders play crucial roles in shaping and reinforcing culture.[44] The five most important elements in managing culture are (1) what leaders pay attention to, (2) how leaders react to crises, (3) how leaders behave, (4) how leaders allocate rewards, and (5) how leaders hire and fire individuals.

The Enron Corporation fiasco illustrates each of these roles. "Enron ethics" is the term applied to the gap between words and deeds, and it illustrates that leader behavior deeply affects organizational culture.[45] Enron created deceptive partnerships and used questionable accounting practices to maintain its investment-grade rating. Employees recorded earnings before they were realized; they thought this

6. Describe five ways leaders reinforce organizational culture.

was merely recording them early, not wrongly. Enron's culture was shaping the ethical boundaries of its employees, and Enron executives bent the rules for personal gain.

■ WHAT LEADERS PAY ATTENTION TO

Leaders in an organization communicate their priorities, values, and beliefs through the themes that consistently emerge from what they focus on. These themes are reflected in what they notice, comment on, measure, and control. If leaders are consistent in what they pay attention to, measure, and control, employees receive clear signals about what is important in the organization. If, however, leaders are inconsistent, employees spend a lot of time trying to decipher and find meaning in the inconsistent signals.

Enron leader Jeffrey Skilling paid attention to money and profit at all costs. Employees could take as much vacation as they wanted as long as they were delivering results; they could deliberately break company rules as long as they were making money.

■ HOW LEADERS REACT TO CRISES

The way leaders deal with crises communicates a powerful message about culture. Emotions are heightened during a crisis, and learning is intense.

Difficult economic times present crises for many companies and illustrate their different values. Some organizations do everything possible to prevent laying off workers. Others may claim that employees are important but quickly institute major layoffs at the first signal of an economic downturn. Employees may perceive that the company shows its true colors in a crisis and thus may pay careful attention to the reactions of their leaders. For example, critics have always predicted that the success of Whole Foods will be short lived and cap out at a certain point because of its insanely high prices. In fact, they point to some jokes that suggest that Whole Foods is sometimes referred to as "Whole Paycheck" as it is so very expensive. However, John Mackey has always proclaimed that not every consumer is driven by the lowest cost appeal and Whole Foods has repeatedly capitalized on this fact.[46]

With mergers and acquisitions, how the leader reacts to change, transparency of the procedures used, and communication quality affect how followers perceive change and ultimately accept any associated changes in the organizational culture.[47]

◄◄think critically►►

Think about any leader that you admire. This could be your boss, CEO, peer group leader, or the coach of your university's athletic team. How does this leader react to crises? What does this leader's behavior do to the culture of that organization? Can this leader change his/her organization's culture through his/her actions/words?

■ HOW LEADERS BEHAVE

Through role modeling, teaching, and coaching, leaders reinforce the values that support the organizational culture. Employees often emulate leaders' behavior and look to the leaders for cues to appropriate behavior. Many companies are encouraging employees to be more entrepreneurial—to take more initiative and be more innovative in their jobs. A study showed that if managers want employees to be more entrepreneurial, they must demonstrate such behaviors themselves.[48] This is the case with any cultural value. Employees observe the behavior of leaders to find out what the organization values.

The behavior of Enron's managers spoke volumes; they broke the law as they created fake partnerships. They ignored and then denied that problems existed. While employees were unable to dump their Enron stocks, managers were hastily getting rid of their shares, all the while telling employees that the company would be fine.

HOW LEADERS ALLOCATE REWARDS

To ensure that values are accepted, leaders should reward behavior that is consistent with the values. Some companies, for example, may claim that they use a pay-for-performance system that distributes rewards on the basis of performance. When the time comes for raises, however, the increases are awarded according to length of service with the company. Imagine the feelings of a high-performing newcomer who has heard leaders espouse the value of rewarding individual performance and then receives only a tiny raise.

Some companies may value teamwork. They form cross-functional teams and empower these teams to make important decisions. However, when performance is appraised, the criteria for rating employees focus on individual performance. This sends a confusing signal to employees about the company's culture: Is individual performance valued, or is teamwork the key?

At Enron, employees were rewarded only if they produced consistent results, with little regard for ethics. Managers were given extremely rich bonuses to keep the stock price up at any cost. Performance reviews were done in public, and poor performers were ridiculed.

HOW LEADERS HIRE AND FIRE INDIVIDUALS

A powerful way that leaders reinforce culture is through the selection of newcomers to the organization. Leaders often unconsciously look for individuals who are similar to current organizational members in terms of values and assumptions. Some companies hire individuals on the recommendation of a current employee; this tends to perpetuate the culture because the new employees typically hold similar values. Promotion-from-within policies also serve to reinforce organizational culture. Jeffrey Schwartz, CEO of Timberland, has a unique way of hiring people. He has his recruiter call the applicant in advance and have them wear anything they feel passionately about other than Timberland shoes. Senior applicants go through a day of community service with Timberland executives because Schwartz claims that anyone can be smarter than him in an interview, but service brings out the real person and this is who they try to hire.[49] With the advent of electronic recruitment practices, applicant perceptions of organizational culture are shaped by what the organization advertises on their recruitment Web site. Typical perception-shaping mechanisms are organizational values, policies, awards, and goals.[50]

The way a company fires an employee and the rationale behind the firing also communicate the culture. Some companies deal with poor performers by trying to find a place within the organization where they can perform better and make a contribution. Other companies seem to operate under the philosophy that those who cannot perform are out quickly.

The reasons for terminations may not be directly communicated to other employees, but curiosity leads to speculation. An employee who displays unethical behavior and is caught may simply be reprimanded even though such behavior is clearly against the organization's values. Other employees may view this as a failure to reinforce the values within the organization.

Enron hired employees who had aggressiveness, greed, a desire to win at all costs, and a willingness to break rules. It fired nonproductive employees, using a "rank and yank" system whereby the bottom 15–20 percent of employees were let go each year. Peers were required to rank each other, which led to cutthroat competition and extreme distrust among employees.

In summary, leaders play a critical role in shaping and reinforcing organizational culture. The Enron case provides an illustration of how powerful, and potentially damaging, that influence can be. The lesson for future managers is to create a positive culture through what they pay attention to, how they react to crises, how they behave, the way they allocate rewards, and how they hire and fire employees. Research results from a sample of finance professionals in Greece seem to support this view. Transformational leaders create a more adaptive culture which in turn affects business unit performance.[51]

: **7.** Describe the three stages of organizational socialization and the ways culture is communicated in each step.

organizational socialization
The process by which newcomers are transformed from outsiders to participating, effective members of the organization.

anticipatory socialization
The first socialization stage, which encompasses all of the learning that takes place prior to the newcomer's first day on the job.

🔳 ORGANIZATIONAL SOCIALIZATION

We have seen that leaders play key roles in shaping an organization's culture. Another process that perpetuates culture is the way it is handed down from generation to generation of employees. Newcomers learn the culture through *organizational socialization*—the process by which newcomers are transformed from outsiders to participating, effective members of the organization.[52] The process is also a vehicle for bringing newcomers into the organizational culture. As we saw earlier, cultural socialization begins with the careful selection of newcomers who are likely to reinforce the organizational culture.[53] Once selected, newcomers pass through the socialization process.

▮ THE STAGES OF THE SOCIALIZATION PROCESS

The organizational socialization process is generally described as having three stages: anticipatory socialization, encounter, and change and acquisition. Figure 15.2 presents a model of the process and the key concerns at each stage of it.[54] It also describes the outcomes of the process, which will be discussed in the next section of the chapter.

ANTICIPATORY SOCIALIZATION

Anticipatory socialization, the first stage, encompasses all of the learning that takes place prior to the newcomer's first day on the job. It includes the newcomer's expectations. The two key concerns at this stage are realism and congruence.

Stages of socialization

FIGURE 15.2

The Organizational Socialization Process: Stages and Outcomes

SOURCE: Reprinted from *Organizational Dynamics,* Autumn 1989, "An Ethical Weather Report: Assessing the Organization's Ethical Climate" by John B. Cullen, et al. Copyright © 1989, with permission from Elsevier Science.

Realism is the degree to which a newcomer holds realistic expectations about the job and about the organization. One thing newcomers should receive information about during entry into the organization is the culture. Information about values at this stage can help newcomers begin to construct a scheme for interpreting their organizational experiences. A deeper understanding of the organization's culture will be possible through time and experience in the organization.

There are two types of *congruence* between an individual and an organization: congruence between the individual's abilities and the demands of the job, and the fit between the organization's values and the individual's values. Organizations disseminate information about their values through their Web pages, annual reports, and recruitment brochures.[55] Value congruence is particularly important for organizational culture. It is also important in terms of newcomer adjustment. Newcomers whose values match the company's values are more satisfied with their new jobs, adjust more quickly, and say they intend to remain with the firm longer.[56]

ENCOUNTER

The second stage of socialization, *encounter*, is when newcomers learn the tasks associated with the job, clarify their roles, and establish new relationships at work. This stage commences on the first day at work and is thought to encompass the first six to nine months on the new job. Newcomers face task demands, role demands, and interpersonal demands during this period.

Task demands involve the actual work performed. Learning to perform tasks is related to the organization's culture. In some organizations, newcomers are given considerable latitude to experiment with new ways to do the job, and creativity is valued. In others, newcomers are expected to learn the established procedures for

encounter

The second socialization stage in which the newcomer learns the tasks associated with the job, clarifies roles, and establishes new relationships at work.

their tasks. Early experiences with trying to master task demands can affect employees' entire careers. Auditors, for example, are often forced to choose between being thorough, on one hand, and being fast in completing their work, on the other. By pressuring auditors in this way, firms often set themselves up for problems later, when these pressures may lead auditors to make less-than-ethical decisions.

Role demands involve the expectations placed on newcomers. Newcomers may not know exactly what is expected of them (role ambiguity) or may receive conflicting expectations from other individuals (role conflict). The way newcomers approach these demands depends in part on the culture of the organization. Are newcomers expected to operate with considerable uncertainty, or is the manager expected to clarify the newcomers' roles? Some cultures even put newcomers through considerable stress in the socialization process, including humility-inducing experiences, so newcomers will be more open to accepting the firm's values and norms. Long hours, tiring travel schedules, and an overload of work are part of some socialization practices.

Interpersonal demands arise from relationships at work. Politics, leadership style, and group pressure are interpersonal demands. All of them reflect the values and assumptions that operate within the organization. Most organizations have basic assumptions about the nature of human relationships. The Korean chaebol LG Group strongly values harmony in relationships and in society, and its decision-making policy emphasizes unanimity.

In the encounter stage, the expectations formed in anticipatory socialization may clash with the realities of the job. It is a time of facing the task, role, and interpersonal demands of the new job.

CHANGE AND ACQUISITION

change and acquisition
The third socialization stage, in which the newcomer begins to master the demands of the job.

In the third and final stage of socialization, *change and acquisition*, newcomers begin to master the demands of the job. They become proficient at managing their tasks, clarifying and negotiating their roles, and engaging in relationships at work. The time when the socialization process is completed varies widely, depending on the individual, the job, and the organization. The end of the process is signaled by newcomers being considered by themselves and others as organizational insiders.

■ OUTCOMES OF SOCIALIZATION

Newcomers who are successfully socialized should exhibit good performance, high job satisfaction, and the intention to stay with the organization. In addition, they should exhibit low levels of distress symptoms.[57] High levels of organizational commitment are also marks of successful socialization.[58] This commitment is facilitated throughout the socialization process by the communication of values into which newcomers can buy. Successful socialization is also signaled by mutual influence; that is, the newcomers have made adjustments in the job and organization to accommodate their knowledge and personalities. Newcomers are expected to leave their mark on the organization and not be completely conforming.

When socialization is effective, newcomers understand and adopt the organization's values and norms. This ensures that the company's culture, including its central values, survives. It also provides employees a context for interpreting and responding to things that happen at work, and it ensures a shared framework of understanding among employees.[59]

Newcomers adopt the company's norms and values more quickly when they receive positive support from organizational insiders. Sometimes this is accomplished through informal social gatherings.[60]

■ SOCIALIZATION AS CULTURAL COMMUNICATION

Socialization is a powerful cultural communication tool. While the transmission of information about cultural artifacts is relatively easy, the transmission of values is more difficult. The communication of organizational assumptions is almost impossible, since organization members themselves may not be consciously aware of them.

The primary purpose of socialization is the transmission of core values to new organization members.[61] Newcomers are exposed to these values through the role models they interact with, the training they receive, and the behavior they observe being rewarded and punished. Newcomers are vigilant observers, seeking clues to the organization's culture and consistency in the cultural messages they receive. If they are expected to adopt these values, it is essential that the message reflect the underlying values of the organization.

One company known for its culture is The Walt Disney Company. Disney transmits its culture to employees through careful selection, socialization, and training. The Disney culture is built around customer service, and its image serves as a filtering process for applicants. Peer interviews are used to learn how applicants interact with each other. Disney tries to secure a good fit between employee values and the organization's culture. To remind employees of the image they are trying to project, employees are referred to as "cast members" and they occupy a "role." They work either "on stage" or "backstage" and wear "costumes," rather than uniforms. Disney operates its own "universities," which are attended by all new employees. Once trained at a Disney university, cast members are paired with role models to continue their learning on-site.

Companies such as Disney use the socialization process to communicate messages about organizational culture. Both individuals and organizations can take certain actions to ensure the success of the socialization process.

◨ CHANGING ORGANIZATIONAL CULTURE

Changing situations may require changes in the existing culture of an organization. With rapid environmental changes such as globalization, workforce diversity, and technological innovation, the fundamental assumptions and basic values that drive the organization may need to be altered. One particular situation that may require cultural change is a merger or acquisition. The blending of two distinct organizational cultures may prove difficult.

Despite good-faith efforts, combining cultures is difficult. When dignified, established media giant Time Warner merged with free-wheeling Internet upstart America Online in 2001, few could imagine the fireworks that would result when these two "oil and water" firms tried to mix. Typical of the conflicts that followed was a client dinner in which AOL executive Neil Davis horrified Time Warner executives by describing how AOL preferred to handle weakened competitors.

Taking a steak knife from the table, Davis raised his arm and drove the knife into the table top, explaining that, "What we like to do to a competitor that is damaged is drive the knife in their heart." The shocked client ultimately declined to buy ads on AOL, and the entire merger was eventually deemed a multibillion-dollar failure due, at least in part, to the culture clash between the two partners.[62]

Alterations in culture may also be required when an organization employs people from different countries. Research indicates that some organizational cultures actually enhance differences in national cultures.[63] One study compared foreign employees working in a multinational organization with employees working in different organizations within their own countries. The assumption was that the employees from various countries working for the same multinational organization would be more similar than employees working in diverse organizations in their native countries. The results were surprising, in that there were significantly greater differences among the employees of the multinational than among managers working for different companies within their native countries. In the multinational, Swedes became more Swedish, Americans became more American, and so forth. It appears that employees enhance their national culture traditions even when working within a single organizational culture.[64] This is more likely to occur when diversity is moderate. When diversity is very high, employees are more likely to develop a shared identity in the organization's culture instead of relying on their own national culture.[65]

Changing an organization's culture is feasible but difficult.[66] One reason for the difficulty is that assumptions—the deepest level of culture—are often unconscious. As such, they are often nonconfrontable and nondebatable. Another reason for the difficulty is that culture is deeply ingrained and behavioral norms and rewards are well learned.[67] In a sense, employees must unlearn the old norms before they can learn new ones. Managers who want to change the culture should look first to the ways culture is maintained.

8. Explain actions managers can take to change organizational culture.

A model for cultural change that summarizes the interventions managers can use is presented in Figure 15.3. In this model, the numbers represent the actions managers can take. There are two basic approaches to changing the existing culture: (1) helping current members buy into a new set of values (actions 1, 2, and 3); or (2) adding newcomers and socializing them into the organization and removing current members as appropriate (actions 4 and 5).[68]

The first action is to change behavior in the organization. Even if behavior does change, however, this change is not sufficient for cultural change to occur. Behavior is an artifact (level 1) of culture. Individuals may change their behavior but not the values that drive it. They may rationalize, "I'm only doing this because my manager wants me to."

Therefore, managers must use action 2, which is to examine the justifications for the changed behavior. Are employees buying into the new set of values, or are they just complying?

The third action, cultural communication, is extremely important. All of the artifacts (personal enactment, stories, rites and ceremonies, rituals, and symbols) must send a consistent message about the new values and beliefs. It is crucial that the communication be credible; that is, managers must live the new values and not just talk about them. The two remaining actions (4 and 5) involve shaping the workforce to fit the intended culture. First, the organization can revise its selection

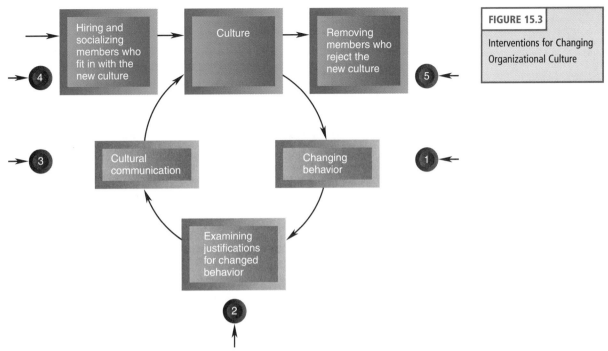

SOURCE: From Vijay Sathe, "How to Decipher and Change Corporate Culture," Chap. 13 in *Gaining Control of the Corporate Culture* (R. H. Kilmann et al., eds.) Fig. 1, p. 245. Copyright © 1985 Jossey-Bass, Inc. Reprinted by permission of Jossey-Bass, Inc., a subsidiary of John Wiley & Sons, Inc.

strategies to more accurately reflect the new culture. Second, the organization can identify individuals who resist the cultural change or who are no longer comfortable with the values in the organization. Reshaping the workforce should not involve a ruthless pursuit of nonconforming employees; it should be a gradual and subtle change that takes considerable time. Changing personnel in the organization is a lengthy process; it cannot be done effectively in a short period of time without considerable problems.

Evaluating the success of cultural change may be best done by looking at behavior. Cultural change can be assumed to be successful if the behavior is intrinsically motivated—on "automatic pilot." If the new behavior would persist even if rewards were not present, and if the employees have internalized the new value system, then the behavior is probably intrinsically motivated. If employees automatically respond to a crisis in ways consistent with the corporate culture, then the cultural change effort can be deemed successful.

One organization that has changed its culture is AT&T. In 1984, the courts ordered the breakup of AT&T. Prior to the breakup, the company operated in a stable environment with low levels of uncertainty. The organization was a highly structured bureaucracy. The culture emphasized lifetime employment, promotion from within, and loyalty. AT&T faced minimal competition, and it offered individual security. When the courts ordered AT&T to divest its Bell operating companies, the old culture was no longer effective. The company had to move toward a culture that holds individuals accountable for their performance. Change at AT&T was painful and slow, but it was necessary for the company to be able to operate in the new competitive environment.[69] Changing environments may bring about changes in organizational culture.

Given the current business environment, managers may want to focus on three particular cultural modifications: (1) support for a global view of business, (2) reinforcement of ethical behavior, and (3) empowerment of employees to excel in product and service quality.

◼ DEVELOPING A GLOBAL ORGANIZATIONAL CULTURE

The values that drive the organizational culture should support a global view of the company and its efforts. To do so, the values should be clear to everyone involved so that everyone understands them. The values should also be strongly supported at the top. Management should embody the shared values and reward employees who support the global view. Finally, the values should be consistent over time. Consistent values give an organization a unifying theme that competitors may be unable to emulate.[70]

Global corporations suffer from the conflicting pressures of centralization and decentralization. An overarching corporate culture that integrates the decentralized subsidiaries in locations around the world can be an asset in the increasingly competitive global marketplace.

Following are six specific guidelines for managers who want to create a global culture:[71]

1. Create a clear and simple mission statement. A shared mission can unite individuals from diverse cultural backgrounds.

2. Create systems that ensure an effective flow of information. Coordination councils and global task forces can be used to ensure that information flows throughout the geographically dispersed organization are consistent.

3. Create "matrix minds" among managers; that is, broaden managers' minds to allow them to think globally. IBM does this through temporary overseas assignments. Managers with international experience share that experience when they return to the home organization.

4. Develop global career paths. This means ensuring not only that home country executives go overseas but also that executives from other countries rotate into service in the home office.

5. Use cultural differences as a major asset. The former Digital Equipment Corporation (now part of Hewlett-Packard), for example, transferred its research and development functions to Italy to take advantage of the free-flowing Italian management style that encouraged creativity. Its manufacturing operations went to Germany, which offered a more systematic management style.

6. Implement worldwide management education and team development programs. Unified training efforts that emphasize corporate values can help establish a shared identity among employees.

These guidelines are specifically aimed at multinational organizations that want to create a global corporate culture, but other organizations can also benefit from them. Companies that want to broaden employees' views or to use the diversity of their workforce as a resource will find several of these recommendations advantageous.

■ DEVELOPING AN ETHICAL ORGANIZATIONAL CULTURE

While a majority of U.S. firms have rushed to create and publicize codes of ethics in an effort to help their employees discern right from wrong, the impact of these codes is not always as positive as might be expected. While the implementation of formal ethics guidelines might be expected to improve ethical behavior, some studies have shown the exact opposite, with institution of formal ethics codes actually leading to less ethical behavior among employees. While the reasons for this are not clear, it appears that in some cases employees see the code of ethics as simply a management showpiece, leading to cynicism and resentment. In other cases, a heavy reliance on a strict set of rules may reduce the perceived need for employees to think about and be involved in ethical decision making, leading to inferior choices in the long run.[72]

The organizational culture, however, can have profound effects on the ethical behavior of organization members.[73] When a company's culture promotes ethical norms, individuals behave accordingly. Managers can encourage ethical behavior by being good role models for employees. They can institute the philosophy that ethical behavior makes good business sense and puts the company in congruence with the larger values of society.[74] Managers can also communicate that rationalizations for unethical behavior are not tolerated. For example, some salespersons justify padding their expense accounts because everyone else does it. Declaring these justifications illegitimate sends a clear message about the lack of tolerance for such behavior.

Trust is another key to effectively managing ethical behavior, especially in cultures that encourage whistle-blowing (as we saw in Chapter 2). Employees must trust that whistle-blowers will be protected, that procedures used to investigate ethical problems will be fair, and that management will take action to solve problems that are uncovered.

At John Deere & Company, a simple idea guides the firm's ethics and decision making: "No smoke, no mirrors, no tricks: just right down the middle of the field," as Robert Lane, chairman and CEO, puts it. John Deere's decision to donate a multimillion-dollar parcel of land to a university, rather than selling it to a developer, demonstrates its values and is one of the reasons the firm made the top 10 in *Business Ethics* magazine's list of the "100 Best Corporate Citizens for 2004."[75]

The reasons most often cited for unethical corporate conduct are interesting.[76] They include the belief that a behavior is not really unethical, that it is in the organization's best interest, that it will not be discovered, and that the organization will support it because it offers a good outcome for the organization. An ethical corporate culture can eliminate the viability of these excuses by clearly communicating the boundaries of ethical conduct, selecting employees who support the ethical culture, rewarding organization members who exhibit ethical behavior, and conspicuously punishing members who engage in unethical behavior.

Organizations that seek to encourage ethical behavior can do so by using their organizational culture. By completing Challenge 15.2, you can assess the ethical culture of an organization you're familiar with.

CHALLENGE 15.2

Organizational Culture and Ethics

Think about the organization you currently work for or one you know something about and complete the following Ethical Climate Questionnaire:

Use the scale below and write the number that best represents your answer in the space next to each item.

To what extent are the following statements true about your company?

Completely false	Mostly false	Somewhat false	Somewhat true	Mostly true	Completely true
0	1	2	3	4	5

_____ **1.** In this company, people are expected to follow their own personal and moral beliefs.

_____ **2.** People are expected to do anything to further the company's interests.

_____ **3.** In this company, people look out for each other's good.

_____ **4.** It is very important here to follow the company's rules and procedures strictly.

_____ **5.** In this company, people protect their own interests above other considerations.

_____ **6.** The first consideration is whether a decision violates any law.

_____ **7.** Everyone is expected to stick by company rules and procedures.

_____ **8.** The most efficient way is always the right way in this company.

_____ **9.** Our major consideration is what is best for everyone in the company.

_____ **10.** In this company, the law or ethical code of the profession is the major consideration.

_____ **11.** It is expected at this company that employees will always do what is right for the customer and the public.

To score the questionnaire, first add up your responses to questions 1, 3, 6, 9, 10, and 11. This is subtotal number 1. Next, reverse the scores on questions 2, 4, 5, 7, and 8 (5 = 0, 4 = 1, 3 = 2, 2 = 3, 1 = 4, 0 = 5). Add the reverse scores to form subtotal number 2. Add subtotal number 1 to subtotal number 2 for an overall score.

Subtotal 1 _____ + Subtotal 2 _____ = Overall Score _____.

Overall scores can range from 0 to 55. The higher the score, the more the organization's culture encourages ethical behavior.

Source: Reprinted from *Organizational Dynamics*, Autumn 1989, "An Ethical Weather Report: Assessing the Organization's Ethical Climate" by John B. Cullen et al. Copyright © 1989, with permission from Elsevier Science.

◢ MANAGERIAL IMPLICATIONS: THE ORGANIZATIONAL CULTURE CHALLENGE

Managing organizational culture is a key challenge for leaders in today's organizations. With the trend toward downsizing and restructuring, maintaining an organizational culture in the face of change is difficult. In addition, such challenges as globalization, workforce diversity, technology, and managing ethical behavior often require that an organization change its culture. Adaptive cultures that can respond to changes in the environment can lead the way in terms of organizational performance.

Managers have at their disposal many techniques for managing organizational culture. These techniques range from manipulating the artifacts of culture, such as ceremonies and symbols, to communicating the values that guide the organization. The socialization process is a powerful cultural communication process. Managers are models who communicate the organizational culture to employees through personal enactment. Their modeled behavior sets the norms for the other employees to follow. Their leadership is essential for developing a culture that values diversity, supports empowerment, fosters innovations in product and service quality, and promotes ethical behavior.

LOOKING BACK :: WHOLE FOODS MARKET, INC.

Is Imitation the Best Form of Flattery?

Several well-established and older grocery retail giants are now planning on store openings that look, feel, and taste exactly like Whole Foods Market, Inc.[77]

The latest to jump on the bandwagon is none other than Wal-Mart. It announced expansion of its organic foods division with organic foods being sold in its Plano, Texas, store. And Wal-Mart is not the only one to follow the high standards set by Whole Foods. Will this imitation kill the competitive advantage that Whole Foods seems to have sustained

for the last 25-plus years? All signs seem to point in the direction of: probably not! Business analysts predict that the key to Whole Foods' success is not just its organic products and snazzy store ambience but its culture, team members, and almost cultlike customer base. They further point out that this loyal and discerning customer base, combined with an "intelligent" workforce, are what sets Whole Foods apart and makes it something that rivals and copycats might have a tough time mimicking.[78]

CHAPTER SUMMARY

1. Organizational (corporate) culture is a pattern of basic assumptions that are considered valid and that are taught to new members as the way to perceive, think, and feel in the organization.

2. The most visible and accessible level of culture is artifacts, which include personal enactment, ceremonies and rites, stories, rituals, and symbols.

3. Organizational culture has four functions: giving members a sense of identity and increasing their commitment, serving as a sense-making device for members, reinforcing organizational values, and serving as a control mechanism for shaping behavior.

4. Three theories about the relationship between culture and performance are the strong culture perspective, the fit perspective, and the adaptation perspective.

5. Leaders shape and reinforce culture by what they pay attention to, how they react to crises, how they behave, how they allocate rewards, and how they hire and fire individuals.

6. Organizational socialization is the process by which newcomers become participating, effective members of the organization. Its three stages are anticipatory socialization, encounter, and change and acquisition. Each stage plays a unique role in communicating organizational culture.

7. It is difficult but not impossible to change organizational culture. Managers can do so by helping current members buy into a new set of values, by adding newcomers and socializing them into the organization, and by removing current members as appropriate.

KEY TERMS

adaptive culture (p. 394)
anticipatory socialization (p. 398)
artifacts (p. 387)
assumptions (p. 392)
change and acquisition (p. 400)

enacted values (p. 391)
encounter (p. 399)
espoused values (p. 391)
organizational (corporate)
culture (p. 387)

organizational socialization
(p. 398)
strong culture (p. 393)

REVIEW QUESTIONS

1. Explain the three levels of organizational culture. How can each level of culture be measured?
2. Describe five artifacts of culture and give an example of each.
3. Explain three theories about the relationship between organizational culture and performance. What does the research evidence say about each one?
4. Contrast adaptive and nonadaptive cultures.

5. How can leaders shape organizational culture?
6. Describe the three stages of organizational socialization. How is culture communicated in each stage?
7. What actions can leaders take to change the organizational culture?
8. How does a manager know that cultural change has been successful?
9. What can managers do to develop a global organizational culture?

Discussion and Communication QUESTIONS

1. Name a company with a visible organizational culture. What do you think are the company's values? Has the culture contributed to the organization's performance? Explain.
2. Name a leader you think manages organizational culture well. How does the leader do this? Use Schein's description of how leaders reinforce culture to analyze the leader's behavior.
3. Suppose you want to change your organization's culture. What sort of resistance would you expect from employees? How would you deal with this resistance?

4. Given Schein's three levels, can we ever truly understand an organization's culture? Explain.
5. To what extent is culture manageable? Changeable?
6. *(communication question)* Select an organization for which you might like to work. Learn as much as you can about that company's culture, using library resources, online sources, contacts within the company, and as many creative means as you can. Prepare a brief presentation to the class summarizing the culture.

ETHICAL DILEMMA

Jean Miller is the managing director of housekeeping at a large, upscale hotel. She feels good about working for an organization that cares a lot about its employees. The hotel respects its employees and does everything possible to create a culture of loyalty and commitment. Throughout Jean's 20 years, the hotel's strong commitment is among the most

positive aspects of her job. Lately, Jean feels this loyalty is going too far, especially when it comes to Mary, one of the housekeeping supervisors.

Housekeeping is a very physical job that Mary excelled at for many years. Now Mary is ready to retire, but she is not in a financial position to do so. This greatly affects Mary's attitude, and unrest is beginning to spread among the people who work for her. There are three openings in Mary's department already and more are expected. The biggest obstacle, from Jean's perspective, is that she feels any new hires sent to Mary would end up quitting. Jean recently hired a very promising new person, Pat. Jean even warned her about Mary's department. Within the first few weeks, Pat was socialized into the negativity of the department. Jean tried to relocate Pat to a different department when she saw what was happening, but it was too late. Even in the new environment, Pat has retained the mindset she had already developed.

The most pressing challenge is what to do about the open positions. Jean is sure that any new person would react as Pat had to Mary, but it isn't fair to those who have to carry a great number of rooms everyday until the positions are filled. Jean has tried to move people from other departments but everyone has threatened to quit if they are transferred. Jean could also go to management and ask that Mary's retirement be enforced, but she doesn't want to do that either, given Mary's financial situation. Jean is unsure how to proceed but knows that she has to do something.

QUESTIONS

1. Is it Jean's responsibility to resolve this conflict?

2. Evaluate Jean's decision using rule, virtue, right, and justice theories.

EXPERIENTIAL EXERCISES

15.1 IDENTIFYING BEHAVIORAL NORMS

This exercise asks you to identify campus norms at your university. Every organization or group has a set of norms that help determine individuals' behavior. A norm is an unwritten rule for behavior in a group. When a norm is not followed, negative feedback is given. It may include negative comments, stares, harassment, and exclusion.

1. As a group, brainstorm all the norms you can think of in the following areas:

   Dress

   Classroom behavior

   Studying

   Weekend activities

   Living arrangements

   Campus activities

   Dating (who asks whom)

   Relationships with faculty

   Eating on campus versus off campus

   Transportation

2. How did you initially get this information?

3. What happens to students who don't follow these norms?

4. What values can be inferred from these norms?

SOURCE: "Identifying Behavioral Norms" by Dorothy Marcic, *Organizational Behavior: Experiences and Cases* (St. Paul, Minn.: West Publishing, 1989). Reprinted by permission.

15.2 CONTRASTING ORGANIZATIONAL CULTURES

To complete this exercise, groups of four or five students should be formed. Each group should select one of the following pairs of organizations:

American Airlines and Northwest Airlines

Anheuser-Busch and Coors

Hewlett-Packard and Xerox

Albertsons and Winn-Dixie

Dayton-Hudson (Target) and JCPenney

Use your university library's resources to gather information about the companies' cultures.

Contrast the cultures of the two organizations using the following dimensions:

> Strength of the culture.

> Fit of the culture with the industry's environment.

> Adaptiveness of the culture.

Which of the two is the better performer? On what did you base your conclusion? How does the performance of each relate to its organizational culture?

SOURCE: Adapted with the permission of The Free Press, a Division of Simon & Schuster, Inc., from *Corporate Culture and Performance* by John P. Kotter and James L. Heskett. Copyright © 1992 by Kotter Associates, Inc., and James L. Heskett. All rights reserved.

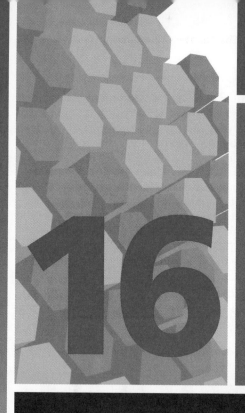

Managing Change

16

THINKING AHEAD :: VIRGIN GROUP, LTD.

Navigating Heated Air Spaces

"Our goal cannot be profit at any cost, because we know that tomorrow's success depends on the trust we build today."[1]

Today's business environment is one in which there is heightened focus on ethical and environmental issues. Some companies have lost their footing because of an inability to stay abreast of constantly changing business perceptions. However, one company seems to have invested an incredible amount of time, money, and energy into anticipating and dealing with these types of changes. Virgin Group, Ltd., lead by Sir Richard Branson, has stayed at the forefront of anticipating and managing change. It created Project Aware as a response to these concerns.

Through this project, Virgin brings together best practices across the world that improve its products, communities, and the environments in which they work. For example, Virgin now has a set of strict codes of ethics that dictate who its partners will be and the standards for quality of life that these partners need to meet. Virgin is a $20 billion corporation spread across five continents and is highly decentralized to help it adapt to local changes. A common unifying goal created by another one of Virgin's landmark charities, Project Unite, brings together all of Virgin's employees and business units in attempting to find ingenious solutions to the most critical challenges facing our times.[2]

▌ FORCES FOR CHANGE IN ORGANIZATIONS

Change has become the norm in most organizations. Plant closings, business failures, mergers and acquisitions, and downsizing have become experiences common to American companies. *Adaptiveness, flexibility,* and *responsiveness* are characteristics of the organizations that will succeed in meeting the competitive challenges that businesses face.[3] In the past, organizations could succeed by claiming excellence in one area—quality, reliability, or cost, for example—but this is not the case today. The current environment demands excellence in all areas and vigilant leaders. A recent survey of CEOs who were facing crises found that 50 percent of them said they believed the problems arrived "suddenly" and that they had not prepared adequately for them. More than 10 percent said they were, in fact, the last to know about the problems.[4]

As we saw in Chapter 1, change is what's on managers' minds. The pursuit of organizational effectiveness through downsizing, restructuring, reengineering, productivity management, cycle-time reduction, and other efforts is paramount. Organizations are in a state of tremendous turmoil and transition, and all members are affected. Continued downsizings may have left firms leaner but not necessarily richer. Though downsizing can increase shareholder value by better aligning costs with revenues, firms may suffer from public criticism for their actions. Laying off employees may be accompanied by increases in CEO pay and stock options, linking the misery of employees with the financial success of owners and management.[5]

Organizations must also deal with ethical, environmental, and other social issues. Sir Richard Branson announced a $25 million prize for scientists who could figure out how to remove billions of tons of carbon dioxide from the atmosphere.

This announcement is seen by many as Virgin proactively dealing with an issue that many claim is created by air travel.[6] Competition is fierce, and companies can no longer afford to rest on their laurels. American Airlines has developed a series of programs to constantly reevaluate and change its operating methods to prevent the company from stagnating. General Electric holds off-site WorkOut sessions with groups of managers and employees whose goal is to make GE a faster, less complex organization that can respond effectively to change. In the WorkOut sessions, employees recommend specific changes, explain why they are needed, and propose ways the changes can be implemented. Top management must make an immediate response: an approval, a disapproval (with an explanation), or a request for more information. The GE WorkOut sessions eliminate the barriers that keep employees from contributing to change.

planned change
Change resulting from a deliberate decision to alter the organization.

unplanned change
Change that is imposed on the organization and is often unforeseen.

There are two basic forms of change in organizations. *Planned change* is change resulting from a deliberate decision to alter the organization. Companies that wish to move from a traditional hierarchical structure to one that facilitates self-managed teams must use a proactive, carefully orchestrated approach. Not all change is planned, however. *Unplanned change* is imposed on the organization and is often unforeseen. Changes in government regulations and changes in the economy, for example, are often unplanned. Responsiveness to unplanned change requires tremendous flexibility and adaptability on the part of organizations. Managers must be prepared to handle both planned and unplanned forms of change in organizations.

Forces for change can come from many sources. Some of these are external, arising from outside the company, whereas others are internal, arising from sources within the organization.

: 1. Examine the major external and internal forces for change in organizations.

■ EXTERNAL FORCES

The four major managerial challenges we have described throughout the book are major external forces for change. Globalization, workforce diversity, technological change, and managing ethical behavior are challenges that precipitate change in organizations.

GLOBALIZATION

The power players in the global market are the multinational and transnational organizations. Conoco, for example, formed a joint venture with Arkhangelskgeoldobycha, a Russian firm, to develop a new oil field in Russia. This partnership, named Polar Lights, was the first Russian-American joint venture to develop an oil field in Russia. The project has been successful, and the production from Polar Lights has now passed the 75 million bbl production milestone.

NAFTA's impact has been felt across numerous industries. American agriculture has been a tremendous beneficiary, with annual U.S. exports of fruits and vegetables to Mexico climbing by more than $1 billion since 1993. This expanded market has been a tremendous windfall for U.S. producers, but trouble may be looming. Mexican farm leaders have accused the United States of unfairly dumping fruits and vegetables into the Mexican market.[7] They also claim that small Mexican farms cannot compete with large industrialized U.S. operations, and they have asked the Mexican government to renegotiate NAFTA to give them greater protection.[8] Because global business implicitly involves multiple governments and legal systems, it carries unique risks not found by firms competing within a single nation. On the other hand, NAFTA has enabled Wal-Mart to enter the Mexican markets, thus driving at least one industry (soaps and detergents) to improve efficiencies in order to compete. Those firms unable to innovate or respond to the presence of Wal-Mart have lost market share and eventually closed.[9]

The United States is but one nation in the drive to open new markets. Japan and Germany are responding to global competition in powerful ways, and the emergence of the European Union as a powerful trading group will have a profound impact on world markets. By joining with their European neighbors, companies in smaller countries will begin to make major progress in world markets, thus increasing the fierce competition that already exists.

◀◀think critically▶▶

What skills should business majors acquire in order to compete in a global market?

Coca-Cola faced a crisis when it introduced its Dasani bottled water in Great Britain. Coke had chosen a particularly compelling theme for its advertising, touting Dasani as even more pure than other bottled waters. After Coke had invested more than £7 million in this project, government regulators found that the water contained illegally high levels of bromate, a potentially cancer-causing chemical. To make matters worse, Coke was forced to admit that the contamination was introduced by its own production process. Coke's response was swift: It quickly pulled half a million bottles of Dasani from London shelves and postponed plans for product launches in France and Germany. Coke is still contemplating how best to respond to this debacle, which some British writers rank among the worst marketing disasters in Britain's history.[10] Kellogg's anticipated warm embrace of its Corn Flakes cereal in India turned out instead to be a cold, soggy response. Kellogg's failed to consider India's breakfast preferences, which are for something hot, fresh, and spicy.

All of these changes, along with others, have led companies to rethink the borders of their markets and to encourage their employees to think globally. Jack Welch, former CEO of GE, was among the first to call for a boundaryless company, in which there are no mental distinctions between domestic and foreign operations or between managers and employees.[11] The thought that drives the boundaryless company is that barriers that get in the way of people's working together should be removed. Globalizing an organization means rethinking the most efficient ways to use resources, disseminate and gather information, and develop people. It requires not only structural changes but also changes in the minds of employees.

WORKFORCE DIVERSITY

Related to globalization is the challenge of workforce diversity. As we have seen throughout this book, workforce diversity is a powerful force for change in organizations. Let us recap the demographic trends contributing to workforce diversity that we discussed at length in Chapter 2. First, the workforce will see increased participation from females, because the majority of new workers will be female.[12]

Second, the workforce will be more culturally diverse than ever. Part of this is attributable to globalization, but in addition, U.S. demographics are changing. The participation of African Americans and Hispanic Americans is increasing in record numbers. Third, the workforce is aging. There will be fewer young workers and more middle-aged Americans working.[13]

A few years ago, Denny's, the restaurant chain, was a name synonymous with racism. In 1994, the company paid $54.4 million to settle two lawsuits brought by black customers who claimed some restaurants refused to seat or serve them. Denny's undertook radical changes led by a blunt-talking CEO and a determined diversity officer in 1995. Because Denny's responded quickly, decisively, and sincerely, it weathered the crisis. Performance appraisals are now based on valuing diversity. A top manager who doesn't do so can have up to 25 percent of his or her bonus withheld. The company's response to a recent incident demonstrates that it takes this issue seriously: a cook and a waiter accused of racist behavior toward an African American customer in Florida were fired within 24 hours of the complaint. Almost half of Denny's 1,011 franchises are owned by minorities, 255 of them by Asian Indians, while one-third of restaurant managers and one-fifth of executives are also minorities. Denny's ranks fifth on *Fortune*'s list of the "50 Best Companies for Minorities."[14]

◀◀ think critically ▶▶

Are diversity training programs in organizations a good idea? What can they accomplish?

TECHNOLOGICAL CHANGE

Rapid technological innovation is another force for change in organizations, and those that fail to keep pace can quickly fall behind. *Smart tags,* for example, are replacing bar codes for tracking and scanning products. Bar codes are passive identification markers whose stripes are unchangeable, and items must be lined up individually for scanning (like in a grocery store checkout line). Manufacturers are starting to use radio-frequency identification (RFID) tags that are as small as two matches laid side by side and hold digital memory chips the size of a pinhead. RFIDs are also used in show dogs and cats. The tags are injected under a pet's skin with a syringe.

RFIDs contain a lot more information than bar codes, and users can alter the information on them. As many as 50 tags per second can be read—40 times faster than bar-code scanners. Ford uses RFIDs to track parts. Data such as a unique ID, part type, plant location, and time/date stamps are included on the tag. Because RFIDs are reusable, the long-term costs are about the same as bar codes.[15]

Technological innovations bring about profound change because they are not just changes in the way work is performed. Instead, the innovation process promotes associated changes in work relationships and organizational structures.[16] The team approach adopted by many organizations leads to flatter structures, decentralized decision making, and more open communication between leaders and team members.

MANAGING ETHICAL BEHAVIOR

Recent ethical scandals have brought ethical behavior in organizations to the forefront of public consciousness. Ethical issues, however, are not always public and monumental. Employees face ethical dilemmas in their daily work lives. The need to manage ethical behavior has brought about several changes in organizations. Most center upon the idea that an organization must create a culture that encourages ethical behavior.

All public companies issue annual financial reports. Gap Inc. has gone a step further by issuing an annual ethical report. The clothing industry is almost synonymous with the use of sweatshops, or low-paying overseas factories in which third-world workers (including children) labor for 50 to 60 hours each week for a few dollars in pay; in this sense, Gap is hardly alone in facing these issues. What sets Gap apart is its candor, beginning with its open admission that none of its 3,000 suppliers fully complies with the firm's ethical code of conduct. But rather than run from these problems, Gap has chosen to work with its suppliers to improve conditions overseas. The firm has more than 90 full-time employees charged with monitoring supplier operations around the world.[17]

The annual report includes extensive descriptions of these workers' activities, including which factories were monitored, what violations were found, and which factories are no longer used by Gap because of violations. It also addresses media reports critical of Gap and its operations.

Gap tries to improve worker conditions by providing training and encouraging suppliers to develop their own conduct codes. For example, in China it has encouraged lunchtime sessions in which workers are advised of their rights. While most facilities respond positively to these efforts, some don't, and Gap pulled its business from 136 factories it concluded were not going to improve. It also terminated contracts with two factories that had verifiable use of child labor. Gap's approach to overseas labor offers a model for other garment firms.[18]

Society expects organizations to maintain ethical behavior both internally and in relationships with other organizations. Ethical behavior is expected in relationships with customers, the environment, and society. These expectations may be informal, or they may come in the form of increased legal requirements.

These four challenges are forces that place pressures to change on organizations. There are other forces as well. Legal developments, changing stakeholder expectations, and shifting consumer demands can also lead to change.[19] And some companies change simply because others are changing.[20] Other powerful forces for change originate from within the organization.

INTERNAL FORCES

Pressures for change that originate inside the organization are generally recognizable in the form of signals indicating that something needs to be altered. A declining effectiveness is a pressure to change. A company that experiences its third quarterly loss within a fiscal year is undoubtedly motivated to do something about it. Some companies react by instituting layoffs and massive cost-cutting programs, whereas others look at the bigger picture, view the loss as symptomatic of an underlying problem, and seek the cause of the problem.

A crisis may also stimulate change in an organization. Strikes or walkouts may lead management to change the wage structure. The resignation of a key decision maker may cause the company to rethink the composition of its management team and its role in the organization. A much-publicized crisis that led to change at Exxon (now ExxonMobil) was the oil spill caused by the *Exxon Valdez* oil tanker. The accident brought about many changes in Exxon's environmental policies.

Changes in employee expectations can also trigger change in organizations. A company that hires a group of young newcomers may find that their expectations are very different from those expressed by older workers. The workforce is more educated than ever before. Although this has its advantages, workers with more education demand more of employers. Today's workers are also concerned with career and family balance issues, such as dependent care. The many sources of workforce diversity hold potential for a host of differing expectations among employees.

Changes in the work climate at an organization can also stimulate change. A workforce that seems lethargic, unmotivated, and dissatisfied is a symptom that must be addressed. This symptom is common in organizations that have experienced layoffs. Workers who have escaped a layoff may grieve for those who have lost their jobs and may find it hard to continue to be productive. They may fear that they will be laid off as well, and many feel insecure in their jobs.

CHANGE IS INEVITABLE

: **2.** Understand *incremental change, strategic change, transformational change,* and *change agent.*

We have seen that organizations face substantial pressures to change from both external and internal sources. Change in organizations is inevitable, but change is a process that can be managed. The scope of change can vary from small to quantum.

THE SCOPE OF CHANGE

incremental change
Change of a relatively small scope, such as making small improvements.

Change can be of a relatively small scope, such as a modification in a work procedure (an *incremental change*). Such changes, in essence, are a fine-tuning of the organization, or the making of small improvements. Intel and other chip producers must continually upgrade their manufacturing equipment just to stay competitive. Intel's 2004 plan to convert an Arizona "fab" or chip-making plant from older to newer technology is expected to cost $2 billion.[21] While radical change is more exciting and interesting to discuss, most research on change has focused on evolutionary (incremental) rather than revolutionary change.[22] Change can also be of a larger scale, such as the restructuring of an organization (a *strategic change*).[23] In strategic change, the organization moves from an old state to a known new state during a controlled period of time. Strategic change usually involves a series of transition steps. AT&T, the granddaddy of long distance companies, made a strategic decision in 2004 to get out of the residential long distance market entirely. Rather than simply cutting off its existing customers, the firm has stopped advertising to consumers and raised residential rates sharply.[24]

strategic change
Change of a larger scale, such as organizational restructuring.

transformational change
Change in which the organization moves to a radically different, and sometimes unknown, future state.

The most massive scope of change is *transformational change*, in which the organization moves to a radically different, and sometimes unknown, future state.[25] In transformational change, the organization's mission, culture, goals, structure, and leadership may all change dramatically.[26] Just over a century ago, two successful bicycle makers decided to leave the safety of the bike business to devote their time to building and selling an amazing new invention—the airplane—which transformed travel, warfare, communications, and the entire world. The Wright brothers transformed not only their bike business but the whole world! Of all the tasks a leader undertakes, many say that changing the form and nature of the organization itself may be the most difficult, an observation supported by research.[27]

One of the toughest decisions faced by leaders is the proper "pace" of change. Some scholars argue that rapid change is more likely to succeed, since it creates momentum,[28] while others argue that these short, sharp changes are actually rare and not experienced by most firms.[29] Still others observe that change in a large organization may occur incrementally in parts of the firm and quickly in others.[30] In summary, researchers agree that the pace of change is important, but they can't quite agree on which pace of change is most beneficial.

Very little long-term research has looked at change over a significant time period. One 12-year study looked at change in the structure of Canadian National Sports Organizations (NSOs). It found that within NSOs, radical transition did not always require a fast pace of change. It also found that successful transitions often involve changing the high-impact elements of an organization (in this case, their decision-making structures) early in the process.[31]

■ THE CHANGE AGENT'S ROLE

The individual or group that undertakes the task of introducing and managing a change in an organization is known as a ***change agent***. Change agents can be internal, such as managers or employees who are appointed to oversee the change process. In her book *The Change Masters,* Rosabeth Moss Kanter notes that at companies like Hewlett-Packard and Polaroid, managers and employees alike are developing the needed skills to produce change and innovation in the organization.[32] Change agents can also be external, such as outside consultants.

Internal change agents have certain advantages in managing the change process. They know the organization's past history, its political system, and its culture. Because they must live with the results of their change efforts, internal change agents are likely to be very careful about managing change. There are disadvantages, however, to using internal change agents. They may be associated with certain factions within the organization and may easily be accused of favoritism. Furthermore, internal change agents may be too close to the situation to have an objective view of what needs to be done.

Change leaders within organizations tend to be young, in the 25–40 age range. They are more flexible than ordinary general managers and much more people oriented. A high number of change leaders are women. The change leaders have a balance of technical and interpersonal skills. They are tough decision makers who focus on performance results. They also know how to energize people and get them aligned in the same direction. They get more out of people than ordinary managers can. In addition, they have the ability to operate in more than one leadership style and can shift from a team mode to command and control, depending on the situation. They are also comfortable with uncertainty.[33]

If change is large scale or strategic in nature, it may take a team of leaders to make change happen. A team assembling leaders with a variety of skills, expertise,

change agent
The individual or group that undertakes the task of introducing and managing a change in an organization.

and influence that can work together harmoniously may be needed to accomplish change of large scope.[34]

External change agents bring an outsider's objective view to the organization. They may be preferred by employees because of their impartiality. External change agents face certain problems, however; not only is their knowledge of the organization's history limited, but they may also be viewed with suspicion by organization members. External change agents have more power in directing changes if employees perceive the change agents as being trustworthy, possessing important expertise, having a track record that establishes credibility, and being similar to them.[35]

Different change agent competencies are required at different stages of the change process. Leadership, communication, training, and participation have varying levels of impact as the change proceeds, meaning change agents must be flexible in how they work through the different phases of the process.[36] Effective change leaders build strong relationships within their leadership team, between the team and organizational members, and between the team and key environmental players. Maintaining all three relationships simultaneously is quite difficult, so successful leaders are continually "coupling" and "uncoupling" with the different groups as the change process proceeds. Adaptability is a key skill for both internal and external change leaders.[37]

THE PROCESS OF CHANGE IN ORGANIZATIONS

Organizations tend to respond to change by continuing to do what they are good at. After all, these strategies have been successful in the past. After periods of success, organizations can lose the ability to recognize when it is necessary to give up past strategies and try something new. Once an organization has made the decision to change, careful planning and analysis must take place. Change processes such as business process reengineering cannot ensure the success of the change. The people aspects of change are the most critically important for successful transformations.[38] Even Michael Hammer, who launched the reengineering movement, admits that he forgot about the "human aspects" of change. "I was reflecting on my engineering background and was insufficiently appreciative of the human dimension. I've learned that it's critical."[39] If people are not taken into account, a change process will be negatively affected or may even fail. Like organizations, people tend to cling to what has worked in the past, especially if they have been successful and they see no need for change.[40] One major aspect that change agents need to consider is the altered psychological contracts that employees perceive with their employer after a merger or an acquisition. Research results indicate that such change agents can typically help people adjust to such corporate culture changes by working with them to enhance their coping abilities.[41]

: 3. Describe the major reasons individuals resist change and discuss methods organizations can use to manage resistance.

RESISTANCE TO CHANGE

People often resist change in a rational response based on self-interest. However, people resist change for countless other reasons. Many of these center around the notion of reactance—that is, a negative reaction that occurs when individuals feel that their personal freedom is threatened.[42] Some of the major reasons for resisting change follow.

FEAR OF THE UNKNOWN

Change often brings with it substantial uncertainty. Employees facing a technological change, such as the introduction of a new computer system, may resist the change simply because it introduces ambiguity into what was once a comfortable situation for them. This is especially a problem when there has been little communication about the change.

FEAR OF LOSS

When a change is impending, some employees may fear losing their jobs; this fear is particularly acute when an advanced technology like robotics is introduced. Employees may also fear losing their status because of a change.[43] Computer systems experts, for example, may feel threatened when they feel their expertise is eroded by the installation of a more user-friendly networked information system. Another common fear is that changes may diminish the positive qualities the individual enjoys in the job. Computerizing the customer service positions at Southwestern Bell (now part of SBC Communications), for example, threatened the autonomy that representatives previously enjoyed.

FEAR OF FAILURE

Some employees fear changes because they fear their own failure. Employees may fear that changes will result in increased workloads or increased task difficulty, and they may question their own competencies for handling these. They may also fear that performance expectations will be elevated following the change, and that they may not measure up.[44] Resistance can also stem from a fear that the change itself will not really take place. In one large library that was undergoing a major automation effort, employees were doubtful that the vendor could really deliver the state-of-the-art system that was promised. In this case, the implementation never became a reality—the employees' fears were well founded.[45]

DISRUPTION OF INTERPERSONAL RELATIONSHIPS

Employees may resist change that threatens to limit meaningful interpersonal relationships on the job. Librarians facing the automation effort described previously feared that once the computerized system was implemented, they would not be able to interact as they did when they had to go to another floor of the library to get help finding a resource. In the new system, with the touch of a few buttons on the computer, they would get their information without consulting another librarian.

PERSONALITY CONFLICTS

When the change agent's personality engenders negative reactions, employees may resist the change. A change agent who appears insensitive to employee concerns and feelings may meet considerable resistance, because employees perceive that their needs are not being taken into account.

POLITICS

Organizational change may also shift the existing balance of power in the organization. Individuals or groups who hold power under the current arrangement may be threatened with losing these political advantages in the advent of change.

CULTURAL ASSUMPTIONS AND VALUES

Sometimes cultural assumptions and values can be impediments to change, particularly if the assumptions underlying the change are alien to employees. This form of resistance can be very difficult to overcome, because some cultural assumptions are unconscious. As we discussed in Chapter 2, some cultures tend to avoid uncertainty. In Mexican and Greek cultures, for example, change that creates a great deal of uncertainty may be met with great resistance.

Some individuals are more tolerant of ambiguity than others. You can assess your own attitude toward ambiguity in Challenge 16.1.

C H A L L E N G E 16.1

Tolerance for Ambiguity

Tolerance for Ambiguity Survey Form

Read each of the following statements carefully. Then rate each of them in terms of the extent to which you either agree or disagree with the statement using the following scale:

Completely Disagree			Neither Agree nor Disagree			Completely Agree
1	2	3	4	5	6	7

Place the number that best describes your degree of agreement or disagreement in the blank to the left of each statement.

_____ 1. An expert who doesn't come up with a definite answer probably doesn't know much.

_____ 2. I would like to live in a foreign country for a while.

_____ 3. The sooner we all acquire similar values and ideals, the better.

_____ 4. A good teacher is one who makes you wonder about your way of looking at things.

_____ 5. I like parties where I know most of the people more than ones where all or most of the people are complete strangers.

_____ 6. Teachers or supervisors who hand out vague assignments give a chance for one to show initiative and originality.

_____ 7. A person who leads an even, regular life in which few surprises or unexpected happenings arise really has a lot to be grateful for.

_____ 8. Many of our most important decisions are based upon insufficient information.

_____ 9. There is really no such thing as a problem that cannot be solved.

_____ 10. People who fit their lives to a schedule probably miss most of the joy of living.

_____ 11. A good job is one where what is to be done and how it is to be done are always clear.

_____ 12. It is more fun to tackle a complicated problem than to solve a simple one.

_____ 13. In the long run, it is possible to get more done by tackling small, simple problems rather than large and complicated ones.

_____ 14. Often the most interesting and stimulating people are those who don't mind being different and original.

_____ 15. What we are used to is always preferable to what is unfamiliar.

(continued)

Scoring:

For even-numbered questions, add the total points.

For odd-numbered questions, use reverse scoring and add the total points.

Your score is the total of the even- and odd-numbered questions.

Norms Using the Tolerance for Ambiguity Scale

Source: The Tolerance for Ambiguity Scale

Basis: The survey asks 15 questions about personal and work-oriented situations with ambiguity. You were asked to rate each situation on a scale from one (tolerant) to seven (intolerant). (Alternating questions have the response scale reversed.) The index scores the items. A perfectly tolerant person would score 15 and a perfectly intolerant person 105. Scores between 20 and 80 are reported, with means of 45. The responses to the even-numbered questions with 7 minus the score are added to the response for the odd-numbered questions.

Source: "Tolerance for Ambiguity" from D. Marcic, *Organizational Behavior: Experiences and Cases* (St. Paul, Minn.: West Publishing, 1992): 339–340. Adapted from Paul Nutt. Used with permission.

We have described several sources of resistance to change. The reasons for resistance are as diverse as the workforce itself and vary with different individuals and organizations. The challenge for managers is introducing change in a positive manner and managing employee resistance.

MANAGING RESISTANCE TO CHANGE

The traditional view of resistance to change treated it as something to be overcome, and many organizational attempts to reduce the resistance have only served to intensify it. The contemporary view holds that resistance is simply a form of feedback and that this feedback can be used very productively to manage the change process.[46] One key to managing resistance is to plan for it and to be ready with a variety of strategies for using the resistance as feedback and helping employees negotiate the transition. Three key strategies for managing resistance to change are communication, participation, and empathy and support.[47]

Communication about impending change is essential if employees are to adjust effectively.[48] The details of the change should be provided, but equally important is the rationale behind the change. Employees want to know why change is needed.

If there is no good reason for it, why should they favor the change? Providing accurate and timely information about the change can help prevent unfounded fears and potentially damaging rumors from developing. Delaying the announcement of a change and handling information in a secretive fashion can serve to fuel the rumor mill. Open communication in a culture of trust is a key ingredient for successful change.[49] It is also beneficial to inform people about the potential consequences of the change. Educating employees on new work procedures is often helpful. In addition, mentors and mentees both derive benefits from going through the process of organizational change. Mentees are aided in their sensemaking of change while mentors experience satisfaction in having helped the mentee through the change process.[50] Studies on the introduction of computers in the workplace indicate that providing employees with opportunities for hands-on practice helps alleviate fears about the new technology. Employees who have experience with computers display more positive attitudes and greater efficacy—a sense that they can master their new tasks.[51] Another key ingredient that can help employees adjust to change is a supervisor that they can trust. When employees trust their supervisors, it serves as a social support mechanism and they are more committed to the organization even if they feel they can't control the change process.[52]

Substantial research support underscores the importance of participation in the change process. Employees must be engaged and involved in order for change to work—as supported by the notion "That which we create, we support." Participation helps employees become involved in the change and establish a feeling of ownership in the process. When employees are allowed to participate, they are more committed to the change. Designer retailer Prada, famous for its extravagant clothing, decided to create an equally amazing retail location. When the company opened perhaps the world's most advanced boutique in New York City, it had spent one-fourth of the company's IT budget on the experiment. Wireless networks linked each item in inventory to a single database, allowing staff to walk the floor armed with wireless PDAs to check inventory. Automated dressing rooms with touchscreens offered additional information to customers. Within a couple of years, most of the technology sat abandoned, some of it malfunctioning, some of it simply too difficult to use. Like many other firms before it, Prada appears to have fallen in love with the "idea" of going high tech, without bothering to get the actual users (its employees) onboard.[53]

Another strategy for managing resistance is providing empathy and support to employees who have trouble dealing with the change. Active listening is an excellent tool for identifying the reasons behind resistance and for uncovering fears. An expression of concern about the change can provide important feedback that managers can use to improve the change process. Emotional support and encouragement can help an employee deal with the anxiety that is a natural response to change. Employees who experience severe reactions to change can benefit from talking with a counselor. Some companies provide counseling through their employee assistance plans.

Open communication, participation, and emotional support can go a long way toward managing resistance to change. Managers must realize that some resistance is inevitable, however, and should plan ways to deal with resistance early in the change process. In the Thinking Ahead feature, Sir Branson seems to have created a culture of low resistance to change by engendering trust through participation and his own tolerance (and appetite) for the unknown.

The Hartford Financial Services Group encountered some resistance to change in going global. When the company attempted to enter the lucrative British and

Dutch insurance markets by acquiring British and Dutch companies, the overseas staff resisted changes suggested by Hartford, such as using laptops and introducing new financial products. The introduction of such U.S. business practices is often referred to as "economic imperialism" by employees who feel they are being forced to substitute corporate values for personal or national values.

Hartford needed its European staff to understand that they were part of a transnational company. Its solution was to offer a stock ownership plan that tied the personal fortunes of the staff to the company. This gave employees a considerable interest in Hartford's success and helped them identify with the company.[54]

■ BEHAVIORAL REACTIONS TO CHANGE

In spite of attempts to minimize the resistance to change in an organization, some reactions to change are inevitable. Negative reactions may be manifested in overt behavior or through more passive resistance to change. People show four basic, identifiable reactions to change: disengagement, disidentification, disenchantment, and disorientation.[55] Managers can use interventions to deal with these reactions, as shown in Table 16.1.

Disengagement is psychological withdrawal from change. The employee may appear to lose initiative and interest in the job. Disengagement can be recognized by behaviors such as being hard to find or doing only the basics to get the job done. Typical disengagement statements include "No problem" or "This won't affect me." The basic managerial strategy for dealing with disengaged individuals is to confront them with their reactions and draw them out so that they can identify the concerns that need to be addressed. Disengaged employees may not be aware of the change in their behavior, and they need to be assured of your intentions. Drawing them out and helping them air their feelings can lead to productive discussions.

Another reaction to change is *disidentification*. Individuals reacting in this way feel that their identity has been threatened by the change, and they feel very vulnerable. Many times they cling to a past procedure because they had a sense of mastery over it, and it gave them a sense of security. "My job is completely changed" and "I used to . . ." are verbal indications of disidentification. Managers can help them through the transition by encouraging them to explore their feelings and helping them transfer their positive feelings into the new situation. One way to do this is to help them identify what they liked in the old situation and then show them how it is possible to have the same positive experience in the new situation.

disengagement
Psychological withdrawal from change.

disidentification
Feeling that one's identity is being threatened by a change.

REACTION	EXPRESSION	MANAGERIAL INTERVENTION
Disengagement	Withdrawal	Confront, identify
Disidentification	Sadness, worry	Explore, transfer
Disenchantment	Anger	Neutralize, acknowledge
Disorientation	Confusion	Explain, plan

TABLE 16.1

Reactions to Change and Managerial Interventions

SOURCE: Table adapted from H. Woodward and S. Buchholz, *Aftershock: Helping People through Corporate Change*, p. 15. Copyright © 1987 John Wiley & Sons, Inc. Reprinted by permission of John Wiley & Sons, Inc.

disenchantment

Feeling negativity or anger toward a change.

Disenchantment is also a common reaction to change. It is usually expressed as negativity or anger. Disenchanted employees realize that the past is gone, and they are mad about it. They may try to enlist the support of other employees by forming coalitions. Destructive behaviors like sabotage and backstabbing may result. More often, however, cultures view the expression of emotion at work as improper and unbusinesslike. In these cultures, the anger is suppressed and emerges in more passive-aggressive ways, such as badmouthing and starting rumors. One of the particular dangers of disenchantment is that it is quite contagious in the workplace. Managers should try to bring the employee to a more neutral emotional state and acknowledge that their anger is valid.

disorientation

Feelings of loss and confusion due to a change.

A final reaction to change is *disorientation.* Disoriented employees are lost and confused, and often they are unsure of their feelings. They waste energy trying to figure out what to do instead of how to do things. The managerial strategy for dealing with this reaction is to explain the change in a way that minimizes the ambiguity that is present. Information about the change needs to be put into a framework or an overall vision so that the disoriented individual can see where he or she fits into the grand scheme of things.[56]

Managers need to be able to diagnose these four reactions to change. Because each reaction brings with it significant and different concerns, no single universal strategy can help all employees adjust. By recognizing each reaction and applying the appropriate strategy, it is possible to help even strong resisters work through a transition successfully. Open communication from top management, sufficient resources, and positive peer reactions greatly facilitate the acceptance of change. Skilled middle management is a key factor in successful implementation of change.

: **4.** Apply force field analysis to a problem.

■ LEWIN'S CHANGE MODEL

Kurt Lewin developed a model of the change process that has stood the test of time and continues to influence the way organizations manage planned change. Lewin's model is based on the idea of force field analysis.[57] Figure 16.1 shows a force field analysis of a decision to engage in exercise behavior.

This model contends that a person's behavior is the product of two opposing forces; one force pushes toward preserving the status quo, and the other force pushes for change. When the two opposing forces are approximately equal, current behavior

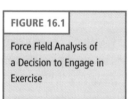

FIGURE 16.1

Force Field Analysis of a Decision to Engage in Exercise

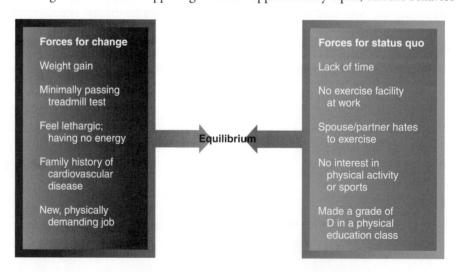

CHALLENGE 16.2

Applying Force Field Analysis

Think of a problem you are currently facing. An example would be trying to increase the amount of study time you devote to a particular class.

1. Describe the problem, as specifically as possible.
2. List the forces driving change on the arrows at the left side of the diagram.
3. List the forces restraining change on the arrows at the right side of the diagram.
4. What can you do, specifically, to remove the obstacles to change?
5. What can you do to increase the forces driving change?
6. What benefits can be derived from breaking a problem down into forces driving change and forces restraining change?

Forces driving change | Forces restraining change

is maintained. For behavioral change to occur, the forces maintaining the status quo must be overcome. This can be accomplished by increasing the forces for change, by weakening the forces for the status quo, or by a combination of these actions. Challenge 16.2 asks you to apply force field analysis to a problem in your life.

Lewin's change model is a three-step process, as shown in Figure 16.2. The process begins with *unfreezing*, which is a crucial first hurdle in the change process. Unfreezing involves encouraging individuals to discard old behaviors by shaking up the equilibrium state that maintains the status quo. Organizations often accomplish unfreezing by eliminating the rewards for current behavior and showing that current behavior is not valued. By unfreezing, individuals accept that change needs to occur. In essence, individuals surrender by allowing the boundaries of their status quo to be opened in preparation for change.[58]

5. Explain Lewin's organizational change model.

unfreezing
The first step in Lewin's change model, in which individuals are encouraged to discard old behaviors by shaking up the equilibrium state that maintains the status quo.

Unfreezing	Moving	Refreezing
Reducing forces for status quo	Developing new attitudes, values, and behaviors	Reinforcing new attitudes, values, and behaviors

FIGURE 16.2

Lewin's Change Model

moving

The second step in Lewin's change model, in which new attitudes, values, and behaviors are substituted for old ones.

refreezing

The final step in Lewin's change model, in which new attitudes, values, and behaviors are established as the new status quo.

The second step in the change process is *moving*. In the moving stage, new attitudes, values, and behaviors are substituted for old ones. Organizations accomplish moving by initiating new options and explaining the rationale for the change, as well as by providing training to help employees develop the new skills they need. Employees should be given the overarching vision for the change so that they can establish their roles within the new organizational structure and processes.[59]

Refreezing is the final step in the change process. In this step, new attitudes, values, and behaviors are established as the new status quo. The new ways of operating are cemented in and reinforced. Managers should ensure that the organizational culture and formal reward systems encourage the new behaviors and avoid rewarding the old ways of operating. Changes in the reward structure may be needed to ensure that the organization is not rewarding the old behaviors and merely hoping for the new behaviors. A study by Exxon Research and Engineering showed that framing and displaying a mission statement in managers' offices may eventually change the behavior of 2 percent of the managers. In contrast, changing managers' evaluation and reward systems will change the behavior of 55 percent of the managers almost overnight.[60]

The approach used by Monsanto to increase opportunities for women within the company is an illustration of how to use Lewin's model effectively. First, Monsanto emphasized unfreezing by helping employees debunk negative stereotypes about women in business. This also helped overcome resistance to change. Second, Monsanto moved employees' attitudes and behaviors by diversity training in which differences were emphasized as positive, and supervisors learned ways of training and developing female employees. Third, Monsanto changed its reward system so that managers were evaluated and paid according to how they coached and promoted women, which helped refreeze the new attitudes and behaviors.

One frequently overlooked issue is whether or not the change is consistent with the company's deeply held core values. Value consistency is critical to making a change "stick." Organizations whose members perceive the changes to be consistent with the firm's values adopt the changes much more easily and fully. Conversely, organizations whose members' values conflict with the changes may display "superficial conformity," in which members pay lip service to the changes, but ultimately revert to their old behaviors.[61]

Organizations that wish to change can select from a variety of methods to make a change become reality. Organization development is a method that consists of various programs for making organizations more effective.

ORGANIZATION DEVELOPMENT INTERVENTIONS

organization development (OD)

A systematic approach to organizational improvement that applies behavioral science theory and research in order to increase individual and organizational well-being and effectiveness.

Organization development (OD) is a systematic approach to organizational improvement that applies behavioral science theory and research in order to increase individual and organizational well-being and effectiveness.[62] This definition implies certain characteristics. First, OD is a systematic approach to planned change. It is a structured cycle of diagnosing organizational problems and opportunities and then applying expertise to them. Second, OD is grounded in solid research and theory. It involves the application of our knowledge of behavioral

Diagnosis and needs analysis

Intervention

Follow-up

FIGURE 16.3

The Organization Development Cycle

science to the challenges that organizations face. Third, OD recognizes the reciprocal relationship between individuals and organizations. It acknowledges that for organizations to change, individuals must change. Finally, OD is goal oriented. It is a process that seeks to improve both individual and organizational well-being and effectiveness.

Organization development has a rich history. Some of the early work in OD was conducted by Kurt Lewin and his associates during the 1940s. This work was continued by Rensis Likert, who pioneered the use of attitude surveys in OD. During the 1950s, Eric Trist and his colleagues at the Tavistock Institute in London focused on the technical and social aspects of organizations and how they affect the quality of work life. These programs on the quality of work life migrated to the United States during the 1960s. During this time, a 200-member OD network was established, and it has grown to more than 4,100 members worldwide. As the number of practitioners has increased, so has the number of different OD methods. One compendium of organizational change methods estimates that more than 300 different methods have been used.[63]

Organization development is also being used internationally. OD has been applied in Canada, Sweden, Norway, Germany, Japan, Australia, Israel, and Mexico, among others. Some OD methods are difficult to implement in other cultures. As OD becomes more internationally widespread, we will increase our knowledge of how culture affects the success of different OD approaches.

Prior to deciding on a method of intervention, managers must carefully diagnose the problem they are attempting to address. Diagnosis and needs analysis is a critical first step in any OD intervention. Following this, an intervention method is chosen and applied. Finally, a thorough follow-up of the OD process is conducted. Figure 16.3 presents the OD cycle, a continuous process of moving the organization and its employees toward effective functioning.

■ DIAGNOSIS AND NEEDS ANALYSIS

Before any intervention is planned, a thorough organizational diagnosis should be conducted. Diagnosis is an essential first step for any organization development intervention.[64] The term *diagnosis* comes from *dia* (through) and *gnosis* (knowledge of). Thus, the diagnosis should pinpoint specific problems and areas in need of improvement. Problems can arise in any part of the organization. Six areas to examine carefully are the organization's purpose, structure, reward system, support systems, relationships, and leadership.[65]

: 6. Describe the use of organizational diagnosis and needs analysis as a first step in organizational development.

Harry Levinson's diagnostic approach asserts that the process should begin by identifying where the pain (the problem) in the organization is, what it is like, how long it has been happening, and what has already been done about it.[66] Then a four-part, comprehensive diagnosis can begin. The first part of the diagnosis involves achieving an understanding of the organization's history. In the second part, the organization as a whole is analyzed to obtain data about its structure and processes. In the third part, interpretive data about attitudes, relationships, and current organizational functioning are gathered. In the fourth part of the diagnosis, the data are analyzed and conclusions are reached. In each stage of the diagnosis, the data can be gathered using a variety of methods, including observation, interviews, questionnaires, and archival records.

The diagnostic process may yield the conclusion that change is necessary. As part of the diagnosis, it is important to address the following issues:

> What are the forces for change?

> What are the forces preserving the status quo?

> What are the most likely sources of resistance to change?

> What are the goals to be accomplished by the change?

This information constitutes a force field analysis, as discussed earlier in the chapter.

A needs analysis is another crucial step in managing change. This is an analysis of the skills and competencies that employees must have to achieve the goals of the change. A needs analysis is essential because interventions such as training programs must target these skills and competencies.

Hundreds of alternative OD intervention methods exist. One way of classifying these methods is by the target of change. The target of change may be the organization, groups within the organization, or individuals.

: 7. Discuss the major organization development interventions.

■ ORGANIZATION- AND GROUP-FOCUSED TECHNIQUES

Some OD intervention methods emphasize changing the organization itself or changing the work groups within the organization. Intervention methods in this category include survey feedback, management by objectives, product and service quality programs, team building, and process consultation.

SURVEY FEEDBACK

survey feedback
A widely used method of intervention whereby employee attitudes are solicited using a questionnaire.

Survey feedback is a widely used intervention method whereby employee attitudes are solicited using a questionnaire. Once the data are collected, they are analyzed and fed back to the employees to diagnose problems and plan other interventions. Survey feedback is often used as an exploratory tool and then is combined with some other intervention. The effectiveness of survey feedback in actually improving outcomes (absenteeism or productivity, for example) increases substantially when this method is combined with other interventions.[67] Furthermore, the effectiveness of this technique is contingent upon trust between management and subordinates, and this can be reinforced through the anonymity and confidentiality of survey responses.

MANAGEMENT BY OBJECTIVES

As an organization-wide technique, *management by objectives (MBO)* involves joint goal setting between employees and managers. MBO is a valuable intervention because it meets three needs. First, it clarifies what is expected of employees. This reduces role conflict and ambiguity. Second, MBO provides knowledge of results, an essential ingredient in effective job performance. Finally, MBO provides an opportunity for coaching and counseling by the manager. The problem-solving approach encourages open communication and discussion of obstacles to goal achievement.[68]

management by objectives (MBO)
An organization-wide intervention technique that involves joint goal setting between employees and managers.

PRODUCT AND SERVICE QUALITY PROGRAMS

Quality programs—programs that embed product and service quality excellence in the organizational culture—are assuming key roles in the organization development efforts of many companies. For example, the success or failure of a service company may depend on the quality of customer service it provides.[69]

quality program
A program that embeds product and service quality excellence in the organizational culture.

TEAM BUILDING

Team building programs can improve the effectiveness of work groups. Team building usually begins with a diagnostic process through which team members identify problems, and it continues with the team's planning actions to take in order to resolve those problems. The OD practitioner in team building serves as a facilitator, and the work itself is completed by team members.[70]

Team building is a very popular OD method. A survey of *Fortune 500* companies indicated that human resource managers considered team building the most successful OD technique.[71] Managers are particularly interested in building teams that can learn. To build learning teams, members must be encouraged to seek feedback, discuss errors, reflect on successes and failures, and experiment with new ways of performing. One popular technique for team building is the use of outdoor challenges. Participants go through a series of outdoor activities, such as climbing a 14-foot wall. Similar physical challenges require the participants to work as a team and focus on trust, communication, decision making, and leadership.

team building
An intervention designed to improve the effectiveness of a work group.

PROCESS CONSULTATION

Pioneered by Edgar Schein, *process consultation* is an OD method that helps managers and employees improve the processes that are used in organizations.[72] The processes most often targeted are communication, conflict resolution, decision making, group interaction, and leadership.

One of the distinguishing features of the process consultation approach is that an outside consultant is used. The role of the consultant is to help employees help themselves. In this way, the ownership of a successful outcome rests with the employees.[73] The consultant guides the organization members in examining the processes in the organization and in refining them. The steps in process consultation are entering the organization, defining the relationship, choosing an approach, gathering data and diagnosing problems, intervening, and gradually leaving the organization.

process consultation
An OD method that helps managers and employees improve the processes that are used in organizations.

All the preceding OD methods focus on changing the organization or the work group. Other OD methods are aimed at facilitating change within individuals.

■ INDIVIDUAL-FOCUSED TECHNIQUES

Organization development efforts that are targeted toward individuals include skills training, leadership training and development, executive coaching, role negotiation, job redesign, health promotion programs, and career planning.

SKILLS TRAINING

skills training
Increasing the job knowledge, skills, and abilities that are necessary to do a job effectively.

The key question addressed by *skills training* is "What knowledge, skills, and abilities are necessary to do this job effectively?" Skills training is accomplished either in formal classroom settings or on the job. The challenge of integrating skills training into organization development is the rapid change that most organizations face. The job knowledge in most positions requires continual updates to keep pace with rapid change.

LEADERSHIP TRAINING AND DEVELOPMENT

leadership training and development
A variety of techniques that are designed to enhance individuals' leadership skills.

Companies invest millions of dollars in *leadership training and development*, a term that encompasses a variety of techniques that are designed to enhance individuals' leadership skills. One popular technique is sending future leaders to off-site training classes. Research shows that this type of education experience can have some impact, but participants' enthusiastic return to work may be short-lived due to the challenges and realities of work life. Classroom learning alone thus has a limited effect on leadership skills.

At IBM, managers are strongly held accountable for leadership development. In fact, IBM's managers will not be considered for promotion into senior executive positions unless they have a record of developing leaders. Top management must be committed to the process of leadership training and development if they want to create a pipeline of high-potential employees to fill leadership positions.[74]

EXECUTIVE COACHING

executive coaching
A technique in which managers or executives are paired with a coach in a partnership to help the executive perform more efficiently.

Executive coaching is a technique in which managers or executives are paired with a coach in a partnership to help the executive perform more effectively at work and, sometimes, even in personal life. Although coaching is usually done in a one-on-one manner, it is sometimes attempted in groups. The popularity of executive coaching has increased dramatically in recent years. The International Coach Federation, a group that trains and accredits executive coaches, in just two years of existence doubled its membership, which is now at 7,000 members in 35 countries.

ROLE NEGOTIATION

role negotiation
A technique whereby individuals meet and clarify their psychological contract.

Individuals who work together sometimes have differing expectations of one another within the working relationship. *Role negotiation* is a simple technique whereby individuals meet and clarify their psychological contract. In doing this, the expectations of each party are clarified and negotiated. The outcome of role negotiation is a better understanding between the two parties of what each can be expected to give and receive in the reciprocal relationship. When both parties have a mutual agreement on expectations, there is less ambiguity in the process of working together.

JOB REDESIGN

As an OD intervention method, *job redesign* emphasizes the fit between individual skills and the demands of the job. Chapter 13 outlined several approaches to job design. Many of these methods are used as OD techniques for realigning task demands and individual capabilities or for redesigning jobs to fit new techniques or organizational structures better.

Another form of job redesign is telecommuting, in which employees perform some or all of their work from home. Companies including American Express, AT&T, and Merrill Lynch have significant numbers of employees who work this way. When AT&T surveyed its managers to assess the impact of telecommuting, 76 percent were happier with their jobs, and 79 percent were happier with their careers in general since they began telecommuting.[75]

job redesign
An OD intervention method that alters jobs to improve the fit between individual skills and the demands of the job.

HEALTH PROMOTION PROGRAMS

As organizations have become increasingly concerned with the costs of distress in the workplace, health promotion programs have become a part of larger organization development efforts. The American Psychological Association recently began recognizing companies for innovative programs that support psychologically healthy work environments. Winners included Small Dog Electronics, Inc., of Vermont and ARUP Laboratories, located in Utah. Small Dog Electronics, Inc., works hard to create a relaxing work environment. Employee work areas are painted in brilliant colors, while employees choose the music played in the office. Breaks are encouraged, pets are allowed in the office, and pet insurance is offered as an employee benefit.

CAREER PLANNING

Matching an individual's career aspirations with the opportunities in the organization is career planning. This proactive approach to career management is often part of an organization's development efforts. Career planning is a joint responsibility of organizations and individuals. Companies like IBM, Travelers Life & Annuity (part of Citigroup), and 3M have implemented career-planning programs.

Managers can choose from a host of organization development techniques to facilitate organizational change. Some of these techniques are aimed toward organizations or groups, and others focus on individuals. Large-scale changes in organizations require the use of multiple techniques. For example, implementing a new technology like robotics may require simultaneous changes in the structure of the organization, the configuration of work groups, and individual attitudes.

We should recognize at this point that the organization development methods just described are means to an end. Programs do not drive change; business needs do. The OD methods are merely vehicles for moving the organization and its employees in a more effective direction.

☛ ETHICAL CONSIDERATIONS IN ORGANIZATION DEVELOPMENT

Organization development is a process of helping organizations improve. It may involve resistance to change, shifts in power, losses of control, and redefinition of tasks.[76] These are all sensitive issues. Further, the change agent, whether a

8. Identify the ethical issues that must be considered in organization development efforts.

manager from within the organization or a consultant from outside, is in a position of directing the change. Such a position carries the potential for misuse of power. The ethical concerns surrounding the use of organization development center around four issues.[77]

The first issue is the selection of the OD method to be used. Every change agent has inherent biases about particular methods, but these biases must not enter into the decision process. The OD method used must be carefully chosen in accordance with the problem as diagnosed, the organization's culture, and the employees concerned. All alternatives should be given fair consideration in the choice of a method. In addition, the OD practitioner should never use a method he or she is not skilled in delivering. Using a method you are not an expert in is unethical, because the client assumes you are.

The second ethical issue is voluntary participation. No employee should be forced to participate in any OD intervention.[78] To make an informed decision about participation, employees should be given information about the nature of the intervention and what will be expected of them. They should also be afforded the option to discontinue their participation at any time they so choose.

The third issue of ethical concern is confidentiality. Change agents gather a wealth of information during organizational diagnoses and interventions. Successful change agents develop a trusting relationship with employees. They may receive privileged information, sometimes unknowingly. It is unethical for a change agent to reveal information in order to give some group or individual political advantage or to enhance the change agent's own standing. Consultants should not reveal information about an organization to its competitors. The use of information gathered from OD efforts is a sensitive issue and presents ethical dilemmas.

A final ethical concern in OD is the potential for manipulation by the change agent. Because any change process involves influence, some individuals may feel manipulated. The key to alleviating the potential for manipulation is open communication. Participants should be given complete knowledge of the rationale for change, what they can expect of the change process, and what the intervention will entail. No actions should be taken that limit the participants' freedom of choice.[79]

◢ ARE ORGANIZATION DEVELOPMENT EFFORTS EFFECTIVE?

Because organization development is designed to help organizations manage change, it is important to evaluate the effectiveness of these efforts. The success of any OD intervention depends on a host of factors, including the technique used, the competence of the change agent, the organization's readiness for change, and top management commitment. No single method of OD is effective in every instance. Instead, multiple-method OD approaches are recommended because they allow organizations to capitalize on the benefits of several approaches.[80]

Efforts to evaluate OD efforts have focused on outcomes such as productivity. One review of more than 200 interventions indicated that worker productivity improved in 87 percent of the cases.[81] A separate analysis of 98 of these interventions revealed impressive productivity increases.[82] We can conclude that when properly applied and managed, organization development programs have positive effects on performance.[83]

❑ MANAGERIAL IMPLICATIONS: MANAGING CHANGE

Several guidelines can be used to facilitate the success of management change efforts.[84] First, managers should recognize the forces for change. These forces can come from a combination of sources both internal and external to the organization.

A shared vision of the change should be developed that includes participation by all employees in the planning process. Top management must be committed to the change and should visibly demonstrate support, because employees look to these leaders to model appropriate behavior. A comprehensive diagnosis and needs analysis should be conducted. The company then must ensure that there are adequate resources for carrying out the change.

Resistance to change should be planned for and managed. Communication, participation, and empathetic support are ways of helping employees adjust. The reward system within the organization must be carefully evaluated to ensure that new behaviors, rather than old ones, are being reinforced. Participation in the change process should also be recognized and rewarded.

The organization development technique used should be carefully selected to meet the goals of the change. Finally, organization development efforts should be managed in an ethical manner and should preserve employees' privacy and freedom of choice. Employees must be treated fairly, and management's explanations for change must be congruent with their actions. The congruence between talk and actions, or "walking the talk," is critical in managing organizational change.[85] By using these guidelines, managers can meet the challenges of managing change while enhancing productivity in their organizations.

LOOKING BACK :: VIRGIN GROUP, LTD.

On Crises and Charities

Virgin Group is not immune to accidents that plague any major transportation company. Recently, one of its trains derailed, leaving one person dead and several injured. Virgin Trains reacted to the crisis in a prompt fashion with emergency and rescue services in place. Sir Branson highlighted that his immediate concern was the recovery of those injured and pinpointing the cause of the derailment in order to improve future safety regulations. He further commended his own on-board crew for responding in an "exemplary fashion" and thereby preventing further damages. The impact of this accident is yet to be determined; however, for now Virgin Group seems secure and competent enough to handle such accidents. The company's reaction to the crisis says a lot about its culture. Furthermore, its response is in keeping with its Project Aware philosophy that every step in business should lead to better solutions for the communities in which it serves and operates.[86]

C H A P T E R   S U M M A R Y

1. Organizations face many pressures to change. Some forces are external, including globalization, workforce diversity, technological innovation, and ethics. Other forces are internal, such as declining effectiveness, crises, changing employee expectations, and a changing work climate.

2. Organizations face both planned and unplanned change. Change can be of an incremental, strategic, or transformational nature. The individual who directs the change, known as a change agent, can be internal or external to the organization.

3. Individuals resist change for many reasons, and many of these reasons are rooted in fear. Organizations can help manage resistance by educating workers and openly communicating the change, encouraging worker participation in the change efforts, and providing empathy and support to those who have difficulty dealing with change.

4. Reactions to change may be manifested in behaviors reflecting disengagement, disidentification, disenchantment, and disorientation. Managers can use separate interventions targeted toward each reaction.

5. Force field analysis states that when the forces for change are balanced by the forces restraining change, an equilibrium state exists. For change to occur, the forces for change must increase, or the restraining forces must decrease.

6. Lewin's change model proposes three stages of change: unfreezing, moving, and refreezing.

7. A thorough diagnosis and needs analysis is a critical first step in any organization development (OD) intervention.

8. OD interventions targeted toward organizations and groups include survey feedback, management by objectives, product and service quality programs, team building, and process consultation.

9. OD interventions that focus on individuals include skills training, leadership training and development, executive coaching, role negotiation, job redesign, health promotion programs, and career planning.

10. OD efforts should be managed ethically and should preserve individual freedom of choice and privacy.

11. When properly conducted, organization development can have positive effects on performance.

K E Y   T E R M S

change agent (p. 417)
disenchantment (p. 424)
disengagement (p. 423)
disidentification (p. 423)
disorientation (p. 424)
executive coaching (p. 430)
incremental change (p. 416)
job redesign (p. 431)
leadership training and development (p. 430)

management by objectives (MBO) (p. 429)
moving (p. 426)
organization development (OD) (p. 426)
planned change (p. 412)
process consultation (p. 429)
quality program (p. 429)
refreezing (p. 426)
role negotiation (p. 430)

skills training (p. 430)
strategic change (p. 416)
survey feedback (p. 428)
team building (p. 429)
transformational change (p. 416)
unfreezing (p. 425)
unplanned change (p. 412)

R E V I E W   Q U E S T I O N S

1. What are the major external and internal forces for change in organizations?

2. Contrast incremental, strategic, and transformational change.

3. What is a change agent? Who plays this role?

4. What are the major reasons individuals resist change? How can organizations deal with resistance?

5. Name the four behavioral reactions to change. Identify an organizational strategy for dealing with each reaction.

6. Describe force field analysis and its relationship to Lewin's change model.

7. What is organization development? Why is it undertaken by organizations?

8. Name six areas to be critically examined in any comprehensive organizational diagnosis.

9. What are the major organization-focused and group-focused OD intervention methods? The major individual-focused methods?

10. Which OD intervention is most effective?

Discussion and Communication QUESTIONS

1. What are the major external forces for change in today's organizations?

2. What are the advantages of using an external change agent? An internal change agent?

3. Review Challenge 16.1. What can you learn from this challenge about how individuals' tolerance for ambiguity can lead to resistance?

4. Can organizations prevent resistance to change? If so, how?

5. What organization development techniques are the easiest to implement? What techniques are the most difficult to implement? Why?

6. Suppose your organization experiences a dramatic increase in turnover. How would you diagnose the underlying problem?

7. Downsizing has played a major role in changing U.S. organizations. Analyze the internal and external forces for change regarding downsizing an organization.

8. If you were in charge of designing the ideal management development program, what topics would you include? Why?

9. *(communication question)* Find an article that describes an organization that has gone through change and managed it well. Prepare a brief oral presentation about this organization's change experience for your class.

10. *(communication question)* Think of a change you would like to make in your life. Using Figure 16.1 as a guide, prepare your own force field analysis for that change. How will you overcome the forces for the status quo? How will you make sure to "refreeze" following the change? Summarize your analysis in an action plan.

ETHICAL DILEMMA

Tom Wood cannot contain his feelings of sadness. He is sitting at his desk considering the dismissal of his best department supervisor: Liz Williams. Liz has always been one of his best employees. She ran an efficient department and was always well within budget. Best of all, her employees were the happiest and most productive in the company. Tom had spent many days wishing that he had several more supervisors like Liz Williams working for him.

But that was the old Liz. Since the merger, Liz has become a very different employee. She has resented some of the changes that have taken place since the company has merged with a large multinational corporation. Tom has spoken with Liz on several occasions about the changes that have taken place. He knows Liz is struggling with the new management philosophy, and he does not want to lose her. Liz liked the way the previous company operated and is not making the necessary adjustments to become part of the new organization. She disagrees with the new company's procedures, and she is not afraid to let people know it. On more than one occasion in the last six months, Tom has had to defend his decision to keep Liz as part of the team.

Recently, Tom believed things were getting better for Liz. She seemed to be settling down and adjusting to the new culture. At least that is what he thought until yesterday when Liz had a major dispute with her counterpart at the home office in Germany. It had been the last straw for upper management. Tom had gotten the phone message this morning that Liz needs to go. Tom needs to decide if he is pushing his luck too far by going to bat for Liz one more time. He isn't sure how much more his superiors are willing to listen to him defend Liz. Even he agrees that she is beginning to be a real problem. But she is also a good friend and under normal circumstances a very good worker. Does she deserve another chance?

QUESTIONS

1. How long does Tom need to defend Liz's behaviors?
2. What is Liz's responsibility to Tom?
3. Using rule, virtue, right, and justice theories, evaluate Tom's decision.

EXPERIENTIAL EXERCISES

16.1 ORGANIZATIONAL DIAGNOSIS OF THE UNIVERSITY

The purpose of this exercise is to give you experience in organizational diagnosis. Assume that your team has been hired to conduct a diagnosis of problem areas in your university and to make preliminary recommendations for organization development interventions.

Each team member should complete the following University Profile. Then, as a team, evaluate the strengths and weaknesses within each area (academics, teaching, social, cultural, and administrative) using the accompanying University Diagnosis form. Finally, make recommendations concerning organization development interventions for each area. Be as specific as possible in both your diagnosis and your recommendations. Each team should then present its diagnosis to the class.

University Profile

Not True	1	2	3	4	5	Very True

I. Academics

1 2 3 4 5   1. There is a wide range of courses to choose from.
1 2 3 4 5   2. Classroom standards are too easy.
1 2 3 4 5   3. The library is adequate.
1 2 3 4 5   4. Textbooks are helpful.

II. Teachers

1 2 3 4 5   1. Teachers here are committed to quality instruction.
1 2 3 4 5   2. We have a high-quality faculty.

III. Social

1 2 3 4 5   1. Students are friendly to one another.
1 2 3 4 5   2. It is difficult to make friends.
1 2 3 4 5   3. Faculty get involved in student activities.
1 2 3 4 5   4. Too much energy goes into drinking and goofing off.

IV. Cultural Events

1 2 3 4 5   1. There are ample activities on campus.
1 2 3 4 5   2. Student activities are boring.
1 2 3 4 5   3. The administration places a high value on student activities.
1 2 3 4 5   4. Too much emphasis is placed on sports.
1 2 3 4 5   5. We need more "cultural" activities.

V. Organizational/Management

1 2 3 4 5   1. Decision making is shared at all levels of the organization.
1 2 3 4 5   2. There is unity and cohesiveness among departments and units.
1 2 3 4 5   3. Too many departmental clashes hamper the organization's effectiveness.
1 2 3 4 5   4. Students have a say in many decisions.
1 2 3 4 5   5. The budgeting process seems fair.
1 2 3 4 5   6. Recruiting and staffing are handled thoughtfully with student needs in mind.

UNIVERSITY DIAGNOSIS

	STRENGTH	WEAKNESS	INTERVENTION
1. Academic			
2. Teaching			
3. Social			
4. Cultural			
5. Administrative			

SOURCE: "Organizational Diagnosis of the University" by D. Marcic, *Organizational Behavior: Experiences and Cases* (St. Paul, Minn.: West Publishing Company, 1989): 326–329. Reprinted by permission.

16.2 TEAM BUILDING FOR TEAM EFFECTIVENESS

This exercise will allow you and your team to engage in an organization development activity for team building. The two parts of the exercise are diagnosis and intervention.

Part 1. Diagnosis

Working as a team, complete the following four steps:

1. Describe how you have worked together this semester as a team.
2. What has your team done especially well? What has enabled this?
3. What problems or conflicts have you had as a team? (Be specific.) What was the cause of the problems your team experienced? Have the conflicts been over ideas, methods, or people?
4. Would you assess the overall effectiveness of your team as excellent, good, fair, poor, or a disaster? Explain your effectiveness rating.

Part 2. Intervention

A diagnosis provides the basis for intervention and action in organization development. Team building is a way to improve the relationships and effectiveness of teams at work. It is concerned with the results of work activities and the relationships among the members of the team. Complete the following three steps as a team.

Step 1. Answer the following questions with regard to the relationships within the team:

a. How could conflicts have been handled better?
b. How could specific relationships have been improved?
c. How could the interpersonal atmosphere of the team have been improved?

Step 2. Answer the following questions with regard to the results of the team's work:

a. How could the team have been more effective?
b. Are there any team process changes that would have improved the team's effectiveness?
c. Are there any team structure changes that would have improved the team's effectiveness?

Step 3. Answer the following questions with regard to the work environment in your place of employment:

a. What have you learned about team building that you can apply there?
b. What have you learned about team building that would not be applicable there?

Chapter 1

1. O. Malik, "The New Phone Company," *Business 2.0* 4 (November 2003): 82–89, http://www.business2.com/b2/subscribers/articles/0,17863,541290-1,00.html.

2. H. Schwartz, "The Clockwork or the Snakepit: An Essay on the Meaning of Teaching Organizational Behavior," *Organizational Behavior Teaching Review* 11, No. 2 (1987): 19–26.

3. M. Matcho, "Idea Fest," *Fast Company* 66 (January 2003): 95–105, http://www.fastcompany.com/online/66/ideafest.html.

4. H. G. Barkem, J. A. C. Baum, and E. A. Mannix, "Management Challenges in a New Time," *Academy of Management Journal* 45 (2002): 916–930.

5. K. Lewin, "Field Theory in Social Science," selected theoretical papers (edited by Dorin Cartwright) (New York: Harper, 1951).

6. N. Schmitt, ed., Industrial/Organizational Section in *Encyclopedia of Psychology* (Washington, D.C.: American Psychological Association, and New York: Oxford University Press, 2000).

7. R. M. Yerkes, "The Relation of Psychology to Military Activities," *Mental Hygiene* 1 (1917): 371–376.

8. N. Gross, W. Mason, and A. McEachen, *Explorations in Role Analysis: Studies of the School Superintendency Role* (New York: Wiley, 1958).

9. J. S. Adams, A. Tashchian, and T. H. Stone, "Codes of Ethics as Signals for Ethical Behavior," *Journal of Business Ethics* 29 (2001): 199–211.

10. F. W. Taylor, *The Principles of Scientific Management* (New York: Norton, 1911).

11. E. A. Locke and G. P. Latham, *A Theory of Goal Setting and Task Performance* (Englewood Cliffs, N.J.: Prentice-Hall, 1990).

12. A. L. Wilkins and W. G. Ouchi, "Efficient Cultures: Exploring the Relationship between Culture and Organizational Performance," *Administrative Science Quarterly* 28 (1983): 468–481.

13. M. F. R. Kets de Vries and D. Miller, "Personality, Culture, and Organization," *Academy of Management Review* 11 (1986): 266–279.

14. H. Schwartz, *Narcissistic Process and Corporate Decay: The Theory of the Organizational Ideal* (New York: NYU Press, 1990).

15. J. G. March and H. A. Simon, *Organizations* (New York: Wiley, 1958).

16. H. B. Elkind, *Preventive Management: Mental Hygiene in Industry* (New York: B. C. Forbes, 1931).

17. J. C. Quick, "Occupational Health Psychology: Historical Roots and Future Directions," *Health Psychology* 18 (1999).

18. K. R. Pelletier, *Mind as Healer, Mind as Slayer: A Holistic Approach to Preventing Stress Disorders* (New York: Delacorte, 1977).

19. D. R. Ilgen, "Health Issues at Work," *American Psychologist* 45 (1990): 273–283.

20. B. M. Staw, L. E. Sandelands, and J. E. Dutton, "Threat-Rigidity Effects in Organizational Behavior: A Multilevel Analysis," *Administrative Science Quarterly* 26 (1981): 501–524.

21. E. V. Brown, President of Proline International, Inc., "Commencement Address—College of Business Administration, the University of Texas at Arlington" (December 2003).

22. F. J. Roethlisberger and W. J. Dickson, *Management and the Worker* (Cambridge, Mass.: Harvard University Press, 1939).

23. W. L. French and C. H. Bell, *Organization Development*, 4th ed. (Englewood Cliffs, N.J.: Prentice-Hall, 1990).

24. J. P. Kotter, "Managing External Dependence," *Academy of Management Review* 4 (1979): 87–92.

25. H. K. Steensma and D. G. Corley, "Organizational Context as a Moderator of Theories on Firm Boundaries for Technology Sourcing," *Academy of Management Journal* 44 (2001): 271–291.

26. Cisco Systems 2004 Annual Report, http://cisco.com, accessed February 6, 2006.

27. "Pixar Reports Record Results for 2005." Pixar Press Box. http://www.pixar.com/companyinfo/press_box/news/20060307-189666.htm, accessed February 6, 2005.

28. Hoover's Online, "Virgin Group Ltd.—Fact Sheet," http://www.hoovers.com/; B. Morris, "Richard Branson: What a Life," *Fortune* 7 (October 6, 2003), http://www.fortune.com/fortune/personalfortune/articles/0,15114,488581,00.html.

29. Whole Foods Market, Inc. 2004 Annual Report, http://wholefoodsmarket.com, accessed February 6, 2006.

30. T. B. Lawrence and V. Corwin, "Being There: The Acceptance and Marginalization of Part-Time Professional Employees," *Journal of Organizational Behavior* 24 (2003): 923–943.

31. M. K. Gowing, J. D. Kraft, and J. C. Quick, *The New Organizational Reality: Downsizing, Restructuring and Revitalization* (Washington, D.C.: American Psychological Association, 1998); T. Tang and R. M. Fuller, "Corporate Downsizing: What Managers Can Do to Lessen the Negative Effects of Layoffs," *SAM Advanced Management Journal* 60 (1995): 12–15, 31.

32. S. London, "Xerox Runs off a New Blueprint—Cultural Change," *Financial Times* (September 23, 2005): 13.

33. L. R. Offermann and M. K. Gowing, "Organizations of the Future," *American Psychologist* 45 (1990): 95–108.

34. J. Chatman, J. Polzer, S. Barsade, and M. Neale, "Being Different Yet Feeling Similar: The Influence of Demographic Composition and Organizational Culture on Work Processes and Outcomes," *Administrative Science Quarterly* 43 (1998): 749–780.

35. L. E. Thurow, *Head to Head: The Coming Economic Battle among Japan, Europe, and America* (New York: William Morrow, 1992).

36. J. E. Patterson, *Acquiring the Future: America's Survival and Success in the Global Economy* (Homewood, Ill.: Dow Jones-Irwin, 1990); H. B. Stewart, *Recollecting the Future: A View of Business, Technology, and Innovation in the Next 30 Years* (Homewood, Ill.: Dow Jones-Irwin, 1989).

37. D. Ciampa, *Total Quality* (Reading, Mass.: Addison-Wesley, 1992).

38. T. J. Douglas and W. Q. Judge, Jr., "Total Quality Management Implementation and Competitive Advantage: The Role of Structural Control and Exploration," *Academy of Management Journal* 44 (2001): 158–169.

39. American Management Association, *Blueprints for Service Quality: The Federal Express Approach* (New York: American Management Association, 1991); P. R. Thomas, L. J. Gallace, and K. R. Martin, *Quality Alone Is Not Enough* (New York: American Management Association, 1992).

40. J. de Mast, "A Methodological Comparison of Three Strategies for Quality Improvement," *International Journal of Quality & Reliability Management* 21 (2004): 198–213.

41. M. Barney, "Motorola's Second Generation," *Six Sigma Forum Magazine* 1 (3) (May 2002): 13.

42. London, "Xerox Runs off Blueprint," 13.

43. J. A. Edosomwan, "Six Commandments to Empower Employees for Quality Improvement," *Industrial Engineering* 24 (1992): 14–15.

44. M. Baer and W. Frese, "Innovation Is Not Enough: Climates for Initiative and Psychological Safety Advantage: The Role of Structural Control and Exploration," *Journal of Organizational Behavior* 24 (2003): 45–68.

45. See also the five articles in the Special Research Forum on Teaching Effectiveness in the Organizational Sciences, *The Academy of Management Journal* 40 (1997): 1265–1398.

46. R. M. Steers, L. W. Porter, and G. A. Bigley, *Motivation and Leadership at Work* (New York: McGraw-Hill, 1996).

47. H. Levinson, *Executive Stress* (New York: New American Library, 1975).

48. D. L. Whetzel, "The Department of Labor Identifies Workplace Skills," *Industrial/Organizational Psychologist* 29 (1991): 89–90.

49. D. A. Whetton and K. S. Cameron, *Developing Management Skills*, 3rd ed. (New York: HarperCollins, 1995).

50. C. Argyris and D. A. Schon, *Organizational Learning: A Theory of Action Perspective* (Reading, Mass.: Addison-Wesley, 1978).

51. D. Kirkpatrick, "Where the Action Is," *Fortune* 147 (May 12, 2003): 78, http://www.fortune.com/fortune/subs/article/0,15114,447123,00.html.

Chapter 2

1. J. Larsen, "The New Disney?" *The American Enterprise* 14 (July/August 2003): 50.
2. M. A. Hitt, R. E. Hoskisson, and J. S. Harrison, "Strategic Competitiveness in the 1990s: Challenges and Opportunities for U.S. Executives," *Academy of Management Executive* 5 (1991): 7–22.
3. H. G. Barkem, J. A. C. Baum, and E. A. Mannix, "Management Challenges in a New Time," *Academy of Management Journal* 45 (2002): 916–930.
4. S. C. Harper, "The Challenges Facing CEOs: Past, Present, and Future," *Academy of Management Executive* 6 (1992): 7–25.
5. T. R. Mitchell and W. G. Scott, "America's Problems and Needed Reforms: Confronting the Ethic of Personal Advantage," *Academy of Management Executive* 4 (1990): 23–25.
6. B. Spindle, "Sinking in Sync—The Global Slowdown Surprises Economists and Many Companies," *The Wall Street Journal* (December 21, 2000): A1–A10.
7. D. A. Harrison, J. H. Gavin, and A. T. Florey, "Time, Teams, and Task Performance: Changing Effects of Surface- and Deep-Level Diversity on Group Functioning," *Academy of Management Journal* 45 (2003): 1029–1045.
8. J. H. Gavin, J. C. Quick, C. L. Cooper, and J. D. Quick, "A Spirit of Personal Integrity: The Role of Character in Executive Health," *Organizational Dynamics* 32 (2003): 165–179.
9. K. Sera, "Corporate Globalization: A New Trend," *Academy of Management Executive* 6 (1992): 89–96.
10. K. Ohmae, *Borderless World: Power and Strategies in the Interlinked Economy* (New York: Harper & Row, 1990).
11. C. A. Bartlett and S. Ghoshal, *Managing across Borders: The Transnational Solution* (Boston: Harvard Business School Press, 1989).
12. F. Warner, "Learning How to Speak to Gen Y," *Fast Company* 72 (July 2003): 36–37, http://www.fastcompany.com/magazine/72/smartcompany.html.
13. K. R. Xin and J. L. Pearce, "Guanxi: Connections as Substitutes for Formal Institutional Support," *Academy of Management Journal* 39 (1996): 1641–1658.
14. P. S. Chan, "Franchise Management in East Asia," *Academy of Management Executive* 4 (1990): 75–85.
15. H. Weihrich, "Europe 1992: What the Future May Hold," *Academy of Management Executive* 4 (1990): 7–18.
16. E. H. Schein, "Coming to a New Awareness of Organizational Culture," *MIT Sloan Management Review* 25 (1984): 3–16.
17. S. S. Sarwano and R. M. Armstrong, "Microcultural Differences and Perceived Ethical Problems: An International Business Perspective," *Journal of Business Ethics* 30 (2001): 41–56.
18. R. Sharpe, "Hi-Tech Taboos," *The Wall Street Journal* (October 31, 1995): A1.

19. G. Hofstede, *Culture's Consequences: International Differences in Work-Related Values* (Beverly Hills, Calif.: Sage Publications, 1980).
20. G. Hofstede, "Motivation, Leadership, and Organization: Do American Theories Apply Abroad?" *Organizational Dynamics* (Summer 1980): 42–63.
21. R. Buda and S. M. Elsayed-Elkhouly, "Cultural Differences between Arabs and Americans," *Journal of Cross-Cultural Psychology* 29 (1998): 487–492.
22. G. Hofstede, "Gender Stereotypes and Partner Preferences of Asian Women in Masculine and Feminine Countries," *Journal of Cross Cultural Psychology* 27 (1996): 533–546.
23. G. Hofstede, "Cultural Constraints in Management Theories," *Academy of Management Executive* 7 (1993): 81–94.
24. G. M. Spreitzer, M. W. McCall, Jr., and J. D. Mahoney, "Early Identification of International Executive Potential," *Journal of Applied Psychology* 82 (1997): 6–29.
25. A. J. Michel, "Goodbyes Can Cost Plenty in Europe," *Fortune* (April 6, 1992): 16.
26. M. Adams, "Building a Rainbow One Stripe at a Time," *HR Magazine* 9 (August 1999): 72–79. Intel, "Diversity at Intel: Our Commitment," 2003, http://www.intel.com/intel/diversity/divcommit.htm.
27. E. Brandt, "Global HR," *Personnel Journal* 70 (1991): 38–44.
28. P. Chattopadhyay, "Can Dissimilarity Lead to Positive Outcomes: The Influence of Open versus Closed Minds," *Journal of Organizational Behavior* 24 (2003): 295–312.
29. J. C. Quick, J. H. Gavin, C. L. Cooper, and J. D. Quick, "Working Together: Balancing Head and Heart," in R. H. Rozensky, N. G. Johnson, C. D. Goodheart, and W. R. Hammond, eds., *Psychology Builds a Healthy World: Opportunities for Research and Practice* (Washington, D.C.: American Psychological Association, 2004): 219–232.
30. J. A. Gilbert and J. M. Ivancevich, "Valuing Diversity: A Tale of Two Organizations," *Academy of Management Executive* 4 (2000): 93–105.
31. R. W. Judy and C. D'Amico, *Workforce 2020* (Indianapolis, Ind.: Hudson Institute, 1997), U.S. Department of Labor, "Usual Weekly Earnings Summary," *Labor Force Statistics from the Current Population Survey* (Washington D.C.: U.S. Government, 2002).
32. S. Caudron, "Task Force Report Reveals Coke's Progress on Diversity," *Workforce* 82 (2003): 40, http://www.workforceonline.com/section/03/feature/23/42/44/234246.html.
33. L. S. Gottfredson, "Dilemmas in Developing Diversity Programs," in S. E. Jackson, ed., *Diversity in the Workplace: Human Resources Initiatives* (New York: Guilford Press, 1992): 279–305.
34. U.S. Department of Labor, "Employment Status of the Civilian Population by Sex and Age" (July 2004).

Accessed online at http://stats.bls.gov/news.release/empsit.t01.htm.
35. Catalyst, *Catalyst Census of Women Corporate Officers and Top Earners*, 2005.
36. D. Jones, "Not-So-Good Year for Female CEOs: Fortune 500 Sees Count Go from 9 to 7," *USA Today* (December 22, 2005): B3.
37. U.S. Department of Labor, "Highlights of Women's Earnings in 2002," *Report 972* (September 2003).
38. A. M. Morrison, R. P. White, E. Van Velsor, and the Center for Creative Leadership, *Breaking the Glass Ceiling: Can Women Reach the Top of America's Largest Corporations?* (Reading, Mass.: Addison-Wesley, 1987).
39. D. E. Arfken, S. L. Bellar, and M. M. Helms, "The Ultimate Glass Ceiling Revisited: The Presence of Women on Corporate Boards," *Journal of Business Ethics* 50 (March 2004): 177–186.
40. N. J. Adler, "Global Leadership: Women Leaders," *Management International Review* 37 (1997): 171–196.
41. A. Eyring and B. A. Stead, "Shattering the Glass Ceiling: Some Successful Corporate Practices," *Journal of Business Ethics* 17 (1998): 245–251.
42. Catalyst, *Advancing Women in Business: The Catalyst Guide* (San Francisco: Jossey-Bass, 1998).
43. D. L. Nelson and M. A. Hitt, "Employed Women and Stress: Implications for Enhancing Women's Mental Health in the Workplace," in J. C. Quick, L. R. Murphy, and J. J. Hurrell, Jr., eds., *Stress and Well-Being at Work* (Washington, D.C.: American Psychological Association, 1992): 164–177.
44. L. E. Atwater and D. D. Van Fleet, "Another Ceiling: Can Males Compete for Traditionally Female Jobs?" *Journal of Management* 23 (1997): 603–626.
45. U.S. Department of Health and Human Services, *Profile of Older Americans* (Washington, D.C.: U.S. Government, 1997).
46. W. B. Johnston, "Global Workforce 2000: The New World Labor Market," *Harvard Business Review* 69 (1991): 115–127.
47. S. E. Jackson and E. B. Alvarez, "Working through Diversity as a Strategic Imperative," in S. E. Jackson, ed., *Diversity in the Workplace: Human Resources Initiatives* (New York: Guilford Press, 1992): 13–36.
48. "Managing Generational Diversity," *HR Magazine* 36 (1991): 91–92.
49. M. Dittmann, "Generational Differences at Work," *Monitor on Psychology* 36: 54.
50. C. M. Solomon, "Managing the Baby Busters," *Personnel Journal* (March 1992): 52–59.
51. S. R. Rhodes, "Age-Related Differences in Work Attitudes and Behavior: A Review and Conceptual Analysis," *Psychological Bulletin* 93 (1983): 338–367.
52. B. L. Hassell and P. L. Perrewe, "An Examination of Beliefs about Older Workers: Do Stereotypes Still Exist?" *Journal of Organizational Behavior* 16 (1995): 457–468.

53. U.S. Bureau of the Census, *Population Profile of the United States, 1997* (Washington, D.C.: U.S. Government Printing Office, 1997).
54. M. P. Bell, *Diversity in Organizations* (Cincinnati: South-Western, February 2006).
55. W. J. Rothwell, "HRD and the Americans with Disabilities Act," *Training and Development Journal* (August 1991): 45–47.
56. M. P. Bell, *Diversity in Organizations* (Cincinnati: South-Western, February 2006).
57. J. Waldrop, "The Cost of Hiring the Disabled," *American Demographics* (March 1991): 12.
58. J. J. Laabs, "The Golden Arches Provide Golden Opportunities," *Personnel Journal* (July 1991): 52–57.
59. L. Winfield and S. Spielman, "Making Sexual Orientation Part of Diversity," *Training and Development* (April 1995): 50–51.
60. N. E. Day and P. Schoenrade, "Staying in the Closet versus Coming Out: Relationships between Communication about Sexual Orientation and Work Attitudes," *Personnel Psychology* 50 (1997): 147–163.
61. J. Landau, "The Relationship of Race and Gender to Managers' Ratings of Promotion Potential," *Journal of Organizational Behavior* 16 (1995): 391–400.
62. P. Barnum, "Double Jeopardy for Women and Minorities: Pay Differences with Age," *Academy of Management Journal* 38 (1995): 863–880.
63. J. E. Rigdon, "PepsiCo's KFC Scouts for Blacks and Women for Its Top Echelons," *The Wall Street Journal* (November 13, 1991): A1.
64. P. A. Galagan, "Tapping the Power of a Diverse Workforce," *Training and Development Journal* 26 (1991): 38–44.
65. C. L. Holladay, J. L. Knight, D. L. Paige, and M. A. Quinones, "The Influence of Framing on Attitudes Toward Diversity Training," *Human Resource Development Quarterly* 14 (2003): 245–263.
66. R. Thomas, "From Affirmative Action to Affirming Diversity," *Harvard Business Review* 68 (1990): 107–117.
67. T. H. Cox, Jr., *Cultural Diversity in Organizations: Theory, Research and Practice* (San Francisco: Berrett-Koehler, 1994).
68. J. Gordon, "Different from What?" *Training* (May 1995): 25–33.
69. M. R. Fusilier, C. D. Aby, Jr., J. K. Worley, and S. Elliott, "Perceived Seriousness of Business Ethics Issues," *Business and Professional Ethics Journal* 15 (1996): 67–78.
70. J. S. Mill, *Utilitarianism, Liberty, and Representative Government* (London: Dent, 1910).
71. K. H. Blanchard and N. V. Peale, *The Power of Ethical Management* (New York: Morrow, 1988).
72. C. Fried, *Right and Wrong* (Cambridge, Mass.: Harvard University Press, 1978).
73. I. Kant, *Groundwork of the Metaphysics of Morals,* trans. H. J. Paton (New York: Harper & Row, 1964).

74. A. Smith, *An Inquiry into the Nature and Causes of the Wealth of Nations,* vol. 10 of The Harvard Classics, ed. C. J. Bullock (New York: P. F. Collier & Son, 1909).
75. R. C. Solomon, "Corporate Roles, Personal Virtues: Aristotelean Approach to Business Ethics," *Business Ethics Quarterly* 2 (1992): 317–339; R. C. Solomon, *A Better Way to Think about Business: How Personal Integrity Leads to Corporate Success* (New York: Oxford University Press, 1999).
76. D. Kemp, "Employers and AIDS: Dealing with the Psychological and Emotional Issues of AIDS in the Workplace," *American Review of Public Administration* 25 (1995): 263–278.
77. J. J. Koch, "Wells Fargo's and IBM's HIV Policies Help Protect Employees' Rights," *Personnel Journal* (April 1990): 40–48.
78. A. Arkin, "Positive HIV and AIDS Policies at Work," *Personnel Management* (December 1994): 34–37.
79. U.S. EEOC, 1980. Discrimination because of sex under Title VII of the 1964 Civil Rights Act as amended: Adoption of interim guidelines—sexual harassment. *Federal Register* 45: 25024–25025; S. J. Adler, "Lawyers Advise Concerns to Provide Precise Written Policy to Employees," *The Wall Street Journal* (October 9, 1991): B1.
80. L. F. Fitzgerald, F. Drasgow, C. L. Hulin, M. J. Gelfand, and V. J. Magley, "Antecedents and Consequences of Sexual Harassment in Organizations: A Test of an Integrated Model," *Journal of Applied Psychology* 82 (1997): 578–589.
81. E. Felsenthal, "Rulings Open Way for Sex-Harass Cases," *The Wall Street Journal* (June 29, 1998): A10.
82. K. T. Schneider, S. Swan, and L. F. Fitzgerald, "Job-Related and Psychological Effects of Sexual Harassment in the Workplace: Empirical Evidence from Two Organizations," *Journal of Applied Psychology* 82 (1997): 401–415.
83. A. M. O'Leary-Kelly, R. L. Paetzold, and R. W. Griffin, "Sexual Harassment as Aggressive Behavior: An Actor-Based Perspective," *Academy of Management Review* 25 (2000): 372–388.
84. L. M. Goldenhar, N. G. Swanson, J. J. Hurrell, Jr., A. Ruder, and J. Deddens, "Stressors and Adverse Outcomes for Female Construction Workers," *Journal of Occupational Health Psychology* 3 (1998): 19–32; C. S. Piotrkowski, "Gender Harassment, Job Satisfaction and Distress Among Employed White and Minority Women," *Journal of Occupational Health Psychology* 3 (1998): 33–42.
85. G. N. Powell and S. Foley, "Something to Talk About: Romantic Relationships in Organizational Settings," *Journal of Management* 24 (1998): 421–448.
86. D. Fields, M. Pang, and C. Chio, "Distributive and Procedural Justice as

Predictors of Employee Outcomes in Hong Kong," *Journal of Organizational Behavior* 21 (2000): 547–562.
87. J. Greenberg, "Stress Fairness to Fare No Stress: Managing Workplace Stress by Promoting Organizational Justice," *Organizational Dynamics* 33 (2004): 352–365.
88. H. L. Laframboise, "Vile Wretches and Public Heroes: The Ethics of Whistleblowing in Government," *Canadian Public Administration* (Spring 1991): 73–78.
89. A. Nyberg, "Whistle-Blower Woes," *CFO Magazine* 19 (October 2003): 50, http://www.cfo.com/article/1,5309,10790,00.html.
90. D. B. Turban and D. W. Greening, "Corporate Social Performance and Organizational Attractiveness to Prospective Employees," *Academy of Management Journal* 40 (1996): 658–672.
91. W. E. Hull, *The Four-Way Test: Core Values of the Rotary Movement* (Birmingham, Ala.: The Rotary Club of Birmingham, 2004).
92. J. Martin, "Inside the Pixar Dream Factory," *Fortune Small Business* 13 (2003): 45, http://www.fortune.com/fortune/smallbusiness/articles/0,15114,411065,00.html.

Chapter 3

1. K. Lewin, "Formalization and Progress in Psychology," in D. Cartwright, ed., *Field Theory in Social Science* (New York: Harper, 1951).
2. N. S. Endler and D. Magnusson, "Toward an Interactional Psychology of Personality," *Psychological Bulletin* 83 (1976): 956–974.
3. J. R. Terborg, "Interactional Psychology and Research on Human Behavior in Organizations," *Academy of Management Review* 6 (1981): 561–576.
4. C. Spearman, "General Intelligence: Objectively Determined and Measured," *American Journal of Psychology* 15 (1904): 201–293.
5. F. L Schmidt and J. Hunter, "General Mental Ability in the World of Work: Occupational Attainment and Job Performance," *Journal of Personality and Social Psychology* 86 (1) (2004): 162–173.
6. C. Bertua, N. Anderson, and J. F. Salgado, "The Predictive Validity of Cognitive Ability Tests: A UK Meta-Analysis," *Journal of Occupational and Organizational Psychology* 78 (2004): 387–409.
7. T. J. Bouchard, Jr., "Twins Reared Together and Apart: What They Tell Us about Human Diversity," in S. W. Fox, ed., *Individuality and Determinism* (New York: Plenum Press, 1984).
8. R. D. Arvey, T. J. Bouchard, Jr., N. L. Segal, and L. M. Abraham, "Job Satisfaction: Environmental and Genetic Components," *Journal of Applied Psychology* 74 (1989): 235–248.

9. J. M. Digman, "Personality Structure: Emergence of a Five-Factor Model," *Annual Review of Psychology* 41 (1990): 417–440.

10. T. A. Judge, J. J. Martocchio, and C. J. Thoresen, "Five-Factor Model of Personality and Employee Absence," *Journal of Applied Psychology* 82 (1997): 745–755.

11. H. J. Bernardin, D. K. Cooke, and P. Villanova, "Conscientiousness and Agreeableness as Predictors of Rating Leniency," *Journal of Applied Psychology* 85 (2000): 232–234.

12. S. E. Seibert and M. L. Kraimer, "The Five-Factor Model of Personality and Career Success," *Journal of Vocational Behavior* 58 (2001): 1–21.

13. T. A. Judge and R. Ilies, "Relationships of Personality to Performance Motivation: A Meta-Analytic Review," *Journal of Applied Psychology* 87 (2002): 797–807.

14. G. M. Hurtz and J. J. Donovan, "Personality and Job Performance: The Big Five Revisited," *Journal of Applied Psychology* 85 (2000): 869–879.

15. J. F. Salgado, S. Moscoso, and M. Lado, "Evidence of Cross-Cultural Invariance of the Big Five Personality Dimensions in Work Settings," *European Journal of Personality* 17 (2003): S67–S76; C. Rodriguez and T. H. Church, "The Structure and Personality Correlates of Affect in Mexico: Evidence of Cross-Cultural Comparability Using the Spanish Language," *Journal of Cross-Cultural Psychology* 34 (2003): 211–230.

16. H. C. Triandis, "Cultural Influences on Personality," *Annual Review of Psychology* 53 (2002): 133–160.

17. M. R. Barrick and M. K. Mount, "The Big Five Personality Dimensions and Job Performance: A Meta-Analysis," *Personnel Psychology* 44 (1991): 1–26.

18. D. D. Clark and R. Hoyle, "A Theoretical Solution to the Problem of Personality-Situational Interaction," *Personality and Individual Differences* 9 (1988): 133–138.

19. D. Byrne and L. J. Schulte, "Personality Dimensions as Predictors of Sexual Behavior," in J. Bancroft, ed., *Annual Review of Sexual Research*, vol. 1 (Philadelphia: Society for the Scientific Study of Sex, 1990).

20. T. A. Judge, E. A. Locke, and C. C. Durham, "The Dispositional Causes of Job Satisfaction: A Core Self-Evaluation Approach," *Research in Organizational Behavior* 19 (1997): 151–188.

21. M. Erez and T. A. Judge, "Relationship of Core Self-Evaluations to Goal Setting, Motivation and Performance," *Journal of Applied Psychology* 86 (2001): 1270–1279.

22. R. F. Piccolo, T. A Judge, K. Takahashi, N. Watanabe, and E. A. Locke, "Core Self-Evaluations in Japan: Relative Effects on Job Satisfaction, Life Satisfaction, and Happiness," *Journal of Organizational Behavior* 26 (8) (2005): 965–984.

23. J. B. Rotter, "Generalized Expectancies for Internal vs. External Locus of Control of Reinforcement," *Psychological Monographs* 80, whole No. 609 (1966).

24. T. A. Judge and J. E. Bono, "Relationship of Core Self-Evaluations Traits—Self-Esteem, Generalized Self-Efficacy, Locus of Control, and Emotional Stability—with Job Satisfaction and Job Performance: A Meta-Analysis," *Journal of Applied Psychology* 86 (2001): 80–92.

25. T. A. Judge and J. E. Bono, "Relationship of Core Self-Evaluations Traits—Self-Esteem, Generalized Self-Efficacy, Locus of Control, and Emotional Stability—with Job Satisfaction and Job Performance: A Meta-Analysis," *Journal of Applied Psychology* 86 (2001): 80–92.

26. S. S. K. Lam and J. Shaubroeck, "The Role of Locus of Control in Reactions to Being Promoted and to Being Passed Over: A Quasi Experiment," *Academy of Management Journal* 43 (2000): 66–78.

27. G. Chen, S. M. Gully, J. Whiteman, and R. N. Kilcullen, "Examination of Relationships Among Trait-Like Individual Differences, State-Like Individual Differences, and Learning Performance," *Journal of Applied Psychology* 85 (2000): 835–847; G. Chen, S. M. Gully, and D. Eden, "Validation of a New General Self-Efficacy Scale," *Organizational Research Methods* 4 (2001): 62–83.

28. A. Bandura, *Self-Efficacy: The Exercise of Control* (San Francisco: Freeman, 1997).

29. D. R. Avery, "Personality as a Predictor of the Value of Voice," *The Journal of Psychology* 137 (2003): 435–447.

30. T. A. Judge and J. E. Bono, "Relationship of Core Self-Evaluations Traits—Self-Esteem, Generalized Self-Efficacy, Locus of Control, and Emotional Stability—with Job Satisfaction and Job Performance: A Meta-Analysis," *Journal of Applied Psychology* 86 (2001): 80–92.

31. B. W. Pelham and W. B. Swann, Jr., "From Self-Conceptions to Self-Worth: On the Sources and Structure of Global Self-Esteem," *Journal of Personality and Social Psychology* 57 (1989): 672–680.

32. A. H. Baumgardner, C. M. Kaufman, and P. E. Levy, "Regulating Affect Interpersonally: When Low Esteem Leads to Greater Enhancement," *Journal of Personality and Social Psychology* 56 (1989): 907–921.

33. J. Schimel, T. Pyszczynski, J. Arndt, and J. Greenberg, "Being Accepted for Who We Are: Evidence that Social Validation of the Intrinsic Self Reduces General Defensiveness," *Journal of Personality and Social Psychology* 80 (2001): 35–52.

34. P. Tharenou and P. Harker, "Moderating Influences of Self-Esteem on Relationships between Job Complexity, Performance, and Satisfaction," *Journal of Applied Psychology* 69 (1984): 623–632.

35. R. A. Ellis and M. S. Taylor, "Role of Self-Esteem within the Job Search Process," *Journal of Applied Psychology* 68 (1983): 632–640.

36. J. Brockner and T. Hess, "Self-Esteem and Task Performance in Quality Circles," *Academy of Management Journal* 29 (1986): 617–623.

37. B. R. Schlenker, M. F. Weingold, and J. R. Hallam, "Self-Serving Attributions in Social Context: Effects of Self-Esteem and Social Pressure," *Journal of Personality and Social Psychology* 57 (1990): 855–863.

38. M. K. Duffy, J. D. Shaw, and E. M. Stark, "Performance and Satisfaction in Conflicted Interdependent Groups: When and How Does Self-Esteem Make a Difference?" *Academy of Management Journal* 43 (2000): 772–782.

39. T. Mussweiler, S. Gabriel, and G. V. Bodenhausen, "Shifting Social Identities as a Strategy for Deflecting Threatening Social Comparisons," *Journal of Personality and Social Psychology* 79 (2000): 398–409.

40. M. Erez and T. A. Judge, "Relationship of Core Self-Evaluations to Goal Setting, Motivation and Performance," *Journal of Applied Psychology* 86 (2001): 1270–1279.

41. M. Snyder and S. Gangestad, "On the Nature of Self-Monitoring: Matters of Assessment, Matters of Validity," *Journal of Personality and Social Psychology* 51 (1986): 123–139.

42. A. Mehra, M. Kilduff, and D. J. Brass, "The Social Networks of High and Low Self-Monitors: Implications for Workplace Performance," *Administrative Science Quarterly* 46 (2001): 121–146.

43. W. H. Turnley and M. C. Bolino, "Achieving Desired Images While Avoiding Undesired Images: Exploring the Role of Self-Monitoring in Impression Management," *Journal of Applied Psychology* 86 (2001): 351–360.

44. M. Kilduff and D. V. Day, "Do Chameleons Get Ahead? The Effects of Self-Monitoring on Managerial Careers," *Academy of Management Journal* 37 (1994): 1047–1060.

45. A. H. Church, "Managerial Self-Awareness in High-Performing Individuals in Organizations," *Journal of Applied Psychology* 82 (1997): 281–292.

46. C. Douglas and W. L. Gardner, "Transition to Self-Directed Work Teams: Implications of Transition Time and Self-Monitoring for Managers' Use of Influence Tactics," *Journal of Organizational Behavior* 25 (2004): 45–67.

47. A. M. Isen and R. A. Baron, "Positive Affect and Organizational Behavior," in B. M. Staw and L. L. Cummings, eds., *Research in Organizational Behavior*, vol. 12 (Greenwich, Conn.: JAI Press, 1990).

48. D. Watson and L. A. Clark, "Negative Affectivity: The Disposition to Experience

Aversive Emotional States," *Psychological Bulletin* 96 (1984): 465–490.

49. R. Ilies and T. Judge, "On the Heritability of Job Satisfaction: The Mediating Role of Personality," *Journal of Applied Psychology* 88 (2003): 750–759.

50. J. M. George, "State or Trait," *Journal of Applied Psychology* 76 (1991): 299–307.

51. J. M. George, "Mood and Absence," *Journal of Applied Psychology* 74 (1989): 287–324.

52. S. Lyubormirsky, L. King, L, & E. Diener, "The Benefits of Frequent Positive Affect: Does Happiness Lead to Success?" *Psychological Bulletin,* 131 (6)(2005): 803–855.

53. M. J. Burke, A. P. Brief, and J. M. George, "The Role of Negative Affectivity in Understanding Relations between Self-Reports of Stressors and Strains: A Comment on the Applied Psychology Literature," *Journal of Applied Psychology* 78 (1993): 402–412.

54. S. Barsade, A. Ward, J. Turner, and J. Sonnenfeld, "To Your Heart's Content: A Model of Affective Diversity in Top Management Teams," *Administrative Science Quarterly* 45 (2000): 802–836.

55. W. Mischel, "The Interaction of Person and Situation," in D. Magnusson and N. S. Endler, eds., *Personality at the Crossroads: Current Issues in Interactional Psychology* (Hillsdale, N.J.: Erlbaum, 1977).

56. C. G. Jung, *Psychological Types* (New York: Harcourt & Brace, 1923).

57. Consulting Psychologists Press.

58. R. Benfari and J. Knox, *Understanding Your Management Style* (Lexington, Mass.: Lexington Books, 1991).

59. O. Kroeger and J. M. Thuesen, *Type Talk* (New York: Delacorte Press, 1988).

60. A. Park and P. Burrows, "What You Don't Know About Dell," *Business Week* (November 3, 2003): 74–84.

61. S. Hirsch and J. Kummerow, *Life Types* (New York: Warner Books, 1989).

62. I. B. Myers and M. H. McCaulley, *Manual: A Guide to the Development and Use of the Myers-Briggs Type Indicator* (Palo Alto, Calif.: Consulting Psychologists Press, 1990).

63. G. P. Macdaid, M. H. McCaulley, and R. I. Kainz, *Myers-Briggs Type Indicator: Atlas of Type Tables* (Gainesville, Fla.: Center for Application of Psychological Type, 1987).

64. A. Thomas, M. Benne, M. Marr, E. Thomas, and R. Hume, "The Evidence Remains Stable: The MBTI Predicts Attraction and Attrition in an Engineering Program," *Journal of Psychological Type* 55 (2000): 35–42.

65. C. Walck, "Training for Participative Management: Implications for Psychological Type," *Journal of Psychological Type* 21 (1991): 3–12.

66. E. C. Webster, *The Employment Interview: A Social Judgment Process* (Schomberg, Canada: SIP, 1982).

67. N. Adler, *International Dimensions of Organizational Behavior*, 2nd ed. (Boston: PWS-Kent, 1991).

68. L. R. Offerman and M. K. Gowing, "Personnel Selection in the Future: The Impact of Changing Demographics and the Nature of Work," in Schmitt, Borman & Associates, eds., *Personnel Selection in Organizations* (San Francisco: Jossey-Bass, 1993).

69. J. Park and M. R. Banaji, "Mood and Heuristics: The Influence of Happy and Sad States on Sensitivity and Bias in Stereotyping," *Journal of Personality and Social Psychology* 78 (2000): 1005–1023.

70. M. W. Levine and J. M. Shefner, *Fundamentals of Sensation and Perception* (Reading, Mass.: Addison-Wesley, 1981).

71. R. L. Dipboye, H. L. Fromkin, and K. Willback, "Relative Importance of Applicant Sex, Attractiveness, and Scholastic Standing in Evaluations of Job Applicant Resumes," *Journal of Applied Psychology* 60 (1975): 39–43.

72. I. H. Frieze, J. E. Olson, and J. Russell, "Attractiveness and Income for Men and Women in Management," *Journal of Applied Social Psychology* 21 (1991): 1039–1057.

73. P. Ekman and W. Friesen, *Unmasking the Face* (Englewood Cliffs, N.J.: Prentice-Hall, 1975).

74. J. E. Rehfeld, "What Working for a Japanese Company Taught Me," *Harvard Business Review* (November–December 1990): 167–176.

75. M. W. Morris and R. P. Larrick, "When One Cause Casts Doubt on Another: A Normative Analysis of Discounting in Causal Attribution," *Psychological Review* 102 (1995): 331–355.

76. G. B. Sechrist and C. Stangor, "Perceived Consensus Influences Intergroup Behavior and Stereotype Accessibility," *Journal of Personality and Psychology* 80 (2001): 645–654; A. Lyons and Y. Kashima, "How Are Stereotypes Maintained Through Communication? The Influence of Stereotype Sharedness," *Journal of Personality and Social Psychology* 85 (2003): 989–1005.

77. L. Copeland, "Learning to Manage a Multicultural Workforce," *Training* (May 1988): 48–56.

78. M. Bertrand and S. Mullainathan, "Are Emily and Greg More Employable than Lakisha and Jamal? A Field Experiment on Labor Market Discrimination," *American Economic Review* 94 (2004): 991–1013.

79. S. Ferrari, "Human Behavior in International Groups," *Management International Review* 7 (1972): 31–35.

80. M. Biernat, "Toward a Broader View of Social Stereotyping," *American Psychologist* 58 (2003): 1019–1027.

81. E. Burnstein and Y. Schul, "The Informational Basis of Social Judgments: Operations in Forming an Impression of Another Person," *Journal of Experimental Social Psychology* 18 (1982): 217–234.

82. D. Eden and Y. Zuk, "Seasickness as a Self-Fulfilling Prophecy: Raising Self-Efficacy to Boost Performance at Sea," *Journal of Applied Psychology* 80 (1995): 628–635.

83. D. Eden, "Pygmalion without Interpersonal Contrast Effects: Whole Groups Gain from Raising Manager Expectations," *Journal of Applied Psychology* 75 (1990): 394–398.

84. R. A. Giacolone and P. Rosenfeld, eds., *Impression Management in Organizations* (Hillsdale, N.J.: Erlbaum, 1990); J. Tedeschi and V. Melburg, "Impression Management and Influence in the Organization," in S. Bacharach and E. Lawler, eds., *Research in the Sociology of Organizations* (Greenwich, Conn.: JAI Press, 1984): 31–58.

85. A. Colella and A. Varma, "The Impact of Subordinate Disability on Leader–Member Exchange Relationships," *Academy of Management Journal* 44 (2001): 304–315.

86. D. C. Gilmore and G. R. Ferris, "The Effects of Applicant Impression Management Tactics on Interviewer Judgments," *Journal of Management* (December 1989): 557–564.

87. C. K. Stevens and A. L. Kristof, "Making the Right Impression: A Field Study of Applicant Impressions Management during Job Interviews," *Journal of Applied Psychology* 80 (1995): 587–606.

88. S. J. Wayne and R. C. Liden, "Effects of Impression Management on Performance Ratings: A Longitudinal Study," *Academy of Management Journal* 38 (1995): 232–260.

89. R. A. Baron, "Impression Management by Applicants during Employment Interviews: The 'Too Much of a Good Thing' Effect," in R. W. Eder and G. R. Ferris, eds., *The Employment Interview: Theory, Research, and Practice* (Newbury Park, Calif.: Sage Publications, 1989).

90. F. Heider, *The Psychology of Interpersonal Relations* (New York: Wiley, 1958).

91. B. Weiner, "An Attributional Theory of Achievement Motivation and Emotion," *Psychological Review* (October 1985): 548–573.

92. P. D. Sweeney, K. Anderson, and S. Bailey, "Attributional Style in Depression: A Meta-Analytic Review," *Journal of Personality and Social Psychology* 51 (1986): 974–991.

93. P. Rosenthal, D. Guest, and R. Peccei, "Gender Differences in Managers' Causal Explanations for Their Work Performance," *Journal of Occupational and Organizational Psychology* 69 (1996): 145–151.

94. J. Silvester, "Spoken Attributions and Candidate Success in Graduate Recruitment Interviews," *Journal of Occupational and Organizational Psychology* 70 (1997): 61–71.

95. L. Ross, "The Intuitive Psychologist and His Shortcomings: Distortions in the Attribution Process," in L. Berkowitz, ed., *Advances in Experimental Social Psychology* (New York: Academic Press, 1977);

M. O'Sullivan, "The Fundamental Attribution Error in Detecting Deception: The Boy-Who-Cried Wolf Effect," *Personality & Social Psychology Bulletin* 29 (2003): 1316–1327.

96.   D. T. Miller and M. Ross, "Self-Serving Biases in the Attribution of Causality: Fact or Fiction?" *Psychological Bulletin* 82 (1975): 313–325.

97.   J. R. Schermerhorn, Jr., "Team Development for High-Performance Management," *Training and Development Journal* 40 (1986): 38–41.

98.   J. G. Miller, "Culture and the Development of Everyday Causal Explanation," *Journal of Personality and Social Psychology* 46 (1984): 961–978.

99.   G. Si, S. Rethorst, and K. Willimczik, "Causal Attribution Perception in Sports Achievement: A Cross-Cultural Study on Attributional Concepts in Germany and China," *Journal of Cross-Cultural Psychology* 26 (1995): 537–553.

Chapter 4

1.   R. Levering and M. Moskowitz, "The 100 Best Companies to Work For," *Fortune* (January 12, 2004): 68.

2.   J. Tarnowski, "Doing What Comes Naturally: A Far-Reaching Philosophy of Interdependence Has Made Whole Foods a Lifestyle Brand for Upscale Shoppers," *Progressive Grocer* (September 1, 2003): 22.

3.   A. H. Eagly and S. Chaiken, *The Psychology of Attitudes* (Orlando, Fla.: Harcourt Brace Jovanovich, 1993).

4.   L. Festinger, *A Theory of Cognitive Dissonance* (Evanston, Ill.: Row, Peterson, 1957).

5.   R. H. Fazio and M. P. Zanna, "On the Predictive Validity of Attitudes: The Roles of Direct Experience and Confidence," *Journal of Personality* 46 (1978): 228–243.

6.   A. Tversky and D. Kahneman, "Judgment under Uncertainty: Heuristics and Biases," in D. Kahneman, P. Slovic, and A. Tversky, eds., *Judgment under Uncertainty* (New York: Cambridge University Press, 1982): 3–20.

7.   D. Rajecki, *Attitudes*, 2nd ed. (Sunderland, Mass.: Sinauer Associates, 1989).

8.   I. Ajzen and M. Fishbein, "Attitude–Behavior Relations: A Theoretical Analysis and Review of Empirical Research," *Psychological Bulletin* 84 (1977): 888–918.

9.   B. T. Johnson and A. H. Eagly, "Effects of Involvement on Persuasion: A Meta-Analysis," *Psychological Bulletin* 106 (1989): 290–314.

10.   K. G. DeBono and M. Snyder, "Acting on One's Attitudes: The Role of History of Choosing Situations," *Personality and Social Psychology Bulletin* 21 (1995): 629–636.

11.   I. Ajzen and M. Fishbein, *Understanding Attitudes and Predicting Social Behavior* (Englewood Cliffs, N.J.: Prentice-Hall, 1980).

12.   I. Ajzen, "From Intentions to Action: A Theory of Planned Behavior," in J. Kuhl and J. Beckmann, eds., *Action-Control: From Cognition to Behavior* (Heidelberg: Springer, 1985).

13.   I. Ajzen, "The Theory of Planned Behavior," *Organizational Behavior and Human Decision Processes* 50 (1991): 1–33.

14.   A. Sagie and M. Krausz, "What Aspects of the Job Have Most Effect on Nurses?" *Human Resource Management Journal* 13 (2003): 46–62.

15.   C. P. Parker, B. B. Baltes, S. A. Young, J. W. Huff, R. A. Altman, H. A. LaCost, and J. E. Roberts, "Relationships between Psychological Climate Perceptions and Work Outcomes: A Meta-Analytic Review," *Journal of Organizational Behavior* 24 (2003): 389–416.

16.   J. Lemmick and J. Mattsson, "Employee Behavior, Feelings of Warmth and Customer Perception in Service Encounters," *International Journal of Retail & Distribution Management* 30 (2002): 18–44.

17.   E. A. Locke, "The Nature and Causes of Job Satisfaction," in M. Dunnette, ed., *Handbook of Industrial and Organizational Psychology* (Chicago: Rand McNally, 1976).

18.   P. C. Smith, L. M. Kendall, and C. L. Hulin, *The Measurement of Satisfaction in Work and Retirement* (Skokie, Ill.: Rand McNally, 1969).

19.   R. Ilies and T. A. Judge, "On the Heritability of Job Satisfaction: The Mediating Role of Personality," *Journal of Applied Psychology* 88 (2003): 750–759.

20.   D. J. Weiss, R. V. Davis, G. W. England, and L. H. Lofquist, *Manual for the Minnesota Satisfaction Questionnaire* (Minneapolis: Industrial Relations Center, University of Minnesota, 1967).

21.   C. D. Fisher, "Why Do Lay People Believe that Satisfaction and Performance Are Correlated? Possible Sources of a Commonsense Theory," *Journal of Organizational Behavior* 24 (2003): 753–777.

22.   M. T. Iaffaldano and P. M. Muchinsky, "Job Satisfaction and Job Performance: A Meta-Analysis," *Psychological Bulletin* 97 (1985): 251–273.

23.   L. A. Bettencourt, K. P. Gwinner, and M. L. Meuter, "A Comparison of Attitude, Personality, and Knowledge Predictors of Service-Oriented Organizational Citizenship Behaviors," *Journal of Applied Psychology* 86 (2001): 29–41.

24.   Aplus.Net, "Aplus.Net Is Put to the Test with Firestorm 2003 and Passes with Flying Colors," http://www.aplus.net/comp_info_20031105.html, accessed November 6, 2003.

25.   D. W. Organ, *Organizational Citizenship Behavior: The Good Soldier Syndrome* (Lexington, Mass.: Lexington Books, 1988).

26.   P. M. Podsakoff, S. B. Mackenzie, and C. Hui, "Organizational Citizenship Behaviors and Managerial Evaluations of Employee Performance: A Review and Suggestions for Future Research," G. Ferris, ed., in *Research in Personnel and Human Resources Management* (Greenwich, Conn.: JAI Press, 1993), 1–40.

27.   K. Lee and N. J. Allen, "Organizational Citizenship Behavior and Workplace Deviance: The Role of Affect and Cognitions," *Journal of Applied Psychology* 87 (1) (2002). 131–142.

28.   O. Christ, R. Van Dick, and U. Wagner, "When Teachers Go the Extra Mile: Foci of Organizational Identification as Determinants of Different Forms of Organizational Citizenship Behavior Among Schoolteachers," *British Journal of Educational Psychology* 73 (2003): 329–341.

29.   G. L. Blakely, M. C. Andrews, and J. Fuller, "Are Chameleons Good Citizens: A Longitudinal Study of the Relationship between Self-Monitoring and Organizational Citizenship Behavior," *Journal of Business & Psychology* 18 (2003): 131–144.

30.   W. H. Bommer, E. W. Miles, and S. L. Grover, "Does One Good Turn Deserve Another? Coworker Influences on Employee Citizenship," *Journal of Organizational Behavior* 24 (2003): 181–196.

31.   C. Ostroff, "The Relationship between Satisfaction, Attitudes and Performance: An Organizational Level Analysis," *Journal of Applied Psychology* 77 (1992): 963–974.

32.   R. Griffin and T. Bateman, "Job Satisfaction and Organizational Commitment," in C. Cooper and I. Robertson, eds., *International Review of Industrial and Organizational Psychology* (New York: Wiley, 1986).

33.   H. Y. Choi and H. Choi, "An Exploratory Study and Design of Cross-Cultural Impact of Information Systems Managers' Performance, Job Satisfaction, and Managerial Values," *Journal of Global Information Management* 11 (2003): 1–30.

34.   X. Huang and E. Van De Vliert, "Where Intrinsic Job Satisfaction Fails to Work: National Moderators of Intrinsic Motivation," *Journal of Organizational Behavior* 24 (2003): 133–250.

35.   S. L. Robinson and R. J. Bennett, "A Typology of Deviant Workplace Behaviors: A Multidimensional Scaling Study," *Academy of Management Journal* 38 (2) (1995): 555.

36.   M. E. Heilman and V. B. Alcott, "What I Think You Think of Me: Women's Reactions to Being Viewed as Beneficiaries of Preferential Selection," *Journal of Applied Psychology* 86 (2001): 574–582.

37.   M. E. Heilman, C. J. Block, and P. Stathatos, "The Affirmative Action Stigma of Incompetence: Effects of Performance Information Ambiguity," *Academy of Management Journal* 40 (1997): 603–625.

38.   R. T. Mowday, L. W. Porter, and R. M. Steers, *Employee–Organization Linkages: The Psychology of Commitment* (New York: Academic Press, 1982).

39. H. S. Becker, "Notes on the Concept of Commitment," *American Journal of Sociology* 66 (1960): 32–40.

40. J. P. Meyer, N. J. Allen, and C. A. Smith, "Commitment to Organizations and Occupations: Extension and Test of a Three-Component Model," *Journal of Applied Psychology* 78 (1993): 538–551.

41. J. P. Curry, D. S. Wakefield, J. L. Price, and C. W. Mueller, "On the Causal Ordering of Job Satisfaction and Organizational Commitment," *Academy of Management Journal* 29 (1986): 847–858.

42. B. Benkhoff, "Ignoring Commitment Is Costly: New Approaches Establish the Missing Link between Commitment and Performance," *Human Relations* 50 (1997): 701–726; N. J. Allen and J. P. Meyer, "Affective, Continuance, and Normative Commitment to the Organization: An Examination of Construct Validity," *Journal of Vocational Behavior* 49 (1996): 252–276.

43. M. J. Somers, "Organizational Commitment, Turnover, and Absenteeism: An Examination of Direct and Interaction Effects," *Journal of Organizational Behavior* 16 (1995): 49–58; L. Lum, J. Kervin, K. Clark, F. Reid, and W. Sirola, "Explaining Nursing Turnover Intent: Job Satisfaction, Pay Satisfaction, or Organizational Commitment?" *Journal of Organizational Behavior* 19 (1998): 305–320.

44. F. Stinglhamber and C. Vandenberghe, "Organizations and Supervisors as Sources of Support and Targets of Commitment," *Journal of Organizational Behavior* 24 (2003): 251–270.

45. R. Eisenberger et al., "Reciprocation of Perceived Organizational Support," *Journal of Applied Psychology* 86 (2001): 42–51; J. E. Finegan, "The Impact of Person and Organizational Values on Organizational Commitment," *Journal of Occupational and Organizational Psychology* 73 (2000): 149–169.

46. E. Snape and T. Redman, "Too Old or Too Young? The Impact of Perceived Age Discrimination," *Human Resource Management Journal* 13 (2003): 78–89.

47. F. Luthans, H. S. McCaul, and N. C. Dodd, "Organizational Commitment: A Comparison of American, Japanese, and Korean Employees," *Academy of Management Journal* 28 (1985): 213–219.

48. C. Wong and I. Wong, "The Role of Perceived Quality of Social Relationships within Organizations in Chinese Societies," *International Journal of Management* 20 (2003): 216–223.

49. D. J. Koys, "The Effects of Employee Satisfaction, Organizational Citizenship Behavior, and Turnover on Organizational Effectiveness: A Unit-Level, Longitudinal Study," *Personnel Psychology* 54 (2001): 101–114.

50. J. A. Conger, "The Necessary Art of Persuasion," *Harvard Business Review* 76 (1998): 84–96.

51. J. Cooper and R. T. Croyle, "Attitudes and Attitude Change," *Annual Review of Psychology* 35 (1984): 395–426.

52. P. Sellers, "The Trials of John Mack," *Fortune* (August 11, 2003): 98–102.

53. D. M. Mackie and L. T. Worth, "Processing Deficits and the Mediation of Positive Affect in Persuasion," *Journal of Personality and Social Psychology* 57 (1989): 27–40.

54. J. W. Brehm, *Responses to Loss of Freedom: A Theory of Psychological Reactance* (New York: General Learning Press, 1972).

55. D. DeSteno, R. E. Petty, and D. D. Rucker, "Discrete Emotions and Persuasion: The Role of Emotion-Induced Expectancies," *Journal of Personality & Social Psychology* 86 (2004): 43–56.

56. R. Petty, D. T. Wegener, and L. R. Fabrigar, "Attitudes and Attitude Change," *Annual Review of Psychology* 48 (1997): 609–647.

57. P. Brinol and R. E. Petty, "Overt Head Movements and Persuasion: A Self-Validation Analysis," *Journal of Personality & Social Psychology* 84 (2003): 1123–1139.

58. W. Wood, "Attitude Change: Persuasion and Social Influence," *Annual Review of Psychology* 51 (2000): 539–570.

59. N. H. Frijda, "Moods, Emotion Episodes, and Emotions," in M. Lewis and J. M. Haviland, eds., *Handbook of Emotions* (New York: Guilford Press, 1993): 381–403.

60. A. Ortony, G. L. Clore, and A. Collins, *The Cognitive Structure of Emotions* (Cambridge, England: Cambridge University Press, 1988).

61. R. S. Lazarus, *Emotion and Adaptation.* (New York: Oxford University Press, 1991).

62. H. M. Weiss, K. Suckow, and R. Cropanzano, "Effects of Justice Conditions on Discrete Emotions," *Journal of Applied Psychology* 84 (1999): 786–794.

63. B. L. Fredrickson and C. Brannigan, "Positive Emotions," in. G. Bonnano and T. Mayne, eds., *Emotions: Current Issues and Future Directions* (New York: Guilford Press, 2001): 123–152.

64. A. M. Isen and R. A. Baron, "Positive Affect as a Factor in Organizational Behavior," *Research in Organizational Behavior* 13 (1991): 1–53.

65. J. E. Dutton, P. J. Frost, M. C. Worline, J. M. Lilius, and J. M. Kanov, "Leading in Times of Trauma," *Harvard Business Review* 80 (1) (2002).

66. T. A. Stewart, "The Highway of the Mind," *Harvard Business Review* 82 (1) (2004): 116.

67. S. G. Barsade, "The Ripple Effect: Emotional Contagion and Its Influence on Group Behavior," *Administrative Science Quarterly* 47 (2002): 644–675.

68. S. Fox and P. E. Spector, "Relations of Emotional Intelligence, Practical Intelligence, General Intelligence, and Trait Affectivity with

Interview Outcomes: It's Not All Just 'G,' *Journal of Organizational Behavior* 21 (2000): 203–220.

69. L. T. Lam and S. L. Kirby, "Is Emotional Intelligence an Advantage? An Exploration of the Impact of Emotional and General Intelligence on Individual Performance," *Journal of Social Psychology* 142 (2002): 133–143.

70. M. M. Tugade and B. L. Fredrickson, "Resilient Individuals Use Positive Emotions to Bounce Back from Negative Emotional Experiences," *Journal of Personality and Social Psychology* 86 (2004): 320–333.

71. A. R. Hochschild, *The Managed Heart: Commercialization of Human Feeling* (Berkeley, Calif.: University of California Press, 1983).

72. A. Rafaeli and R. I. Sutton, "The Expression of Emotion in Organizational Life," *Research in Organizational Behavior* 11 (1989): 1–42.

73. B. Schneider and D. E. Bowen, "Employee and Customer Perceptions of Service in Banks: Replication and Extension," *Journal of Applied Psychology* 70 (1985): 423–433.

74. S. M. Kruml and D. Geddes, "Catching Fire Without Burning Out: Is There an Ideal Way to Perform Emotional Labor?" in N. M. Ashkanasy, C. E. J. Hartel, and W. J. Zerbe, eds., *Emotions in the Workplace: Research, Theory and Practice,* (Westport: Quorum Books, 2000): 177–188.

75. F. Navran, "Your Role in Shaping Ethics," *Executive Excellence* 9 (1992): 11–12.

76. K. Labich, "The New Crisis in Business Ethics," *Fortune* (April 20, 1992): 167–176.

77. L. S. Paine, *Value Shift: Why Companies Must Merge Social and Financial Imperatives to Achieve Superior Performance* (New York: McGraw-Hill, 2003).

78. D. B. Turban and D. M. Cable, "Firm Reputation and Applicant Pool Characteristics," *Journal of Organizational Behavior* 24 (2003): 733–751.

79. E. A. Lind, J. Greenberg, K. S. Scott, and T. D. Welchans, "The Winding Road from Employee to Complainant: Situational and Psychological Determinants of Wrongful-Termination Claims," *Administrative Science Quarterly* 45 (2000): 557–590.

80. Miriam Schulman, "LittleBrother Is Watching You," http://www.scu.edu/ethics/publications/iie/v9n2/brother.html.

81. G. Flynn, "Make Employee Ethics Your Business," *Personnel Journal* (June 1995): 30–40.

82. M. S. Baucus and D. A. Baucus, "Paying the Piper: An Empirical Examination of Longer-Term Financial Consequences of Illegal Corporate Behavior," *Academy of Management Journal* 40 (1997): 129–151.

83. J. O. Cherrington and D. J. Cherrington, "A Menu of Moral Issues: One Week in the Life of *The Wall Street Journal*," *Journal of Business Ethics* 11 (1992): 255–265.

84. B. L. Flannery and D. R. May, "Environmental Ethical Decision Making in the U.S. Metal-Finishing Industry," *Academy of Management Journal* 43 (2000): 642–662.

85. K. R. Andrews, "Ethics in Practice," *Harvard Business Review* (September–October 1989): 99–104.

86. M. Rokeach, *The Nature of Human Values* (New York: Free Press, 1973).

87. M. Rokeach and S. J. Ball-Rokeach, "Stability and Change in American Value Priorities, 1968–1981," *American Psychologist* 44 (1989): 775–784.

88. S. P. Eisner, "Managing Generation Y," *S.A.M. Advanced Management Journal* 70 (4) (2005): 4–15.

89. G. W. England, "Organizational Goals and Expected Behavior of American Managers," *Academy of Management Journal* 10 (1967): 107–117.

90. E. C. Ravlin and B. M. Meglino, "Effects of Values on Perception and Decision Making: A Study of Alternative Work Values Measures," *Journal of Applied Psychology* 72 (1987): 666–673.

91. E. C. Ravlin and B. M. Meglino, "The Transitivity of Work Values: Hierarchical Preference Ordering of Socially Desirable Stimuli," *Organizational Behavior and Human Decision Processes* 44 (1989): 494–508.

92. B. M. Meglino, E. C. Ravlin, and C. L. Adkins, "A Work Values Approach to Corporate Culture: A Field Test of the Value Congruence Process and Its Relationship to Individual Outcomes," *Journal of Applied Psychology* 74 (1989): 424–432.

93. T. A. Judge and R. D. Bretz, Jr., "Effects of Work Values on Job Choice Decisions," *Journal of Applied Psychology* 77 (1992): 261–271.

94. Tony Jones, "Survey Finds Big Business Lacking in Social Responsibility," Australian Broadcasting Corporation (October 13, 2003), http://www.abc.net.au/lateline/content/2003/s966137.htm; and RepuTex, http://www.reputex.com.au.

95. R. H. Doktor, "Asian and American CEOs: A Comparative Study," *Organizational Dynamics* 18 (1990): 46–56.

96. R. L. Tung, "Handshakes across the Sea: Cross-Cultural Negotiating for Business Success," *Organizational Dynamics* (Winter 1991): 30–40.

97. C. Gomez, B. L. Kirkman, and D. L. Shapiro, "The Impact of Collectivism and In-Group/Out-Group Membership on the Evaluation Generosity of Team Members," *Academy of Management Journal* 43 (2000): 1097–1106; J. Zhou and J. J. Martocchio, "Chinese and American Managers' Compensation Award Decisions: A Comparative Policy-Capturing Study," *Personnel Psychology* 54 (2001): 115–145.

98. A. J. Ali and M. Amirshahi, "The Iranian Manager: Work Values and Orientations," *Journal of Business Ethics* 40 (2002): 133–143.

99. R. Neale and R. Mindel, "Rigging Up Multicultural Teamworking," *Personnel Management* (January 1992): 27–30.

100. K. Hodgson, "Adapting Ethical Decisions to a Global Marketplace," *Management Review* 81 (1992): 53–57.

101. J. B. Rotter, "Generalized Expectancies for Internal versus External Control of Reinforcement," *Psychological Monographs* 80 (1966): 1–28.

102. L. K. Trevino and S. A. Youngblood, "Bad Apples in Bad Barrels: A Causal Analysis of Ethical Decision-Making Behavior," *Journal of Applied Psychology* 75 (1990): 378–385.

103. H. M. Lefcourt, *Locus of Control: Current Trends in Theory and Research*, 2nd ed. (Hillsdale, N.J.: Erlbaum, 1982).

104. N. Machiavelli, *The Prince*, trans. George Bull (Middlesex, England: Penguin Books, 1961).

105. R. Christie and F. L. Geis, *Studies in Machiavellianism* (New York: Academic Press, 1970).

106. R. A. Giacalone and S. B. Knouse, "Justifying Wrongful Employee Behavior: The Role of Personality in Organizational Sabotage," *Journal of Business Ethics* 9 (1990): 55–61.

107. S. B. Knouse and R. A. Giacalone, "Ethical Decision Making in Business: Behavioral Issues and Concerns," *Journal of Business Ethics* 11 (1992): 369–377.

108. L. Kohlberg, "Stage and Sequence: The Cognitive Developmental Approach to Socialization," in D. A. Goslin, ed., *Handbook of Socialization Theory and Research* (Chicago: Rand McNally, 1969): 347–480.

109. C. I. Malinowski and C. P. Smith, "Moral Reasoning and Moral Conduct: An Investigation Prompted by Kohlberg's Theory," *Journal of Personality and Social Psychology* 49 (1985): 1016–1027.

110. M. Brabeck, "Ethical Characteristics of Whistleblowers," *Journal of Research in Personality* 18 (1984): 41–53.

111. W. Y. Penn and B. D. Collier, "Current Research in Moral Development as a Decision Support System," *Journal of Business Ethics* 4 (1985): 131–136.

112. Trevino and Youngblood, "Bad Apples in Bad Barrels."

113. G. R. Franke, D. F. Crown, and D. F. Spake, "Gender Differences in Ethical Perceptions of Business Practices: A Social Role Theory Perspective," *Journal of Applied Psychology* 82 (1997): 920–934.

114. B. Horovitz, "Whole Foods Pledges to Be More Humane," *USA Today* (October 21, 2003): B1.

115. J. N. Frank, "VivaUSA Push Forces Whole Foods Change," *PR Week* (November 3, 2003): 4.

Chapter 5

1. L. W. Porter, G. Bigley, and R. M. Steers, *Motivation and Leadership at Work*, 7th ed. (New York: McGraw-Hill, 2002).

2. M. Weber, *The Protestant Ethic and the Spirit of Capitalism* (London: Talcott Parson, tr., 1930).

3. S. Freud, *Civilization and Its Discontents*, trans. and ed. J. Strachey (New York: Norton, 1961).

4. K. J. Sweetman, "Employee Loyalty around the Globe," *Sloan Management Review* 42 (2001): 16.

5. B. S. Frey, *Not Just for the Money: An Economic Theory of Personal Motivation* (Brookfield, Vt.: Edgar Elger, 1997).

6. X. Huang and E. van de Vliert, "Where Intrinsic Job Satisfaction Fails to Work: National Moderators of Intrinsic Motivation," *Journal of Organizational Behavior* 24 (2) (2003): 159–179.

7. A. H. Maslow, "A Theory of Human Motivation," *Psychological Review* 50 (1943): 370–396.

8. L. W. Porter, "A Study of Perceived Need Satisfactions in Bottom and Middle Management Jobs," *Journal of Applied Psychology* 45 (1961): 1–10.

9. E. E. Lawler, III and J. L. Suttle, "A Causal Correlational Test of the Need Hierarchy Concept," *Organizational Behavior and Human Performance* 7 (1973): 265–287.

10. D. M. McGregor, *The Human Side of Enterprise* (New York: McGraw-Hill, 1960).

11. D. M. McGregor, "The Human Side of Enterprise," *Management Review* (November 1957): 22–28, 88–92.

12. E. E. Lawler, G. E. Lawford, S. A. Mohrman, and G. E. Ledford, Jr., *Strategies for High Performance Organizations—The CEO Report: Employee Involvement, TQM, and Reengineering Programs in Fortune 1000 Corporations* (San Francisco: Jossey-Bass, Inc., 1998).

13. J. Boorstin, "No Preservatives. No Unions. Lots of Dough," *Fortune* 148 (September 15, 2003): 127–129.

14. G. E. Forward, D. E. Beach, D. A. Gray, and J. C. Quick, "Mentofacturing: A Vision for American Industrial Excellence," *Academy of Management Executive* 5 (1991): 32–44.

15. D. C. McClelland, "Achievement Motivation Can Be Learned," *Harvard Business Review* 43 (1965): 6–24.

16. R. Eisenberger, J. R. Jones, F. Stinglhamber, L. Shanock, and A. T. Randall, "Flow Experiences at Work: For High Need Achievers Alone?" *Journal of Organizational Behavior* 26 (2005): 755–775.

17. E. A. Ward, "Multidimensionality of Achievement Motivation among Employed Adults," *Journal of Social Psychology* 134 (1997): 542–544.

18. A. Sagie, D. Elizur, and H. Yamauchi, "The Structure and Strength of Achievement Motivation: A Cross-Cultural Comparison," *Journal of Organizational Behavior* 17 (1996): 431–444.

19. D. C. McClelland and D. Burnham, "Power Is the Great Motivator," *Harvard Business Review* 54 (1976): 100–111; J. Hall and J. Hawker, *Power Management Inventory* (The Woodlands, Tex.: Teleometrics International, 1988).

20. F. Luthans, "Successful versus Effective Real Managers," *Academy of Management Executive* 2 (1988): 127–131.

21. S. Schachter, *The Psychology of Affiliation* (Stanford, Calif.: Stanford University Press, 1959).

22. N. W. van Yperen and M. Hagedoorn, "Do High Job Demands Increase Intrinsic Motivation or Fatigue or Both? The Role of Job Control and Job Social Support," *Academy of Management Journal* 46 (2003): 339–348.

23. F. Herzberg, B. Mausner, and B. Snyderman, *The Motivation to Work* (New York: Wiley, 1959).

24. F. Herzberg, *Work and the Nature of Man* (Cleveland: World, 1966).

25. F. J. Leach and J. D. Westbrook, "Motivation and Job Satisfaction in One Government Research and Development Environment," *Engineering Management Journal* 12 (2000): 3–8.

26. P. M. Blau, *Exchange and Power in Social Life* (New York: Wiley, 1964).

27. A. Etzioni, "A Basis for Comparative Analysis of Complex Organizations," in A. Etzioni, ed., *A Sociological Reader on Complex Organizations,* 2nd ed. (New York: Holt, Rinehart & Winston, 1969): 59–76.

28. O. Janssen, "Job Demands, Perceptions of Effort–Reward Fairness and Innovative Work Behavior," *Journal of Occupational & Organizational Psychology* 73 (2000): 287–302.

29. R. Cropanzano, B. Goldman, and R. Folger, "Deontic Justice: The Role of Moral Principles in Workplace Fairness," *Journal of Organizational Behavior* 24 (2003): 1019–1024.

30. C. Dahle, "A Steelmakers's Heart of Gold," *Fast Company* 71 (June 2003): 46, http://www.fastcompany.com/magazine/71/smartcompany.html.

31. S. S. Masterson and C. L. Stamper, "Perceived Organizational Membership: An Aggregate Framework Representing the Employee–Organization Relationship," *Journal of Organizational Behavior* 24 (2003): 473–490.

32. J. S. Adams, "Inequity in Social Exchange," in L. Berkowitz, ed., *Advances in Experimental Social Psychology,* Vol. 2 (New York: Academic Press, 1965): 267–299; J. S. Adams, "Toward an Understanding of Inequity," *Journal of Abnormal and Social Psychology* 67 (1963): 422–436.

33. J. Nelson-Horchler, "The Best Man for the Job Is a Man," *Industry Week* (January 7, 1991): 50–52.

34. P. D. Sweeney, D. B. McFarlin, and E. J. Inderrieden, "Using Relative Deprivation Theory to Explain Satisfaction with Income and Pay Level: A Multistudy Examination," *Academy of Management Journal* 33 (1990): 423–436.

35. R. C. Huseman, J. D. Hatfield, and E. A. Miles, "A New Perspective on Equity Theory: The Equity Sensitivity Construct," *Academy of Management Review* 12 (1987): 222–234.

36. D. McLoughlin and S. C. Carr, "Equity and Sensitivity and Double Demotivation," *Journal of Social Psychology* 137 (1997): 668–670.

37. K. E. Weick, M. G. Bougon, and G. Maruyama, "The Equity Context," *Organizational Behavior and Human Performance* 15 (1976): 32–65.

38. R. Coles, *Privileged Ones* (Boston: Little, Brown, 1977).

39. J. A. Colquitt and J. Greenberg, "Organizational Justice: A Fair Assessment of the State of the Literature," in J. Greenberg, ed., *Organizational Behavior: The State of the Science,* 2nd ed. (Mahwah, N.J.: Erlbaum Associates, 2003).

40. G. P. Latham and C. C. Pinder, "Work Motivation Theory and Research at the Dawn of the Twenty-First Century," *Annual Review of Psychology* 56 (2005): 485–516.

41. J. Greenberg, "Equity and Workplace Status: A Field Experiment," *Journal of Applied Psychology* 73 (1988): 606–613.

42. T. M. Trip, R. J. Bies, and K. Aquino, "Poetic Justice or Petty Jealousy? The Aesthetics of Revenge," *Organizational Behavior and Human Decision Processes* 89 (2002): 966–984.

43. J. Greenberg, "Who Stole the Money, and When? Individual and Situational Determinants of Employee Theft," *Organizational Behavior and Human Decision Processes.* 89 (2002): 985–1003.

44. J. Greenberg, "Losing Sleep over Organizational Justice: Attenuating Insomniac Reactions to Underpayment Inequity with Supervisory Training in Interactional Justice," *Journal of Applied Psychology* 91 (2006): 38–69.

45. M. L. Ambrose, M. A. Seabright, M. Schminke, "Sabotage in the Workplace: The Role of Organizational Justice," *Organizational Behavior and Human Decision Processes* 89 (2002): 947–965.

46. J. Greenberg and B. Alge, "Aggressive Reactions to Workplace Injustice," in R. W. Griffin, A. O'Leary-Kelly, and J. Collins, eds., *Dysfunctional Behavior in Organizations, Vol. 1: Violent Behaviors in Organizations* (Greenwich, Conn.: JAI, 1998), 119–145.

47. J. Greenberg and R. S. Cropanzano, *Advances in Organizational Justice* (Palo Alto, Calif.: Stanford University Press, 2001).

48. J. S. Greenberg and J. Colquitt, *Handbook of Organizational Justice* (Mahwah, N.J.: Lawrence Erlbaum Associates, Inc., 2005).

49. V. H. Vroom, *Work and Motivation* (New York: Wiley, 1964/1970).

50. U. R. Larson, "Supervisor's Performance Feedback to Subordinates: The Effect of Performance Valence and Outcome Dependence," *Organizational Behavior and Human Decision Processes* 37 (1986): 391–409.

51. M. C. Kernan and R. G. Lord, "Effects of Valence, Expectancies, and Goal-Performance Discrepancies in Single and Multiple Goal Environments," *Journal of Applied Psychology* 75 (1990): 194–203.

52. R. J. Sanchez, D. M. Truxillo, and T. N. Bauer, "Development and Examination of an Expectancy-Based Measure of Test-Taking Motivation," *Journal of Applied Psychology* 85 (2000): 739–750.

53. W. VanEerde and H. Thierry, "Vroom's Expectancy Models and Work-Related Criteria: A Meta-Analysis," *Journal of Applied Psychology* 81 (1996): 575–586.

54. E. D. Pulakos and N. Schmitt, "A Longitudinal Study of a Valence Model Approach for the Prediction of Job Satisfaction of New Employees," *Journal of Applied Psychology* 68 (1983): 307–312.

55. F. J. Landy and W. S. Becker, "Motivation Theory Reconsidered," in L. L. Cummings and B. M. Staw, eds., *Research in Organizational Behavior* 9 (Greenwich, Conn.: JAI Press, 1987), 1–38.

56. L. Kohlberg, "The Cognitive-Developmental Approach to Socialization," in D. A. Goslin, ed., *Handbook of Socialization Theory and Research* (Chicago: Rand McNally, 1969).

57. N. J. Adler, *International Dimensions of Organizational Behavior,* 4th ed. (Mason, Ohio: South-Western, 2001).

58. G. Hofstede, "Motivation, Leadership, and Organization: Do American Theories Apply Abroad?" *Organizational Dynamics* 9 (1980): 42–63.

59. G. H. Hines, "Cross-Cultural Differences in Two-Factor Theory," *Journal of Applied Psychology* 58 (1981): 313–317.

60. D. L. Nelson and B. L. Simmons, "Health Psychology and Work Stress: A More Positive Approach," in J. C. Quick and L. E. Tetrick, eds., *Handbook of Occupational Health Psychology* (Washington, D.C.: American Psychological Association, 2003): 97–119.

61. K. S. Cameron, J. E. Dutton, and R. E. Quinn, eds., *Positive Organizational Scholarship: Foundations of a New Discipline* (San Francisco: Berrett-Keohler, 2003).

62. A. Shirom, "Feeling Vigorous at Work? The Construct of Vigor and the Study of Positive Affect in Organizations, in D. Granster and P. L. Perrewe, eds., *Research in Organizational Stress and Well-Being,* Vol. 3 (2003): 135–165.

63.   J. Loehr and T. Schwartz, "The Making of a Corporate Athlete," *Harvard Business Review* 79 (2001): 120–129.

64.   J. Loehr and T. Schwartz, *The Power of Full Engagement: Managing Energy, Not Time, Is the Key to High Performance and Personal Renewal* (New York: Free Press, 2003).

65.   S. Whiting, "Sanjay Patel on How Growing up in a Motel Can Affect Your Creative Impulses," *San Francisco Chronicle* (December 10, 2006): CM-4.

Chapter 6

1.   D. Dearlove, "Do the Hippy, Hippy Shake," in *Business the Richard Branson Way: 10 Secrets of the World's Greatest Brand Builder* (Oxford, UK: Capstone Publishing Ltd., 2002): 44–47.

2.   I. P. Pavlov, *Conditioned Reflexes* (New York: Oxford University Press, 1927).

3.   B. F. Skinner, *The Behavior of Organisms: An Experimental Analysis* (New York: Appleton-Century-Crofts, 1938).

4.   B. F. Skinner, *Science and Human Behavior* (New York: Free Press, 1953).

5.   F. Luthans and R. Kreitner, *Organizational Behavior Modification and Beyond* (Glenview, Ill.: Scott, Foresman, 1985).

6.   A. D. Stajkovic and F. Luthans, "A Meta-Analysis of the Effects of Organizational Behavior Modification on Task Performance, 1975–95," *Academy of Management Journal* 40 (1997): 1122–1149.

7.   A. D. Stajkovic and F. Luthans, "Differential Effects of Incentive Motivators on Work," *Academy of Management Journal* 44 (2001): 580–591.

8.   J. Hale, "Strategic Rewards: Keeping Your Best Talent from Walking Out the Door," *Compensation & Benefits Management* 14 (1998): 39–50.

9.   B. F. Skinner, *Contingencies of Reinforcement: A Theoretical Analysis* (New York: Appleton-Century-Crofts, 1969).

10.   J. P. Chaplin and T. S. Krawiec, *Systems and Theories of Psychology* (New York: Holt, Rinehart & Winston, 1960).

11.   M. Maccoby, J. Hoffer Gittell, and M. Ledeen, "Leadership and the Fear Factor," *Sloan Management Review* 148 (Winter 2004): 14–18.

12.   A. Bandura, *Social Learning Theory* (Englewood Cliffs, N.J.: Prentice-Hall, 1977); A. Bandura, "Self-Efficacy: Toward a Unifying Theory of Behavioral Change," *Psychological Review* 84 (1977): 191–215.

13.   J. J. Martocchio and E. J. Hertenstein, "Learning Orientation and Goal Orientation Context: Relationships with Cognitive and Affective Learning Outcomes," *Human Resource Development Quarterly* 14 (2003): 413–434.

14.   A. Bandura, "Regulation of Cognitive Processes through Perceived Self-Efficacy," *Developmental Psychology* (September 1989): 729–735.

15.   J. M. Phillips and S. M. Gully, "Role of Goal Orientation, Ability, Need for Achievement, and Locus of Control in the Self-Efficacy and Goal-Setting Process," *Journal of Applied Psychology* 82 (1997): 792–802.

16.   C. Tay and L. Van Dyne, "Personality, Biographical Characteristics, and Job Interview Success: A Longitudinal Study of the Mediating Effects of Interviewing Self-Efficacy and the Moderating Effects of Internal Locus of Causality," *Journal of Applied Psychology* 91 (2006): 446–454.

17.   A. D. Stajkovic and F. Luthans, "Social Cognitive Theory and Self-Efficacy: Going Beyond Traditional Motivational and Behavioral Approaches," *Organizational Dynamics* (Spring 1998): 62–74.

18.   A. D. Stajkovic and F. Luthans, "Self-Efficacy and Work-Related Performance: A Meta-Analysis," *Psychological Bulletin* 124 (1998): 240–261.

19.   V. Gecas, "The Social Psychology of Self-Efficacy," *Annual Review of Sociology* 15 (1989): 291–316.

20.   E. A. Locke and G. P. Latham, *A Theory of Goal Setting and Task Performance* (Englewood Cliffs, N.J.: Prentice-Hall, 1990).

21.   J. B. Minor, "The Rated Importance, Scientific Validity, and Practical Usefulness of Organizational Behavior Theories: A Quantitative Review," *The Academy of Management Learning and Education* 2: (2003): 250–268.

22.   E. A. Locke and G. P. Latham, "Building a Practically Useful Theory of Goal Setting and Task Motivation: A 35-Year Odyssey," *American Psychologist* 57 (2002):705–717.

23.   M. L. Ambrose and C. T. Kulik, "Old Friends, New Faces: Motivation Research in the 1990s," *Journal of Management* 25 (1999): 231–292.

24.   E. A. Locke and G. P. Latham, "Building a Practically Useful Theory."

25.   A. Erez and A. M. Isen, "The Influence of Positive Affect on Components of Expectancy Motivation," *Journal of Applied Psychology* 87 (2002): 1055–1067.

26.   J. M. George and J. Zhou, "Understanding When Bad Moods Foster Creativity and Good Ones Don't: The Role of Context and Clarity of Feelings," *Journal of Applied Psychology* 87 (2002): 687–697.

27.   G. P. Latham and C. C. Pinder, "Work Motivation Theory and Research at the Dawn of the Twenty First Century," *Annual Review of Psychology* 56 (2005): 485–516.

28.   G. H. Seijts and G. P. Latham, "Learning Versus Performance Goals: When Should Each Be Used?" *Academy of Management Executive* 19 (2005): 124–131.

29.   T. O. Murray, *Management by Objectives: A Systems Approach to Management* (Fort Worth, Tex.: Western Company, n.d.).

30.   W. T. Brooks and T. W. Mullins, *High Impact Time Management* (Englewood Cliffs, N.J.: Prentice-Hall, 1989).

31.   E. A. Locke, "Toward a Theory of Task Motivation and Incentives," *Organizational Behavior and Human Performance* 3 (1968): 157–189.

32.   J. C. Quick, "Dyadic Goal Setting within Organizations: Role Making and Motivational Considerations," *Academy of Management Review* 4 (1979): 369–380.

33.   D. McGregor, "An Uneasy Look at Performance Appraisal," *Harvard Business Review* 35 (1957): 89–94.

34.   J. R. Hollenbeck, C. R. Williams, and H. J. Klein, "An Empirical Examination of the Antecedents of Commitment to Difficult Goals," *Journal of Applied Psychology* 74 (1989): 18–23.

35.   R. C. Rodgers and J. E. Hunter, "The Impact of Management by Objectives on Organizational Productivity," unpublished paper (Lexington: University of Kentucky, 1989).

36.   E. A. Locke, K. N. Shaw, L. M. Saari, and G. P. Latham, "Goal Setting and Task Performance: 1969–1980," *Psychological Bulletin* 90 (1981): 125–152.

37.   D. B. Fedora, W. D. Davis, J. M. Maslync, and K. Mathiesond, "Performance Improvement Efforts in Response to Negative Feedback: The Roles of Source Power and Recipient Self-Esteem," *Journal of Management* 27 (2001): 79–98.

38.   J. C. Quick, "Dyadic Goal Setting and Role Stress," *Academy of Management Journal* 22 (1979): 241–252.

39.   G. S. Odiorne, *Management by Objectives: A System of Managerial Leadership* (New York: Pitman, 1965).

40.   American Management Association, *Blueprints for Service Quality: The Federal Express Approach* (New York: American Management Association, 1991).

41.   G. P. Latham and G. A. Yukl, "A Review of Research on the Application of Goal Setting in Organizations," *Academy of Management Journal* 18 (1975): 824–845.

42.   P. F. Drucker, *The Practice of Management* (New York: Harper & Bros., 1954).

43.   C. L. Hughes, *Goal Setting: Key to Individual and Organizational Effectiveness* (New York: American Management Association, 1965).

44.   M. E. Tubbs and S. E. Ekeberg, "The Role of Intentions in Work Motivation: Implications for Goal-Setting Theory and Research," *Academy of Management Review* 16 (1991): 180–199.

45.   S. Vatave, "Managing Risk," *Supervision* 65 (2004): 6–9.

46.   J. R. Hollenbeck and A. P. Brief, "The Effects of Individual Differences and Goal Origin on Goal Setting and Performance," *Organizational Behavior and Human Decision Processes* 40 (1987): 392–414.

47.   R. A. Katzell and D. E. Thompson, "Work Motivation: Theory and Practice," *American Psychologist* 45 (1990): 144–153; M. W. McPherson, "Is Psychology the Science of Behavior?" *American Psychologist* 47 (1992): 329–335.

48.   E. A. Locke, "The Ideas of Frederick W. Taylor: An Evaluation," *Academy of Management Review* 7 (1982): 15–16; R. M. Yerkes and J. D. Dodson, "The Relation of Strength of Stimulus to Rapidity of Habit-Formation," *Journal of Comparative Neurology and Psychology* 18 (1908): 459–482.

49.   F. L. Schmidt and J. Hunter, "General Mental Ability in the World of Work: Occupational Attainment and Job Performance," *Journal of Personality and Social Psychology* 86 (2004): 162–173.

50.   R. L. Cardy, *Performance Management: Concepts, Skills, and Exercises* (Armonk, New York and London, England: M.E. Sharpe, 2004).

51.   P. Cappelli and N. Rogovsky, "Employee Involvement and Organizational Citizenship: Implications for Labor Law Reform and 'Lean Production,'" *Industrial & Labor Relations Review* 51 (1998): 633–653.

52.   B. Erdogan, M. L. Kraimer, and R. C. Liden, "Procedural Justice as a Two-Dimensional Construct: An Examination in the Performance Appraisal Account," *Journal of Applied Behavioral Science* 37 (2001): 205–222.

53.   S. E. DeVoe and S. S. Iyengar, "Managers' Theories of Subordinates: A Cross-Cultural Examination of Manager Perceptions of Motivation and Appraisal of Performance," *Organizational Behavior and Human Decision Processes* 93 (2004): 47–61.

54.   I. M. Jawahar and C. R. Williams, "Where All the Children Are Above Average: The Performance Appraisal Purpose Effect," *Personnel Psychology* 50 (1997): 905–925.

55.   M. E. Tubbs and M. L. Trusty, "Direct Reports of Motivation for Task Performance Levels: Some Construct-Related Evidence," *Journal of Psychology* 135 (2001): 185–205.

56.   R. R. Kilburg, *Executive Coaching: Developing Managerial Wisdom in a World of Chaos* (Washington, D.C.: American Psychological Association, 2000).

57.   H. H. Meyer, E. Kay, and J. R. P. French, "Split Roles in Performance Appraisal," *Harvard Business Review* 43 (1965): 123–129.

58.   L. R. Offerman, "When Followers Become Toxic," *Harvard Business Review,* Vol. 82, Issue 82 (2004): 54–60.

59.   W. A. Fisher, J. C. Quick, L. L. Schkade, and G. W. Ayers, "Developing Administrative Personnel through the Assessment Center Technique," *Personnel Administrator* 25 (1980): 44–46, 62.

60.   K. D. Harper, "The Positive Feedback Bias as a Response to Out-Group

Unfriendliness," *Journal of Applied Social Psychology* 34 (2004): 2272–2297.

61.   J. S. Goodman, R. E. Wood, and M. Hendricks, "Feedback Specificity, Exploration, and Learning," *Journal of Applied Psychology* 89 (2004): 248–262.

62.   M. B. DeGregorio and C. D. Fisher, "Providing Performance Feedback: Reactions to Alternative Methods," *Journal of Management* 14 (1988): 605–616.

63.   G. C. Thornton, "The Relationship between Supervisory and Self-Appraisals of Executive Performance," *Personnel Psychology* 21 (1968): 441–455.

64.   A. S. DeNisi and A. N. Kluger, "Feedback Effectiveness: Can 360-Degree Appraisals Be Improved?" *Academy of Management Executive* 14 (2000): 129–140.

65.   F. Luthans and S. J. Peterson, "360-Degree Feedback with Systematic Coaching: Empirical Analysis Suggests a Winning Combination," *Human Resource Management* 42 (2003): 243–256.

66.   G. Toegel and J. A. Conger, "360-Degree Assessment: Time for Reinvention," *Academy of Management Learning and Education* 2 (2003): 297–311.

67.   C. C. Rosen, P. E. Levy, and R. J. Hall, "Placing Perceptions of Politics in the Context of the Feedback Environment, Employee Attitudes, and Job Performance," *Journal of Applied Psychology* 91 (2005): 211–220.

68.   L. Hirschhorn, "Leaders and Followers in a Postindustrial Age: A Psychodynamic View," *Journal of Applied Behavioral Science* 26 (1990): 529–542.

69.   F. M Jablin, "Superior-Subordinate Communication: The State of the Art," *Psychological Bulletin* 86 (1979): 1201–1222.

70.   J. Pfeffer, "Six Dangerous Myths about Pay," *Harvard Business Review* 76 (1998): 108–119.

71.   M. Erez, "Work Motivation from a Cross-Cultural Perspective," in A. M. Bouvy, F. J. R. Van de Vijver, P. Boski, and P. G. Schmitz, eds., *Journeys into Cross-Cultural Psychology* (Amsterdam, Netherlands: Swets & Zeitlinger, 1994): 386–403.

72.   George T. Milkovich and Jerry M. Newman, *Compensation,* 4th ed. (Homewood, Ill.: Irwin, 1993).

73.   J. M. Bardwick, *Danger in the Comfort Zone* (New York: American Management Association, 1991).

74.   N. Wilson, "Rewarding Values at Loop Customer Management," *Strategic HR Review* 3 (January/February 2004): 12–13.

75.   M. J. Martinko and W. L. Gardner, "The Leader/Member Attributional Process," *Academy of Management Review* 12 (1987): 235–249.

76.   K. N. Wexley, R. A. Alexander, J. P. Greenawalt, and M. A. Couch, "Attitudinal Congruence and Similarity as Related to Interpersonal Evaluations in Manager-Subordinate Dyads," *Academy of Management Journal* 23 (1980): 320–330.

77.   M. E. Heilman and M. C. Haynes, "No Credit Where Credit Is Due: Attributional Rationalization of Women's Success in Male-Female Teams," *Journal of Applied Psychology* 90 (2005): 905–906.

78.   H. H. Kelley, *Attribution in Social Interaction* (New York: General Learning Press, 1971).

79.   H. H. Kelley, "The Processes of Causal Attribution," *American Psychologist* 28 (1973): 107–128.

80.   B. Raabe and T. A. Beehr, "Formal Mentoring versus Supervisor and Coworker Relationships: Differences in Perceptions and Impact," *Journal of Organizational Behavior* 24 (2003): 271–293.

81.   A. M. Young and P. L. Perrewe, "What Did You Expect? An Examination of Career-Related Support and Social Support among Mentors and Protégés," *Journal of Management* 26 (2000): 611–633.

82.   K. Doherty, "The Good News about Depression," *Business and Health* 3 (1989): 1–4.

83.   K. E. Kram, "Phases of the Mentor Relationship," *Academy of Management Journal* 26 (1983): 608–625.

84.   T. D. Allen, L. T. Eby, M. L. Poteet, E. Lentz, and L. Lima, "Career Benefits Associated with Mentoring for Protégés: A Meta-Analysis," *Journal of Applied Psychology* 89 (2004): 127–136.

85.   T. N. Bauer and S. G. Green, "Development of Leader–Member Exchange: A Longitudinal Test," *Academy of Management Journal* 39 (1996): 1538–1567.

86.   K. E. Kram and L. A. Isabella, "Mentoring Alternatives: The Role of Peer Relationships in Career Development," *Academy of Management Journal* 28 (1985): 110–132.

87.   J. Greco, "Hey, Coach!" *Journal of Business Strategy* 22 (2001): 28–32.

88.   P. J. Taylor, D. F. Russ-Eft, and D. W. L. Chan, "A Meta-Analytic Review of Behavior Modeling Training," *Journal of Applied Psychology* 90 (2005): 692–709.

89.   H. Begum, "Branson's Force," *The Lawyer* (October 20, 2003): 15, http://www.thelawyer.com/cgi-bin/item.cgi?id=107286&d=11h=24&f=46.

Chapter 7

1.   M. White, "Does Your Intranet Have a Win–Win Strategy?" *EContent Magazine* 3 (March 2004): 41, http://www.ecmag.net/Articles/ArticleReader.aspx?ArticleID=6193&CategoryID=12.

2.   D. L. Whetzel, "The Department of Labor Identifies Workplace Skills," *The Industrial/Organizational Psychologist* (July 1991): 89–90.

3.   M. Macik-Frey, J. C. Quick, and J. D. Quick, "Interpersonal Communication:

The Key to Unlocking Social Support for Preventive Stress Management," in C. L. Cooper, ed., *Handbook of Stress, Medicine, and Health, Revised Edition* (Boca Raton, Fla.: CRC Press), in press.

4. CFO Staff, "Hold that Golden Spike," *CFO Magazine* 20 (Spring 2004): 9, http://www.cfo.com/article/1,5309,12606||M|846,00.html.

5. *Richness* is a term originally coined by W. D. Bodensteiner, "Information Channel Utilization under Varying Research and Development Project Conditions" (Ph.D. diss., University of Texas at Austin, 1970).

6. B. Barry and I. S. Fulmer, "The Medium and the Message: The Adaptive Use of Communication Media in Dyadic Influence," *Academy of Management Review* 29 (2004): 272–292.

7. R. Reik, *Listen with the Third Ear* (New York: Pyramid, 1972).

8. E. Rautalinko and H. O. Lisper, "Effects of Training Reflective Listening in a Corporate Setting," *Journal of Business and Psychology* 18 (2004): 281–299.

9. A. G. Athos and J. J. Gabarro, *Interpersonal Behavior: Communication and Understanding in Relationships* (Englewood Cliffs, N.J.: Prentice-Hall, 1978).

10. K. N. Kinnick and S. R. Parton, "Workplace Communication: What *The Apprentice* Teaches about Communication Skills," *Business Communication Quarterly,* Vol. 68 (2005): 429–456.

11. A. D. Mangelsdorff, "Lessons Learned from the Military: Implications for Management" (Distinguished Visiting Lecture, University of Texas at Arlington, 29 January 1993).

12. J. E. Hale, R. E. Dulek, and D. P. Hale, "Crisis Response Communication Challenges: Building Theory from Qualitative Data," *Journal of Business Communication,* Vol. 42 (2005): 112–134.

13. D. A. Morand, "Language and Power: An Empirical Analysis of Linguistic Strategies Used in Superior–Subordinate Communication," *Journal of Organizational Behavior* 21 (2000): 235–249.

14. F. Luthans, "Successful versus Effective Real Managers," *Academy of Management Executive* 2 (1988): 127–132.

15. L. E. Penley, E. R. Alexander, I. E. Jernigan, and C. I. Henwood, "Communication Abilities of Managers: The Relationship of Performance," *Journal of Management* 17 (1991): 57–76.

16. J. A. LePine and L. Van Dyne, "Voice and Cooperative Behavior as Contrasting Forms of Contextual Performance: Evidence of Differential Relationships with Big Five Personality Characteristics and Cognitive Ability," *Journal of Applied Psychology* 86 (2001): 326–336.

17. F. M. Jablin, "Superior-Subordinate Communication: The State of the Art," *Psychological Bulletin* 86 (1979): 1201–1222; W. C. Reddin, *Communication within the Organization: An Interpretive Review of Theory and Research* (New York: Industrial Communication Council, 1972).

18. B. Barry and J. M. Crant, "Dyadic Communication Relationships in Organizations: An Attribution Expectancy Approach," *Organization Science* 11 (2000): 648–665.

19. J. C. Quick, D. L. Nelson, and J. D. Quick, *Stress and Challenge at the Top: The Paradox of the Successful Executive* (Chichester, England: Wiley, 1990).

20. G. T. Kumkale and D. Albarracin, "The Sleeper Effect in Persuasion: A Meta-Analytic Review," *Psychological Bulletin* 130 (2004): 143–172.

21. A. Furhham and P. Stringfield, "Congruence in Job-Performance Ratings: A Study of 360 Degree Feedback Examining Self, Manager, Peers, and Consultant Ratings," *Human Relations* 51 (1998): 517–530.

22. J. W. Gilsdorf, "Organizational Rules on Communicating: How Employees Are—and Are Not—Learning the Ropes," *Journal of Business Communication* 35 (1998): 173–201.

23. J. J. Lynch, *The Cry Unheard* (Baltimore, Md.: Bancroft Press, 2000).

24. R. Boyatzis and A. McKee, *Resonant Leadership* (Boston: Harvard Business School Press, 2005).

25. D. Tannen, *You Just Don't Understand: Women and Men in Conversation* (New York: William Morrow and Company, Inc., 1990).

26. K. L. Ashcraft, "Empowering 'Professional' Relationships," *Management Communication Quarterly* 13 (2000): 347–393.

27. D. Tannen, *Talking from 9 to 5: Women and Men at Work* (New York: Quill, 1994).

28. G. Hofstede, *Culture's Consequences: International Differences in Work-Related Values* (Beverly Hills, Calif.: Sage Publications, 1980).

29. G. Hofstede, "Motivation, Leadership, and Organization: Do American Theories Apply Abroad?" *Organizational Dynamics* 9 (1980): 42–63.

30. H. Levinson, *Executive* (Cambridge, Mass.: Harvard University Press, 1981).

31. M. J. Gannon and Associates, *Understanding Global Cultures: Metaphorical Journeys through 17 Countries* (Thousand Oaks, Calif.: Sage Publications, 1994).

32. S. Gibson, "Understanding the Indian 'yes,'" *eweek,* Vol. 23 (2006): 32.

33. T. M. Karelitz and D. V. Budescu, "You Say 'Probable' and I Say 'Likely': Improving Interpersonal Communication with Verbal Probability Phrases," *Journal of Experimental Psychology: Applied* 10 (2004): 25–41.

34. T. Wells, *Keeping Your Cool under Fire: Communicating Nondefensively* (New York: McGraw-Hill, 1980).

35. R. D. Laing, *The Politics of the Family and Other Essays* (New York: Pantheon, 1971).

36. M. L. Knapp, *Nonverbal Communication in Human Interaction* (New York: Holt, Rinehart & Winston, 1978); J. McCroskey and L. Wheeless, *Introduction to Human Communication* (New York: Allyn & Bacon, 1976).

37. A. M. Katz and V. T. Katz, eds., *Foundations of Nonverbal Communication* (Carbondale, Ill.: Southern Illinois University Press, 1983).

38. M. D. Lieberman, "Intuition: A Social Cognitive Neuroscience Approach," *Psychological Bulletin* (2000): 109–138.

39. E. T. Hall, *The Hidden Dimension* (Garden City, N.Y.: Doubleday Anchor, 1966).

40. E. T. Hall, "Proxemics," in A. M. Katz and V. T. Katz, eds., *Foundations of Nonverbal Communication* (Carbondale, Ill.: Southern Illinois University Press, 1983).

41. R. T. Barker and C. G. Pearce, "The Importance of Proxemics at Work," *Supervisory Management* 35 (1990): 10–11.

42. R. L. Birdwhistell, *Kinesics and Context* (Philadelphia: University of Pennsylvania Press, 1970).

43. M. G. Frank and P. Ekman, "Appearing Truthful Generalizes Across Different Deception Situations," *Journal of Personality and Social Psychology* 86 (2004): 486–495.

44. P. Ekman and W. V. Friesen, "Research on Facial Expressions of Emotion," in A. M. Katz and V. T. Katz, eds., *Foundations of Nonverbal Communication* (Carbondale, Ill.: Southern Illinois University Press, 1983).

45. H. H. Tan, M. D. Foo, C. L. Chong, and R. Ng, "Situational and Dispositional Predictors of Displays of Positive Emotions," *Journal of Organizational Behavior* 24 (2003): 961–978.

46. C. Barnum and N. Wolniansky, "Taking Cues from Body Language," *Management Review* 78 (1989): 59.

47. Katz and Katz, *Foundations of Nonverbal Communication,* 181.

48. R. Gifford, C. F. Ng, and M. Wilkinson, "Nonverbal Cues in the Employment Interview: Links between Applicant Qualities and Interviewer Judgments," *Journal of Applied Psychology* 70 (1985): 729–736.

49. P. J. DePaulo and B. M. DePaulo, "Can Deception by Salespersons and Customers Be Detected through Nonverbal Behavioral Cues?" *Journal of Applied Social Psychology* 19 (1989): 1552–1577.

50. P. Ekman, *Telling Lies* (New York: Norton, 1985); D. Goleman, "Nonverbal Cues Are Easy to Misinterpret," *New York Times* (September 17, 1991): B5.

51. J. J. Lynch, *A Cry Unheard: New Insights into the Medical Consequences of Loneliness* (Baltimore, Md.: Bancroft Press, 2000).

52. J. C. Quick, J. H. Gavin, C. L. Cooper, and J. D. Quick, "Working Together: Balancing Head and Heart," in N. G. Johnson, R. H. Rozensky, C. D. Goodheart, and R. Hammond,

eds., *Psychology Builds a Healthy World:* (Washington, D.C.: American Psychological Association, 2004), 219–232.

53.   J. C. Quick, C. L. Cooper, J. D. Quick, and J. H. Gavin, *The Financial Times Guide to Executive Health* (London, UK: Financial Times–Prentice Hall, 2003).

54.   K. M. Wasylyshyn, "Coaching the Superkeepers," in L. A. Berger and D. R. Berger, eds., *The Talent Management Handbook: Creating Organizational Excellence by Identifying, Developing, and Positioning Your Best People* (New York, N.Y.: McGraw-Hill, 2003): 320–336.

55.   J. C. Quick and M. Macik-Frey, "Behind the Mask: Coaching through Deep Interpersonal Communication," *Consulting Psychology Journal: Practice and Research* 56 (2004): 67–74.

56.   R. Carter, "Fast Talk: The New IT Agenda," *Fast Company* 69 (April 2003): 53, http://www.fastcompany.com/magazine/69/fasttalk.html.

57.   B. Drake and K. Yuthas, "It's Only Words—Impacts of Information Technology on Moral Dialogue," *Journal of Business Ethics* 23 (2000): 41–60.

58.   N. Frohlich and J. Oppenheimer, "Some Consequences of E-Mail vs. Face-to-Face Communication in Experiment," *Journal of Economic Behavior & Organization* 35 (1998): 389–403.

59.   C. Brod, Technostress: *The Human Cost of the Computer Revolution* (Reading, Mass.: Addison-Wesley, 1984).

60.   S. Kiesler, "Technology and the Development of Creative Environments," in Y. Ijiri and R. L. Kuhn, eds., *New Directions in Creative and Innovative Management* (Cambridge, Mass.: Ballinger Press, 1988).

61.   S. Kiesler, J. Siegel, and T. W. McGuire, "Social Psychological Aspects of Computer-Mediated Communication," *American Psychologist* 39 (1984): 1123–1134.

62.   L. H. Bastin, "All's Well that Starts Well," *Circuits Assembly* 15 (February 2004): 7.

Chapter 8

1.   Whole Foods Market Press Release, "Declaration of Independence," (May 14, 2004), http://www.wholefoodmarket.com/company/declaration.html.

2.   G. Garcia, "Measuring Performance at Northrop Grumman," *Knowledge Management Review* 3 (2001): 22–25.

3.   A. M. Towsend, S. M. DeMarie, and A. R. Hendrickson, "Virtual Teams: Technology and the Workplace of the Future," *Academy of Management Executive* 12 (1998): 17–29.

4.   D. M. McGregor, *The Human Side of Enterprise* (New York: McGraw-Hill, 1960).

5.   J. R. Katzenbach and D. K. Smith, "The Discipline of Teams," *Harvard Business Review* 71 (1993): 111–120.

6.   K. L. Bettenhausen and J. K. Murnighan, "The Development and Stability of Norms in Groups Facing Interpersonal and Structural Challenge," *Administrative Science Quarterly* 36 (1991): 20–35.

7.   D. Tjosvold and Z. Yu, "Goal Interdependence and Applying Abilities for Team In-Role and Extra-Role Performance in China," *Group Dynamics: Theory, Research, and Practice* 8 (2004): 98–111.

8.   V. U. Druskat and S. B. Wolff, "Building the Emotional Intelligence of Groups," *Harvard Business Review* 79 (2001): 80–90.

9.   I. Summers, T. Coffelt, and R. E. Horton, "Work-Group Cohesion," *Psychological Reports* 63 (1988): 627–636.

10.   D. C. Man and S. S. K. Lam, "The Effects of Job Complexity and Autonomy on Cohesiveness in Collectivistic and Individualistic Work Groups: A Cross-Cultural Analysis," *Journal of Organizational Behavior* 24 (2003): 979–1001.

11.   K. H. Price, "Working Hard to Get People to Loaf," *Basic and Applied Social Psychology* 14 (1993): 329–344.

12.   R. Albanese and D. D. Van Fleet, "Rational Behavior in Groups: The Free-Riding Tendency," *Academy of Management Review* 10 (1985): 244–255.

13.   E. Diener, "Deindividuation, Self-Awareness, and Disinhibition," *Journal of Personality and Social Psychology* 37 (1979): 1160–1171.

14.   S. Prentice-Dunn and R. W. Rogers, "Deindividuation and the Self-Regulation of Behavior," in P. Paulus, ed., *Psychology of Group Influence* (Hillsdale, N.J.: Erlbaum, 1989): 87–109.

15.   B. M. Bass and E. C. Ryterband, *Organizational Psychology*, 2nd ed. (Boston: Allyn & Bacon, 1979).

16.   W. G. Bennis and H. A. Shepard, "A Theory of Group Development," *Human Relations* 9 (1956): 415–438.

17.   F. Warner, "GM Goes Off-Road," *Fast Company* 67 (February 2003): 40, http://www.fastcompany.com/magazine/67/smartcompany.html.

18.   S. Caudron, "Monsanto Responds to Diversity," *Personnel Journal* (November 1990): 72–80.

19.   D. L. Fields and T. C. Bloom, "Employee Satisfaction in Work Groups with Different Gender Composition," *Journal of Organizational Behavior* 18 (1997): 181–196.

20.   D. C. Lau and J. K. Murnighan, "Demographic Diversity and Faultlines: The Compositional Dynamics of Organizational Groups," *Academy of Management Review* 23 (1998): 325–340.

21.   B. Tuckman, "Developmental Sequence in Small Groups," *Psychological Bulletin* 63 (1965): 384–399; B. Tuckman and M. Jensen, "Stages of Small-Group Development," *Group and Organizational Studies* 2 (1977): 419–427.

22.   J. Li and D. C. Hambrick, "Factional Groups: A New Vantage on Demographic Faultlines, Conflict, and Disintegration in Work Teams," *Academy of Management Journal* 48 (2005): 794–813.

23.   D. Nichols, "Quality Program Sparked Company Turnaround," *Personnel* (October 1991): 24. For a commentary on Wallace's hard times and subsequent emergence from Chapter 11 bankruptcy, see R. C. Hill, "When the Going Gets Tough: A Baldrige Award Winner on the Line," *Academy of Management Executive* 7 (1993): 75–79.

24.   S. Weisband and L. Atwater, "Evaluating Self and Others in Electronic and Face-to-Face Groups," *Journal of Applied Psychology* 84 (1999): 632–639.

25.   C. J. G. Gersick, "Time and Transition in Work Teams: Toward a New Model of Group Development," *The Academy of Management Journal* 31 (1988): 9–41.

26.   M. Hardaker and B. K. Ward, "How to Make a Team Work," *Harvard Business Review* 65 (1987): 112–120.

27.   C. R. Gowen, "Managing Work Group Performance by Individual Goals and Group Goals for an Interdependent Group Task," *Journal of Organizational Behavior Management* 7 (1986): 5–27.

28.   K. L. Bettenhausen and J. K. Murnighan, "The Emergence of Norms in Competitive Decision-Making Groups," *Administrative Science Quarterly* 30 (1985): 350–372; K. L. Bettenhausen, "Five Years of Groups Research: What We Have Learned and What Needs to Be Addressed," *Journal of Management* 17 (1991): 345–381.

29.   J. E. McGrath, *Groups: Interaction and Performance* (Englewood Cliffs, N.J.: Prentice-Hall, 1984).

30.   K. L. Gammage, A. V. Carron, and P. A. Estabrooks, "Team Cohesion and Individual Productivity," *Small Group Research* 32 (2001): 3–18.

31.   S. E. Seashore, *Group Cohesiveness in the Industrial Work Group* (Ann Arbor, Mich.: University of Michigan, 1954).

32.   K. W. Phillips and D. L. Loyd, "When Surface and Deep-Level Diversity Collide: The Effects on Dissenting Group Members," *Organizational Behavior and Human Decision Processes* 99 (2006): 143–160.

33.   S. M. Klein, "A Longitudinal Study of the Impact of Work Pressure on Group Cohesive Behaviors," *International Journal of Management* 12 (1996): 68–75.

34.   N. Steckler and N. Fondas, "Building Team Leader Effectiveness: A Diagnostic Tool," *Organizational Dynamics* 23 (1995): 20–35.

35. G. Parker, *Team Players and Teamwork* (San Francisco: Jossey-Bass, 1990).
36. N. R. F. Maier, "Assets and Liabilities in Group Problem Solving: The Need for an Integrative Function," *Psychological Review* 74 (1967): 239–249.
37. T. A. Stewart, "The Search for the Organization of Tomorrow," *Fortune* (May 18, 1992): 92–98.
38. J. R. Goktepe and C. E. Schneier, "Role of Sex, Gender Roles, and Attraction in Predicting Emergent Leaders," *Journal of Applied Psychology* 74 (1989): 165–167.
39. W. R. Lassey, "Dimensions of Leadership," in W. R. Lassey and R. R. Fernandez, eds., *Leadership and Social Change* (La Jolla, Calif.: University Associates, 1976): 10–15.
40. J. D. Quick, G. Moorhead, J. C. Quick, E. A. Gerloff, K. L. Mattox, and C. Mullins, "Decision Making among Emergency Room Residents: Preliminary Observations and a Decision Model," *Journal of Medical Education* 58 (1983): 117–125.
41. W. J. Duncan and J. P. Feisal, "No Laughing Matter: Patterns of Humor in the Workplace," *Organizational Dynamics* 17 (1989): 18–30.
42. A. Hunter, "Best Practice Club," *Personnel Today* (April 15, 2003): 8.
43. S. S. Webber and R. J. Klimoski, "Crews: A Distinct Type of Work Team," *Journal of Business and Psychology* 18 (2004): 261–279.
44. P. F. Drucker, "There's More than One Kind of Team," *The Wall Street Journal* (February 11, 1992): A16.
45. B. LaRue, "Getting Things Done Through Action-Learning Teams," *Leadership Excellence*, Vol. 22, Issue 22 (August 2005): 18.
46. B. L. Kirkman, C. B. Gibson, and D. L. Shapiro, "'Exporting' Teams: Enhancing the Implementation and Effectiveness of Work Teams in Global Affiliates," *Organizational Dynamics* 30 (2001): 12–29.
47. R. R. Hirshfeld, M. H. Jordan, H. S. Field, W. F. Giles, and A. A. Armenakis, "Becoming Team Players: Team Members' Mastery of Teamwork Knowledge as a Predictor of Team Task Proficiency and Observed Teamwork Effectiveness," *Journal of Applied Psychology* 91 (2006): 467–474.
48. J. Vowler, "Teamwork Key to Charity's Success," *Computer Weekly* (February 24, 2004): 24.
49. P. M. Podsakoff, M. Ahearne, and S. B. MacKenzie, "Organizational Citizenship Behavior and the Quantity and Quality of Work Group Performance," *Journal of Applied Psychology* 82 (1997): 262–270.
50. L. Hirschhorn, *Managing in the New Team Environment* (Upper Saddle River, N.J.: Prentice-Hall), 521A.

51. G. Chen and R. J. Klimoski, "The Impact of Expectations on Newcomer Performance in Teams as Mediated by Work Characteristics, Social Exchanges, and Empowerment," *Academy of Management Journal* 46 (2003): 591–607.
52. B. Beersma, J. R. Hollenbeck, S. E. Humphrey, H. Moon, D. E. Conlon, and D. R. Ilgen, "Cooperation, Competition, and Team Performance: Toward a Contingency Approach," *Academy of Management Journal* 46 (2003): 572–590.
53. P. Chattopadhyay, M. Tluchowska, and E. George, "Identifying the Ingroup: A Closer Look at the Influence of Demographic Dissimilarity on Employee Social Identity," *Academy of Management Review* 29 (2004): 180–202.
54. E. V. Hobman, P. Bordia, and C. Gallois, "Consequences of Feeling Dissimilar from Others in a Work Team," *Journal of Business and Psychology* 17 (2003): 301–325.
55. A. E. Randel and K. S. Jaussi, "Functional Background Identity, Diversity, and Individual Performance in Cross-Functional Teams," *Academy of Management Journal* 46 (2003): 763–774.
56. J. S. Bunderson, "Team Member Functional Background and Involvement in Management Teams: Direct Effects and the Moderating Role of Power Centralization," *Academy of Management Journal* 46 (2003): 458–474.
57. G. S. Van Der Vegt, E. Van De Vliert, and A. Oosterhof, "Informational Dissimilarity and Organizational Citizenship Behavior: The Role of Intrateam Interdependence and Team Identification," *Academy of Management Journal* 46 (2003): 715–727.
58. A. Pirola-Merlo and L. Mann, "The Relationship between Individual Creativity and Team Creativity: Aggregating Across People and Time," *Journal of Organizational Behavior* 25 (2004): 235–257.
59. L. Thompson, "Improving the Creativity of Organizational Work Groups," *Academy of Management Executive* 17 (2003): 96–111.
60. C. Ford and D. M. Sullivan, "A Time for Everything: How the Timing of Novel Contributions Influences Project Team Outcomes," *Journal of Organizational Behavior* 25 (2004): 279–292.
61. J. W. Pfeiffer and C. Nolde, eds., *The Encyclopedia of Team-Development Activities* (San Diego: University Associates, 1991).
62. J. Boorstin, "No Preservatives. No Unions. Lots of Dough," *Fortune* 148 (September 15, 2003): 127-130; A. Blackman, "Putting a Ceiling on Pay: No Whole Foods Executive Can Earn Cash Pay of More Than 14 Times What Its Average Worker Makes; Will Other Companies Follow?" *The Wall Street Journal* (April 12, 2004): R11.

Chapter 9

1. http://en.wikipedia.org/wiki/Pixar.
2. H. A. Simon, *The New Science of Management Decision* (New York: Harper & Row, 1960).
3. R. Walker, "Brand Blue," *Fortune* (April 28, 2003): 118B–118H, http://www.fortune.com/fortune/smallbusiness/articles/0,15114,426909,00.html.
4. G. Huber, *Managerial Decision Making* (Glenview, Ill.: Scott, Foresman, 1980).
5. H. A. Simon, *Administrative Behavior* (New York: Macmillan, 1957).
6. E. F. Harrison, *The Managerial Decision-Making Process* (Boston: Houghton Mifflin, 1981).
7. R. L. Ackoff, "The Art and Science of Mess Management," *Interfaces* (February 1981): 20–26.
8. R. M. Cyert and J. G. March, eds., *A Behavioral Theory of the Firm* (Englewood Cliffs, N.J.: Prentice-Hall, 1963).
9. M. D. Cohen, J. G. March, and J. P. Olsen, "A Garbage Can Model of Organizational Choice," *Administrative Science Quarterly* 17 (1972): 1–25.
10. J. G. March and J. P. Olsen, "Garbage Can Models of Decision Making in Organizations," in J. G. March and R. Weissinger-Baylon, eds., *Ambiguity and Command* (Marshfield, Mass.: Pitman, 1986): 11–53.
11. D. van Knippenberg, B. van Knippenberg, and E. van Dijk, "Who Takes the Lead in Risky Decision Making? Effects of Group Members' Risk Preferences and Prototypicality," *Organizational Behavior and Human Decision Processes* 83 (2000): 213–234.
12. K. R. MacCrimmon and D. Wehrung, *Taking Risks* (New York: Free Press, 1986).
13. T. S. Perry, "How Small Firms Innovate: Designing a Culture for Creativity," *Research Technology Management* 28 (1995): 14–17.
14. B. M. Staw, "Knee-Deep in the Big Muddy: A Study of Escalating Commitment to a Chosen Course of Action," *Organizational Behavior and Human Performance* 16 (1976): 27–44; B. M. Staw, "The Escalation of Commitment to a Course of Action," *Academy of Management Review* 6 (1981): 577–587.
15. B. M. Staw and J. Ross, "Understanding Behavior in Escalation Situations," *Science* 246 (1989): 216–220.
16. T. Freemantle and M. Tolson, "Space Station Had Political Ties in Tow," *Houston Chronicle* (August 4, 2003), http://www.chron.com/cs/CDA/ssistory.mpl/space/2004947.
17. L. Festinger, *A Theory of Cognitive Dissonance* (Evanston, Ill.: Row, Peterson, 1957).
18. B. M. Staw, "The Escalation of Commitment: An Update and Appraisal," in Z. Shapira, ed., *Organizational Decision Making* (Cambridge, England: Cambridge University Press, 1997).

19. D. M. Boehne and P. W. Paese, "Deciding Whether to Complete or Terminate an Unfinished Project: A Strong Test of the Project Completion Hypothesis," *Organizational Behavior and Human Decision Processes* 81 (2000): 178–194; H. Moon, "Looking Forward and Looking Back: Integrating Completion and Sunk Cost Effects within an Escalation-of-Commitment Progress Decision," *Journal of Applied Psychology* 86 (2000): 104–113.

20. D. M. Rowell, "Concorde: An Untimely and Unnecessary Demise" (April 11, 2003), http://www.thetravelinsider.info/2003/0411.htm.

21. G. McNamara, H. Moon, and P. Bromiley, "Banking on Commitment: Intended and Unintended Consequences of an Organization's Attempt to Attenuate Escalation of Commitment," *Academy of Management Journal* 45 (2002): 443–452.

22. G. Whyte, "Diffusion of Responsibility: Effects on the Escalation Tendency," *Journal of Applied Psychology* 76 (1991): 408–415.

23. A. Saleh, "Brain Hemisphericity and Academic Majors: A Correlation Study," *College Student Journal* 35 (2001): 193–200.

24. N. Khatri, "The Role of Intuition in Strategic Decision Making," *Human Relations* 53 (2000): 57–86.

25. H. Mintzberg, "Planning on the Left Side and Managing on the Right," *Harvard Business Review* 54 (1976): 51–63.

26. D. J. Isenberg, "How Senior Managers Think," *Harvard Business Review* 62 (1984): 81–90.

27. R. N. Beck, "Visions, Values, and Strategies: Changing Attitudes and Culture," *Academy of Management Executive* 1 (1987): 33–41.

28. K. G. Ross, G. A. Klein, P. Thunholm, J. F. Schmitt, and H. C. Baxter, "The Recognition-Primed Decision Model," *Military Review* 84 (2004): 6–10.

29. C. I. Barnard, *The Functions of the Executive* (Cambridge, Mass.: Harvard University Press, 1938).

30. R. Rowan, *The Intuitive Manager* (New York: Little, Brown, 1986).

31. W. H. Agor, *Intuition in Organizations* (Newbury Park, Calif.: Sage, 1989).

32. Isenberg, "How Senior Managers Think," 81–90.

33. H. A. Simon, "Making Management Decisions: The Role of Intuition and Emotion," *Academy of Management Executive* 1 (1987): 57–64.

34. J. L. Redford, R. H. McPhierson, R. G. Frankiewicz, and J. Gaa, "Intuition and Moral Development," *Journal of Psychology* 129 (1994): 91–101.

35. R. Wild, "Naked Hunch; Gut Instinct Is Vital to Your Business," *Success* (June 1998), http://www.findarticles.com/cf_dls/m3514/n6_v45/20746158/p1/article.jhtml.

36. W. H. Agor, "How Top Executives Use their Intuition to Make Important Decisions," *Business Horizons* 29 (1986): 49–53.

37. O. Behling and N. L. Eckel, "Making Sense Out of Intuition," *Academy of Management Executive* 5 (1991): 46–54.

38. L. R. Beach, *Image Theory: Decision Making in Personal and Organizational Contexts* (Chichester, England: Wiley, 1990).

39. E. Bonabeau, "Don't Trust Your Gut," *Harvard Business Review* 81 (2003): 116–126.

40. L. Livingstone, "Person-Environment Fit on the Dimension of Creativity: Relationships with Strain, Job Satisfaction, and Performance" (Ph.D. diss., Oklahoma State University, 1992).

41. M. A. West and J. L. Farr, "Innovation at Work," in M. A. West and J. L. Farr, eds., *Innovation and Creativity at Work: Psychological and Organizational Strategies* (New York: Wiley, 1990): 3–13.

42. G. Morgan, *Riding the Waves of Change* (San Francisco: Jossey-Bass, 1988).

43. G. Wallas, *The Art of Thought* (New York: Harcourt Brace, 1926).

44. H. Benson and W. Proctor, *The Break-Out Principle* (Scribner: New York, 2003).

45. G. L. Fricchione, B. T. Slingsby, and H. Benson, "The Placebo Effect and the Relaxation Response: Neural Processes and Their Coupling to Constitutive Nitric Oxide," *Brain Research Reviews* 35 (2001): 1–19.

46. M. D. Mumford and S. B. Gustafson, "Creativity Syndrome: Integration, Application, and Innovation," *Psychological Bulletin* 103 (1988): 27–43.

47. T. Poze, "Analogical Connections—The Essence of Creativity," *Journal of Creative Behavior* 17 (1983): 240–241.

48. I. Sladeczek and G. Domino, "Creativity, Sleep, and Primary Process Thinking in Dreams," *Journal of Creative Behavior* 19 (1985): 38–46.

49. F. Barron and D. M. Harrington, "Creativity, Intelligence, and Personality," *Annual Review of Psychology* 32 (1981): 439–476.

50. R. J. Sternberg, "A Three-Faced Model of Creativity," in R. J. Sternberg, ed., *The Nature of Creativity* (Cambridge, England: Cambridge University Press, 1988): 125–147.

51. G. L. Clore, N. Schwartz, and M. Conway, "Cognitive Causes and Consequences of Emotion," in R. S. Wyer and T. K. Srull, eds., *Handbook of Social Cognition* (Hillsdale, N.J.: Erlbaum, 1994): 323–417.

52. B. L. Frederickson, "What Good Are Positive Emotions?" *Review of General Psychology* 2 (1998): 300–319.

53. B. L. Frederickson, "The Role of Positive Emotions in Positive Psychology," *American Psychologist* 56 (2001): 218–226.

54. T. M. Amabile, S. G. Barsade, J. S. Mueller, and B. M. Staw, "Affect and Creativity at Work," *Administrative Science Quarterly* 50 (3) (2005): 367–403.

55. E. R. Hirt, G. M. Levine, H. E. McDonald, R. J. Melton, and L. L. Martin, "The Role of Mood in Quantitative and Qualitative Aspects of Performance: Single or Multiple Mechanisms?" *Journal of Experimental Social Psychology* 33 (1997): 602–629.

56. J. M. George and Z. Zhou, "Understanding When Bad Moods Foster Creativity and Good Ones Don't: The Role of Context and Clarity of Feelings," *Journal of Applied Psychology* 87 (2002): 687–697.

57. J. Zhou, "When the Presence of Creative Coworkers Is Related to Creativity: Role of Supervisor Close Monitoring, Developmental Feedback, and Creative Personality," *Journal of Applied Psychology* 88 (2003): 413–422.

58. C. Axtell, D. Holman, K. Unsworth, T. Wall, and P. Waterson, "Shopfloor Innovation: Facilitating the Suggestion and Implementation of Ideas," *Journal of Occupational Psychology* 73 (2000): 265–285.

59. T. M. Amabile, R. Conti, H. Coon, J. Lazenby, and M. Herron, "Assessing the Work Environment for Creativity," *Academy of Management Journal* 39 (1996): 1154–1184.

60. T. Tetenbaum and H. Tetenbaum, "Office 2000: Tear Down the Wall," *Training* (February 2000): 58–64.

61. D. M. Harrington, "Creativity, Analogical Thinking, and Muscular Metaphors," *Journal of Mental Imagery* 6 (1981): 121–126; R. M. Kanter, *The Change Masters* (New York: Simon & Schuster, 1983).

62. T. M. Amabile, B. A. Hennessey, and B. S. Grossman, "Social Influences on Creativity: The Effects of Contracted-for Reward," *Journal of Personality and Social Psychology* 50 (1986): 14–23.

63. Livingstone, "Person-Environment Fit."

64. R. L. Firestein, "Effects of Creative Problem-Solving Training on Communication Behaviors in Small Groups," *Small Group Research* (November 1989): 507–521.

65. R. Von Oech, *A Whack on the Side of the Head* (New York: Warner, 1983).

66. A. G. Robinson and S. Stern, *How Innovation and Improvement Actually Happen* (San Francisco: Berrett Koehler, 1997).

67. K. Unsworth, "Unpacking Creativity," *Academy of Management Review* 26 (2001): 289–297.

68. M. F. R. Kets de Vries, R. Branson, and P. Barnevik, "Charisma in Action: The Transformational Abilities of Virgin's Richard Branson and ABBS's Percy Barnevik," *Organizational Dynamics* 26 (1998): 7–21.

69. M. Kostera, M. Proppe, and M. Szatkowski, "Staging the New Romantic Hero in the Old Cynical Theatre: On Managers, Roles, and Change in Poland," *Journal of Organizational Behavior* 16 (1995): 631–646.

70. J. Pfeffer, "Seven Practices of Successful Organizations," *California Management Review* 40 (1998): 96–124.

71. L. A. Witt, M. C. Andrews, and K. M. Kacmar, "The Role of Participation in Decision Making in the Organizational Politics—Job Satisfaction Relationship," *Human Relations* 53 (2000): 341–358.

72. C. R. Leana, E. A. Locke, and D. M. Schweiger, "Fact and Fiction in Analyzing Research on Participative Decision Making: A Critique of Cotton, Vollrath, Froggatt, Lengnick-Hall, and Jennings," *Academy of Management Review* 15 (1990): 137–146; J. L. Cotton, D. A. Vollrath, M. L. Lengnick-Hall, and K. L. Froggatt, "Fact: The Form of Participation Does Matter—A Rebuttal to Leana, Locke, and Schweiger," *Academy of Management Review* 15 (1990): 147–153.

73. G. Hamel, "Reinvent Your Company," *Fortune* 141 (June 12, 2000): 98–118.

74. T. W. Malone, "Is Empowerment Just a Fad? Control, Decision Making, and Information Technology," *Sloan Management Review* 38 (1997): 23–35.

75. IBM Customer Success Stories, "City and County of San Francisco Lower Total Cost of Ownership and Build on Demand Foundation" (February 3, 2004), http://www-306.ibm.com/software/success/cssdb.nsf/cs/LWRT-5VTLM2?OpenDocument&Site=lotusmandc.

76. G. Stasser, L. A. Taylor, and C. Hanna, "Information Sampling in Structured and Unstructured Discussion of Three- and Six-Person Groups," *Journal of Personality and Social Psychology* 57 (1989): 67–78.

77. E. Kirchler and J. H. Davis, "The Influence of Member Status Differences and Task Type on Group Consensus and Member Position Change," *Journal of Personality and Social Psychology* 51 (1986): 83–91.

78. R. F. Maier, "Assets and Liabilities in Group Problem Solving," *Psychological Review* 74 (1967): 239–249.

79. M. E. Shaw, *Group Dynamics: The Psychology of Small Group Behavior*, 3rd ed. (New York: McGraw-Hill, 1981).

80. P. W. Yetton and P. C. Bottger, "Individual versus Group Problem Solving: An Empirical Test of a Best Member Strategy," *Organizational Behavior and Human Performance* 29 (1982): 307–321.

81. W. Watson, L. Michaelson, and W. Sharp, "Member Competence, Group Interaction, and Group Decision Making: A Longitudinal Study," *Journal of Applied Psychology* 76 (1991): 803–809.

82. M. A. Serva, M. A. Fuller, and R. C. Mayer, "The Reciprocal Nature of Trust: A Longitudinal Study of Interacting Teams," *Journal of Organizational Behavior* 26 (2005): 625–649.

83. I. Janis, *Victims of Groupthink* (Boston: Houghton Mifflin, 1972).

84. M. A. Hogg and S. C. Hains, "Friendship and Group Identification: A New Look at the Role of Cohesiveness in Groupthink," *European Journal of Social Psychology* 28 (1998): 323–341.

85. P. E. Jones and H. M. P. Roelofsma, "The Potential for Social Contextual and Group Biases in Team Decision Making: Biases, Conditions, and Psychological Mechanisms," *Ergonomics* 43 (2000): 1129–1152; J. M. Levine, E. T. Higgins, and H. Choi, "Development of Strategic Norms in Groups," *Organizational Behavior and Human Decision Processes* 82 (2000): 88–101.

86. A. L. Brownstein, "Biased Predecision Processing," *Psychological Bulletin* 129 (2003): 545–568.

87. C. P. Neck and G. Moorhead, "Groupthink Remodeled: The Importance of Leadership, Time Pressure, and Methodical Decision-Making Procedures," *Human Relations* 48 (1995): 537–557.

88. J. Schwartz and M. L. Ward, "Final Shuttle Report Cites 'Broken Safety Culture' at NASA," *New York Times* (August 26, 2003), http://www.nytimes.com/2003/08/26/national/26CND-SHUT.html?ex=1077253200&en=882575f2c17ed8ff&ei=5070.

89. C. Ferraris and R. Carveth, "NASA and the Columbia Disaster: Decision Making by Groupthink?" in Proceedings of the 2003 Convention of the Association for Business Communication Annual Convention, http://www.businesscommunication.org/conventions/Proceedings/2003/PDF/03ABC03.pdf.

90. G. Moorhead, R. Ference, and C. P. Neck, "Group Decision Fiascoes Continue: Space Shuttle *Challenger* and a Revised Groupthink Framework," *Human Relations* 44 (1991): 539–550.

91. J. R. Montanari and G. Moorhead, "Development of the Groupthink Assessment Inventory," *Educational and Psychological Measurement* 49 (1989): 209–219.

92. P. t'Hart, "Irving L. Janis' Victims of Groupthink," *Political Psychology* 12 (1991): 247–278.

93. J. A. F. Stoner, "Risky and Cautious Shifts in Group Decisions: The Influence of Widely Held Values," *Journal of Experimental Social Psychology* 4 (1968): 442–459.

94. S. Moscovici and M. Zavalloni, "The Group as a Polarizer of Attitudes," *Journal of Personality and Social Psychology* 12 (1969): 125–135.

95. G. R. Goethals and M. P. Zanna, "The Role of Social Comparison in Choice of Shifts," *Journal of Personality and Social Psychology* 37 (1979): 1469–1476.

96. A. Vinokur and E. Burnstein, "Effects of Partially Shared Persuasive Arguments on Group-Induced Shifts: A Problem-Solving Approach," *Journal of Personality and Social Psychology* 29 (1974): 305–315.

97. L. Armstrong, "Toyota's Scion: A Siren to Young Buyers?" *Business Week* (March 4, 2002), http://www.businessweek.com/bwdaily/dnflash/mar2002/nf2002034_8826.htm.

98. Edmunds.com, Inc., "Toyota Courts NetGen Youth with Echo Subcompact" (January 1, 1999), http://www.edmunds.com/news/autoshows/articles/44460/page020.html.

99. Bloomberg.com, "Toyota Puts Hipness Ahead of Sales for New Scion Cars," (February 8, 2007) http://www.bloomberg.com/apps/news?pid=20601080&sid=at0Lm7MV8QFI&refer=asia

100. K. Dugosh, P. Paulus, E. Roland, and H. Yang, "Cognitive Stimulation in Brainstorming," *Journal of Personality and Social Psychology* 79 (2000): 722–735.

101. B. A. Nijstad, W. Stroebe, and H. F. M. Lodewijkx, "Production Blocking and Idea Generation: Does Blocking Interfere with Cognitive Processes?" *Journal of Experimental Social Psychology* 39 (2003): 531–549.

102. W. H. Cooper, R. B. Gallupe, S. Pollard, and J. Cadsby, "Some Liberating Effects of Anonymous Electronic Brainstorming," *Small Group Research* 29 (1998): 147–178.

103. A. Van de Ven and A. Delbecq, "The Effectiveness of Nominal, Delphi and Interacting Group Decision-Making Processes," *Academy of Management Journal* 17 (1974): 605–621.

104. A. L. Delbecq, A. H. Van de Ven, and D. H. Gustafson, *Group Techniques for Program Planning: A Guide to Nominal, Group, and Delphi Processes* (Glenview, Ill.: Scott, Foresman, 1975).

105. R. A. Cosier and C. R. Schwenk, "Agreement and Thinking Alike: Ingredients for Poor Decisions," *Academy of Management Executive* 4 (1990): 69–74.

106. D. M. Schweiger, W. R. Sandburg, and J. W. Ragan, "Group Approaches for Improving Strategic Decision Making: A Comparative Analysis of Dialectical Inquiry, Devil's Advocacy, and Consensus," *Academy of Management Journal* 29 (1986): 149–159.

107. G. Whyte, "Decision Failures: Why They Occur and How to Prevent Them," *Academy of Management Executive* 5 (1991): 23–31.

108. N. Adler, *International Dimensions of Organizational Behavior*, 3rd ed. (Cincinnati, Ohio: South-Western, 1997).

109. S. C. Peppas, "Attitudes of Hispanics and Non-Hispanics in the U.S.: A Comparative Study of Business Ethics," *Management Research News* 29 (3) (2006):, 92–105.

110. G. K. Stephens and C. R. Greer, "Doing Business in Mexico: Understanding Cultural Differences," *Organization Dynamics* 24 (1995): 39–55.

111. C. R. Greer and G. K. Stephens, "Escalation of Commitment: A Comparison of Differences between Mexican and U.S. Decision Makers," *Journal of Management* 27 (2001): 51–78.

112. K. W. Phillips and D. L. Lloyd, "When Surface and Deep-Level Diversity Collide: The Effects on Dissenting Group Members," *Organizational Behavior and*

Human Decision Processes 99 (2) (2006): 143–160.

113.   T. Simons, L. H. Pelled, and K. A. Smith, "Making Use of Difference: Diversity, Debate, and Decision Comprehensiveness in Top Management Teams," *Academy of Management Journal* 42 (6) (1999): 662–673.

114.   A. M. Townsend, S. M. DeMarie, and A. R. Hendrickson, "Virtual Teams: Technology and the Workplace of the Future," *Academy of Management Executive* 12 (1998): 17–29.

115.   M. S. Poole, M. Holmes, and G. DeSanctis, "Conflict Management in a Computer-Supported Meeting Environment," *Management Science* 37 (1991): 926–953.

116.   S. S. K. Lam and J. Schaubroeck, "Improving Group Decisions by Better Pooling Information: A Comparative Advantage of Group Decision Support Systems," *Journal of Applied Psychology* 85 (2000): 565–573.

117.   L. M. Jessup and J. F. George, "Theoretical and Methodological Issues in Group Support Systems," *Small Group Research* 28 (1997): 394–413.

118.   E. Bonabeau, "Predicting the Unpredictable," *Harvard Business Review* 80 (2002): 109–117.

119.   K. Blanchard and N. V. Peale, *The Power of Ethical Management* (New York: Fawcett Crest, 1988).

120.   C. Schneider, "War Dance: Will SEC Go Light on DOD Contractors?" *CFO Magazine* (April 7, 2003), http://www.cfo.com/article/1,5309,9121,00.htmlz?f=related.

121.   https://renderman.pixar.com/products/whatsrenderman/release.html.

122.   P. R. La Monica, "Disney Buys Pixar," CNNmoney.com (January 25, 2006). http://money.cnn.com/2006/01/24/news/companies/disney_pixar_deal/.

Chapter 10

1.   G. Baum, "Cisco's CEO: John Chambers," *Forbes* (February 23, 1998): 52, http://www.forbes.com/asap/1998/0223/052.html.

2.   John Chambers, "Guts and Glory," *Forbes* (May 5, 2007). http://members.forbes.com/global/2007/0507/060.html.

3.   P. Burrows, "Cisco's Comeback," *Business Week* (November 24, 2003): 116, http://www.businessweek.com/magazine/content/03_47/b3859008.htm.

4.   John Chambers, "Productivity, Labor and Capital." http://newsroom.cisco.com/dlls/tln/exec_team/chambers/perspectives.html.

5.   G. C. Homans, "Social Behavior as Exchange," *American Journal of Sociology* 63 (1958): 597–606.

6.   R. D. Middlemist and M. A. Hitt, *Organizational Behavior: Managerial Strategies for Performance* (St. Paul, Minn.: West Publishing, 1988).

7.   C. Barnard, *The Functions of the Executive* (Cambridge, Mass.: Harvard University Press, 1938).

8.   J. B Wade, C. A O'Reilly III, T. G Pollock. "Overpaid CEOs and Underpaid Managers: Fairness and Executive Compensation." *Organization Science* Vol.17 (5) (2006): 527–548.

9.   PBS online news hour. "Unions agree to pay cuts as American's CEO resigns." (April 25, 2003) http://www.pbs.org/newshour/updates/american_04-25-03.html.

10.   J. R. P. French and B. Raven, "The Bases of Social Power," in D. Cartwright, ed., *Group Dynamics: Research and Theory* (Evanston, Ill.: Row, Peterson, 1962); T. R. Hinkin and C. A. Schriesheim, "Development and Application of New Scales to Measure the French and Raven (1959) Bases of Social Power," *Journal of Applied Psychology* 74 (1989): 561–567.

11.   K. D. Elsbach and G. Elofson, "How the Packaging of Decision Explanations Affects Perceptions of Trustworthiness," *Academy of Management Journal* 43, No. 1 (2000): 80–89.

12.   P. M. Podsakoff and C. A. Schriesheim, "Field Studies of French and Raven's Bases of Power: Critique, Reanalysis, and Suggestions for Future Research," *Psychological Bulletin* 97 (1985): 387–411.

13.   M. A. Rahim, "Relationships of Leader Power to Compliance and Satisfaction with Supervision: Evidence from a National Sample of Managers," *Journal of Management* 15 (1989): 545–556.

14.   C. Argyris, "Management Information Systems: The Challenge to Rationality and Emotionality," *Management Science* 17 (1971): 275–292; J. Naisbitt and P. Aburdene, *Megatrends 2000* (New York: Morrow, 1990).

15.   P. P. Carson, K. D. Carson, E. L. Knight, and C. W. Roe, "Power in Organizations: A Look through the TQM Lens," *Quality Progress* (November 1995): 73–78.

16.   M. Velasquez, D. J. Moberg, and G. F. Cavanaugh, "Organizational Statesmanship and Dirty Politics: Ethical Guidelines for the Organizational Politician," *Organizational Dynamics* 11 (1982): 65–79.

17.   J. Pfeffer and G. Salancik, *The External Control of Organizations* (New York: Harper & Row, 1978).

18.   T. M. Welbourne and C. O. Trevor, "The Roles of Departmental and Position Power in Job Evaluation," *Academy of Management Journal* 43, No. 4 (2000): 761–771.

19.   R. H. Miles, *Macro Organizational Behavior* (Glenview, Ill.: Scott, Foresman, 1980).

20.   D. Hickson, C. Hinings, C. Lee, R. E. Schneck, and J. M. Pennings, "A Strategic Contingencies Theory of Intraorganizational Power," *Administrative Science Quarterly* 14 (1971): 219–220.

21.   C. R. Hinings, D. J. Hickson, J. M. Pennings, and R. E. Schneck, "Structural Conditions of Intraorganizational Power," *Administrative Science Quarterly* 19 (1974): 22–44.

22.   B. T. Mayes and R. T. Allen, "Toward a Definition of Organizational Politics," *Academy of Management Review* 2 (1977): 672–678.

23.   M. Valle and P. L. Perrewe, "Do Politics Perceptions Relate to Political Behaviors? Tests of an Implicit Assumption and Expanded Model," *Human Relations* 53 (2000): 359–386.

24.   W. A. Hochwarter, "The Interactive Effects of Pro-Political Behavior and Politics Perceptions on Job Satisfaction and Affective Commitment," *Journal of Applied Social Psychology* 33 (2003): 1360–1378.

25.   W. A. Hochwarter, K. M. Kacmar, D. C. Treadway, and T. S. Watson, "It's All Relative: The Distinction and Prediction of Political Perceptions Across Levels," *Journal of Applied Social Psychology* 33 (2003): 1955–2016.

26.   D. A. Ralston, "Employee Ingratiation: The Role of Management," *Academy of Management Review* 10 (1985): 477–487; D. R. Beeman and T. W. Sharkey, "The Use and Abuse of Corporate Politics," *Business Horizons* (March–April 1987): 25–35.

27.   C. O. Longnecker, H. P. Sims, and D. A. Gioia, "Behind the Mask: The Politics of Employee Appraisal," *Academy of Management Executive* 1 (1987): 183–193.

28.   M. Valle and P. L. Perrewe, "Do Politics Perceptions Relate to Political Behaviors? Tests of an Implicit Assumption and Expanded Model," *Human Relations* 53, No. 3 (2000): 359–386.

29.   D. Butcher and M. Clarke, "Organizational Politics: The Cornerstone for Organizational Democracy," *Organizational Dynamics* 31 (2002): 35–46.

30.   D. Kipnis, S. M. Schmidt, and I. Wilkinson, "Intraorganizational Influence Tactics: Explorations in Getting One's Way," *Journal of Applied Psychology* 65 (1980): 440–452; D. Kipnis, S. Schmidt, C. Swaffin-Smith, and I. Wilkinson, "Patterns of Managerial Influence: Shotgun Managers, Tacticians, and Bystanders," *Organizational Dynamics* (Winter 1984): 60–67; G. Yukl and C. M. Falbe, "Influence Tactics and Objectives in Upward, Downward, and Lateral Influence Attempts," *Journal of Applied Psychology* 75 (1990): 132–140.

31.   G. R. Ferris and T. A. Judge, "Personnel/Human Resources Management: A Political Influence Perspective," *Journal of Management* 17 (1991): 447–488.

32.   G. Yukl, P. J. Guinan, and D. Sottolano, "Influence Tactics Used for Different Objectives with Subordinates, Peers, and Superiors," *Groups & Organization Management* 20 (1995): 272–296.

33. C. A. Higgins, T. A. Judge, and G. R. Ferris, "Influence Tactics and Work Outcomes: A Meta-Analysis," *Journal of Organizational Behavior* 24 (2003): 89–106.

34. K. K. Eastman, "In the Eyes of the Beholder: An Attributional Approach to Ingratiation and Organizational Citizenship Behavior," *Academy of Management Journal* 37 (1994): 1379–1391.

35. R. A. Gordon, "Impact of Ingratiation on Judgments and Evaluations: A Meta-Analytic Investigation," *Journal of Personality and Social Psychology* 71 (1996): 54–70.

36. A. Drory and D. Beaty, "Gender Differences in the Perception of Organizational Influence Tactics," *Journal of Organizational Behavior* 12 (1991): 249–258.

37. S. Wellington, M. B. Kropf, and P. R. Gerkovich, "What's Holding Women Back?" *Harvard Business Review* (June 2003): 2–4.

38. P. Perrewe and D. Nelson, "Gender and Career Success: The Facilitative Role of Political Skill," *Organizational Dynamics,* in press.

39. R. Y. Hirokawa and A. Miyahara, "A Comparison of Influence Strategies Utilized by Managers in American and Japanese Organizations," *Communication Quarterly* 34 (1986): 250–265.

40. P. David, M. A. Hitt, and J. Gimeno, "The Influence of Activism by Institutional Investors on R&D," *Academy of Management Journal* 44, No. 1 (2001): 144–157.

41. G. R. Ferris, P. L. Perrewe, W. P. Anthony, and D. C, Gilmore, "Political Skill at Work," *Organizational Dynamics* 28 (2000): 25–37.

42. D. C. Treadway, W. A. Hochwarter, G. R. Ferris, C. J. Kacmar, C. Douglas, A. P. Ammeter, and M. R. Buckley, "Leader Political Skill and Employee Reactions," *Leadership Quarterly* 15 (2004): 493–513.

43. K. K. Ahearn, G. R. Ferris, W. A. Hochwarter, C. Douglas, and A. P. Ammeter, "Leader Political Skill and Team Performance," *Journal of Management* 30 (3) (2004): 309–327.

44. P. L. Perrewé, K. L. Zellars, G. R. Ferris, A. M. Rossi, C. J. Kacmar, and D. A. Ralston, "Neutralizing Job Stressors: Political Skill as an Antidote to the Dysfunctional Consequences of Role Conflict Stressors," *Academy of Management Journal* 47 (2004): 141–152.

45. G. R. Ferris, D. C. Treadway, R. W. Kolodinsky, W. A. Hochwarter, C. J. Kacmar, C. Douglas, and D. D. Frink, "Development and Validation of the Political Skill Inventory," *Journal of Management* 31 (2005): 126–152.

46. G. Ferris, S. Davidson, and P. Perrewé, "Developing Political Skill at Work," *Training* 42 (2005): 40–45.

47. K. Kumar and M. S. Thibodeaux, "Organizational Politics and Planned Organizational Change," *Group and Organization Studies* 15 (1990): 354–365.

48. D. E. McClelland, *Power: The Inner Experience* (New York: Irvington, 1975).

49. Beeman and Sharkey, "Use and Abuse of Corporate Politics," 37.

50. C. P. Parker, R. L. Dipboye, and S. L. Jackson, "Perceptions of Organizational Politics: An Investigation of Antecedents and Consequences," *Journal of Management* 21 (1995): 891–912.

51. S. J. Ashford, N. P. Rothbard, S. K. Piderit, and J. E. Dutton, "Out on a Limb: The Role of Context and Impression Management in Selling Gender-Equity Issues," *Administrative Science Quarterly* 43 (1998): 23–57.

52. J. Zhou and G. R. Ferris, "The Dimensions and Consequences of Organizational Politics Perceptions: A Confirmatory Analysis," *Journal of Applied Social Psychology* 25 (1995): 1747–1764.

53. M. L. Seidal, J. T. Polzer, and K. J. Stewart, "Friends in High Places: The Effects of Social Networks on Discrimination in Salary Negotiations," *Administrative Science Quarterly* 45 (2000): 1–24.

54. J. J. Gabarro and J. P. Kotter, "Managing Your Boss," *Harvard Business Review* (January–February 1980): 92–100.

55. P. Newman, "How to Manage Your Boss," Peat, Marwick, Mitchell & Company's *Management Focus* (May–June 1980): 36–37.

56. F. Bertolome, "When You Think the Boss Is Wrong," *Personnel Journal* 69 (1990): 66–73.

57. J. Conger and R. Kanungo, *Charismatic Leadership: The Elusive Factor in Organizational Effectiveness* (New York: Jossey-Bass, 1988).

58. G. M. Spreitzer, M. A. Kizilos, and S. W. Nason, "A Dimensional Analysis of the Relationship between Psychological Empowerment and Effectiveness, Satisfaction, and Strain," *Journal of Management* 23 (1997): 679–704.

59. J. Simons, "Merck's Man in the Hot Seat," *Fortune* (February 23, 2004): 111–114.

60. S. Finkelstein, *Why Smart Executives Fail: And What You Can Learn from Their Mistakes* (New York: Portfolio, 2003).

61. J. P. Kotter, "Power, Dependence, and Effective Management," *Harvard Business Review* 55 (1977): 125–136; J. P. Kotter, *Power and Influence* (New York: Free Press, 1985).

62. http://newsroom.cisco.com/dlls/index.html.

Chapter 11

1. http://www.forbes.com/static/bill2005/LIR2Y7I.html?passListId=10&passYear=2005&passListType=Person&uniqueId=2Y7I&datatype=Person.

2. M. Broad, "The Greatest Briton in Management and Leadership," *Personnel Today* (February 18, 2003): 20–21.

3 T. Hall and agencies, "Branson launches stem-cell storage venture," http://www.telegraph.co.uk/news/main.jhtml?xml=/news/2007/02/01/nstem101.xml.

4. J. P. Kotter, "What Leaders Really Do," *Harvard Business Review* 68 (1990): 103–111.

5. M. Roman, "In Biz This Week," *BusinessWeek* (January 12, 2004) http://www.businessweek.com/magazine/content/04_02/c3865035.htm

6. A. Zaleznik, "HBR Classic—Managers and Leaders: Are They Different?" *Harvard Business Review* 70 (1992): 126–135.

7. http://www.telegraph.co.uk/news/main.jhtml?xml=/news/2007/01/29/nba129.xml.

8. W. G. Rowe, "Creating Wealth in Organizations: The Role of Strategic Leadership," *Academy of Management Executive* 15 (2001): 81–94.

9. R. M. Stogdill, "Personal Factors Associated with Leadership: A Survey of the Literature," *Journal of Psychology* 25 (1948): 35–71.

10. K. Lewin, R. Lippitt, and R. K. White, "Patterns of Aggressive Behavior in Experimentally Created 'Social Climates,'" *Journal of Social Psychology* 10 (1939): 271–299.

11. R. M. Stogdill and A. E. Coons, eds., *Leader Behavior: Its Description and Measurement*, research monograph no. 88 (Columbus, Ohio: Bureau of Business Research, The Ohio State University, 1957).

12. A. W. Halpin and J. Winer, "A Factorial Study of the Leader Behavior Description Questionnaire," in R. M. Stogdill and A. E. Coons, eds., *Leader Behavior: Its Description and Measurement*, research monograph no. 88 (Columbus, Ohio: Bureau of Business Research, The Ohio State University, 1957): 39–51.

13. E. A. Fleishman, "Leadership Climate, Human Relations Training, and Supervisory Behavior," *Personnel Psychology* 6 (1953): 205–222.

14. R. Kahn and D. Katz, "Leadership Practices in Relation to Productivity and Morale," in D. Cartwright and A. Zander, eds., *Group Dynamics, Research and Theory* (Elmsford, N.Y.: Row, Paterson, 1960).

15. R. R. Blake and J. S. Mouton, *The Managerial Grid III: The Key to Leadership Excellence* (Houston: Gulf, 1985).

16. W. Vandekerckhove and R. Commers, "Downward Workplace Mobbing: A Sign of the Times?" *Journal of Business Ethics* 45 (2003): 41–50.

17. F. E. Fiedler, *A Theory of Leader Effectiveness* (New York: McGraw-Hill, 1964).

18. F. E. Fiedler, *Personality, Motivational Systems, and Behavior of High and Low LPC Persons*, tech. rep. no. 70-12 (Seattle: University of Washington, 1970).

19.   J. T. McMahon, "The Contingency Theory: Logic and Method Revisited," *Personnel Psychology* 25 (1972): 697–710; L. H. Peters, D. D. Hartke, and J. T. Pohlman, "Fiedler's Contingency Theory of Leadership: An Application of the Meta-Analysis Procedures of Schmidt and Hunter," *Psychological Bulletin* 97 (1985): 224–285.

20.   F. E. Fiedler, "The Contingency Model and the Dynamics of the Leadership Process," in L. Berkowitz, ed., *Advances in Experimental and Social Psychology*, Vol. 11 (New York: Academic Press, 1978).

21.   S. Arin and C. McDermott, "The Effect of Team Leader Characteristics on Learning, Knowledge Application, and Performance of Cross-Functional New Product Development Teams," *Decision Sciences* 34 (2003): 707–739.

22.   F. E. Fiedler, "Engineering the Job to Fit the Manager," *Harvard Business Review* 43 (1965): 115–122.

23.   R. J. House, "A Path–Goal Theory of Leader Effectiveness," *Administrative Science Quarterly* 16 (1971): 321–338; R. J. House and T. R. Mitchell, "Path–Goal Theory of Leadership," *Journal of Contemporary Business* 3 (1974): 81–97.

24.   C. A. Schriescheim and V. M. Von Glinow, "The Path–Goal Theory of Leadership: A Theoretical and Empirical Analysis," *Academy of Management Journal* 20 (1977): 398–405; E. Valenzi and G. Dessler, "Relationships of Leader Behavior, Subordinate Role Ambiguity, and Subordinate Job Satisfaction," *Academy of Management Journal* 21 (1978): 671–678; N. R. F. Maier, *Leadership Methods and Skills* (New York: McGraw-Hill, 1963).

25.   J. P. Grinnell, "An Empirical Investigation of CEO Leadership in Two Types of Small Firms," *S.A.M. Advanced Management Journal* 68 (2003): 36–41.

26.   G. B. Graen and M. Uhl-Bien, "Relationship-Based Approach to Leadership: Development of Leader–Member Exchange (LMX) Theory of Leadership over 25 Years," *Leadership Quarterly* 6 (1995): 219–247; C. R. Gerstner and D. V. Day, "Meta-Analytic Review of Leader–Member Exchange Theory: Correlates and Construct Issues," *Journal of Applied Psychology* 82 (1997): 827–844; R. C. Liden, S. J. Wayne, and R. T. Sparrowe, "An Examination of the Mediating Role of Psychological Empowerment on the Relations between the Job, Interpersonal Relationships, and Work Outcomes," *Journal of Applied Psychology* 85 (2001): 407–416.

27.   J. Townsend, J. S. Phillips, and T. J. Elkins, "Employee Retaliation: The Neglected Consequence of Poor Leader–Member Exchange Relations," *Journal of Occupational Health Psychology* 5 (2000): 457–463.

28.   D. Nelson, R. Basu, and R. Purdie, "An Examination of Exchange Quality and Work Stressors in Leader–Follower Dyads," *International Journal of Stress Management* 5 (1998): 103–112.

29.   K. M. Kacmar, L. A. Witt, S. Zivnuska, and S. M. Gully, "The Interactive Effect of Leader–Member Exchange and Communication Frequency on Performance Ratings," *Journal of Applied Psychology* 88 (2003): 764–772.

30.   P. Hersey and K. H. Blanchard, "Life Cycle Theory of Leadership," *Training and Development* 23 (1969): 26–34; P. Hersey, K. H. Blanchard, and D. E. Johnson, *Management of Organizational Behavior: Leading Human Resources*, 8th ed. (Upper Saddle River, N.J.: Prentice-Hall, 2001).

31.   B. M. Bass, *Bass and Stogdill's Handbook of Leadership: Theory, Research, and Managerial Applications*, 3rd ed. (New York: Free Press, 1990).

32.   J. M. Burns, *Leadership* (New York: Harper & Row, 1978); T. O. Jacobs, *Leadership and Exchange in Formal Organizations* (Alexandria, Va.: Human Resources Research Organization, 1971).

33.   B. M. Bass, "From Transactional to Transformational Leadership: Learning to Share the Vision," *Organizational Dynamics* 19 (1990): 19–31; B. M. Bass, *Leadership and Performance beyond Expectations* (New York: Free Press, 1985).

34.   P. M. Podsakoff, S. B. MacKenzie, and W. H. Bommer, "Transformational Leader Behaviors and Substitutes for Leadership as Determinants of Employee Satisfaction, Commitment, Trust, and Organizational Citizenship Behaviors," *Journal of Management* 22 (1996): 259–298.

35.   T. A. Judge and R. F. Piccolo, "Transformational and Transactional Leadership: A Meta-Analytic Test of Their Relative Validity," *Journal of Applied Psychology* 89 (2004): 755–768.

36.   L. G. Bolman and T. E. Deal. "Wizard and warrior: neglected leadership roles," *Strategy & Leadership* (2006) 34 (5):46.

37.   R. J. House and M. L. Baetz, "Leadership: Some Empirical Generalizations and New Research Directions," in B. M. Staw, ed., *Research in Organizational Behavior*, Vol. 1 (Greenwood, Conn.: JAI Press, 1979): 399–401.

38.   J. A. Conger and R. N. Kanungo, "Toward a Behavioral Theory of Charismatic Leadership in Organizational Settings," *Academy of Management Review* 12 (1987): 637–647.

39.   A. R. Willner, *The Spellbinders: Charismatic Political Leadership* (New Haven, Conn.: Yale University Press, 1984).

40.   D. Waldman, G. G. Ramirez, R. J. House, and P. Puranam, "Does Leadership Matter? CEO Leadership Attributes and Profitability under Conditions of Perceived Environmental Uncertainty," *Academy of Management Journal* 44 (2001): 134–143.

41.   J. M. Howell, "Two Faces of Charisma: Socialized and Personalized Leadership in Organizations," in J. A. Conger, ed., *Charismatic Leadership: Behind the Mystique of Exceptional Leadership* (San Francisco: Jossey-Bass, 1988).

42.   F. Luthans, and B. J. Avolio, "Authentic Leadership: A Positive Development Approach," in K. S. Cameron, J. E. Dutton, and R. E. Quinn, eds., *Positive Organizational Scholarship: Foundations of a New Discipline* (San Francisco, Calif.: Berrett-Koehler, 2004): 241–261.

43.   W. L. Gardner, B. J. Avolio, F. Luthans, D. R. May, and F. O. Walumbwa, "Can You See the Real Me?" A Self-Based Model of Authentic Leader and Follower Development," *The Leadership Quarterly* 16 (2005): 343–372.

44.   B. J. Avolio, W. L. Gardner, F. O. Walumbwa, F. Luthans, and D. R May, "Unlocking the Mask: A Look at the Process by Which Authentic Leaders Impact Follower Attitudes and Behaviors," *The Leadership Quarterly* 15 (2004): 801–823.

45.   S. Michie and J. Gooty, "Values, Emotions and Authentic Leadership Behaviors: Will the Real Leader Please Stand Up?" *The Leadership Quarterly* 16 (2005): 441–457.

46.   S. Michie and D. L. Nelson, "The Effects of Leader Compassion Display on Follower Attributions: Building a Socialized Leadership Image," Paper presented at the Academy of Management Conference in Honolulu, Hawaii (2005).

47.   D. Goleman, "What Makes a Leader?" *Harvard Business Review* 82 (2004): 82–91.

48.   D. Goleman, "Never Stop Learning," *Harvard Business Review* 82 (2004): 28–30.

49.   C. L. Gohm, "Mood Regulation and Emotional Intelligence: Individual Differences," *Journal of Personality and Social Psychology* 84 (2003): 594–607.

50.   J. Useem, "A Manager for All Seasons," *Fortune* (April 30, 2001): 66–72.

51.   R. C. Mayer, J. H. Davis, and F. D. Schoorman, "An Integrative Model of Organizational Trust," *Academy of Management Review* 20 (1995): 709–734.

52.   R. S. Dooley and G. E. Fryxell, "Attaining Decision Quality and Commitment from Dissent: The Moderating Effects of Loyalty and Competence in Strategic Decision-Making Teams," *Academy of Management Journal* 42 (1999): 389–402.

53.   S. W. Lester and H. H. Brower, "In the Eyes of the Beholder: The Relationship between Subordinates' Felt Trustworthiness and Their Work Attitudes and Behaviors," *Journal of Leadership & Organizational Studies* 10 (2003): 17–33.

54.   Saj-nicole A. Joni, "The Geography of Trust," *Harvard Business Review* 82 (2003): 82–88.

55.   M. E. Heilman, C. J. Block, R. F. Martell, and M. C. Simon, "Has Anything Changed? Current Characteristics of Men, Women, and Managers," *Journal of Applied Psychology* 74 (1989): 935–942.

56. A. H. Eagly, S. J. Darau, and M. Makhijani, "Gender and the Effectiveness of Leaders: A Meta-Analysis," *Psychological Bulletin* 117 (1995): 125–145.

57. E. P. Hollander and L. R. Offerman, "Power and Leadership in Organizations: Relationships in Transition," *American Psychologist* 45 (1990): 179–189.

58. H. P. Sims, Jr., and C. C. Manz, *Company of Heroes: Unleashing the Power of Self-Leadership* (New York: John Wiley & Sons, 1996).

59. C. C. Manz and H. P. Sims, "Leading Workers to Lead Themselves: The External Leadership of Self-Managing Work Teams," *Administrative Science Quarterly* 32 (1987): 106–128.

60. L. Hirschhorn, "Leaders and Followers in a Postindustrial Age: A Psychodynamic View," *Journal of Applied Behavioral Science* 26 (1990): 529–542.

61. R. E. Kelley, "In Praise of Followers," *Harvard Business Review* 66 (1988): 142–148.

62. C. C. Manz and H. P. Sims, "SuperLeadership: Beyond the Myth of Heroic Leadership," *Organizational Dynamics* 20 (1991): 18–35.

63. W. J. Crockett, "Dynamic Subordinancy," *Training and Development Journal* (May 1981): 155–164.

64. N. J. Adler, *International Dimensions in Organizational Behavior* (Boston: PWS-Kent, 1991).

65. F. C. Brodback *et al.*, "Cultural Variation of Leadership Prototypes across 22 European Countries," *Journal of Occupational and Organizational Psychology* 73 (2000): 1–29.

66. B. Alimo-Metcalfe and R. J. Alban-Metcalfe, "The Development of a New Transformational Leadership Questionnaire," *Journal of Occupational and Organizational Psychology* 74 (2001): 1–27.

67. T. Lenartowicz and J. P. Johnson, "A Cross-National Assessment of the Values of Latin American Managers: Contrasting Hues or Shades of Gray?" *Journal of International Business Studies* 34 (2003): 266–281.

68. Y. Hui-Chun and P. Miller, "The Generation Gap and Cultural Influence: A Taiwan Empirical Investigation," *Cross Cultural Management* 10 (2003): 23–42.

69. G. A. Yukl, *Leadership in Organizations,* 2nd ed. (Upper Saddle River, N.J.: Prentice-Hall, 1989).

70. Harvard Business School, "James E. Burke," *Working Knowledge* (October 27, 2003), http://hbswk.hbs.edu/pubitem.jhtml?id=3755&t=leadership.

71. B. Morris, "Sir Richard's Rules," *Fortune* (2003) http://money.cnn.com/magazines/fortune/fortune_archive/2003/10/06/350384/index.htm.

Chapter 12

1. Whole Foods Market® Soars to Number 5 Spot on FORTUNE's "100 Best Companies to Work For" List. http://www.wholefoods.com/company/pr_01-09-07.html. retrieved 07/05/07.

2. Definition adapted from D. Hellriegel, J. W. Slocum, Jr., and R. W. Woodman, *Organizational Behavior* (St. Paul: West, 1992) and from R. D. Middlemist and M. A. Hitt, *Organizational Behavior* (St. Paul: West, 1988).

3. D. Tjosvold, *The Conflict-Positive Organization* (Reading, Mass.: Addison-Wesley, 1991).

4. K. Thomas and W. Schmidt, "A Survey of Managerial Interests with Respect to Conflict," *Academy of Management Journal* 19 (1976): 315–318; G. L. Lippitt, "Managing Conflict in Today's Organizations," *Training and Development Journal* 36 (1982): 66–74.

5. M. Rajim, "A Measure of Styles of Handling Interpersonal Conflict," *Academy of Management Journal* 26 (1983): 368–376.

6. D. Goleman, *Emotional Intelligence* (New York: Bantam Books, 1995); J. Stuller, "Unconventional Smarts," *Across the Board* 35 (1998): 22–23.

7. Tjosvold, *The Conflict-Positive Organization,* 4.

8. R. A. Cosier and D. R. Dalton, "Positive Effects of Conflict: A Field Experiment," *International Journal of Conflict Management* 1 (1990): 81–92.

9. D. Tjosvold, "Making Conflict Productive," *Personnel Administrator* 29 (1984): 121–130.

10. A. C. Amason, W. A. Hochwarter, K. R. Thompson, and A. W. Harrison, "Conflict: An Important Dimension in Successful Management Teams," *Organizational Dynamics* 24 (1995): 25–35.

11. T. L. Simons and R. S. Peterson, "Task Conflict and Relationship Conflict in Top Management Teams: The Pivotal Role of Intergroup Trust," *Journal of Applied Psychology* 85 (2000): 102–111.

12. R. Nibler and K. L. Harris, "The Effects of Culture and Cohesiveness on Intragroup Conflict and Effectiveness," *The Journal of Social Psychology* 143 (2003): 613–631.

13. I. Janis, *Groupthink,* 2nd ed. (Boston: Houghton Mifflin, 1982).

14. J. D. Thompson, *Organizations in Action* (New York: McGraw-Hill, 1967).

15. G. Walker and L. Poppo, "Profit Centers, Single-Source Suppliers, and Transaction Costs," *Administrative Science Quarterly* 36 (1991): 66–87.

16. R. Miles, *Macro Organizational Behavior* (Glenview, Ill.: Scott, Foresman, 1980).

17. H. Levinson, "The Abrasive Personality," *Harvard Business Review* 56 (1978): 86–94.

18. J. C. Quick and J. D. Quick, *Organizational Stress and Preventive Management* (New York: McGraw-Hill, 1984).

19. F. N. Brady, "Aesthetic Components of Management Ethics," *Academy of Management Review* 11 (1986): 337–344.

20. J. R. Ogilvie and M. L. Carsky, "Building Emotional Intelligence in Negotiations," *The International Journal of Conflict Management* 13 (2002): 381–400.

21. A. M. Bodtker and R. L. Oliver, "Emotion in Conflict Formation and Its Transformation: Application to Organizational Conflict Management," *International Journal of Conflict Management* 12 (2001): 259–275.

22. D. E. Conlon and S. H. Hunt, "Dealing with Feeling: The Influence of Outcome Representations on Negotiation," *International Journal of Conflict Management* 13 (2002): 35–58.

23. V. K. Raizada, "Multi-Ethnic Corporations and Inter-Ethnic Conflict," *Human Resource Management* 20 (1981): 24–27; T. Cox, Jr., "The Multicultural Organization," *Academy of Management Executive* 5 (1991): 34–47.

24. G. Hofstede, *Culture's Consequences: International Differences in Work-Related Values* (Beverly Hills, Calif.: Sage, 1980); G. Hofstede and M. H. Bond, "The Confucius Connection: From Cultural Roots to Economic Growth," *Organizational Dynamics* (Spring 1988): 4–21; G. Hofstede, "Cultural Constraints in Management Theories," *Academy of Management Executive* 7 (1993): 81–94.

25. T. H. Cox, S. A. Lobel, and P. L. McLead, "Effects of Ethnic Group Cultural Differences on Cooperative and Competitive Behavior in a Group Task," *Academy of Management Journal* 34 (1991): 827–847.

26. J. Schopler, C. A. Insko, J. Wieselquist, *et al.,* "When Groups Are More Competitive than Individuals: The Domain of the Discontinuity Effect," *Journal of Personality and Social Psychology* 80 (2001): 632–644.

27. M. Sherif and C. W. Sherif, *Social Psychology* (New York: Harper & Row, 1969).

28. C. Song, S. M. Sommer, and A. E. Hartman, "The Impact of Adding an External Rater on Interdepartmental Cooperative Behaviors of Workers," *International Journal of Conflict Management* 9 (1998): 117–138.

29. W. Tsai and S. Ghoshal, "Social Capital and Value Creation: The Role of Intrafirm Networks," *Academy of Management Journal* 41 (1998): 464–476.

30. M. A. Zarate, B. Garcia, A. A. Garza, and R. T. Hitlan, "Cultural Threat and Perceived Realistic Group Conflict as Dual Predictors of Prejudice," *Journal of Experimental Social Psychology* 40 (2004): 99–105.

31. M. L. Maznevski and K. M. Chudoba, "Bridging Space over Time: Global

Virtual-Team Dynamics and Effectiveness," *Organization Science* 11 (2000): 473–492.

32.   J. L. Badaracco, Jr., "The Discipline of Building Character," *Harvard Business Review* (March–April 1998): 115–124.

33.   B. Schneider, "The People Make the Place," *Personnel Psychology* 40 (1987): 437–453.

34.   C. A. O'Reilly, J. Chatman, and D. F. Caldwell, "People and Organizational Culture: A Profile Comparison Approach to Assessing Person-Organization Fit," *Academy of Management Journal* 34 (1991): 487–516.

35.   I. Dayal and J. M. Thomas, "Operation KPE: Developing a New Organization," *Journal of Applied Behavioral Science* 4 (1968): 473–506.

36.   R. H. Miles, "Role Requirements as Sources of Organizational Stress," *Journal of Applied Psychology* 61 (1976): 172–179.

37.   K. Thomas, "Conflict and Conflict Management," in M. D. Dunnette, ed., *Handbook of Industrial and Organizational Psychology* (New York: Wiley, 1976).

38.   H. H. Meyer, E. Kay, and J. R. P. French, "Split Roles in Performance Appraisal," *Harvard Business Review* 43 (1965): 123–129.

39.   T. W. Costello and S. S. Zalkind, *Psychology in Administration: A Research Orientation* (Englewood Cliffs, N.J.: Prentice-Hall, 1963).

40.   Snapshot Spy, "Employee Computer & Internet Abuse Statistics," http://www.snapshotspy.com/employee-computer-abuse-statistics.htm; Data sources include U.S. Department of Commerce—Economics and Statistics Administration and the National Telecommunications and Information Administration—Greenfield and Rivet, "Employee Computer Abuse Statistics."

41.   P. F. Hewlin, "And the Award for Best Actor Goes to . . . : Facades of Conformity in Organizational Settings," *Academy of Management Review* 28 (2003): 633–642.

42.   C. A. Insko, J. Scholper, L. Gaertner, *et al.,* "Interindividual–Intergroup Discontinuity Reduction through the Anticipation of Future Interaction," *Journal of Personality and Social Psychology* 80 (2001): 95–111.

43.   D. Tjosvold and M. Poon, "Dealing with Scarce Resources: Open-Minded Interaction for Resolving Budget Conflicts," *Group and Organization Management* 23 (1998): 237–255.

44.   R. Steers, *Introduction to Organizational Behavior,* 4th ed. (Glenview, Ill.: Harper-Collins, 1991).

45.   C. Morrill, M. N. Zold, and H. Rao, "Covert Political Conflict in Organizations: Challenges from Below," *Annual Review of Sociology* 29 (2003): 391–415.

46.   A. Tyerman and C. Spencer, "A Critical Text of the Sheriff's Robber's Cave Experiments: Intergroup Competition and

Cooperation between Groups of Well-Acquainted Individuals," *Small Group Behavior* 14 (1983): 515–531; R. M. Kramer, "Intergroup Relations and Organizational Dilemmas: The Role of Categorization Processes," in B. Staw and L. Cummings, eds., *Research in Organizational Behavior* 13 (Greenwich, Conn.: JAI Press, 1991): 191–228.

47.   A. Carmeli, "The Relationship between Emotional Intelligence and Work Attitudes, Behavior and Outcomes: An Examination among Senior Managers," *Journal of Managerial Psychology* 18 (2003): 788–813.

48.   R. Blake and J. Mouton, "Overcoming Group Warfare," *Harvard Business Review* 64 (1984): 98–108.

49.   D. G. Ancona and D. Caldwell, "Improving the Performance of New Product Teams," *Research Technology Management* 33 (1990): 25–29.

50.   C. K. W. DeDreu and L. R. Weingart, "Task versus Relationship Conflict, Team Performance, and Team Member Satisfaction: A Meta-Analysis," *Journal of Applied Psychology* 88 (2003): 741–749.

51.   R. J. Lewicki, J. A. Litterer, J. W. Minton, and D. M. Saunders, *Negotiation,* 2nd ed. (Burr Ridge, Ill.: Irwin, 1994).

52.   C. K. W. De Dreu, S. L. Koole, and W. Steinel, "Unfixing the Fixed Pie: A Motivated Information-Processing Approach to Integrative Negotiation," *Journal of Personality and Social Psychology* 79 (2000): 975–987.

53.   M. H. Bazerman, J. R. Curhan, D. A. Moore, and K. L. Valley, "Negotiation," *Annual Review of Psychology* 51 (2000): 279–314.

54.   I. Ayers and P. Siegelman, "Race and Gender Discrimination in Bargaining for a New Car," *American Economic Review* 85 (1995): 304–321.

55.   L. J. Kray, L. Thompson, and A. Galinsky, "Battle of the Sexes: Gender Stereotype Confirmation and Reactance in Organizations," *Journal of Personality and Social Psychology* 80 (2001): 942–958.

56.   K. W. Thomas, "Conflict and Conflict Management," in M. D. Dunnette, ed., *Handbook of Industrial and Organizational Psychology* (Chicago: Rand McNally, 1976): 900.

57.   C. K. W. De Dreu and A. E. M. Van Vianen, "Managing Relationship Conflict and the Effectiveness of Organizational Teams," *Journal of Organizational Behavior* 22 (2001): 309–328.

58.   R. A. Baron, S. P. Fortin, R. L. Frei, L. A. Hauver, and M. L. Shack, "Reducing Organizational Conflict: The Role of Socially Induced Positive Affect," *International Journal of Conflict Management* 1 (1990): 133–152.

59.   S. L. Phillips and R. L. Elledge, *The Team Building Source Book* (San Diego: University Associates, 1989).

60.   T. N. Gladwin and I. Walter. "How Multinationals Can Manage Social and Political Forces," *Journal of Business Strategy,* Summer 1980a: 54-68.

61.   K. W. Thomas, "Toward–Multidimensional Values in Teaching: The Example of Conflict Behaviors," *Academy of Management Review* 2 (1977): 484–490.

62.   S. Alper, D. Tjosvold, and K. S. Law, "Conflict Management, Efficacy, and Performance in Organizational Teams," *Personnel Psychology* 53 (2000): 625–642.

63.   W. King and E. Miles, "What We Know and Don't Know about Measuring Conflict," *Management Communication Quarterly* 4 (1990): 222–243.

64.   J. Barker, D. Tjosvold, and I. R. Andrews, "Conflict Approaches of Effective and Ineffective Project Managers: A Field Study in a Matrix Organization," *Journal of Management Studies* 25 (1988): 167–178.

65.   M. Chan, "Intergroup Conflict and Conflict Management in the R&D Divisions of Four Aerospace Companies," *IEEE Transactions on Engineering Management* 36 (1989): 95–104.

66.   M. K. Kozan, "Cultural Influences on Styles of Handling Interpersonal Conflicts: Comparisons among Jordanian, Turkish, and U.S. Managers," *Human Relations* 42 (1989): 787–799.

67.   S. McKenna, "The Business Impact of Management Attitudes towards Dealing with Conflict: A Cross-Cultural Assessment," *Journal of Managerial Psychology* 10 (1995): 22–27.

68.   Tjosvold, *The Conflict-Positive Organization.*

69.   P. J. Frost, *Toxic Emotions at Work: How Compassionate Managers Handle Pain and Conflict* (Harvard Business School Press, 2003).

70.   J. R. Ogilvie and M. L. Carsky, "Building Emotional Intelligence in Negotiations," *The International Journal of Conflict Management* 13 (2002): 381–400.

71.   M. Rothschild, "Whole Foods Unionized," *The Progressive* (July 9, 2002), http://www.progressive.org/webex/wx071602.html.

Chapter 13

1.   S. P. Means, "Playing at Pixar," *The Salt Lake Tribune* (May 30, 2003): D1.

2.   F. Warner, "Employees Choosing Work over Perks," *Management Services* 48 (March 2004): 3.

3.   F. W. Taylor, *The Principles of Scientific Management* (New York: Norton, 1911).

4.   T. Bell, *Out of This Furnace* (Pittsburgh: University of Pittsburgh Press, 1941).

5.   P. Cappelli, "A Market-Driven Approach to Retaining Talent," *Harvard Business Review* 78 (2000): 103–111.

6. N. D. Warren, "Job Simplification versus Job Enlargement," *Journal of Industrial Engineering* 9 (1958): 435–439.

7. C. R. Walker, "The Problem of the Repetitive Job," *Harvard Business Review* 28 (1950): 54–58.

8. T. Moller, S. E. Mathiassen, H. Franzon, and S. Kihlberg, "Job Enlargement and Mechanical Exposure Variability in Cyclic Assembly Work," *Ergonomics* 47 (2004): 19–40.

9. C. R. Walker and R. H. Guest, *The Man on the Assembly Line* (Cambridge, Mass.: Harvard University Press, 1952).

10. M. A. Campion, L. Cheraskin, and M. J. Stevens, "Career-Related Antecedents and Outcomes of Job Rotation," *Academy of Management Journal* 37 (1994): 1518–1542.

11. E. Santora, "Keep Up Production Through Cross-Training," *Personnel Journal* (June 1992): 162–166.

12. R. P. Steel and J. R. Rentsch, "The Dispositional Model of Job Attitudes Revisited: Findings of a 10-Year Study," *Journal of Applied Psychology* 82 (1997): 873–879; C. S. Wong, C. Hui, and K. S. Law, "A Longitudinal Study of the Job Perception–Job Satisfaction Relationship: A Text of the Three Alternative Specifications," *Journal of Occupational & Organizational Psychology* 71 (Part 2, 1998): 127–146.

13. F. Herzberg, "One More Time: How Do You Motivate Employees?" *Harvard Business Review* 46 (1968): 53–62.

14. R. N. Ford, "Job Enrichment Lessons from AT&T," *Harvard Business Review* 51 (1973): 96–106.

15. R. J. House and L. A. Wigdor, "Herzberg's Dual-Factor Theory of Job Satisfaction and Motivation: A Review of the Evidence and a Criticism," *Personnel Psychology* 20 (1967): 369–389.

16. A. N. Turner and P. R. Lawrence, *Industrial Jobs and the Worker* (Cambridge, Mass.: Harvard University Press, 1965).

17. J. R. Hackman and G. R. Oldham, "The Job Diagnostic Survey: An Instrument for the Diagnosis of Jobs and the Evaluation of Job Redesign Projects," *Technical Report No. 4* (New Haven, Conn.: Department of Administrative Sciences, Yale University, 1974).

18. J. R. Hackman and G. R. Oldham, "Development of the Job Diagnostic Survey," *Journal of Applied Psychology* 60 (1975): 159–170.

19. E. Sadler-Smith, G. El-Kot, and M. Leat, "Differentiating Work Autonomy Facets in a Non-Western Context," *Journal of Organizational Behavior* 24 (2003): 709–731.

20. P. H. Birnbaum, J. L. Farh, and G. Y. Y. Wong, "The Job Characteristics Model in Hong Kong," *Journal of Applied Psychology* 71 (1986): 598–605.

21. J. R. Hackman and G. R. Oldham, *Work Design* (Reading, Mass.: Addison-Wesley, 1980).

22. H. P. Sims, A. D. Szilagyi, and R. T. Keller, "The Measurement of Job Characteristics," *Academy of Management Journal* 19 (1976): 195–212.

23. H. P. Sims and A. D. Szilagyi, "Job Characteristic Relationships: Individual and Structural Moderators," *Organizational Behavior and Human Performance* 17 (1976): 211–230.

24. Y. Fried, "Meta-Analytic Comparison of the Job Diagnostic Survey and Job Characteristic Inventory as Correlates of Work Satisfaction and Performance," *Journal of Applied Psychology* 76 (1991): 690–698.

25. D. R. May, R. L. Gilson, and L. M. Harter, "The Psychological Conditions of Meaningfulness, Safety, and Availability and the Engagement of the Human Spirit at Work," *Journal of Occupational and Organizational Psychology* 77 (2004): 11–37.

26. R. Wagner, "Nourishing Employee Engagement," *Gallup Management Journal* (February 12, 2004): 1–7, http://gmj.gallup.com/content/default.asp?ci=10504.

27. J. Loehr and T. Schwartz, *The Power of Full Engagement: Managing Energy, Not Time, Is the Key to High Performance and Personal Renewal* (New York: Free Press, 2003).

28. M. F. R. Kets de Vries, "Creating Authentizotic Organizations: Well-Functioning Individuals in Vibrant Companies," *Human Relations* 54 (2001): 101–111.

29. G. R. Salancik and J. Pfeffer, "A Social Information Processing Approach to Job Attitudes and Task Design," *Administrative Science Quarterly* 23 (1978): 224–253.

30. J. Pfeffer, "Management as Symbolic Action: The Creation and Maintenance of Organizational Paradigms," in L. L. Cummings and B. M. Staw, eds., *Research in Organizational Behavior,* Vol. 3 (Greenwich, Conn.: JAI Press, 1981): 1–52.

31. J. Thomas and R. Griffin, "The Social Information Processing Model of Task Design: A Review of the Literature," *Academy of Management Review* 8 (1983): 672–682.

32. D. J. Campbell, "Task Complexity: A Review and Analysis," *Academy of Management Review* 13 (1988): 40–52.

33. D. R. May, K. Reed, C. E. Schwoerer, and P. Potter, "Ergonomic Office Design and Aging: A Quasi-Experimental Field Study of Employee Reactions to an Ergonomics Intervention Program," *Journal of Occupational Health Psychology* 9 (2004): 123–135.

34. M. A. Campion and P. W. Thayer, "Job Design: Approaches, Outcomes, and Trade-Offs," *Organizational Dynamics* 16 (1987): 66–79.

35. J. Teresko, "Emerging Technologies," *Industry Week* (February 27, 1995): 1–2.

36. M. A. Campion and C. L. McClelland, "Interdisciplinary Examination of the Costs and Benefits of Enlarged Jobs: A Job Design Quasi-Experiment," *Journal of Applied Psychology* 76 (1991): 186–199.

37. B. Kohut, *Country Competitiveness: Organizing of Work* (New York: Oxford University Press, 1993).

38. J. C. Quick and L. E. Tetrick, eds., *Handbook of Occupational Health Psychology* (Washington, D.C.: American Psychological Association, 2002).

39. W. E. Deming, *Out of the Crisis* (Cambridge, Mass.: MIT Press, 1986).

40. L. Thurow, *Head to Head: The Coming Economic Battle among Japan, Europe, and America* (New York: Morrow, 1992).

41. M. A. Fruin, *The Japanese Enterprise System—Competitive Strategies and Cooperative Structures* (New York: Oxford University Press, 1992).

42. W. Niepce and E. Molleman, "Work Design Issue in Lean Production from a Sociotechnical System Perspective: Neo-Taylorism or the Next Step in Sociotechnical Design?" *Human Relations* 51 (1998): 259–287.

43. S. K. Parker, "Longitudinal Effects of Lean Production on Employee Outcomes and the Mediating Role of Work Characteristics," *Journal of Applied Psychology* 88 (2003): 620–634.

44. E. Furubotn, "Codetermination and the Modern Theory of the Firm: A Property-Rights Analysis," *Journal of Business* 61 (1988): 165–181.

45. H. Levinson, *Executive: The Guide to Responsive Management* (Cambridge, Mass.: Harvard University Press, 1981).

46. B. Gardell, "Scandinavian Research on Stress in Working Life" (Paper presented at the IRRA Symposium on Stress in Working Life, Denver, September 1980).

47. L. Levi, "Psychosocial, Occupational, Environmental, and Health Concepts; Research Results and Applications," in G. P. Keita and S. L. Sauter, eds., *Work and Well-Being: An Agenda for the 1990s* (Washington, D.C.: American Psychological Association, 1992): 199–211.

48. Y. Baruch, "The Status of Research on Teleworking and an Agenda for Future Research," *International Journal of Management Review* 3 (2000): 113–129.

49. K. E. Pearlson and C. S. Saunders, "There's No Place Like Home: Managing Telecommuting Paradoxes," *Academy of Management Executive* 15 (2001): 117–128.

50. S. Caudron, "Working at Home Pays Off," *Personnel Journal* (November 1992): 40–47.

51. D. S. Bailey and J. Foley, "Pacific Bell Works Long Distance," *HRMagazine* (August 1990): 50–52.

52. S. M. Pollan and M. Levine, "Asking for Flextime," *Working Women* (February 1994): 48.

53. S. A. Rogier and M. Y. Padgett, "The Impact of Utilizing a Flexible Work Schedule on the Perceived Career Advancement Potential of Women," *Human

Resource Development Quarterly 15 (2004): 89–106.

54.   S. Zuboff, In the Age of the Smart Machine: The Future of Work and Power (New York: Basic Books, 1988).

55.   B. A. Gutek and S. J. Winter, "Computer Use, Control over Computers, and Job Satisfaction," in S. Oskamp and S. Spacapan, eds., People's Reactions to Technology in Factories, Offices, and Aerospace: The Claremont Symposium on Applied Social Psychology (Newbury Park, Calif.: Sage, 1990): 121–144.

56.   L. M. Schleifer and B. C. Amick III, "System Response Time and Method of Pay: Stress Effects in Computer-Based Tasks," International Journal of Human-Computer Interaction 1 (1989): 23–39.

57.   K. Voight, "Virtual Work: Some Telecommuters Take Remote Work to the Extreme," The Wall Street Journal Europe (February 1, 2001): 1.

58.   M. Lasswell, "Pixar—To Infinity and Beyond," Management Today (May 1, 2004): 64–67.

Chapter 14

1.   "Cisco Systems Announces New Organizational Structure," Cisco News Release, http://newsroom.cisco.com, accessed August 23, 2001.

2.   "Cisco Systems to Invest Over US $1 Billion in India over Next Three Years," Cisco News Release, http://newsroom.cisco.com, accessed October 19, 2005.

3.   J. Flint, "When Car Guys Ran GM," Forbes 173 (April 19, 2004): 77, http://www.forbes.com/columnists/business/forbes/2004/0419/077.html.

4.   J. Child, Organization (New York: Harper & Row, 1984).

5.   P. Lawrence and J. Lorsch, "Differentiation and Integration in Complex Organizations," Administrative Science Quarterly 12 (1967): 1–47.

6.   R. Dewar and J. Hage, "Size, Technology, Complexity, and Structural Differentiation: Toward a Theoretical Synthesis," Administrative Science Quarterly 23 (1978): 111–136.

7.   Lawrence and Lorsch, "Differentiation and Integration," 1–47.

8.   J. R. R. Galbraith, Designing Complex Organizations (Reading, Mass.: Addison-Wesley-Longman, 1973).

9.   D. Pugh, D. Hickson, C. Hinnings, and C. Turner, "Dimensions of Organization Structure," Administrative Science Quarterly 13 (1968): 65–91; B. Reimann, "Dimensions of Structure in Effective Organizations: Some Empirical Evidence," Academy of Management Journal 17 (1974): 693–708; S. Robbins, Organization Theory: The Structure and Design of Organizations, 3rd ed. (Englewood Cliffs, N.J.: Prentice-Hall, 1990).

10.   J. Shenn, "RBC Idea for Processing Mortgages: Decentralize," American Banker 169 (April 12, 2004): 1.

11.   H. Mintzberg, The Structuring of Organizations (Englewood Cliffs, N.J.: Prentice-Hall, 1979).

12.   J. A. Kuprenas, "Implementation and Performance of a Matrix Organization Structure," International Journal of Project Management 21 (2003): 51–62.

13.   Mintzberg, Structuring of Organizations.

14.   K. Weick, "Educational Institutions as Loosely Coupled Systems," Administrative Science Quarterly (1976): 1–19.

15.   D. Miller and C. Droge, "Psychological and Traditional Determinants of Structure," Administrative Science Quarterly 31 (1986): 540; H. Tosi, Jr., and J. Slocum, Jr., "Contingency Theory: Some Suggested Directions," Journal of Management 10 (1984): 9–26.

16.   C. B. Clott, "Perspectives on Global Outsourcing and the Changing Nature of Work," Business and Society Review 109 (2004): 153–170.

17.   D. Mack and J. C. Quick, "EDS: An Inside View of a Corporate Life Cycle Transition," Organizational Dynamics 30 (2002): 282–293.

18.   M. Meyer, "Size and the Structure of Organizations: A Causal Analysis," American Sociological Review 37 (1972): 434–441; J. Beyer and H. Trice, "A Reexamination of the Relations between Size and Various Components of Organizational Complexity," Administrative Science Quarterly 24 (1979): 48–64; B. Mayhew, R. Levinger, J. McPherson, and T. James, "Systems Size and Structural Differentiation in Formal Organizations: A Baseline Generator for Two Major Theoretical Propositions," American Sociological Review 37 (1972): 26–43.

19.   M. Gowing, J. Kraft, and J. C. Quick, The New Organizational Reality: Downsizing, Restructuring, and Revitalization (Washington, D.C.: American Psychological Association, 1998).

20.   B. A. Pasternack and A. J. Viscio, The Centerless Corporation: A New Model for Transforming Your Organization for Growth and Prosperity (New York: Simon & Schuster, 1999).

21.   J. Woodward, Industrial Organization: Theory and Practices (London: Oxford University Press, 1965).

22.   C. Perrow, "A Framework for the Comparative Analysis of Organizations," American Sociological Review 32 (1967): 194–208; D. Rosseau, "Assessment of Technology in Organizations: Closed versus Open Systems Approaches," Academy of Management Review 4 (1979): 531–542.

23.   Perrow, "A Framework for the Comparative Analysis of Organizations," 194–208.

24.   J. D. Thompson, Organizations in Action (New York: McGraw-Hill, 1967).

25.   P. Nemetz and L. Fry, "Flexible Manufacturing Organizations: Implication for Strategy Formulation and Organization Design," Academy of Management Review 13 (1988): 627–638; G. Huber, "The Nature and Design of Post-Industrial Organizations," Management Science 30 (1984): 934.

26.   E. Feitzinger and H. L. Lee, "Mass Customization at Hewlett-Packard: The Power of Postponement," Harvard Business Review 75 (1997): 116–121.

27.   S. M. Davis, Future Perfect (Reading, Mass.: Addison-Wesley, 1987).

28.   J. R. Baum and S. Wally, "Strategic Decision Speed and Firm Performance," Strategic Management Journal 24 (2003): 1107–1129.

29.   Thompson, Organizations in Action.

30.   H. Downey, D. Hellriegel, and J. Slocum, Jr., "Environmental Uncertainty: The Construct and Its Application," Administrative Science Quarterly 20 (1975): 613–629.

31.   T. Burns and G. Stalker, The Management of Innovation (London: Tavistock, 1961); Mintzberg, Structuring of Organizations.

32.   M. L. Ambrose and M. Schminke, "Organization Structure as a Moderator of the Relationship between Procedural Justice, Interactional Justice, Perceived Organizational Support, and Supervisory Trust," Journal of Applied Psychology 88 (2003): 293–303.

33.   M. Chandler and L. Sayles, Managing Large Systems (New York: Harper & Row, 1971).

34.   G. Dess and D. Beard, "Dimensions of Organizational Task Environments," Administrative Science Quarterly 29 (1984): 52–73.

35.   J. Courtright, G. Fairhurst, and L. Rogers, "Interaction Patterns in Organic and Mechanistic Systems," Academy of Management Journal 32 (1989): 773–802.

36.   R. Daft, Organization Theory and Design, 7th ed. (Mason, OH: South-Western/Thomson Learning, 2000).

37.   D. Miller, "The Structural and Environmental Correlates of Business Strategy," Strategic Management Journal 8 (1987): 55–76.

38.   W. R. Scott, Organizations: Rational, Natural, and Open Systems, 4th ed. (Upper Saddle River, N.J.: Prentice-Hall, 1997).

39.   D. Miller and P. Friesen, "A Longitudinal Study of the Corporate Life Cycle," Management Science 30 (1984): 1161–1183.

40.   M. H. Overholt, "Flexible Organizations: Using Organizational Design as a Competitive Advantage," Human Resource Planning 20 (1997): 22–32; P. W. Roberts and R. Greenwood, "Integrating Transaction Cost and Institutional Theories: Toward a Constrained-Efficiency Framework for Understanding Organizational Design

Adoption," *Academy of Management Review* 22 (1997): 346–373.

41. C. W. L. Hill and G. R. Jones, *Strategic Management Theory,* 5th ed. (Boston: Houghton Mifflin, 2000).

42. Daft, *Organization Theory and Design.*

43. C. M. Savage, *5th Generation Management, Revised Edition: Cocreating through Virtual Enterprising, Dynamic Teaming, and Knowledge Networking* (Boston: Butterworth-Heinemann, 1996).

44. S. M. Davis, *Future Perfect* (Perseus Publishing, 1997).

45. A. Boynton and B. Victor, "Beyond Flexibility: Building and Managing a Dynamically Stable Organization," *California Management Review* 8 (Fall 1991): 53–66.

46. P. J. Brews and C. L. Tucci, "Exploring the Structural Effects of Internetworking," *Strategic Management Journal* 25 (2004): 429–451.

47. J. Fulk, "Global Network Organizations: Emergence and Future Prospects," *Human Relations* 54 (2001): 91–100.

48. The use of the theatrical troupe as an analogy for virtual organizations was first used by David Mack, circa 1995.

49. E. C. Kasper-Fuehrer and N. M. Ashkanasy, "Communicating Trustworthiness and Building Trust in Interorganizational Virtual Organizations," *Journal of Management* 27 (2001): 235–254.

50. R. Teerlink and L. Ozley, *More than a Motorcycle: The Leadership Journey at Harley-Davidson* (Boston: Harvard Business School Press, 2000).

51. W. A. Cohen and N. Cohen, *The Paranoid Organization and 8 Other Ways Your Company Can Be Crazy: Advice from an Organizational Shrink* (New York: American Management Association, 1993).

52. P. E. Tetlock, "Cognitive Biases and Organizational Correctives: Do Both Disease and Cure Depend on the Politics of the Beholder?" *Administrative Science Quarterly* 45 (2000): 293–326.

53. M. F. R. Kets de Vries and D. Miller, "Personality, Culture, and Organization," *Academy of Management Review* 11 (1986): 266–279.

54. "Fortune 100 Best Companies to Work for 2006," CNNMoney.com, http://money.cnn.com/magazines/fortune/bestcompanies.

Chapter 15

1. Quote from Cindy Bradley, vice president of Human Resources and Team Member Services at Whole Foods Market, Inc.

2. http://www.wholefoodsmarket.com/company/corevalues.html.

3. T. E. Deal and A. A. Kennedy, *Corporate Cultures* (Reading, Mass.: Addison-Wesley, 1982).

4. W. Ouchi, *Theory Z* (Reading, Mass.: Addison-Wesley, 1981).

5. T. J. Peters and R. H. Waterman, *In Search of Excellence* (New York: Harper & Row, 1982).

6. M. Gardner, "Creating a Corporate Culture for the Eighties," *Business Horizons* (January–February 1985): 59–63.

7. Definition adapted from E. H. Schein, *Organizational Culture and Leadership* (San Francisco: Jossey-Bass, 1985): 9.

8. C. D. Sutton and D. L. Nelson, "Elements of the Cultural Network: The Communicators of Corporate Values," *Leadership and Organization Development* 11 (1990): 3–10.

9. http://www.google.com/corporate/culture.html.

10. http://www.eskimojoes.com/index.php?module=pagemaster&PAGE_user_op=view_page&PAGE_id=13&MMN_position=16:16

11. A. Bandura, *Social Learning Theory* (Englewood Cliffs, N.J.: Prentice-Hall, 1977).

12. J. A. Chatman, "Leading by Leveraging Culture," *California Management Review* 45 (2003): 20–34.

13. J. M. Beyer and H. M. Trice, "How an Organization's Rites Reveal Its Culture," *Organizational Dynamics* 16 (1987): 5–24.

14. H. M. Trice and J. M. Beyer, "Studying Organizational Cultures through Rites and Ceremonials," *Academy of Management Review* 9 (1984): 653–669.

15. M. J. Schneider, "The Wal-Mart Annual Meeting: From Small-Town America to a Global Corporate Culture," *Human Organization* 57 (1998): 292–299.

16. H. Levinson and S. Rosenthal, *CEO: Corporate Leadership in Action* (New York: Basic Books, 1984).

17. V. Sathe, "Implications of Corporate Culture: A Manager's Guide to Action," *Organizational Dynamics* 12 (1987): 5–23.

18. "Wal-Mart Culture Stories—The Sundown Rule," http://www.wal-martchina.com/english/walmart/rule/sun.htm.

19. J. Martin, M. S. Feldman, M. J. Hatch, and S. B. Sitkin, "The Uniqueness Paradox in Organizational Stories," *Administrative Science Quarterly* 28 (1983): 438–453.

20. B. Durrance, "Stories at Work," *Training and Development* (February 1997): 25–29.

21. B. Siuru, "2003 Saturn L Series," http://www.autowire.net/2002-40.html.

22. R. Goffee and G. Jones, "What Holds the Modern Company Together?" *Harvard Business Review* (November–December 1996): 133–143.

23. C. Argyris and D. A. Schon, *Organizational Learning* (Reading, Mass.: Addison-Wesley, 1978).

24. D. J. McAllister and G. A. Bigley, "Work Context and the Definition of Self: How Organizational Care Influences Organization-Based Self-Esteem," *Academy of Management Journal* 45 (2002): 894–905.

25. "Sounds Like a New Woman," *New Woman* (February 1993): 144.

26. M. Peterson, "Work, Corporate Culture, and Stress: Implications for Worksite Health Promotion," *American Journal of Health Behavior* 21 (1997): 243–252.

27. R. Targos, "Big Bad Hog—Harley-Davidson Customer Service," *Child Care Business,* http://www.childcarebusiness.com/articles/161cover.html.

28. J. Rosenthal and M. A. Masarech, "High-Performance Cultures: How Values Can Drive Business Results," *Journal of Organizational Excellence* (Spring 2003): 3–18.

29. "Earthlink—Core Values and Beliefs," http://www.earthlink.net/about/cvb.

30. L. Smircich, "Concepts of Culture and Organizational Analysis," *Administrative Science Quarterly* (1983): 339–358.

31. Y. Weiner and Y. Vardi, "Relationships between Organizational Culture and Individual Motivation: A Conceptual Integration," *Psychological Reports* 67 (1990): 295–306.

32. M. R. Louis, "Surprise and Sense Making: What Newcomers Experience in Entering Unfamiliar Organizational Settings," *Administrative Science Quarterly* 25 (1980): 209–264.

33. D. Ravasi and M. Schultz, "Responding to Organizational Identity Threats: Exploring the Role of Organizational Culture," *Academy of Management Journal* 49 (3) (2006): 433–458.

34. T. L. Doolen, M. E. Hacker, and E. M. van Aken, "The Impact of Organizational Context on Work Team Effectiveness: A Study of Production Teams," *IEEE Transactions on Engineering Management* 50 (2003): 285–296.

35. D. D. Van Fleet and R. W. Griffin, "Dysfunctional Organization Culture: The Role of Leadership in Motivating Dysfunctional Work Behaviors," *Journal of Managerial Psychology* 21 (8) (2006): 698.

36. J. P. Kotter and J. L. Heskett, *Corporate Culture and Performance* (New York: Free Press, 1992).

37. Deal and Kennedy, *Corporate Cultures.*

38. D. R. Katz, *The Big Store* (New York: Viking, 1987).

39. G. G. Gordon, "Industry Determinants of Organizational Culture," *Academy of Management Review* 16 (1991): 396–415.

40. G. Donaldson and J. Lorsch, *Decision Making at the Top* (New York: Basic Books, 1983).

41. R. H. Kilman, M. J. Saxton, and R. Serpa, eds., *Gaining Control of the Corporate Culture* (San Francisco: Jossey-Bass, 1986).

42. J. P. Kotter, *A Force for Change: How Leadership Differs from Management* (New York: Free Press, 1990); R. M. Kanter, *The Change Masters* (New York: Simon & Schuster, 1983).

43. T. Peters and N. Austin, *A Passion for Excellence: The Leadership Difference* (New York: Random House, 1985).

44. Schein, *Organizational Culture and Leadership.*

45. R. R. Sims and J. Brinkmann, "Enron Ethics (or Culture Matters More than Codes)," *Journal of Business Ethics* 45 (2003): 243–256.

46. "Eating Too Fast at Whole Foods" (October 24, 2005), http://www.businessweek.com/magazine/content/05_43/b3956106.htm.

47. M. H. Kavanagh and N. M. Ashkanasy, "The Impact of Leadership and Change Management Strategy on Organizational Culture and Individual Acceptance of Change during a Merger," *British Journal of Management: Supplement* 17 (1) (2006): S81–S103.

48. J. A. Pearce II, T. R. Kramer, and D. K. Robbins, "Effects of Managers' Entrepreneurial Behavior on Subordinates," *Journal of Business Venturing* 12 (1997): 147–160.

49. Kate Bonamici, "Timberland: The Shoe-In" (January 23, 2006), http://money.cnn.com/magazines/fortune/fortune_archive/2006/01/23/8366992/index.htm.

50. P. W. Braddy, A. W. Meade, and C. M. Kroustalis, "Organizational Recruitment Website Effects on Viewers' Perceptions of Organizational Culture," *Journal of Business and Psychology* 20 (4) (2006): 525–543.

51. A. Xenikou and M. Simosi, "Organizational Culture and Transformational Leadership as Predictors of Business Unit Performance," *Journal of Managerial Psychology* 21 (6) (2006): 566–579.

52. D. C. Feldman, "The Multiple Socialization of Organization Members," *Academy of Management Review* 6 (1981): 309–318.

53. R. Pascale, "The Paradox of Corporate Culture: Reconciling Ourselves to Socialization," *California Management Review* 27 (1985): 26–41.

54. D. L. Nelson, "Organizational Socialization: A Stress Perspective," *Journal of Occupational Behavior* 8 (1987): 311–324.

55. D. M. Cable, L. Aiman-Smith, P. W. Mulvey, and J. R. Edwards, "The Sources and Accuracy of Job Applicants' Beliefs about Organizational Culture," *Academy of Management Journal* 43 (2000): 1076–1085.

56. J. Chatman, "Matching People and Organizations: Selection and Socialization in Public Accounting Firms," *Administrative Science Quarterly* 36 (1991): 459–484.

57. D. L. Nelson, J. C. Quick, and M. E. Eakin, "A Longitudinal Study of Newcomer Role Adjustment in U.S. Organizations," *Work and Stress* 2 (1988): 239–253.

58. N. J. Allen and J. P. Meyer, "Organizational Socialization Tactics: A Longitudinal Analysis of Links to Newcomers' Commitment and Role Orientation," *Academy of Management Journal* 33 (1990): 847–858.

59. T. N. Bauer, E. W. Morrison, and R. R. Callister, "Organizational Socialization: A Review and Directions for Future Research," *Research in Personnel and Human Resources Management* 16 (1998): 149–214.

60. D. M. Cable and C. K. Parsons, "Socialization Tactics and Person–Organization Fit," *Personnel Psychology* 54 (2001): 1–23.

61. M. R. Louis, "Acculturation in the Workplace: Newcomers as Lay Ethnographers," in B. Schneider, ed., *Organizational Climate and Culture* (San Francisco: Jossey-Bass, 1990): 85–129.

62. C. Yang, "Merger of Titans, Clash of Cultures," *BusinessWeek Online* (July 14, 2003), http://www.businessweek.com/magazine/content/03_28/b3841042_mz005.htm.

63. N. J. Adler, *International Dimensions of Organizational Behavior,* 2nd ed. (Boston: PWS Kent, 1991).

64. A. Laurent, "The Cultural Diversity of Western Conceptions of Management," *International Studies of Management and Organization* 13 (1983): 75–96.

65. P. C. Earley and E. Mosakowski, "Creating Hybrid Team Cultures: An Empirical Test of Transnational Team Functioning," *Academy of Management Journal* 43 (2000): 26–49.

66. P. Bate, "Using the Culture Concept in an Organization Development Setting," *Journal of Applied Behavior Science* 26 (1990): 83–106.

67. K. R. Thompson and F. Luthans, "Organizational Culture: A Behavioral Perspective," in B. Schneider, ed., *Organizational Climate and Culture* (San Francisco: Jossey-Bass, 1990).

68. V. Sathe, "How to Decipher and Change Corporate Culture," in R. H. Kilman et al., *Managing Corporate Cultures* (San Francisco: Jossey-Bass, 1985).

69. J. B. Shaw, C. D. Fisher, and W. A. Randolph, "From Maternalism to Accountability: The Changing Cultures of Ma Bell and Mother Russia," *Academy of Management Executive* 5 (1991): 7–20.

70. D. Lei, J. W. Slocum, Jr., and R. W. Slater, "Global Strategy and Reward Systems: The Key Roles of Management Development and Corporate Culture," *Organizational Dynamics* 19 (1990): 27–41.

71. S. H. Rhinesmith, "Going Global from the Inside Out," *Training and Development Journal* 45 (1991): 42–47.

72. A. Pater and A. van Gils, "Stimulating Ethical Decision Making in a Business Context: Ethics of Ethical and Professional Codes," *European Management Journal* 21 (December 2003): 762–772.

73. L. K. Trevino and K. A. Nelson, *Managing Business Ethics: Straight Talk about How to Do It Right* (New York: John Wiley & Sons, 1995).

74. A. Bhide and H. H. Stevenson, "Why Be Honest if Honesty Doesn't Pay?" *Harvard Business Review* (September–October 1990): 121–129.

75. "Business Ethics Names 100 Best Corporate Citizens," *Business Ethics* (Spring 2004), http://www.business-ethics.com/100best.htm.

76. S. W. Gellerman, "Why Good Managers Make Bad Ethical Choices," *Harvard Business Review* 64 (1986): 85–90.

77. Bruce Horovitz, "Supermarkets Copy Whole Foods' Shopping List" (June 28, 2006) http://www.usatoday.com/money/industries/food/2006-06-28-whole-mimics-usat_x.htm.

78. Parija Bhatnagar, "Wal-Mart's Next Conquest: Organics" (May 1, 2006) http://money.cnn.com/2006/05/01/news/companies/walmart_organics/.

Chapter 16

1. A quote on Virgin Group, Ltd.'s corporate Web site at http://www.virgin.com/RBP/WhatisProjectAware.aspx.

2. Virgin Group, corporate Web site, http://www.virgin.com/RBP/WhatisProjectAware.aspx.

3. M. A. Verespej, "When Change Becomes the Norm," *Industry Week* (March 16, 1992): 35–38.

4. P. Mornell, "Nothing Endures But Change," *Inc. Magazine* 22 (July 2000): 131–132, http://www.inc.com/magazine/20000701/19555.html.

5. H. J. Van Buren III, "The Bindingness of Social and Psychological Contracts: Toward a Theory of Social Responsibility in Downsizing," *Journal of Business Ethics* 25 (2000): 205–219.

6. http://www.realclimate.org/index.php/archives/2007/02/save-the-world-earn-25-million/.

7. United States Embassy in Mexico Press Release, "Response to Criticism of U.S. Agricultural Policy and NAFTA" (December 5, 2002), http://www.usembassy-mexico.gov/releases/ep021205realitiesNAFTA.htm.

8. M. Stevenson, "Mexican Farmers Renew NAFTA Protests," *Yahoo! News* (January 20, 2003).

9. B. S. Javorcik, W. Keller, and J. Tybout, "Openness and Industrial Response in a Wal-Mart World: A Case Study of Mexican Soaps, Detergents and Surfactant Producers," NBER Working Paper No. 12457 (August 2006), JEL No. F1, F23, L65, L81, http://www.nber.org/papers/w12457.pdf.

10. M. McCarthy, "PR Disaster as Coke Withdraws 'Purest' Bottled Water in Britain," *The New Zealand Herald* (March 20, 2004), http://www.nzherald.co.nz/business/businessstorydisplay.cfm?storyID=3555911&thesection=business&thesubsection=world&thesecondsubsection=europe.

11. L. Hirschhorn and T. Gilmore, "The New Boundaries of the 'Boundaryless'

Company," *Harvard Business Review* (May–June 1992): 104–115.

12. L. R. Offerman and M. Gowing, "Organizations of the Future: Changes and Challenges," *American Psychologist* (February 1990): 95–108.

13. W. B. Johnston, "Global Work Force 2000: The New World Labor Market," *Harvard Business Review* (March–April 1991): 115–127.

14. "50 Best Companies for Minorities: Full List," *Fortune* (June 28, 2004), http://money.cnn.com/magazines/fortune/fortune_archive/2004/06/28/374393/index.htm.

15. G. Bylinsky, "Hot New Technologies for American Factories," *Fortune* (June 26, 2000): 288A–288K.

16. R. M. Kanter, "Improving the Development, Acceptance, and Use of New Technology: Organizational and Interorganizational Challenges," in *People and Technology in the Workplace* (Washington, D.C.: National Academy Press, 1991): 15–56.

17. Gap Inc. Press Release, "Gap Inc. Joins the Ethical Trading Initiative," *CSRwire* (April 28, 2004), http://www.csrwire.com/article.cgi/2683.html.

18. "Gap Inc. 2003 Social Responsibility Report," *Gap Inc.* (September 17, 2004), http://ccbn.mobular.net/ccbn/7/645/696/index.html.

19. S. A. Mohrman and A. M. Mohrman, Jr., "The Environment as an Agent of Change," in A. M. Mohrman, Jr., et al., eds., *Large-Scale Organizational Change* (San Francisco: Jossey-Bass, 1989): 35–47.

20. T. D'Aunno, M. Succi, and J. A. Alexander, "The Role of Institutional and Market Forces in Divergent Organizational Change," *Administrative Science Quarterly* 45 (2000): 679–703.

21. Intel press release (Santa Clara, Calif.: April 21, 2004), http://www.intel.com/pressroom.

22. Q. N. Huy, "Emotional Balancing of Organizational Continuity and Radical Change: The Contribution of Middle Managers," *Administrative Science Quarterly* 47 (March 1, 2002): 31–69.

23. D. Nadler, "Organizational Frame-Bending: Types of Change in the Complex Organization," in R. Kilmann and T. Covin, eds., *Corporate Transformation* (San Francisco: Jossey-Bass, 1988): 66–83.

24. K. Belson, "AT&T Plans to Raise Its Rates for Residential Calling Plans," *The New York Times* (August 4, 2004), http://www.nytimes.com/2004/08/04/business/04phone.html.

25. L. Ackerman, "Development, Transition, or Transformation: The Question of Change in Organizations," *OD Practitioner* (December 1986): 1–8.

26. T. D. Jick, *Managing Change* (Homewood, Ill.: Irwin, 1993): 3.

27. J. M. Bloodgood and J. L. Morrow, "Strategic Organizational Change: Exploring the Roles of Environmental Structure, Internal Conscious Awareness, and Knowledge," *Journal of Management Studies* 40 (2003): 1761–1782.

28. D. Miller and M. J. Chen, "Sources and Consequences of Competitive Inertia. A Study of the U.S. Airline Industry," *Administrative Science Quarterly* 39 (1994): 1–23.

29. S. L. Brown and K. M. Eisenhardt, "The Art of Continuous Change: Linking Complexity Theory and Time-Paced Evolution in Relentlessly Shifting Organizations," *Administrative Science Quarterly* 42 (1997): 1–34.

30. J. Child and C. Smith, "The Context and Process of Organizational Transformation: Cadbury Ltd. in Its Sector," *Journal of Management Studies* 12 (1987): 12–27.

31. J. Amis, T. Slack, and C. R. Hinings, "The Pace, Sequence, and Linearity of Radical Change," *Academy of Management Journal* 47 (2004): 15–39.

32. R. M. Kanter, *The Change Masters* (New York: Simon & Schuster, 1983).

33. J. R. Katzenbach, *Real Change Leaders* (New York: Times Business, 1995).

34. J. L. Denis, L. Lamothe, and A. Langley, "The Dynamics of Collective Leadership and Strategic Change in Pluralistic Organizations," *Academy of Management Journal* 44 (2001): 809–837.

35. M. Beer, *Organization Change and Development: A Systems View* (Santa Monica, Calif.: Goodyear, 1980): 78.

36. K. Whalen-Berry and C. R. Hinings, "The Relative Effect of Change Drivers in Large-Scale Organizational Change: An Empirical Study," in W. Passmore and R. Goodman, eds., *Research in Organizational Change and Development* 14 (New York: JAI Press, 2003): 99–146.

37. J. L. Denis, L. Lamothe, and A. Langley, "The Dynamics of Collective Leadership and Strategic Change in Pluralistic Organizations," *Academy of Management Journal* 44 (2001): 809–837.

38. F. Cheyunski and J. Millard, "Accelerated Business Transformation and the Role of the Organizational Architect," *Journal of Applied Behavioral Science* 34 (1998): 268–285.

39. N. A. M. Worren, K. Ruddle, and K. Moore, "From Organizational Development to Change Management: The Emergence of a New Profession," *Journal of Applied Behavioral Science* 35 (1999): 273–286.

40. P. G. Audia, E. A. Locke, and K. G. Smith, "The Paradox of Success: An Archival and a Laboratory Study of Strategic Persistence Following Radical Environmental Change," *Academy of Management Journal* 43 (2000): 837–853.

41. V. Bellou, "Psychological Contract Assessment After a Major Organizational Change: The Case of Mergers and

Acquisitions," *Employee Relations* 29 (1) (2007): 68–88.

42. J. W. Brehm, *A Theory of Psychological Reactance* (New York: Academic Press, 1966).

43. J. A. Klein, "Why Supervisors Resist Employee Involvement," *Harvard Business Review* 62 (1984): 87–95.

44. B. L. Kirkman, R. G. Jones, and D. L. Shapiro, "Why Do Employees Resist Teams? Examining the 'Resistance Barrier' to Work Team Effectiveness," *International Journal of Conflict Management* 11 (2000): 74–92.

45. D. L. Nelson and M. A. White, "Management of Technological Innovation: Individual Attitudes, Stress, and Work Group Attributes," *Journal of High Technology Management Research* 1 (1990): 137–148.

46. D. Klein, "Some Notes on the Dynamics of Resistance to Change: The Defender Role," in W. G. Bennis, K. D. Benne, R. Chin, and K. E. Corey, eds., *The Planning of Change,* 3rd ed. (New York: Holt, Rinehart & Winston, 1969): 117–124.

47. T. G. Cummings and E. F. Huse, *Organizational Development and Change* (St. Paul, Minn.: West, 1989).

48. N. L. Jimmieson, D. J. Terry, and V. J. Callan, "A Longitudinal Study of Employee Adaptation to Organizational Change: The Role of Change-Related Information and Change-Related Self Efficacy," *Journal of Occupational Health Psychology* 9 (2004): 11–27.

49. N. DiFonzo and P. Bordia, "A Tale of Two Corporations: Managing Uncertainty during Organizational Change," *Human Resource Management* 37 (1998): 295–303.

50. J. de Vries, C. Webb, and J. Eveline, "Mentoring for Gender Equality and Organizational Change," *Employee Relations* 28 (6) (2006): 573–587.

51. L. P. Livingstone, M. A. White, D. L. Nelson, and F. Tabak, "Delays in Technological Innovation Implementations: Some Preliminary Results on a Common but Understudied Occurrence," working paper, Oklahoma State University.

52. P. Neves and A. Caetano, "Social Exchange Processes in Organizational Change: The Roles of Trust and Control," *Journal of Change Management* 6 (4) (2006): 351.

53. G. Lindsay, "Prada's High-Tech Misstep," *Business 2.0* (March 1, 2004): 72–75, http://money.cnn.com/magazines/business2/business2_archive/2004/03/01/363574/index.htm.

54. M. Hickins, "Reconcilable Differences," *Management Review* 87 (1998): 54–58.

55. J. P. Kotter and L. A. Schlesinger, "Choosing Strategies for Change," *Harvard Business Review* 57 (1979): 109–112; W. Bridges, *Transitions: Making Sense of Life's Changes* (Reading, Mass.: Addison-Wesley, 1980); H. Woodward and S. Buchholz, *Aftershock: Helping People through Corporate Change* (New York: Wiley, 1987).

56.   S. E. Herzig, and N. L. Jimmieson, "Middle Managers' Uncertainty Management During Organizational Change," *Leadership & Organization Development Journal* 27 (8) (2006): 628–645.

57.   K. Lewin, "Frontiers in Group Dynamics," *Human Relations* 1 (1947): 5–41.

58.   W. McWhinney, "Meta-Praxis: A Framework for Making Complex Changes," in A. M. Mohrman, Jr., et al., eds., *Large-Scale Organizational Change* (San Francisco: Jossey-Bass, 1989): 154–199.

59.   M. Beer and E. Walton, "Developing the Competitive Organization: Interventions and Strategies," *American Psychologist* 45 (1990): 154–161.

60.   B. Bertsch and R. Williams, "How Multinational CEOs Make Change Programs Stick," *Long Range Planning* 27 (1994): 12–24.

61.   J. Amis, T. Slack, and C. R. Hinings, "Values and Organizational Change," *Journal of Applied Behavioral Science* 38 (2002): 356–385.

62.   W. L. French and C. H. Bell, *Organization Development: Behavioral Science Interventions for Organization Improvement,* 4th ed. (Englewood Cliffs, N.J.: Prentice-Hall, 1990); W. W. Burke, *Organization Development: A Normative View* (Reading, Mass.: Addison-Wesley, 1987).

63.   A. Huczynski, *Encyclopedia of Organizational Change Methods* (Brookfield, Vt.: Gower, 1987).

64.   A. O. Manzini, *Organizational Diagnosis* (New York: AMACOM, 1988).

65.   M. R. Weisbord, "Organizational Diagnosis: Six Places to Look for Trouble with or without a Theory," *Group and Organization Studies* (December 1976): 430–444.

66.   H. Levinson, *Organizational Diagnosis* (Cambridge, Mass.: Harvard University Press, 1972).

67.   J. Nicholas, "The Comparative Impact of Organization Development Interventions," *Academy of Management Review* 7 (1982): 531–542.

68.   E. Huse, "Putting in a Management Development Program that Works," *California Management Review* 9 (1966): 73–80.

69.   L. L. Berry and A. Parasuraman, "Prescriptions for a Service Quality Revolution in America," *Organizational Dynamics* 20 (1992): 5–15.

70.   W. G. Dyer, *Team Building: Issues and Alternatives,* 2nd ed. (Reading, Mass.: Addison-Wesley, 1987).

71.   E. Stephan, G. Mills, R. W. Pace, and L. Ralphs, "HRD in the Fortune 500: A Survey," *Training and Development Journal* (January 1988): 26–32.

72.   E. Schein, *Its Role in Organization Development,* Vol. 1 of Process Consultation (Reading, Mass.: Addison-Wesley, 1988).

73.   H. Hornstein, "Organizational Development and Change Management: Don't Throw the Baby Out with the Bath Water," *Journal of Applied Behavioral Science* 37 (2001): 223–226.

74.   D. A. Ready and J. A. Conger, "Why Leadership Development Efforts Fail," *MIT Sloan Management Review* 44 (2003): 83–89.

75.   "Occupational Stress and Employee Stress," *American Psychological Association* (November 3, 2003), http://www.psychologymatters.org/karasek.html.

76.   D. A. Nadler, "Concepts for the Management of Organizational Change," in J. R. Hackman, E. E. Lawler III, and L. W. Porter, eds., *Perspectives on Organizational Behavior* (New York: McGraw-Hill, 1983).

77.   Cummings and Huse, *Organizational Development;* P. E. Connor and L. K. Lake, *Managing Organizational Change* (New York: Praeger, 1988).

78.   R. L. Lowman, "Ethical Human Resource Practice in Organizational Settings," in D. W. Bray, ed., *Working with Organizations* (New York: Guilford Press, 1991).

79.   H. Kelman, "Manipulation of Human Behavior: An Ethical Dilemma for the Social Scientist," in W. Bennis, K. Benne, and R. Chin, eds., *The Planning of Change* (New York: Holt, Rinehart, & Winston, 1969).

80.   A. M. Pettigrew, R. W. Woodman, and K. S. Cameron, "Studying Organizational Change and Development: Challenges for Future Research," *Academy of Management Journal* 44 (2001): 697–713.

81.   R. A. Katzell and R. A. Guzzo, "Psychological Approaches to Worker Productivity," *American Psychologist* 38 (1983): 468–472.

82.   R. A. Guzzo, R. D. Jette, and R. A. Katzell, "The Effects of Psychologically Based Intervention Programs on Worker Productivity," *Personnel Psychology* 38 (1985): 275–291.

83.   I. L. Goldstein, *Training in Organizations,* 3rd ed. (Pacific Grove, Calif.: Brooks/Cole, 1993).

84.   T. Covin and R. H. Kilmann, "Participant Perceptions of Positive and Negative Influences on Large-Scale Change," *Group and Organization Studies* 15 (1990): 233–248.

85.   C. M. Brotheridge, "The Role of Fairness in Mediating the Effects of Voice and Justification on Stress and Other Outcomes in a Climate of Organizational Change," *International Journal of Stress Management* 10 (2003): 253–268.

86.   http://www.virgintrains.co.uk/news/default.aspx#news_132.

A

adaptive culture An organizational culture that encourages confidence and risk taking among employees, has leadership that produces change, and focuses on the changing needs of customers.

adhocracy A selectively decentralized form of organization that emphasizes the support staff and mutual adjustment among people.

administrative orbiting Delaying action on a conflict by buying time.

affective commitment The type of organizational commitment that is based on an individual's desire to remain in an organization.

anthropocentric Placing human considerations at the center of job design decisions.

anthropology The science of the learned behavior of human beings.

anticipatory socialization The first socialization stage, which encompasses all of the learning that takes place prior to the newcomer's first day on the job.

artifacts Symbols of culture in the physical and social work environment.

assumptions Deeply held beliefs that guide behavior and tell members of an organization how to perceive and think about things.

attitude A psychological tendency expressed by evaluating an entity with some degree of favor or disfavor.

attribution theory A theory that explains how individuals pinpoint the causes of their own behavior and that of others.

authentic leader A leader who is guided by explicit values that emphasize collective interest, enabling them to operate at high levels of moral integrity.

authority The right to influence another person.

authority-compliance manager (9,1) A leader who emphasizes efficient production.

autocratic style A style of leadership in which the leader uses strong, directive, controlling actions to enforce the rules, regulations, activities, and relationships in the work environment.

B

barriers to communication Aspects of the communication content and context that can impair effective communication in a workplace.

benevolent An individual who is comfortable with an equity ratio less than that of his or her comparison other.

bounded rationality A theory that suggests that there are limits upon how rational a decision maker can actually be.

brainstorming A technique for generating as many ideas as possible on a given subject, while suspending evaluation until all the ideas have been suggested.

C

centralization The degree to which decisions are made at the top of the organization.

challenge The call to competition, contest, or battle.

change The transformation or modification of an organization and/or its stakeholders.

change agent The individual or group that undertakes the task of introducing and managing a change in an organization.

change and acquisition The third socialization stage, in which the newcomer begins to master the demands of the job.

character assassination An attempt to label or discredit an opponent.

character theory An ethical theory that emphasizes the character, personal virtues, and integrity of the individual.

charismatic leadership A leader's use of personal abilities and talents in order to have profound and extraordinary effects on followers.

classical conditioning Modifying behavior so that a conditioned stimulus is paired with an unconditioned stimulus and elicits an unconditioned response.

coercive power Power that is based on an agent's ability to cause an unpleasant experience for a target.

cognitive dissonance A state of tension that is produced when an individual experiences conflict between attitudes and behavior.

cognitive moral development The process of moving through stages of maturity in terms of making ethical decisions.

collectivism A cultural orientation in which individuals belong to tightly knit social frameworks, and they depend strongly on large extended families or clans.

communication The evoking of a shared or common meaning in another person.

communicative disease The absence of heartfelt communication in human relationships leading to loneliness and social isolation.

communicator The person originating a message.

compensation A compromise mechanism in which an individual attempts to make up for a negative situation by devoting himself or herself to another pursuit with increased vigor.

complexity The degree to which many different types of activities occur in the organization.

conflict Any situation in which incompatible goals, attitudes, emotions, or behaviors lead to disagreement or opposition between two or more parties.

consensus An informational cue indicating the extent to which peers in the same situation behave in a similar fashion.

consequential theory An ethical theory that emphasizes the consequences or results of behavior.

consideration Leader behavior aimed at nurturing friendly, warm working relationships, as well as encouraging mutual trust and interpersonal respect within the work unit.

consistency An informational cue indicating the frequency of behavior over time.

contextual variables A set of characteristics that influence the organization's design processes.

continuance commitment The type of organizational commitment that is based on the fact that an individual cannot afford to leave.

conversion A withdrawal mechanism in which emotional conflicts are expressed in physical symptoms.

Core self-evaluation (CSE) A broad set of personality traits that refers to self-concept, comprised of locus of control, self-esteem, generalized self-efficacy, and emotional stability.

counter-role behavior Deviant behavior in either a correctly or incorrectly defined job or role.

country club manager (1,9) A leader who creates a happy, comfortable work environment.

creativity A process influenced by individual and organizational factors that results in the production of novel and useful ideas, products, or both.

cross-training A variation of job enlargement in which workers are trained in different specialized tasks or activities.

cultural theory An ethical theory that emphasizes respect for different cultural values.

data Uninterpreted and unanalyzed facts.

defensive communication Communication that can be aggressive, attacking, and angry, or passive and withdrawing.

Delphi technique Gathering the judgments of experts for use in decision making.

democratic style A style of leadership in which the leader takes collaborative, responsive, interactive actions with followers concerning the work and work environment.

devil's advocacy A technique for preventing groupthink in which a group or individual is given the role of critic during decision making.

dialectical inquiry A debate between two opposing sets of recommendations.

differentiation The process of deciding how to divide the work in an organization.

discounting principle The assumption that an individual's behavior is accounted for by the situation.

disenchantment Feeling negativity or anger toward a change.

disengagement Psychological withdrawal from change.

disidentification Feeling that one's identity is being threatened by a change.

disorientation Feelings of loss and confusion due to a change.

displacement An aggressive mechanism in which an individual directs his or her anger toward someone who is not the source of the conflict.

distinctiveness An informational cue indicating the degree to which an individual behaves the same way in other situations.

distributive bargaining A negotiation approach in which the goals of the parties are in conflict, and each party seeks to maximize its resources.

distributive justice The fairness of the outcomes that individuals receive in an organization.

diversity All forms of individual differences, including culture, gender, age, ability, race, religion, personality, social status, and sexual orientation.

divisionalized form A moderately decentralized form of organization that emphasizes the middle level and standardization of outputs.

due process nonaction A procedure set up to address conflicts that is so costly, time consuming, or personally risky that no one will use it.

dynamic follower A follower who is a responsible steward of his or her job, is effective in managing the relationship with the boss, and practices self-management.

dysfunctional conflict An unhealthy, destructive disagreement between two or more people.

effective decision A timely decision that meets a desired objective and is acceptable to those individuals affected by it.

empowerment Sharing power within an organization.

emotional contagion A dynamic process through which the emotions of one person are transferred to another either consciously or unconsciously through nonverbal channels.

emotional intelligence An individual difference that reflects the ability to recognize and manage one's own emotions and those of others.

emotional labor The act of managing one's emotions in accordance with an organization's display rules.

emotions Mental states that typically include feelings, physiological changes, and the inclination to act.

enacted values Values reflected in the way individuals actually behave.

encounter The second socialization stage in which the newcomer learns the tasks associated with the job, clarifies roles, and establishes new relationships at work.

engagement The expression of oneself as one performs in work or other roles.

engineering The applied science of energy and matter.

entitled An individual who is comfortable with an equity ratio greater than that of his or her comparison other.

environment Anything outside the boundaries of an organization.

environmental uncertainty The amount and rate of change in the organization's environment.

equity sensitive An individual who prefers an equity ratio equal to that of his or her comparison other.

ergonomics The science of adapting work and working conditions to the employee or worker.

escalation of commitment The tendency to continue to support a failing course of action.

espoused values What members of an organization say they value.

ethical behavior Acting in ways consistent with one's personal values and the commonly held values of the organization and society.

eustress Healthy, normal stress.

executive coaching A technique in which managers or executives are paired with a coach in a partnership to help the executive perform more efficiently.

expatriate manager A manager who works in a country other than his or her home country.

expectancy The belief that effort leads to performance.

expert power The power that exists when an agent has specialized knowledge or skills that the target needs.

extinction The attempt to weaken a behavior by attaching no consequences to it.

extraversion A preference indicating that an individual is energized by interaction with other people.

fantasy A withdrawal mechanism that provides an escape from a conflict through daydreaming.

feedback Information fed back that completes two-way communication.

feeling Making decisions in a personal, value-oriented way.

femininity The cultural orientation in which relationships and concern for others are valued.

first-impression error The tendency to form lasting opinions about an individual based on initial perceptions.

fixation An aggressive mechanism in which an individual keeps up a dysfunctional behavior that obviously will not solve the conflict.

flextime An alternative work pattern that enables employees to set their own daily work schedules.

flight/withdrawal A withdrawal mechanism that entails physically escaping a conflict (flight) or psychologically escaping (withdrawal).

followership The process of being guided and directed by a leader in the work environment.

formal leadership Officially sanctioned leadership based on the authority of a formal position.

formal organization The official, legitimate, and most visible part of the system.

formalization The degree to which the organization has official rules, regulations, and procedures.

functional conflict A healthy, constructive disagreement between two or more people.

fundamental attribution error The tendency to make attributions to internal causes when focusing on someone else's behavior.

G

garbage can model A theory that contends that decisions in organizations are random and unsystematic.

gateways to communication Pathways through barriers to communication and antidotes to communication problems.

general self-efficacy An individual's general belief that he or she is capable of meeting job demands in a wide variety of situations.

glass ceiling A transparent barrier that keeps women from rising above a certain level in organizations.

goal setting The process of establishing desired results that guide and direct behavior.

group Two or more people with common interests, objectives, and continuing interaction.

group cohesion The "interpersonal glue" that makes members of a group stick together.

group polarization The tendency for group discussion to produce shifts toward more extreme attitudes among members.

groupthink A deterioration of mental efficiency, reality testing, and moral judgment resulting from pressures within the group.

guanxi The Chinese practice of building networks for social exchange.

H

Hawthorne studies Studies conducted during the 1920s and 1930s that discovered the existence of the informal organization.

heuristics Shortcuts in decision making that save mental activity.

hierarchy of authority The degree of vertical differentiation across levels of management.

hygiene factor A work condition related to dissatisfaction caused by discomfort or pain.

I

identification A compromise mechanism whereby an individual patterns his or her behavior after another's.

impoverished manager (1,1) A leader who exerts just enough effort to get by.

impression management The process by which individuals try to control the impressions others have of them.

incremental change Change of a relatively small scope, such as making small improvements.

individual differences The way in which factors such as skills, abilities, personalities, perceptions, attitudes, values, and ethics differ from one individual to another.

individualism A cultural orientation in which people belong to loose social frameworks, and their primary concern is for themselves and their families.

inequity The situation in which a person perceives he or she is receiving less than he or she is giving, or is giving less than he or she is receiving.

influence The process of affecting the thoughts, behavior, and feelings of another person.

informal leadership Unofficial leadership accorded to a person by other members of the organization.

informal organization The unofficial and less visible part of the system.

information Data that have been interpreted, analyzed, and have meaning to some user.

Information communication technology (OCT) The various new technologies, such as electronic mail, voice mail, teleconferencing, and wireless access, which are used for interpersonal communication.

information power Access to and control over important information.

initiating structure Leader behavior aimed at defining and organizing work relationships and roles, as well as establishing clear patterns of organization, communication, and ways of getting things done.

instrumental values Values that represent the acceptable behaviors to be used in achieving some end state.

instrumentality The belief that performance is related to rewards.

integrated involvement Closeness achieved through tasks and activities.

integration The process of coordinating the different parts of an organization.

integrative approach The broad theory that describes personality as a composite of an individual's psychological processes.

integrative negotiation A negotiation approach that focuses on the merits of the issues and seeks a win-win solution.

interactional justice The fairness of the interpersonal treatment given in the course of explaining procedures and outcomes.

interactional psychology The psychological approach that emphasizes that in order to understand human behavior, we must know something about the person and about the situation.

intergroup conflict Conflict that occurs between groups or teams in an organization.

interorganizational conflict Conflict that occurs between two or more organizations.

interpersonal communication Communication between two or more people in an organization.

interpersonal conflict Conflict that occurs between two or more individuals.

intragroup conflict Conflict that occurs within groups or teams.

intrapersonal conflict Conflict that occurs within an individual.

introversion A preference indicating that an individual is energized by time alone.

intuiting Gathering information through "sixth sense" and focusing on what could be rather than what actually exists.

intuition A fast, positive force in decision making that is utilized at a level below consciousness and involves learned patterns of information.

job A set of specified work and task activities that engage an individual in an organization.

Job Characteristics Model A framework for understanding person-job fit through the interaction of core job dimensions with critical psychological states within a person.

Job Diagnostic Survey (JDS) The survey instrument designed to measure the elements in the Job Characteristics Model.

job enlargement A method of job design that increases the number of activities in a job to overcome the boredom of overspecialized work.

job enrichment Designing or redesigning jobs by incorporating motivational factors into them.

job redesign An OD intervention method that alters jobs to improve the fit between individual skills and the demands of the job.

job rotation A variation of job enlargement in which workers are exposed to a variety of specialized jobs over time.

job satisfaction A pleasurable or positive emotional state resulting from the appraisal of one's job or job experiences.

job sharing An alternative work pattern in which more than one person occupies a single job.

judging preference Preferring closure and completion in making decisions.

jurisdictional ambiguity The presence of unclear lines of responsibility within an organization.

laissez-faire style A style of leadership in which the leader fails to accept the responsibilities of the position.

language The words, their pronunciation, and the methods of combining them used and understood by a group of people.

leader An advocate for change and new approaches to problems.

leader–member exchange theory (LMX) A theory that recognizes that leaders form two groups of followers, an in-group and an out-group.

leader–member relations The quality of interpersonal relationships among a leader and the group members.

leadership The process of guiding and directing the behavior of people in the work environment.

Leadership Grid An approach to understanding a leader's or manager's concern for results (production) and concern for people.

leadership training and development A variety of techniques that are designed to enhance individuals' leadership skills.

lean production Using committed employees with ever-expanding responsibilities to achieve zero waste, 100 percent good product, delivered on time, every time.

learning A change in behavior acquired through experience.

least preferred coworker (LPC) The person a leader has least preferred to work with over his or her career.

legitimate power Power that is based on position and mutual agreement; agent and target agree that the agent has the right to influence the target.

locus of control An individual's generalized belief about internal control (self-control) versus external control (control by the situation or by others).

loss of individuality A social process in which individual group members lose self-awareness and its accompanying sense of accountability, inhibition, and responsibility for individual behavior.

Machiavellianism A personality characteristic indicating one's willingness to do whatever it takes to get one's own way.

machine bureaucracy A moderately decentralized form of organization that emphasizes the technical staff and standardization of work processes.

maintenance function An activity essential to effective, satisfying interpersonal relationships within a team or group.

management The study of overseeing activities and supervising people in organizations.

management by objectives (MBO) A goal-setting program based on interaction and negotiation between employees and managers.

manager An advocate for stability and the status quo.

masculinity The cultural orientation in which assertiveness and materialism are valued.

mechanistic structure An organizational design that emphasizes structured activities, specialized tasks, and centralized decision making.

medicine The applied science of healing or treatment of diseases to enhance an individual's health and well-being.

mentoring A work relationship that encourages development and career enhancement for people moving through the career cycle.

message The thoughts and feelings that the communicator is attempting to elicit in the receiver.

moral maturity The measure of a person's cognitive moral development.

motivation The process of arousing and sustaining goal-directed behavior.

motivation factor A work condition related to satisfaction of the need for psychological growth.

moving The second step in Lewin's change model, in which new attitudes, values, and behaviors are substituted for old ones.

Myers-Briggs Type Indicator (MBTI)®instrument An instrument developed to measure Carl Jung's theory of individual differences.

need for achievement A manifest (easily perceived) need that concerns individuals' issues of excellence, competition, challenging goals, persistence, and overcoming difficulties.

need for affiliation A manifest (easily perceived) need that concerns an individual's need to establish and maintain warm, close, intimate relationships with other people.

need for power A manifest (easily perceived) need that concerns an individual's need to make an impact on others, influence others, change people or events, and make a difference in life.

need hierarchy The theory that behavior is determined by a progression of physical, social, and psychological needs by higher order needs.

negative affect An individual's tendency to accentuate the negative aspects of himself or herself, other people, and the world in general.

negative consequences Results of a behavior that a person finds unattractive or aversive.

negativism An aggressive mechanism in which a person responds with pessimism to any attempt at solving a problem.

nominal group technique (NGT) A structured approach to group decision making that focuses on generating alternatives and choosing one.

nonaction Doing nothing in hopes that a conflict with disappear.

nondefensive communication Communication that is assertive, direct, and powerful.

nonprogrammed decision A new, complex decision that requires a creative solution.

nonverbal communication All elements of communication that do not involve words.

normative commitment The type of organizational commitment that is based on an individual's perceived obligation to remain with an organization.

norms of behavior The standards that a work group uses to evaluate the behavior of its members.

objective knowledge Knowledge that results from research and scholarly activities.

one-way communication Communication in which a person sends a message to another person and no feedback, questions, or interaction follow.

operant conditioning Modifying behavior through the use of positive or negative consequences following specific behaviors.

opportunistic "what's in it for me" manager (Opp) A leader whose style aims to maximize self-benefit.

opportunities Favorable times or chances for progress and advancement.

organic structure An organizational design that emphasizes teamwork, open communication, and decentralized decision making.

organization development (OD) A systematic approach to organizational improvement that applies behavioral science theory and research in order to increase individual and organizational well-being and effectiveness.

organization man manager (5,5) A middle-of-the-road leader.

organizational behavior The study of individual behavior and group dynamics in organizations.

organizational citizenship behavior Behavior that is above and beyond the call of duty.

organizational commitment The strength of an individual's identification with an organization.

organizational (corporate) culture A pattern of basic assumptions that are considered valid and that are taught to new members as the way to perceive, think, and feel in the organization.

organizational design The process of constructing and adjusting an organization's structure to achieve its goals.

organizational life cycle The differing stages of an organization's life from birth to death.

organizational politics The use of power and influence in organizations.

organizational socialization The process by which newcomers are transformed from outsiders to participating, effective members of the organization.

organizational structure The linking of departments and jobs within an organization.

participative decision making Decision making in which individuals who are affected by decisions influence the making of those decisions.

paternalistic "father knows best" manager (9+9) A leader who promises reward and threatens punishment.

perceiving preference Preferring to explore many alternatives and flexibility.

perceptual screen A window through which we interact with people that influences the quality, accuracy, and clarity of the communication.

performance appraisal The evaluation of a person's performance.

performance management A process of defining, measuring, appraising, providing feedback on, and improving performance.

personality A relatively stable set of characteristics that influence an individual's behavior.

planned change Change resulting from a deliberate decision to alter the organization.

political behavior Actions not officially sanctioned by an organization that are taken to influence others in order to meet one's personal goals.

political skill The ability to get things done through favorable interpersonal relationships outside of formally prescribed organizational mechanisms.

position power The authority associated with the leader's formal position in the organization.

positive affect An individual's tendency to accentuate the positive aspects of himself or herself, other people, and the world in general.

positive consequences Results of a behavior that a person finds attractive or pleasurable.

power The ability to influence another person.

power distance The degree to which a culture accepts unequal distribution of power.

powerlessness A lack of power.

procedural justice The fairness of the process by which outcomes are allocated in an organization.

process consultation An OD method that helps managers and employees improve the processes that are used in organizations.

professional bureaucracy A decentralized form of organization that emphasizes the operating core and standardization of skills.

programmed decision A simple, routine matter for which a manager has an established decision rule.

projection Overestimating the number of people who share our own beliefs, values, and behaviors.

psychological intimacy Emotional and psychological closeness to other teams or group members.

psychology The science of human behavior.

punishment The attempt to eliminate or weaken undesirable behavior by either bestowing negative consequences or withholding positive consequences.

quality program A program that embeds product and service quality excellence in the organizational culture.

R

rationality A logical, step-by-step approach to decision making, with a thorough analysis of alternatives and their consequences.

rationalization A compromise mechanism characterized by trying to justify one's behavior by constructing bogus reasons for it.

receiver The person receiving a message.

referent power An elusive power that is based on interpersonal attraction.

reflective listening A skill intended to help the receiver and communicator clearly and fully understand the message sent.

refreezing The final step in Lewin's change model, in which new attitudes, values, and behaviors are established as the new status quo.

reinforcement The attempt to develop or strengthen desirable behavior by either bestowing positive consequences or withholding negative consequences.

reward power Power based on an agent's ability to control rewards that a target wants.

richness The ability of a medium or channel to elicit or evoke meaning in the receiver.

risk aversion The tendency to choose options that entail fewer risks and less uncertainty.

role negotiation A technique whereby individuals meet and clarify their psychological contract.

rule-based theory An ethical theory that emphasizes the character of the act itself rather than its effects.

S

satisfice To select the first alternative that is "good enough," because the costs in time and effort are too great to optimize.

secrecy Attempting to hide a conflict or an issue that has the potential to create conflict.

selective perception The process of selecting information that supports our individual viewpoints while discounting information that threatens our viewpoints.

self-esteem An individual's general feeling of self-worth.

self-fulfilling prophecy The situation in which our expectations about people affect our interaction with them in such a way that our expectations are fulfilled.

self-interest What is in the best interest and benefit to an individual.

self-monitoring The extent to which people base their behavior on cues from other people and situations.

self-serving bias The tendency to attribute one's own successes to internal causes and one's failures to external causes.

sensing Gathering information through the five senses.

simple structure A centralized form of organization that emphasizes the upper echelon and direct supervision.

Six Sigma A high-performance system to execute business strategy that is customer-driven, emphasizes quantitative decision making, and places a priority on saving money.

skill development The mastery of abilities essential to successful functioning in organizations.

skills training Increasing the job knowledge, skills, and abilities that are necessary to do a job effectively.

social decision schemes Simple rules used to determine final group decisions.

social information-processing (SIP) model A model that suggests that the important job factors depend in part on what others tell a person about the job.

social learning The process of deriving attitudes from family, peer groups, religious organizations, and culture.

social loafing The failure of a group member to contribute personal time, effort, thoughts, or other resources to the group.

social perception The process of interpreting information about another person.

social power Power used to create motivation or to accomplish group goals.

social responsibility The obligation of an organization to behave in ethical ways.

sociology The science of society.

sociotechnical systems (STS) Giving equal attention to technical and social considerations in job design.

specialization The degree to which jobs are narrowly defined and depend on unique expertise.

standardization The degree to which work activities are accomplished in a routine fashion.

status structure The set of authority and task relations among a group's members.

stereotype A generalization about a group of people.

strategic change Change of a larger scale, such as organizational restructuring.

strategic contingencies Activities that other groups depend on in order to complete their tasks.

strong culture An organizational culture with a consensus on the values that drive the company and with an intensity that is recognizable even to outsiders.

strong situation A situation that overwhelms the effects of individual personalities by providing strong cues for appropriate behavior.

superordinate goal An organizational goal that is more important to both parties in a conflict than their individual or group goals.

survey feedback A widely used method of intervention whereby employee attitudes are solicited using a questionnaire.

synergy A positive force that occurs in groups when group members stimulate new solutions to problems through the process of mutual influence and encouragement within the group.

T

task environment The elements of an organization's environment that are related to its goal attainment.

task function An activity directly related to the effective completion of a team's work.

task structure The degree of clarity, or ambiguity, in the work activities assigned to the group.

task-specific self-efficacy An individual's beliefs and expectancies about his or her ability to perform a specific task effectively.

team building An intervention designed to improve the effectiveness of a work group.

team manager (9,9) A leader who builds a highly productive team of committed people.

teamwork Joint action by a team of people in which individual interests are subordinated to team unity.

technocentric Placing technology and engineering at the center of job design decisions.

technological interdependence The degree of interrelatedness of the organization's various technological elements.

technostress The stress caused by new and advancing technologies in the workplace.

terminal values Values that represent the goals to be achieved or the end states of existence.

Theory X A set of assumptions of how to manage individuals who are motivated by lower order needs.

Theory Y A set of assumptions of how to manage individuals who are motivated by higher order needs.

thinking Making decisions in a logical, objective fashion.

360-degree feedback A process of self-evaluation and evaluations by a manager, peers, direct reports, and possibly customers.

time orientation Whether a culture's values are oriented toward the future (long-term orientation) or toward the past and present (short-term orientation).

transformational change Change in which the organization moves to a radically different, and sometimes unknown, future state.

transformational leaders Leader who inspire followers to transcend their self-interests and achieve exceptional performance.

transnational organization An organization in which the global viewpoint supersedes national issues.

two-way communication A form of communication in which the communicator and receiver interact.

uncertainty avoidance The degree to which a culture tolerates ambiguity and uncertainty.

unfreezing The first step in Lewin's change model, in which individuals are encouraged to discard old behaviors by shaking up the equilibrium state that maintains the status quo.

unplanned change Change that is imposed on the organization and is often unforeseen.

valence The value or importance one places on a particular reward.

values Enduring beliefs that a specific mode of conduct or end state of existence is personally or socially preferable to an opposite or converse mode of conduct or end state of existence.

vigor Physical strength, emotional energy, and cognitive aliveness.

virtual office A mobile platform of computer, telecommunication, and information technology and services.

whistle-blower An employee who informs authorities of the wrongdoings of his or her company or coworkers.

work Mental or physical activity that has productive results.

work simplification Standardization and the narrow, explicit specification of task activities for workers.

work team A group of people with complementary skills who are committed to a common mission, performance goals, and approach for which they hold themselves mutually accountable

workplace deviance behavior (WDB) Any voluntary counterproductive behavior that violates organizational norms and causes some degree of harm to organizational functioning.

zone of indifference The range in which attempts to influence a person will be perceived as legitimate and will be acted on without a great deal of thought.

COMPANY INDEX

SUBJECT INDEX

Task-specific self-efficacy, 150
Team building, 429
Team manager (9,9), 280
Team reward systems, individual versus, 161–162
Teams, 212
    diversity and creativity in, 214–215
    or groups, task and maintenance functions in, 211
Teamwork, 212
    for productivity and quality, managerial implications, 216–217
Techniques
    conflict management strategies and, 314–318
    effective, 316–318
    for group decision making, 239–241
    individual-focused, 430–431
    ineffective, 315–316
    organization- and group-focused, 428–429
Technocentric, 346
Technological change, 414
Technological interdependence, 367
Technology, 366–369
    and basic design dimensions, summary of Perrow's findings about the relationship between, 368
    at work, 350
    changes in information-processing, 375
    communicating through new, 192–195
Technostress, 350
Telecommuting, 347–349
Terminal values, 111–112
Territorial space, 188
The Four-Way Test for doing business, 56
Theory of motivation, motivation-hygiene, 129
Theory X, 125–126
Theory Y, 125–126
Thinking, 77
Thorndike's law of effect, 148
360-degree feedback, 160
    e orientation, 37
    lues, 309
    y management (TQM), 13
    nal

Trust, 288–289
Tuckman's five-stage model of group development, 205
Two-factor theory
    critique of, 128–129
    Herzberg's, 127–129
Two-way communication, 179
Type theory preferences and descriptions, 76

Uncertainty avoidance, 37, 308
Uncertainty, environmental, 369–370
Unfair and injustice treatment, unintended consequences of, 134–135
Unfreezing, 425
Unknown, fear of, 419
Unplanned change, 412
Unwanted sexual attention, 52
Utilitarian romances, 54
Utilitarianism, 49

Valence, 135
Values, 111–116, 391–392
    at work, managerial implications, 116
    cultural assumptions and, 419–421
    cultural differences in, 113–114
    enacted, 391
    espoused, 391
    ethics and, 307
    instrumental and terminal, 111–112
    international differences in work-related, 184
    time orientation of, 309
    work, 112–113
Valuing Diversity, 204
Variables influencing individual behavior, 67
Variables, contextual, 358, 364–373
Verbal communication, characteristics of the target, 80
Vertical differentiation, 358–359
    level of, 374
Vigor, 139
Virtual
    office, 350
    organizations, 377
    teams, 201, 242–243
    work, 182–183
    workplace, decision making in, 242–243

Voice mail systems, 193
VOIP (voice over Internet protocol), 21

Whistle-blower, 54
Whistle-blowing, 54–55
Wi-Fi, 21
Win–Lose vs. Win–Win strategies, 314
Withdrawal. *See* Flight/withdrawal
Women, gender diversity in workforce, 42–44
Work, 333
    behavior and quality at, 13–14
    contemporary issues in the design of, 347–350
    defensive communication at, 185
    emotions at, 105–111
    equity and inequity at, 132
    international perspectives on the design of, 345–347
    justice and fair treatment at, 133–135
    managerial implications: changing nature of, 351
    technology at, 350
    unintended consequences of injustice and unfair treatment, 134–135
    virtual, 182–183
Work attitudes, 96–103
Work behavior, motivation and, 122–123
Work in organizations, 333–334
Work motivation and task performance, increasing, 155
Work patterns, alternative, 349–350
Work simplification, 335
Work team, 202
    in organizations, 212–214
    structure and work team process, 213–214
Work values, 112–113
Workforce
    diversity, 11, 41–49, 413–414
    feminization of, 42–44
    managing a diverse, 33
Workplace deviance behavior (WDB), 101
Work-related tension, cohesiveness and, 208
Work-related values, international differences in, 184

Zone of indifference, 251
Zones of territorial space in U.S. culture, 188